Research Findings in the Economics of Aging

A National Bureau
of Economic Research
Conference Report

Research Findings in the Economics of Aging

Edited by   **David A. Wise**

The University of Chicago Press

Chicago and London

DAVID A. WISE is the John F. Stambaugh Professor of Political
Economy at the John F. Kennedy School of Government, Harvard
University, and director of the program on the economics of aging at
the National Bureau of Economic Research.

The University of Chicago Press, Chicago 60637
The University of Chicago Press, Ltd., London
© 2010 by the National Bureau of Economic Research
All rights reserved. Published 2010
Printed in the United States of America

19 18 17 16 15 14 13 12 11 10   1 2 3 4 5
ISBN-13: 978-0-226-90306-4 (cloth)
ISBN-10: 0-226-90306-0 (cloth)

Library of Congress Cataloging-in-Publication Data

Research findings in the economics of aging / edited by David A. Wise.
        p. cm. — (National Bureau of Economic Research conference
    report)
        Includes bibliographical references and indexes.
        ISBN-13: 978-0-226-90306-4 (alk. paper)
        ISBN-10: 0-226-90306-0 (alk. paper)
        1. Aging—Economic aspects—Congresses. 2. Older people—
    Economic conditions—Congresses. 3. Old age pensions—
    Congresses. 4. Disability retirement—Congresses. 5. Medicare—
    Congresses. I. Wise, David A. II. Series: National Bureau of
    Economic Research conference report.
        HQ1061.R438 2010
        305.26—dc22
                                                        2009021117

Relation of the Directors to the
Work and Publications of the
National Bureau of Economic Research

1. The object of the NBER is to ascertain and present to the economics profession, and to the public more generally, important economic facts and their interpretation in a scientific manner without policy recommendations. The Board of Directors is charged with the responsibility of ensuring that the work of the NBER is carried on in strict conformity with this object.

2. The President shall establish an internal review process to ensure that book manuscripts proposed for publication DO NOT contain policy recommendations. This shall apply both to the proceedings of conferences and to manuscripts by a single author or by one or more co-authors but shall not apply to authors of comments at NBER conferences who are not NBER affiliates.

3. No book manuscript reporting research shall be published by the NBER until the President has sent to each member of the Board a notice that a manuscript is recommended for publication and that in the President's opinion it is suitable for publication in accordance with the above principles of the NBER. Such notification will include a table of contents and an abstract or summary of the manuscript's content, a list of contributors if applicable, and a response form for use by Directors who desire a copy of the manuscript for review. Each manuscript shall contain a summary drawing attention to the nature and treatment of the problem studied and the main conclusions reached.

4. No volume shall be published until forty-five days have elapsed from the above notification of intention to publish it. During this period a copy shall be sent to any Director requesting it, and if any Director objects to publication on the grounds that the manuscript contains policy recommendations, the objection will be presented to the author(s) or editor(s). In case of dispute, all members of the Board shall be notified, and the President shall appoint an ad hoc committee of the Board to decide the matter; thirty days additional shall be granted for this purpose.

5. The President shall present annually to the Board a report describing the internal manuscript review process, any objections made by Directors before publication or by anyone after publication, any disputes about such matters, and how they were handled.

6. Publications of the NBER issued for informational purposes concerning the work of the Bureau, or issued to inform the public of the activities at the Bureau, including but not limited to the NBER Digest and Reporter, shall be consistent with the object stated in paragraph 1. They shall contain a specific disclaimer noting that they have not passed through the review procedures required in this resolution. The Executive Committee of the Board is charged with the review of all such publications from time to time.

7. NBER working papers and manuscripts distributed on the Bureau's web site are not deemed to be publications for the purpose of this resolution, but they shall be consistent with the object stated in paragraph 1. Working papers shall contain a specific disclaimer noting that they have not passed through the review procedures required in this resolution. The NBER's web site shall contain a similar disclaimer. The President shall establish an internal review process to ensure that the working papers and the web site do not contain policy recommendations, and shall report annually to the Board on this process and any concerns raised in connection with it.

8. Unless otherwise determined by the Board or exempted by the terms of paragraphs 6 and 7, a copy of this resolution shall be printed in each NBER publication as described in paragraph 2 above.

Contents

Preface   xi

Introduction   1
David A. Wise

I. DISABILITY, WORK, AND RETIREMENT

1. **New Age Thinking: Alternative Ways of
   Measuring Age, Their Relationship to Labor
   Force Participation, Government Policies,
   and GDP**   17
   John B. Shoven
   Comment: Erzo F. P. Luttmer

2. **Work Disability: The Effects of Demography,
   Health, and Disability Insurance**   37
   Axel Börsch-Supan
   Comment: Robert J. Willis

3. **Labor Market Status and Transitions
   during the Pre-Retirement Years: Learning
   from International Differences**   63
   Arie Kapteyn, James P. Smith, Arthur van Soest,
   and James Banks
   Comment: Michael Hurd

II. EDUCATION AND DISABILITY

    4. The Education Gradient in Old Age Disability   101
    David M. Cutler and Adriana Lleras-Muney
    Comment: Anne Case

    5. Social Interactions and Smoking   123
    David M. Cutler and Edward L. Glaeser
    Comment: Arie Kapteyn

    6. Education and the Prevalence of Pain   145
    Steven J. Atlas and Jonathan Skinner

III. ECONOMIC CIRCUMSTANCES AND HEALTH

    7. Aging and Death under a Dollar a Day   169
    Abhijit V. Banerjee and Esther Duflo
    Comment: Amitabh Chandra and
    Heidi Williams

    8. What's Past Is Prologue: The Impact of
    Early Life Health and Circumstance on
    Health in Old Age   211
    Anne Case
    Comment: James P. Smith

    9. Income, Aging, Health, and Well-Being
    around the World: Evidence from the Gallup
    World Poll   235
    Angus Deaton
    Comment: Amitabh Chandra and
    Heidi Williams

IV. RETIREMENT SAVING

    10. The Rise of 401(k) Plans, Lifetime Earnings,
    and Wealth at Retirement   271
    James M. Poterba, Steven F. Venti, and
    David A. Wise
    Comment: Robert J. Willis

    11. The Impact of Employer Matching on Savings
    Plan Participation under Automatic Enrollment   311
    John Beshears, James J. Choi, David Laibson,
    and Brigitte C. Madrian
    Comment: Daniel McFadden

12. **Housing Price Volatility and Downsizing in Later Life**   337
James Banks, Richard Blundell, Zoë Oldfield, and James P. Smith
Comment: Steven F. Venti

V. MEDICARE

13. **The Narrowing Dispersion of Medicare Expenditures 1997 to 2005**   387
Jay Bhattacharya, Alan M. Garber, and Thomas MaCurdy
Comment: Jonathan Skinner

14. **Mind the Gap! Consumer Perceptions and Choices of Medicare Part D Prescription Drug Plans**   413
Florian Heiss, Daniel McFadden, and Joachim Winter
Comment: Amy Finkelstein

Contributors   485
Author Index   489
Subject Index   493

Preface

This volume consists of papers presented at a conference held in Carefree, Arizona, in May 2007. Most of the research was conducted as part of the program on the Economics of Aging at the National Bureau of Economic Research. The majority of the work was sponsored by the U.S. Department of Health and Human Services, through the National Institute on Aging grants P01-AG05842 and P30-AG12810 to the National Bureau of Economic Research. Any other funding sources are noted in the individual chapters.

Any opinions expressed in this volume are those of the respective authors and do not necessarily reflect the views of the National Bureau of Economic Research or the sponsoring organizations.

Introduction

David A. Wise

The next twenty years mark a new phase in the demographic transition of the United States, as the baby boom generation becomes eligible for Social Security and Medicare. This large population mass, which has been in a prime working and earning phase of their careers, and supporting a comparatively smaller population of older retirees, reaches an age when they too may retire. Whatever social and economic transitions may accompany this demographic shift depend a lot on the labor market decisions of this population, how much they will have saved for their retirement, and what health care they will need.

We consider these issues in this, the twelfth in a series of NBER volumes on the Economics of Aging. The previous volumes are *The Economics of Aging, Issues in the Economics of Aging, Topics in the Economics of Aging, Studies in the Economics of Aging, Advances in the Economics of Aging, Inquiries in the Economics of Aging, Frontiers in the Economics of Aging, Themes in the Economics of Aging, Perspectives on the Economics of Aging, Analyses in the Economics of Aging,* and *Developments in the Economics of Aging.* This introduction provides an overview of the studies contained in the volume, relying to a significant extent on the authors' own language to summarize their findings.

Disability, Work, and Retirement

The first three chapters in the volume consider work and retirement behavior, work disability, and their relationship to the structure of retirement

David A. Wise is the John F. Stambaugh Professor of Political Economy at the John F. Kennedy School of Government, Harvard University, and director of the program on the economics of aging at the National Bureau of Economic Research.

and disability policies. These issues are central to discussions of population aging and its impact, because the ages at which people leave the labor force, whether through retirement or disability, define the effective dependency ratio in the population and, by consequence, the associated economic strain that we collectively confront. Even modest changes in when people leave the labor force, on average, could have a very substantial impact on the productive output of the economy as a whole. Moreover, with continual improvements in functional health at older ages, there is an increased capacity for work at older ages that people may or may not choose to do. A common feature of all three studies is their attention to health and disability trends, and the extent to which public policies are structured in ways that reflect health and functional ability as they evolve over time.

In chapter 1, "New Age Thinking: Alternative Ways of Measuring Age, Their Relationship to Labor Force Participation, Government Policies, and GDP," John Shoven develops several innovative approaches to thinking about age. The traditional measure of age is a measure of years-since-birth. Shoven suggests that for some purposes, age measures that are more closely associated with health and longevity might be more appropriate. For example, a simple alternative to years since birth would be a measure of age based on mortality risk. Groups whose mortality risk is high would be considered old, those with low mortality risk would be classified as young and those with the same mortality risk would be considered to be the same age. Another approach would be to measure age from the other end of life, based on remaining life expectancy, or RLE. Those with a short RLE would be considered elderly and those with a long RLE would be considered young. Shoven notes one advantage of the RLE approach over the mortality risk approach is that it is measured in years, units that are widely understood.

One can apply alternative measures of age in the context of different population groups at any one time, or to compare populations over the course of time. For example, using RLE or mortality risk as a measure of age, one would conclude that a man at the conventionally defined age of sixty-five is roughly the same "age" as a woman of age seventy. The differences across time may be even more dramatic, as mortality rates decline and as longevity increases. For example, fifty-one-year-old men in 1970 had the same mortality risk as fifty-eight-year-old men in 2000, suggesting that they are the same "age," if age is defined as mortality risk. The mortality risk approach to measuring age would define each of the following groups as being the same age: seventy-year-old women in 2000, sixty-five-year-old men in 2000, and fifty-nine-year-old men in 1970. These kinds of comparative age measurements are presented in detail in chapter 1.

An interesting extension of alternative age measurement applies to population forecasts. By using alternative age measures in population forecasts, the huge wave of elderly forecast for the first half of this century does not look like a huge wave at all. By conventional sixty-five and over standards, for example, the fraction of the population that is elderly will grow by about 66 percent in the coming decades. By contrast, the fraction of the population that is above a mortality rate that corresponds to sixty-five and over today will grow by only 20 percent. Needless to say, the aging of the society is a lot less dramatic with the alternative mortality-based age measures.

In yet another application of alternative age measurement, Shoven explores the consequences of stabilizing labor force participation rates by age, again using alternative definitions of age. If labor force participation were to remain as it is today with respect to remaining life expectancy (i.e., if the length of retirement stayed where it is today) rather than labor force participation remaining fixed by conventionally-defined age, then there would be almost 10 percent more total labor supply by 2050 in the United States. This additional labor supply would be very helpful in terms of meeting the challenges of financing entitlement programs, among other things. Gross domestic product (GDP) might be almost 10 percent higher by 2050 if retirement lengths stabilize. Several policies are examined in the chapter that would encourage longer work careers, based in part on the redefinition of policy parameters to a new definition of age.

Chapters 2 and 3 focus on the wide variation in enrollment and spending in disability insurance programs across countries, even among countries with similar levels of economic development and comparable access to modern medical technology and treatment. The range of per capita expenditures is enormous, even after correcting for purchasing power differences across countries. The question is, how much of the variation is based on underlying differences in health and functional ability across countries and how much is based on the policies and institutions that provide disability benefits?

The study in chapter 2, "Work Disability: The Effects of Demography, Health, and Disability Insurance," by Axel Börsch-Supan, points to a trade-off in the provision of disability insurance. On the one hand, disability insurance is a welcome and necessary part of the social safety net as it prevents income losses for those who lose their ability to work before the normal retirement age. On the other hand, disability insurance may be used instead as a shortcut to early retirement even if an individual's ability to work is not impaired. Understanding the trade-off between its role as a health-dependent social safety net and its use as a broader early retirement program is important for the design of a modern social security system, particularly at a time of financial strain on income support systems in most countries.

Börsch-Supan notes three explanations commonly offered for the large variation in disability insurance spending across countries: demographics, health, and institutions. First, while all European countries are aging, the specific age demographics of the population vary considerably from one country to another. A second potential cause for the cross-national variation is international variation in health and disability status, beyond just the difference in demographic composition. Third, public pension and disability support systems exert large incentive effects which, according to each country's legislation and policies, significantly increase or decrease the take-up of benefits.

The results of the cross-country study indicate that demographic and health-related differences explain very little of the cross-national variation in disability enrollment rates. By contrast, more than 75 percent of the cross-national variation can be explained by the generosity of, and the ease of access to, disability insurance. The most influential institutional variable is the minimum level of disability required to obtain full benefits. According to the study, this variable alone explains more than 60 percent of the cross-national variation.

In chapter 3, "Labor Market Status and Transitions during the Pre-Retirement Years: Learning from International Differences," Arie Kapteyn, James Smith, Arthur van Soest, and James Banks conduct a similar analysis and reach similar conclusions. Both studies analyze variations in work disability and enrollment in disability insurance in Europe and the United States. Both studies highlight the importance of institutional and policy variation as the primary cause of varying enrollments and spending. Chapter 2 analyzes the issue using data from the Survey of Health, Aging, and Retirement in Europe (SHARE), the English Longitudinal Study on Aging (ELSA), and the Health and Retirement Study (HRS). Chapter 3 uses data from the Panel Study of Income Dynamics (PSID) and the European Community Household Panel (ECHP).

An additional aspect of chapter 3 is a simulation analysis that applies U.S. institutional variables to the population characteristics of other countries to see how self-reported work disability would change in the other countries in the study. These institutional differences include program eligibility rules, workplace accommodation of older or sick workers, and generosity of benefits. Kapteyn, Smith, and van Soest find that by simulating work disability using U.S. parameters (i.e., U.S. institutions and norms), but applied to European countries, there is often a considerable reduction in self-reported disability rates.

Education and Disability

In many past studies of disability trends, a consistent finding is the strong correlation between education and functional ability. Those with more education are less likely to develop functional limitations and appear to cope more effectively with functional limitations when they do develop. The question is, why? What is it about education that reduces disability? The next three chapters in the volume consider aspects of this question.

Chapter 4, by David M. Cutler and Adriana Lleras-Muney, analyzes "The

Education Gradient in Old Age Disability." The authors note that nearly half of elderly people with less than a high school degree report some difficulty caring for themselves; whereas only about a quarter of college graduates report that they are disabled. The lower disability rate among those who are better educated results in substantial differences in health and medical spending, in employment and earnings, and in many aspects of functional independence. Understanding why education is related to disability and whether changes in education have contributed to disability declines is thus a central policy concern.

There are many theories about the link between education and disability, ranging from childhood conditions that affect both education and disability, occupational differences in the working years, differential health behaviors, differential access to medical care, and differential living situations as a senior. Cutler and Lleras-Muney focus on each of them.

Three factors are highlighted in the chapter as particularly strong influences on the education gradient in disability. The first is health behaviors. Better educated people are significantly less likely to smoke than are less educated people; they are also less obese. Smoking and obesity are both strongly related to disability, and explain a good part of the education effect. In the case of smoking, the difference is not so much smoking initiation (a decision made early in life), but smoking cessation. The share of people who ever smoked is roughly similar by education; quitting behavior, in contrast, is very different. About one-third of the education gradient in disability is found to be associated with differential health behaviors. Another third is explained by differences in lifetime occupation. People are, in perhaps a literal sense, broken down by hard work. Finally, differential rates of medical conditions explain another fifth of the education gradient in disability. Stroke, heart disease, and chronic conditions such as diabetes and arthritis are highly related to disability. Less educated people are more likely to have suffered from these conditions, partly as a result of their greater propensity to smoke and to be obese.

All told, differences in occupation, health behaviors, and their disease consequences explain essentially all of the differences between those with a high school degree and college graduates. However, the factors we analyze can only explain about 55 percent of the differences in disability rates between those with a high school degree and high school dropouts. Interestingly, childhood conditions, use of preventive care after age sixty-five, and living arrangements after age sixty-five do not explain a large share of the education gradient in disability. Based on these results, Cutler and Lleras-Muney suggest that the increased education of recent cohorts will result in lower disability rates in the future and, if lowering education gradients are the policy objective, then efforts should concentrate on modifying the health behaviors of less educated individuals.

Chapter 5 considers one health behavior in particular, smoking, and the effect of peer behavior in influencing smoking rates. "Social Interactions and Smoking," by David M. Cutler and Edward L. Glaeser, asks whether people are more likely to smoke when they are surrounded by smokers. Cutler and Glaeser suggest several reasons that peers might matter for health-related behaviors. In many cases, health-related behaviors are more fun to do when others are doing them too (drinking, for example). Peers are also a source of information about health (the benefits of a mammogram) or about what is acceptable in society (the approbation accorded smokers). These interpersonal complementarities can have enormous social impact. They may also relate to the differences in health behavior by education described in chapter 4.

In addition to helping us understand how health behaviors operate, peer effects also magnify the impact of policy interventions. The existence of social interactions implies that a policy intervention has both a direct effect on the impacted individual and an indirect effect, as that person's behavior impacts those around them. These indirect effects create a social multiplier where the predicted impact of interventions will be greater when the interventions are imposed in larger geographic areas.

Cutler and Glaeser find that individuals whose spouse faced a workplace smoking ban were less likely to smoke themselves. Put the other way, individuals whose spouses smoke are estimated to be 40 percent more likely to smoke themselves. Interestingly, the variation in smoking rates across states and metropolitan areas is estimated to be seven times higher than it would be if there were no social interactions and if there were no exogenous variables differing across geographic regions. The study also finds a significant social multiplier in the impact of smoking bans. The bans have a much stronger impact at higher levels of geographic aggregation. This social multiplier could explain the large time series drop in smoking among some demographic groups.

Chapter 6, by Steven J. Atlas and Jonathan Skinner, is entitled "Education and the Prevalence of Pain." The study begins by documenting the dramatic differences across educational groups in the prevalence of pain. The authors find significant differences across educational groups, with rates of people aged fifty to fifty-nine troubled by pain ranging from 26 percent for women with a college education to 55 percent for those without a high school diploma. More surprisingly, the prevalence of pain declined with age.

One might think that these differences result from those with lower education being more likely to have worked in manual jobs, or to experience other types of health impairments. This motivated a second component of the study, which followed patients with intervertebral disk herniation (IDH) over a ten-year follow-up period after treatment. The study provided detailed clinical baseline information for a homogeneous sample of people with a common clinical complaint of lower back pain associated with sciatica (referred pain down the leg) arising from IDH. Atlas and Skinner consider education-based differences in the long-term prevalence of pain with treatment, and whether these differences can be explained by underlying clinical health at baseline, or by access to surgical or other medical treatments. The initial severity of the IDH, as measured by imaging or clinical diagnosis, explains just a small degree of variation in outcomes. The most important predictive factor of long-term pain outcomes is education. Even after ten years, the percentage of people who experience leg or back pain "almost always" or "always" is 34 percent for high school dropouts but just 9 percent for college graduates.

Why then is pain so much greater among lower educational (or income) groups? One explanation may be that people report pain to justify nonemployment and disability. According to Atlas and Skinner, however, there is scant evidence for this explanation from the economics literature, and a growing clinical and neurological literature rejecting the idea of people falsely reporting pain. Instead, this new view recognizes the importance of the brain in generating *real* pain even in the absence of a specific physical injury. The strong association between education and pain in both the survey data and the clinical data are supportive of the view that educational attainment has an independent association with the neurological mediators of pain, or for social or even economic factors that may be associated with the perception of pain.

Economic Circumstances and Health

There is a well-established relationship between economic circumstances, health and mortality across the full continuum of economic circumstances. The next three chapters in the volume deal with aspects of this relationship. In chapter 7, "Aging and Death under a Dollar a Day," Abhijit V. Banerjee and Esther Duflo consider this relationship among those with extremely low incomes around the world. Their research compares the consumption patterns and mortality outcomes of the very poor (living on less than one dollar per day), the poor (less than two dollars per day) and the somewhat less poor (two to four dollars per day, or six to ten dollars per day). As a point of comparison, the poverty line for a family of five in the United States amounts to $13 per person per day.

Much of these investigators' prior research has focused on the effects of poverty on relative consumption patterns. At least in some countries, there is evidence that the extremely poor are short on calories and other nutrients, relative to the standard norms for their country. In India, the poorest live on less than 1,500 calories a day compared to a norm of over 2,000, and even this number seems to be going down over time. Where there is more detailed health information, such as in a survey carried out by the authors in a rural Udaipur district, it is also clear that the very poor are undernourished: 65 percent of adult men and 40 percent of adult women have body mass indexes (BMIs) of less than 18.5, which is the standard cut-off for being underweight. Compared to the poor, the less poor are more likely to send their children to school, more likely to see a doctor when they feel sick, and more inclined to see a private doctor rather than a public practitioner. They also have greater access to water, sanitation, and public infrastructure.

The additional focus of chapter 7 is on the implications of relative poverty for mortality. Based on multiple pieces of evidence, the results all point in the same direction: the poor, and particularly the very poor, have a lower chance of survival than those who are somewhat better off. The proxy measure of longevity used in the study is the probability that an adult's mother and father are alive. The mother of someone who is not poor is more likely to be alive than the mother of someone who is poor. Using panel data for Indonesia and Vietnam, the authors also find that older adults are more likely to have died five years later if they are poor.

Chapter 8 also explores the relationship between economic circumstances and health, focusing on health and environment in early childhood and its long-term effect on health and functioning in old age. In "What's Past is Prologue: The Impact of Early Life Health and Circumstance on Health in Old Age," Anne Case uses two markers of health and environment in early life to assess their impact on health in later life. First, Case documents the extent to which height, as a measure of early life health and nutrition, is associated with more favorable outcomes in old age. Second, she investigates whether conditions that might have affected a mother's nutrition while pregnant—specifically, the success of corn crop production while she was pregnant—are predictive of health in later life, and whether this marker of mother's nutrition can explain the association between height and health outcomes in old age.

The study finds that height is protective of health. On average, taller men and women are more likely to report themselves to be in better health, and are less likely to report that a doctor has told them that they have hypertension. They report fewer difficulties with activities of daily living (ADLs) and better fine motor skills. Height appears to become more protective against hypertension, ADLs, and loss of fine motor skills at the oldest ages, when there is a higher risk of poor health. The study also finds that height is predicted by the success of the corn crop in the year before birth, and that, taken together, height and corn production both have large and significant effects on health in old age. Corn production, like height, appears to be protective against hypertension, the loss of fine motor skills, the loss of large muscle group skills, and the ability to carry out activities of daily living.

The third study on economic circumstances and health is authored by Angus Deaton and is reported in chapter 9. "Income, Aging, Health, and Well-Being around the World: Evidence from the Gallup World Poll" looks at the effects of income and age on self-reported well-being in more than a hundred countries. It addresses in particular self-reports of life satisfaction, health, and disability, how these measures change with age, and how the effects of age differ across countries according to their level of development and their region of the world. The analysis is based on the Gallup World Poll, which collected data from samples of people in each of 132 countries during 2006. With few exceptions, the samples are nationally representative of people aged fifteen and older. Because the survey used the same questionnaire in all countries, it provides an opportunity to make cross-country comparisons while, at the same time, providing enough data to permit within-country disaggregation; for example, by age, gender, ethnicity, or education.

Deaton finds that the citizens of richer countries are on average more satisfied with their lives than the citizens of poorer countries. Unlike most earlier studies, this effect of income is not confined to poor, unhappy countries, but extends across the range of the income distribution, from Cambodia, Sierra Leone, Togo, Niger, and Chad, which are among the bottom ten countries in both income and life-satisfaction, to Norway, Switzerland, Denmark, Australia, and Canada, which rank in the top ten in both income and life-satisfaction. Each doubling of national income is associated with a near one unit increase in average life-satisfaction measured on an eleven point scale from 0 ("the worst possible life") to 10 ("the best possible life"). If anything, the effect of national income on national happiness is found to be *stronger* in the rich countries than in the poor countries.

Deaton also looks at the pattern of life satisfaction at different ages. He finds that the results differ according to the level of economic development. Life satisfaction was much worse among the elderly than among the young in poor and middle-income countries. By contrast, in rich countries, especially the English-speaking rich countries, the elderly were relatively satisfied with their lives, sometimes more satisfied than those in midlife. The elderly in the countries of Eastern Europe and the former Soviet Union are particularly dissatisfied with their lives and with their health. In almost all countries and for all age groups, satisfaction with health declines with age, and is lowest among the elderly. The rate of deterioration is much faster in poor than in rich countries, and in some of the richest, satisfaction with health actually *rises* toward the end of life. Thus it appears that one of the benefits of being rich, or at least of living in a rich country, is that wealth slows the ravages of age on health, or at least on satisfaction with health.

While the results of the study are powerful at some level, Deaton cautions that the links between life-satisfaction and life expectancy or HIV prevalence, or even between health-satisfaction and these measures, show too many anomalies to make life-satisfaction a good indicator of health and income combined. For example, HIV prevalence appears to have little or no effect on the fraction of the population reporting dissatisfaction with their health. Indeed, the fraction of Kenyans who are satisfied with their personal health is the same as the fraction of Britons and higher than the fraction of Americans.

Retirement Saving

The next three chapters look at two of the largest asset categories of older households: retirement saving accounts and housing equity. Over the past two decades, personal retirement accounts have replaced defined benefit pension plans as the primary means of retirement saving, and contributions to 401(k)-type plans have expanded dramatically. More than 80 percent of private retirement plan contributions in 2000 and 2001 were to 401(k) and other personal accounts. Housing equity is the most significant nonretirement asset for a majority of households. Together with Social Security wealth, these asset categories represent a large fraction of the resources available to most households at older ages.

In chapter 10, James M. Poterba, Steven F. Venti, and I analyze "The Rise of 401(k) Plans, Lifetime Earnings, and Wealth at Retirement." Because 401(k) plans have not existed for the full careers of currently retiring workers, their impact is becoming more significant with each retiring cohort. The typical 401(k) participant retiring in 2000, for example, contributed only for about seven years. By 2040, many more people will have participated, and they will have contributed for most or all of their working careers. In past work, we have projected the impact of 401(k) growth in aggregate, and on average, across households. For example, if equity returns between 2006 and 2040 are comparable to those observed historically, by 2040 average projected 401(k) assets of all persons age sixty-five will be over six times larger than the maximum level ever achieved by traditional defined-benefit pension plans. If equity returns average 300 basis points below their historical value, we project average 401(k) assets that are 3.7 times as large as the peak value of defined benefits (DB).

While these projections highlight aggregate trends, asset accumulation will vary across households. In this study, we look at how Social Security, 401(k) participation, and other asset accumulation fit together for households with different lifetime earnings and different Social Security wealth accumulations. We focus initially on two broad categories of wealth: (a) dedicated retirement assets, which are made up of Social Security wealth, accrued benefits in traditional pension plans, 401(k) savings, and IRAs and Keogh plans; and (b) undedicated assets, including nonretirement financial savings and housing equity.

We find that while 401(k) participation varies substantially by income, broader measures of retirement assets show a "retirement replacement rate" (inclusive of both Social Security and retirement saving) and a "total saving rate" (including both dedicated and undedicated assets) that varies only moderately by lifetime earnings and by Social Security wealth. Combining projections of 401(k) assets with estimated Social Security wealth, the study finds that the combined rate of growth is surprisingly similar across earnings deciles, and translates to at least a doubling of retirement resources in most earnings and Social Security wealth deciles. The growth rate is lower in the bottom two deciles of lifetime earnings. These various results are indicative of a very dramatic shift in the landscape of financial resources available to retirees in the future.

In Chapter 11, "The Impact of Employer Matching on Savings Plan Participation under Automatic Enrollment," John Beshears, James J. Choi, David Laibson, and Brigitte C. Madrian present the next in a continuing series of studies on the structural features of 401(k) plans. Companies have used a variety of approaches to encourage participation in employer-sponsored savings plans. The most common approach, the provision of an employer matching contribution, is now offered by the vast majority of large firms. Even with a match, however, savings plan participation rates are often surprisingly low, and their effect on participation is found to be relatively small. Automatic enrollment is an alternative mechanism for increasing savings plan participation. Under automatic enrollment, employees are enrolled in their employer's savings plan at a default contribution rate and asset allocation unless they actively make an alternative choice. Relative to the standard opt-in approach, automatic enrollment dramatically increases plan participation, particularly among younger, low-tenure, and lower-income employees.

All of the companies in which automatic enrollment has been studied to date have also offered an employer matching contribution. This raises a question about how effective automatic enrollment would be by itself, without an employer match. The extent to which automatic enrollment's effectiveness relies on the presence of a match is an open question.

The study disentangles the effects of matching and automatic enrollment in two ways. The first is to study a large firm with automatic enrollment that replaced its employer match with a noncontingent employer contribution to the plan, thereby eliminating the incentive that was provided by the match. Among new hires with six months of tenure, savings plan participation rates are found to decrease by, at most, 5 to 6 percentage points after the firm eliminated the employer match. The second approach is to pool the participation data from nine firms, all with automatic enrollment, but with varying matching provisions. The findings from this approach suggest that moving from a typical matching structure (50 percent on the first 6 percent of pay) to no match reduces participation under automatic enrollment by 5 to 11 percentage points. These results lead the authors to conclude that automatic enrollment participation rates are positively related to match generosity, but that the incremental effect is modest. Thus, companies with automatic enrollment need not offer a match in order to achieve broad-based participation.

In chapter 12, we turn our attention from targeted retirement saving to another important asset of older households, their home. In "Housing Price Volatility and Downsizing in Later Life," James Banks, Richard Blundell, Zoë Oldfield, and James P. Smith model several types of housing transitions made at older ages in Britain and the United States. They consider the extent of residential mobility and the extent of downsizing across multiple dimensions, including housing size (number of rooms), housing value, and ownership (as compared with renting). They also look at some of the determinants of mobility, with a particular focus on house price volatility, but also the role of major life events, such as retirement or widowhood. A particular contribution of the chapter is its analysis of a longer time horizon, in which there is more likely to be evidence of downsizing if it exists in the data.

The authors find that on balance, looking over a number of dimensions and over a number of transition intervals, downsizing is an important part of life for older households in both countries, but particularly in the United States. For example, over a decade, almost one in every three American homeowners who were at least fifty years old moved out of their originally owned home. Mobility is also found to be higher among renters. And when people do move, they tend to downsize their housing consumption. This downsizing takes multiple forms, including reductions in the number of rooms per dwelling and the value of the home. Among the explanations offered for lower housing mobility and lower downsizing in Britain, the authors note differences in transactions costs associated with moving in Britain, the nature of bequests and inheritance tax bases, and the role of housing wealth in the means test for long-term care.

A second contribution of the chapter is to assess the role of house price volatility in the mobility decisions of the elderly. In addition to any type of downsizing in housing consumption that may occur, some housing transitions at older ages may reflect an attempt to escape from the risk associated with a highly volatile asset. For example, housing price risk at older ages may encourage relocation to less volatile markets. The study finds suggestive evidence that downsizing is greater when house price volatility is greater, and that American households may moderate house price volatility by moving to markets that are more stable.

Medicare

The last two chapters in the volume look at two of the more significant Medicare policy reforms of the last decade. The first was a part of the Balanced Budget Act of 1997. The second was the implementation of Medicare Part D prescription drug coverage in late 2005.

The 1997 Balanced Budget Act (BBA) was one of the most far-reaching attempts to control Medicare expenditure growth. The changes included direct reductions to the Prospective Payment System, affecting nearly all hospitals that care for Medicare inpatients; cuts in both direct and indirect medical education payments; changes in the formulas for disproportionate share payments; the implementation of prospective payment systems for outpatient hospital care, skilled nursing facilities, and home health agencies; and the creation of Medicare + Choice managed care plans. The BBA also expanded the Medicare transfer policy, which reduces payments for transfers of short-term acute patients to a Skilled Nursing Facility, PPS-exempt facilities, or a home health agency.

Chapter 13, "The Narrowing Dispersion of Medicare Expenditures 1997 to 2005," by Jay Bhattacharya, Alan Garber, and Thomas MaCurdy, investigates how BBA affected Medicare expenditure trends. In the immediate post-BBA period, the most important effects were on inpatient services and home health services, where the intention was unambiguously to reduce Medicare payments. Other features of BBA, such as the introduction of prospective payment for some outpatient services and the creation of Medicare + Choice plans, involved new payment mechanisms with the prospect for long-term expenditure control. The study assesses whether expenditures grew more or less rapidly for high-expenditure Medicare beneficiaries (as compared with people who used few Medicare-covered services) in the period following BBA's implementation. In particular, did it selectively reduce cost growth at the high end, where many of its provisions were targeted?

The study finds that after 1997, the growth in expenditures among the highest-cost users of Medicare-reimbursed care was less than growth among lower-cost users. Thus, the overall dispersion in expenditures fell over time. These findings suggest that the main effects of the BBA were realized as intended. The authors make the point that piecemeal changes to Medicare policy—those that target only some components of Medicare—cannot be assumed to control overall expenditure growth, since substitution of services can offset some of the savings. In the case of the BBA, however, the targeting of high-cost users is likely to have led to a compression of the expenditure distribution and an overall containment of cost growth.

Chapter 14, "Mind the Gap! Consumer Perceptions and Choices of Medicare Part D Prescription Drug Plans," by Florian Heiss, Daniel McFadden, and Joachim Winter, analyzes an Internet-based survey of individuals who became eligible for prescription drug coverage through Medicare Part D. Decision making in Medicare Part D can be complicated, because of the diversity of plan options and plan features, combined with uncertainty about future medical needs. The complexity of the program was a source of concern before its introduction. Thus, the design of the program raises questions about how seniors made a decision about whether to enroll in

Medicare Part D and, if they did enroll, how they chose among the available plan options.

The data collection was done in three waves. The initial survey took place in the week before Medicare Part D enrollment began in November 2005, and focused on respondents' knowledge of the program, their perceptions, and their preferences regarding prescription drug use, cost, and insurance. A key finding from the initial data was that a majority of the Medicare population had at least some knowledge of Part D and intended to enroll. However, those with lower income, less education, and poorer health were less well-informed. After the initial enrollment period closed on May 15, 2006, the same respondents were reinterviewed to learn about the actual Medicare Part D enrollments that had taken place. Widespread enrollment was confirmed (though sizable numbers of older people remained uncovered); consumer opinions about the program were mixed. A year later, respondents were interviewed a third time to learn about their experiences in the first year of the program.

The study in chapter 14 focuses on the decisions made in the initial enrollment period, and the influence on plan choice of previous prescription drug use, health risks, health-related expectations, and subjective factors. It draws on all three waves of survey data. The study finds generally that seniors' choices respond in predictable ways to the incentives provided by their own health status and the plan options available to them. In some circumstances, however, consumers selected inexpensive plans even though more expensive and comprehensive alternatives were actuarially favorable. The model developed in the study also suggests that given the subsidies to the program, as well as the penalties for late enrollment, not enrolling immediately in a plan in 2006 would have been the optimal choice for just 2.5 percent of the sample. Despite these caveats, however, the proportion of individuals who appear not to have made an optimal choice is relatively small.

I

Disability, Work, and Retirement

1

New Age Thinking
Alternative Ways of Measuring Age, Their Relationship to Labor Force Participation, Government Policies, and GDP

John B. Shoven

This chapter is not about what you think it is. It is about how to measure age. I argue that there are better alternatives to the standard measure of years-since-birth. In fact, I claim that public policy would be better if age were more appropriately specified in the law. A particularly simple alternative to years-since-birth would be a measure of age based on mortality risk. Groups whose mortality risk is high would be considered old, those with low mortality risk would be classified as young, and those with the same mortality risk would be considered to be the same age. Another closely related approach would be to measure age from the other end of life, at least in expected terms. That is, remaining life expectancy (RLE) would be the measure of age—those with a short RLE would be considered elderly and those with a long RLE would be considered young. One advantage of the RLE approach is that it is measured in years, units that are widely understood, unlike mortality risk, which is measured in the percentage chance of dying within a year.

Even at a point in time, there are differences between the various ways of measuring age. For instance, RLE and mortality risk would reflect that a man at the conventionally defined age of sixty-five is roughly the same age as a woman of age seventy. The real differences between the proposed mortality-based measures and the conventional years-since-birth measure

John B. Shoven is the Charles R. Schwab Professor of Economics at Stanford University, director of the Stanford Institute for Economic Policy Research, and a research associate of the National Bureau of Economic Research.

The author would like to thank Gopi Shah Goda and Matthew Gunn for discussing these matters with me and helping with the analysis. Also, he would like to thank Erzo Luttmer for his insightful discussion of the paper at the Boulders conference and the other participants in the conference for their ideas and reactions. Victor Fuchs, my long time colleague and friend, was on this tack long before me. The remaining flaws in the logic are all mine.

comes when comparing populations at different points in time, such as comparing the 1965 population with the 2007 population or the projected 2050 population. The different measures will, for instance, give a very different answer to how many elderly people there will be in 2050. Later in the chapter we will look at how these various ways of measuring age would apply to labor force participation and also how different old-age dependency ratios might look under the alternative approaches.

To the best of my knowledge, there is not a large existing literature on alternative ways of measuring age. The paper that contains ideas most similar to mine was written by my Stanford colleague Victor Fuchs (1984). In his paper, Victor discusses using remaining life expectancy as a better measure of age and noted that when Social Security was designed in 1935, the gender-blended remaining life expectancy at age sixty-five was 12.5 years. By 1984, those who had 12.5 years of remaining life expectancy were seventy-two years of age. Victor went on to say that if sixty-five was the appropriate entry age for being categorized as elderly in 1935, then the entry age for that status should have been seventy-two in 1984. Thus, Victor already had the idea of an alternative measure of age and suggested that "nominal ages" could or perhaps should be adjusted to "real ages" based on mortality or remaining life expectancy.

Another paper that is closely related is Cutler and Sheiner (2001). The authors are concerned with the impact of demographic changes on medical spending both in the past and in future projections. They note that for acute care and nursing home care, demand is more a function of remaining life expectancy than it is of age. They also note the high medical costs associated with the last year of life and that, on average, the last year of life has been occurring at older and older ages. They do not quite reach the conclusion that I have—namely, that age itself could be defined as something other than years-since-birth—but their analysis suggests the need for a new measure of age.

In order to get started, figures 1.1 and 1.2 introduce the concept of mortality milestones—the first age at which men and women reach 1, 2, and 4 percent mortality risk. Figure 1.1 shows that in the year 2000, men first reached a mortality risk of 1 percent at age fifty-eight, they first reached a 2 percent mortality risk at age sixty-five, and they reached the 4 percent milestone at age seventy-three. The corresponding ages in 1970 were fifty-one, fifty-nine, and sixty-eight. The figure says that fifty-one-year-olds in 1970 and fifty-eight-year-olds in 2000 had the same mortality risk (1 percent), fifty-nine-year-olds in 1970 and sixty-five-year-olds in 2000 similarly had the same mortality (2 percent), and sixty-eight-year-olds in 1970 had the same mortality risk as seventy-three-year-olds in 2000. In just the thirty years between 1970 and 2000, the age at which 1 percent mortality is reached advanced seven years, the age at which 2 percent mortality risk is reached advanced six years, and the age at which 4 percent is reached advanced five

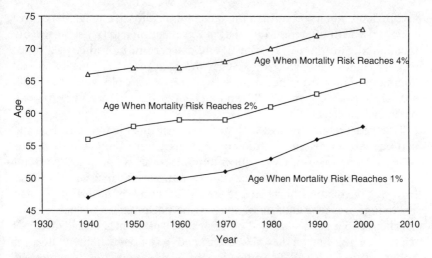

Fig. 1.1   Age of mortality milestones for men, 1940–2000
Note: Sixty-five-year-olds in 2000 had the same mortality risks as fifty-nine-year-olds in 1970.

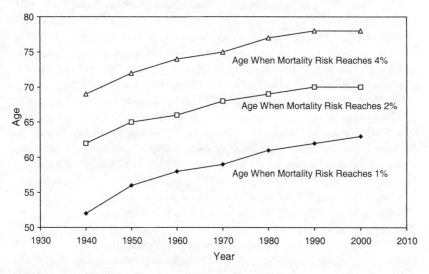

Fig. 1.2   Age of mortality milestones for women, 1940–2000
Note: Sixty-three-year-olds in 2000 had the same mortality risks as fifty-nine-year-olds in 1970.

years. Any way you look at it, there was remarkable progress in age-specific mortality. A mortality-based age system would suggest that fifty-nine-year-old men in 1970 and sixty-five-year-old men in 2000 were the same age.

Figure 1.2 has the corresponding information for women. Two things are immediately apparent. First, women at the same number of years since birth are effectively younger than men of the same conventionally defined age. In 2000, women first reach a 1 percent mortality risk at age sixty-three (compared with fifty-eight for men), a 2 percent mortality risk at seventy (compared with sixty-five for men) and a 4 percent mortality risk at age seventy-eight (compared with seventy-three for men). The mortality risk approach to measuring age would have seventy-year-old women in 2000, sixty-five-year-old men in 2000, and fifty-nine-year-old men in 1970 as all being the same age.

The measurement of age with different measures is not like choosing between measuring temperature on a Fahrenheit or Centigrade scale. The connection between the two temperature measures is linear and constant through time. In a very real sense, it does not matter which scale you use. However, the relationships between the different ways of measuring human age change over time and some apparently important phenomenon are primarily due to a particular method of age measurement. For instance, it is reasonably well-known that Medicare spends more on men than it does on women of the same age. The difference (being of the order of 30 percent) is not small. But, this result is a function of how age is measured. Medicare spends roughly the same amount on men and women with the same mortality risk or with the same remaining life expectancy (Shoven 2004). Of course, the fact that reconciles these observations is that seventy-five-year-old women are younger than seventy-five-year-old men, at least according to an age system based on mortality risk or remaining life expectancy.

Figures 1.1 and 1.2 also show that the rate of mortality progress was somewhat slower for women than for men, at least for the last thirty years of the twentieth century. The age at which women first reach a 1 percent mortality risk went up four years between 1970 and 2000 (versus seven years for men), the age at which mortality risk reaches 2 percent advanced two years for women (versus six for men) and the age where 4 percent mortality is "achieved" advanced three years for women (versus five years for men).

Figures 1.3 and 1.4 illustrate the same phenomenon slightly differently. They show mortality risk by years-since-birth for men and women in 1965 and 2005. Once again, we see that there was more mortality progress for men than women over this period. One way to look at it is the amount you would have to shift the 1965 curve to the right in order for it to overlap the 2005 curve. If you do it so that the curves match at roughly 3.5 percent for men (about at age sixty-five in 1965), then the required shift is about seven years. This is similar to the fact we saw in figure 1.1, but here we learn that seventy-two-year-old men in 2005 had about the same mortality risk as sixty-five-year-olds in 1965. The mortality curve for women would need to shift to the right far less to coincide between 1965 and 2005. The mortality risk of sixty-five-year-old women in 1965 was about 1.75 percent, roughly the same as sixty-nine-year-old women in 2005. So, at these ages we see that men in 2005 are effectively seven years younger than someone of the same age in 1965, whereas women are effectively about four years younger.

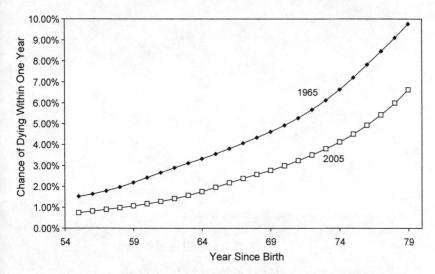

Fig. 1.3   Male mortality risk by age in 1965 and 2005, age fifty-five through seventy-nine

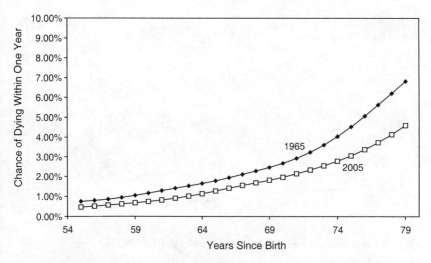

Fig. 1.4   Female mortality by age in 1965 and 2005, age fifty-five through seventy-nine

There are plenty of other demographic statistics we could look at regarding the measurement of age, but I will simply present one more relationship, the relationship between remaining life expectancy and mortality risk for men and women. The data are plotted in figures 1.5 and 1.6. You might have thought that the relationship between mortality risk and remaining life expectancy would be pretty stable across time (I did), since they are

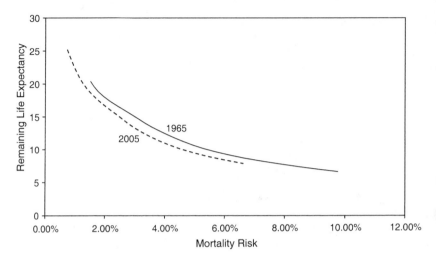

Fig. 1.5   **Remaining life expectancy by mortality risk for males**

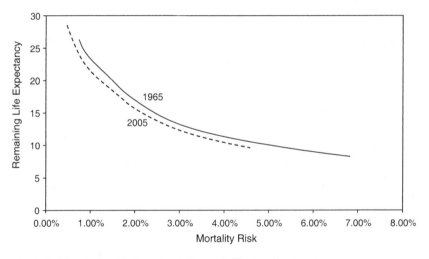

Fig. 1.6   **Remaining life expectancy by mortality risk for females**

alternative mortality-related measures of age. However, the figures show that the relationship has changed considerably in the forty years between 1965 and 2005. The basic pattern has a positive interpretation. The charts are drawn for people between age fifty-five and seventy-nine, just like for figures 1.3 and 1.4. At least for this age range, for any given remaining life expectancy, people had a lower mortality risk in 2005 than they did in 1965. For instance, men with a fifteen-year remaining life expectancy in 1965 had about a 3.00 mortality risk, whereas such a man in 2005 had about a 2.45

percent mortality risk. For women with fifteen years of expected remaining life, the corresponding mortality risks were 2.45 percent in 1965 and 2.15 percent in 2005. At least to me, this suggests that even with the same remaining life expectancy, people are healthier in 2005 than they were in 1965. This is consistent with a mild squaring of the survival curves and a concentration of high mortality in the last years of life.

1.1   How Much Aging Will Occur in the U.S. Population between Now and 2050?

There probably is as much attention paid to the anticipated aging of the U.S. population and how the economy will adjust to it as any demographic fact. Some of the predictions of the aging of the population are simply due to the use of the conventional years-since-birth measure of age. Consider two alternative definitions of who is elderly in the population, those who are currently sixty-five or older, and those who have a mortality risk of 1.5 percent or worse. Today, at least on a gender blended basis, the two definitions of elderly are equivalent, since the average mortality risk faced by sixty-five-year-olds is 1.5 percent. However, going forward being sixty-five and over and having a mortality risk of 1.5 percent and over will not be equivalent. Figure 1.7 tells the story. The Census Department predicts that the sixty-five and over population will increase from about 12.5 percent of the population today to about 20.5 percent between 2035 to 2050. In 2050, the Census predicts that the percent of the population that is elderly will continue to gradually increase. On the other hand, the percent of the population with mortality risks higher than 1.5 percent (currently also 12.5

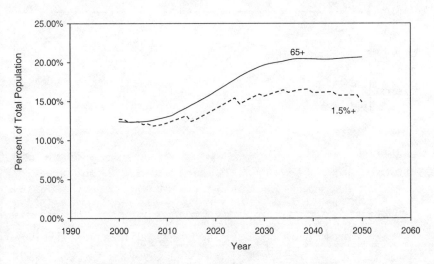

Fig. 1.7   Elderly as a percent of the U.S. population, 2000 to 2050

percent of the population) never gets above 16.5 percent and is projected to be just slightly below 15 percent and declining by 2050. With the sixty-five and over criterion, the fraction of the population that is classified as elderly is projected to grow by approximately 66 percent by 2050; whereas with the 1.5 percent and above mortality criterion, the fraction of the population classified as elderly is projected to grow by only 20 percent. The point is the great aging of our society is partly a straightforward consequence of how we measure age. Another interpretation of figure 1.7 is that by 2050 there will be approximately 6 percent of the population that are over sixty-five years of age but who are young enough to have a mortality risk of less than 1.5 percent. By the standard criterion used today they would be classified as elderly but by any mortality-based definition of who is elderly they would not. This naturally leads to the topic of labor force participation by age.

1.2   Labor Force Participation

There have been significant changes in labor force participation by age over the past forty years. I am going to concentrate on male labor force participation because the dramatic increase of women in the workforce masks to some degree what is going on in the retirement behavior of women. The conventional graph of male labor force participation by age is shown in figure 1.8. There was a dramatic decrease in labor force participation by age between 1965 and 1985 with the labor force participation at age sixty-two falling from 79 percent to 51 percent and at age sixty-five falling from 56 percent to 30 percent. The change between 1985 and 2005 was less dramatic, with labor force falling slightly from ages fifty-five to sixty-one, but rising

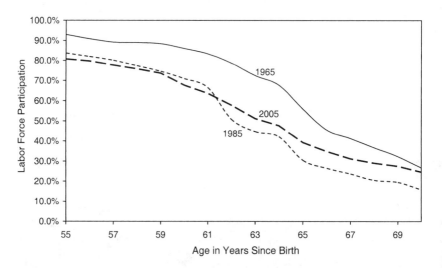

Fig. 1.8   Male labor force participation by age, fifty-five to seventy

somewhat from sixty-two through seventy. On average, men were retiring almost three years earlier in 2005 than they were in 1965.

If we look at male labor force participation by age with one of the two mortality-based definitions of age, we get a somewhat different picture. Figures 1.9 and 1.10 plot male labor force participation by mortality risk and by remaining life expectancy, respectively. First, the figures show that with either mortality-based age measure, the fact that men are working more at older ages essentially disappears. In figure 1.9, we see that men of a given

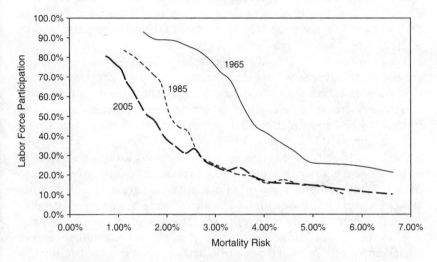

Fig. 1.9   Male labor force participation by mortality risk

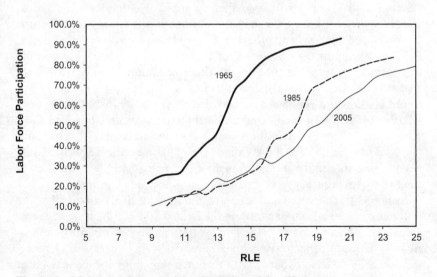

Fig. 1.10   Male labor force participation by remaining life expectancy

mortality risk have dramatically lower labor force participation in 2005 than in 1965, and that the shift from 1985 to 2005 was generally toward lower labor force participation. Figure 1.10 perhaps is the most revealing. While the conventional chart (figure 1.8) shows that men are retiring two-and-a-half to three years earlier than they did in 1965, figure 1.10 displays the more interesting fact that men are living roughly six years longer in retirement than they did in 1965. The six-year figure comes from noting that labor force participation was 50 percent in 1965 for men with a RLE of thirteen years, but in 2005 it was 50 percent for men with a RLE of nineteen years. Those that exit the labor force relatively early are leaving with even more than six extra years of remaining life relative to their counterparts in 1965, whereas those that exit relatively late are leaving with an extra five years of life expectancy. The overall average is that the RLE of male retirees increased six years over the forty years between 1965 and 2005 for an overall increase in the expected length of male retirement of nearly 50 percent. This percentage increase in the length of male retirement is right in the data, but it is not a well-known fact. Such a dramatic increase in the length of the average retirement has quite a bit to do with the financial strains faced by Social Security and defined benefit pension plans. Providing for a nineteen- or twenty-year retirement with a thirty-five- or forty-year career is much more difficult than providing for a thirteen-year retirement. Unless retirement ages begin to adjust with RLE, today's young people could spend 40 percent of their adult life out of the workforce.

All of the increase in life expectancy of adult men in the twentieth century was taken as retirement and not work. The expected length of retirement of men increased from approximately two years in 1900 to about nineteen years in 2000. It appears to be financially impossible that the same allocation of increased life expectancy to continue in the twenty-first century. However, pension laws and programs feature lots of conventionally defined ages that have not been adjusted for improvements in mortality and life expectancy. For instance, the 59.5 age after which money can be withdrawn from tax deferred retirement accounts has not changed since it was introduced decades ago. Similarly, the age of early eligibility for Social Security (sixty-two), the age of Medicare entitlement (sixty-five), and the age that one must begin withdrawing from tax-deferred saving accounts (70.5) have not changed in at least the past forty years, if ever. These critical ages will likely need to be adjusted if we expect much of the increase in life expectancy in the twenty-first century to be devoted to work instead of retirement.

In a book I wrote with George Shultz (Shultz et al. 2008), we calculate the difference in the total labor supply in the United States in 2050 between two scenarios: (a) people retire in the same pattern as they do today by conventionally defined ages, and (b) people retire with the same lengths of retirement as they do today; that is, with the same remaining life expectancy at the time of retirement. Obviously, the difference between retiring at the same ages and retiring with the same retirement lengths depends on the amount of mortality progress between now and 2050. If we use the official Census forecast for mortality improvement, then the total labor supply (in aggregate hours of work) would be about 9.6 percent higher if labor force participation stayed constant relative to remaining life expectancy (that is, the 2050 graph in figure 1.10 looks like the 2005 one) than it would be if labor force participation stays constant in terms of age (if the 2050 curve in figure 1.8 were to look like the 2005 one). We do not think of this 9.6 percent number as precisely estimated by any means—it might be 8 percent or it might be 10 percent. On the other hand, 9.6 percent is our best estimate and we think that an increase in the size of the labor force by such a magnitude is rather enormous. The estimate takes account not only the change in the labor force participation by age under the two scenarios, but also takes account of the number of hours worked per week at different stages of the life cycle. One way to think about it is that in one scenario, all labor force behavior (both work week and retirement) remains constant as a function of years since birth between now and 2050 and in the other scenario, all labor force behavior remains constant as a function of age. But in the second scenario, age is defined as remaining life expectancy. A simple Cobb-Douglas aggregate production function would suggest that 9.6 percent more labor would result in about 7 percent more gross domestic product (GDP), even if the extra labor was not accompanied with a larger capital stock. If investment were correspondingly higher so that the capital stock was also 9.6 percent higher in 2050 under the second scenario, then GDP could also be 9.6 percent higher. These figures of an extra 7 to 10 percent of GDP are worth pursuing, particularly given the forecasts of how much more we will be spending as a society on health care by 2050. The question is how to encourage people to balance work and retirement relative to their age and guide them on how to think of age.

There are lots of policies within Social Security, Medicare, and the tax law that actually discourage long careers. In a paper coauthored with Gopi Shah Goda and Sita Nataraj (2007), I analyzed three changes in Social Security that would level the playing field with respect to career length. Currently, Social Security counts only the highest thirty-five years of indexed earnings in computing the initial monthly benefit for someone commencing benefits. With each year of work for the first thirty-five years, the year's earnings replace a zero in the benefit calculation. Once an individual has worked for thirty-five years, additional years either replace earlier nonzero indexed earnings or they do not count at all, because they are lower than the previous best thirty-five. In all cases, the thirty-sixth, thirty-seventh, and thirty-eight years (etc.) count far less than the thirty-third, thirty-fourth, and thirty-fifth years of work. The modal age at which men reach thirty-five years of covered service in Social Security is fifty-two. That is an incredibly young age to reduce or eliminate the connection between additional work and contributions and higher benefits. So, one possible reform would be to raise the thirty-five years that go into the benefit formula to forty years and then index the number of years for improvements in life expectancy. A second reform would be to create a new category of workers, those that are "paid up" in terms of Social Security and Medicare contributions. After completing the years that count (forty under reform one plus whatever increase comes from further increases in life expectancy), workers would achieve this new paid-up status. They would be exempt from all payroll taxes if they choose to work further. Today, most of these workers face a pure tax with no increase in benefits to offset the additional payroll taxes that they face for working. Under this reform, they would neither pay taxes nor improve their benefits from further work. The third reform we examined was to have all of the years that count (forty), count the same. Currently, short careers are favored relative to long careers. For instance, someone who works for seventeen-and-a-half years instead of thirty-five years at the same real indexed wage rate will get significantly more than half the benefits of the full career. Social Security uses the same formula to achieve progressivity that it uses to treat people with different career lengths. Effectively, those with less than full careers are treated as if they are lower income and benefit from the progressivity of the system. There is a relatively simple fix for confounding these two effects. Progressivity can be set in terms of the average salary earned over the years worked. If one works a full career (thirty-five years under current law, forty under the first reform we examine), then the progressive formula would be used to calculate monthly benefits. However, if one works less than a full career, benefits would be reduced proportionately. A twenty-year career would generate half of the benefits of a forty-year career under the proposed reform. All of these proposals could be implemented in such a way as to preserve average benefits at today's levels.

The impact of the three proposals would be a rather dramatic change in the net payroll tax from continued work. The current law has long-career people facing a 10.4 percent payroll tax, whereas short career people actually face a Social Security wage subsidy. What is going on is that Social Security is a net subsidy (the extra benefits are worth more than the extra payroll taxes) as long as you remain on the first segment (the 90 percent segment) of the primary insurance amount-average indexed monthly earnings (PIA-AIME) formula. When you work enough to "graduate" onto the second segment of the PIA formula (the 32 percent section), you face an immediate 10 percentage point jump in marginal tax rates. Those relatively high income people who work long careers and "graduate" to the third segment of the PIA formula (the 15 percent segment) face yet another 3 percent jump in marginal tax rates. Finally, once the additional work stops qualifying in the "high 35" aspect of the PIA formula, the payroll tax becomes simply a tax with no offsetting benefit increases. All of these facts are shown on the left-hand graph in figure 1.11. Our concern is that those with long careers face high marginal tax rates while those with short careers are subsidized. The three relatively simple reforms that we examine change everything in terms of work incentives, as shown on the right-hand side of the graph. All of the jumps are eliminated as is the predominate fact of increasing marginal tax rates for those with longer careers. To us, it makes sense to try to level the playing field for those with long careers.

Figure 1.12 is another way to look at the three reforms. It shows the benefit

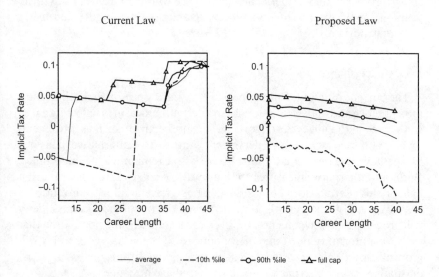

Fig. 1.11   Current law; proposed law

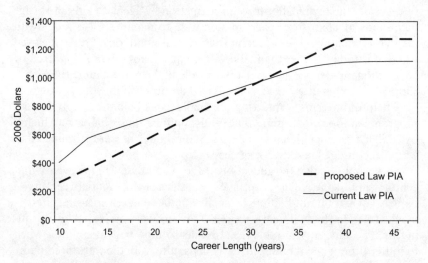

Fig. 1.12   Monthly primary insurance amount under current and proposed law, average income earner

levels for a person with average earnings for different career lengths under current law and under the three alternative benefit rules. What should be clear is that under the revised rules, each of the first forty years has the same marginal improvement of benefits. The current system has lower and declining marginal benefits (the flat region corresponds to the 32 percent bracket in the PIA formula) from lengthening a career. The net impact of the three rule changes would be to offer lower benefits for those with careers shorter than thirty years and higher benefits for those who work longer than thirty years. Given the improvements in life expectancy, these changes in incentives seem appropriate.

1.3   Conclusion

The current practice of measuring age as years-since-birth, both in common practice and in the law, rather than alternative measures reflecting a person's stage in the life cycle, distorts important behavior such as retirement, saving, and the discussion of dependency ratios. Two alternative measures of age have been explored, mortality risk and remaining life expectancy. With these alternative measures, the huge wave of elderly forecast for the first half of this century does not look like a huge wave at all. By conventional sixty-five and over standards, the fraction of the population that is elderly will grow by about 66 percent. However, the fraction of the population that is above a mortality rate that corresponds to sixty-five and over today will grow by only 20 percent. Needless to say, the aging of the society is a lot less dramatic with the alternative mortality-based age measures.

In a separate application of age measurement, I examined the consequences of stabilizing labor force participation by age with alternative age definitions. If labor force participation were to remain as it is today with respect to remaining life expectancy (i.e., if the length of retirement stayed where it is today) rather than labor force participation remaining fixed by conventionally-defined age, then there would be 9.6 percent more total labor supply by 2050 in the United States. This additional labor supply would be very helpful in terms of meeting the challenges of financing entitlement programs, among other things. The GDP might be almost 10 percent higher by 2050 if retirement lengths stabilize. Several policies were examined that would encourage longer work careers.

It is my opinion that the allocation of the extra lifetime in the twenty-first century cannot and will not continue the pattern of the twentieth century— namely, all extra adult lifetime is taken as retirement. Even average retirement ages today look like early retirement when age is measured by remaining life expectancy or mortality risk. In order to allow people to choose when to retire without encouraging an early departure from the workforce, many ages in the laws should be indexed for demographic changes. It is time to consider a new way to measure age.

References

Cutler, D. M., and L. Sheiner. 2001. Demographics and medical care spending: Standard and non-standard effects. In *Demographic change and fiscal policy,* ed. A. Auerbach and R. Lee, 253–91. Cambridge: Cambridge University Press.

Fuchs, V. R. 1984. "Though much is taken": Reflections on aging, health, and medical care. *The Milbank Memorial Fund Quarterly: Health and Society, Special Issue, Financing Medicare: Explorations in Controlling Costs and Raising Revenues* 62 (2): 142–66.

Goda, G. S., J. B. Shoven, and S. N. Slavov. 2007. Removing the disincentives for long careers in Social Security. NBER Working Paper no. 13110. Cambridge, MA: National Bureau of Economic Research, May.

Shoven, J. B. 2004. The impact of major improvement in life expectancy on the financing of Social Security, Medicare, and Medicaid. In *Coping with Methuselah: The impact of molecular biology on medicine and society,* ed. H. J. Aaron and W. B. Schwartz, 166–97. Washington, DC: The Brookings Institution.

Shultz, G. P., and J. B. Shoven, with M. Gunn and G. Shah Goda. 2008. *A citizen's guide to Social Security and health care reform.* New York: W.W. Norton & Company.

Comment   Erzo F. P. Luttmer

The key contribution of this chapter is a straightforward but profound insight. For policies that are age dependent because functioning depends on age, years-since-birth is generally not the best measure of age. For example, we might want to set the retirement age at an age where workers' health on average becomes too poor to reasonably expect work or where a worker has a certain number of remaining years to live. The chronological age at which this occurs is generally not constant over time or across groups. Thus, rather than defining retirement age as years-since-birth, this chapter argues it should depend on a "new age" measure such as mortality risk or remaining life expectancy. More generally, this chapter argues that in many policy settings the relevant measure of age is not chronological age but a measure of age that captures an individual's functioning. In short, it is a thought-provoking chapter that challenges the reader to think at a more conceptual level about what aging really means, rather than narrowly counting the years since birth.

The chapter also discusses a proposal to remove the incentives for early retirement in the Social Security system. This is a sensible proposal, but it is somewhat disconnected from the rest of the chapter because most of the substantive elements of this proposal have little to do with the switch

Erzo F. P. Luttmer is an associate professor of economics at the Kennedy School of Government, Harvard University, and a faculty research fellow at the National Bureau of Economic Research.

from chronological age to a "new age" measure such as the remaining life expectancy. Because the proposal has been more thoroughly presented and analyzed in Goda, Shoven, and Slavov (2009) and has been discussed by me in that same volume, I will not discuss it further here.

Shoven motivates the case for new age measures by noting the tremendous decreases in age-specific mortality between 1970 and 2000. A fifty-nine-year-old male in 1970 had roughly the same mortality risk as a sixty-five-year-old male in 2000. Thus, using mortality risk as a measure of age, a fifty-nine-year-old male in 1970 was as old as a sixty-five-year-old in 2000. Thus, using mortality risk as a measure of age, men have effectively become six years younger in the span of three decades. Women also experienced a substantive decrease in age-specific mortality, and the age-specific mortality is much lower for women than for men. If age is measured by age-specific mortality, a seventy-year-old female in 2000 is as old as a sixty-five-year-old male.

These decreases in the effective age are remarkably insensitive to the new age measure chosen. Using an alternative measure of mortality risk, Cutler, Liebman, and Smyth (2006) find that a sixty-eight-year-old person in 2000 has effectively the same age as a sixty-two-year-old individual in 1960. Furthermore, a sixty-seven-year-old in 2000 has the same remaining life expectancy as a sixty-two-year old in 1960. In other words, also for these alternative measures, individuals have effectively become about 1.5 years younger per decade in the last four decades. One might be concerned that a large fraction of the age-specific mortality reductions can be attributed to medical interventions keeping people in very poor health alive. If this were the case, we would observe decreases in age-specific health. In fact, the opposite appears to be happening. Cutler, Liebman, and Smyth (2006) show that, conditional on age, both subjective and objective indicators of health have increased substantially over the last couple of decades. In other words, people not only live longer, but are also healthy longer.

The increases in life expectancy, however, are unequally distributed. Meara, Richards, and Cutler (2008) show that between 1990 and 2000, the life expectancy at age twenty-five of those with any college increased by about 1.6 years while the life expectancy of those with a high school degree or less increased by less than a month. This pattern also occurs in each of the four race-by-gender groups. Within each group, the life expectancy at age twenty-five of those with at least some college increased significantly more than that of those with a high school degree or less. Thus, while the aggregate reductions in age-specific mortality may indicate that the Social Security retirement age could be increased, such an increase would harm the less educated groups, who have not experienced reductions in age-specific mortality.

The chapter makes a compelling case that it is worthwhile to think about age in terms of mortality risk or remaining life expectancy, especially in light of the large changes in age-specific mortality risk in the last several decades.

The chapter also claims that policy would be better if age were measured by a new age measure such as mortality risk or remaining life expectancy. It would be worthwhile to develop the underpinnings of this claim. In principle, the same policy can be implemented independently of how age is measured. For example, the Personal-Security Accounts (PSA) plan (1994 to 1996 advisory council on Social Security [SS]) set the rise in the retirement age (in years-since-birth) such that the ratio of years in retirement to years working remained constant. Here the proposed adjustment was automatic, but in principle the adjustments could also be made periodically by the policymakers. Shoven's claim that policy would be better if based on a new age measure thus rests on the assumption that in practice, policymakers seldom make such adjustments. This assumption seems reasonable, but it would be good to explore what underpins it. What is the model of the political process that makes political change easier with the new measure of age than with chronological age? Even if change is easier with the new age measure, does it imply that the policy would be closer to the optimal policy?

Two major implementation issues need to be resolved in order to base policy on a new age measure. First, new age measures are not observed at the individual level—we do not observe an individual's true mortality risk or true remaining life expectancy. Instead, we estimate these variables conditional on chronological age and, possibly, other demographics. On which of the other demographics, if any, should the new age measure be conditioned? Not conditioning on any other demographic variable would lead to rather imprecisely estimated new age measures given the large differences in mortality and longevity by race, gender, and education.[1] Even accepting such level differences, the differences in trends in the new age measures by demographic group could have politically sensitive impacts. For example, an increase in retirement age linked to average increases in life expectancy would reduce the absolute number of years of retirement benefits for those groups, such as those with a high school education or less, that have not experienced an increase in life expectancy. Conditioning on demographics creates a more accurate estimate of the new age measure but also raises issues. Even though everyone would be eligible for the policy at the same level of the new age measure (e.g., a given remaining life expectancy), eligibility in terms of chronological age would depend on the conditioning demographics. Would it be acceptable to have the chronological retirement age depend on conditioning demographics such as gender, race, or educa-

1. The differences in life expectancy across demographic groups are very large. For example, Meara, Richards, and Cutler (2008) document that life expectancy at age twenty-five is roughly five years higher for women than for men, five years higher for whites than for blacks, and five years higher for those with some college or more than for those with a high school degree or less. Moreover, these effects are roughly additive. Thus, while a black male with a high school degree or less has a remaining life expectancy of forty-two years at age twenty-five, a white female with some college or more has a remaining life expectancy of fifty-nine years.

tion? Another possibility is to try to get market-based estimates of the new age measure. For example, the government could solicit bids for annuity or life insurance contracts for each individual (and purchase a fraction of these contracts to make the bids incentive compatible). The winning bid price of the contract for a given individual would allow one to calculate the market-based mortality or longevity expectation for that individual. This expectation would implicitly be based on all observable individual-specific characteristics.

Second, it needs to be decided when an individual's new age is estimated. Again, consider the example of eligibility for Social Security benefits being determined by an individual reaching a given remaining life expectancy, say fifteen years. The estimate of remaining life expectancy may change over time. For example, when the individual has a chronological age of twenty-five, we might estimate that at age sixty-nine the individual will have a remaining life expectancy of fifteen years. However, due to changing mortality patterns over time, at age sixty, the estimate of the age at which the remaining life expectancy is fifteen years may have increased to seventy-three years. For planning purposes, it is useful to know one's retirement eligibility in terms of chronological age. Thus, when would the individual learn his chronological retirement age? This involves a trade-off between the benefit of having an accurate measure of remaining life expectancy (the case for informing the individual relatively late) and the benefit of giving the individual more time to plan (the case for informing the individual relatively early).

Finally, it strikes me that using a new age measure rather than chronological age is fundamentally about fairness rather than efficiency. For example, a new age measure does not give much guidance about what the efficient retirement age is, or even how the efficient retirement age changes. However, basing policy on a new age measure rather than chronological age changes which individuals are treated similarly (because those who share the same new age do not generally share the same chronological age). Thus, the choice between basing policy on new age versus chronological age has large equity implications across generations and, if new age measures are conditioned on demographics, within generations.

In conclusion, Shoven makes a compelling case that we should think about aging in terms of measures of functioning (such as mortality risk or remaining life expectancy) rather than simply chronological age. This is important because the remarkable increase in life expectancy indeed requires a reevaluation of policies defined in terms of chronological age. Similarly, the chapter raises the question of the equity of policies based on chronological age given the tremendous disparities in new age measures across population groups of the same age. Since new age measures offer limited guidance on the optimal level of a policy itself, their greatest contribution is that they give guidance on the fairness of policies. The implementation of new age measures is harder than chronological age, but the implementation issues do not seem insurmountable.

References

Cutler, D. M., J. B. Liebman, and S. Smyth. 2006. How fast should the Social Security eligibility age rise? Harvard University. Unpublished Manuscript.

Goda, G. S., J. B. Shoven, and S. N. Slavov. 2009. Removing the disincentives in Social Security for long careers. In *Social Security policy in a changing environment,* ed. J. R. Brown, J. B. Liebman, and D. A. Wise, 21–38. Chicago: University of Chicago Press.

Meara, E., S. Richards, and D. M. Cutler. 2008. The gap gets bigger: Changes in mortality and life expectancy, by education, 1981–2000. *Health Affairs* 27 (2): 350–60.

Work Disability
The Effects of Demography,
Health, and Disability Insurance

Axel Börsch-Supan

2.1 Introduction

Disability insurance—the insurance against the loss of the ability to work—is a substantial part of public social expenditures and an important part of the social safety net of all developed countries. Like almost all elements of modern social security systems, disability insurance faces a trade-off. On the one hand, disability insurance is a welcome and necessary part of the social safety net, as it prevents income losses for those who lose their ability to work before the normal retirement age. On the other hand, disability insurance may be misused to serve as an early retirement route even if the normal ability to work is not affected at all.

Understanding the trade-off between social safety provision and its misuse is important for the design of a modern social security system that maximizes social safety provision under increasingly tight financial budget constraints (Aarts, Burkhauser, and de Jong 1996). The aim of this chapter is to use the newly collected SHARE data (the Survey of Health, Aging, and

Axel Börsch-Supan is a professor of economics at the University of Mannheim, director of the Mannheim Research Institute for the Economics of Aging, and a research associate of the National Bureau of Economic Research.

I am grateful to Stephanie Stuck for generating the SHARE data extract, to Fabian Terner for merging ELSA and HRS data to it, and to Christian Goldammer who collected additional institutional data and did an extraordinary job as research assistant. I thank Angus Deaton, Dana Goldman, Martin Prince, Susann Rohwedder, David Weir, and Bob Willis for their helpful comments on previous versions. Financial support by the Deutsche Forschungsgemeinschaft, the Land of Baden Württemberg, the Gesamtverband der deutschen Versicherungswirtschaft, and the National Institute on Aging through grant 5 P01 AG022481-04 are gratefully acknowledged. The findings and conclusions expressed are solely those of the author and do not represent the views of any agency of the German and U.S. Governments, the NBER, the RAND Corporation, or any other sponsor.

Retirement in Europe) together with data from its sister surveys in England (ELSA, the English Longitudinal Study on Aging) and the United States (HRS, the Health and Retirement Study) to shed light on this trade-off. A starting point for this chapter is the striking variation of the expenditures on disability insurance across European countries and the United States (see figure 2.1). This and the two following figures are based on the official figures provided by the European Union, collected as part of the European System of Integrated Social Protection Statistics, which employ a harmonized definition of disability insurance. The data for the United States in figures 2.1 and 2.2 are taken from the Organization for Economic Cooperation and Development (OECD 2003) and uses a comparable definition. Unfortunately, it is only available for 1999.

While the EU15 countries (i.e., the fifteen countries that formed the European Union before its enlargement in 2005) spend, on average, about 8 percent of their social expenditures on disability insurance, it is much higher—about 14 percent—in the Scandinavian countries and also higher in the two Anglo-Saxon countries (about 10 percent in the United Kingdom and the United States). In turn, some countries, such as France, Greece, and Ireland, spend only about 5 percent.

Figure 2.2 shows that this variation is not a matter of rich and poor countries: the order of countries and the range is about the same when correcting for gross domestic product (GDP) differences across countries. The only substantial change is the United States. Since U.S. total social expenditures are about half of what they are in Europe, disability insurance expenditures as percentage of GDP are much smaller in the United States than the share of disability insurance in social expenditures.

Absolute expenditures have risen in all EU15 countries (see figure 2.3). The pattern over time, however, is quite different across countries. Especially Sweden and Denmark exhibit a sharp increase since about the year 2000, while the Netherlands and Finland have about stabilized their very large expenditures on disability insurance until the mid-1990s.

The range of per capital expenditures is enormous, even after correcting for purchasing power differences within the European Union.[1] Sweden and Denmark spend four to five times more on disability insurance than France and the Mediterranean countries. The U.S. spending corresponds to 89 percent of the EU15 average.

The remainder of the chapter is devoted to isolating the causes underlying the large cross-national variation of disability insurance expenditures and the different expenditure patterns over time visible in figures 2.1 through 2.3.

Three causes are commonly mentioned to explain the large variation: demographics, health, and institutions. First, while all European countries are aging, the extent of population varies considerably. Hence, the first

---

1. This correction includes differential purchasing power in the euro zone.

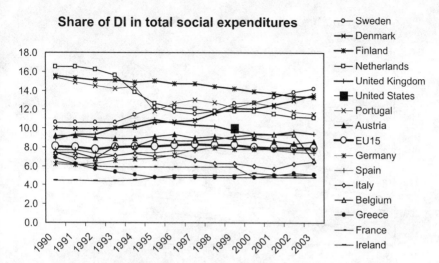

Fig. 2.1   Share of disability insurance expenditures in total expenditures (percentages)
Source: Eurostat Data Archive 2005 and OECD 2003.

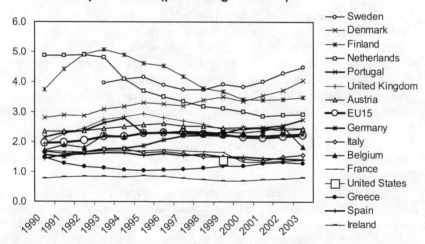

Fig. 2.2   Disability insurance expenditures as percent of GDP (percentages)
Source: Eurostat Data Archive 2005 and OECD 2003.

explanation claims that a country with an older population also has a higher prevalence of disability insurance uptake. A second potential cause for the cross-national variation is international variation in health status. One might hypothesize that in countries that have lower physical and mental health, disability insurance is taken up more frequently than in countries with better health status.

DI Expenditures (Euro per capita, PPP)

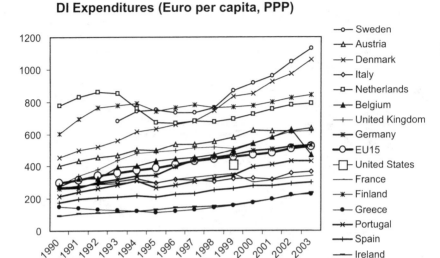

Fig. 2.3   **Disability insurance expenditures per capita (Euro, purchasing power parity)**
Source: Eurostat Data Archive 2005.

Third, recent studies such as the string of international comparisons by Gruber and Wise (1999, 2004, and 2005) and the OECD study by Blöndal and Scarpetta (1998), based on the Gruber and Wise (1999) methodology, have shown that public old-age pension systems exert large incentive effects which, according to each country's legislation, significantly increase the uptake of early retirement provisions. Similar incentive effects may also arise from disability insurance. Figure 2.4 may indicate that this is the case. It shows early and normal eligibility age for public old-age pension, and the actual average age of withdrawal from the labor force. Some countries have an average withdrawal age that is considerably lower than the earliest eligibility age for old-age pensions. Because few people can afford to retire without public retirement income, disability insurance or other transfer income may fill the gap in these countries. Particular striking examples are Austria, Belgium, and France, where the average withdrawal age is younger than age sixty. But also in Denmark and the United Kingdom, countries with a generally much higher retirement age, the average withdrawal age is below the earliest eligibility age for old-age pensions.

The chapter proceeds as follows. Section 2.2 introduces the Survey of Health, Aging, and Retirement in Europe (SHARE) and describes how we merged comparable data from the English Longitudinal Study on Aging (ELSA) and the U.S. Health and Retirement Study (HRS). The section ends with a set of descriptive statistics characterizing our sample.

The richness of these microdata permits us to estimate regressions that

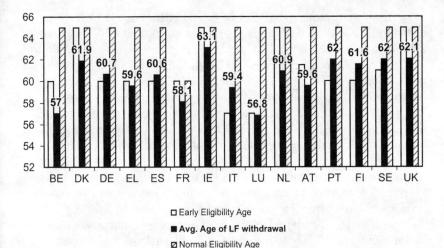

□ Early Eligibility Age

■ Avg. Age of LF withdrawal

▨ Normal Eligibility Age

Fig. 2.4   Retirement age in Europe
Source: European Commission (2004).

relate the uptake of disability insurance to demographic and health characteristics of the respondents in these surveys. Section 2.3 reports the result of these regressions, and section 2.4 applies them to a counterfactual exercise: what would disability uptake rates look like if there were no demographic and health-related differences among the twelve European countries and the United States in our sample? As it turns out, demographic and health-related differences across countries do not explain much of the cross-national variation in disability enrolment rates.

Section 2.5 therefore turns to the institutional details of the disability schemes and regresses disability insurance enrollment on a set of institutional variables derived from recent OECD work. Our main result is that more than 75 percent of the cross-national variation can be explained by a parsimonious set of a few variables describing the generosity of, and the ease of access to, disability insurance. Section 2.6 concludes.

2.2   The Data: SHARE, ELSA, and HRS

The SHARE is modeled closely after the U.S. HRS (see Juster and Suzman 1995)—the first survey of this kind—and the ELSA (see Marmot et al. 2003), which followed the lead by HRS. Researchers from HRS and ELSA have been participating in the design process of SHARE at all stages. About two-thirds of the variables in SHARE are identical to variables in ELSA and HRS, and most of the remainder is closely comparable, so one can map these variables into each other. The longitudinal sequence of waves is synchronized among SHARE, ELSA, and HRS. The SHARE started in 2004 and 2005 when HRS already had five waves, and ELSA started the first reinterview. This is the data on which this chapter is based. In 2006 and 2007 HRS collected its sixth wave, ELSA the third, and SHARE the second wave of data.

The SHARE, HRS, and ELSA are truly multidisciplinary surveys. Variables include health variables (e.g., self-reported health, physical functioning, cognitive functioning, physical measures such as grip strength and walking speed, health behavior, use of health care facilities); psychological variables (e.g., psychological health, well-being, life satisfaction); economic variables (e.g., current work activity, job characteristics, opportunities to work past retirement age, employment history, pension rights, sources and composition of current income, wealth and consumption, housing, education); and social support variables (e.g., assistance within families, transfers of income and assets, social networks, volunteer activities, time use).

The SHARE, as opposed to HRS and ELSA, has one additional dimension. Unlike these one-country surveys, SHARE is ex-ante harmonized cross-national. The first wave in 2004 involved eleven countries, representing Europe's economic, social, institutional, and cultural diversity from Scandinavia (Denmark, Sweden) across Western and Central Europe (Austria, Germany, France, Belgium, the Netherlands, Switzerland) to the Mediterranean (Greece, Italy, Spain). In 2006, additional data came from the Czech Republic, Ireland, Israel, and Poland. The SHARE is the first European data set to combine extensive cross-national information on socioeconomic status, health, and family relationships of the elderly population.

This chapter uses the first release of the SHARE baseline data. It contains 22,777 individuals age fifty and older (including spouses, irrespective of age) in ten countries; see table 2.1 for a detailed breakdown. We augment this sample by the recent release of the Belgian SHARE data.

Table 2.1 shows the unit response rates of SHARE in comparison to other recent multinational surveys in Europe. It compares favorably to the other surveys, although the weighted average (62 percent, unweighted 60 percent) is still lower than what is typically seen in the United States. The appropriate comparison is probably with the newest HRS cohort (the early baby boomers cohort drawn in 2004), which has a response rate at baseline of 69 percent. Earlier, the HRS has experienced much higher, but declining response rates. For the initial cohort of HRS in 1992, a response rate of 82 percent could be achieved, while the samples drawn in 1998 had a response rate of 70 percent. There is no directly comparable response rate of ELSA, since the sample of ELSA was based on those who were successfully interviewed in the Health Survey of England (HSE). The response rate was lowest in Switzerland, which is typical for this country, and highest in France, where the National Institute for Statistics and Economic Studies (INSEE) conducted the survey.

Table 2.1   **Sample size and response rate of SHARE and other European surveys**

	SHARE 2004		Eurostat		Scientific surveys					
	Sample size	Response rate	ECHP 1994	EU-LFS 1996	ESS 2002	ESS 2004	EVS 1999–2000	EES 1999	ISSP 2002	Avg.
Austria	1,986	58.1	—	—	—	62.4	77	49	63.9	63.1
Denmark	1,732	63.2	62	75	68	65.1	57	59	66.1	64.6
France	1,842	73.6	79	(a)	—	—	42	44	20.3	46.3
Germany	3,020	63.4	47	(a)	57	50.0	42	49	42.7	47.9
Greece	2,142	61.4	(a)	—	80	78.8	82	28	—	67.2
Italy	2,559	55.1	(a)	—	44	—	68	—	—	56.0
Netherlands	3,000	61.3	(a)	59	68	—	40	30	46.6	48.7
Spain	2,419	53.3	67	(a)	53	54.8	24	—	(a)	49.7
Sweden	3,067	50.2	—	(a)	69	65.8	41	31	57.2	52.8
Switzerland	1,010	37.6	—	—	34	46.9	—	—	32.8	37.9
Total*	22,777	61.8	62.0	63.2	55.6	54.9	46.4	43.9	36.7	50.8

Source: De Luca and Peracchi (2005).
Notes: (a) no prescreening response rate reported, (—) country not in sample, (*) weighted average. ECHP: European Community Household Panel; EU-LFS: European Labour Force Survey; ESS: European Social Survey; EVS: European Values Study; EES: European Election Study; ISSP: International Social Survey Project.

Unit nonresponse was compensated by adjusting the design weights. This was done in a calibration approach. In most countries the weights were calibrated against national population totals stratified by narrow age bands and gender. In two countries more information could be used (including economic status), while in two other countries only the national totals of the fifty and over population, stratified by gender, could enter the calibration of weights. Details are reported by Klevmarken, Swensson, and Hesselius (2006).

The SHARE has made great efforts to deliver truly comparable data in order to permit a reliable study of how differences in cultures, living conditions, and policy approaches are shaping the life of Europeans just before and after retirement. The questionnaire has been translated according to a protocol ensuring functional equivalence and was administered by a Computer Assisted Personal Interview (CAPI) plus a drop-off self-completion part. Interview procedures have been harmonized with the help of a joint case management system. Methodological details of the study are reported by Börsch-Supan and Jürges (2005), and first results summarized in Börsch-Supan et al. (2005). The SHARE data is available at http://www .share-project.org. Further data processing and record matching are still ongoing. A second data release was published in 2007 with more than 30,000 individuals.

This chapter is based on an extract of variables of SHARE 2004, ELSA

2004, and HRS 2004, which include whether a person receives disability insurance or not, basic demographic characteristics, and a broad set of health variables. These health variables include self-reported health; functional status measured by indicators of (instrumental) activities of daily living; a set of mental health questions (including the Center for Epidemiologic Studies Depression Scale [CES-D]) indicating dementia and depression; and physical measurements such as body mass index, walking speed, and grip strength. Most variables are identical in all three surveys. Weight and height (to compute body mass index) are self-reported in HRS and SHARE, while ELSA had interviewers actually measure the respondents. Grip strength is only available in the eleven SHARE countries.

Disability insurance is defined as all branches of publicly-financed insurances against the loss of the ability to perform gainful employment. Table 2.2 lists the institutions in each country by their proper name.

Figure 2.5 shows the enrollment in disability insurance by age for the eleven SHARE countries. Enrollment rises steeply from 4 percent, on average, across all SHARE countries at age fifty to almost 10 percent at age sixty-five. Disability insurance enrollment declines sharply after age sixty-five to a percentage lower than at age fifty. The reason for this sharp decline is that in most countries disability insurance benefits are automatically converted to old-age pension benefits at age sixty-five.

We therefore restrict our analysis to individuals in the time window from

Table 2.2	Disability insurance schemes considered
Austria (AT)	Staatliche Invaliditätspension
Belgium (BE)	Assurance invalidité légale/Wettelijke uitkering wegens arbeidsongeval of beroepsziekte; Pension de maladie, d'invalidité, maladie professionnelle/Wettelijke uitkering wegens ziekte of invaliditeit of tegemoetkoming aan personen met een handicap
Switzerland (CH)	Invalidenrente aus IV, assurance invalidité légale (AI) and Rendità invalidità (AI)
Germany (DE)	Erwerbsminderungsrente and Beamtenpension wegen Dienstunfähigkeit
Denmark (DK)	Offentlig sygedagpenge and offentlig førtidspension
Spain (ES)	Pensión pública contributiva y no contributiva de invalidez/incapacidad
France (FR)	Prestation publique d'invalidité (AAH, APA)
Greece (GR)	Σύνταξη αναπερίας
Italy (IT)	Assicurazione pubblica di disabilità (anche assegno di accompagnamento) and pnsione pubblica di invalidità o di inabilità
Netherlands (NL)	WAO, Waz of invaliditeitspensioen and Algemene bijstandswet (Abw), IOAW/IOAZ, aanvullende bijstandsuitkering, Toeslagenwet (TW)
Sweden (SE)	Förtidspension (sjukersättning), yrkesskadepension, and sjukbidrag
England (UK)	Incapacity benefits (previously invalidity benefits)
United States (US)	SSDI and SSI disability pension

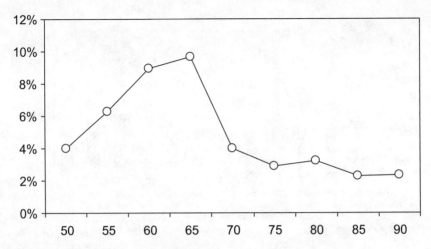

Fig. 2.5   Disability insurance enrollment by age
Note: Percentage of individuals enrolled in disability insurance by age. SHARE 2004.
Weighted data.

age fifty to age sixty-five. Our SHARE release covers 15,808 individuals of this age. The ELSA and HRS contribute 6,732 and 4,270 individuals, respectively, to the joint sample, which therefore consists of 26,810 individuals. For joint descriptive statistics, the calibrated weights in SHARE, ELSA, and HRS have been renormalized to give each country equal weight.

Our introductory finding of a striking variation across European countries in the number of persons who receive disability insurance benefits is echoed in the SHARE-ELSA-HRS microdata (see figure 2.6).

We can distinguish four country groups. Very high enrollment rates exist in Denmark, the Netherlands, and Sweden. Between 13 and 16 percent of individuals between fifty and sixty-five years of age receive disability insurance benefits in this first group of countries. The second group has enrollment rates around the average enrollment rate of 7.5 percent. This group consists of Switzerland, Spain, the United Kingdom, and the United States, with the United Kingdom substantially above this average. Here the enrollment ranges from 6 to almost 10 percent. Belgium, Germany, France, and Italy, the third group, have below-average enrollment rates between 4 and 6 percent. In Austria and Greece, less than 3 percent of individuals between fifty and sixty-five years of age receive disability insurance benefits.

Disability insurance enrollment is only slightly higher among men than among women (see table 2.3).

There are, however, striking international differences. In Sweden and Denmark, it is mainly women who contribute to the very high enrollment rates, relative to the rest of Europe. In the Netherlands, the third country with very high enrollment rates, it is the other way around and more men enroll

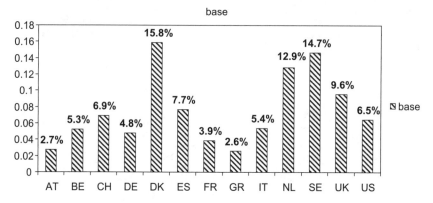

Fig. 2.6   Disability insurance enrollment in Europe, 2004
Note: SHARE 2004, ELSA 2004, and HRS 2004. Age fifty to sixty-five. Weighted data.

Table 2.3   **Disability insurance enrollment by country and gender**

	Austria	Germany	Sweden	Netherlands	Spain	Total
Male	4.65	6.15	9.39	15.79	11.44	8.40
Female	1.88	3.41	20.12	11.78	5.82	8.00

	Italy	France	Denmark	Switzerland	Belgium	
Male	5.21	4.92	11.18	5.81	6.82	8.40
Female	3.87	2.35	17.20	4.10	4.63	8.00

Source: SHARE 2004. Weighted data.

than women. This may point to institutional features; we will come back to this point in section 2.6.

Self-reported health is much worse among those who are on disability insurance; see the left panels of figure 2.7. While 19.7 percent report poor health among the enrolled, only 2.9 are among the not enrolled. In turn, only 9.8 percent report excellent or very good health among the enrolled, while this share is 42.5 percent among the not enrolled. Nonetheless, it is a striking finding that almost 10 percent report excellent or very good health in spite of being on disability insurance.

The health differences are less pronounced when measured more objectively as grip strength. Respondents use a little machine that they have to press two times with each hand; the maximum is reported in the right panels of figure 2.7. Average grip strength is 38.1 kilograms among the not enrolled, while individuals on disability insurance have lower grip strength of 34.4 kilograms. Grip strength has a fairly large standard deviation (about 13 kilograms), but the difference is statistically significant in this large sample.

The discrepancy between very large self-reported health differences

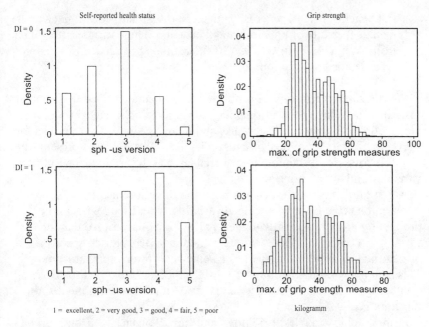

Fig. 2.7   Health by disability insurance status
Source: SHARE 2004. Weighted data.

and significant but less pronounced differences in the more objective grip strength measure may hint at justification bias of self-reported health (Sen 2002). Individuals who have enrolled in disability insurance may justify this by reporting a lower health status than what can be measured more objectively by grip strength.

2.3   Explaining Microdata Variation in Disability Insurance Enrollment

Our aim is to look at which weight each of the three potential causes—demographics, health, and institutions—has in explaining disability enrollment in Europe. We exploit the richness of the SHARE, ELSA, and HRS microdata to relate individual disability insurance enrollment probabilities to three types of variables:

* Demographic characteristics (age and gender)
* A broad set of health measures, ranging from self-reported health to more objective measurements of the functional physical (ADL: activities of daily living, IADL: instrumental activities of daily living) and mental health status (CES-D test battery of mental health).
* A set of variables characterizing the generosity of the disability insurance in each country (coverage, minimum disability level required for

full benefits, benefit generosity, medical assessment, vocational assessment, generosity of unemployment benefits). These variables are taken
from Annex A.2.1 in OECD (2003), see the appendix to this chapter
for a detailed description.

We run three regressions: a probit model of being enrolled in disability
insurance, a Weibull proportional hazards model of the age when an individual enrolls in disability insurance, and finally, a simple linear model for
the probability to be enrolled into disability insurance. Table 2.4 presents the
results in four blocks: demographic variables, health variables, institutional
variables, and interactions among them.

A first finding is the similarity among the three specifications. A second
observation is the large unexplained variation. The (Pseudo-)R^2 in the two
probability models is slightly higher than 0.25; a quarter of the individual
variation in our microdata is not explained in spite of a rich specification
of health. The duration model has a somewhat lower explanatory power.
This is in line with the findings of OECD (2003) where only little correlation between "medical disability status" and "disability enrollment status"
was found.

Demographic variables are jointly significant. Women have a lower probability to enroll into disability insurance, conditional on health. Also this was
a finding of OECD (2003). Older age increases to probability to be enrolled
until about age sixty-three. We apply a piecewise linear specification, with
breakpoints at ages fifty-five and sixty. Notable is the sharp increase in the
enrollment probability between ages fifty and fifty-five.

All health variables are strongly significant. Since we do not have grip
strength and walking speed in all three surveys, these variables are not
included. Including them in the SHARE sample reduces the significance of
the self-reported health measure considerably, but leaves the overall results
unaffected; this corresponds to the findings reported in figure 2.7. Noteworthy is the significant effect of mental illness, measured by the CES-D
battery, conditional on physical health, and the strong effect of instrumental
activities of daily living (IADLs) probably picking up work-related disability. Given these functional measures, self-reported health remains highly
significant and quantitatively large.

Demographics and health explain, in isolation, about a sixth of the total
variation of the linear model. This is not much, and corresponds to the
already cited OECD findings.

The institutional variables are also highly jointly significant. Since they
are country-specific and thus have much less variation than the microdata,
we use the "cluster" specification to correct the t-statistics accordingly. All
measures are scored by the OECD from 0 to 5. Coverage measures on a 0
to 5 scale which population groups are eligible for insurance. The highest
score is given if disability insurance covers the entire population; the low-

Table 2.4   **Regression results**

	Probit	z	Weibull	z	Linear	T
Female	−0.661	−1.91	0.430	−1.71	−0.078	−1.39
Age < 55	−1.068	−0.58	2.602	0.19	−0.094	−0.31
Age > 60	0.385	0.1	12.949	0.49	0.123	0.25
Age-lin1	0.027	2.05	0.940	−1.84	0.003	2.29
Age-lin2	0.006	0.15	0.955	−0.56	0.001	0.12
Age-lin3	−0.006	−0.09	0.960	−0.45	−0.002	−0.22
SRH-excellent	−0.896	−6.86	0.141	−8.14	−0.063	−2.62
SRH-very good	−0.534	−4.28	0.324	−7.5	−0.041	−2.15
SRH-fair	−0.007	−0.06	1.417	0.68	−0.192	−4.73
SRH-poor	0.361	2.49	2.206	1.55	−0.078	−1.53
CES-D (sum)	0.058	4.88	1.087	4.33	0.008	2.84
ADL (sum)	0.054	1.33	1.052	1.04	0.022	1.9
IADL (sum)	0.221	4.6	1.257	4.42	0.061	3.7
Coverage	0.039	0.68	1.320	1.96	−0.023	−2.19
Min. benefits	0.361	4.39	1.992	3.09	0.036	2.39
Full benefits	−0.184	−2.18	0.616	−2.87	0.003	0.26
Generosity	−0.329	−5.03	0.546	−2.71	−0.028	−3.12
Permanent	0.049	1.87	1.175	2.59	−0.006	−0.81
Medical	0.069	2.71	1.106	1.46	0.006	1.4
Vocational	−0.121	−1.79	0.943	−0.31	−0.040	−3.29
UI-Benefits	0.106	4.02	1.120	1.3	0.022	3.02
covg_fem	0.205	4.87	1.447	4.46	0.027	3.18
minl_fem	0.015	0.15	1.025	0.14	0.000	−0.03
Full_fem	−0.086	−1.17	0.810	−1.71	−0.005	−0.52
geno_fem	−0.018	−0.23	0.908	−0.53	−0.002	−0.2
covg_old	−0.032	−0.92	0.922	−0.99	0.000	0
minl_old	−0.118	−1.65	0.819	−1.08	−0.003	−0.37
full_old	−0.048	−1.12	0.882	−1.25	−0.010	−1.94
geno_old	0.173	2.72	1.353	1.6	0.011	1.32
covg_hfpoor	0.110	5.27	1.008	0.09	0.078	14.63
minl_hfpoor	0.091	2.12	0.918	−0.45	0.072	7.95
full_hfpoor	0.063	1.32	1.430	2.67	−0.024	−2.88
geno_hfpoor	−0.036	−0.95	1.111	0.53	−0.030	−7.68
Constant	−1.827	−0.71	1.256	35.76	0.182	0.49
(Pseudo-)R^2		0.2588		0.1957		0.2667

Note: Based on 9,388 individuals age fifty through sixty-five in SHARE 2004, ELSA 2002, and HRS 2004.

est score if only employees are covered. A broad coverage increases disability enrollment, but the effect is surprisingly small and insignificant. A lenient minimum disability level to claim benefits has more influence on disability insurance uptake and is significant in all three specifications. The generosity of benefits is significant, but with an unexpected negative sign, as is the disability level required for full benefits. The strictness of a medical exam reduces disability uptake. Whether vocational considerations play a role in the eligibility process or not is insignificant, as is the permanence of benefits.

The last institutional variable measures the duration and benefit level of unemployment compensation, a possible alternative to disability insurance as an early retirement device. It is scored 5 for a short duration and lower unemployment benefits than disability insurance benefits. Indeed, tight unemployment insurance increases disability insurance enrollment in a highly significant and quantitatively important way.

Finally, we also interact the institutional variables with selected demographic and health variables. These interactions explain 20.6 percent of the total variation in the linear model, thus more than demographics and health together. They exhibit some interesting features, especially when compared to the institutional variables alone. They explain some of the surprising findings just discussed. For example, the surprisingly small influence of coverage turns into a very large effect for women and those of poor health. The latter is a straightforward to explain; the former may be a result of the low labor force participation of European women who have difficulties to be eligible for a normal old-age pension and thus may seek disability pensions. This corresponds to the very high female enrollment in some countries (see table 2.3). In Germany, a lenient eligibility to disability insurance for women was explicitly a policy instrument in the early 1980s.

Another example is the generosity variable, which carries an unexpected negative sign in the overall regression, but is strongly positive for the older part of the sample (age sixty and over).

2.4   Counterfactual Simulations: Controlling for Demography and Health

This section predicts what enrollment rates would look like if demographics and health were equal across countries. If demographic differences were the main cause for enrolling into disability insurance, enrollment rates should be very similar after taking demographic differences out. We then go through the same procedure for differences in health status.

Our first step is to normalize disability insurance enrollment with respect to demographic differences across countries. Italy, for instance, has an older population than the European average, while Denmark has a younger population. We use the regression results of table 2.4 to establish the influence of age and gender on disability insurance take up. We then predict, in a counterfactual simulation exercise, which share of our sample individuals would take up disability insurance if all countries had the same age and gender distribution as the average of the SHARE countries. The result is shown in figure 2.8, comparing the counterfactual simulation results to the baseline results depicted in figure 2.6.

Quite clearly, taking account of demographic differences does not make a substantive difference. Italy, featuring the highest average age of individu-

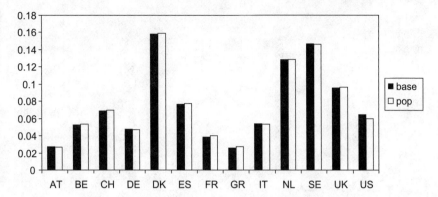

Fig. 2.8   Actual and predicted disability insurance enrollment if age and gender were identical in all countries

Note: Based on linear regression specification in table 2.3.

als between fifty and sixty-five years of age among the thirteen countries, would have a slightly lower disability insurance enrollment if it had the age distribution of the average country. In Denmark, which is younger than average, the opposite would happen. The effects, however, are very small. Demographic differences across Europe cannot explain why the enrollment rates in disability insurance are so different in Europe.

Our second step is, therefore, to account for difference in the health status of the population. The health status differs along many dimensions across countries. A first dimension is self-assessed health. Self-assessed health is relatively poor in Italy and Spain; it is best in Switzerland. One major concern with the self-assessed health ratings, however, is that respondents do not perceive the health self-assessment scale given to them as absolute. Individuals with the same true health status may have different reference levels against which they judge their health. This sheds doubt on the comparability of such measures across countries (e.g., Groot 2000; Sen 2002). We therefore also included more objective measures such as the physical performance in daily activities (e.g., walking or bathing) in the regression reported in table 2.4. In this second dimension, Germany exhibits the most limitations and Greece the least. A third dimension is mental health. Depression, an often named reason for taking up disability insurance, varies quite substantially across the SHARE countries. Spain, Italy, and France show the worst scores on the CES-D depression scale, while Denmark, Germany, and Switzerland have the lowest share of depression cases. Hence, the cross-national variation in health status looks like a good candidate to explain the variation in disability insurance enrollment.

We use the same methodology to correct for the influence of the multidimensional health differences as we did with demographics. We first establish the influence of health on disability insurance take up, and then predict

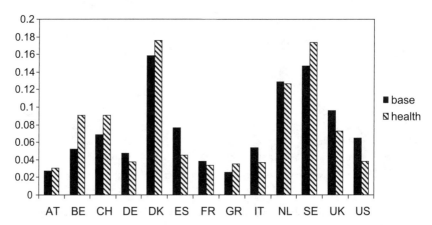

Fig. 2.9   Predicted disability insurance enrollment if health status were identical
Note: Based on linear regression specification in table 2.3.

which share of our sample individuals would take up disability insurance if the health status measured along the aforementioned four dimensions would be identical to the average of our thirteen countries. The results are shown in figure 2.9.

The differences between enrollment rates under the actual and a hypothetically identical health status are now more pronounced. In general, the counterfactual enrollment rates go up in countries with good health, and down in countries with lower health status than the average, as expected. If the Italians and Spaniards had the same health status as the average person in our sample, their disability insurance enrollment would be much lower. The same holds, notably, for the two Anglo-Saxon countries. In Switzerland, Denmark, and Sweden, it would be considerably higher.

If health would be the dominant explanation for disability insurance enrollment, the predicted shares should be equal across countries, once health is identical in all countries. As figure 2.9 shows, this is clearly not the case. There are still pronounced differences. The high enrollment rates in Sweden, Denmark, and the Netherlands, especially, remain either relatively stable after correcting for health differences (Netherlands), or they increase even further (Sweden and Denmark). We conclude that differences in health across Europe cannot explain the cross-national variation in the European disability insurance enrollment; in fact, it is just the opposite. In Sweden and Denmark, enrollment rates are high in spite of a very good health status of the fifty- to sixty-five-year-olds in our sample.

A logical next step is to correct for differences in demographics and health simultaneously, using the same methodology as before. Figure 2.10 shows the results.

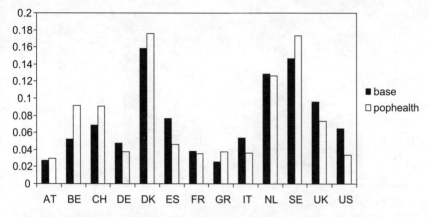

Fig. 2.10   Predicted disability insurance enrollment if age, gender, and health status were identical in all countries

Note: Based on linear regression specification in table 2.3.

The picture changes only slightly from the last one. Hence, counterfactually assigning the same age, gender, and health distributions to all countries does not make the striking variation in the uptake of disability insurance across the thirteen countries go away. The large enrollment rates in Sweden, Denmark, and the Netherlands, especially, must have different reasons than an older population or a worse health status in these countries.

2.5   The Effects of Disability Insurance

By exclusion of the first two of the three popular explanations—demographic and health-related differences—the third popular explanation remains; namely, institutional differences, specifically enrollment and eligibility rules that make disability insurance benefits easier to receive and more generous in some countries than in others. Such rules may create incentive effects similar to those exerted by old-age pensions, which often provide a financial incentive to retire early. In many countries, health requirements for disability insurance eligibility are weak. Under such circumstances, disability insurance may work as a labor market exit route to early retirement (Börsch-Supan 2001). Many countries have established very lenient work disability eligibility rules under the conditions of high unemployment.

Alternatively, the large unexplained variation may include factors not measured by the three sets of variables corresponding to the three main causal attributions: demographics, health, and institutions. Ideally, we would model the entire complex set of eligibility and benefit rules in each country as they apply to each individual in the sample, as the exercises in the Gruber and Wise (1999, 2004, 2005) volumes did. This is a massive project

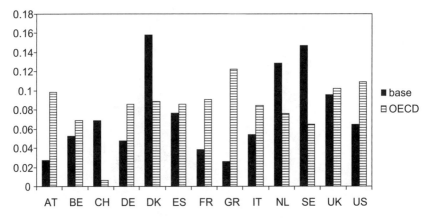

Fig. 2.11   Predicted disability insurance enrollment if eligibility and benefit rules were equally generous in all countries

Note: Based on linear regression specification in table 2.3.

only possible in a large team such as the team assembled by Gruber and Wise. Instead, we employ the institutional indicators provided by OECD (2003) that already entered the regression in table 2.4, and run a third counterfactual simulation that makes these indicators identical for all individuals in our cross-national sample. We then predict the take up outcomes in the same sprit as we did in figures 2.8 through 2.10.

The results are striking (see figure 2.11). The counterfactual simulation holding eligibility and benefit generosity indicators constant produces much more similar disability uptake rates than holding demographics and health constant. The only outlier is Switzerland, where uptake rates would be extremely low under average generosity.

A simple back-of-the-envelope regression confirms the aforementioned results. Regressing the aggregate enrollment rates in the small sample of thirteen countries on five of the previous indicator variables (coverage, minimum disability level required, benefit generosity, medical assessment, vocational assessment) yields an R^2 of 89 percent (adjusted 78 percent) and highly significant coefficients. Hence, more than three-quarters of the cross-national variation in enrollment rates can be explained by the institutional factors embedded in the five OECD indicators.

2.6   Summary and Conclusions

The variation in disability insurance take up rates across European countries is striking. It reaches from some 15 percent of individuals between fifty- and sixty-five-years-old in Denmark, Sweden, and the Netherlands to less than 3 percent in Austria and Greece.

In order to find out which popular explanation is most convincing, we

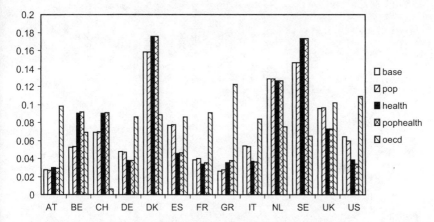

Fig. 2.12   Baseline enrollment rates and counterfactual simulations
Note: Based on linear regression specification in table 2.3.

counterfactually equalize each potential cause among the thirteen countries in our joint SHARE-ELSA-HRS data set and then see whether disability insurance enrollments are also equal. Figure 2.12 summarizes the sequence of our results in a single chart.

Correcting for differences in the age, gender, and health distribution across countries does not explain this striking variation. The large enrollment rates in Sweden, Denmark, and the Netherlands, especially, have different reasons than an older population or a worse health status than in the other European countries.

Institutional factors—some of them creating strong incentives to enroll in disability insurance as an early retirement device—are a more likely explanation. The counterfactual simulation holding eligibility and benefit generosity rules approximately constant (the leftmost bars in figure 2.12) produces much more similar disability uptake rates than holding demographics and health constant.

The most influential institutional variable in our regressions is the minimum level of disability to obtain full benefits. This variable alone explains more than 60 percent of the cross-national variation. It seems to be the most powerful policy variable when countries such as the Netherlands, Denmark, and Sweden want to bring their disability insurance enrollment rates closer to the average European and U.S. level.

Appendix

Table 2A.1   Definition of the OECD variables used in the regressions of table 2.4

Dimension	5 points	4 points	3 points	2 points	1 point	0 points
X. Compensation						
x1. Coverage	Total population (residents)	Some of those out of the labor force (e.g., congenital)	Labor force plus means-tested noncontrib. scheme	Labor force with voluntary self-insurance	Labor force	Employees
x2. Minimum disability level	0–25%	26–40%	41–55%	56–70%	71–85%	86–100%
x3. Disability level for full benefit	< 50%	50–61%	62–73%	74–85%	86–99%	100%
x4. Maximum benefit level	RR ≥ 75%, Reasonable minimum	RR ≥ 75%, Minimum not specified	75 > RR ≥ 50%, Reasonable minimum	75 > RR ≥ 50%, Minimum not specified	RR < 50%, Reasonable minimum	RR < 50%, Minimum not specified
x5. Permanence of benefits	Strictly permanent	De facto permanent	Self-reported review only	Regulated review procedure	Strictly temporary, unless fully (= 100%) disabled	Strictly temporary in all cases
x6. Medical assessment	Treating doctor exclusively	Treating doctor predominantly	Insurance doctor predominantly	Insurance doctor exclusively	Team of experts in the insurance	Insurance team and two-step procedure
x7. Vocational assessment	Strict own or usual occupation assessment	Reference is made to one's previous earnings	Own-occupation assessment for partial benefits	Current labor market conditions are taken into account	All jobs available are taken into account, leniently applied	All jobs available are taken into account, strictly applied
x8. Sickness benefit level	RR = 100% also for long-term sickness absence	RR = 100% (short-term) ≥ 75% (long-term) sickness absence	RR ≥ 75% (short-term) ≥ 50% (long-term) sickness absence	75 > RR ≥ 50% for any type of sickness absence	RR ≥ 50% (short-term) < 50% (long-term) sickness absence	RR < 50% also for short-term sickness absence
x9. Sickness benefit duration	One year or more, short or no wage payment period	One year or more, significant wage payment period	Six-twelve months, short or no wage payment period	Six-twelve months, significant wage payment period	Less than 6 months, short or no wage payment period	Less than 6 months, significant wage payment period
x10. Unemployment benefit level and duration	DI > UE level, short duration of unemployment	DI > UE level, long duration of unemployment	Similar levels, short duration of unemployment	Similar levels, long duration of unemployment	DI < UE level, short duration of unemployment	DI < UE level, long duration of unemployment

Source: OECD.

References

Aarts, L. J. M., R. V. Burkhauser, and P. R. de Jong, eds. 1996. *Curing the Dutch disease. An international perspective on disability policy reform.* Aldershot: Avebury.

Banks, J., A. Kapteyn, J. P., Smith, and A. van Soest. 2004. International comparisons of work disability. RAND Working Paper no. WR-155.

Bardage, C., S. M. F. Plujim, N. L. Pedersen, D. J. H. Deeg, M. Jylhä, M. Noale, T. Blumstein, and A. Otero. 2005. Self-rated health among older adults: A crossnational comparison. *European Journal of Aging* 2:149–58.

Blöndal, S., and S. Scarpetta. 1998. The retirement decision in OECD countries. OECD Economics Department Working Paper. Paris: Organization for Economic Cooperation and Development.

Börsch-Supan, A. 2001. Incentive effects of social security under an uncertain disability option. In *Themes in the economics of aging,* ed. D. A. Wise, 281–310. Chicago: University of Chicago Press.

———. 2005. Work disability and health. In *Health, aging, and retirement in Europe: First results from SHARE,* ed. A. Börsch-Supan, A. Brugiavani, H. Jurges, J. Mackenbach, J. Siegrist, and G. Weber, 253–59. Mannheim: MEA.

Börsch-Supan, A., A. Brugiavini, H. Jürges, J. Mackenbach, J. Siegrist, and G. Weber, eds. 2005. *Health, aging, and retirement in Europe: First results from SHARE.* Mannheim: Mannheim Research Institute for the Economics of Aging.

Börsch-Supan, A., and H. Jürges, eds. 2005. *The survey of health, aging, and retirement in Europe: Methodology.* Mannheim: MEA.

De Luca, G., and F. Peracchi. 2005. Survey participation in the first wave of SHARE. In *Health, Aging, and Retirement in Europe: Methodology,* ed. Börsch-Supan, A., and H. Jürges. Mannheim: MEA.

Dewey, M. E., and M. J. Prince. 2005. Mental health. In *Health, aging and retirement in Europe: First results from SHARE,* ed. A. Börsch-Supan, A. Brugiavani, H. Jurges, J. Mackenbach, J. Siegrist, and G. Weber, 108–17. Mannheim: MEA.

European Commission. 2004. *Adequate and sustainable pensions.* Joint report by the Commission and the Council.

Eurostat. 2005. Eurostat Data Archive. Available at: http://europa.eu.int/comm/eurostat/.

Groot, W. 2000. Adaptation and scale of reference bias in self-assessments of quality of life. *Journal of Health Economics* 19 (3): 403–20.

Gruber, J., and D. Wise, eds. 1999. *Social Security and retirement around the world.* Chicago: University of Chicago Press.

———. 2004. *Social Security and retirement around the world: Micro estimation of early retirement incentives.* Chicago: University of Chicago Press.

———. 2005. *Social Security and retirement around the world: Budget impacts of early retirement incentives.* Chicago: University of Chicago Press.

Hayward, M. D., and Z. Zhang. 2001. Demography of aging. In *Handbook of aging and the social sciences,* 5th ed., ed. R. H. Binstock, and L. K. George, 69–85. San Diego: Academic Press.

Jürges, H. 2005. Cross-country differences in general health. In *Health, aging, and retirement in Europe: First results from SHARE,* ed. Börsch-Supan, A. Brugiavani, H. Jurges, J. Mackenbach, J. Siegrist, and G. Weber. Mannheim: MEA.

Juster, F. T., and R. Suzman. 1995. An overview of the Health and Retirement Study. *Journal of Human Resources* 30 (Special Issue): S7–S56.

Kapteyn, A., J. P. Smith, and A. van Soest. 2004. Self-reported Work Disability in the US and The Netherlands. RAND Working Paper WR-206.

King, G., C. Murray, J. Salomon, and A. Tandon. 2004. Enhancing the validity and cross-cultural comparability of measurement in survey research. *American Political Science Review* 98 (1): 567–83.

Klevmarken, N. A., B. Swensson, and P. Hesselius. 2006. The SHARE sampling procedures and calibrated design weights. In *Health, aging, and retirement in Europe: Methodology*, ed. A. Börsch-Supan, and H. Jürges. Mannheim: MEA.

Kohli, M., M. Rein, A.-M. Guillemard, and H. van Gunsteren, eds. 1991. *Time for retirement: Comparative studies of early exit from the labor force*. Cambridge: Cambridge University Press.

Lan, T. Y., D. J. H. Deeg, J. M. Guralnik, and D. Melzer. 2003. Responsiveness of the index of mobility limitation: Comparison with gait speed alone in the longitudinal aging study Amsterdam. *Journal of Gerontology: Medical Science* 58A:721–28.

Mackenbach, J., M. Avendano, K. Andersen-Ranberg, and A. R. Aro. 2005. Physical health. In *Health, Aging, and Retirement in Europe: First results from SHARE*, ed. A. Börsch-Supan, A. Brugiavani, H. Jurges, J. Mackenbach, J. Siegrist, and G. Weber. Mannheim: MEA.

Marmot, M., J. Banks, R. Blundell, C. Lessof, and J. Nazroo. 2003. *Health, wealth, and lifestyles of the older population in England: The 2002 English longitudinal study of aging*. London: The Institute for Fiscal Studies.

National Research Council. 2001. *Preparing for an aging world: The case for cross-national research*, Panel on a Research Agenda and New Data for an Aging World, Committee on Population and Committee on National Statistics, Division of Behavioral and Social Sciences and Education. Washington, DC: National Academies Press.

Organization for Economic Cooperation and Development. 2003. *Transforming disability into ability*. Paris: OECD.

———. 2005. *OECD health data*. Paris: OECD.

Sen, A. 2002. Health: Perception versus observation. *British Medical Journal* 324 (April): 860–61.

World Health Organization. 2002. *Active aging: A policy framework*. Geneva: WHO.

Comment   Robert J. Willis

The tension between a political desire to maintain welfare state benefits and the fact of rapid population aging generates many of the key problems facing European policymakers. Not only does population aging directly increase the costs of pension, health, and disability programs that benefit the elderly, but economic theory and analysis has shown that these costs may be exacerbated by unintended incentive effects. This point was made dramatically in the cross-national project of Gruber and Wise (1999, 2004, 2005) which showed powerful effects of pension and disability plans on retirement behavior. Their initial analysis, based on country-level administrative and

Robert J. Willis is a professor of economics at the University of Michigan, where he is also a research professor in the Survey Research Center and the Population Studies Center of the Institute for Social Research.

aggregate data, provided important motivation for the development of comparable cross-national microlevel survey data in Europe in order to advance understanding of the effects of social and economic policies in the countries of the European Union.

Under the leadership of Axel Börsch-Supan, a remarkable group of researchers from across Europe and across disciplines have come together to design and carry out the SHARE project (Survey of Health, Aging, and Retirement in Europe). The SHARE collects longitudinal data on persons age fifty and over using a design that attempts to maximize comparability both across countries within SHARE and with its sister studies, the Health and Retirement Study (HRS) in the United States and the English Longitudinal Study of Aging (ELSA) in the United Kingdom. While the current chapter by Börsch-Supan uses cross-section data from SHARE's first survey wave of eleven countries in 2004 (together with 2004 cross-sections from HRS and ELSA), researchers can look forward to longitudinal data beginning with the 2006 wave and to the expansion of SHARE to include fourteen countries in 2008 and, ultimately, all EU countries by 2010. In addition, researchers from HRS, ELSA, and SHARE have been active collaborators in supporting the creation of similar surveys in Latin America (Mexico, Costa Rica, Chile) and Asia (Korea, Japan, China). These efforts are creating a truly global data system that will allow researchers to study behavior of individuals and families in their own country's policy environment, in contrast to the behavior of comparable people in the policy environments of other countries.

This chapter provides a first hint of the potential of the SHARE data to produce useful insights into important policy questions. Disability rates vary substantially across countries within the EU. Popular explanations for these variations include cross-country differences in demographic composition, in the health status of their populations, and in institutions that provide disability benefits for those who apply and are deemed eligible. In this chapter, SHARE, HRS, and ELSA data are pooled in order to examine the importance of demographic, health, and institutional variables in microlevel regressions on individual disability status. Not surprisingly, many variables in each of these categories are statistically significant predictors of disability status in the expected direction.

To me, two results from the micro regressions are of most interest. One is the strong interaction between gender and generosity of disability program, which the author explains plausibly as a consequence of the relative attractiveness of disability programs to older women whose pension options are poor because of short work histories. The second result is the finding that the impact of poor health on disability enrollment can be demonstrated using an objective measure—grip strength—in addition to its relationship to subjective self-reported health measures, which may suffer from justification and cultural biases. The fact that this pooled regression can be estimated is testimony to the remarkable scientific collaboration among the designers of these surveys to ensure harmonization of questionnaires and survey methods in order to maximize the comparability of economic and health measures across countries.

Next, Börsch-Supan uses these regression estimates to answer a set of "counterfactual" questions about which cross-country variations in disability rates are due to demographic, health, or institutional differences. Although demographic and health variables do affect the chances of individual disability enrollment, he finds that cross-country differences in the distribution of these variables have essentially no power to explain cross-country variation in aggregate disability rates. In contrast, he finds that most systematic cross-country variation is eliminated under the counterfactual assumption that all individuals face the same policy regime. Given the strong interaction effect between gender and policy already noted, it would be interesting to redo this analysis using sex-specific aggregate rates and regression coefficients to see if cross-country differences are eliminated for both sexes.

Clearly, the analysis of this chapter is but a first step. The chapter convincingly shows that policy matters in determining disability rates, but it leaves open critical questions about precisely what features of policy are important in determining disability status. These, of course, are the questions to which policymakers would wish to know the answers in thinking about reforms to the disability systems in their country. More generally, policymakers would want to know how to balance deadweight losses borne by society due to distortions of retirement incentives created by a disability policy against the gain in the welfare of those who become disabled. These are difficult questions. To answer some of them may require, as Börsch-Supan notes, a major project analogous to the Gruber-Wise project to infer quantitative policy parameters such as implicit tax rates on work from the disability policies in each country that could be appended to the pooled HRS/ELSA/SHARE microdata. Even without such a project, SHARE and its sister surveys provide the raw material to address disability policy issues in much more depth. For example, in a series of papers, Benitez-Silva et al. (1999, 2004) and Benitez-Silva et al. (2006) utilize HRS self-reported health conditions to examine the determinants of the decision to enroll in disability programs and the degree to which the U.S. disability system correctly enrolls the truly disabled and excludes the nondisabled. It would be both feasible and fascinating to examine these questions across different countries using SHARE data.

References

Benitez-Silva, H., M. Buchinsky, H. Chan, and J. Rust. 2006. How large are the classification errors in the Social Security disability award process? Unpublished Manuscript.

Benitez-Silva, H., M. Buchinsky, H. Chan, J. Rust, and S. Sheidvasser. 1999. An empirical analysis of the Social Security Disability application, appeal, and award process. *Labour Economics* 6 (2): 147–78.

———. 2004. How large is the bias in self-reported disability? *Journal of Applied Econometrics* 19 (6): 649–70.

Gruber, J., and D. Wise, eds. 1999. *Social Security and retirement around the world.* Chicago: University of Chicago Press.

———. 2004. *Social Security and retirement around the world: Micro estimation of early retirement incentives.* Chicago: University of Chicago Press.

———. 2005. *Social Security and retirement around the world: Budget impacts of early retirement incentives.* Chicago: University of Chicago Press.

3

Labor Market Status and Transitions during the Pre-Retirement Years
Learning from International Differences

Arie Kapteyn, James P. Smith, Arthur van Soest, and James Banks

3.1 Introduction

Increasing labor force participation among older workers is an important issue on the scientific and policy agenda in the United States and other industrialized countries. Major categories of individuals who are out of the labor force at later ages consist of persons drawing disability benefits, unemployment benefits, and early retirement benefits. Cross-country differences in the prevalence of early retirement are clearly related to differences in financial incentives (Gruber and Wise 2003; Börsch-Supan 2007). The fraction of workers on disability insurance is vastly different across countries with similar levels of economic development and comparable access to modern medical technology and treatment.

Health is also a major determinant of economic inactivity, and those who have a health problem that limits them in their daily activities or in the amount or kind of work they can do (a "work disability") are much less likely to work for pay than others (Stapleton and Burkhauser 2003). In view of the aging of the workforce in developed countries, reducing work disability among the working population and particularly among older workers may have a major impact on the sustainability of social security and health care systems, among other things. Institutional differences in eligibility rules,

Arie Kapteyn is a senior economist at the RAND Corporation and director of the RAND Labor and Population Program. James P. Smith is a senior economist at the RAND Corporation. Arthur van Soest is a professor of econometrics at Netspar Tilburg University and a researcher at the RAND Corporation. James Banks is a professor of economics at University College London, and deputy research director of the Institute for Fiscal Studies.

We are grateful to Tania Andreyeva for research assistance, to Michael Hurd for comments, and to the National Institutes on Aging (Grant# P01-AG022481-01) and the Social Security Administration, through the Michigan Retirement Research Center, for research support.

workplace accommodation of older or sick workers, or generosity of benefits, contribute to explaining the differences in disability rolls (cf., e.g., Bound and Burkhauser 1999; Autor and Duggan 2003; and Börsch-Supan 2007). Recent survey data show, however, that significant differences between countries are also found in self-reports of work-limiting disabilities and general health (Banks et al. 2009).

In this chapter we use data from the Panel Study of Income Dynamics (PSID) and the European Community Household Panel (ECHP) to study the labor force dynamics in the United States and in thirteen European countries. To focus on labor market dynamics in the pre-retirement years and because these dynamics are likely to differ by gender, we concentrate on the age group between forty and sixty-five and consider males and females separately. We also investigate the dynamics of work disability (i.e., the extent to which work disability varies over time and its reversibility) and how this varies across countries. One of the questions we address is whether we can explain the prevalence of self-reported work disability as a function of individual characteristics, including general health.

The remainder of the chapter is organized as follows. In section 3.2 the details of the data that are used are described. Section 3.3 discusses some pertinent characteristics of institutions in Europe and the United States that relate especially to the incentives and institutions of work disability programs. Section 3.4 presents the model that is used to describe labor force dynamics in the various countries. The model is estimated for each country separately. Section 3.5 presents the estimation results. In section 3.6, we summarize the implications of these results by showing simulations, where we assign U.S. parameter values to the models for the European countries. The implied differences in outcomes can be seen as a counterfactual simulation of the impact U.S. policies and institutions would have when implemented in European countries. Section 3.7 concludes.

3.2   Data

Our data come from two sources: the European Community Household Panel (ECHP) and the Panel Study of Income Dynamics (PSID). Both data sets have reasonably comparable measures of labor force activity and self-assessed work disability for the countries that will be included in our analysis. We discuss some issues related to the comparability of measurement of these key concepts in section 3.5.

The ECHP is an annual longitudinal survey of households in the EU.[1] Data were collected by national statistical agencies under the supervision and coordination of Eurostat (the statistical office of the EU). Table 3A.1,

---

1. See Nicoletti and Peracchi (2002) and Peracchi (2002) for more information on ECHP.

taken from Eurostat (2003, 15), gives an overview of the waves of ECHP in all fifteen countries that participated in the ECHP project.

The ECHP started in 1994 and was terminated in 2001. The first wave covered some 60,500 households and some 130,000 adults age sixteen and above from all countries except Austria, Finland, and Sweden. Austria and Finland were added in the second and third waves. As of the fourth wave, the original ECHP survey was terminated in Germany, Luxembourg, and the United Kingdom. Comparable data for these countries were obtained from existing national panels. For the United Kingdom this was the British Household Panel Survey (BHPS), for Germany the Socio-Economic Panel (SOEP), and for Luxembourg the PSELL (Panel socio-économique Liewen zu Lëtzebuerg). For these countries we will use the existing national panels rather than the few waves of the ECHP. As of the fourth wave, data for Sweden were obtained from the Swedish Living Conditions Survey. Since this is not a panel, we will exclude Sweden from our analysis. We will also not use the Luxembourg data, since it provides no information on self-reported disability.

The Panel Study of Income Dynamics (PSID) has gathered almost thirty years of extensive economic and demographic data on a nationally representative sample of approximately 5,000 (original) families and 35,000 individuals who live in these families. Details on labor market activity and family income and its components have been gathered in each wave since the inception of PSID in 1968. The PSID has been collecting information on self-reported general health status (the standard five-point scale from excellent to poor) since 1984 and has always collected good information on work-related disabilities. To provide comparability in the time period with the EHCP, our analysis will use the PSID waves between 1995 and 2003. It should be noted that after the 1999 wave the PSID is no longer annual, but biannual.

3.3   Institutions

There exists great variation in labor market institutions across the Organization for Economic Cooperation and Development (OECD) countries; regulations with respect to disability insurance are certainly no exception. To get a very broad overview for a majority of countries in our sample, figure 3.1 reports a crude measure of the generosity of disability benefits—the fraction of gross domestic product (GDP) accounted for by public expenditures on disability benefits. Considerable variation across OECD countries is readily apparent, with France and Italy spending less than 1 percent of GDP and three countries—Sweden, Denmark, and the Netherlands—spending more than twice that level. Using this metric, the United States ranks lower than any of the OECD countries listed in figure 3.1. The variation in spending

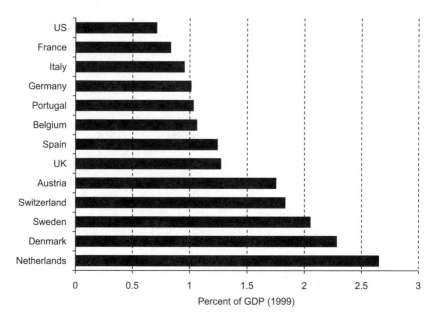

Fig. 3.1   Public expenditure on disability benefits
Source: OECD (2003b, chapter 2).

levels can of course be due to variation in benefit levels or variation in eligibility, or some combination of both.

Looking more deeply into international variation than the simple generosity measure previously presented, various dimensions can be distinguished. The main ones are the loss of earnings capacity required to qualify for benefits and the way in which such loss of earnings capacity is assessed, eligibility requirements based on work or contribution history, and benefit levels in relation to loss of earnings capacity. Table 3A.2 provides an overview of the main features of disability insurance systems in the countries we study in this chapter.

Table 3A.2 illustrates the complexity of these disability programs across countries. For example, while many countries have a basic five year's minimum period of eligibility (e.g., Germany, Austria, Italy, Portugal), basic eligibility is as low as six months in Belgium and one year in France, while one is not fully covered unless one has worked for ten years in the United States. Similarly, while the loss of normal earnings capacity is sufficient to qualify for eligibility in Spain, one must have a loss of two-thirds of earnings capacity in France, Belgium, and Portugal.

Not surprisingly, the variation in Disability Insurance (DI) systems identified in table 3A.2 is correlated with differences in prevalence of DI receipt across countries and in the disability status of individuals receiving DI. Börsch-Supan (2007) showed that a cross-sectional context variation in

Table 3.1   **Expenditures on disability insurance and self-reported male work disability, 2001**

	DI expenditure as a % of GDP	Self-reported male work disability, 40–65, 2001 (%)
Germany	1.6	40.3
Denmark	2.7	22.0
Netherlands	4.0	24.5
Belgium	2.2	14.3
France	1.7	20.5
United Kingdom	2.2	13.1
Ireland	1.3	15.7
Italy	2.0	8.0
Greece	1.6	13.3
Spain	2.3	15.5
Portugal	2.4	22.9
Austria	2.3	17.8
Finland	3.1	29.0
United States	1.1	19.3

Source: DI expenditures: World Bank (2006). Self-reported male disability: ECHP and PSID data used in this chapter; unbalanced panels, weighted.

incentives and institutional rules across a series of European countries and the United States can account for differences across these countries in the fractions of individuals on work disability programs. In contrast, variation in demographic attributes and health across these countries did little to explain these differences.

In this chapter, we do not attempt to analyze being on the disability rolls but instead aim at explaining the cross-sectional and dynamic variation across countries in self-assessed work disability and work. Table 3.1 shows for 2001 the relation between what is probably the best single measure of the scope of a country's disability program, the fraction of disability benefits as a fraction of GDP, and the fraction of men who self-report that they have a work disability.[2] There appears to be almost no correlation between these two measures. Although the incentives and institutions across countries appear to have a great deal to do with the fraction of workers who are on disability programs, these incentives and institutions appear to be only weakly related to the fraction of men who claim that they are work disabled.

Table 3A.3, taken from a recent OECD study, provides information on some characteristics of DI recipients for most of the countries we are considering in this chapter. The first column shows that a substantial fraction

2. The exact question on work disability in ECHP is: "Are you hampered in your daily activities by any physical or mental health problem, illness or disability?" In the PSID, it is: "Do you have any physical or nervous condition that limits the type of work or the amount of work you can do?"

of the people on DI declare that they have no work disability. This fraction varies a lot across countries and is particularly large in Sweden (48.9 percent) and the United States (46.7 percent). Either people are granted DI benefits while not acknowledging disability status, or those who recover from their disability are not able to find a job and instead stay on DI, or some combination of both. The third column of table 3A.3 shows indeed that exit rates from DI are extremely low. The United Kingdom and the Netherlands seem to be the exceptions in this respect, but this might have to do with reforms in the disability insurance system in these countries.

The second column of table 3A.3 shows the other side of the coin—many people who report to have a (moderate or severe) work disability receive neither earnings nor DI or other benefits. Again, variation across countries is substantial. In Sweden, almost everyone with a work disability has earnings from work or receives benefits, but in Spain and Italy, 28 or 29 percent receive neither of the two. The United States has an intermediate position in this respect.

Column (4) shows that the expected negative relation between disability and the chances of being employed holds in all countries: the relative employment rate is always less than one. Still, there are substantial differences across countries. In Spain, someone with a work disability is 0.41 times as likely to do paid work as someone without a work disability, compared to 0.79 in Switzerland. Again, the United States is somewhere in the middle with 0.58. Column (5) shows that there is an earnings differential between workers with and without a work disability, but in most countries, it is not very large. Here the United States and (surprisingly) Sweden are the exceptions—with workers with a disability earning almost 30 percent less than workers without disability.[3]

On the other hand, for those with a work disability, working seems to be an effective way of increasing income, as is borne out by column (6). This is particularly true in the United States, where the disabled who work have an average income that is 2.84 times as high as the average income of disabled who do not work. In Europe, the differences are smaller, but even in Sweden and Denmark, the countries with the lowest income differentials between working and nonworking disabled persons, the difference is still 37 or 38 percent. These cross-country differences seem to be in line with the generosity of disability insurance systems (as indicated by figure 3.1, for example).

3.4   The Model

In this section, we outline our model of the interrelated dynamics of self-reported work disability and labor force status (work versus no work). The equation for disability of individual i in time period t is specified as:

---

3. A complete analysis of this effect would need to account additionally for differential selection into the labor market across countries.

(1) $D_{it}^* = X_{it}'\beta^D + \gamma_D^{D'}D_{i,t-1} + \gamma_W^D W_{i,t-1} + \alpha_i^D + \varepsilon_{it}^D$

$D_{it} = 1[D_{it}^* > 0].$

Here D_{it} indicates the presence of self-reported work disability; 0 means no disability and 1 means disability. Lagged labor force status is denoted by an indicator variable $W_{i,t-1} = 1$ if the respondent worked in the previous period and $W_{i,t-1} = 0$ otherwise. The error terms ε_{it}^D are assumed to be independent standard normal; α_i^D is an individual effect, normally distributed with variance σ_α^2. The ε_{it}^D and α_i^D are assumed mutually independent and independent of the vector of explanatory variables X_{it}.

Thus, there are two direct sources of persistence in the disability equation: the lagged dependent variable $D_{i,t-1}$ and the unobserved heterogeneity term α_i^D. We allow for a lagged effect of workforce status on work disability, but not for a contemporaneous effect. That is, we are effectively assuming no contemporaneous "justification bias" in self-reported disability (justification bias would imply that people say they have a work disability to justify their nonwork status).

The second equation explains whether respondents do paid work or not. Labor force status W_{it} is explained by a Probit equation as follows:

(2) $W_{it}^* = X_{it}'\beta^W + \gamma_D^W D_{i,t-1} + \gamma_W^W W_{i,t-1} + \delta_d^W D_{i,t} + \alpha_i^W + \varepsilon_{it}^W$

$W_{it} = 1[W_{it}^* > 0].$

Thus, we allow for both a contemporaneous and a lagged effect of work disability on labor force status. The assumptions about individual effects and error terms are the same as before. We do not allow for correlation between the error terms in the two equations, but we do allow for correlated individual effects. Also here, there are two direct sources of persistence: lagged labor force status $W_{i,t-1}$ and the individual effect α_i^W.

The variance-covariance matrix of the individual effects is unrestricted. For estimation purposes we parameterize it as follows. Let $u_i = (u_i^D, u_i^W) \sim N_2(0,I)$. Then we specify the vector of individual effects $\alpha_i = (\alpha_i^D, \alpha_i^W)$ as $\alpha = \Lambda u$, with

(3) $\Lambda = \begin{pmatrix} \lambda_D^D & 0 \\ \lambda_D^W & \lambda_W^W \end{pmatrix},$

a lower triangular matrix. The parameter estimates summarized in the next section include the estimates of the entries in Λ.

To account for the initial conditions problem, we follow Heckman (1981), Hyslop (1999), and Vella and Verbeek (1999) and specify separate equations for wave 1. These equations have the same exogenous regressors and contemporaneous dependent variables on the right-hand side as the dynamic equations just presented, but do not include the lagged dependent variables. No restrictions are imposed on the coefficients or their relation to the coefficients in the dynamic equations. These coefficients are estimated jointly with the parameters in the dynamic equations and can be seen as nuisance parameters.

In the initial condition equations, we include arbitrary linear combinations of the individual effects in the two dynamic equations. This is the same as including an arbitrary linear combination of the two entries in u_i. The estimated coefficients of these linear combinations can be seen as nuisance parameters.

The previous equations must be slightly adapted for the PSID data. In the PSID, the frequency of interviewing was reduced from once a year to once every two years starting in 1997.[4] As a result, for the more recent years a lagged variable in the PSID model refers to a value two years ago. Hence, in the model for the PSID data we include separate coefficients for the lagged variables for the case that the previous wave is one year ago and the case that the previous wave is two years ago.[5]

3.5   Results

Our focus in this research is on the dynamics of disability and labor force activity during the pre-retirement years. These labor market dynamics are likely to be very different than those that characterize the period of labor market entry when people are first entering the labor market. Therefore, we estimate our models on samples of people who are age forty and over. Separate models are estimated for men and women given that the dynamics of labor force behavior are potentially very different.

A problem that requires special attention in an exercise like this is the international comparability of variable definitions. For example, if schools are organized in very different ways in different countries (as they are), it would be very difficult to know what it would mean to make comparisons across countries that "assume" that the schooling levels of workers are the same.

For that reason we have only used a very limited set of covariates: age dummies for the age groups forty to forty-four, forty-five to forty-nine, fifty to fifty-four, fifty-five to fifty-nine, sixty to sixty-four; year dummies; marital status (married or not, where married includes cohabitation), and two health dummies.

International comparability of self-reported health is a very difficult problem in itself. Because of this, we have adopted the following simple approach: in the United States and European data, respectively, we find the weighted frequency distributions for ages forty to sixty-five (balanced panel) in the top

4. To be precise, we use PSID waves 1994, 1995, 1996, 1997, 1999, 2001, and 2003.
5. To be precise, for the years 1995, 1996, and 1997, only the one-year lags are included; for the years 1999, 2001, and 2003, only the two-year lags are included.

Table 3.2   **Self-reported health in the PSID and the ECHP data**

	United States		European Union	
	Original classification			
Excellent	21.3%	Very good	16.2%	
Very good	26.6%	Good	43.4%	
Good	29.5%	Fair	29.8%	
Fair	10.1%	Bad	8.6%	
Poor	2.5%	Very bad	2.0%	
	Combined classification			
Excellent	57.8%	Excellent	59.6%	
Good	29.5%	Good	29.8%	
Fair	12.7%	Fair	10.6%	

panel of table 3.2. Based on this we collapse the five categories into three; combining the first two and the last two, essentially ignoring the wording differences. This leads to the distribution of self-reported health in the bottom panel of table 3.2. The health distribution is now similar in the United States and the European countries. In the analysis section following, we discuss what the implications for work disability and labor market participation would be if health were "the same" in all countries.

Table 3A.4 summarizes for men and women separately some of the key dynamic parameters (relating disability and work) estimated from our empirical models. While there are differences between our estimates for men and women, these tend to be concentrated in the "off-diagonal" terms—the effects of disability on work status or vice versa. In most countries (but not all), the effects of lagged disability on current disability is similar for men and women within each country. To the extent that the effect of lagged disability on current disability measures the pure transitions of work-related health between the waves, the similarity between men and women may not be that surprising. In most countries, the effects of lagged employment on current employment are higher for men than for women. The traditionally more transitory nature of employment for women would imply a smaller estimated impact of lagged employment.

With the exception of Belgium and Finland, the estimated effects of disability on employment are somewhat larger (in absolute value) for men than for women. Disability programs whose generosity depends on a past series of contributions would imply greater generosity for men compared to women, and this is what we find. Finally, the effects of lagged employment on disability may reflect in part the health effects of work. More likely this is picking up the unobserved effects of health, which is very incompletely captured in this data. Better health increases the likelihood of work and makes disability less likely.

Both disability and work status are highly persistent, and significantly so, across all countries. Current disability is negatively associated with current work status in most countries, and the relationship is particularly strong in the United States (and for women in Belgium). The evidence for lagged disability affecting current work status over and above the contemporaneous effect is weaker. There is evidence of lagged employment status affecting current work disability, however.

As one would probably expect, the parameter estimates for the effects of lagged work status on current work status tend to be relatively low in the United States, reflecting a higher turnover than in the European countries (both from working to not working and from not working to working). At the low end of the European scale in this respect are the United Kingdom and Spain, with the other European countries demonstrating somewhat larger effects.

3.6   Discussion

To gain a better understanding of the differences between the countries, we carry out four simulations. The first simulation simply generates values of work and self-reported disability over the sample period in each country, using the estimated models. The second simulation replaces the country-specific parameter estimates for the disability equation by the corresponding U.S. coefficients, but retains the own country work parameters. Conversely, the third simulation replaces the country-specific parameter estimates of the work equation by U.S. coefficients, but retains the own country disability equation. Finally, the fourth simulation replaces the country-specific parameters in both equations by U.S. coefficients. In all simulations the initial conditions are generated according to the country-specific estimates.

The figures in the appendix present time paths of two variables: the percentage of individuals with a work disability and the percentage of individuals working. For each of these variables we produce four values, according to the four scenarios sketched previously.

Let us first concentrate on work disability. The lines represent the scenarios where the U.S. disability parameters are used (the lines with triangles) or where both the disability parameters and the work parameters come from the United States (the lines with the x). The graphs suggest that the initial conditions only have an effect during the first couple of years of the simulations. The path of disability moves away from its initial position very quickly.

In countries where self-reported disability tends to be low, moving to U.S. parameters will lead to an increase in self-reported work disability. This is the case for female disability in Belgium, United Kingdom, and the Southern European countries, and for disability among males in the United Kingdom, Italy, and Spain. In some other cases the simulations with U.S. parameters do not lead to very different time paths of disability, like for Belgian, Greek, and Portuguese males. In a number of countries, adopting U.S. parameters leads to a dramatic fall in disability. These cases include males and females in Germany and Finland, and females in Denmark and the Netherlands.

Another noteworthy aspect of the graphs is that these lines tend to be on top of each other for most countries. This suggests that the feedback from work to disability is quantitatively similar to that in the United States (since the line with triangles uses country-specific work parameters this should generate deviations from the all-U.S. parameters if work had an appreciably different effect on disability in Europe compared to the United States). Cases where the feedback from work to disability appears to make a difference include females in the Netherlands, Belgium, Ireland, Italy, Greece, Spain, and Austria. For males the difference in feedback from work to disability seems to be essentially immaterial, with the possible exception of Belgium. Inspecting the second column of table 3A.4 suggests that the cases with the biggest differences between the triangled and x lines are indeed the cases where the estimated values of γ_W^D, the effect of lagged work on disability, deviate most from the U.S. estimate.

Now consider the bottom part of the graphs; that is, the simulation of employment under the different scenarios. The simulations with all U.S. coefficients lead to final values that are quite similar across countries: from 0.66 (Portugal) to 0.75 (Belgium, Ireland) for women, and from 0.76 (Germany) to 0.86 (several countries) for men. The main sources of differences are initial conditions and demographic and health differences. A second observation is that the simulation with all U.S. coefficients leads to the highest employment rate in almost all countries, although often it makes only a negligible difference whether European or U.S. coefficients are used for the work disability equation. Exceptions are Italy and the United Kingdom, where replacing EU disability coefficients by U.S. coefficients leads to higher work disability and thus lowers employment. As a consequence, the highest employment rate is attained with U.S. work and EU disability coefficients.

This argument, however, does not always work: to further isolate the effect of labor market institutions from the effect of disability, it is of interest to consider the difference between the line with triangles (only disability parameters from the United States) and the lines with x (all parameters from the United States) in more countries. It is instructive to take the Netherlands as an example. When looking at females, we note that the simulation with U.S. disability coefficients but Dutch work coefficients yields essentially the same employment rate, despite the fact that disability is much lower with U.S. disability coefficients. Table 3A.4 tells us immediately why this is so. The parameter γ_D^W is close to zero for Dutch females. We also note, however, that the line with x (all U.S. parameters) is about 25 percentage points higher than the line with triangles. This suggests that independent of the disability status of Dutch women, American institutions would generate a much higher employment rate. The story for Dutch males is qualitatively similar, but since the employment rate is already high, adopting U.S. coefficients can only have a limited effect. With this example in mind we observe that in all countries, with the possible exception of Denmark, the United Kingdom, and Ireland, labor market institutions, rather than disability, cause the employment rate to be low relative to the United States.

One can further investigate this by looking at the lines with squares (EU disability parameters, but U.S. work parameters). The relevant comparison now is between the lines with squares and the lines with diamonds (all EU parameters). Once again we find that labor market institutions explain the differences in employment rates, rather than differences in disability.

A different way to obtain insight into the different dynamics across the various countries is to consider transition matrices. These are given in table 3A.5 (for disability) and table 3A.6 (for work). These key dynamics relate to the transitions between work and nonwork and disability and nondisability. Each can be summarized by two off-diagonal transitions. For work, the two transitions are the transition from work to nonwork and the transition from nonwork to work. Similarly, for disability the off-diagonal transitions are from not disabled to disabled and from disabled to not disabled. Because our interest concerns how all these transition patterns vary across our set of countries, tables 3A.7 (for disability) and 3A.8 (for work) summarize the key parameters by organizing them by the magnitude of the transitions with the country names attached. Finally, since the United States will be the benchmark for all countries in our simulations, we list the U.S. parameter at the bottom of each list.

Consider first the disability transitions. We observe considerable variation in the inflow rates into disability (the transition from being not disabled in one period to being disabled the next period). For men these rates vary from 18 percent in Germany to 4 percent in the United States, United Kingdom, and Italy. For women the rates vary from 21 percent in Germany to 5 percent in Ireland, Italy, and Belgium. The United States is near the bottom with 6 percent. On the other hand, outflow rates out of disability (the transition from being disabled in one period and not disabled in the next period) vary less, at least in relative terms. For men the rates vary from 42 percent in Italy to 23 percent in Germany and Denmark, while for women the rates vary from 49 percent in Italy to 22 percent in Germany.

There are a number of salient patterns to these disability transitions. First, while the levels differ between men and women, the country rankings are remarkably similar by gender, suggesting that the variation across countries is at least partly due to institutional variation affecting men and women in a similar way. To illustrate, Germany ranks highest on the transition into disability for both sexes, while Italy ranks highest in the transition from work disability into nonwork disability. Second, for almost all the countries listed there exists considerable churning between work and nonwork disability, indicating that work disability is far from a permanent condition even at these older ages (cf. Kapteyn, Smith, and Van Soest 2007). Consequently, cross-sectional analysis of work disability status will not be able to capture some of the main features of work disabilities during the pre-retirement years. Third, compared to the European countries, the United States ranks very low on the transition into work disability, while it ranks in the middle of the pack in the transitions out of work disability.

Work disability will tend to be high when the transition into work disability is high, while the transition out of work disability is low. Germany, Denmark, and Finland would be the best prototypes of such behavior. On the other hand, other countries have a relatively low transition into disability, matched with a relatively high transition out of disability. Italy, Greece, and Spain would be good illustrations of that behavior and in those countries the steady-state levels of work disability will be low.

Consider next the ranking of the transitions between work and nonwork for countries listed in table 3A.8. First, we note that the variation in transitions from work to nonwork varies less across countries than the transitions from nonwork to work. Thus, most of the variation across countries in labor market dynamics relates to whether persons who are out of the labor force are likely to transit back into the labor force. To illustrate, for men, transition rates from nonwork to work vary from 31 percent in the United Kingdom to as low as 3 percent in Austria and Belgium. Indeed, the countries where moving back into the labor force appears to be least likely are very similar for men and women alike. These countries would include Italy, France, Belgium, and Austria.

In contrast, the United States has a relatively high rate of transition back into the labor force for both sexes compared to all countries. It is in comparisons between the United States and Italy, France, Belgium, and Austria, that the effects on employment are quite dramatic. For example, the chart for Austria in the appendix shows a very low employment rate toward the end of the observation period. For women, among the European countries the United Kingdom has the highest inflow into employment (16 percent), while Belgium has the lowest inflow (3 percent). The chart for Belgium in the appendix confirms that female employment in Belgium is very low in comparison with other countries.

In sharp contrast, table 3A.8 shows much less variation in transitions from work to nonwork, especially for men. The full range of values for men in table 3A.8 is only from 0.03 (Denmark) to 0.08 (Germany), with the United States at a value of 0.07. In fact, eight of the thirteen European countries in table 3A.8 for men lie within 2 percentage points of the U.S. transition value from work to not work. Thus, the source of the labor market dynamic differences among these countries appears not to lie in the ease or difficulty of the transition from work to not-work. Instead, it is the relative rigidity of some European countries in discouraging reentry into the labor force that appears to be the major issue.

This is further illustrated by table 3A.9. The last four columns of table 3A.9 contain the same transition rates as table 3A.8, but in addition, the first two columns contain measures of employment protection and replacement rates at retirement. The employment protection measure is taken from OECD (2004) and is the sum of three main components reflecting, respectively, (a) difficulty of dismissal, (b) procedural inconveniences an employer faces in the dismissal process, and (c) severance pay provisions (OECD 2004, 65). The measure presented here is "version 2, late 1990s" (see table 2.A2.4 in OECD [2004]). The replacement rate shown in the table is the replacement rate of a worker with average earnings in a country, as calculated in OECD (2005). The countries in table 3A.9 have been ranked according to the employment protection measure. Somewhat remarkably, it is particularly the transitions from nonwork to work that are affected by the employment protection index: for both women and men, more employment protection implies a smaller transition rate back into employment. A similar finding is reported in OECD (2004). On the other hand, the protective effect seems to be limited; transition rates out of employment do not correlate significantly with the employment protection measure.

In view of the age range we are considering, a measure of a retirement replacement rate has been included, since one would expect that some workers who are temporarily out of the labor force will transit into retirement rather than back into employment if that alternative is sufficiently attractive. Table 3A.9 indeed shows the expected negative correlation. However, when regressing the transition rates on both the employment protection measure and the replacement rate measure we find the former to be significant, but not the latter.

3.7   Conclusion

In this chapter, we have investigated the dynamics of labor force and work disability behavior among individuals between forty and sixty-five in several Western European countries and the United States. We estimated the dynamics of labor force and disability behavior separately for men and women using high quality panel data in thirteen European countries and the United States. We find substantial differences in labor force dynamics between the countries. Adopting U.S. parameters (i.e., U.S. institutions and norms) often leads to considerable reductions in self-reported disability. Although this has some effect on employment rates, most of the action is in the labor market institutions themselves, where adopting U.S. coefficients may generate substantially higher employment rates. Comparison of transition rates with aggregate measures of employment protection suggests that these play a major role in generating the observed differences across countries.

Appendix

Simulated Time Paths of Mild and Severe Disability and of Labor Force Status

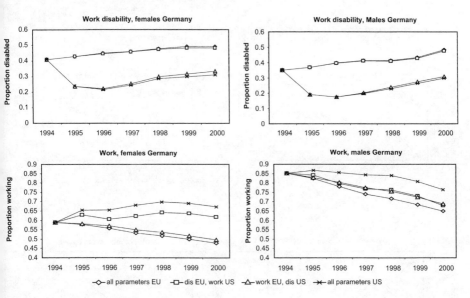

Fig. 3A.1   Germany

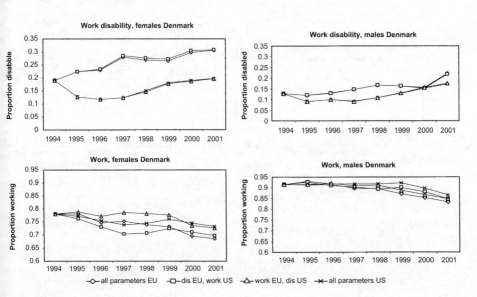

Fig. 3A.2   Denmark

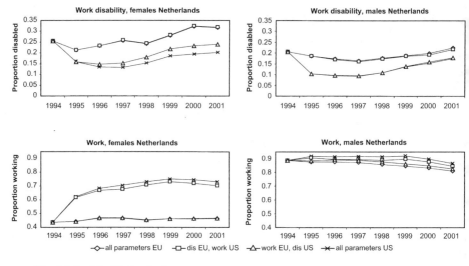

Fig. 3A.3   The Netherlands

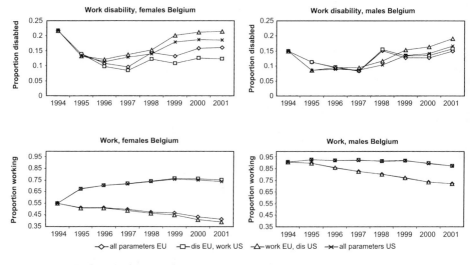

Fig. 3A.4   Belgium

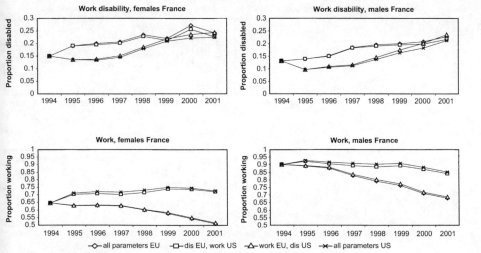

Fig. 3A.5   France

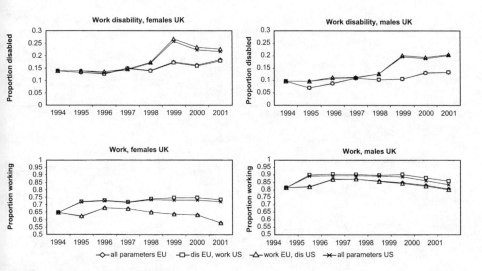

Fig. 3A.6   United Kingdom

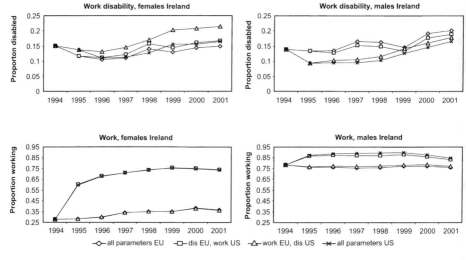

Fig. 3A.7 Ireland

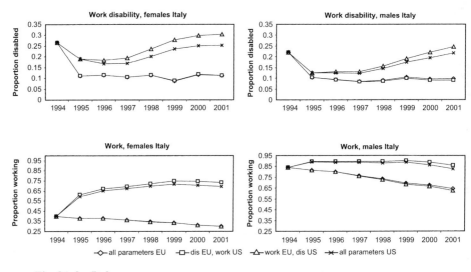

Fig. 3A.8 Italy

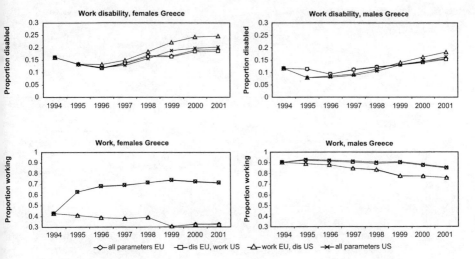

Fig. 3A.9　Greece

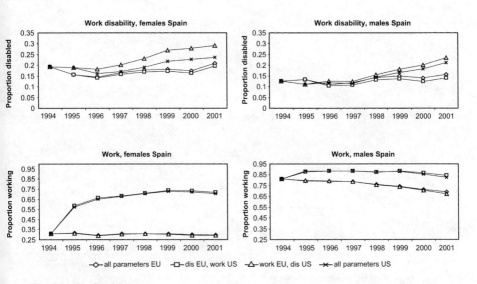

Fig. 3A.10　Spain

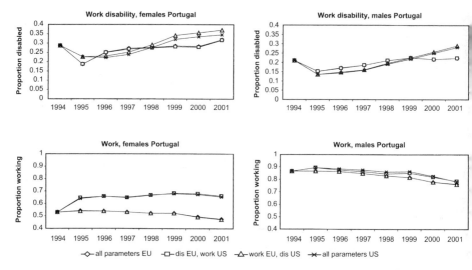

Fig. 3A.11   Portugal

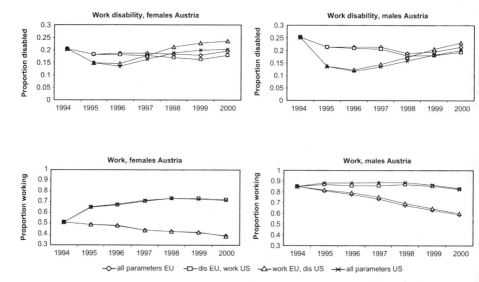

Fig. 3A.12   Austria

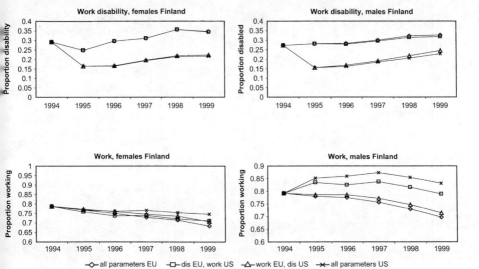

Fig. 3A.13 Finland

Fig. 3A.13   Finland

Table 3A.1   **Overview of ECHP waves**

								Subsample									
		D							L							UK	
	B	DK	ECHP	SOEP	EL	E	F	IrI	I	ECHP	PSELL	NL	A	P	Fin	S	ECHP	BHPS
1994											—		—		—	—		
1995													—			—		
1996													—					
1997		—								—							—	
1998		—								—							—	
1999		—								—							—	
2000		—								—							—	
2001		—								—							—	

Note: ECHP = European Community Household Panel; SOEP = Socio-Economic Panel; PSELL = Panel socio-économique Liewen zu Lëtzebuerg; BHPS = British Household Panel Survey. Dashed cells denote missing waves.

Table 3A.2   Selected characteristics of disability pension policies across countries

	Qualifying conditions		Permanent disability benefits
	Loss of earning capacity	Minimum period of contributions	
Austria	≥ 50% compared to person with the same education	60 months + 1 month for each month (from age 50) in the last 10 years (plus 2 months for each month from age 50)	60% of assessment base (= average earnings in the best 16 years, up to an annual maximum of €3,013)
Belgium	2/3 in the usual occupation	6 months, incl. 120 days of actual/credited work	65% of lost earnings (s.t. ceiling) for an insured w/ dependents; 40% if no dependents; 50% if no dependents but living w/ others with no income. Payable > 1 year disability (1st year-sickness benefit)
Denmark	Reduced working capacity and inability to assure subsistence	Disability pension and supplement (both income-tested) payable age 18 = 64 w/ ≥ 3 years' residence from age 15	13,895 kroner monthly for single, 11,810 kroner if not living alone; disability supplement (income test): 6,000 kroner a year
Finland	60% if earnings-related disability pension	Universal disability pension (income-tested) permanent incapacity for suitable work	Universal disability—Income tested €11.21 to €496.38 a month; earnings-related disability: 1.5% of wage for each year of service up to disability onset
France	2/3 of earning capacity in any occupation under age 60	12 months insurance before disability onset and 800 hrs. employment in last 12 months	50% of average earnings in the best 10 years if incapable of any professional activity, up to a maximum of €1,238 a month. Partial disability 30% of average earnings in best yrs., min. pension €241/month
Germany	Full reduction (cannot work > 3 hours/day in any form of employment) or partial reduction (cannot work > 6 hours/day in any form of employment)	5 years of contributions and 36 months of compulsory contributions in the last 5 years	Total of individual earnings points (individual annual earnings divided by the average earnings of all contributors multiplied by the entry factor) multiplied by pension factor and pension value
Greece	At least 80% disabled	Max 4,500 days of contributions (1,500 days if the insured began working after 1993); 300 days if younger than 21	For an assessed degree of disability of 80% or more (severe), 100% of the pension is paid; for an assessed degree of disability of 67% to 79.9% (ordinary), 75% of the pension paid; min. pension €392.16/month.
Ireland	Invalidity pension—permanent incapacity for work; disability allowance (means-tested): aged 16–66, physically/mentally disabled	260 weeks of paid contributions with 48 weeks paid or credited in the last tax year	Invalidity pension: €140.30 a week; €167.30 a week if aged 65 or older; disability allowance (means-tested): up to €134.80 a week, + €89.40 a week for a qualified adult and €16.80 for each dependent child

Italy	Total and permanent inability to perform any work	5 years of contributions, including 3 in the 5 years before the claim. No other forms of income, including earnings from self-employment and unemployment benefits	Pension based on a progressive percentage (0.9% to 2%) of salary multiplied by the number of years of contributions, up to a maximum of 40
Netherlands	At least 80% of earning capacity in the current occupation for full pension	Partial pension: The loss of 15% to 80% of earning capacity for employed workers	Up to 70% of earnings for loss of earning capacity of at least 80%; 14% to 50.75% of earnings for a loss of earning capacity of 15% to 80%. €167.70 a day maximum
Portugal	2/3 of earning capacity	5 years of contributions (120 days of registered pay)	2% of average adjusted lifetime salary for each year of contributions
Spain	Loss of normal earning capacity	1/4 of period from age 20 to the onset of disability, with at least 5 years of contributions and at least 1/5 of the required contributions in the last 10 years	Permanent total disability, pension 100% of the benefit base (min €411.76). For permanent occupational disability, award 55% of benefit base, plus 20% if aged 55+ & not employed (min €411.76).
Sweden	Work capacity reduced by at least one-quarter	Earnings-related sickness compensation independent of insurance periods	94,320 kronor for an insured person with 40 years of residence and without an earnings-related benefit
Switzerland	At least 40% disabled	Contributions in all years from age 21. Special pension for nationals not meeting required min. contribution period for disability base pension	9,146 francs a year plus a variable amount calculated by multiplying annual income by 13/600 if income < 37,080
United Kingdom	Long-term incapacity benefit and disability living allowance (noncontributory, no means test)	3 years before the claim, age before 65	Long-term incapacity benefit £72.15 a week, plus £43.15 a week for a dependent adult; Allowance £57.20, £38.30, or £15.15 a week according to needs
United States	Disability pension: Incapable of permanent substantial gainful activity; Disability supplemental income benefit (means-tested): disabled and blind persons age < 65 low income	Quarter of coverage for each year since age 21 up to the year of the onset of disability, up to a maximum of 40 quarters of coverage, 20 quarters of coverage in the 10-year period	Pension based on the average covered earnings since 1950 (or age 21, if later) and indexed for past wage inflation, up to the onset of disability, excluding up to 5 years with the lowest earnings. Max. monthly pension $2,036 (certain conditions)

Source: SSA, Social Security Programs Throughout the World: Europe, 2004. Available at: http://www.ssa.gov/policy/docs/progdesc/ssptw/2004–2005/europe/.

Table 3A.3   **Characteristics of DI recipients: men, late 1990s**

	% of disability benefit recipients declaring that they are not disabled	% of disabled persons ages 20–64 with neither income from work nor income from benefits	Annual rates of outflow from disability benefits	Relative employment rate of disabled persons age 20–64 vs. nondisabled ages 20–64	Relative income from work of disabled over nondisabled persons working	Relative average personal income of disabled persons working over disabled persons not working
Austria	27.7	14.2	1.04	0.60	0.97	1.96
Germany	n.a.	11.9	1.25	0.67	0.92	1.79
Sweden	48.9	1.1	n.a.	0.69	0.70	1.37
Netherlands	30.6	19.5	3.34	0.60	0.87	1.45
Spain	18.3	28.0	0.57	0.41	0.86	2.07
Italy	43.9	28.8	n.a.	0.60	0.94	1.94
Portugal	28.6	20.9	0.97	0.59	n.a.	1.81
France	33.3	11.7	n.a.	0.72	n.a.	1.83
Denmark	26.2	6.3	n.a.	0.61	0.88	1.38
United Kingdom	43.3	9.1	5.64	0.53	0.84	1.61
United States	46.7	18.8	1.16	0.58	0.71	2.84
Switzerland	29.8	14.2	n.a.	0.79	0.98	n.a.
Belgium	43.4	16.2	n.a.	0.54	0.90	1.91

Notes: n.a. = data not available. These tables are summaries of more detailed information in OECD (2003b). The underlying data sources are ECHP 1996 or 1997 for the European countries and SIPP for the United States.

Source: OECD (2003a, chapter 3, tables 3.7 and 3.8).

Table 3A.4   **Work disability and employment dynamics: Key parameter estimates**

		Disability equation		Work equation		
		Lagged disability γ_D^D	Lagged employment γ_W^D	Lagged disability γ_D^W	Lagged employment γ_W^W	Current disability δ_D^W
Germany	Men	0.725	−0.422	−0.432	1.973	−0.200
	Women	0.572	−0.244	−0.285	1.356	−0.143
Denmark	Men	1.011	−0.763	−0.587	1.841	−0.575
	Women	0.780	−0.743	−0.559	1.826	−0.497
Netherlands	Men	0.842	−0.789	−0.236	2.007	−0.762
	Women	0.854	0.041	−0.068	1.516	−0.095
Belgium	Men	1.225	0.231	−0.193	3.105	−0.211
	Women	0.983	−1.344	−0.500	2.452	−1.221
France	Men	0.814	−0.348	−0.234	2.541	−0.306
	Women	0.875	−0.446	−0.184	2.495	−0.139
United Kingdom	Men	1.153	−0.249	−0.037	1.541	−0.157
	Women	0.835	−0.244	−0.075	1.418	0.037
Ireland	Men	0.948	−0.728	−0.197	2.034	−0.670
	Women	1.133	−0.030	−0.073	1.723	−0.532
Italy	Men	1.023	−0.315	−0.198	2.093	−0.403
	Women	0.683	0.011	0.012	1.725	−0.076
Greece	Men	0.935	−0.255	0.165	2.063	−0.411
	Women	0.931	−0.122	−0.021	1.510	−0.161
Spain	Men	0.738	−0.665	−0.650	1.701	−0.541
	Women	0.749	−0.147	−0.239	1.175	−0.416
Portugal	Men	1.021	−0.104	0.127	2.316	−0.459
	Women	0.958	−0.097	−0.108	1.920	−0.110
Austria	Men	0.758	−0.437	−0.375	2.863	−0.444
	Women	0.936	−0.266	−0.413	2.213	−0.199
Finland	Men	0.977	−0.348	−0.284	1.765	−0.284
	Women	0.978	−0.038	−0.363	1.403	−0.524
United States	Men	1.064	−0.643	−0.308	1.643	−0.995
	Women	0.841	−0.558	−0.202	1.447	−0.778

Notes: Results for the United States are coefficients on one-year lagged variables, although two-year lags are also included to control for the varying periodicity of PSID data. All specifications also include year dummies, controls for education, age group, marital status, self-reported general health status, and (in the U.S. case) ethnicity. Equations for the initial conditions use the same variable.

Table 3A.5   **Transition probabilities for disability status actual**

	Men		Women	
	Not disabled	Disabled	Not disabled	Disabled
Germany				
Not disabled	0.82	0.18	0.79	0.21
Disabled	0.23	0.77	0.22	0.78
Denmark				
Not disabled	0.82	0.12	0.88	0.12
Disabled	0.23	0.77	0.28	0.72
Netherlands				
Not disabled	0.92	0.08	0.89	0.11
Disabled	0.29	0.71	0.26	0.74
Belgium				
Not disabled	0.95	0.05	0.95	0.05
Disabled	0.34	0.66	0.29	0.71
France				
Not disabled	0.91	0.09	0.90	0.10
Disabled	0.31	0.69	0.30	0.70
United Kingdom				
Not disabled	0.96	0.04	0.93	0.07
Disabled	0.26	0.74	0.31	0.69
Ireland				
Not disabled	0.93	0.07	0.95	0.05
Disabled	0.31	0.69	0.34	0.65
Italy				
Not disabled	0.96	0.04	0.95	0.05
Disabled	0.42	0.58	0.49	0.51
Greece				
Not disabled	0.94	0.06	0.93	0.07
Disabled	0.37	0.63	0.37	0.63
Spain				
Not disabled	0.93	0.07	0.91	0.09
Disabled	0.37	0.63	0.40	0.60
Portugal				
Not disabled	0.92	0.08	0.90	0.10
Disabled	0.28	0.72	0.27	0.74
Austria				
Not disabled	0.91	0.09	0.91	0.09
Disabled	0.35	0.65	0.36	0.64
Finland				
Not disabled	0.88	0.12	0.87	0.13
Disabled	0.25	0.75	0.26	0.74
United States				
Not disabled	0.96	0.04	0.94	0.06
Disabled	0.26	0.74	0.29	0.71

Table 3A.6   **Transition probabilities for labor force status actual**

	Men		Women	
	Does not work	Works	Does not work	Works
Germany				
Does not work	0.89	0.11	0.91	0.09
Works	0.08	0.92	0.10	0.90
Denmark				
Does not work	0.84	0.16	0.86	0.14
Works	0.03	0.97	0.06	0.94
Netherlands				
Does not work	0.86	0.14	0.92	0.08
Works	0.04	0.96	0.09	0.91
Belgium				
Does not work	0.97	0.03	0.97	0.03
Works	0.04	0.96	0.07	0.93
France				
Does not work	0.92	0.08	0.94	0.05
Works	0.05	0.95	0.06	0.93
United Kingdom				
Does not work	0.69	0.31	0.84	0.16
Works	0.06	0.94	0.10	0.90
Ireland				
Does not work	0.87	0.13	0.93	0.07
Works	0.04	0.96	0.11	0.89
Italy				
Does not work	0.91	0.09	0.97	0.03
Works	0.07	0.93	0.10	0.90
Greece				
Does not work	0.88	0.12	0.94	0.07
Works	0.05	0.95	0.15	0.85
Spain				
Does not work	0.85	0.15	0.94	0.06
Works	0.07	0.93	0.14	0.86
Portugal				
Does not work	0.89	0.12	0.92	0.08
Works	0.04	0.96	0.09	0.91
Austria				
Does not work	0.97	0.03	0.96	0.04
Works	0.07	0.93	0.09	0.91
Finland				
Does not work	0.87	0.13	0.87	0.13
Works	0.06	0.94	0.07	0.93
United States				
Does not work	0.80	0.20	0.74	0.2603
Works	0.07	0.93	0.037	0.97

Table 3A.7   **Ordering of transitions in disability states by country**

Men		Women	
Transition	Countries	Transition	Countries
	A Not disabled to disabled		
.18	Germany	.21	Germany
.12	Denmark, Finland	.13	Finland
.09	France, Austria	.12	Denmark
.08	Netherlands, Portugal	.11	Netherlands
.07	Ireland, Spain	.10	France, Portugal
.06	Greece	.09	Austria, Spain
.05	Belgium	.07	Greece, United Kingdom
.04	Italy, United Kingdom	.05	Belgium, Ireland, Italy
	United States = .04		United States = .06
	B Disabled to not disabled		
.42	Italy	.49	Italy
.37	Greece, Spain	.40	Spain
.35	Austria	.37	Greece
.34	Belgium	.36	Austria
.31	France, Ireland	.34	Ireland
.29	Netherlands	.31	United Kingdom
.28	Portugal	.30	France
.26	United Kingdom	.29	Belgium
.25	Finland	.28	Denmark
.23	Germany, Denmark	.27	Portugal
		.26	Netherlands, Finland
		.22	Germany
	United States = .26		United States = .29

Table 3A.8   Ordering of work transitions by country

Men		Women	
Transition	Countries	Transition	Countries

A Work to not work

Men		Women	
.08	Germany	.15	Greece
.07	Italy, Spain, Austria	.14	Spain
.06	United Kingdom, Finland	.11	Ireland
.05	France, Greece	.10	Germany, United Kingdom, Italy
.04	Netherlands, Belgium	.09	Netherlands, Portugal, Austria
	Ireland, Portugal	.07	Belgium, Finland
.03	Denmark	.06	Denmark, France
	United States = .07		United States = .04

B Not work to work

Men		Women	
.31	United Kingdom		
.16	Denmark	.16	United Kingdom
.15	Spain	.14	Denmark
.14	Netherlands	.13	Finland
.13	Ireland, Finland	.09	Germany
.12	Greece, Portugal	.08	Portugal, Netherlands
.11	Germany	.07	Ireland, Greece
.09	Italy	.06	Spain
.08	France	.05	France
.03	Belgium, Austria	.04	Austria
		.03	Belgium, Italy
	United States = .20		United States = .26

Table 3A.9   Transition rates, employment protection, and retirement replacement rates

	OECD employment protection measure	Replacement rate at median	Men		Women	
			Work to not work	Not work to work	Work to not work	Not work to work
Portugal	3.7	79.8	0.04	0.12	0.09	0.08
Greece	3.5	99.9	0.05	0.12	0.15	0.07
Italy	3.1	88.8	0.07	0.09	0.10	0.03
Spain	3.0	88.3	0.07	0.15	0.14	0.06
France	2.8	68.8	0.05	0.08	0.06	0.05
Germany	2.6	71.8	0.08	0.11	0.10	0.09
Belgium	2.5	63.1	0.04	0.03	0.07	0.03
Austria	2.4	93.2	0.07	0.03	0.09	0.04
Netherlands	2.3	84.1	0.04	0.14	0.09	0.08
Finland	2.2	78.8	0.06	0.13	0.07	0.13
Denmark	1.8	54.1	0.03	0.16	0.06	0.14
Ireland	1.2	36.6	0.04	0.13	0.11	0.07
United Kingdom	1.0	47.6	0.06	0.31	0.10	0.16
United States	0.7	51.0	0.07	0.20	0.04	0.26
correlation with OECD measure[a]		0.81 [.001]	−0.02 [.96]	−0.57 [.03]	0.45 [.10]	−0.70 [.005]
correlation with replacement rate[a]		0.28 [.32]	−0.46 [.09]	0.46 [.10]	−0.50 [.07]	

Note: See text for explanation.

[a]Significance level in square brackets.

References

Autor, D., and M. Duggan. 2003. The rise in the disability rolls and the decline in unemployment. *Quarterly Journal of Economics* 118 (1): 157–206.

Banks, J., A. Kapteyn, J. P. Smith, and A. van Soest. 2009. Work disability is a pain in the *****, especially in England, the Netherlands, and the United States. In *Health in older ages: The causes and consequences of declining disability among the elderly*, ed. D. Cutler and D. Wise, 251–94.

Börsch-Supan, A. 2007. Work disability, health, and incentive effects. Paper presented at NBER Economics of Aging Conference. August, Carefree, Arizona.

Bound, J., and R. Burkhauser. 1999. Economic analysis of transfer programs targeted on people with disabilities. In *Handbook of labor economics,* vol. 3C, ed. O. Ashenfelter and D. Card, 3417–528.

Eurostat. 2003. *ECHP UDB description of variables data dictionary, codebook and differences between countries and waves.* European Commission, Brussels.

Gruber, J., and D. Wise, eds. 2003. *Social Security programs and retirement around the world: Micro estimation.* Chicago: University of Chicago Press.

Heckman, J. J. 1981. The incidental parameters problem and the problem of initial conditions in estimating a discrete time-discrete data stochastic process. In *Structural analysis of discrete data with econometric applications,* ed. C. F. Manski and D. L. McFadden, 179–95. London: MIT Press.

Hyslop, D. R. 1999. State dependence, serial correlation and heterogeneity in intertemporal labor force participation of married women. *Econometrica* 67:1255–94.

Kapteyn, A., J. P. Smith, and A. van Soest. 2007. Dynamics of pain and work disability. *Journal of Health Economics* 27 (2): 496–509.

Nicoletti, C., and F. Peracchi. 2002. Aging in Europe: What can we learn from the Europanel? In *Pensions: More information, less ideology,* ed. T. Boeri, A. Börsch-Supan, A. Brugiavini, R. Disney, A. Kapteyn, and F. Peracchi, 153–88. Dordrecht: Kluwer.

Organization for Economic Cooperation and Development. 2003a. *OECD employment outlook 2003: Towards more and better jobs.* Paris: OECD.

———. 2003b. *Transforming disability into ability: Policies to promote work and income security for the disabled.* Paris: OECD.

———. 2004. *OECD employment outlook 2004: Employment protection regulation and labour market performance.* Paris: OECD.

———. 2005. *Pensions at a glance; public policies across OECD countries.* Paris: OECD.

Peracchi, F. 2002. The European community household panel: A review. *Empirical Economics* 27 (1): 63–90.

Stapleton, D.C., and R. V. Burkhauser, eds. 2003. *The decline in employment of people with disabilities: A policy puzzle.* Kalamazoo, MI: W. E. Upjohn Institute for Employment Research.

Vella, F., and M. Verbeek. 1999. Two-step estimation of panel data models with censored endogenous variables and selection bias. *Journal of Econometrics* 90 (2): 239–63.

World Bank. 2006. Social safety nets in OECD countries. *Social Safety Nets in OECD Countries, no. 25.*

Comment   Michael Hurd

We observe across Europe and between Europe and the United States differing levels of labor market activity and differing levels of participation in state disability programs as a function of age. For example, as shown in table 3C.1, the employment rates of men age fifty to fifty-four are similar in Sweden, France, and the United States. But then they drop sharply with age in France, reaching just 4.1 percent among those sixty to sixty-four, whereas they are 61 percent in Sweden and 57 percent in the United States. Almost no men age sixty-five or over work in Sweden or France, whereas 19.8 percent work in the United States. The table reveals that there is large variation across Europe, possibly as much as between Europe and the United States. Thus, it is inaccurate to think solely of a distinction between Europe and the United States. The table also reveals that differences are not due to a country fixed effect that is additive at all ages; rather, there are country-specific interactions with age that are surely due to public policies that induce or facilitate the employment patterns and to societal attitudes toward working at particular ages. Indeed, in countries with mandatory retirement the relationship between age and employment will be very sharp.

Because the levels of employment by age differ across countries, the rates of transition from working to not working will also differ. For example, the transition rate from working to not working of men fifty to fifty-four as they age to fifty-five to fifty-nine is approximately 17 percent in Sweden (1 − 73.9 ÷ 88.9), 38 percent in France, and 10 percent in the United States. Broadly speaking, the differing levels of employment at age fifty-five or over are due to differing transition rates, not to differing initial levels at younger ages; that is, France has much lower employment rates at older ages because of high transition rates out of employment, not because men fifty to fifty-four work substantially less. Establishing this fact is an important point of studying the dynamics. The fraction of the population with self-reported disabilities also varies across countries. For example, about 12 percent of fifty-seven-year-olds in the Netherlands report that they are disabled versus just 4 percent in Denmark and 3 percent in Sweden.[1] There is similarly large variation in the transition rates.

A natural question is what causes these differing transition rates. A pos-

Michael Hurd is senior principal researcher and director of the RAND Center for the Study of Aging and a research associate of the National Bureau of Economic Research.

1. Based on figure 1, chapter 5.3, Börsch-Supan et al. (2005). The figure is based on a question in SHARE about current job status (EP005). Possible responses are permanently sick or disabled, employed, retired, unemployed, homemaker, or other. I imagine that most respondents would think about disability in the context of working and so tend to equate disability with participation in the state disability program.

Table 3C.1   **Employment rate of men**

Age	Sweden	France	United States
50–54	88.9	82.5	83.6
55–59	73.9	51.5	75.2
60–64	60.7	4.1	57.0
65 or over	2.0	0.3	19.8

Sources: Sweden and Europe: SHARE wave 1 (2004 table 5a3); Börsch-Supan et al. (2005); U.S.: CPS data for 2006, accessed Dec. 28, 2007 at www.bls.gov/cps/cpsaat3.pdf.

sible answer might be differences in health; however, it seems unlikely that health could explain the employment transition rates. What could cause actual health in France to decline rapidly beginning at age fifty-five even as health remained good in Sweden and the United States? And what could cause health at sixty-five to decline in Sweden relative to the United States? A more plausible explanation is incentives. Individuals face different public programs and private pension systems with respect to generosity and structure. Employers also face differing public programs to facilitate the transition of their employees into retirement. The chapter by Kapteyn, Smith, van Soest, and Banks is the beginning of a research program to relate transition rates to the detailed structure of public retirement and disability policy. Eventually they would aim to quantify how changes in policy will affect the transition rates.

In my view, a natural and simple way of addressing the problem is to estimate hazard models or vector auto regressions (VAR) country by country as

$$\begin{bmatrix} D_t \\ W_t \end{bmatrix} = \begin{bmatrix} \pi_{11} & \pi_{12} \\ \pi_{21} & \pi_{22} \end{bmatrix} \begin{bmatrix} D_{t-1} \\ W_{t-1} \end{bmatrix} + \begin{bmatrix} \varepsilon_d \\ \varepsilon_w \end{bmatrix},$$

where D_t is a self-reported disability indicator and W_t is a work indicator.[2] Then one could relate the π_{ij} to policy variables such as the generosity of the disability system. One would think that in countries where access to the disability program is easy and generosity is high, π_{12} would be large and π_{22} would be (relatively) small. However, table 3C.1 suggests that age interactions would be required so that the π_{ij} would vary by country and by age.

Kapteyn, Smith, van Soest, and Banks use a more complex model

$$\begin{bmatrix} 1 & 0 \\ -\alpha & 1 \end{bmatrix} \begin{bmatrix} D_t \\ W_t \end{bmatrix} = \Gamma \begin{bmatrix} D_{t-1} \\ W_{t-1} \end{bmatrix} + \begin{bmatrix} \lambda_{11} & 0 \\ \lambda_{21} & \lambda_{22} \end{bmatrix} \begin{bmatrix} u_d \\ u_w \end{bmatrix} + \begin{bmatrix} \varepsilon_d \\ \varepsilon_w \end{bmatrix},$$

---

2. The actual specification leads to probit estimation, but to simplify the discussion I will illustrate with linear models.

where the ε and u are all independent and individual heterogeneity is generated by the u. This specification leads to a reduced form that has a lower triangular structure in the coefficient matrices on the error terms. That is, it is a recursive model, and, except for the heterogeneity, could be estimated by ordinary least squares.

One question concerns the use of this model and the complications about interpretations that accompany it. The model has the character of a structural model but it is not embedded in a theoretical structure, and so the interpretation is difficult. It imposes some restrictions: what difference do they make? For example, the specification for working is

$$W_t = \gamma_{21} W_{t-1} + \gamma_{22} D_{t-1} + \alpha D_t + v_t.$$

This could be simply descriptive, summarizing the fact that the transition from employment to employment is smaller (holding D_{t-1} constant) if a person reports $D_t = 1$. Empirically that is the case, as shown by the coefficients in table 3A.4. But to interpret beyond that one would need to say where the specification comes from. The authors do not interpret the coefficients except in a descriptive manner; rather, they present the implications via simulation. I would expect similar simulation results from the simple hazard model.

A second question about the specification is that it lacks an interaction between W_{t-1} and D_{t-1}. In that state disability programs are aimed at accommodating workers who become disabled, I would think that work transitions would be different for disabled workers than for disabled nonworkers. The difference would be revealing about the effects of public programs.

Unemployment is an important intermediate point in the transition from working to retired in some European countries. For example, according to Survey of Health, Aging, and Retirement in Europe (SHARE) data, about 12 percent of fifty-seven-year-olds in Denmark are unemployed, compared with just 3 percent in the Netherlands. The sum of the fraction disabled and the fraction unemployed is about 15 percent in the two countries, but the division is quite different, illustrating how policy can lead to a substitution between disability and unemployment.

The actual measurement of disability could use more discussion. Some of the data on Europe come from the European Community Household Panel (ECHP), but some come from national surveys after the ECHP was discontinued in some countries. It would be useful to have some information about the comparability of measurement of disability across Europe. But even in the ECHP the measurement is far from ideal. It is based on the following:

158. Do you have any chronic physical or mental health problem, illness or disability?

Table 3C.2   **Average transition rates, disabled**

		Age $t+1$	
	Age t	Not disabled	Disabled
Europe	Not disabled	90.8	9.1
	Disabled	31.4	68.6
United States	Not disabled	95.0	5.0
	Disabled	27.5	72.5

Source: Author's calculations based on tables 3A.5 and 3A.6, Chapter 3 in this volume.

159. Are you hampered in your daily activities by this physical or mental health problem, illness or disability?

I have taken the previous material from the 1997 ECHP wave 4 individual questionnaire.[3] I presume someone is coded with a work disability if he or she affirms both questions. The Panel Study of Income Dynamics (PSID) question is

H2. Do you have any physical or nervous condition that limits the type of work or the amount of work you can do?

I have taken this question from the 1997 PSID questionnaire.[4] Because work activities are a subset of daily activities, we would expect to find higher prevalence levels in response to the ECHP question than in response to the PSID question. This difference could explain the higher levels of disability between Europe and the United States. A second issue is that the ECHP question does not directly mention work. Someone who does not work may not be hampered in his or her daily activities but would be should he or she work. Thus, it is unclear how the ECHP question relates to work disability, and makes comparability with the PSID tenuous.

To summarize the actual transitions into and out of disability, I have taken the simple average of the European rates in table 3A.5. Table 3C.2 shows those rates along with similar rates from the United States. With respect to disabled status, the main difference between Europe and the United States is a considerably higher transition rate from not disabled to disabled in Europe, about 4 percentage points, or 80 percent, higher. Among those disabled, the transition rates from disabled to not disabled are a little higher in Europe. The structure of the ECHP questions could also explain some of the disability dynamics: in Europe people who work and are disabled with respect to their jobs could retire and not have any disability with respect to their activi-

3. See http://circa.europa.eu/Public/irc/dsis/echpanel/library?1=/doc_pan/1_survey_design/1_1_questionnaires/pan080_97questw4/_EN_1.0_&a=d.
4. See http://psidonline.isr.umich.edu/Data/Documentation/cai_doc/1997_Interview_Year/Section_B_C_D_E__Employment.htm.

ties in their retired state. Such people would have recovered from a disability. In the PSID I take the question to cover the hypothetical state of working even among nonworkers, so that such people would not have recovered from a disability. These differences in transition rates imply substantially different rates of disability in steady-state: 15 percent of the population would be disabled in the United States, compared with 23 percent in Europe.

Conclusion

International comparisons of disability and work have considerable promise for increasing our understanding of the effect of public policy on individual and firm behavior. Although cross-section analyses are useful, they have inherent limitations that can be substantially reduced in panel. Kapteyn, Smith, van Soest, and Banks have embarked on a research program whose aim is to relate transition rates to the details of public programs. This chapter represents a useful first step.

Reference

Börsch-Supan, A., A. Brugiavani, H. Jurges, J. Mackenbach, J. Siegrist, and G. Weber. 2005. *Health, aging, and retirement in Europe: First results from SHARE.* Mannheim: Mannheim Institute for the Economics of Aging.

II

Education and Disability

The Education Gradient
in Old Age Disability

David M. Cutler and Adriana Lleras-Muney

Disability among older adults has a clear socioeconomic gradient. Nearly half of elderly people with less than a high school degree report some difficulty caring for themselves, whereas only about a quarter of college graduates report that they are disabled. The lower disability rate among the better educated results in substantial differences in health and medical spending. Of disabled people, 10 percent live in a nursing home.[1] In addition, disabled people spend as much as five times more on medical care than the nondisabled (Chernew et al. 2005), and mortality rates are significantly higher for the disabled (Manton 1988). Disability rates have been falling in the United States (Cutler 2001). Understanding why education is related to disability and whether changes in education have contributed to disability declines is thus a central policy concern.

There are many theories about the link between education and disability, ranging from childhood conditions that affect both education and disability, occupational differences in the working years, differential health behaviors, differential access to medical care, and differential living situations as a senior. In this chapter, we examine this range of theories. Our empirical analysis is straightforward: we relate disability to education first with only basic demographic controls, and then with a series of controls for life course

David M. Cutler is the Otto Eckstein Professor of Applied Economics at Harvard University and a research associate of the National Bureau of Economic Research. Adriana Lleras-Muney is an associate professor of economics at the University of California, Los Angeles, and a faculty research fellow of the National Bureau of Economic Research.

This chapter was prepared for the NBER Conference on the Economics of Aging, May 2007. We are grateful to Doug Norton for research assistance, to Anne Case and conference participants for helpful comments, and to the National Institutes on Aging and the Lasker Foundation for research support.

1. This reflects authors' calculations from the 2004 Medicare Current Beneficiary Survey.

events. We see how each of these controls affects the education gradient in disability.

Our data come from the Health and Retirement Study (HRS). Because the HRS is focused on the elderly, our sample sizes are large; we have 9,157 observations in the 2002 survey. With the exception of measures of lifetime occupation, our control variables are also very good. Three factors emerge from our results as particularly associated with the education gradient in disability. The first is health behaviors. Better educated people are significantly less likely to smoke than are less educated people; they are also less obese. Smoking and obesity are both strongly related to disability, and explain a good part of the education effect. Our results show that about one-third of the education gradient in disability is associated with differential health behaviors. Another third is explained by differences in lifetime occupation. Finally, differential rates of medical conditions explain another fifth of the education gradient in disability. Stroke, heart disease, and chronic conditions such as diabetes and arthritis are highly related to disability. Less educated people are more likely to have suffered from these conditions, partly as a result of their greater propensity to smoke and be obese. All told, differences in occupation, health behaviors, and their disease consequences explain essentially all of the differences between those with high school degrees and college graduates. However, the factors we analyze can only explain about 55 percent of the differences in disability rates between those with a high school degree and high school dropouts. Interestingly, childhood conditions, use of preventive care after age sixty-five, and living arrangements after age sixty-five do not explain a large share of the education gradient in disability.

We present these findings, and also note their limitations. Most importantly, we do not explain why better educated people have healthier lifestyles. To what extent is that nature, nurture, or their interaction? What in nurture explains these differences? Our ongoing work focuses on this issue (Cutler and Lleras-Muney 2007a, 2007b), but we do not address it here. Nevertheless, these results suggest that the increased education of recent cohorts will result in lower disability rates in the future and that if lowering education gradients is the policy objective, then efforts should concentrate on modifying the health behaviors of less educated individuals.

Our chapter is structured as follows. The first section discusses measures of disability and shows the education gradient in disability. The second section elucidates theories for the education gradient. The third section presents our empirical results. The last section concludes.

4.1   The Education Gradient in Disability

To measure population disability, we use data from the 2002 Health and Retirement Study. Since the HRS is longitudinal, data from any year should be similar. The 2002 data are recent, and can be linked to extensive prior information. In addition, the initial HRS sample (1992 and 1993) was of the community-dwelling population only. By 2002, however, many of those people will have moved into an institution, and so our sample is nationally representative.[2] We consider people age sixty-five and older. We focus on the elderly to avoid reporting issues associated with collection of Disability Insurance. Other surveys of disability are also focused on the elderly (e.g., the National Long-Term Care Survey, and the Medicare Current Beneficiary Survey), making our results comparable with previous studies. The 2002 survey contains complete information on 9,155 elderly people.

Disability refers to whether a person can function independently in society (Verbrugge 1994). Functioning is both physical and cognitive; an ideal measure picks up both. In practice, most researchers use a measure of disability defined by Nagi (1965) in the 1960s: whether a person has impairments in physical Activities of Daily Living (ADLs) or social Instrumental Activities of Daily Living (IADLs). A typical set of ADL impairments includes difficulty eating, bathing, dressing, walking across a room, and getting in and out of bed. Typical IADL impairments include difficulty using a telephone, taking medication, managing money, shopping for groceries, and preparing meals. The ADL questions in the HRS are as follows: "Here are a few more everyday activities. Please tell me if you have any difficulty with these because of a physical, mental, emotional, or memory problem. Again exclude any difficulties you expect to last less than three months. Because of a health or memory problem do you have any difficulty with. . . ." Possible answers are "yes," "no," "can't do," and "don't do." We define a disability as it is usually done in the literature: an individual is coded as disabled if he answers yes or that he cannot or does not do any of the ten activities.

We examine the link between education and disability.[3] Consistent with most of the literature, we group education into four categories: less than a high school degree, high school graduate, some college, and a college degree or more. In our sample, 28 percent of people have less than a high school degree, 36 percent have exactly a high school education, 18 percent have some college, and 18 percent completed college.

Table 4.1 shows summary statistics for the sample. The first row shows that 34 percent of people report being disabled. Figure 4.1 shows the age and sex adjusted share of people reporting disability by education. There is a clear gradient in disability. The disability rate among people without a high school degree is 47 percent. The share declines to 31 percent for people with a high school degree, and 27 percent for people with some college or a college degree.

---

2. The vast bulk of people in a nursing home will have been in for less than a decade, so the 2002 survey should be nationally representative by living arrangement.

3. We could alternatively look at the relation between income and disability, but education is more consistent with past research, and perhaps measures permanent income better.

Table 4.1   Summary statistics

Variable	Percent	Variable	Percent
Disability rate	34	Smoker: current	15
Education		Smoker: former	42
< High school	28	Smoker: never	43
High school	36	Drinker: heavy	3
Some college	18	Drinker: light	43
College grad	18	Drinker: never	32
Childhood health and SES		Drinker: missing	22
Needed financial help	11	Health conditions	
Moved for financial reasons	19	High blood pressure	58
Father unemployed	23	Diabetes	18
SES: Well-off	5	Stroke	8
SES: Average	60	Cancer	18
SES: Poor	34	Heart condition	32
Health: Excellent	48	Arthritis	67
Health: Very good	27	Chronic lung disease	11
Health: Good	19	Psychiatric	14
Health: Fair	4	Preventive care	
Health: Poor	2	Cholesterol test	77
Height (meters)	1.7	Flu shot	70
Major occupation		Breast self exam (women)	59
Professional/managerial	27	Mammogram (women)	71
Sales worker	8	Pap smear (women)	55
Clerical worker	14	Prostate exam (men)	76
Farmer	5	Living status	
Machine operator	9	Socialize daily	17
Other	20	Friends live nearby	74
Missing/No profession	17	Family lives nearby	32
Behaviors		Marital status: married	55
BMI: obese	19	Marital status: unmarried,	
BMI: overweight	42	living with others	12
BMI: normal weight	39	Marital status: unmarried,	
BMI: missing	0	living alone	33

Note: Data are from the 2002 HRS. The sample is 9,155 people.

As previously noted, disability in this scale reflects both physical and social functioning. It may be that one is more responsive to education than the other. Figure 4.2 considers this by looking separately at ADL and IADL disability. Both measures of disability decline markedly with education. The decline is uniform with ADL disability, and continuous up to any college experience for IADL disability. The implication is that the trend in figure 4.1 is not a result of a simple process such as a particular physical limitation or impairment in a single aspect of living. We turn to alternative theories of the education gradient in disability in the next section.

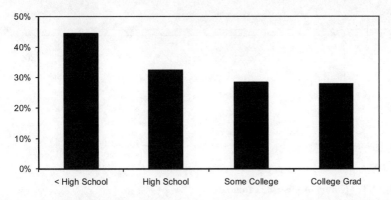

Fig. 4.1   Disability by education
Source: Authors' calculations from the 2002 HRS.

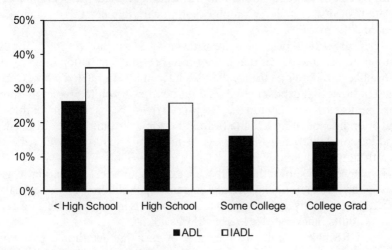

Fig. 4.2   ADL and IADL disability by education
Source: Authors' calculations from the 2002 HRS.

4.2   Theories of Differential Disability

There are a number of possible explanations for the marked difference in disability by education. We discuss the theories by their timing over the life course—from earlier in life to later in life. In each case, we also note the data in the HRS that will allow us to test each theory. The schematic in figure 4.3 shows the timing of the different theories.

4.2.1   Childhood Health and Economic Status

A substantial literature shows that people who are less healthy as a child continue to be less healthy as an adult. Childhood disease is also associated

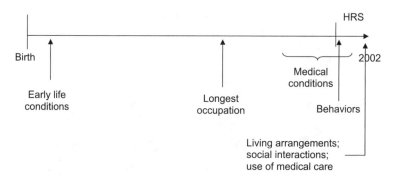

Fig. 4.3   Timing of possible explanations

with receipt of less education. Thus, education and late life health may be related because of their common origin in early life health and socioeconomic differences.

There are several possible reasons this may occur. Barker (1992), for example, argues that babies that do not receive enough nutrition in utero are more likely to develop chronic diseases later in life. In related work, Costa (2002) shows that exposure to infectious disease as a child predicts chronic disease development later in life. Fogel (1994) argues for the general role of nutrition in explaining late life health and longevity, and Case, Lubotsky, and Paxson (2002) show that average income while a child is correlated with health status as a child.

Evidence also shows that health as a child can affect education. Case, Fertig, and Paxson (2005) present evidence that children in worse health receive significantly less education than their peers in better health, and earn less as adults. They are also less healthy as adults.

The HRS has a number of measures of early life health and economic status. On the financial end, people are asked if their family needed financial help as a child, whether they moved for financial reasons, or whether their father was unemployed for a significant time before age sixteen. In addition, people were asked to rate their socioeconomic status as a child: well-off, average, poor, or other. People were also asked to rate their health as a child: excellent, very good, good, fair, or poor. Finally, we include height, which has been shown to reflect nutritional intake as a young child (Fogel 1994). The main limitation of these measures is that they are retrospective and subjective evaluations.

Figure 4.4 shows how these measures of childhood health and economic status are related to subsequent education. Adults with higher education were substantially less likely to have had a father unemployed during their childhood, and were substantially less likely to be poor while growing up. They are also more likely to report that their health status was better in childhood.

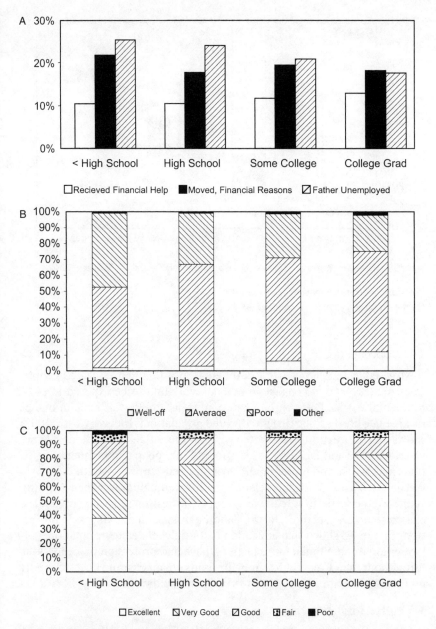

Fig. 4.4 Childhood health and economic status measures: *A*, **Financial status;** *B*, **self-rated SES;** *C*, **self-rated health**

Source: Authors' calculations from the 2002 HRS.

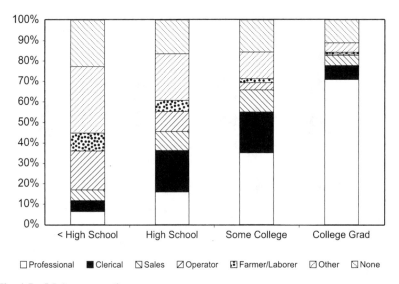

Fig. 4.5   Major occupation
Source: Authors' calculations from the 2002 HRS.

4.2.2   Occupation

More educated people work in different jobs than less educated people. They are less likely to engage in manual work and to be exposed to environmental toxins. Differential work experience could thus explain higher rates of late life disability in less educated populations. Indeed, Costa (2002) shows that occupation is associated with late life health among Union Army veterans. Case and Deaton (2005) also find that people in manual occupations have worse and more rapidly declining self-reported health.

The HRS asks about the person's major occupation over their working years. We code these into seven groups: professional/managerial, sales, clerical, machine operator, farmer/laborer, other, and missing or no profession. Figure 4.5 shows that education is strongly related to occupation: college graduates are much more likely to have had professional occupations throughout their lives. High school dropouts are much more likely to report no major occupation or to have worked in manual work.

4.2.3   Health Behaviors

Several behaviors are known to affect health status, and could thus be related to disability. The most common such risky behaviors are smoking, obesity, and drinking. Smoking is the most important behavioral cause of mortality, accounting for an estimated 435,000 deaths annually (Mokdad et al. 2004). Obesity is the second leading behavioral cause of mortality, accounting for 100,000 to 400,000 deaths annually, depending on the estimate. Alcohol is the third most common cause, accounting for nearly 90,000 deaths (Mokdad et al. 2004).

Health behaviors can affect disability directly, or through the diseases they lead to. For example, obese people may have difficulty with mobility, which might be compounded by arthritis or heart disease. We include both medical conditions and health behaviors, with the understanding that the two may be related.

Health behaviors can change over time. Many people will stop smoking after having a heart attack or cancer, for example. Since most behaviors have a lasting effect on health (i.e., former smokers do not have the mortality risk of never smokers), one would ideally like to know about health behaviors over the course of a person's life. The HRS does not ask about long-term weight or drinking. To partly adjust for this, we include health behaviors as of the first year the person was interviewed—in most cases 1992 or 1993. This allows us to have nearly a decade between the behaviors and the measure of disability. While this does not completely eliminate the endogeneity concern about health behaviors, it reduces its importance.[4]

Figure 4.6 shows how age and sex adjusted health behaviors are related to education. The differences are large. The share of people who ever smoked is similar across education groups, but many more highly educated people have quit smoking. The current smoking rate is half as large for college graduates compared to high school dropouts. Obesity is also related to education. Of high school dropouts, 24 percent are obese, compared to 14 percent of college graduates (though the relationship is larger for women). High school dropouts are substantially more likely to never drink, while college graduates are more likely to be light drinkers. Recent evidence suggests that light drinking may be good for health, so this difference does not necessarily indicate poorer health among the better educated. Although heavy drinking is a health risk, there appear to be no differences in self-reported heavy drinking across education groups.

4.2.4   Medical Conditions

Many medical conditions lead directly into disability. Conditions such as stroke, arthritis, and heart disease are very disabling. Stroke, for example, often results in mobility limitations and cognitive impairment. If these conditions are less common in the better educated, they could account for education-related differences in disability.

Of course, to the extent that differences in medical conditions are a significant part of the explanation for differential disability by education, one wants to understand why they differ. For example, it may be that the less educated are more likely to suffer from heart disease because of the nature

---

4. The trade-off is that because we have measures at only one point in time, measurement error may be more of a concern.

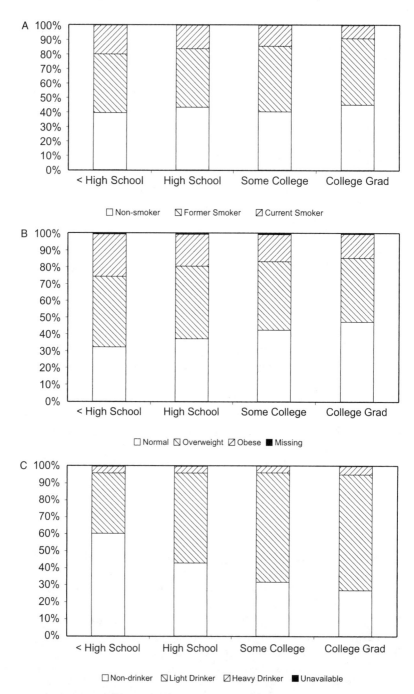

Fig. 4.6   Health behaviors: *A*, Smoking status; *B*, BMI; *C*, Drinking
Source: Authors' calculations from the 2002 HRS.

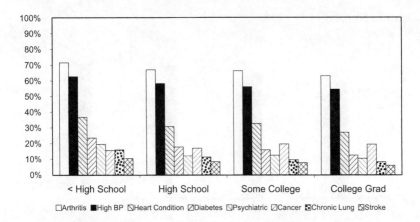

Fig. 4.7   Medical conditions
Source: Authors' calculations from the 2002 HRS.

of their work, or their nutritional intake as a child. It may also be that differences in health behaviors explain disease incidence. In our analysis, we speculate about the reasons for differences in medical conditions, but we do not address the issue definitively.

The HRS asks a number of questions about medical conditions. People are asked if they have ever been told they have hypertension, high cholesterol, diabetes, arthritis, (all chronic diseases) and a heart condition, cancer, stroke, chronic lung disease, or psychiatric problems (acute diseases). We include nine dummies for each of these conditions. The main limitation of these indicators is that they are affected by interactions with the health care system: for example, there may be individuals with hypertension that are not aware of their condition because they have not seen the doctor.

Figure 4.7 shows how disease incidence varies by education. Arthritis is the most common condition in the elderly. Of people without a high school degree, 70 percent report a diagnosis of arthritis, compared to 60 percent of those who are college graduates. Hypertension is nearly as prevalent, and also declines with education. The remaining conditions have lower prevalence, but in virtually every case disease prevalence declines with education. This is somewhat surprising given that the more educated are possibly more likely to be diagnosed conditional on having the disease, and it suggests that the actual differences in disease rates might be even higher. It is thus possible that differential rates of medical conditions explain the education gradient in health behaviors.

4.2.5   Interaction with the Medical System

Regular medical interaction may prevent the onset of disability. Medications for hypertension or high cholesterol can reduce their impact on sub-

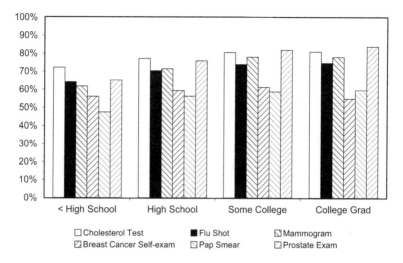

Fig. 4.8   Preventive behavior in last two years
Source: Authors' calculations from the 2002 HRS.

sequent health. Regular screening can catch cancers early and thus extend disease-free survival. Greater use of preventive care may thus explain the lower rate of disability among the better educated.

In addition to its direct effect on health, use of preventive care might be a signal about the importance people attach to health. People who go for regular cancer screenings may also exercise more or otherwise live in environments more suited to maintaining independence. We include preventive care receipt in our regressions, but do not attribute it to either of these two explanations.

The HRS includes a number of measures of prevention. The questions are asked about the time since the previous interview (approximately two years prior). Everyone is asked about cholesterol testing and receipt of a flu shot. Women are asked about breast self-examination, mammography, and receipt of a pap smear. Men are asked about receipt of a prostate-specific antigen (PSA) test.

Figure 4.8 shows how preventive care is related to education. In almost every case, better educated people are more likely to receive preventive medical care. Cholesterol testing, for example, is 10 percent higher for those with a college degree than for high school dropouts. Mammography rates are even more different.

4.2.6   Living Arrangements

Disability is not a measure of just physical performance; it reflects what a person needs to do as well. A person with fewer demands will be less disabled than a person with more demands, health status held constant. An important factor influencing need is the person's living status. A married person will (often) have help from their spouse lifting grocery bags, managing money, and cleaning house. Thus, at the same level of physical performance, a married person is less likely to be disabled than a person living alone. Similarly, people who socialize regularly or have many friends may have implicit help managing usual activities. All of this could lead to lower disability.

While living arrangements will affect disability, they might be influenced by disability as well. People who are disabled will need help from others; they might choose to live near their children. On the other hand, people in poor health may find remarriage difficult after a spouse dies, and keeping up with friends may be too taxing. Disability may thus cause a person to remain alone. Sorting out the causal relation between living arrangements and disability is difficult without a good instrument for living arrangements. We do not have such an instrument. As a result, we include living arrangements only as the last variable, and without a strong causal interpretation.

Figure 4.9 shows the education gradient in living arrangements. Better

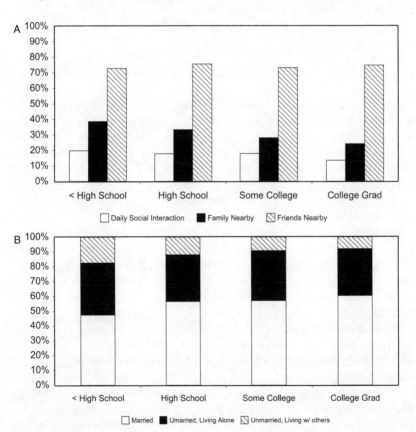

Fig. 4.9   Social interactions (yes/no) and living arrangements: *A*, **Social interactions;** *B*, **Living arrangements**

Source: Authors' calculations from the 2002 HRS.

educated people live farther away from family, but are more likely to be married. The implication for disability is not entirely clear.

4.3   Empirical Analysis of Disability

Having discussed our different variables possibly mediating the link between education and disability, in this section we examine them empirically. Our methodology is relatively simple: we start with a basic regression of disability on five year age by sex dummy variables and education:

$$(1) \qquad \text{Disability}_i = \beta_0 + \frac{\text{age}}{\text{sex}_i}, \text{region}_i + \beta_1 {}^*\text{Education}_i + \varepsilon_i.$$

For expositional ease, equation (1) shows education entered linearly, though our actual empirical models divide education into four groups. From our earlier means, we know that the coefficient β_1 will be negative: better educated people are less likely to be disabled.

We then augment this equation by including the other mediating variables, in sequence:

$$(2) \qquad \text{Disability}_i = \alpha_0 + \frac{\text{age}}{\text{sex}_i}, \text{region}_i + \alpha_1 {}^*\text{Education}_i + \mathbf{X}_i \alpha + \varepsilon_i.$$

To the extent that these variables explain the education gradient in disability, the coefficient α_1 will be smaller than the corresponding coefficient β_1. We measure the importance of each variable to the education gradient by calculating $(1 - \alpha_1)/\beta_1$, the decline in the education coefficient relative to the coefficient without any controls.

Because disability is a dichotomous variable, we estimate equations (1) and (2) as probit models. For interpretation, we report the implied change in the probability of being disabled.

Table 4.2 shows our regression results. The first column includes education and the age/sex and region controls, but no other variables. The coefficients match those in the figures. Relative to people with just a high school degree, high school dropouts have a 12 percent higher risk of being disabled. College graduates, in contrast, have a 5 percent lower risk of being disabled.

The second column includes the childhood social and economic measures. Including these measures has relatively little effect on the education gradient in disability. The coefficient on high school dropouts declines by only 7 percent, and the coefficient on college graduates falls by only 8 percent.

The most important variables to include are the longest occupation, health behaviors, and medical conditions. In each case, including these variables has a significant impact on the education gradient in disability. Including major occupation, for example, reduces the coefficient on college graduates by 32 percent. Adding health behaviors accounts for an additional

Table 4.2   **Explaining disability among the elderly change in probability from logit model**

Independent variable	(1)	(2)	(3)	(4)	(5)	(6)	(7)
Education[a]							
< High school	0.122	0.114	0.095	0.081	0.065	0.059	0.056
	(0.014)	(0.014)	(0.015)	(0.016)	(0.015)	(0.015)	(0.014)
Some college	–0.042	–0.040	–0.030	–0.021	–0.024	–0.020	–0.018
	(0.017)	(0.017)	(0.018)	(0.018)	(0.018)	(0.018)	(0.018)
College grad	–0.052	–0.048	–0.032	–0.012	–0.001	0.000	0.004
	(0.017)	(0.017)	(0.019)	(0.020)	(0.022)	(0.022)	(0.021)
Share of no control effect							
< High school	—	93%	78%	66%	53%	48%	46%
Some college	—	96%	73%	49%	56%	48%	43%
College grad	—	92%	60%	23%	2%	–1%	–7%
Childhood health and SES[b]							
Needed financial help	—	0.021	0.021	0.023	0.017	0.017	0.015
		(0.017)	(0.017)	(0.017)	(0.017)	(0.018)	(0.018)
Moved for financial	—	0.011	0.011	0.012	0.007	0.007	0.008
reasons		(0.014)	(0.014)	(0.014)	(0.015)	(0.015)	(0.015)
Father unemployed	—	–0.017	–0.017	–0.016	–0.018	–0.017	–0.017
		(0.014)	(0.014)	(0.014)	(0.014)	(0.014)	(0.014)
SES: Well-off	—	–0.030	–0.032	–0.028	–0.031	–0.029	–0.031
		(0.030)	(0.030)	(0.029)	(0.028)	(0.028)	(0.028)
SES: Poor	—	–0.005	–0.006	0.000	0.005	0.007	0.008
		(0.014)	(0.014)	(0.013)	(0.014)	(0.014)	(0.014)
Health: Excellent	—	–0.057	–0.055	–0.059	–0.044	–0.044	–0.042
		(0.016)	(0.016)	(0.016)	(0.016)	(0.017)	(0.017)
Health: Very good	—	–0.059	–0.058	–0.056	–0.051	–0.050	–0.049
		(0.020)	(0.020)	(0.020)	(0.019)	(0.019)	(0.020)
Health: Fair	—	0.062	0.060	0.057	0.040	0.040	0.046
		(0.031)	(0.032)	(0.032)	(0.031)	(0.031)	(0.032)
Health: Poor	—	0.067	0.075	0.071	0.025	0.020	0.030
		(0.039)	(0.038)	(0.035)	(0.035)	(0.034)	(0.035)
Height (meters)	—	0.025	0.034	0.083	0.029	0.036	0.046
		(0.076)	(0.076)	(0.074)	(0.075)	(0.076)	(0.077)
Missing height	—	0.207	0.209	0.296	0.250	0.286	0.288
		(0.310)	(0.310)	(0.320)	(0.330)	(0.330)	(0.330)
Major occupation[c]							
Professional/managerial	—	—	–0.051	–0.049	–0.054	–0.050	–0.044
			(0.031)	(0.031)	(0.034)	(0.034)	(0.034)
Sales worker	—	—	–0.058	–0.056	–0.058	–0.056	–0.047
			(0.035)	(0.035)	(0.036)	(0.037)	(0.037)
Clerical worker	—	—	–0.068	–0.060	–0.065	–0.062	–0.055
			(0.038)	(0.039)	(0.041)	(0.042)	(0.042)
Machine operator	—	—	–0.001	–0.008	–0.010	–0.008	–0.002
			(0.041)	(0.041)	(0.043)	(0.044)	(0.043)
Other	—	—	–0.007	–0.015	–0.019	–0.015	–0.009
			(0.031)	(0.030)	(0.033)	(0.034)	(0.034)
Missing/No profession	—	—	0.027	0.027	0.018	0.017	0.023
			(0.034)	(0.034)	(0.037)	(0.036)	(0.037)

(continued)

Table 4.2 (continued)

Independent variable	(1)	(2)	(3)	(4)	(5)	(6)	(7)
Behavior[d]							
BMI: obese	—	—	—	0.138	0.105	0.101	0.098
				(0.015)	(0.015)	(0.015)	(0.015)
BMI: overweight	—	—	—	0.033	0.023	0.021	0.022
				(0.010)	(0.010)	(0.010)	(0.010)
BMI: missing	—	—	—	0.047	0.022	0.020	0.024
				(0.100)	(0.097)	(0.096)	(0.098)
Smoker: current	—	—	—	0.104	0.071	0.062	0.056
				(0.020)	(0.021)	(0.021)	(0.022)
Smoker: former	—	—	—	0.020	−0.003	−0.003	−0.004
				(0.013)	(0.014)	(0.014)	(0.014)
Drinker: heavy	—	—	—	−0.017	0.009	0.005	0.006
				(0.024)	(0.025)	(0.025)	(0.025)
Drinker: light	—	—	—	−0.077	−0.066	−0.063	−0.060
				(0.014)	(0.014)	(0.015)	(0.015)
Drinker: missing	—	—	—	−0.012	0.003	0.006	0.007
				(0.016)	(0.016)	(0.016)	(0.016)
Health conditions							
High blood pressure	—	—	—	—	−0.027	−0.021	−0.023
					(0.011)	(0.011)	(0.011)
Diabetes	—	—	—	—	0.052	0.054	0.050
					(0.020)	(0.020)	(0.020)
Stroke	—	—	—	—	0.199	0.196	0.189
					(0.022)	(0.021)	(0.021)
Cancer	—	—	—	—	0.022	0.027	0.028
					(0.013)	(0.013)	(0.013)
Heart condition	—	—	—	—	0.072	0.073	0.073
					(0.014)	(0.014)	(0.014)
Arthritis	—	—	—	—	0.067	0.072	0.073
					(0.012)	(0.013)	(0.013)
Chronic lung disease	—	—	—	—	0.067	0.070	0.067
					(0.018)	(0.017)	(0.017)
Psychiatric	—	—	—	—	0.162	0.161	0.158
					(0.018)	(0.018)	(0.018)
Preventive care							
Cholesterol test	—	—	—	—	—	−0.015	−0.011
						(0.014)	(0.014)
Flu shot	—	—	—	—	—	0.007	0.009
						(0.013)	(0.013)
Breast self exam (women)	—	—	—	—	—	−0.049	−0.047
						(0.015)	(0.015)
Mammogram (women)	—	—	—	—	—	−0.039	−0.033
						(0.022)	(0.023)
Pap smear (women)	—	—	—	—	—	−0.044	−0.045
						(0.016)	(0.017)
Prostate exam (men)	—	—	—	—	—	−0.054	−0.054
						(0.019)	(0.018)

Table 4.2   (continued)

Independent variable	(1)	(2)	(3)	(4)	(5)	(6)	(7)
Living status[e]							
Socialize daily	—	—	—	—	—	—	−0.018
							(0.015)
Friends live nearby	—	—	—	—	—	—	−0.040
							(0.015)
Family lives nearby	—	—	—	—	—	—	0.033
							(0.013)
Marital status: unmarried, living with others	—	—	—	—	—	—	0.084
							(0.017)
Marital status: unmarried, living alone	—	—	—	—	—	—	−0.020
							(0.015)
Observations	9,155	9,155	9,155	9,155	9,155	9,155	9,155

Notes: Data are from the 2002 HRS. All regressions control for give year age-sex dummy variables, and dummy variables for region of residence. Standard errors are in parentheses. Dashed cells indicate not included in regression.
[a]Omitted education is high school graduate.
[b]Childhood SES is relative to average and health is relative to good.
[c]Professions are relative to farmers and laborers.
[d]BMI is relative to normal weight, smoker is relative to never smoker, and drinker is relative to non-drinker.
[e]Living status is relative to married.

37 percent, and medical conditions is another 21 percent. In the fifth column of the table, the residual difference in disability for people who are college graduates is positive, although not statistically significant. Adding either preventive care or living arrangements measures does not significantly affect the results, once occupation, medical conditions, and health behaviors are accounted for.

Occupation, health behaviors, and medical conditions reduce the impact of low education as well, although the impact is somewhat smaller. Compared to the 7 percent reduction from including childhood socioeconomic status (SES) and health factors, the impact of occupation, health behaviors, and medical conditions is each 12 to 15 percent. Including living status and preventive care is associated with modest further reductions in the education effect, especially for high school dropouts. The combined impact is 7 percent. In total, however, only 54 percent of the higher disability rate for high school dropouts is a result of the factors we identify.

The impact of major occupation on disability is largely along white-collar and blue-collar lines. Farmers/laborers (the omitted category) and machine operators have the highest disability rates. Professional/managerial, clerical, and sales workers all have disability rates that are 5 to 7 percent lower. In this sense, our results are different from those of Marmot and colleagues, who find a graded difference in mortality rates throughout the occupational distribution.

Obesity and current smoking are the health behaviors most associated with disability. In column (4), obese people are 14 percent more likely to be disabled than normal weight people, all else constant. Smokers are 10 percent more likely to be disabled. Heavy drinking is not associated with a statistically significantly higher disability rate; indeed, the coefficient is negative, but not significant. Further results (not shown) indicate that smoking and obesity contribute approximately equally to the education gradient in disability; both are key behaviors in understanding the education gradient in health.

Stroke is the most disabling medical condition. People who suffer a stroke are 20 percent more likely to be disabled than similar people without a stroke. Heart conditions, arthritis, and chronic lung disease each add 7 percent to disability rates. These conditions are to a great extent a product of smoking and obesity. Thus, we suspect that a high percentage of the impact of medical conditions on disability is a reflection of underlying health behaviors and the bad events that flow from them. The exception to this is psychiatric problems, which are very disabling (16 percent), but much less a product of smoking or weight management.

We included the explanatory variables with a particular ordering—from early life influences to later life influences. This generally makes temporal sense, but one also wonders whether the results differ if the later life variables are included without the early life variables. In general, the results are very similar. Consider, for example, the difference in disability between high school graduates and college graduates. Relative to the regression with age/sex and region controls only, the impact of including just preventive care receipt is a reduction of 2 percent and the impact of including living conditions is 13 percent. In contrast, including just occupation reduces the college/high school gap by 29 percent, including just health behaviors reduces the gap by 44 percent, and including just health conditions reduces the gap by 35 percent. Thus, our results are largely unaffected by the temporal ordering that we present.

4.4 Implications

Our results suggest three factors as being most important in explaining the education gradient in disability. The first is a lifetime of blue-collar work. People are, in perhaps a literal sense, broken down by hard work. Occupation explains 15 to 30 percent of the education differential in disability.

An equally large factor is health behaviors. Better educated people are less likely to smoke and are less likely to be obese. In the case of smoking, the difference is not so much smoking initiation (a decision made early in life), but smoking cessation. The share of people who ever smoked is roughly similar by education; quitting behavior, in contrast, is very different. Different health behaviors, and their disease consequences, explain another third of the education gradient in disability.

The final important factor is medical conditions that are not attributable to these risk behaviors. Psychiatric problems have a major effect on disability, but the pathway is almost certainly not through smoking and weight management. Similarly, receipt of preventive care mildly affects disability, and this too would be through a different channel. The reason for the education gradient in mental health is not entirely clear.

The major issue raised by our results is why better educated people behave better. What explains the fact that better educated people can quit smoking more or not succumb to the temptations of ready food? We do not have the answers to these questions, but they are high priorities for future research.

References

Barker, D. J. P. 1992. *Fetal and infant origins of adult disease.* London: BMJ Books.

Case, A. C., and A. Deaton. 2005. Broken down by age and sex: How our health declines. In *Analyses in the economics of aging,* ed. D. Wise, 185–205. Chicago: University of Chicago Press.

Case, A. C., A. Fertig, and C. Paxson. 2005. The lasting impact of childhood health and circumstance. *Journal of Health Economics* 24 (2): 365–89.

Case, A. C., D. Lubotsky, and C. Paxson. 2002. Economic status and health in childhood: The origins of the gradient. *American Economic Review* 92 (5): 1308–34.

Chernew, M., D. Goldman, F. Pan, and B. Shang. 2005. Disability and health care expenditures among Medicare beneficiaries. *Health Affairs,* September 26 (Web Exclusive).

Costa, D. 2002. Changing chronic disease rates and long-term declines in functional limitation among older men. *Demography* 39 (1): 119–38.

Cutler, D. M. 2001. Declining disability among the elderly. *Health Affairs* 20 (6): 11–27.

Cutler, D. M., and A. Lleras-Muney. 2007a. Education and health: Evaluating theories and evidence. In *The effects of social and economic policy on health,* ed. J. House, R. Schoeni, G. Kaplan, and H. Pollack, 29–60. New York: Russell Sage Foundation.

———. 2007b. Understanding health differences by education. Unpublished Manuscript.

Fogel, R. W. 1994. Economic growth, population theory, and physiology: The bearing of long-term processes on the making of economic policy. *American Economic Review* 84 (3): 369–95.

Manton, K. G. 1988. A longitudinal study of functional change and mortality in the United States. *Journal of Gerontology* 43 (5): S153–S161.

Mokdad, A. H., J. S. Marks, D. F. Stroup, and J. L. Gerberding. 2004. Actual causes of death in the United States, 2000. *Journal of the American Medical Association* 291 (10): 1238–45.

Nagi, S. Z. 1965. Some conceptual issues in disability and rehabilitation. In *Sociology and rehabilitation,* ed. M. B. Sussman, 100–13. Washington, DC: American Sociological Association.
Verbrugge, L. 1994. The disablement process. *Social Science and Medicine* 38 (1): 1–14.

Comment   Anne Case

This chapter provides an interesting quantification of the causes of the education gradient observed in disability in the U.S. elderly population. Using data from the Health and Retirement Study (HRS), the authors find that three factors can explain more than half of difference in disability found between high-school graduates and high-school dropouts: high school graduates were less likely to have worked in blue collar jobs during their working years, which may have protected them against wear and tear; they report better health behaviors, especially those related to smoking and obesity; and they are significantly less likely to report chronic conditions linked to disability. I found the chapter very interesting and thought provoking, and so my comments reflect thoughts on where this work might go from here.

Difficulties in Quantifying Causal Effects of Education

I think there is a fair amount of agreement that education is of first-order importance in protecting health status. However, that said, there are real hurdles in ruling out "third factor" explanations for the associations found between higher levels of education and better health. For example, we know that children who are sickly generally complete fewer years of schooling. Persistence in health processes could then lead to a positive association between health and education in adulthood that is really attributable to the impact of poor health in childhood on both educational attainment and health in adulthood. Relatedly, if parents are themselves in poor health, this could lead to lower family socioeconomic status (SES) and both family SES and parents' health could lead to poorer schooling outcomes and poorer health for their children. We could have poorer health and lower educational attainment echoing down the generations, without having much with which to identify the size of the effects leading from health to education, and those leading from education to health. It is also possible that some individuals embody certain characteristics that could lead to both better education and better health. For example, more patient people may take the time to wash

Anne Case is the Alexander Stewart 1886 Professor of Economics and Public Affairs and a Professor of Economics and Public Affairs at the Woodrow Wilson School of Public and International Affairs and the Economics Department at Princeton University, and a research associate of the National Bureau of Economic Research.

their hands and get to the gym and, being more patient, they may also have greater success at school.

Over the past decade, researchers have tried a number of interesting approaches to pin down the causal effects of schooling on health. Some have chosen to instrument for years of schooling in regressions of schooling on health. Unfortunately, it is often challenging to come up with instruments that affect completed schooling that we could reasonably agree would not have direct effects on health outcomes. Other researchers have begun randomized control trials (RCTs), looking at the impact of changes in the school environment, and in turn the impact this has on children's long term outcomes (including health in adulthood). This is a very exciting area of research. Unfortunately, not all research questions related to schooling and health can be readily answered using RCTs, and, of those that can, it will be forty to sixty years before the impact of schooling on health outcomes of the elderly could be evaluated within this framework. In this chapter, Cutler and Lleras-Muney take a different tack, using the temporal order of events (from birth to old age) to estimate the impact of earlier life events on later life outcomes. I find this life-course approach to estimating the impact of education on disability that these authors choose to use here quite appealing.

There are (at least) four interesting questions raised by this approach. Two of these I will mention in passing (since I have nothing to useful to say about them). The first is the question of how selective mortality could influence the gradient found between education and disability in the elderly. My guess is that less well-educated individuals who live into old age must be quite hardy. If this is the case, selective mortality might lead to a flattening of the education-health gradient as cohort members age. The second question that I will have little to say about (here echoing what David and Adriana themselves note) is whether education is proxying for permanent income. In old age, reported income could be a very weak measure of an individual's income in early and middle adulthood. Education may provide a better measure of permanent income than does current income at older ages. If the focus was on how to protect against disability, the question of whether it was education or income that was protective would be quite important.

This leaves two questions that came up as I read through the authors' results. The first is the role of heterogeneity between people, which is related to the potential "third factors" previously discussed. The authors note that better educated people are less likely to smoke. In the HRS, better educated people are equally likely to report that they ever smoked, but they are more likely to have quit. I was curious how the current authors thought about this result in comparison with those from the interesting paper on smoking and schooling by Farrell and Fuchs (which appeared in the first volume of the *Journal of Health Economics* in 1982). Farrell and Fuchs demonstrate that the education gradient in smoking observed at age twenty-four in data collected by the Stanford Heart Disease Prevention Program could be explained by differences in smoking at age seventeen, when all respondents were still in the same grade. It would be really interesting to know what David and Adriana think of the potential role of heterogeneity between individuals as a determinant of both educational attainment and smoking habits.

The last issue I wanted to raise is on their fascinating obesity results. Obesity rates are very different between race and sex in the United States. Using data I had on hand from the National Health Interview Survey from 1986 to 1994, I found white non-Hispanic women are significantly less likely to be obese than are white non-Hispanic men. However, African American women were fully 8 percentage points more likely to be obese than were African American men. Globally, men and women face markedly different risks of obesity. In all but a handful of (primarily Western European) countries, obesity is more prevalent among women. Case and Menendez (2007) provide some evidence that these sex differences may be related to sex-specific effects of early-life deprivation. The interaction between early-life deprivation and later-life obesity, and the role played by education in this, is a fascinating topic for future research.

References

Case, A., and A. Menendez. 2007. Sex differences in obesity rates in poor countries: Evidence from South Africa. NBER Working Paper no. 13541. Cambridge, MA: National Bureau of Economic Research.

Farrell, P., and V. R. Fuchs. 1982. Schooling and health: The cigarette connection. *Journal of Health Economics* 1:217–30.

5

Social Interactions and Smoking

David M. Cutler and Edward L. Glaeser

5.1 Introduction

A large and growing literature suggests that individual choices are influenced by the choices of their friends and neighbors. These peer effects have been found in dropping out, unemployment, crime, pregnancy, and many other settings (Crane 1991; Case and Katz 1991; Glaeser Sacerdote, and Scheinkman 1996; Topa 2001; Brock and Durlauf 2001; Kuziemko 2006). The older work in this literature was criticized because the company you keep is rarely random (Manski 1993). Newer work in this area has documented peer effects in settings where there is real random assignment, such as college dormitories (Sacerdote 2001).

There are many reasons to think that peers matter for health-related behaviors. In many cases, health-related behaviors are more fun to do when others are doing them too (drinking, for example). Peers are also a source of information (the benefits of a mammogram) or about what is acceptable in society (the approbation accorded smokers). A recent study suggested that a good part of the obesity "epidemic" in the United States is spread from person to person, in a manner reminiscent of viral infections (Christakis and Fowler 2007).

These interpersonal complementarities can have enormous social impact. In addition to helping us understand how health behaviors operate, they magnify the impact of policy interventions. The existence of social inter-

David M. Cutler is the Otto Eckstein Professor of Applied Economics at Harvard University and a research associate of the National Bureau of Economic Research. Edward L. Glaeser is the Fred and Eleanor Glimp Professor of Economics at Harvard University and a research associate of the National Bureau of Economic Research.

We are grateful to Alice Chen for research assistance, to Arie Kapteyn for comments, and to the National Institutes on Aging (Grant# P01 AG005842) for research support.

actions implies that a policy intervention has both a direct effect on the impacted individual and an indirect, as that person's behavior impacts everyone around. These indirect effects create a social multiplier where the predicted impact of interventions will be greater when the interventions occur at large geographic levels than when they occur individually (Glaeser, Sacerdote, and Scheinkman 2003). The social multiplier also suggests that parameter estimates from aggregate regressions can mislead us about individual level parameters.

In this chapter, we assess the evidence on social interactions in one particularly important health-related behavior: smoking. There are a number of reasons we might expect to see social interactions in smoking, as we discuss in section 5.2. These include direct social interactions (where one person's utility is affected by whether others are doing the same thing); the social formation of beliefs; and supply-side interactions from market creation in a situation in fixed costs.

Section 5.3 lays out the empirical implications of social interactions. The most straightforward implication of social interactions is that an exogenous variable that increases the costs of a behavior for one person will decrease the prevalence of that behavior is his or her peers. Social interactions models also predict excess variance in smoking rates across aggregates. Finally, the existence of social interactions implies that the measured impact of an exogenous variable on an outcome becomes larger at higher levels of aggregation.

In sections 5.3 and 5.4, we look at these three empirical predictions. At the individual level, we examine the impact of workplace smoking bans on spousal smoking. Evans, Farrelly, and Montgomery (1999) show that workplace bans have a significant impact on the probability that an individual will smoke and that these bans survive various estimation strategies that address selection of smokers into smoke-friendly workplaces. We look at whether people are more likely to smoke if their spouse smokes, using workplace smoking bans as an instrument for spousal smoking. The independent variable (IV) estimate is large: we estimate that an individual whose spouse smokes is 40 percent more likely to smoke. The instrumental variables estimate is higher for men than for women, suggesting that men are more influenced by spousal smoking. These effects are also stronger for people with some college than for people with college degrees or people who were high school dropouts.

In section 5.5, we turn to the other empirical implications of social interactions. We first show that the impact of smoking bans appears to be greater at the area level than at the individual level. At an individual level, a workplace ban reduces the probability of smoking by about 5 percent. At the metropolitan area level, a 10 percent increase in the share of workers facing workplace bans reduces the share of people who smoke by more than 3 percent—six times greater than the .5 percent predicted by the individual model. At the state level, the social multiplier rises to more than ten.

We also examine the prediction that social interactions create excess variance of aggregate smoking rates. We find that the standard deviation of smoking rates across metropolitan areas or states are about seven times higher than the rates that would be predicted if there were no social interactions and if there were no exogenous variables that differed across space. Since there are significant exogenous variables that differ across space, we do not put complete stock in these numbers. Still, these high variances provide evidence supporting the existence of social interactions in smoking.

Section 5.6 turns to the question of whether social interactions can help us make sense of the time series of smoking. Social interactions predict s-shaped adoption curves and changes are a function of current levels of smoking. A simple regression suggests that social interactions are not obvious in the national dynamics of cigarette prevalence, but our samples for this regression are small. Section 5.7 concludes.

5.2   Sources of Social Interactions

Why should one person's smoking increase his neighbor's tendency to smoke? There are three broad categories of reasons for such social interactions: (a) direct social interactions, including social approval and stigma; (b) the social formation of beliefs, and (c) market-mediated spillovers that occur because of fixed costs in the provision of healthy or unhealthy behavior. In this section, we briefly review these three possible reasons for interpersonal complementarities in smoking and other health-related behaviors.

The first reason that one person's smoking, or eating or exercise, might positively influence a neighbor's choices is that it is more pleasant to do something together than alone. This is most obvious in the context of eating, where it is more pleasurable (most of the time) to eat with others rather than eating alone. Because of the desire to eat together, people are more likely to go to donut shops, steak houses, or McDonald's, if their friends are also doing so. Drinking is also a social activity; if one's friends like to drink in bars, the returns from going to bars rises. Smoking and exercise may be somewhat less social activities, but many people like to exercise or smoke with friends around.

Conversely, smoking around a nonsmoker can be much less pleasant because of the discomfort caused by secondhand smoke to a nonsmoker. While there may be debate about the health consequences of secondhand smoke, there is less disagreement about whether nonsmokers dislike smoke. If a smoker has some degree of altruism for the uncomfortable nonsmoker, or if the nonsmoker chooses to reciprocate his discomfort by scolding the smoker, then this will decrease the returns to smoking around nonsmokers.

A second reason for social interactions in health behaviors is that beliefs may themselves be formed through social learning. One type of social learning model suggests that people infer truth from the behavior of others (e.g., Ellison and Fudenberg 1993). A person may not know whether moderate drinking is good or bad, but they can get guidance on this by watching others they believe have more information. In these models, the presence of friends and neighbors who smoke, drink, or exercise will provide evidence about the benefits of these activities. Conversely, the absence of smoking will be taken to mean that there is something wrong with lighting up.

Of course, conversation also transmits information (e.g., DeMarzo, Vayanos, and Zweibel 2003). If smoking, or any other harmful activity, increases one's belief in the net benefits of that activity—perhaps because of cognitive dissonance—then smokers are likely to articulate the view that cigarettes are pleasurable or not harmful. These views will then be transmitted in conversation and perhaps persuade some peers that smoking is less harmful. The power of these views will depend, of course, on the extent to which other messages about the benefits or harms of the activity are being regularly broadcast.

The third reason for social interactions works through the market. The typical assumption about markets is that supply curves slope up: when more people consume a good, the price of that good rises. This creates a negative social interaction; more people smoking will drive up the price of cigarettes, and discourage some marginal smokers from smoking. However, as George and Waldfogel (2003, 2006) have recently emphasized, in the presence of fixed costs these negative market-based social interactions can be reversed. Suppliers are only likely to pay the fixed costs to set up if the market size is sufficiently high. In that case, the market creates a strong positive social interaction.

This market-based interpersonal complementarity is more likely in goods with fixed costs, such as restaurants, grocery stores, bars, or health clubs. Cigarettes production itself has large fixed costs, but since transport costs are low, cigarette availability does not depend on local market size. However, several studies have shown that healthy foods are hard to buy in low income areas, presumably because of limited demand. The presence of health clubs and bars also depend on the presence of sizable local demand.

The relative importance of these different types of social interactions will differ across behaviors. Direct interactions and belief formation seem more important for smoking. Market-based interactions are more likely to be important for exercise and consumption of healthy food. In the next section, we will not distinguish between these different sources of social interactions but discuss more generally the empirical implications of interpersonal complementarities in health-related behaviors.

5.3   Empirical Tests of Social Interactions

The literature on social interactions has broadly identified four different empirical implications of social interactions. First, social interactions imply that a person is more likely to undertake an activity when his or her peers are also undertaking that activity. Second, the existence of social interactions implies a social multiplier, where the impact of some exogenous characteristic on the outcome at an individual level is much smaller than the impact of that same characteristic on the outcome at an aggregate level. Third, social interactions imply high levels of variance in the activity across space (Glaeser, Sacerdote, and Scheinkman 1996). Fourth, in a dynamic setting, social interactions lead to an S-shaped adoption curve. In this section, we present a particularly simple social interaction model that illustrates the first three points. In section 5.6, we discuss a dynamic model.

We start with a simple model of social interactions. We assume that individual i receives private benefits from an activity, X_i, of $A_i X_i$, where A_i differs across individuals. The cost of the activity is $.5X^2$. To capture social interactions, we assume that benefits increase by b times that average consumption of X among person i's friends, which we denote $\hat{X}_i$. The utility of individual i is therefore $(A_i + b\hat{X}_i)X_i - X_i^2$. When individuals set marginal benefits equal to marginal costs, the optimal level of X will satisfy $X_i = A_i + b\hat{X}_i$.

Aggregating this relationship implies that $\hat{X}_i = \hat{A}_i/(1 - b)$, where $\hat{A}_i$ refers to the average value of A in i's peer group. Substituting this term in implies that individual X will equal $A_i + b\hat{A}_i/(1 - b)$. If b is greater than 1/2, then the impact of average "A" is greater than the impact of individual "A".

These calculations deliver the basic empirical implications of social interactions models. First, there will be greater variation in the outcome across space than would be predicted based on individual differences alone. Within groups, the variance of the outcome will be $Var(A_i)$ while the variance of outcomes across groups will equal $Var(\hat{A}_i)/(1 - b)^2$. If there are N people in each group who are allocated randomly, then $Var(\hat{A}_i) = Var(A_i)/N$, so in that case, the ratio of the aggregate variance to the individual within group variance should equal $1/[N(1 - b)^2]$. High group level variance is a sign that "b" is high.[1]

While we implement this test, we note one obvious difficulty with it: the ratio of across to within group variance is likely to be biased upwards because of omitted characteristics that differ at the group level. For example, if exogenous tastes for smoking differ across areas and we cannot control for tastes, we will attribute the variation in smoking rates across areas to social spillovers rather than tastes. One method of dealing with this problem is to control extensively for observable characteristics and then to assume that the heterogeneity across groups in the unobservable characteristics is some multiple of the heterogeneity across groups in observable characteristics.

A second implication of the model is the existence of a social multiplier.

---

1. We conduct our test using standard deviations: the ratio of the standard deviation at the group level, to the standard deviation at the individual level divided by the square root of N is an estimate of $1/(1 - b)$.

To see this, assume that $A_i = a_i + \delta z_i$ where δ is a constant and z_i is an exogenous characteristic such as income or public policy regulations. In this case, regressing the outcome on z at the individual level will give a coefficient of δ, while the same regression at the aggregate level will give a coefficient of $\delta/(1 - b)$. Thus, the group level relationship will be stronger than individual relationship, which is the definition of a social multiplier.

The most common empirical approach to social interactions has been at the individual level, estimating a regression of one person's outcomes on the outcomes of a neighbor. The reflection problem (Manski 1993) means that a direct regression of this sort does not recover the parameter b. For example, assume a peer group of two people, i and j. Then, person i's outcome is $A_i + bX_j$ and person j's outcome is $A_j + bX_i$. Solving these two equations implies that person i's outcome equals $(A_i + bA_j)/(1 - b^2)$ and person j's outcome equals $(A_j + bA_i)/(1 - b^2)$. Straightforward analysis shows that a univariate regression where person i's outcome is regressed on person j's outcome does not yield the parameter b, but rather $2b/(1 + b^2)$.

External factors can help us with this problem, however. Specifically, if $A_i = a_i + \delta z_i$ and z_j is used as an instrument for A_j then the instrumental variables estimate of the social interaction $(\mathrm{Cov}(A_i, z_j)/\mathrm{Cov}(A_j, z_j))$ will equal b. We will follow this approach in our analysis.

5.4 Social Interactions in Smoking: Direct Tests

Surely a spouse is among the most important of all social influences. For all of the reasons previously discussed, we would expect the influence of behaviors to be particularly large within a family. In addition, smoking might be sensitive to peers or other people similarly situated. In this section, we look at the influence of one spouse's smoking decisions on the smoking propensity of the other spouse. We also look at the influence of smoking rates for people with similar demographic characteristics. Clearly the decision of two married people or friends to smoke is endogenous. To address the endogeneity issues just discussed, we follow Evans, Farrelly, and Montgomery (1999) and use the presence of workplace smoking bans as an instrument for the smoking of one spouse.

We use the Current Population Survey (CPS) tobacco supplement data for information on smoking rates and workplace smoking bans. The CPS asks about smoking and smoking bans in four periods: 1992 and 1993, 1995, 1998, and 2002. We sample people between the ages of fifteen and sixty-four. The smoking data is asked of everyone. The smoking ban question is asked only of indoor workers. We discuss this more in the following.

Table 5.1 shows the means and standard deviations from this data source. Between 1992 and 2002, the overall smoking rate declined from 25 percent to 20 percent, a reduction of one-fifth. The decline for indoor workers, who

Table 5.1   **Trends in smoking rates and smoking bans (%)**

Measure	1992–1993	1995	1998	2002
Smoking rate, overall	25	25	24	20
Smoking rate, indoor workers	24	24	23	20
Percent with smoking ban, overall	35	42	44	45
Percent with smoking ban, indoor workers	66	75	78	79

Note: The sample is self-respondents aged fifteen to sixty-four from the Current Population Survey. Data are weighted using sample weights.

are those effected by smoking bans, was similar: 24 percent in 1992 and 1993 to 20 percent in 2002.

Smoking bans for indoor workers were spreading rapidly in the 1990s. While the overall share of the sample with a smoking ban increases from 35 percent in 1992 and 1993 to 45 percent in 2002, the share of the indoor workers with smoking bans increased from 66 percent in 1992 and 1993 to 79 percent ten years later. The current omnipresence of workplace bans represents a remarkable change over twenty-five years. Evans, Farrelly, and Montgomery (1999) report that as late as 1985, only one-quarter of workplaces banned smoking.

As Evans, Farrelly, and Montgomery (1999) discuss, the estimated impact of smoking bans on smoking may be biased because of sorting across jobs. Smokers may choose jobs that are particularly smoke-friendly, and this will cause a negative correlation between workplace bans and smoking that does not reflect the impact of the bans. Their own instrumentation strategy suggests that this selection (within indoor jobs) is relatively weak. We have no comparable sources of exogenous variation. As such, we will look at the impact of workplace bans directly without using instruments.

We start by looking at the impact of smoking bans on the smoking rates of people affected by them. To do this, we estimate a model of smoking rates as a function of demographics and the presence of a smoking ban:

$$(1) \qquad \text{Smoke}_i = \beta_0 + \beta_1 \cdot \text{Smoking Ban}_i + Z_i\beta + \varepsilon_i,$$

where i denotes individuals and Z is the control variables. We include a number of standard controls: age and its square, gender, family size, family income, a dummy for missing income, education (< high school, high school, some college, college grad, > college), race/ethnicity (white, black, Hispanic, other race), marital status (married, divorced, separated, widowed, never married), industry dummies, occupation dummies, a dummy for whether the person is employed, and a dummy for whether the person is an indoor worker. We also control for metropolitan area and year fixed effects so that our results reflect changes in smoking bans within regions over time.

The first column in table 5.2 shows our basis results. Since the dependent variable is dichotomous, we report marginal effects from a Probit regression. We estimate that workers who face workplace smoking bans are 4.6 percent less likely to be smokers. The coefficient is highly statistically significant. The magnitude here is similar to that found in Evans, Farrelly, and Montgomery (1999), who estimated that smoking bans reduce workplace smoking by 5 percent.

We are less concerned with the other variables, but some are worthy of note. Surprisingly, we do not find a significant effect of cigarette taxes on smoking. The coefficient is negative, as expected, but not statistically significant. It may be that by the late 1990s, the most price sensitive smokers have already left the market. More education is negatively related to smoking, with large coefficients. College graduates are 15 percent less likely to smoke than high school graduates. Blacks and Hispanics are less likely to smoke than are whites, and employed people smoke less.

We now turn to the models including spillovers. In regression (2), we show the ordinary least squares regression when individual smoking is regressed on all of the variables in the first regression and on an indicator variable for whether the spouse smokes.[2] The regression shows that people whose spouse smokes are 21 percent more likely to smoke themselves. We would normally expect this coefficient to be biased upwards both because of the endogeneity of spousal smoking and because of selection of spouses.

Regression (3) looks at the spillovers of smoking in a more general peer group. As is common in the literature, we define the peer group as people in the same metropolitan area and cohort group within the same metropolitan area and with the same age (fourteen to thirty, thirty-one to fifty, and fifty-one to sixty-four) and education level (< high school, high school, come college, college graduate). There is a very high correlation of smoking rates across people in a common reference group. The coefficient on reference group smoking is 0.8, which means that as the share of peers that smokes increases by 10 percent, the probability that an individual will himself smoke increases by 8 percent. As in the case of the spousal smoking coefficient, we expect this coefficient to be biased upwards because individuals influence their peers and because of omitted variables that are correlated across peers.

The obvious solution in each case is instrumental variables. In the case of spousal smoking, we instrument with whether the spouse has a smoking ban at work. In the case of peer group smoking, we instrument with the share of the peer group that has a smoking ban at work. Regressions (4) and (5) show these results—the former for spousal smoking only, and the latter for spousal and reference group smoking.

---

2. Since this is a prelude to the instrumental variables estimates, we also include dummies for whether the spouse is employed, and whether the spouse is an indoor worker.

Table 5.2   **Explaining smoking decisions**

Independent variable	Individual ban only OLS (1)	With peer effects OLS (2)	OLS (3)	IV (4)	IV (5)
Smoking					
Smoking ban	−0.046	−0.043	−0.042	−0.041	−0.041
	(0.005)***	(0.005)***	(0.005)***	(0.005)***	(0.005)***
Spouse smokes	—	0.211	0.180	0.401	0.400
		(0.005)***	(0.006)***	(0.082)***	(0.084)***
Reference group smoking rate	—	—	0.880	—	0.050
			(0.012)***		(0.285)
Cigarette tax	−0.005	−0.006	0.006	−0.006	−0.005
	(0.009)	(0.009)	(0.009)	(0.010)	(0.010)
Demographics					
Age	0.025	0.024	0.013	0.023	0.023
	(0.001)***	(0.001)***	(0.001)***	(0.001)***	(0.004)***
Age^2	−0.0003	−0.0003	−0.0002	−0.0003	−0.0003
	(9.4E-6)***	(1.1E-5)***	(1.1E-5)***	(1.2E-5)***	(4.5E-5)***
Female	−0.036	−0.04	−0.039	−0.044	−0.044
	(0.003)***	(0.003)***	(0.003)***	(0.003)***	(0.004)***
Family size	−0.018	−0.017	−0.016	−0.017	−0.017
	(0.001)***	(0.001)***	(0.001)***	(0.001)***	(0.001)***
Ln(family inc)	−0.047	−0.044	−0.038	−0.041	−0.041
	(0.002)***	(0.002)***	(0.002)***	(0.003)***	(0.004)***
Income missing	−0.524	−0.487	−0.421	−0.458	−0.455
	(0.024)***	(0.026)***	(0.026)***	(0.030)***	(0.038)***
< High school	0.019	0.017	0.016	0.016	0.014
	(0.006)***	(0.006)***	(0.005)***	(0.006)***	(0.006)**
Some college	−0.05	−0.045	0.015	−0.041	−0.036
	(0.004)***	(0.004)***	(0.004)***	(0.004)***	(0.020)
College grad	−0.148	−0.137	0.034	−0.127	−0.114
	(0.005)***	(0.005)***	(0.005)***	(0.006)***	(0.056)**
> College	−0.17	−0.156	0.014	−0.143	−0.13
	(0.005)***	(0.005)***	(0.006)**	(0.008)***	(0.055)**
Black	−0.078	−0.073	−0.067	−0.069	−0.069
	(0.005)***	(0.005)***	(0.005)***	(0.005)***	(0.006)***
Hispanic	−0.13	−0.122	−0.096	−0.116	−0.114
	(0.005)***	(0.005)***	(0.005)***	(0.006)***	(0.011)***
Other race	−0.056	−0.052	−0.051	−0.049	−0.049
	(0.007)***	(0.006)***	(0.006)***	(0.006)***	(0.007)***
Divorced	0.098	0.125	0.113	0.154	0.153
	(0.005)***	(0.006)***	(0.006)***	(0.014)***	(0.014)***
Separated	0.108	0.135	0.122	0.165	0.164
	(0.010)***	(0.010)***	(0.011)***	(0.017)***	(0.017)***
Widowed	0.066	0.093	0.083	0.122	0.122
	(0.010)***	(0.012)***	(0.011)***	(0.016)***	(0.017)***
Never married	0.03	0.055	0.048	0.082	0.082
	(0.004)***	(0.005)***	(0.005)***	(0.012)***	(0.013)***

(*continued*)

Table 5.2 (continued)

Independent variable	Individual ban only OLS (1)	With peer effects OLS (2)	OLS (3)	IV (4)	IV (5)
Employed	−0.074	−0.071	−0.059	−0.068	−0.068
	(0.008)***	(0.008)***	(0.008)***	(0.008)***	(0.008)***
Indoor worker	0.041	0.038	0.037	0.035	0.036
	(0.006)***	(0.006)***	(0.006)***	(0.006)***	(0.007)***
Spouse employed	—	−0.009	−0.008	−0.012	−0.012
		(0.005)**	(0.004)	(0.005)**	(0.005)**
Spouse indoor worker	—	−0.009	−0.005	−0.014	−0.014
		(0.004)**	(0.003)	(0.004)***	(0.005)***
Percent reference group employed	—	—	−0.074	—	0.004
			(0.013)***		(0.030)
Percent reference group indoor worker	—	—	−0.03	—	−0.031
			(0.011)***		(0.012)**
MSA dummy variables	Yes	Yes	Yes	Yes	Yes
Year dummy variables	Yes	Yes	Yes	Yes	Yes
N	195,579	195,579	195,579	195,579	195,579
R^2	0.10	0.11	0.17	0.10	0.11

Notes: Data are from CPS Sept. 1992/May 1993, Sept. 1995, Sept. 1998, and Feb. 2002 Tobacco Supplement Surveys. Sample composition is of people aged fifteen to sixty-four. All regressions also include major industry (twenty-one dummies) and major occupation (thirteen dummies) effects, and are weighted by the self-response supplement sample weight. Models for individuals and spouses are clustered by family id. Models including cohort effects are clustered by the MSA cohort education level with cohort ages of fourteen to thirty, thirty-one to fifty, and fifty-one to sixty-four and education levels of less than high school, high school, some college, and college graduates or higher. Spouse smokes instrumented by spouse smoking ban, and reference group smoking rate instrumented by share of reference group with a smoking ban. OLS = ordinary least squares; IV = independent variable. Dashed Cells = not included in regression.
***Significant at the 1 percent level.
**Significant at the 5 percent level.

The instrumentation has very different effects on the estimated spouse and reference group coefficients. When we instrument using smoking bans facing one's spouse, we find that the estimated impact of spousal smoking increases to .4, so that people whose spouses smoke are 40 percent more likely to smoke themselves. While the magnitude of this coefficient is not unreasonable, we are somewhat skeptical about the fact that the estimated coefficient rises. One interpretation of this might be that we are not measuring the intensity of spousal smoking, and working in a place without a ban might be particularly correlated with intensive smoking. An alternative interpretation is that spouse's workplace smoking bans are correlated with other characteristics, like the prosmoking atmosphere in one's social group, that we cannot adequately control for.

In regression (5), we see that the instrumental variables approach completely eliminates the estimated impact of peer smoking on an individual's decision to smoke. While the standard error is large (29 percent), the coefficient is very small (5 percent). The coefficient on spousal smoking, in contrast, is essentially unchanged. One interpretation of these results is that spousal smoking does have spillovers, but peer group smoking does not. Another view is that our instrumental variables peer group coefficient is not precisely estimated enough to really say much about the impact of peers on smoking.

One question commonly speculated about is how spillovers differ by demographic group. One often hears that less educated groups might be more responsive to peer influences, though information dissemination is perhaps greater in better educated groups. In table 5.3, we estimate the spillover effects separately for different population subgroups. The regressions are all similar to those in table 5.2, though we only report the coefficients on

Table 5.3 **Examining the response to smoking bans by demographic group (instrumental variable estimates)**

Group	Smoking ban	Spouse smokes	Reference group smoking rate	N	R^2
All	−0.041	0.400	0.050	195,579	0.11
	(0.005)***	(0.084)***	(0.285)		
By gender					
Men	−0.052	0.502	−0.002	86,321	0.1
	(0.008)***	(0.196)**	(0.416)		
Women	−0.029	0.365	−0.264	109,258	0.04
	(0.006)***	(0.073)***	(0.628)		
By education					
< High school	−0.033	−0.0080	−0.054	29,392	0.18
	(0.014)**	(0.525)	(2.235)		
High school	−0.050	0.289	−3.198	61,744	—
	(0.012)***	(0.261)	(5.203)		
Some college	−0.042	0.663	−0.269	52,175	—
	(0.011)***	(0.177)***	(0.668)		
College +	−0.020	0.346	1.201	52,268	0.07
	(0.008)***	(0.191)	(1.148)		

Notes: The reference group is based on the MSA cohort education level. All regressions include age, age squared, family size, log(family income), missing income dummy, three indicators for ethnicity, four indicators for marital status, cigarette tax (state + federal), twenty-one industry indicators, and thirteen occupation indicators. Regression for all, men, and women also include four indicators for educational attainment. Regressions for all and education bins include indicator for gender. Spouse smokes instrumented by spouse smoking ban, and reference group smoking rate instrumented by share of reference group with a smoking ban. Regressions weighted by self-response supplement weight.

***Significant at the 1 percent level.

**Significant at the 5 percent level.

workplace bans, spousal smoking, and peer group smoking. The first row in the table reports our benchmark results from column (5) of table 5.2.

The next two rows report these results separately for men and women. Workplace smoking bans have a larger impact on men (5.2 percent) than on women (2.9 percent). This may be because men are more likely to work full time, or because men infer more from a workplace smoking ban than do women. Men are also more sensitive to spousal smoking than are women. The coefficient on (instrumented) spousal smoking is 0.50 for men and 0.37 for women. According to these findings, wives have a bigger impact on husbands than husbands have on wives. The reference group smoking rate is insignificant for both genders.

The next four rows show the results for four separate education groups: high school dropouts, high school graduates with no college, people with some college education, and people with college degrees. The impact on workplace bans is strongest for those individuals in the middle education categories. The impact of spousal smoking is strongest for people with some college and weakest for people who are high school dropouts. The reference group effects differ substantially across education subgroups but are never statistically significant.

Overall, these findings support the idea of a substantial social interaction in smoking between spouses. While we are not confident that the right coefficient is .4, rather than .2, we are reassured by the fact that the positive social spillover is robust to our instrumental variables strategy. The reference group may also be important, but the fact that it is not robust to our instrumental variables strategy makes us less confident about its strength.

5.5 Social Multipliers and Excess Variance in Smoking

We now turn to other evidence for social spillovers in smoking: variability across groups and social multipliers. We start with nonparametric evidence: the variability in smoking rates across groups. At the individual, our estimated smoking rate of 24 percent implies a standard deviation of .43. If there were no omitted variables across metropolitan areas and if there were no social interactions, then this variance should decline substantially with group size. Specifically, the standard deviation of smoking rates across a group of size N should equal $.42/\sqrt{N}$.

Our metropolitan area samples have, on average, 3,238 individuals, which implies that the standard deviation of smoking rates across groups should equal approximately .008. As table 5.4 shows, this is approximately one-sixth of the actual variation in smoking rates across our metropolitan area samples. At the state level, our average sample size is 10,684, which implies that the standard deviation of smoking rates across state groups should equal approximately .004. Again, the actual standard deviation is almost seven times larger than this amount.

Table 5.4   **The variability of smoking across areas**

	Average observations per unit	Predicted standard deviation	Actual standard deviation	Ratio: Actual/predicted
Individual	1	0.427	0.427	—
MSA	3,238	0.008	0.046	6.1
State	10,684	0.004	0.027	6.5

Note: The sample is self-respondents aged fifteen to sixty-four from the Current Population Survey. Data are weighted using sample weights. Dashed cell = ratio not appropriate.

Using the calculations in section 5.2, an aggregate to individual standard deviation of 6 suggests a value of b of .83. Surely, this estimate is biased upwards because of omitted group level characteristics. Nonetheless, there is a high level of variation at the group level, which supports the idea that social interactions may be important in smoking.

A third test for social multipliers is to look at the impact of external factors on smoking rates at the individual and group level. As section 5.2 pointed out, in a situation of social multipliers, the aggregate impact of a particular factor will be greater than the individual impact. We test this using the individual, metropolitan statistical area (MSA), and state-level samples. The basic approach of these regressions is to regress smoking on the same characteristics at the individual, metropolitan area and state level. If social interactions are important then we should expect the impact of characteristics to become more important at higher levels of aggregation (Glaeser, Sacerdote, and Scheinkman 2003).

In principle, a social multiplier could show up in any variable, but we would be less inclined to see it in variables that are strongly correlated with social groupings. For example, even though age is correlated with smoking, we might not expect to find a large social multiplier in age, because people of similar age groups tend to sort together. Thus, the presence of a large number of young smokers in a particular locale would not have a large impact on the smoking habits of older people. With this in mind, we focus most heavily on our key variable—the presence of smoking bans—and look at whether the impact of this variable increases at higher levels of aggregation. We also look at the spillovers associated with years of education, income, and basic demographics (age and gender).

Table 5.5 shows the results of this estimation. The first column of table 5.5 shows our basic individual level specification. The coefficient is similar to table 5.2, though slightly larger, reflecting the restriction to 2001 and the compression of education into a single variable. The second and third columns repeat this specification at the metropolitan area level and the state level. The coefficient on the smoking ban variable increases across columns.

Table 5.5   The spillover effects of smoking

Independent Variable	Individual	MSA	State
Smoking ban	–0.061	–0.257	–0.713
	(0.007)***	(0.112)**	(0.312)**
Years of education	–0.013	–0.011	0.010
	(0.001)***	(0.009)	(0.026)
Log (income)	–0.053	–0.156	–0.271
	(0.003)***	(0.039)***	(0.082)***
N	64,660	243	51
R^2	0.05	0.26	0.59

Notes: Data are from CPS June 2001 Tobacco Supplement Survey. Sample composition is respondents eighteen years and older. Regressions weighted by self-response supplement weight. Regressions include controls for age, gender, employed, indoor worker, and a dummy for missing income. For years of education, first, second, third, and fourth grades were averaged to 2.5 years. Fifth and sixth grades were averaged to 5.5 years, seventh and eighth grades were averaged to 7.5 years, high school diploma and GEDs were treated as 12 years, some college and associates degrees were treated as 14 years, bachelors degrees were treated as 16 years, masters degrees were treated as 18 years, professional degrees (such as MD's, DD's) were treated as 20 years, and doctorate degrees (such as PhD's or EdD's) were treated as 21 years. For income, < \$5,000 was coded as \$2,500, and > \$75,000 was coded as \$75,000. All other categories were averaged over the range in the choice.

***Significant at the 1 percent level.
**Significant at the 5 percent level.

The individual coefficient of –.061 increases to –.257 at the metropolitan area level and –.713 at the state level.

A social multiplier of four at the metropolitan area level and twelve at the state level gives us another estimate of $1/(1 - b)$, which is again compatible with an estimate of "*b*" ranging from .75 to .9. Of course, just as the variance estimates can potentially be biased by omitted area level characteristics, the social multiplier numbers are also likely to be biased upwards. Nonetheless, this provides suggestive support for significant social interactions in the smoking.

Perhaps the other two most natural candidates for variables in which to look for social multipliers are income and education. The years of education measure shows essentially no social multiplier. The logarithm of income shows a much stronger social multiplier of three at the metropolitan level and five at the state level. Again, this is compatible with high levels of social interactions, between .67 and .8.

Table 5.6 looks at these social multipliers within education categories. In this case, we just look at the social multiplier on the smoking ban variable. We find the largest social multipliers for high school graduates and the smallest for college graduates. In these regressions, social influence in smoking is more important for less educated people.

Table 5.6   **Spillover effects by education**

Education group	Impact of smoking ban		
	Individual	MSA	State
< High school	−0.028	0.075	−0.859
	(0.025)	(0.202)	(0.469)
High school grad	−0.059	−0.223	−1.303
	(0.013)***	(0.129)*	(0.423)***
Some college	−0.081	−0.426	−0.573
	(0.013)***	(0.123)***	(0.320)
College grad	−0.027	−0.075	−0.347
	(0.011)**	(0.079)	(0.187)

Notes: Data are from CPS June 2001 Tobacco Supplement Survey. The sample is individuals aged eighteen and older. Regressions are weighted and control for age, gender, employed, and indoor working.
***Significant at the 1 percent level.
**Significant at the 5 percent level.
*Significant at the 10 percent level.

5.6   The Smoking Time Series

In the previous two sections, we focused on cross-sectional implications of social interactions. In this section, we turn to the dynamic implications of social interaction models and their connection with the time series of cigarette consumption. The basic structure of dynamic social interactions models is to assume that the rate at which individuals choose a behavior is an increasing function of the share of the population that is already selecting that behavior.

For example, if the population was fixed and infinitely lived, and if people who started smoking never stopped, then a dynamic social interaction model might take the form:

$$(2) \qquad S(t + 1) - S(t) = (a_0 + a_1 S(t))(1 - S(t)),$$

where $S(t)$ is the share of the population that smokes at time t and a_0 and a_1 are parameters. In this framework, all nonsmokers have some probability of switching to become smokers (a_0) and this probability increases with the share of the population that is already smoking. The parameter a_1 determines the power of the social interactions.

In this formulation, higher values of $S(t)$ are associated with a more S-shaped curve, and it is this S-shaped curve that is the hallmark of dynamic social interaction models. For example, figure 5.1 shows the time paths implied by three different values of a_1. In all three cases, we assume that $S(0) = .05$, and $a_0 = .02$. We show results for $a_1 = .1$, $a_1 = .2$ and $a_1 = .3$.

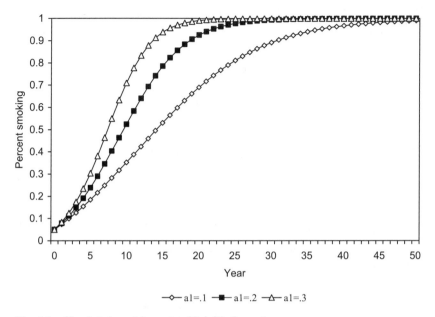

Fig. 5.1 Simulated smoking rate with initiation only

Higher values of a_1 imply both a faster convergence to everyone smoking and also a more s-shaped curve.

While this one-sided model might be appropriate for a time period when smoking was rising—the first half of the century, for example—it seems ill-suited for the last forty years, when cigarette smoking has been declining. A more sensible model might assume that both smokers and nonsmokers have a probability of transitioning into the other group. For example, we might assume that a nonsmoker becomes a smoker between time t and $t + 1$ with probability $a_0 + a_1 S(t)$, and a smoker becomes a nonsmoker between time t and time $t + 1$ with probability $b_0 + b_1(1 - S(t))$. In this formulation, both the constant transition probabilities and the social impacts of smoking may differ. A particularly natural assumption might be that $a_1 = b_1$ so that the social impacts of smoking and nonsmoking are identical, but that the basic transition probabilities (a_0 and b_0) differ. We think of changes in beliefs about the health consequences of smoking as reflecting changes in those parameters.

With these assumptions, the new difference equation characterizing smoking rates is:

$$(3) \quad S(t + 1) - S(t) = (a_0 + a_1 S(t))(1 - S(t)) - (b_0 + b_1(1 - S(t)))S(t).$$

The change in smoking includes nonsmokers who become smokers (the first term on the right-hand side) and smokers who become nonsmokers (the second term on the right-hand side). This equation can be rewritten:

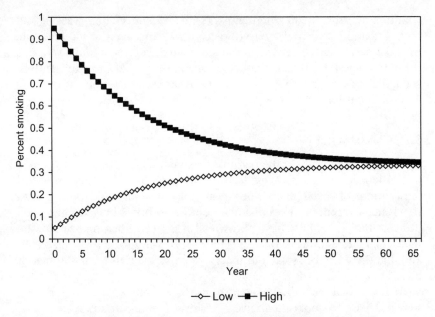

Fig. 5.2   Simulated smoking rate with quitting and initiation

$S(t + 1)$–$S(t) = a_0 + (a_1 - a_0 \; b_0 - b_1)S(t) + (b_1 - a_1)S(t)^2$. In the case that social interactions are the same for smoking and nonsmoking ($a_1 = b_1$), this equation reduces to:

(4) $S(t + 1) - S(t) = a_0 - (a_0 + b_0)S(t)$.

In this case, the system will converge to a steady-state $\overline{S} = a_0/(a_0 + b_0)$. Figure 5.2 shows two cases where the impact of social interactions on both transitions is the same.[3] In the first case, $S(t)$ converges to the steady-state level from below (starting at a smoking rate of 5 percent), and in the second case it converges from above (starting at a rate of 95 percent).

Our modest empirical implementation of this is to regress changes in the smoking rates since 1965 on the initial share of the population that smokes and the square of that share. We use data from 1965 because that is when data on adult prevalence are first available from the National Health Interview Survey (NHIS). Not all years of the NHIS asked about smoking; we use data from all the years that do, and consider adjacent years of the data. When we estimate this equation, we find:

(5) ΔRate = 2.88 − .23 × Lagged Rate + .004 × Lagged Rate^2.
              (5.57) (.38)   (.56)

---

3. We assume $a_0 = .02$ and $b_0 = .04$, so that the steady-state smoking rate is 33 percent.

Standard errors are in parentheses. There are eighteen observations and the r-squared is essentially zero (2 percent). Changes in the smoking rate over the past twenty-five years are uncorrelated with the initial level. This seems to suggest that social interactions operate weakly at an aggregate level, though clearly the number of observations makes us cautious of drawing strong conclusions.

5.7 Conclusion

This chapter discusses the possible reasons why the decision to smoke might depend on the smoking decisions of one's peers, and the empirical implications of social interactions in smoking. The most obvious implication is that exogenous forces that make one person's smoking less likely will decrease the probability that a peer will also smoke. Other implications are that social interactions will create high levels of variance across aggregates, and that there will be social multipliers, where exogenous attributes matter more at higher levels of aggregation.

We found that individuals whose spouse faced a workplace smoking ban were less likely to smoke themselves. The instrumental variables estimate of the impact of spousal smoking suggests a 40 percent reduction in the probability of being an individual smoking if a spouse quits. These impacts were greatest for people with modest levels of education, although not uniformly so. The variance in smoking rates across states and metropolitan areas is about seven times higher than it would be if there were no social interactions and if there were no exogenous variables differing across space. We also find a significant social multiplier in the impact of smoking bans. The bans have a much stronger impact at higher levels of aggregation.

These results suggest that policy interventions that impact an individual's smoking habit will have both direct effects and also indirect effects on the smoking of peers. Workplace bans seem not only to have reduced worker smoking but also the smoking of the worker's spouse. Our results also suggest that interventions are likely to have larger impacts when they are imposed at higher levels of aggregation, although we found little evidence suggesting that social interactions can explain the shape of the time series of smoking rates.

References

Brock, W. A., and S. N. Durlauf. 2001. Discrete choice with social interactions. *The Review of Economic Studies* 68 (2); 235–60.
Case, A. C., and L. F. Katz. 1991. The company you keep: The effects of family and

neighborhood on disadvantaged youths. NBER Working Paper no. 3705. Cambridge, MA: National Bureau of Economic Research, May.

Christakis, N. A., and J. H. Fowler. 2007. The spread of obesity in a large social network over 32 years. *New England Journal of Medicine* 357 (4): 370–79.

Crane, J. 1991. The epidemic theory of ghettos and neighborhood effects on dropping out and teenage childbearing. *American Journal of Sociology* 96 (5): 1226–59.

DeMarzo, P. M., D. Vayanos, and J. Zweibel. 2003. Persuasion bias, social influence, and unidimensional opinions. *Quarterly Journal of Economics* 118 (3): 909–68.

Ellison, G., and D. Fudenberg. 1993. Rules of thumb for social learning. *Journal of Political Economy* 101 (4): 612–43.

Evans, W. N., M. C. Farrelly, and E. B. Montgomery. 1999. Do workplace smoking bans reduce smoking? *American Economic Review* 89 (5): 729–47.

George, L., and J. Waldfogel. 2003. Who affects whom in daily newspaper markets? *Journal of Political Economy* 111 (4): 765–84.

———. 2006. The *New York Times* and the market for local newspapers. *American Economic Review* 96 (1): 435–47.

Glaeser, E., B. Sacerdote, and J. Scheinkman. 1996. Crime and social interactions. *Quarterly Journal of Economics* 111 (2): 507–48.

———. 2003. The social multiplier. *Journal of the European Economics Association* 1 (2): 345–53.

Kuziemko, I. 2006. Is having babies contagious? Fertility peer effects between adult siblings. Princeton University. Unpublished Manuscript.

Manski, C. 1993. Identification of endogenous social effects: The reflection problem. *Review of Economic Studies* 60 (3): 531–42.

Sacerdote, B. 2001. Peer effects with random assignment: Results for Dartmouth roommates. *Quarterly Journal of Economics* 116 (2): 681–704.

Topa, G. 2001. Social interactions, local spillovers and unemployment. *Review of Economic Studies* 68 (2): 261–95.

Comment   Arie Kapteyn

It is gratifying to see that economics is catching up quickly with other social sciences (particularly sociology and social psychology) by incorporating social interactions into models of behavior. One contribution economics may make is to bring rigor to the field and to characterize in particular what is and what is not identifiable in the models that we consider (as in Manski [1993]). Smoking is clearly an example where we would expect social interactions to be important, but also one where social interactions are hard to distinguish from other reasons for observing clusters of smokers or nonsmokers. The most obvious problem is that smokers (or nonsmokers) may flock together. So if we see that smokers often have friends or spouses who smoke, this may point to social interactions, but it may also simply indicate correlated preferences.

Arie Kapteyn is a senior economist at RAND Labor and Population.

In their chapter, Cutler and Glaeser implement an independent variable (IV) strategy, where the existence of workplace smoking bans is used as an instrument. They also consider various other pieces of evidence for the existence of social interactions, to which I will return later.

To set the stage, I find it useful to write down a simple linear model that is akin to theirs, but with slightly more detail. Thus, consider the following structure:

$$(1) \qquad X_1 = a_1 + bX_2 + \varepsilon_1$$
$$X_2 = a_2 + bX_1 + \varepsilon_2$$

Here, X_1 and X_2 are indicators for smoking by spouses 1 and 2, respectively; a_1, a_2, and b are parameters; ε_1 and ε_2 are random i.i.d. error terms, with variances σ_1^2 and σ_2^2 and covariance σ_{12}. I will assume that $0 < b < 1$. In principle, the parameters a_1 and a_2 can be made functions of other explanatory variables and I will return to that later. For now we note that the system (1) implies the following reduced form

$$(2) \qquad X_1 = \frac{1}{1 - b^2}[a_1 + a_2b + b\varepsilon_2 + \varepsilon_1]$$
$$X_2 = \frac{1}{1 - b^2}[a_2 + a_1b + b\varepsilon_1 + \varepsilon_2].$$

Thus, if we regress X_1 on X_2, for instance, then the regression coefficient in the population would be equal to:

$$(3) \qquad \frac{\text{cov}(X_1, X_2)}{\text{var}(X_2)} = \frac{(1 + b^2)\sigma_{12} + b(\sigma_1^2 + \sigma_2^2)}{b^2\sigma_1^2 + 2b\sigma_{12} + \sigma_2^2}.$$

For $\sigma_1^2 = \sigma_2^2 = \sigma^2$ this simplifies to

$$(4) \qquad \frac{\text{cov}(X_1, X_2)}{\text{var}(X_2)} = \frac{(1 + b^2)\sigma_{12} + 2b\sigma^2}{(1 + b^2)\sigma^2 + 2b\sigma_{12}}.$$

And finally, if we assume $\sigma_{12} = 0$ then the regression coefficient is equal to $2b/(1 + b^2)$, which is the result given in the chapter.

It is easy to see that for $\sigma_{12} \geq 0$ the regression of X_1 on X_2 will lead to an overestimate of b, no matter if we apply (3), (4), or the result obtained in the chapter (i.e., with $\sigma_{12} = 0$). It seems very unlikely that σ_{12} would be negative. Hence, we would expect a consistent estimation method for b to yield a smaller value than ordinary least squares (OLS). Yet the chapter finds the opposite: the IV estimate of b is roughly double the OLS estimate.

Cutler and Glaeser offer a number of possible explanations for this finding. I would like to suggest one additional possibility: assortative mating. Suppose that spouses search each other out partly on the basis of smoking preferences. This would suggest that an individual who does not smoke may be more likely to select a spouse who is subject to a smoking ban. This, then, is likely to introduce a correlation between the smoking ban variable and the error term in this individual's smoking equation and thereby invalidating this variable as an instrumental variable. This possibility also suggests a simple, though perhaps crude, test. Given that the prevalence of smoking bans has increased over time, one would expect the correlation of the instrument with the error term to be less for couples who have been together longer. The reasoning for this is that for a couple that got married when there were no smoking bans, this cannot have affected their marriage decision. If this suspicion is correct, the IV estimate of b should be higher for recently weds than for couples that married a long time ago. As a first approximation, one can use age as a proxy for the duration of the marriage.

There is a more general question as to why one needs to use the smoking ban variable as an instrumental variable at all. Let us consider the IV estimation a little closer. In particular, assume that $a_1 = \alpha_1 + \delta_1 z_1$ and $a_2 = \alpha_2 + \delta_2 z_2$, where z_1 and z_2 are exogenous variables that can be used as instruments. Clearly, 2SLS will yield consistent estimates of the parameters in the model, including b. The model used in the chapter includes a large number of controls, which are assumed exogenous, or at least predetermined. In the logic of simultaneous equations, all of these can be used as instruments. There does not seem to be a need, therefore, to use workplace smoking bans.

An interesting second approach to the analysis of social interactions is to consider "social multipliers" and "excess variance" across groups. This is easily illustrated in the framework previously introduced. Let us first consider social multipliers. Suppose that in (1) both a_1 and a_2 are increased by an amount Δa. Ignoring social interaction, both X_1 and X_2 would increase by the same amount Δa. Taking into account social interactions, that is, using (2), we find that both X_1 and X_2 increase by $\Delta a/(1-b)$, which is larger. The social multiplier is equal to $1/(1-b)$. Although I illustrate the social multiplier in the model for two spouses, the same idea applies to other groups in which social interactions may take place, like metropolitan areas or states. It is found that the effect of smoking bans on smoking goes up quite strongly when moving from individual level data to metropolitan level data and then to state level data. Qualitatively similar increases in the social multiplier are found for log-income, but not for years of education. Within the context of the model that finding is problematic, since the simple set-up used in the chapter (and in the previous equations) would imply identical social multipliers for any exogenous variable (any variable on which a_1 and a_2 would depend).

I will also illustrate the notion of excess variance in the context of the spouses model. For simplicity, consider the case $\sigma_1^2 = \sigma_2^2 = \sigma^2$. We then have for $b = 0$ that the conditional variance of "mean smoking" in the household is equal to

$$(5) \qquad \mathrm{Var}\!\left(\frac{X_1 + X_2}{2} \mid a_1, a_2\right) = \frac{1}{2}\{\sigma^2 + \sigma_{12}\}.$$

For $0 < b < 1$ we have that

$$(6) \qquad \mathrm{Var}\!\left(\frac{X_1 + X_2}{2} \mid a_1, a_2\right) = \frac{1}{2(1-b)^2}\{\sigma^2 + \sigma_{12}\},$$

which is clearly larger. Again, the same idea can be applied to larger groups than just couples. The data suggest a substantial amount of excess variance. It would have been interesting to see the same idea applied to couples, as in this example. The formulas also suggest a cautionary note (acknowledged in the chapter): if one were to incorrectly assume that the errors are uncorrelated then the presence of σ_{12} in (5) would suggest excess variance, where only correlated effects are to blame for the larger than expected variance.

A final exercise in the chapter involves a simple dynamic model of adoption of smoking and nonsmoking. It turns out that the dynamic model provides a poor fit of the aggregate data. It is not clear why that is, and I would hesitate at this moment to take that as evidence against social interactions.

So where does this leave us? The chapter presents an elegant framework suggesting various patterns in the data if social interactions are present. By and large, the predicted patterns are indeed found in the data and I am inclined to interpret this as solid evidence of social interactions in smoking. One might argue that social interactions in smoking are so obvious, that empirical evidence to support it is hardly necessary. Apart from the obvious rejoinder that obtaining a quantitative estimate of the extent of interactions in smoking is important by itself, perhaps the most important contribution of the chapter is to show how the analytic framework used helps to interpret and understand data. At the same time, the patterns in the data are not all consistent with the model predictions. The largest marginal value of future work may therefore be found in adaptations of the analytic framework, to be able to accommodate richer patterns in the data. The chapter provides an excellent illustration of the value of a powerful analytic framework for understanding the extent and nature of social interactions.

Reference

Manski, C. 1993. Identification of endogenous social effects: The reflection problem. *Review of Economic Studies* 60 (3): 531–42.

Education and the Prevalence of Pain

Steven J. Atlas and Jonathan Skinner

6.1 Introduction

There is considerable evidence that low educational attainment is associated with poor health. Life cycle models of human capital model (e.g., Case and Deaton 2005) imply that lower education workers will depreciate their physical health more rapidly, leading to strong education-based differentials in health and disability for older ages. Also, there are educational differences in nutritional habits, access to health care, and differences in cognition and the understanding of health risks (Cutler and Lleras-Muney 2006). In this chapter, we consider pain, which is associated with poor health and reflects an important dimension of well-being (Krueger and Stone 2008; Kahneman and Krueger 2006). Many clinical health conditions can cause pain, but in practice the link between pain and organic bodily disorders, such as disc herniation of the spinal column, are tenuous at best. For example, one-half of asymptomatic people—those who are not in pain and function normally—exhibit objective signs of spinal abnormalities on their MRIs (Jensen et. al. 1994). The reverse is also true; people without any discernable clinical evidence of back disorder may be immobilized by excruciating pain (Chou et al. 2007).

Steven J. Atlas is an assistant professor of medicine at Harvard Medical School and an Associate Physician at Massachusetts General Hospital. Jonathan Skinner is the John Sloan Dickey Third Century Professor in Economics at Dartmouth College, professor of community and family medicine at Dartmouth Medical School, and a research associate of the National Bureau of Economic Research.

We thank Amitabh Chandra, Joyce DeLeo, Edward Glaeser, Kathy Stroffolino, James Weinstein, and participants at the NBER Conference on Aging in May 2007 for insightful comments and suggestions. We are grateful to NIAMS (P60-AR048094), the National Institute on Aging (P01-AG19783), and the Robert Wood Johnson Foundation for financial support. Samuel Marshall provided superb research assistance.

One of the few studies in economics to consider the role of pain is Kapteyn, Smith, and van Soest (2006), who find that people "troubled with pain" are far more likely to report a disability that prevents them from working, which in turn substantially raises the likelihood of leaving the labor force.[1] Another study by Krueger and Stone (2008) used a twenty-four-hour diary survey to find one-third of respondents between ages fifty to fifty-nine reporting some pain, with higher rates among people with lower income. In this chapter, we first use the 2004 Health and Retirement Study (HRS) to document the dramatic differences across educational groups in the prevalence of pain. We find differences across educational groups, with rates of people age fifty to fifty-nine troubled by pain, ranging from 26 percent for women with a college education to 55 percent for those without a high school diploma.

An obvious explanation for these differences is that people with lower education are more likely to have worked in manual jobs, or to experience other types of poor health. We can partially control for such differences using controls in the HRS for occupation and industry, factors that appear to matter but that do not dislodge the fundamental result that education matters a great deal for the realization of pain. But we are still concerned with the possibility of long-term unobserved health factors that may be associated with education. As well, we would like to test the hypothesis that education affects *changes* over time in pain.

For this reason, we also consider the importance of pain using data from the Maine Lumbar Spine Study, which followed patients with intervertebral disk herniation (IDH) over a ten-year follow-up period. This unique study provided detailed clinical baseline information for a sample of people with a common clinical complaint of lower back pain associated with sciatica (referred pain down the leg) arising from IDH.[2] We consider education-based differences in the long-term prevalence of pain with treatment, and whether these differences can be explained by underlying clinical health at baseline, or by access to surgical or other medical treatments.

The initial severity of the IDH, as measured by imaging or clinical diagnosis, explains just a small degree of variation in outcomes. Surgery has limited explanatory power in long-term pain, although surgery has been associated with modest outcome benefits (Atlas et. al. 2005; Weinstein, Tosteson, et al., 2006; Weinstein, Lurie, et al. 2006). The most important predictive factor of long-term pain outcomes is education. Even after ten years, the percentage of people who experience leg or back pain "almost always" or "always" is 34 percent for high school dropouts, but just 9 percent for college graduates.

---

1. Blanchflower (2008) has also considered pain as a dependent variable; his results are discussed in more detail following.

2. We therefore exclude all patients who do not have clear objective evidence of a specific cause for their lower back pain. All patients were required to have symptoms of sciatica that were thought due to a herniated disc. Eligibility criteria did not require imaging data for enrollment, however.

Why then is pain so much greater among lower educational (or income) groups? One explanation is that people report pain to justify nonemployment and disability. However, there is modest evidence for this explanation from the economics literature (e.g., Benitez-Silva et al. 2004), as well as a growing clinical and neurological literature rejecting the idea of people falsely reporting pain. Instead, this new view recognizes the importance of the brain in generating *real* pain in specific areas of the brain, even in the absence of a specific physical injury (Melzack 1993; Apkarian, Baliki, and Geha 2009).

As well, there is evidence that this complex process of pain may respond to psychosocial factors or even economic factors that are likely to be associated with education, for example in the repetition strain injury (RSI) epidemic in Australia, which swept across some (but not all) regions before disappearing in the late 1980s (Gawande 2002). The strong association between education and the prevalence of pain in both the HRS and the Maine IDH data are supportive of the view that educational attainment is associated with social or even economic factors that affect the neurobiological processing and perception of pain.

6.2   The Prevalence of Pain in the Health and Retirement Study

The Health and Retirement Study (HRS) is a nationally based longitudinal study of people age fifty and over. The simplest comparisons focus on the question: "Are you often troubled by pain?" The initial sample size for people age fifty and over was $N = 10,561$ (women) and $N = 7,841$ (men) providing valid answers to the pain question. The unadjusted comparisons are shown in table 6.1 by three educational groups: eleven or fewer years of education, high school graduates and some college (twelve to fifteen years), and college graduates (sixteen or more years).

Overall, the prevalence of pain among women fifty to fifty-nine-years-old is substantially higher among those who did not finish school (55 percent), more than double the rate for women of the same age with a college degree (25 percent, $p < .01$), and still substantially higher than for women with high school degrees (36 percent). In general, the prevalence of pain is lower among men, which may be the consequence of differences in disease prevalence. But a similar educational gradient is observed for them as well, with a rate of 42 percent among those who did not graduate from high school, compared to 19 percent for college graduates.

Individuals reporting pain were also asked in more detail about the severity of the pain. These tabulations are shown in figure 6.1 (panel A for women and panel B for men) for ages fifty to fifty-nine. The percentage of "no pain" respondents is simply 100 minus the percentage of people reporting pain in table 6.1, but with more detailed gradation of whether the pain is mild, moderate, or severe. The educational gradient carries over with regard to

Table 6.1   The prevalence of pain, by education and age

Age	High school dropouts	High school graduates +	College graduates +	Sample size
		Females		
50–59	55.12	35.72	25.39	2,776
60–69	44.04	36.60	28.63	3,588
70–79	38.15	34.15	30.14	2,518
80–89	33.23	33.33	30.00	1,430
90+	36.65	33.44	32.95	249
Sample size	2,644	6,105	1,812	10,561
		Males		
50–59	42.20	35.15	19.40	1,956
60–69	40.85	31.36	22.30	2,828
70–79	28.51	26.84	21.06	2,061
80–89	28.64	31.10	27.65	883
90+	27.34	36.91	23.14	119
Sample size	1,976	3,841	2,030	7,847

Source: Health and Retirement Study, 2004.

severity of pain. For women in this age group, mild pain is similar across education groups (10.8 percent for those without a high school diploma, compared to 10.1 percent for college graduates), moderate pain is substantially greater (28.2 percent for the lowest education group, compared with 21 percent for high school graduates and 12 percent for college graduates), and there is a five-to-one difference for severe pain (15.9 percent for those not finishing high school, compared to 2.9 percent for college graduates). A similar pattern is shown for men; for the lowest education group, 10.5 percent report severe pain, compared to 1.6 percent for college graduates.

One might expect rates of reported pain to rise with age, but the opposite pattern is observed, at least among those with lower educational attainment. (Rates rise somewhat for college graduates.) Also, the education gradient largely disappears among older ages. For example, among women age eighty to eighty-nine, 33 percent of those not finishing high school report pain, compared to 30 percent for college graduates.[3] Somewhat more report severe pain, 8.6 for the lowest education group compared to 5.4 for college graduates. For men age eighty to eighty-nine, the rates are nearly identical; 29 percent in the lowest and 28 percent in the highest education groups report pain, with 6.9 versus 6.6 percent reporting severe pain.

One could explain these differences as a cohort effect, that these younger people were more likely to experience pain because of differential labor market experiences, although this hypothesis does not receive support from

3. See also Krueger and Stone (2008), who consider a broader sample of age groups; they find pain rising again among people ninety and older.

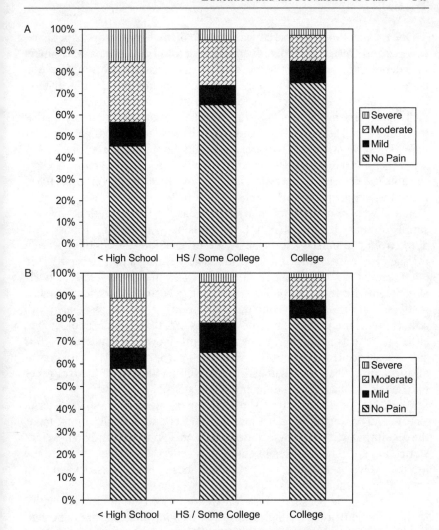

Fig. 6.1   Rates of pain by education group, 2004: *A*, **Females;** *B*, **Males**
Source: Health and Retirement Study, 2004, ages fifty to fifty-nine (*N* = 2,772).

additional waves of the HRS.[4] Another possibility is differential mortality rates, so that there are simply fewer (and healthier) people who did not finish high school in the sample by age eighty to eighty-nine, but selection bias would have to be extreme to cause the large gradient observed at age fifty to fifty-nine (and age sixty to sixty-nine) to disappear so quickly.

4. One might also speculate about an experiential difference between younger and older cohorts if the cultural acceptance of pain (pain as the "fifth vital sign") may be more ingrained in younger cohorts. It is less likely that younger patients have received less care for their pain than older individuals.

One explanation for these educational gradients is past work experience. In Case and Deaton (2005), individuals with lower educational attainment may depreciate human capital more rapidly. For example, working in physically demanding occupations earns a wage premium, but the longer-term impact will adversely affect general health; for example, through injuries, arthritis, or chronic back pain by the time they reach age fifty, implying that low educational attainment workers would experience much higher rates of pain. Thus, we attempt to control for occupation and industry, as well as other factors, in explaining the education-based gradients in pain.

Table 6.2 presents a regression analysis, stratified by age group (fifty to fifty-nine, sixty to sixty-nine, and seventy to seventy-nine) but including men and women in the same analysis. For ease of interpretation, we use a simple ordinary least squares (OLS) regression analysis, with robust standard errors. Column (1) shows the simplest regression analysis by education for age fifty to fifty-nine. Black respondents were less likely to report pain (–4.7 percent, $p < .05$), while female gender, as noted earlier, was positively associated with reported pain (9.3 percent, $p < .01$). Marital status also matters; relative to married couples, widowhood is positively associated with pain (4.2 percent, $p < .05$), but only for ages fifty to fifty-nine; at older ages either the effects are small or not significant. However, being divorced is strongly associated with reported pain (15.8 percent, $p < .01$), with gradually declining effects for older age groups. Neither being separated, or never married, is associated with differential levels of pain.

We also included the log of weight (in pounds), along with a squared term. The impact of weight on pain is minimized at 117 pounds (the minimum of the quadratic), with large associations between low-weight and high-weight status on pain. The low-weight status may reflect a wasting disease (there are relatively few in this category), while obesity is likely associated with arthritis and other ailments.

The association between education and reported pain is strong. Relative to those who did not finish high school, high school graduates are 13 percent less likely to report pain ($p < .01$), and college graduates are 25 percent less likely ($p < .01$). The disparities decline at older ages; Column (3) shows 4.2 lower reported pain for high school graduates (8.5 percent lower for college graduates) among those age seventy to seventy-nine.

Columns (4) and (5) in table 6.2 report coefficients from regressions that include individual occupational and industry variables in the HRS. Occupation matters a great deal; figure 6.2 shows the marginal impact of occupation on the prevalence of pain for the age fifty to fifty-nine group, evaluated at the sample means for education, race, marital status, and weight. (Industry effects were more modest and are not reported here.) These predicted pain measures ranged from 25 percent (managerial) and 29 percent (professional and sales) to 43 percent (services: private households, cleaning, and building support) and 58 percent (armed forces). While the educational gradient is

Table 6.2	Regression analysis explaining prevalence of pain: Health and Retirement Study, 2004				
Age groups	(1) 50–59	(2) 60–69	(3) 70–79	(4) 50–59	(5) 60–69
HS graduate	–0.133	–0.093	–0.042	–0.096	–0.078
	(5.45)***	(5.22)***	(2.38)**	(3.52)***	(3.94)***
College +	–0.252	–0.172	–0.085	–0.168	–0.157
	(9.72)***	(8.24)***	(3.94)***	(5.38)***	(6.04)***
Black	–0.047	–0.080	–0.044	–0.069	–0.093
	(2.20)**	(4.05)***	(1.76)	(3.05)***	(4.60)***
Other race/ethnicity	0.019	0.009	–0.042	0.011	0.001
	(0.64)	(0.23)	(1.14)	(0.36)	(0.04)
Sex	0.093	0.111	0.138	0.129	0.107
	(5.45)***	(7.02)***	(7.80)***	(6.66)***	(5.59)***
Divorced	0.158	0.087	–0.024	0.163	0.064
	(3.34)***	(1.53)	(0.31)	(3.23)***	(1.07)
Widowed	0.042	0.008	0.050	0.023	0.001
	(2.00)**	(0.35)	(1.69)	(1.10)	(0.06)
Separated	–0.004	–0.038	–0.020	–0.018	–0.059
	(0.10)	(1.76)	(1.08)	(0.48)	(2.62)***
Never married	0.019	–0.060	–0.047	0.007	–0.070
	(0.57)	(1.67)	(1.09)	(0.21)	(1.88)
Log (weight) in lbs	–3.350	–3.321	–4.246	–3.583	–3.108
	(3.33)***	(3.33)***	(3.53)***	(3.43)***	(3.06)***
Log (weight)^2	0.352	0.352	0.442	0.373	0.333
	(3.63)***	(3.66)***	(3.76)***	(3.71)***	(3.39)***
Age 55–59	0.030			0.034	
	(2.00)**			(2.22)**	
Age 65–69		–0.034			–0.033
		(2.53)**			(2.39)**
Age 75–79			–0.012		
			(0.79)		
Constant	8.290	8.137	10.425	8.861	7.455
	(3.17)***	(3.15)***	(3.39)***	(3.27)***	(2.83)***
Industry and occupation dummy variables	No	No	No	Yes	Yes
Observations	4,617	6,290	4,533	4,354	5,880
R^2	0.06	0.05	0.03	0.08	0.06

Note: Robust *t*-statistics in parentheses.
***Significant at the 1 percent level.
**Significant at the 5 percent level.

attenuated, there still remains a substantial difference of 10 percent in pain between the lowest educational group and high school graduates, and a 17 percent gap for college graduates age fifty to fifty-nine. Including occupation and industry dummy variables had almost no impact on the educational gradients for age sixty to sixty-nine.

Table 6.3 presents additional ordered probit regressions with the ordering

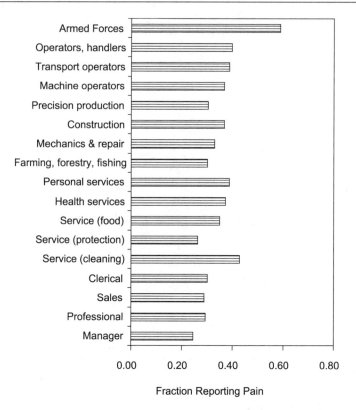

Fig. 6.2   Fraction reporting pain by occupation in the HRS: 2004

Notes: Age fifty to fifty-nine, adjusting for education, marital status, race, weight, and industry; based on Column (4) in table 6.2. See the HRS Codebook for the complete definitions of occupation.

equivalent to no pain (0) through severe pain (3), controlling for occupation and industry. The coefficients on education remain significant, although the magnitude of the coefficients is (again) smaller for ages seventy to seventy-nine. While the interpretation of marginal effects are complicated in ordered probits, note that the coefficient on college education, roughly one-half for ages fifty to fifty-nine and ages sixty to sixty-nine, is more than double the difference in the index between mild and moderate pain (cut point 2 minus cut point 1) and half the difference between moderate and severe pain (cut point 3 minus cut point 2). Thus education remains a key factor in both the presence and severity of pain.

These measures are consistent with an independent association between education and pain, but we acknowledge that this analysis is more suggestive than definitive. For example, income may be the important mediating factor that is correlated with education. However, concerns about the endogeneity of income are particularly important here—especially in light of Kapteyn,

Table 6.3   Ordered probits explaining the intensity of pain: Health and Retirement Study, 2004

Age groups	(1) 50–59	(2) 60–69	(3) 70–79
HS graduate	−0.310	−0.248	−0.135
	(4.63)***	(4.95)***	(2.39)**
College +	−0.542	−0.498	−0.227
	(6.46)***	(7.05)***	(2.76)***
Black	−0.116	−0.245	−0.108
	(1.79)	(4.20)***	(1.39)
Other race/ethnicity	0.069	0.068	−0.143
	(0.80)	(0.54)	(1.03)
Sex	0.398	0.307	0.399
	(7.34)***	(6.00)***	(6.09)***
Divorced	0.492	0.204	−0.081
	(3.81)***	(1.28)	(0.30)
Widowed	0.098	0.059	0.121
	(1.74)	(0.99)	(1.50)
Separated	−0.010	−0.136	−0.040
	(0.10)	(2.13)	(0.66)
Never married	0.046	−0.221	−0.062
	(0.47)	(1.97)**	(0.43)
Log (weight) in lbs	−9.170	−9.258	−6.905
	(3.29)***	(3.37)***	(2.05)**
Log (weight)^2	0.946	0.975	0.747
	(3.55)***	(3.69)***	(2.28)**
Age 55–59	0.109		
	(2.58)***		
Age 65–69		−0.062	
		(1.66)	
Age 75–79			−0.079
			(1.70)
Industry and occupation dummy variables	Yes	Yes	Yes
Cut point 1 (mild)	−21.45	−21.25	−15.40
Cut point 2 (moderate)	−21.11	−20.96	−15.14
Cut point 3 (severe)	−20.12	−20.02	−14.22
Observations	4,346	5,874	3,852

Note: Robust z statistics in parentheses.
***Significant at the 1 percent level.
**Significant at the 5 percent level.

Smith, and van Soest's (2006) finding that pain is a key mediating factor for leaving the labor force. Similarly, we may be missing other measures of underlying health, but again these are potentially endogenous (self-reported health is likely to be affected by the perception of pain) or the consequence of ready access to primary care (knowing that one suffers from hypertension). For these reasons, we turn to data on changes over time in the prevalence of pain for patients, all of whom are suffering from herniated discs, and with detailed baseline data on the severity of their disease.

6.3   Changes over Time in Back Pain: The Maine Lumbar Spine Study

There is an extensive literature describing the epidemiology of back pain. One study of Michigan workers found compensable back strains occurred in 1.7 percent of handlers and laborers annually, compared to just 0.04 percent among executives (Gluck and Oleinick 1998). But most studies do not find that physical tasks are the primary cause for chronic back pain. Even after controlling carefully for differences in occupation, low-education workers in Norway were far more likely to leave the labor force disabled (Hagen et al. 2000). Similarly, there is a strong impact of education and income on days lost for homemakers, a difference that seems unlikely to be explained entirely by differences in types of work performed by homemakers with, for example, high versus low education (Deyo and Tsui-Wu 1987). One study of San Francisco transit workers suggest that while job tasks have some impact on spinal injuries, other factors related to stress and psychosocial issues have more important predictive powers (Krause et al. [1998]; also see Waddell [2004]).

The Maine study was a prospective observational study of patients presenting with sciatica due to an IDH or lumbar spinal stenosis. Patients were treated by orthopedic surgeons, neurosurgeons, and occupational medicine physicians in community-based practices throughout the state of Maine. Details about the study design, methods, and outcomes have been published elsewhere (Keller et al. 1996; Atlas et al. 1996; Atlas et al. 2005). Our primary interest is in the 403 patients enrolled in the trial with sciatica due to an IDH enrolled between 1990 and 1992, and who were followed up after ten years (or who died during the ten-year period).[5] Because the objective of the original study was to compare surgery with nonsurgical treatments, enrollment was stratified to obtain roughly equal numbers in these treatment groups. In addition, oversampling of patients with IDH receiving workers' compensation was achieved by enrolling patients from occupational medicine practices. (Thus, the sample was not designed to be representative of the general population with sciatica.) Specific radiographic findings were not required for study entry but were available for about half of the patients.

For eligible consenting patients, baseline interviews were conducted in person by trained research assistants, with follow-up obtained by mailed questionnaires. Physicians completed a baseline questionnaire including history, physical examination findings, diagnostic procedure results, and planned treatment. Patient data collected at baseline included demographic information, employment and disability status, comorbid conditions, past

---

5. There were 507 patients in the original sample.

spine history, symptoms, and functional status. Generic health status was assessed at baseline with the Medical Outcomes Study Short Form 36-item questionnaire (SF-36). The SF-36 describes eight domains of health, with each scored from 0 (poor health) to 100 (optimal health).

We assessed two measures of pain and functioning specific to low back or leg pain, which for editorial ease will be referred to as generic "back pain." (The leg pain arises from sciatica, a common symptom of IDH.) The first measure, the modified Roland-Morris Score, assesses back-specific functional status, which ranges from 0 to 23 depending on the number of "true" responses to statements about how the patient's life has been affected by back pain (Patrick et al. 1995). Items include: "I stay at home most of the time because of my back," "I stand up for only short periods because of my back," and "Because of back pain, I am more irritable and bad tempered with people than usual." (See the appendix for the full set of questions.) Questions may ask about difficulty in doing jobs around the house, but questions about job issues or whether the back pain makes it difficult to work are avoided. Thus, these questions are not subject to the usual potential endogeneity arising from people reporting illness to justify their nonworking status.[6]

The second measure is the frequency of low back pain, leg pain, leg or foot weakness, leg numbness, and leg pain after walking. There is a 7-point scale that we collapse to focus just on the two most severe answers: "almost always" and "always."[7] Follow-up from year five to year ten for the sample was very good, 352 of the original 403 people remained at the end of the sample, with a small degree of attrition (3 percent) owing to death.

Table 6.4 presents summary statistics of key variables in the analysis, stratified by education: no high school diploma ($N = 47$ at baseline, $N = 35$ for the ten-year follow-up), high school graduates plus some college ($N = 249$ at baseline, 204 at follow-up), and college graduates ($N = 122$ at baseline, 113 at follow-up). The average age in the sample was forty, with little difference across educational groups. However, 15 percent of those without a high school degree were female, compared to 39 percent among college graduates.

The Quebec Severity Score, a standard way to grade the severity of spine disorders (Atlas et al. 1996), did not differ substantially at baseline across educational groups. However, severe IDH based on an imaging test was higher for college graduates (15 percent) compared to people who had not finished high school (2 percent). These percentages are relative to the entire population, including those for whom imaging tests were not available, but the ratio of those with missing data was similar across educational groups;

---

6. Although such reverse causation appears modest at best (see Benitez-Silva et al. 2004).

7. We first find the part of the body with the most severe pain and use that measure as our summary score.

Table 6.4   Summary statistics for Maine IDH study: By education

Variable (baseline unless noted)	Less than high school	High school graduates +	College graduates	Entire sample
Average age	42.6	38.70	42.87	40.37
	(13.7)	(9.24)	(10.0)	(10.2)
Sex (female = 1)	0.149	0.325	0.390	0.325
	(0.36)	(0.47)	(0.49)	(0.47)
Quebec severity score (1 = evidenc)	0.565	0.567	0.658	0.593
	(0.50)	(0.50)	(0.48)	(0.49)
Fraction severe imaging score	0.021	0.108	0.154	0.112
	(0.15)	(0.31)	(0.36)	(0.32)
Fraction missing imaging score	0.447	0.522	0.520	0.513
	(0.50)	(0.50)	(0.50)	(0.50)
Smoker	0.574	0.510	0.287	0.452
	(0.50)	(0.50)	(0.45)	(0.50)
Neurological weakness (score of 0 through 4)	1.370	1.300	1.197	1.277
	(0.80)	(1.00)	(0.96)	(0.96)
Comorbidities[a]	0.277	0.181	0.285	0.222
	(0.45)	(0.39)	(0.45)	(0.42)
Roland-Morris score (average at baseline)	16.83	16.33	14.55	15.86
	(4.89)	(5.13)	(5.65)	(5.32)
Fraction pain always or almost always (Baseline)	0.787	0.787	0.732	0.771
	(0.41)	(0.41)	(0.44)	(0.42)
SF36 bodily pain score (scale of 1 to 100)	21.91	24.07	30.37	25.69
	(20.18)	(18.54)	(24.00)	(20.66)
SF36 physical function score (scale of 1 to 100)	29.67	36.20	44.70	38.03
	(23.49)	(25.59)	(28.71)	(26.72)
Fraction died in 10-year period	0.06	0.03	0.03	0.03
	(0.25)	(0.17)	(0.18)	(0.18)
Fraction surgical treatment	0.404	0.402	0.350	0.387
	(0.50)	(0.49)	(0.48)	(0.49)
Prescription narcotics	0.426	0.474	0.504	0.477
	(0.50)	(0.50)	(0.50)	(0.50)
Roland-Morris score (10-year follow-up)	10.83	7.99	3.40	6.72
	(7.88)	(7.37)	(4.65)	(7.08)
Fraction pain always or almost always (10-year follow-up)	0.343	0.196	0.088	0.176
	(0.48)	(0.40)	(0.29)	(0.38)
Sample size at baseline	47	249	122	419
Sample size at 10-year follow-up	35	204	113	352

Note: [a]Comorbidities include pulmonary disorders, cardiac problems, stroke, cancer, or diabetes. Standard deviation in parentheses.

45 percent for people not finishing high school compared to 52 percent for high school and college graduates.[8]

Baseline factors likely to predict poorer health outcomes were higher

8. Missing data means that the researchers were not able to obtain records of the images, not that the physician did not perform the imaging test. But even when imaging information is not available, there are well-established clinical methods for diagnosing IDH based on, for example, the presence of sciatica and physical examination findings.

for those with lower educational attainment. Of those without high school graduates, 57 percent were smokers, significantly greater than 29 percent among college graduates. Similarly, other markers of health, such as the SF36 bodily pain score and the SF36 physical function score, were higher among people with more education. The baseline Roland-Morris score was slightly worse among high school dropouts (16.8) and high school graduates (16.3) than college graduates (14.6), but back pain was clearly disrupting normal life among all education groups. The percentage of people who "always" or "almost always" experienced back or leg pain was 79 percent for those with high school education (or less), and 73 percent for college graduates.[9]

Surgery is often used to treat IDH, although the clinical effects moderate over one to two years (Atlas et al. 1996, Weinstein, Tosteson et al. 2006; Weinstein, Lurie, et al. 2006), and the benefits largely dissipate over a ten-year period (Atlas et al. 2005, Weber 1983). Surgical procedure rates were 40 percent among high school dropouts and 35 percent for those with college education ($p = 0.78$), so it is unlikely that access to surgery per se can explain the educational gradient. Similarly, the percentage of patients taking narcotic pain medicine did not differ significantly between the lowest and highest education groups ($p = 0.18$).

The bottom of table 6.4 includes the identical Roland-Morris and pain measures, measured ten years later. On average, respondents are far better off than they were at baseline. And here the educational gradient becomes quite pronounced ($p < .01$), with an average Roland-Morris Score of 3.4 for college graduates, half the value for high school graduates (8.0), and one-third the average for those not finishing high school (10.8). Similarly, the percentage reporting pain always or almost always ranges from 34 percent for people without a high school degree to just 9 percent for college graduates ($p < .01$).

The differences in pain outcomes by education hold across the entire distribution of disabling pain. Figure 6.3 shows the distribution of Roland-Morris measures by education, broken into four groups; little pain (< four questions answered in the affirmative), mild (four to nine questions), moderate (ten to fifteen) and severe (sixteen to twenty-three). Just 27 percent of respondents without a high school degree report little pain, fewer than those reporting severe pain (30 percent). By contrast, among college graduates 68 percent report little pain, substantially more than the 5 percent who continue with severe pain.

We therefore consider the association between pain and education in a multivariate context, with the general model written as

$$Y_i = X_i\beta + Z_i\gamma + E_i\alpha + u_i$$

---

9. There was also a higher ten-year rate of mortality among the lowest education group (6 percent compared to the average of 3 percent).

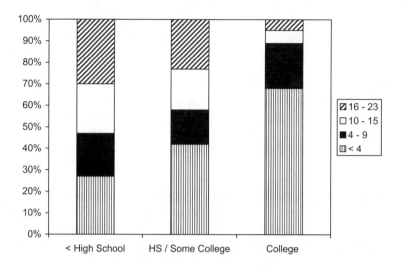

Fig. 6.3   Roland-Morris score ten years after baseline: By education

Notes: A Roland-Morris score of 23 is the most severe, 0 the least severe. See appendix for details of the questions.

where Y_i is the pain outcome at year 10 following baseline for individual i, X_i represents individual-specific characteristics such as age and sex, Z_i is the set of baseline severity characteristics such as imaging results, initial pain levels, and comorbidities, while E_i is a matrix of categorical measures of education.

Least squares regression results are presented in table 6.5, with the excluded educational category corresponding to eleven years of education or fewer. In column (1), which controls just for sex and age, the coefficient for college graduates is –7.32 ($p < .01$), and for high school graduates, –2.69 ($p < .05$). Column (2), which adds a limited set of baseline covariates (Z) raises the R^2 from 0.15 to 0.25, with smoking, the presence of comorbidities, and the baseline Roland-Morris Score, significant and in the expected direction. (One might interpret the baseline Roland-Morris Score as also capturing individual-level heterogeneity in the overall perception of pain.) The education gradient is somewhat less steep; the coefficient for college graduates is now –5.83 ($p < .01$). Finally, adding all baseline and treatment covariates (column [3]) has little impact on the coefficient for college education (–5.32, $p < .01$).

The Roland-Morris pain measure may be a little difficult to interpret, but the measure of whether one experiences back/leg pain "almost always" or "always" (that is, severe pain) may be easier to intuit. (Least-squares regression is used for ease of interpretation, but probit regressions yielded similar results.) As shown in column (4) in table 6.5, the education gradient is a 24 percentage point difference in the percentage of people reporting severe pain between those in the highest and lowest education group. After controlling

Table 6.5   Regression coefficients explaining the endpoint Roland-Morris Score and severe pain measure in the Maine Lumbar Spine Study

Independent variables	Roland (1)	Roland (2)	Roland (3)	Pain (4)	Pain (5)
HS education	−2.686	−1.715	−1.173	−0.136	−0.043
	(1.98)**	(1.29)	(0.86)	(1.92)	(0.58)
College graduate	−7.340	−5.833	−5.239	−0.244	−0.133
	(5.24)***	(4.21)***	(3.70)***	(3.29)***	(1.69)
Sex	0.049	−0.210	−0.231	−0.033	−0.053
	(0.06)	(0.27)	(0.29)	(0.77)	(1.24)
Age 30–39	−2.326	−1.275	−1.473	−0.015	−0.013
	(1.84)	(1.02)	(1.17)	(0.24)	(0.20)
Age 40–49	−1.232	−0.229	−0.768	0.039	0.038
	(0.94)	(0.18)	(0.60)	(0.59)	(0.56)
Age 50–59	−3.829	−2.992	−3.328	−0.078	−0.079
	(2.52)**	(1.99)**	(2.22)**	(1.00)	(0.98)
Age 60+	−1.961	−0.533	−0.642	−0.015	0.022
	(0.91)	(0.25)	(0.30)	(0.13)	(0.19)
Quebec imaging score		2.376	2.188		−0.019
		(0.64)	(0.59)		(0.09)
Severe imaging score		−1.480	−1.250		−0.039
		(1.26)	(1.06)		(0.59)
Smoker (1 = yes)		2.259	2.112		0.112
		(2.83)***	(2.64)***		(2.59)***
Neuro. weakness = 1		−0.574	−0.202		0.075
		(0.58)	(0.20)		(1.36)
Neuro. weakness = 2		−0.255	−0.424		−0.060
		(0.07)	(0.11)		(0.28)
Neuro. weakness = 3		0.039	0.004		0.016
		(0.01)	(0.00)		(0.07)
Comorbidities[a]		2.714	2.979		0.145
		(3.11)***	(3.37)***		(2.96)***
Baseline Roland		0.243	0.101		−0.006
		(3.25)***	(0.80)		(0.83)
Baseline pain			1.133		0.031
			(1.09)		(0.53)
Baseline BF36			−0.025		−0.001
			(0.94)		(0.81)
Baseline PF36			−0.020		−0.001
			(0.95)		(0.92)
Surgery (1 = yes)			1.412		−0.052
			(1.69)		(1.13)
Baseline narcotics			−0.399		−0.000
			(0.48)		(0.01)
Constant	12.630	7.091	9.630	0.349	0.493
	(7.69)***	(1.62)	(1.88)	(4.29)***	(1.68)
Observations	301	293	288	348	332
R^2	0.15	0.25	0.28	0.05	0.11

Note: t-statistics in parentheses.

[a]Comorbidities include pulmonary disorders, cardiac problems, stroke, cancer, or diabetes.

***Significant at the 1 percent level.

**Significant at the 5 percent level.

for all baseline measures, the corresponding gap is still 13 percentage points, as shown in column (5). This coefficient is marginally significant for those with college education, and not significant at all for high school graduates. However, when using an ordered probit equation with all responses to the question (from never experiencing back or leg pain to always experiencing it), the corresponding estimates are highly significant.

6.4   Discussion and Conclusion

In this chapter, we have explored the association between pain and education, and found first that the prevalence of pain exhibits a strong association with education among older (age fifty and over) Americans in the HRS. While previous occupation and industry, as well as marital status, accounts for some of this correlation, there remains a strong and persistent association, at least among ages fifty to seventy-nine.

We also considered how education was associated with the resolution of pain over time. The Maine study included patients with an IDH, a condition that has a specific pain complex that is verifiable in most cases based upon examination and imaging findings (Atlas et al. 2006). Thus, unlike nonspecific low back pain in which examination and imaging findings are less reliable, IDH represents a specific low back disorder in which it is more difficult for patients to report sciatic pain without evidence for an underlying clinical disorder (Atlas et al. 2007). Nevertheless, after ten years, patients with lower educational levels report more pain and functional disability despite objective evidence for the same underlying clinical condition and similar or less severe findings. These effects suggest that education matters for *changes* over time in pain, and swamp any impact of medical or surgical treatments for IDH.

Economists and other social scientists have become increasingly interested in the measurement of both health and well-being. Typically health has been measured using diseases known to the respondent (such as hypertension or diabetes), actual measures of blood pressure, hemoglobin A_1c,(e.g., Banks et al. 2006), and activities of daily living (ADLs) and instrumental activities of daily living (IADLs). These are relatively objective measures that, absent measurement error, should be stable, trend with age, or shift in response to health events. At the other end of the spectrum is "well-being," which is inherently subjective, and is typically measured by asking respondents about their happiness or satisfaction with their life, or with more focused approaches such as day reconstruction diaries, which asks respondents to describe their day and how they felt during each episode (Kahneman et al. 2004). Subjective measures have their drawbacks, however, as they can be sensitive to seemingly irrelevant factors such as whether the weather was nice on the day of the survey (Kahneman and Krueger 2006).

Pain lies somewhere between these two approaches. The study of pain, both in clinical and laboratory settings, occupies a very large literature, with several journals devoted solely to this topic, but economists do not typically consider it.[10] Though pain is self-reported, quantitative measures of pain and its impact have been validated and are widely used (Patrick et al. 1995; Deyo et al. 1998; Bombardier 2000), and prospects for more objective measures of pain using scans of brain activity are improving but are still controversial (Miller 2009).

In an analysis of country-level averages of pain and happiness, countries with the highest reported pain levels (e.g., Poland, Slovakia, Czech Republic, Slovenia, and Bulgaria) also tended to do worse on measures of happiness and life satisfaction (Blanchflower 2008). It is perhaps not surprising that there is a close association between pain and subjective well-being, as in Krueger and Stone (2008). Krueger et al. (2009) have recently proposed a new index measuring the fraction of time spent in an "unpleasant" state, which includes episodes of pain. Furthermore, there is neurological evidence that chronic pain has long-lasting effects on the organization and functioning of the brain, including atrophy (Apkarian et al. 2004; Apkarian, Baliki, and Geha 2009).

Subjective measures of pain have been viewed with suspicion by economists, given the possibility of people who are not working or eligible for disability insurance justifying their work status by claiming disabling pain. Questions are often framed to encourage such an interpretation—for example, asking the respondent whether they have a disability that prevents them from working. Most recently, Benitez-Silva et al. (2004) suggests little self-reporting bias, and in any case none of the questions considered here are related to work decisions. Instead they ask about general pain (HRS) or specific aspects of back pain with respect to sleeping, walking, or household tasks (see appendix).

In the clinical and neurological literature, there is an increased recognition that organic signs of injury are not necessary for real pain to occur (Chou et al. 2007). Atul Gawande (2002) described the case of Rowland Scott Quinlan, an architect who in his fifties was stricken with recurring back pain. Numerous physicians could find no physical explanation. There was no financial reason for him to fake pain, but Gawande nonetheless asked his wife about whether she thought he ever faked it.

> She has seen the pain defeat him in ways that she knows he is too proud to fake. He'll try to carry the groceries, and then, shamefaced, have to hand them back a few moments later. Though he loves movies, they have not been to the cinema in years. There have been times when the pain of

---

10. For example, the eponymous journal *Pain* publishes twenty-one issues per year. A jstor .org search of the word "pain" in all economics journals (in either the abstract or the title) yielded no relevant matches; a typical unrelated match was an 1894 article in the *Quarterly Journal of Economics* by David I. Green entitled "Pain-Cost and Opportunity-Cost."

movement has been so severe that he has soiled his pants rather than make his way to the bathroom. (117)

While Mr. Quinlin continued to work as best he could, for most people this type of pain leads to disability, which in turn leads to a total withdrawal from the labor force (Kapteyn, Smith, and van Soest 2006).

Recall in the Maine study that nearly everyone in the sample was in severe pain at baseline, with most making the transition from acute pain to recovery. The key puzzle is why the fraction of people making the unhappy transition into long-term chronic pain (and often permanent disability) is so much higher for people with lower educational attainment. A number of studies have pointed to psychological factors as being of primary importance for this transition; for example, depressive symptoms and a belief that the pain being experienced will remain permanent (Casey et al. 2008), and these might be associated with education.

Others have pointed to more fundamental differences in brain functioning between chronic pain sufferers and those who recover. Using fMRI scans and other approaches, neuroscientists have argued that chronic back pain (CBP) is associated with fundamental chemical changes in the brain that leads to heightened activity in the medial prefrontal cortex (along with a decline in gray matter density in other parts of the prefrontal cortex), with these factors accounting for roughly three-quarters of the variation in the intensity and duration of chronic back pain (Balaki et al. 2006). That areas of the brain affected by chronic pain are also regions associated with emotion and memory is particularly intriguing. While there is some suggestive evidence suggesting that brain structure differs by socioeconomic status (see Hackman and Farah 2009), the differences do not appear to be sufficiently consistent and large to explain the results we find in the data.

Perhaps a more fruitful explanation for the observed socioeconomic differences in pain is the idea that it is affected by social norms or economic factors, perhaps drawing on the insight that regions of the brain affected by pain are also associated with emotion. Gawande (2002) recounted the "epidemic" of repetition strain injury (RSI) in Australia during the 1980s:

> This was not a mild case of writer's cramp but a matter of severe pain, which started with minor discomfort during typing or other repetitive work and progressed to invalidism. The average time that a sufferer lost from work was seventy-four days. As with chronic back pain, no consistent physical abnormality or effective treatment could be found, yet the arm pain spread like a contagion. (128)

There were widespread outbreaks of this syndrome, with some factories or states being affected in large numbers and others passed by. However, by 1987 the epidemic was over, with observers viewing the most important reasons being that the syndrome was out of favor with physicians, and that it became harder to receive disability payments because of the RSI. While the evidence presented here is suggestive rather than definitive, it does raise questions about the interaction between the Social Security Disability Insurance (SSDI) program, the perception of pain, and social norms. Indeed, Hadler, Tait, and Chibnall (2007) have proposed that chronic back pain often evolves in response to the strong incentives inherent in the U.S. workers' compensation system, while Gawande's description of the Australian RSI epidemic is explicit in pointing to a social contagion model along the lines of Glaeser, Sacerdote, and Scheinkman (1996, 2003) or Rege, Telle, and Vortruba (2008).

This chapter is just a first step in trying to better understand the economic and social implications of pain. Our ongoing research is focusing on changes over time in the prevalence of pain and how these trends may be associated with social programs such as the SSDI program (Autor and Duggan 2003, 2006). The evidence from this chapter suggests that we need to better understand why low educational attainment translates into something more than the risk of a dead-end job—the risk also of a life ruined by chronic long-term pain.

Appendix

The Roland-Morris Questionnaire

1. I stay at home most of the time because of my back.
2. I change position frequently to try and get my back comfortable.
3. I walk more slowly than usual because of my back.
4. Because of my back I am not doing any of the jobs that I usually do around the house.
5. Because of my back, I use a handrail to get upstairs.
6. Because of my back, I have to hold on to something to get out of an easy chair.
7. I get dressed more slowly than usual because of my back.
8. I only stand up for short periods of time because of my back.
9. Because of my back, I try not to bend or kneel down.
10. I find it difficult to get out of a chair because of my back.
11. My back is painful almost all the time.
12. I find it difficult to turn over in bed because of my back.
13. I have trouble putting on my sock (or stockings) because of the pain in my back.
14. I only walk short distances because of my back pain.
15. I sleep less well because of my back.

16. I avoid heavy jobs around the house because of my back.

17. Because of my back pain, I am more irritable and bad tempered with people than usual.

18. Because of my back, I go upstairs more slowly than usual.

19. I stay in bed most of the time because of my back.

20. Because of my back problem, my sexual activity is decreased.

21. I keep rubbing or holding areas of my body that hurt or are uncomfortable.

22. Because of my back, I am doing less of the daily work around the house than I would usually do.

23. I often express concern to other people about what might be happening to my health.

Source: Trout et al. (2005).

References

Apkarian, A. V., Y. Sosa, S. Sonty, R. E. Levy, R. Harden, T. B. Parrish, and D. R. Gitelman. 2004. Chronic back pain is associated with decreased prefrontal and thalamic gray matter density. *Journal of Neuroscience* 24 (46): 10410–5.

Apkarian, A. V., M. N. Baliki, and P. Y. Geha. 2009. Towards a theory of chronic pain. *Progress in Neurobiology* 87 (2): 81–97.

Atlas, S. J., Y. Chang, R. B. Keller, D. E. Singer, Y. A. Wu, and R. A. Deyo. 2006. The impact of disability compensation on long-term treatment outcomes of patients with sciatica due to a lumbar disc herniation. *Spine* 31 (26): 3061–9.

Atlas, S. J., R. A. Deyo, K. B. Keller, A. M. Chapin, D. L. Patrick, J. M. Long, and D. E. Singer. 1996. The Maine Lumbar Spine Study, part II: 1-year outcomes of surgical and nonsurgical management of sciatica. *Spine* 21 (15): 1777–86.

Atlas, S. J., D. E. Singer, Y. A. Wu, R. A. Deyo, and R. B. Keller. 2005. Long-term outcomes of surgical and nonsurgical management of sciatica secondary to a lumbar disc herniation: 10 year results from the Maine Lumbar Spine Study. *Spine* 30 (8): 927–35.

Atlas, S. J., T. D. Tosteson, B. Hanscom, E. A. Blood, G. S. Pransky, B. A. Abdu, G. B. Andersson, and J. N. Weinstein. 2007. What is different about workers' compensation patients? Socioeconomic predictors of baseline disability status among patients with lumbar radiculopathy. *Spine* 32 (18): 2019–26.

Autor, D. H., and M. G. Duggan. 2003. The rise in the disability rolls and the decline in unemployment. *Quarterly Journal of Economics* 118 (1): 157–206.

———. 2006. The growth in the disability insurance roles: A fiscal crisis unfolding. *Journal of Economic Perspectives* 20 (3): 71–96.

Balaki, M., D. R. Chialvo, P. Y. Geha, R. M. Levy, R. N. Harden, T. B. Parrish, and A. V. Apkarian. 2006. Chronic pain and the emotional brain: Specific brain activity associated with spontaneous fluctuations of intensity of chronic back pain. *Journal of Neuroscience* 26 (47): 12165–73.

Banks, J., M. Marmot, Z. Oldfield, and J. P. Smith. 2006. Disease and disadvantage in the United States and in England. *Journal of the American Medical Association* 295 (7): 2037–45.

Benitez-Silva, H., M. Buchinsky, H. M. Chan, S. Cheidvasser, and J. P. Rust. 2004. How large is the bias in self-reported disability? *Journal of Applied Econometrics* 19 (6): 649–70.

Blanchflower, D. G. 2008. International evidence on well-being. NBER Working Paper no. 14318. Cambridge, MA: National Bureau of Economic Research, September.

Bombardier, C. 2000. Outcome assessments in the evaluation of treatment of spinal disorders: Summary and general recommendations. *Spine* 25 (24): 3100–3.

Case, A., and A. Deaton. 2005. Broken down by work and sex: How our health declines. In *Analyses in the economics of aging,* ed. D. Wise, 185–212. Chicago: University of Chicago Press.

Casey, C. Y., M. A. Greenberg, P. M. Nicassio, R. E. Harpin, and D. Hubbard. 2008. Transition from acute to chronic pain and disability: A model including cognitive, affective, and trauma factors. *Pain* 134 (1–2): 69–79.

Chou, R. A. Qaseem, V. Snow, D. Casey, J. T. Cross, P. Shekelle, and D. K. Owens. 2007. Diagnosis and treatment of low back pain: A joint clinical practice guideline from the American College of Physicians and the American Pain Society. *Annals of Internal Medicine* 147 (7): 478–91.

Cutler, D., and A. Lleras-Muney. 2006. Education and health: Evaluating theory and evidence. NBER Working Paper no. 12352. Cambridge, MA: National Bureau of Economic Research, July.

Deyo, R. A., M. Battie, A. J. Beurskens, C. Bombardier, P. Croft, B. Koes, A. Malmivaara, M. Roland, M. Von Korff, and G. Waddell. 1998. Outcome measures for low back pain research. A proposal for standardized use. *Spine* 23 (18): 2003–13.

Deyo, R. A., and Y. Tsui-Wu. 1987. Functional disability due to back pain: A population-based study indicating the importance of socioeconomic factors. *Arthritis and Rheumatism* 30 (11): 1247–53.

Gawande, A. 2002. *Complications.* New York: Henry Holt and Company.

Glaeser, E., B. Sacerdote, and J. Scheinkman. 1996. Crime and social interactions. *Quarterly Journal of Economics* 111 (2): 507–48.

———. 2003. The social multiplier. *Journal of the European Economic Association* 1 (2–3): 345–53.

Gluck, J., and A. Oleinick. 1998. Claim rates of compensable back injuries by age, gender, occupation, and industry. *Spine* 23 (14): 1572–87.

Hackman, D. A., and M. J. Farah. 2009. Socioeconomic status and the developing brain. *Trends in Cognitive Sciences* 13 (2): 65–73.

Hadler, N. M., R. C. Tait, and J. T. Chibnall. 2007. Back pain in the workplace. *Journal of the American Medical Association* 297 (14): 1594–6.

Hagen, K. B., H. H. Holte, K. Tambs, and T. Bjerkedal. 2000. Socioeconomic factors and disability retirement from back pain: A 1983–1993 population-based prospective study in Norway. *Spine* 25 (19): 2480–87.

Jensen, M. C., M. N. Brant-Zawadzki, N. Obuchowski, M. T. Modic, D. Malkasian, and J. S. Ross. 1994. Magnetic resonance imaging of the lumbar spine in people without back pain. *New England Journal of Medicine* 331 (2): 69–73.

Kahneman, D., and A. B. Krueger. 2006. Developments in the measurement of subjective well-being. *Journal of Economic Perspectives* 20 (1): 3–24.

Kahneman, D., A. B. Krueger, D. A. Schkade, N. Schwarz, and A. A. Stone. 2004. A survey method for characterizing daily life experience: The day reconstruction method. *Science* 306 (5702): 1776–780.

Kapteyn, A., J. Smith, and A. van Soest. 2006. Dynamics of work disability and pain. The RAND Corporation. Working Paper, March.

Keller, R. B., S. J. Atlas, D. E. Singer, A. M. Chapin, N. A. Mooney, D. L. Patrick, and R. A. Deyo. 1996. The Maine lumbar spine study, part I: Background and concepts. *Spine* 21 (15): 1769–76.

Krause, N., D. R. Rayland, J. M. Fisher, and S. L. Syme. 1998. Psychosocial job factors, physical workload, and incidence of work-related spinal injury: A 5-year prospective study of urban transit operators. *Spine* 23 (23): 2507–16.

Krueger, A. B., D. Kahneman, D. Schkade, N. Schwarz, and A. A. Stone. 2009. National time accounting: The currency of life. In *Measuring the subjective well-being of nations: National accounts of time use and well-being,* ed. A. B. Krueger, 9–86. Chicago: University of Chicago Press.

Krueger, A. B., and A. A. Stone. 2008. Assessment of pain: A community-based diary survey in the USA. *The Lancet* 371 (9623): 1519–25.

Melzack, R. 1993. Pain: past, present, and future. *Canadian Journal of Experimental Psychology* 47 (4): 615–29.

Miller, G. 2009. Brain scans of pain raise questions for the law. *Science* 323 (January): 195.

Patrick, D. L., R. A. Deyo, S. J. Atlas, D. E. Singer, A. Chapin, and R. B. Keller. 1995. Assessing health-related quality of life in patients with sciatica. *Spine* 20 (17): 1899–908.

Rege, M., K. Telle, and M. Vortruba. 2008. Social interaction effects in disability pension participation: Evidence from plant downsizing. Case Western Reserve University. Working Paper, June.

Trout, A. T., D. F. Kallmes, L. A. Gray, B. A. Goodnature, S. L. Everson, B. A. Comstock, and J. G. Jarvik. 2005. Evaluation of vertebroplasty with a validated outcome measure: The Roland-Morris Disability Questionnaire. *American Journal of Neuroradiology* 26 (November/December): 2652–57.

Waddell, G. 2004. *The back pain revolution,* 2nd ed. New York: Churchill Livingston.

Weber, H. 1983. Lumbar disc herniation: A controlled, prospective study with ten years of observation. *Spine* 8 (2): 131–40.

Weinstein, J. N., J. D. Lurie, T. D. Tosteson, J. S. Skinner, B. Hanscom, A. N. Tosteson, H. Herkowitz, et al. 2006. Surgical vs. nonoperative treatment for lumbar disk herniation: The Spine Patient Outcomes Research Trial (SPORT) observational cohort. *Journal of the American Medical Association* 296 (20): 2451–9.

Weinstein, J. N., T. D. Tosteson, J. D. Lurie, A. N. Tosteson, B. Hanscom, J. S. Skinner, B. Hanscom, et al. 2006. Surgical vs. nonoperative treatment for lumbar disk herniation: The Spine Patient Outcomes Research Trial (SPORT): A randomized trial. *Journal of the American Medical Association* 296 (20): 2441–50.

III

Economic Circumstances and Health

Aging and Death under a Dollar a Day

Abhijit V. Banerjee and Esther Duflo

He who is contented is rich.
—Lao Tzu, Chinese Taoist philosopher

I've been rich and I've been poor. Believe me, rich is better.
—Mae West, American actress

7.1 Introduction

Despite the many assurances from many wise men that being rich is not all that it is made out to be, most economists remain firmly in Ms. West's camp. This is partly no doubt an item of faith not unrelated to what makes people want to be economists. But mostly it reflects the suspicion that, at least up to a point, what are usually called necessities of life are really necessary, and having to do without them cannot be pleasant.

To what extent are the poor deprived of the necessities of life? Obviously this turns on who we call the poor. One popular definition, which we adopt, is to focus on those who have a daily per capita expenditure of a dollar a day (at purchasing power parity [PPP]) or less. We call them the very (or extremely) poor to distinguish them from the merely poor, who live on less than two dollars a day. In a previous essay (Banerjee and Duflo 2007b), we used household surveys from thirteen countries and draw on existing research to look at what the poor can afford. From these it appears that even the extremely poor can afford to buy enough calories to keep going, though whether they always prioritize that over other things they could buy is not entirely clear. At least in some countries there seems to be evidence

Abhijit V. Banerjee is the Ford Foundation International Professor of Economics at the Massachusetts Institute of Technology, and a research associate of the National Bureau of Economic Research. Esther Duflo is the Abdul Latif Jameel Professor of Poverty Alleviation and Development Economics at the Massachusetts Institute of Technology, and a research associate of the National Bureau of Economic Research.

We warmly thank the National Institute of Aging (Grant #P01-AG005842), MIT, the Center for Health and Well-being at Princeton University, and the World Bank for funding. Dhruva Kothari, Remi Jedwab, and Stefana Stancheva provided outstanding research assistance. Many thanks to Angus Deaton for providing important comments on an early draft.

that the extremely poor are actually short on calories and other nutrients, relative to the standard norms for their country. In India, the poorest seem to live on less than 1,500 calories a day compared to a norm of over 2,000, and moreover, this number seems to be going down over time. Where there is more detailed health information, such as in a survey we carried out in the rural Udaipur district (Banerjee, Deaton, and Duflo 2004), it is also clear that the very poor betray signs of undernourishment: 65 percent of adult men and 40 percent of adult women have body mass indexes (BMIs) under 18.5, which is the standard cut-off for being underweight.

How do the very poor do in terms of other necessities? Most of them seem to have a place to stay and some minimal clothing—what else should we be looking for? Perhaps one way to answer that is to look at some of the things that the people immediately richer than them seem to have, that they may not. This is one of things that we did in Banerjee and Duflo (2007a): we used the same surveys to compare the poor with two groups of slightly richer people in the same countries. These are households whose daily per capita expenditures (DPCE) valued at purchasing power parity are between two and four dollars and those whose DPCE are between six and ten dollars. While clearly much better off than the very poor, and much better placed in the consumption distribution of their respective countries, these are still poor households by developed country standards: the poverty line in the United States for someone who lives in a family of five, for example, works out to be about $13 per day.

Compared to the poor, the less poor spend more per visit to the doctor and more per child educated. They are more likely to send their children to school, more likely to see a doctor when they feel sick, and more inclined to see a private doctor rather than a public practitioner. They also have much greater access to water, sanitation, and public infrastructure: the fraction with tap water at home increases with DPCE in most countries (and in some countries by quite a large margin): from 12 percent (for the extremely poor) to 73 percent (for those with DPCE between six and ten dollars) in rural Ivory Coast, 2 percent to 63 percent in rural Tanzania, and 12 percent to 55 percent in Nicaragua. In urban areas, in seven countries out of the nine for which we have data, 70 percent or more of the households with DPCE between six and ten dollars have tap water, whereas the share is below 50 percent in all countries but one for the extremely poor. The same pattern holds for latrines (where the share of those who have latrines among the households with DPCE between six and ten dollars is above 80 percent in seven countries) and electricity (the share that has access to electricity in this group is above 90 percent in seven countries).

These differences obviously suggest a better quality of life for the less poor, though these surveys cannot tell us what, if anything, they are giving up in terms of connectedness in the community or the consumption of leisure (for all it is worth, when asked in surveys, the non-poor always report more life satisfaction than the poor). Do we also see cruder, more tangible, differences between them, say in terms of differences in the risk of dying? And if so, by how much? It is known (see, e.g., Wagstaff 2002) that infant mortality is greater among the poor than among the richer households. Is the same true among adults? This is the set of questions that we set out to answer here.

7.2   Data Sources

We mainly used the Living Standard Measurement Surveys (LSMS) conducted by the World Bank and the "Family Life Surveys" conducted by the Rand Corporation, all of which are publicly available.[1] We have data for fifteen countries from these sources: Brazil, Bangladesh, Ivory Coast, Guatemala, India, Indonesia, Mexico, Nicaragua, Pakistan, Panama, Papua New Guinea, Peru, South Africa, Tanzania, and East Timor. In addition, we also use two surveys that we conducted in India with our collaborators. The first was carried out in 2002 and 2003 in 100 hamlets of Udaipur District, Rajasthan (Banerjee, Deaton, and Duflo 2004). Rural Udaipur is one of the poorer areas of India, with a large population of tribals (the term used in India to designate people who used to be so low in the Hindu caste hierarchy that they had no official place in it) and an unusually high level of female illiteracy (at the time of the 1991 census, only 5 percent of women were literate in rural Udaipur). Our second survey covered 2,000 households in "slums" (or informal neighborhoods) of Hyderabad, the capital of the state of Andhra Pradesh and one of the boomtowns of post-liberalization India (Banerjee, Duflo, and Glennerster 2006). We chose these countries and surveys because they provide detailed information on extremely poor households around the world, from Asia to Africa to Latin America, including information on what they consume, where they work, and how they save and borrow.

From each of these surveys we compute the consumption per capita in PPP terms, using the 1993 PPP as the benchmark.[2] We identify the extremely poor as those living in households where the consumption per capita is less than $1.08 per person per day, as well as the merely "poor," defined as those who live under $2.16 a day using 1993 PPP as benchmark. In keeping with convention, we call these the one and two dollar poverty lines, respectively. For comparison, we then added two additional groups: those living between two and four dollars a day, and those living between six and ten dollars a day.

1. See Frankenberg and Karoly (1995); Frankenberg and Thomas (2000); Strauss et al. (2004).
2. The use of consumption, rather than income, is motivated by the better quality of the consumption data in these surveys (Deaton 2004).

7.3   Age Pyramids: Missing Old People?

One first approach (although we are going to see its limitations shortly) to get at the question of "excess" mortality is to look at the age distribution of the population: is the number of older people in the population unusually low?

Tables 7A.1 and 7A.2 in the appendix show the fraction of the sample that lives under one dollar a day, under two dollars a day, between two and four dollars a day, and between six and ten dollars a day, in different age groups.[3] Tables 7.1 and 7.2 show summary ratios: the fraction of young people (less than eighteen) in the population, and the ratio of those over fifty over all adults (twenty-one and over), broken down by gender and for the overall population.

The first striking (and well-known) fact is that the very poor form a remarkably young group. The ratio of the population under eighteen over the total population among the rural extremely poor range from 40 percent (Indonesia) to 60 percent (Panama). In urban areas it ranges from 34 percent (Indonesia again, in 2000) to 63 percent. This ratio falls substantially in all countries as people get slightly richer, although it remains high even then (it ranges between 35 percent and 42 percent for those with DPCE between six and ten dollars a day in rural areas, and 28 percent to 42 percent for the urban areas).

Part of the reason is, of course, that fertility is high among the poor, and as a result there are a lot of children. But there are also comparably few older people. The ratio of people age fifty and above to adults over twenty among the rural extremely poor ranges between 15 percent (in Papua New Guinea) to 34 percent (Indonesia, 1997). Compared to other indicators of how the poor live, it is actually strikingly similar across these countries, clustered around 20 percent for most of them. In the United States, the corresponding ratio was 38 percent in 2000 (2000 census). This in itself is, however, not sufficient to conclude that the poor die more in developing countries than people do in the United States, since the fertility rates are also higher in poorer countries. As a result, the number of younger people at any point in time is mechanically higher, compared to the number of older people in those countries, compared to in the United States. So these "missing old people" may just be people who were never born.

Is there an income gradient in the ratio of older people over the total number of adults within countries? In most countries, the ratio of old people over all adults is similar when we look at either the poor or the extremely poor. However, in nine countries out of fifteen, in the rural areas, there

---

3. In this and all that follows, the observations are weighted by the survey weights if appropriate (multiplied by household size when the data is first aggregated at the household level) so that these should be estimate of population means.

Table 7.1 **Old and young in the population**

	Fraction of individuals aged less than 18				Fraction of individuals aged 51 or more			
	< $1	< $2	$2–$4	$6–$10	< $1	< $2	$2–$4	$6–$10
Rural								
Bangladesh	0.51	0.49	0.42	0.38	0.13	0.13	0.16	0.21
Brazil	0.61	0.54	0.39	0.31	0.06	0.1	0.19	0.19
East Timor	0.56	0.54	0.45	0.35	0.07	0.07	0.12	0.2
Ecuador	0.61	0.56	0.47	0.34	0.07	0.08	0.1	0.16
Guatemala	0.55	0.57	0.55	0.53	0.08	0.07	0.07	0.07
Indonesia00	0.4	0.41	0.37	0.3	0.13	0.13	0.13	0.14
Indonesia93	0.47	0.46	0.43	0.39	0.16	0.15	0.15	0.15
Indonesia97	0.44	0.43	0.4	0.34	0.18	0.18	0.17	0.17
Ivory Coast	0.44	0.46	0.47	0.42	0.1	0.08	0.06	0.04
Mexico	0.46	0.47	0.41	0.34	0.13	0.12	0.15	0.16
Nicaragua	0.58	0.55	0.47	0.32	0.07	0.08	0.12	0.21
Pakistan*	0.44	0.43	0.4	n.a.	0.09	0.1	0.12	n.a.
Panama	0.6	0.56	0.48	0.34	0.07	0.09	0.13	0.21
Papua New Guinea	0.52	0.51	0.47	0.42	0.06	0.06	0.08	0.08
Peru	0.55	0.53	0.43	n.a.	0.09	0.1	0.16	n.a.
South Africa	0.56	0.54	0.47	0.32	0.27	0.25	0.2	0.16
Tanzania	0.55	0.54	0.47	0.46	0.11	0.1	0.1	0.15
Udaipur	0.54	0.5	0.37	n.a.	0.08	0.1	0.18	n.a.
Vietnam9293	0.46	0.44	0.38	0.35	0.03	0.03	0.05	0.04
Vietnam9798	0.62	0.54	0.45	0.37	0.07	0.11	0.15	0.19
Urban								
Bangladesh	n.a.	n.a.	n.a.	n.a.	n.a.	n.a.	n.a.	n.a.
Brazil	0.63	0.54	0.44	0.33	0.06	0.11	0.13	0.17
East Timor	0.57	0.53	0.47	0.4	0.07	0.07	0.07	0.04
Ecuador	0.57	0.53	0.42	0.37	0.13	0.14	0.16	0.18
Hyderabad	0.48	0.42	0.37	0.32	0.07	0.08	0.09	0.08
Indonesia00	0.34	0.36	0.32	0.25	0.18	0.13	0.13	0.15
Indonesia93	0.44	0.45	0.43	0.38	0.16	0.14	0.12	0.13
Indonesia97	0.44	0.4	0.38	0.34	0.17	0.17	0.16	0.13
Ivory Coast	0.44	0.45	0.45	0.42	0.09	0.1	0.1	0.09
Mexico	0.54	0.5	0.44	0.43	0.1	0.12	0.16	0.14
Nicaragua	0.57	0.54	0.47	0.35	0.09	0.09	0.1	0.13
Pakistan*	0.46	0.44	0.38	0.4	0.09	0.09	0.1	0.14
Panama	n.a.	0.59	0.49	0.38	n.a.	0.1	0.1	0.13
Papua New Guinea	0.6	0.49	0.45	0.45	0.05	0.06	0.07	0.03
Peru	0.57	0.55	0.43	0.35	0.05	0.08	0.12	0.15
South Africa	0.11	0.11	0.11	0.11	0.15	0.2	0.2	0.18
Tanzania	0.51	0.51	0.47	0.39	0.19	0.13	0.09	0.07
Udaipur	n.a.	n.a.	0.42	n.a.	n.a.	n.a.	0.22	n.a.
Vietnam9293	0.48	0.4	0.35	0.28	0.03	0.03	0.06	0.09
Vietnam9798	n.a.	0.45	0.41	0.3	n.a.	0.15	0.17	0.2

Table 7.2 Ratio elderly/prime age: Ratio of individuals over 51/all adults

	All				Women				Men			
	<$1	<$2	$2–$4	$6–$10	<$1	<$2	$2–$4	$6–$10	<$1	<$2	$2–$4	$6–$10
Rural areas												
Bangladesh	0.27	0.27	0.3	0.36	0.25	0.25	0.29	0.36	0.29	0.28	0.31	0.37
Brazil	0.18	0.24	0.33	0.29	0.13	0.24	0.35	0.27	0.22	0.23	0.31	0.31
East Timor	0.19	0.19	0.24	0.31	0.16	0.16	0.26	0.34	0.23	0.21	0.23	0.28
Ecuador	0.19	0.19	0.2	0.26	0.17	0.19	0.21	0.26	0.2	0.18	0.19	0.25
Guatemala	0.2	0.19	0.18	0.19	0.18	0.17	0.16	0.16	0.23	0.21	0.2	0.22
Indonesia00	0.24	0.25	0.23	0.22	0.25	0.25	0.24	0.23	0.24	0.24	0.23	0.21
Indonesia93	0.33	0.29	0.28	0.27	0.32	0.29	0.28	0.28	0.33	0.29	0.27	0.25
Indonesia97	0.34	0.33	0.3	0.27	0.36	0.34	0.3	0.27	0.32	0.32	0.3	0.27
Ivory Coast	0.29	0.22	0.17	0.1	0.27	0.2	0.14	0.08	0.32	0.24	0.21	0.12
Mexico	0.26	0.23	0.24	0.23	0.29	0.22	0.23	0.23	0.22	0.23	0.25	0.23
Nicaragua	0.22	0.22	0.28	0.35	0.18	0.2	0.26	0.36	0.26	0.24	0.29	0.34
Pakistan*	0.24	0.25	0.28	0.23	0.24	0.26	0.28	0.28	0.24	0.25	0.28	0.18
Panama	0.2	0.25	0.29	0.35	0.15	0.23	0.27	0.35	0.26	0.28	0.3	0.34
Papua New Guinea	0.15	0.15	0.18	0.17	0.1	0.11	0.16	0.16	0.21	0.2	0.19	0.17
Peru	0.24	0.24	0.31	n.a.	0.23	0.23	0.31	n.a.	0.25	0.25	0.32	n.a.
South Africa	0.27	0.26	0.24	0.19	0.27	0.26	0.24	0.19	0.27	0.26	0.26	0.23
Tanzania	0.29	0.26	0.23	0.3	0.26	0.23	0.2	0.34	0.32	0.29	0.27	0.24
Udaipur	0.21	0.22	0.32	n.a.	0.22	0.23	0.34	n.a.	0.19	0.21	0.3	n.a.
Vietnam9293	0.13	0.13	0.2	0.17	0.13	0.11	0.18	0.22	0.13	0.15	0.23	0.11
Vietnam9798	0.2	0.25	0.29	0.34	0.25	0.27	0.32	0.34	0.14	0.21	0.27	0.34

Urban areas												
Bangladesh	n.a.	n.a.	n.a.	n.a.	n.a.	n.a.	n.a.	n.a.	n.a.	n.a.	n.a.	n.a.
Brazil	0.19	0.26	0.25	0.28	0.19	0.26	0.27	0.29	0.2	0.26	0.23	0.26
East Timor	0.18	0.17	0.15	0.07	0.19	0.17	0.15	0.07	0.18	0.18	0.15	0.08
Ecuador	0.32	0.32	0.3	0.3	0.31	0.32	0.31	0.27	0.33	0.32	0.3	0.33
Hyderabad	0.16	0.16	0.16	0.14	0.15	0.16	0.15	0.15	0.18	0.17	0.16	0.13
Indonesia00	0.32	0.23	0.2	0.21	0.31	0.25	0.22	0.2	0.33	0.22	0.18	0.22
Indonesia93	0.31	0.28	0.22	0.23	0.34	0.3	0.23	0.21	0.28	0.25	0.2	0.25
Indonesia97	0.33	0.3	0.28	0.21	0.36	0.33	0.28	0.23	0.29	0.27	0.27	0.2
Ivory Coast	0.25	0.27	0.27	0.19	0.21	0.24	0.23	0.15	0.33	0.33	0.31	0.23
Mexico	0.24	0.25	0.26	0.23	0.24	0.24	0.24	0.22	0.23	0.26	0.29	0.24
Nicaragua	0.24	0.23	0.22	0.23	0.26	0.23	0.22	0.26	0.22	0.23	0.21	0.2
Pakistan*	0.23	0.23	0.21	0.3	0.22	0.22	0.2	0.26	0.25	0.23	0.22	0.34
Panama	n.a.	0.27	0.23	0.23	n.a.	0.14	0.23	0.24	n.a.	0.4	0.24	0.22
Papua New Guinea	0.15	0.14	0.16	0.06	0.09	0.1	0.14	0.05	0.2	0.18	0.18	0.07
Peru	0.13	0.2	0.25	0.26	0.08	0.17	0.23	0.25	0.19	0.24	0.26	0.26
South Africa	0.26	0.23	0.22	0.18	0.26	0.23	0.22	0.18	0.32	0.25	0.23	0.18
Tanzania	0.45	0.32	0.19	0.13	0.41	0.28	0.17	0.1	0.5	0.36	0.22	0.15
Udaipur	n.a.	n.a.	0.42	n.a.	n.a.	0.44	n.a.	n.a.	n.a.	n.a.	0.4	n.a.
Vietnam9293	0.11	0.1	0.2	0.21	0.11	0.17	0.08	0.2	0.11	0.12	0.22	0.21
Vietnam9798	n.a.	0.29	0.31	0.3	n.a.	0.31	0.31	0.31	n.a.	0.27	0.3	0.3

are comparatively more old people among the slightly more well-off people (two to four dollars and six to ten dollars) than among the poorer people. For example, in Udaipur district (rural India) the ratio of old to adults increases from 22 percent among the poor to 34 percent among those living on between two and four dollars a day. Likewise in Peru, the ratio increases from 24 percent to 31 percent in the same categories (in both countries, we have too few people with DPCE between six and ten dollars to give meaningful statistics). We get similar numbers for Pakistan and Vietnam. In Nicaragua and Panama, respectively, it increases from 22 percent to 35 percent between the extremely poor and those living between six and ten dollars, and in Panama it increases from 25 percent to 35 percent in the same categories. In all those countries, the ratio of old to prime-age adults among the more well-off is almost similar to what it is in the United States, despite the fact that these people are still very poor by U.S. standards, and despite the much better public health environment in the United States.

In four other countries (Guatemala, Indonesia, Mexico, and Tanzania), the ratio does not change with income. In the remaining two—South Africa and Ivory Coast—it actually falls sharply (from 27 percent to 19 percent in rural South Africa, for example). One thing that is common across these six countries is that the ratio of people in the zero to eighteen age group compared to older people does not vary a lot between the extremely poor and those living between six and ten dollars a day. This difference ranges from 2 percent (South Africa and Guatemala) to 10 percent (Indonesia) in these six countries, whereas it ranges from 10 percent (Papua New Guinea) to 30 percent (Brazil) in the other countries. While the share of those less than eighteen today is a very imperfect proxy for the difference in fertility rates in the past, this suggests the possibility that a part of the reason why some countries have many more young adults compared to older adults among poorer people, is that the poorer people in those countries have relatively more children.

The fact that three of the countries where we see a distinct pattern are in Africa points to another general limitation of this exercise: we may be confusing the location decision of the older people with the fact that they may be alive or not. For example, in South Africa, older people may live with their grandchildren while the parents are away working. Unless they are receiving a pension (which is available after sixty for women and sixty-five for men), the per capita consumption of such households might be particularly low (since they have many children and no prime-age worker) compared to households without older people.

A different choice of location may in turn explain the pattern we found in the other countries: it is conceivable that older people choose to live with their richer children, which would make the ratio of older people to adults artificially low among the poorest.

Of course, since we find the ratios are similar among the extremely poor and the poor, and they start to differ only when we look at various categories, this does not seem very likely, since it is not very likely that many old people have some children living under one dollar a day and others above two dollars. But since we have no data, this remains a possibility.

7.4   A New Measure of Adult Mortality: Are Your Parents Alive?

Given that the age structure data turns out to be quite hard to interpret, it is fortunate that, for a subset of countries, there is a way to address this problem: in some of the household surveys (eleven countries in total), the household roster contains a question on whether each member's father and mother are alive. For these countries, we present in table 7.3 the fraction of those age thirty-five to fifty whose father and mother are alive. These fathers and mothers are likely to be above fifty (if they are alive), giving us a handle, albeit approximate, on how the entire population of those age fifty and above changes across the different income categories. Note that to the extent that richer people have children later, and that the children of richer people are rich as well, this will underestimate any difference in the age-adjusted mortality, since the parents of richer people between thirty-five and fifty will tend to be older.

In table 7.3, we show the data for urban and rural households together (although in some countries the data is available only for rural households. For women, there is a fairly clear pattern: in four countries (Udaipur, Pakistan, South Africa, and Bangladesh), the probability that the mother of the respondent is alive does not really change between the richest category for which we have data and the poorest one. In all the other countries, it goes up with DPCE, and the difference between the richest and the poorest category for which we have data ranges from 6 percentage points in Vietnam to 23 percentage points in East Timor.

In most of the last group of countries (countries where the probability of a person's mother being alive is higher in the richest group than in the poorest), the pattern is one of a monotonic increase. The probability that the respondents' mother is alive goes up as DPCE goes up, though in some countries we only see a sizable gap among the most well-off (e.g., Brazil), while in others the critical break seems to be in the two- and four-dollar range (e.g., Mexico), and yet in others there is a steady increase across all the groups (e.g., Indonesia in 1993).

For fathers, there is no clear picture: in seven surveys (but only five countries, since Indonesia appears three times), the probability of the father being alive increases between the richest and the poorest category. In four countries it declines. In two it is roughly constant.

The gender gap here might reflect differences in the nature of the health problems faced by men and women in their fifties and sixties. First, those men are older (since men have children older than women), and their

Table 7.3 **Out of the individuals age 31–50, fraction whose mother and father is alive**

	Fraction whose father is alive				Fraction whose mother is alive			
	< $1	< $2	$2–$4	$6–$10	< $1	< $2	$2–$4	$6–$10
All								
Bangladesh	0.25	0.23	0.19	n.a.	0.65	0.65	0.66	n.a.
Brazil	0.46	0.44	0.41	0.42	0.61	0.60	0.63	0.69
East Timor	0.09	0.17	0.23	0.30	0.29	0.29	0.33	0.51
Indonesia93	0.15	0.15	0.17	0.17	0.26	0.27	0.29	0.33
Indonesia97	0.31	0.33	0.33	0.36	0.55	0.56	0.59	0.65
Indonesia00	0.30	0.36	0.34	0.35	0.50	0.62	0.63	0.61
Ivory Coast	0.22	0.26	0.29	0.38	0.44	0.48	0.54	0.55
Mexico	0.50	0.51	0.52	0.58	0.67	0.68	0.75	0.75
Nicaragua	0.57	0.54	0.51	0.56	0.68	0.71	0.75	0.74
Pakistan	0.39	0.39	0.34	n.a.	0.54	0.55	0.54	n.a.
South Africa	0.32	0.30	0.30	0.37	0.61	0.60	0.60	0.60
Udaipur	0.46	0.44	0.37	n.a.	0.58	0.58	0.56	n.a.
Vietnam 92	0.41	0.39	0.41	n.a.	0.60	0.62	0.66	n.a.
Rural								
Bangladesh	0.25	0.23	0.19	n.a.	0.65	0.65	0.66	n.a.
Brazil	0.48	0.47	0.45	0.50	0.62	0.63	0.64	0.70
East Timor	0.08	0.15	0.18	0.25	0.27	0.28	0.26	0.35
Indonesia93	0.15	0.15	0.17	0.18	0.26	0.26	0.28	0.37
Indonesia97	0.30	0.33	0.34	0.34	0.53	0.55	0.58	0.65
Indonesia00	0.30	0.36	0.34	0.36	0.53	0.61	0.61	0.65
Ivory Coast	0.36	0.31	0.28	0.28	0.49	0.54	0.60	0.74
Mexico	0.55	0.48	0.50	0.60	0.57	0.67	0.77	0.74
Nicaragua	0.58	0.54	0.55	0.62	0.64	0.69	0.75	0.75
Pakistan	0.39	0.40	0.33	n.a.	0.53	0.55	0.54	n.a.
South Africa	0.31	0.29	0.32	0.33	0.61	0.60	0.63	0.66
Udaipur	0.46	0.44	0.37	n.a.	0.58	0.58	0.56	n.a.
Vietnam92	0.33	0.43	0.43	n.a.	0.33	0.55	0.70	n.a.
Urban								
Urban	n.a.	n.a.	n.a.	n.a.	n.a.	n.a.	n.a.	n.a.
Brazil	0.39	0.40	0.39	0.42	0.57	0.56	0.63	0.69
East Timor	0.13	0.21	0.30	0.31	0.34	0.31	0.43	0.56
Indonesia93	0.15	0.14	0.17	0.16	0.28	0.30	0.31	0.32
Indonesia97	0.35	0.34	0.32	0.37	0.65	0.62	0.62	0.65
Indonesia00	0.31	0.34	0.33	0.35	0.44	0.64	0.66	0.60
Ivory Coast	0.21	0.25	0.30	0.44	0.43	0.48	0.52	0.44
Mexico	0.49	0.51	0.54	0.54	0.69	0.69	0.72	0.77
Nicaragua	0.55	0.54	0.49	0.55	0.82	0.73	0.76	0.74
Pakistan	0.40	0.39	0.36	n.a.	0.55	0.55	0.54	n.a.
South Africa	0.22	0.31	0.29	0.37	0.61	0.58	0.56	0.58
Vietnam92	0.41	0.39	0.40	n.a.	0.61	0.63	0.63	n.a.

Notes: The data for Bangladesh, Guatemala, and Udaipur covers only rural areas. Cells with fewer than 100 observations are eliminated.

mortality naturally catches up across the age group (since eventually everybody dies). Second, in these age groups, men often die of heart disease, lung cancer, diabetes, and high blood pressure, all of which may be related to their pattern of consumption, and therefore potentially be more of a risk for those who can afford to consume more. This is less true of women. Alternatively, it could be pointing to a reverse causation. Young adults whose father is alive may be younger and hence poorer, while since mothers tend to be younger and in any case have a higher life expectancy at forty, having a mother alive may not be a signal of her son's age. Following, we solve this problem by controlling for the respondent's age.

Looking at urban and rural dwellers separately (the interpretation of which is complicated, since the urban dwellers may be migrants whose parents were themselves rural dwellers), we reach similar conclusions: in rural areas in Pakistan, Udaipur, and Bangladesh the probability of an individual's mother being alive is roughly constant between the poorest and those with DPCE between two and four dollars (we do not have richer people in the surveys in rural areas in those countries). It increases across category everywhere else, and the difference usually lies between 10 and 20 percentage points. For example, in Brazil the proportion of rural dwellers whose mother is alive increases from 63 percent to 72 percent across those two categories. In Indonesia it increases from 52 percent to 65 percent. In Mexico it increases from 57 percent to 74 percent, and so forth.

For fathers, once again, there is no obvious pattern: the probability of the father being alive is greater among the richer households in seven surveys (and five countries), roughly constant in two, and decreasing in four countries.

And finally, for urban dwellers, in Nicaragua and South Africa the probability of the mother being alive declines somewhat as we go toward richer households; it is roughly constant in three surveys, and increases in six. For men, we have a clearer pattern than for the rural areas: the probability decreases only in Pakistan. Elsewhere it is either roughly constant (Indonesia in 1993, Nicaragua and Vietnam) or increasing (everywhere else).

Another way to look at this data is to perform simple descriptive regressions. We present in tables 7.4 and 7.5 the results of logit regressions where a dummy indicating whether a respondent's mother (or father) is alive is regressed on the respondent's age and age squared, as well as country dummies and indication of the economic welfare of the household. We present country-by-country regressions in table 7.4 and, to save space, we focus on the pooled rural and urban data and one specification: economic welfare is regressed on the log of total monthly per capita expenditure expressed in 1993 PPP dollars. This table confirms the pattern revealed by the descriptive statistics for mothers, and gives somewhat stronger results for men: there is an insignificant, sometime mildly negative, relationship between the probability that a respondents' mother and father are alive in Udaipur, Pakistan,

Table 7.4   Logit regressions: Coefficient of ln(total expenditure per capita)

	Mother alive (1)	Father alive (2)
Bangladesh	–0.004	–0.010
	(0.041)	(0.053)
Brazil	0.207	0.152
	(0.051)	(0.049)
East Timor	0.176	0.592
	(0.103)	(0.117)
Indonesia93	0.018	0.040
	(0.024)	(0.028)
Indonesia97	0.097	0.117
	(0.041)	(0.043)
Indonesia00	0.069	0.060
	(0.040)	(0.040)
Ivory Coast	0.108	0.236
	(0.083)	(0.090)
Mexico	0.127	0.119
	(0.049)	(0.045)
Nicaragua	0.217	0.163
	(0.070)	(0.069)
Pakistan	0.070	–0.090
	(0.058)	(0.060)
South Africa	0.204	0.308
	(0.031)	(0.032)
Udaipur	0.095	–0.326
	(0.131)	(0.135)

Note: Regressions control for age of respondent, age squared, and rural dummy.

and Bangladesh (except for a significant *negative* relationship between the probability that the father is alive and monthly per capita expenditure in Udaipur). Elsewhere, the coefficients are positive, and in most cases significant at least at the 10 percent level (except in the first wave of the Indonesian Family Life Survey [IFLS] for both mothers and fathers, for mothers in Ivory Coast, and for fathers in Indonesia, 2000).

Finally, to summarize all the patterns in this section, we present in table 7.5 regression using data from all the countries pooled together (all the regressions control for a set of country dummies).[4] In panel A, death is regressed on the logarithm of monthly capita expenditure (expressed in 1993 PPP dollars), and the consumption categories in panel B. In panel B, we exclude the "below 2" dollars a day category, so that the coefficients should all be read in relation to those between one and two dollars a day. Overall, we do see a strong association between log (monthly per capita expenditure) and the probability that one's mother is alive, with similar coefficients in rural and urban areas. For fathers, the relationship is also strong overall,

4. As well as the IFLS wave for Indonesia.

Table 7.5   **Logit regression: Pooling countries**

	Mother alive (1)	Father alive (2)
Panel A		
1. All		
ln(expenditure pc)	0.12	0.10
	(.016)	(.016)
2. Rural		
ln(expenditure pc)	0.08	0.04
	(.024)	(.026)
3. Urban		
ln(expenditure pc)	0.15	0.19
	(.022)	(.023)
Panel B		
1. All		
Below 1	−0.08	−0.06
	(.053)	(.055)
2 to 4	0.11	0.00
	(.041)	(.043)
6 to 10	0.24	0.18
	(.057)	(.059)
2. Rural		
Below 1	−0.08	−0.05
	(.053)	(.054)
2 to 4	0.11	−0.01
	(.041)	(.043)
6 to 10	0.36	0.14
	(.098)	(.097)
3. Urban		
Below 1	−0.08	−0.06
	(.053)	(.054)
2 to 4	0.11	0.00
	(.041)	(.043)
6 to 10	0.18	0.18
	(.061)	(.063)

Notes: All countries are pooled. Expenditure per capita expressed in 1993 PPP dollars. All observations are weighted using country weights, such that weights some to 1 for each country. Regressions control for age of respondent, age squared, and when relevant, rural dummy. In panel B, only individuals living in households with dpce between 0 and 4 or between 6 and 10 are included. The excluded category is "below $2."

but insignificant in rural areas. Even in rural areas, however, those with DPCE between six and ten dollars are more likely to have their father alive, relative to the poor.

This data, which does not suffer from the obvious problems of fertility differential and endogenous locations, suggests that, conditional on reaching adulthood, the poor are significantly less likely to reach old age than the less poor.

This obviously does not rule out the possibility that the dearth of older people in poorer households is also partly driven by the decision of which child to live with. Table 7.3 looks at this question directly: we ask whether poorer or richer adults are likely to have their parents live with them, conditional, obviously, on the parents being alive. The answer to this question, interestingly, turns out to vary quite a lot across countries. In the rural areas of six countries out of twelve, mothers are more likely to live with their grown-up children among households with DPCE between two and four dollars. In one country (Pakistan), the ratio is more or less constant. Within countries, the effect of income is not monotonous: out of the seven countries where children who are between two and four dollars a day are more likely to have their mother living with them than the poor, in all but one of the ones for which we have data for the six to ten dollars a day group, the share is lower for that last group than for the two to four dollar group. The pattern for men is somewhat different: there are in fact two cases (Bangladesh and East Timor) where the probability of coresidence decreases in income for men while increasing for women.

Note that out of the six countries where the ratio of old to young among adults was lower among the rich than among the poor, we have information for five on whether parents are alive and where they live. Out of these five countries, four (Mexico, Indonesia, South Africa, and Ivory Coast) are also countries where richer children were less likely to live with their mother than the extremely poor. This suggests that the choice of residence among the old people might have explained at least a part of why there seem to be "missing" older people in poorer households.

To our knowledge, there is very little evidence on adult mortality by income groups in developing countries. For the reasons previously discussed, age pyramids cannot be used to generate such evidence, and it is rare to have data on mortality and on poverty status in the same data sets. This quick panorama based on whether parents are alive seems to establish that in many countries, at least among women, the poor have higher adult mortality than the non-poor (of course it does not tell us anything about the key question of causality—do the poor die or are the dying poor?)

The best way to establish whether the poor really die more than the non-poor, however, is to use a panel data set to measure the mortality of those identified as poor over the next few years. It is not possible for most of our countries, but there are three where the necessary panel data is available: Udaipur (India), Indonesia (IFLS), and Vietnam.

7.5   Age-Specific Mortality Rates: Indonesia-Vietnam-India

The Indonesian Family Life Survey is a panel, of which three waves have already been completed: the first one was fielded in 1993, the second in 1997, and the last one in 2000. For all waves, a lot of effort went into tracking down most of the respondent households (Frankenberg, Thomas, and Smith 2003). When a household was reinterviewed in the second or third phase, the entire household roster was carefully updated: the interviewers worked with a preprinted list of household members, and asked for each member whether he or she still lived in the household and whether he or she is still alive. In addition, we know if all the members of a given household died.

The Vietnam living standard measurement survey is a two-wave panel, fielded in 1992 and 1993 and 1997 and 1998. As in the Indonesian family life survey, the 1992 and 1993 household roster was updated for all households that were part of the panel in 1997 and 1998, with information for each member of whether they died in the intervening period.

Finally, the Udaipur survey will eventually also be a five-year panel, allowing us to carry out the same exercise, but the endline survey has not been collected yet. Two data sources are available for now: first, a comprehensive update of the household roster was completed after one year. Second, each household is interviewed once a month to monitor health status and health seeking behavior, and if anyone died, this is also indicated in this survey. This survey has been going on for two years (in this version, we only use the one year out mortality).

For all three surveys, we adopted the same method: we determine poverty status in the first wave of the survey; then we compute the probability to have died by the next survey, in different age groups, and notably among the older members.

Table 7.6 presents the results for Indonesia: in all age groups, there is very little difference in death rates between the poor and the extremely poor, but the non-poor are less likely to die than the poor and the extremely poor. This is true both five years out and ten years out, and in both rural and urban areas. In rural areas, depending on the age group and whether we look at five to ten years out, the extremely poor are 1.4 to 5 times more likely to die than those who live between six and ten dollars a day.

In terms of percentage points (and even in terms of ratio of percentages, for the rural areas at least) the largest difference between the poor and the non-poor is seen for the five-years out death rates of those age fifty and over in rural areas. Overall, 15.3 percent of those who were fifty and above in 1993 have died by 1997 among the extremely poor. The number is very similar among all the poor (15.8 percent) but much lower among those who were living between six and ten dollars a day (7 percent). The difference is particularly striking in rural areas (15 percent versus 3 percent) and still large in urban areas (18 percent versus 11 percent).

By 2000, the ratios are much less skewed (22 percent versus 17 percent in the overall population), suggesting that, among the richer households, many of the people who did not die by 1997 have died in the meantime. This is as we might have expected. Clearly by 2050, for example, the ratio would be 100 percent in all income groups.

The patterns are strikingly similar in Vietnam (table 7.7). There again, the percentage who died decline with economic welfare in all age groups, and this decline is particularly steep among the older age group, in the rural areas.

	All	Rural	Urban
Table 7.6			

	All	Rural	Urban
A. Dead by 1997, order than 50 in 1993			
Less than 1 dollar a day	0.154	0.148	0.184
Less than 2 dollars a day	0.158	0.155	0.170
2 to 4 dollars a day	0.135	0.126	0.155
6 to 10 dollars a day	0.073	0.029	0.117
B. Dead by 2000, order than 50 in 1993			
Less than 1 dollar a day	0.222	0.210	0.284
Less than 2 dollars a day	0.229	0.216	0.279
2 to 4 dollars a day	0.222	0.215	0.239
6 to 10 dollars a day	0.178	0.146	0.209
C. Dead by 1997, order than 45 in 1993			
Less than 1 dollar a day	0.137	0.129	0.183
Less than 2 dollars a day	0.141	0.136	0.164
2 to 4 dollars a day	0.119	0.114	0.131
6 to 10 dollars a day	0.069	0.030	0.106
D. Dead by 2000, order than 45 in 1993			
Less than 1 dollar a day	0.204	0.192	0.269
Less than 2 dollars a day	0.208	0.193	0.266
2 to 4 dollars a day	0.196	0.192	0.205
6 to 10 dollars a day	0.153	0.125	0.180
E. Dead by 1997, aged between 15 and 45 in 1993			
Less than 1 dollar a day	0.021	0.023	0.012
Less than 2 dollars a day	0.037	0.033	0.052
2 to 4 dollars a day	0.009	0.007	0.011
6 to 10 dollars a day	0.010	0.009	0.012
F. Dead by 2000, aged between 15 and 45 in 1993			
Less than 1 dollar a day	0.053	0.056	0.038
Less than 2 dollars a day	0.060	0.053	0.082
2 to 4 dollars a day	0.013	0.012	0.015
6 to 10 dollars a day	0.014	0.011	0.017
G. Dead by 1997, aged between 5 and 15 in 1993			
Less than 1 dollar a day	0.014	0.017	0.018
Less than 2 dollars a day	0.030	0.029	0.037
2 to 4 dollars a day	0.003	0.004	0.002
6 to 10 dollars a day	0.011	0.010	0.011
H. Dead by 2000, aged between 5 and 15 in 1993			
Less than 1 dollar a day	0.044	0.046	0.034
Less than 2 dollars a day	0.050	0.045	0.067
2 to 4 dollars a day	0.009	0.011	0.006
6 to 10 dollars a day	0.013	0.010	0.016
I. Dead by 1997, aged less than 5 in 1993			
Less than 1 dollar a day	0.027	0.031	0.000
Less than 2 dollars a day	0.038	0.040	0.032
2 to 4 dollars a day	0.008	0.005	0.011
6 to 10 dollars a day	0.010	0.018	0.000
J. Dead by 2000, aged less than 5 in 1993			
Less than 1 dollar a day	0.046	0.048	0.030
Less than 2 dollars a day	0.055	0.054	0.057
2 to 4 dollars a day	0.013	0.011	0.018
6 to 10 dollars a day	0.012	0.018	0.006

Note: Data is from the IFLS panel. Each cell is the fraction of people found in 1993 who have died by the indicated year.

Table 7.7   **Death rates by age and consumption category, VLSS panel**

	All	Rural	Urban
A. Dead by 1997, order than 50 in 1993			
Less than 1 dollar a day	0.145	0.149	
Less than 2 dollars a day	0.131	0.131	0.132
2 to 4 dollars a day	0.111	0.115	0.100
6 to 10 dollars a day	0.098	0.053	0.108
B. Dead by 1997, order than 45 in 1993			
Less than 1 dollar a day	0.120	0.124	
Less than 2 dollars a day	0.112	0.112	0.110
2 to 4 dollars a day	0.096	0.098	0.090
6 to 10 dollars a day	0.080	0.040	0.090
C. Dead by 1997, aged between 15 and 45 in 1993			
Less than 1 dollar a day	0.010	0.010	
Less than 2 dollars a day	0.010	0.010	0.007
2 to 4 dollars a day	0.008	0.006	0.014
6 to 10 dollars a day	0.000	0.000	0.000
D. Dead by 1997, aged between 5 and 15 in 1993			
Less than 1 dollar a day	0.007	0.008	
Less than 2 dollars a day	0.006	0.006	0.000
2 to 4 dollars a day	0.004	0.003	0.005
6 to 10 dollars a day	0.000	0.000	0.000
E. Dead by 1997, aged less than 5 in 1993			
Less than 1 dollar a day	0.015	0.012	n.a.
Less than 2 dollars a day	0.012	0.012	0.014
2 to 4 dollars a day	0.007	0.005	0.011
6 to 10 dollars a day	0.000	0.000	0.000

Notes: Data is from the Vietnam Living Standard Survey (VLSS). Each cell is the fraction of people found in 1992 who have died by 1997.

Overall, 14.4 percent of those age fifty and above who lived in extremely poor households in 1992 and 1993 have died by 1997 and 1998, versus 9.8 percent among those who were living in households with DPCE between six and ten dollars. In rural areas, the probabilities are, respectively, 15 percent and 5 percent. These numbers are very close to the Indonesian numbers, and suggest that those numbers are unlikely to be just due to chance: above fifty, it seems the rural extremely poor are at least three times more likely to die than the less poor.

It should be noted that those ratios indicate high mortality rates among the old, compared to the United States: For example, in the Health and Retirement Study (HRS), 6 percent of the sample aged between fifty and fifty-nine in the first wave had died by 1998 (in six years).[5]

5. It should be noted that the HRS 1992 sample is younger, since only individuals ages fifty to fifty-nine were sampled. The unweighted average age in the HRS 1992 sample is 55.26, versus 62.6 among all those age fifty-five or above in the Vietnamese survey.

Table 7.8   Udaipur

	Mortality one year out	Mortality two years out
A. Aged 50 or more at baseline		
Less than 1 dollar a day	0.053	0.0659
Less than 2 dollars a day	0.0462	0.0489
More than 2 dollars a day	0.0349	0.0535
B. Aged 46 or more at baseline		
Less than 1 dollar a day	0.0488	0.0521
Less than 2 dollars a day	0.0406	0.0405
More than 2 dollars a day	0.0321	0.045
C. Aged 16 to 45 at baseline		
Less than 1 dollar a day	0.0099	0.0098
Less than 2 dollars a day	0.0058	0.0057
More than 2 dollars a day	0	0.0184
D. Aged 6 to 15 at baseline		
Less than 1 dollar a day	0.0014	0.0066
Less than 2 dollars a day	0.0046	0.0087
More than 2 dollars a day	0.0159	0
E. Aged less than 5 at baseline		
Less than 1 dollar a day	0.0354	0.0273
Less than 2 dollars a day	0.0228	0.0279
More than 2 dollars a day	0	0

Note: Data is from the Udaipur survey.

The results we have for Udaipur are not directly comparable to the results for Vietnam and Indonesia for two reasons: the mortality is only after one year, and there are almost no households in the sample with consumption per capita between six and ten dollars a day. Given the number of observations in each group, and for more clarity, we present the results for three groups: the extremely poor, those with DPCE between one and two dollars, and those with DPCE above two dollars.

Despite these differences, the patterns we find in Udaipur are entirely consistent with those for Indonesia and Vietnam. Here again, in all age groups, the mortality is higher for the extremely poor than for the poor and the non-poor. And once again, the largest difference in percentage point are found among the older people. The probability of dying within a year is 5.8 percent for the extremely poor, 4.6 percent for the poor, and 3.4 percent for those with DPCE above two dollars.

In all three countries, death rates are thus higher for the poor at all consumption levels, and in particular for the old. This higher mortality among the old is particularly striking given that the poor tend to die more at every age, and therefore the surviving old poor might be selected to be particularly healthy. One possible interpretation is that the difference in lifestyle in this group, albeit incremental, does generate these differences in mortality rates. Another possibility (and possibly both coexist) is that poor health is disabling, and responsible for maintaining those households in poverty.

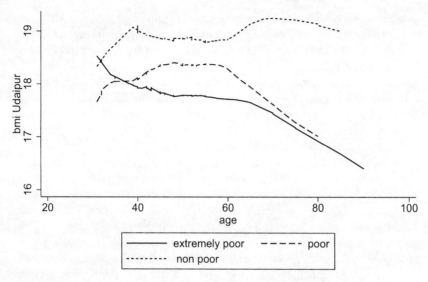

Fig. 7.1   Udaipur: Relationship between BMI and age, by expenditure categories, females

7.6   Aging, Health, and Poverty in India and Indonesia

To shed more light on these rather concerning statistics about death, we now examine the correlation of age and health status among the poor and the less poor in two of the surveys where we conducted the mortality analysis, where we also have detailed health data: Udaipur and Indonesia.

For the two countries, we simply plot nonparametric regressions of a number of health and mental health indicators on age separately by gender and by income groups: in Udaipur we plot these graphs for the extremely poor (less than a dollar a day), the poor (one to two dollars a day) and the non-poor (more than two dollars a day). In Indonesia, we plot these graphs for the extremely poor, the poor, those with DPCE between two and four dollars and those with DPCE between six and ten dollars. Note that this cross-sectional correlation may underestimate the deterioration of health with age (relative to a panel where people would be compared over time), since the weakest people presumably disappear from the sample as they age. Given the differential mortality we have described among the poor and non-poor, this implies that there is a stronger negative bias among the poor than the non-poor, and therefore, everything else equal, we will tend to underestimate any differences in the slope of health with respect to age between the groups.

The indicators we look at are body mass index, hemoglobin (Hb) levels, and anemia (defined as less Hb below 12 g/dl for women and 13g/dl for men), lung capacity (measured as the maximum of three peak flow meters reading), self-reported health status, number of activities of daily living that the person carries out with difficulty or not at all (excluding eating, dressing, and going to the bathroom), and self-reported well-being (which is available only in Udaipur). In addition we have signs of depression, measured differently in both surveys. In Udaipur it is defined as the answer to the question, "In the last twelve months, was there a period of at least one month where you felt worried, tense or anxious?" In Indonesia it is the number of symptoms over the last four weeks from among the following: having difficulty sleeping, being bothered by things, feeling lonely, being sad, being anxious, having difficulty concentrating, and finding everything an effort.

In Udaipur (Udaipur figures, figures 7.2 and 7.3), for most indicators health seems to deteriorate more strongly with age among the poor than the non-poor. Starting with women, BMI, for example, decreases with age for the poorer categories, while it does not among the non-poor. Anemia rises much more steeply with age among the extremely poor than among the poor and it does not increase with age for the non-poor. The same pattern can also be seen for self-reported health status, number of symptoms of acute morbidity, self-reported well-being, and symptoms of depression over the last year. The only variables that do not follow this pattern are the activities of daily living (ADL) limitations, the peak flow meter reading, and the time spent in squatting and getting up for five times (as well as the inability or refusal to do it). Interestingly, the patterns for males are similar for all the objective measures, and different for the self-reported measures (self-reported health status, number of symptoms, symptoms of depressions). The responses to this last set of questions do not always indicate a deterioration with age, and when they do, the slopes are similar for the extremely poor, the poor and the non-poor. The only exception is self-reported well-being, which actually is positively correlated with age for the sixty and eighty age group for the two richer categories, and negatively for the poorest. It could be because men, and in particular older men, are more reluctant to complain. Alternatively, given the Indian context, it is quite likely that older women are substantially less well treated than older men, which could increase both their likelihood of being depressed and their vulnerability to various ailments.

On the whole, in Udaipur, a simple story can be told: as they get older, the poor get comparably weaker and weaker, and they are also more likely to die. Again, it could be that they were always frail (which is why they were poor), and so support age less well, or it could be that poverty accelerates age's damage on the body.

The same analysis for Indonesia does not reveal a similar pattern for all the objective variables, where the slopes are very similar for the poor and non-poor. Hemoglobin levels, if anything, are positively correlated with age among the poor, and negatively among the non-poor. But here again, we find that women's self-reported health status, depression symptoms, and number of health complaints over the last months all worsen more with age

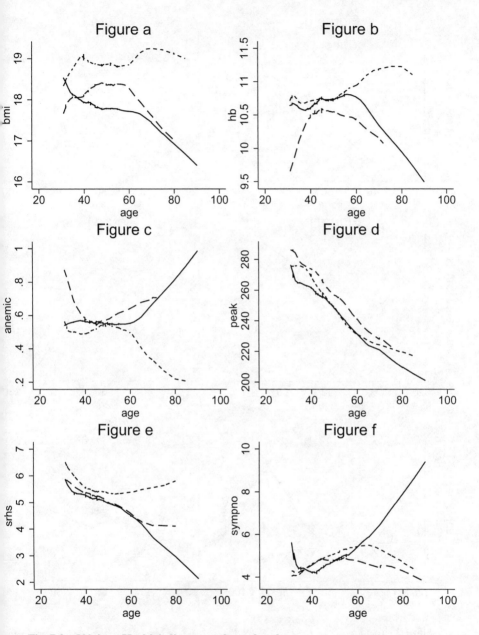

Fig. 7.2   Udaipur: Health indicators and age, females

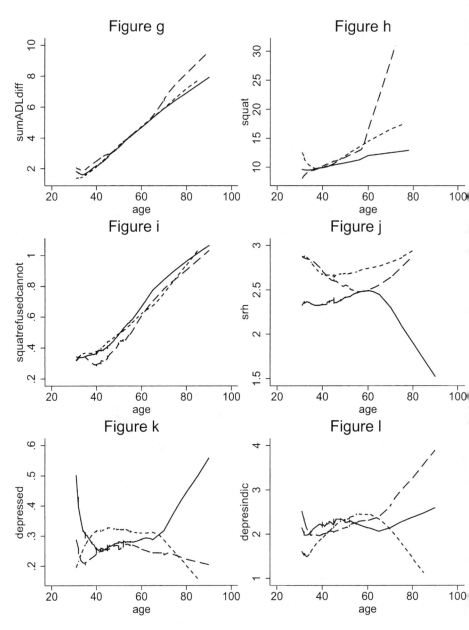

Fig. 7.2 (cont.)

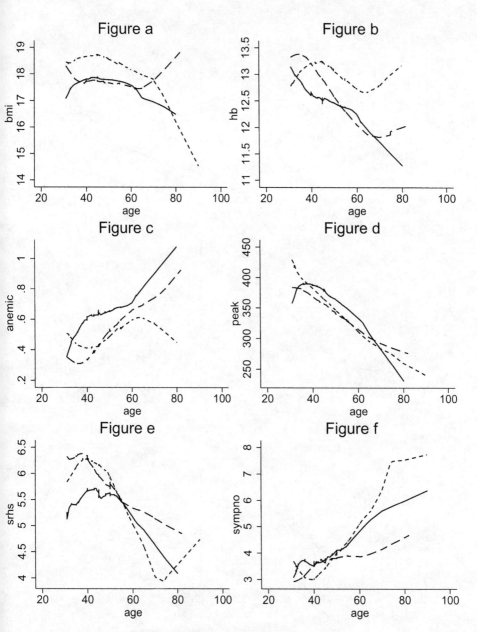

Fig. 7.3   Udaipur: Health indicators and age, males

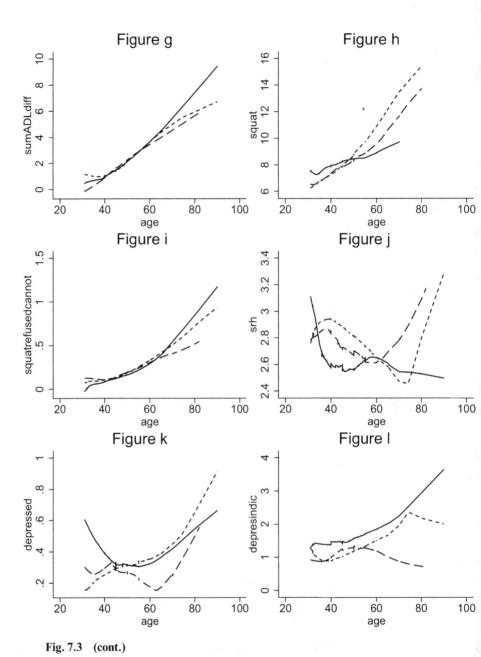

Fig. 7.3 **(cont.)**

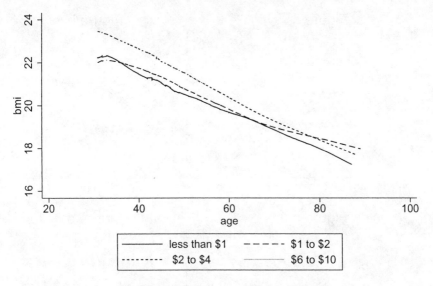

Fig. 7.4   Rural Indonesia: Relationship between BMI and age, by expenditure categories, females

for the poor than for the non-poor (note that in this data, a higher value for self-reported health status variables indicate *worse* health, not better). And once again, this is not true for men.

Unlike Udaipur, there seems to be some tension between the health indicators and the actual mortality in rural Indonesia. One can offer different conjectures for this phenomenon. If one is prepared to take the subjective indicators seriously, one possible explanation is that the "objective" indicators we have here (anemia, BMI, lung capacity, time to squat, and ADLs) are indicative of chronic conditions that are often incurable, at least for older people. However, because of their better access to sanitation and good health care, the rich are less likely to be susceptible to acute conditions (hence the differential age slopes for the number of symptoms they report), and also perhaps less likely to die from them, in part because they are more likely to be treated (for example, an untreated cold for an older person may turn into a pneumonia and kill them, while a younger person would recover from it). Another possibility, if one thinks that the "subjective" measures reveal more about the psychology of the respondent than about their real health status, is that the older poor people become comparatively unhappier with age (the IFLS do not seem to have self-reported happiness indexes, but they do have depression indicators for the past month and the old poor women are much more likely to have those symptoms (see figure 7.5, panel i), which is also why they report more symptoms and worse self-reported health status. If this is true, they may then be less likely to effectively fight illnesses, which, in turn, make him or her more likely to die.

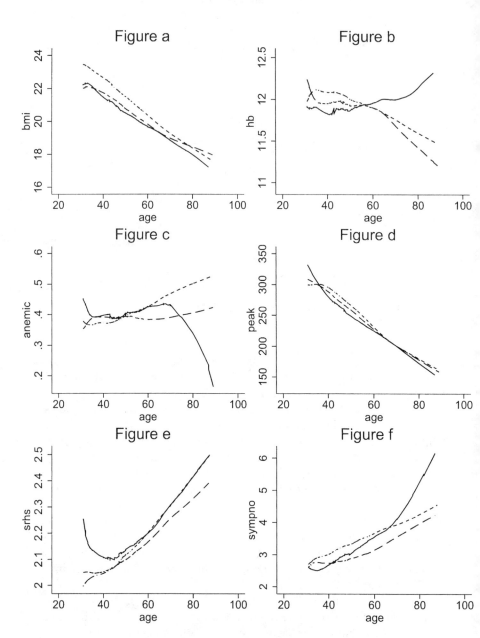

Fig. 7.5   Rural Indonesia: Health indicators and age, females

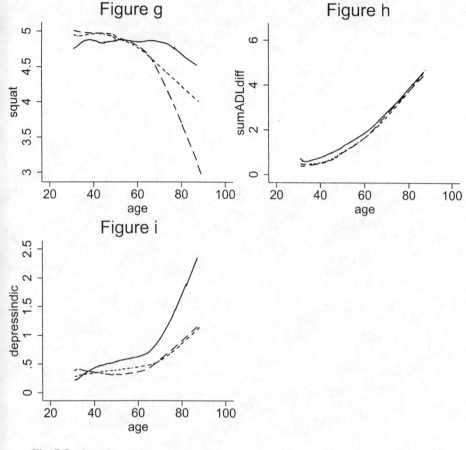

Fig. 7.5   (cont.)

7.7   Discussion and Interpretation

This chapter brings together various pieces of evidence that all point in the same direction: the poor, and particularly the extremely poor, have a lower chance of survival than those who are somewhat more well-off. We have not tried to disentangle the direction of the causality: these adults could be poor because they are in poor health, which would then in turn explain why they are more likely to die. Or alternatively, being poor could make them more likely to die. And of course, both directions of causality may be true at the same time. It is worth pointing out, however, that most old people in developing countries live with other, younger, adults: in Vietnam, for example, this is true of 80 percent of the older adults. And if we restrict the sample to

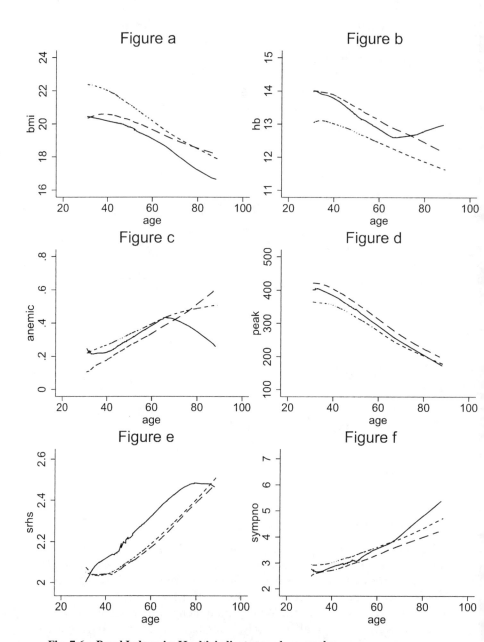

Fig. 7.6   Rural Indonesia: Health indicators and age, males

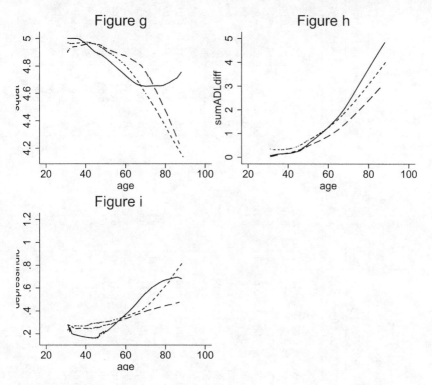

Fig. 7.6 (cont.)

only those people who do live with a younger adult, we find the same excess mortality rate among the poorer old people than in the entire sample.

This weakens the case for a direct link going only from the health of the old people to the poverty status of the household. This point is further strengthened by the fact that when we look at older women in households where there are prime-age adults, we continue to find the same pattern (in Vietnam, for example, for women above fifty who live with prime-age adults, the five-year mortality rate goes from 12 percent among the poor to 7.7 percent among those with DPCE between six and ten dollars). Since older women in households with prime-age adults are very unlikely to be engaged in any market work, it is unlikely that it is because they are unhealthy that the household is poor. To the extent poor health is in part inherited, it could, of course, be the case that unhealthy old people live with unhealthy younger adults, and this is the reason why the household is poor.

On balance, we are tempted to interpret the evidence accumulated in this chapter as revealing, at least in part, that poverty does kill.

Appendix

Table 7A.1 Share of women in different age group in the population, by consumption category

	Girls age 0–12				Girls age 13–18				Women age 20–50				Women age 51 and above			
	<$1	<$2	$2–$4	$6–$10	<$1	<$2	$2–$4	$6–$10	<$1	<$2	$2–$4	$6–$10	<$1	<$2	$2–$4	$6–$10
Rural																
Bangladesh	0.19	0.18	0.14	0.1	0.06	0.06	0.06	0.08	0.18	0.19	0.2	0.17	0.06	0.06	0.08	0.09
Brazil	0.22	0.18	0.13	0.09	0.07	0.07	0.06	0.08	0.15	0.16	0.19	0.24	0.02	0.05	0.1	0.09
East Timor	0.22	0.2	0.17	0.23	0.06	0.06	0.04	0	0.16	0.17	0.18	0.24	0.03	0.03	0.06	0.12
Ecuador	0.14	0.19	0.16	0.11	0.03	0.07	0.07	0.06	0.16	0.17	0.21	0.25	0.03	0.04	0.05	0.09
Guatemala	0.22	0.23	0.21	0.19	0.07	0.06	0.07	0.09	0.16	0.16	0.17	0.19	0.03	0.03	0.03	0.04
Hyderabad	n.a.	n.a.	n.a.	n.a.	n.a.	n.a.	n.a.	n.a.	n.a.	n.a.	n.a.	n.a.	n.a.	n.a.	n.a.	n.a.
Indonesia00	0.13	0.13	0.12	0.08	0.08	0.07	0.07	0.08	0.19	0.2	0.2	0.23	0.06	0.07	0.06	0.07
Indonesia93	0.17	0.17	0.15	0.11	0.06	0.06	0.07	0.06	0.18	0.19	0.21	0.23	0.09	0.08	0.08	0.09
Indonesia97	0.16	0.14	0.12	0.12	0.07	0.07	0.08	0.06	0.18	0.19	0.2	0.23	0.1	0.1	0.09	0.09
Ivory Coast	0.1	0.09	0.1	0.08	0.06	0.08	0.09	0.11	0.16	0.16	0.16	0.17	0.06	0.04	0.03	0.01
Mexico	0.15	0.17	0.13	0.12	0.08	0.06	0.08	0.05	0.17	0.21	0.24	0.3	0.07	0.06	0.07	0.09
Nicaragua	0.2	0.19	0.16	0.1	0.07	0.07	0.07	0.08	0.14	0.14	0.16	0.19	0.03	0.04	0.06	0.1
Pakistan*	0.09	0.09	0.08	n.a.	0.06	0.06	0.08	n.a.	0.13	0.14	0.15	n.a.	0.04	0.05	0.06	n.a.
Panama	0.2	0.2	0.16	0.11	0.08	0.06	0.06	0.05	0.15	0.14	0.15	0.19	0.03	0.04	0.06	0.1
Papua New Guinea	0.2	0.18	0.14	0.12	0.08	0.07	0.07	0.06	0.18	0.18	0.19	0.2	0.02	0.02	0.04	0.04
Peru	0.23	0.21	0.14	n.a.	0.06	0.07	0.06	n.a.	0.15	0.15	0.18	n.a.	0.04	0.05	0.08	n.a.
South Africa	0.04	0.04	0.03	0.03	0.02	0.02	0.02	0.01	0.18	0.19	0.23	0.25	0.08	0.09	0.09	0.08
Tanzania	0.2	0.2	0.17	0.2	0.07	0.07	0.08	0.07	0.15	0.16	0.18	0.19	0.05	0.05	0.04	0.1
Udaipur	0.21	0.19	0.12	n.a.	0.06	0.06	0.08	n.a.	0.15	0.16	0.17	n.a.	0.04	0.05	0.09	n.a.
Vietnam9293	0.19	0.17	0.13	0.12	0.04	0.05	0.06	0.04	0.08	0.1	0.09	0.09	0.01	0.01	0.02	0.02
Vietnam9798	0.26	0.2	0.14	0.08	0.08	0.08	0.08	0.09	0.14	0.17	0.19	0.19	0.05	0.06	0.09	0.1

Urban

Bangladesh	n.a.	n.a.	n.a.	n.a.	n.a.	n.a.	n.a.	n.a.	n.a.	n.a.	n.a.	n.a.	n.a.	n.a.
Brazil	0.06	0.07	0.07	0.07	0.11	0.15	0.16	0.17	0.19	0.23	0.04	0.06	0.07	0.1
East Timor	0.05	0.07	0.08	0.06	0.14	0.16	0.16	0.16	0.18	0.22	0.04	0.03	0.03	0.02
Ecuador	0.07	0.07	0.07	0.06	0.11	0.14	0.14	0.15	0.18	0.21	0.06	0.07	0.08	0.08
Hyderabad	0.07	0.07	0.07	0.07	0.09	0.1	0.19	0.21	0.23	0.21	0.03	0.04	0.04	0.04
Indonesia00	0.05	0.06	0.06	0.05	0.07	0.1	0.18	0.19	0.24	0.27	0.08	0.07	0.07	0.07
Indonesia93	0.1	0.07	0.07	0.06	0.1	0.14	0.19	0.19	0.21	0.23	0.1	0.08	0.07	0.06
Indonesia97	0.08	0.07	0.08	0.08	0.09	0.11	0.18	0.17	0.22	0.24	0.1	0.1	0.09	0.07
Ivory Coast	0.06	0.07	0.06	0.06	0.08	0.1	0.17	0.19	0.16	0.21	0.05	0.05	0.05	0.04
Mexico	0.08	0.07	0.08	0.09	0.14	0.14	0.17	0.16	0.24	0.27	0.05	0.06	0.07	0.08
Nicaragua	0.07	0.08	0.07	0.07	0.1	0.15	0.15	0.14	0.19	0.24	0.05	0.05	0.06	0.08
Pakistan*	0.08	0.08	0.07	0.07	0.07	0.07	0.14	0.17	0.17	0.16	0.04	0.04	0.04	0.06
Panama	0.06	0.07	0.06	n.a.	0.13	0.18	n.a.	0.17	0.17	0.22	n.a.	0.03	0.05	0.07
Papua New Guinea	0.04	0.07	0.07	0.11	0.16	0.15	0.14	0.17	0.21	0.18	0.01	0.02	0.03	0.01
Peru	0.08	0.08	0.08	0.08	0.1	0.14	0.17	0.2	0.21	0.24	0.01	0.04	0.06	0.08
South Africa	0.02	0.02	0.02	0.01	0.03	0.03	0.19	0.16	0.23	0.25	0.09	0.07	0.07	0.06
Tanzania	0.07	0.08	0.07	0.08	0.14	0.16	0.14	n.a.	0.19	0.22	0.1	0.06	0.04	0.03
Udaipur	n.a.	0.11	n.a.	n.a.	n.a.	0.11	n.a.	n.a.	0.14	n.a.	n.a.	n.a.	0.11	n.a.
Vietnam9293	0.04	0.06	0.06	0.05	0.09	0.12	0.1	0.11	0.13	0.19	0.01	0.01	0.03	0.05
Vietnam9798	0.07	0.08	0.05	n.a.	0.08	0.13	n.a.	0.18	0.21	0.25	n.a.	0.08	0.1	0.11

Table 7A.2   Share of men in different age group in the population, by consumption category

	Boys age 0–12				Boys age 13–18				Men age 20–50				Men age 51 and above			
	<$1	<$2	$2–$4	$6–$10	<$1	<$2	$2–$4	$6–$10	<$1	<$2	$2–$4	$6–$10	<$1	<$2	$2–$4	$6–$10
Rural																
Bangladesh	0.18	0.17	0.15	0.07	0.07	0.08	0.08	0.13	0.16	0.16	0.18	0.21	0.06	0.06	0.08	0.12
Brazil	0.23	0.2	0.13	0.1	0.09	0.08	0.07	0.05	0.14	0.16	0.2	0.23	0.04	0.05	0.09	0.11
East Timor	0.21	0.22	0.18	0.06	0.06	0.06	0.06	0.06	0.14	0.15	0.18	0.21	0.04	0.04	0.05	0.08
Ecuador	0.34	0.22	0.17	0.12	0.1	0.07	0.07	0.06	0.14	0.16	0.19	0.22	0.04	0.04	0.05	0.07
Guatemala	0.21	0.22	0.21	0.2	0.05	0.06	0.06	0.06	0.14	0.14	0.14	0.13	0.04	0.04	0.04	0.04
Hyderabad	n.a.	n.a.	n.a.	n.a.	n.a.	n.a.	n.a.	n.a.	n.a.	n.a.	n.a.	n.a.	n.a.	n.a.	n.a.	n.a.
Indonesia00	0.13	0.14	0.12	0.09	0.06	0.06	0.06	0.05	0.2	0.2	0.23	0.27	0.06	0.06	0.07	0.07
Indonesia93	0.18	0.17	0.15	0.13	0.06	0.06	0.07	0.09	0.16	0.17	0.18	0.19	0.08	0.07	0.07	0.07
Indonesia97	0.16	0.15	0.12	0.09	0.06	0.07	0.08	0.06	0.16	0.17	0.19	0.22	0.08	0.08	0.08	0.08
Ivory Coast	0.21	0.21	0.19	0.15	0.07	0.08	0.09	0.08	0.09	0.11	0.14	0.18	0.04	0.04	0.04	0.03
Mexico	0.14	0.16	0.14	0.11	0.09	0.08	0.06	0.05	0.19	0.19	0.22	0.25	0.05	0.06	0.07	0.07
Nicaragua	0.21	0.2	0.16	0.07	0.1	0.09	0.08	0.07	0.12	0.14	0.16	0.2	0.04	0.05	0.07	0.1
Pakistan*	0.22	0.21	0.17	0.14	0.07	0.07	0.07	0.06	0.14	0.15	0.17	0.19	0.05	0.05	0.07	0.04
Panama	0.23	0.22	0.18	0.12	0.09	0.08	0.08	0.06	0.12	0.14	0.17	0.21	0.04	0.05	0.07	0.11
Papua New Guinea	0.17	0.19	0.19	0.16	0.07	0.07	0.08	0.09	0.15	0.16	0.18	0.21	0.04	0.04	0.04	0.04
Peru	0.21	0.2	0.15	n.a.	0.05	0.06	0.07	n.a.	0.14	0.15	0.17	n.a.	0.05	0.05	0.08	n.a.
South Africa	0.04	0.04	0.04	0.03	0.01	0.02	0.02	0.02	0.14	0.15	0.2	0.37	0.06	0.06	0.06	0.07
Tanzania	0.21	0.21	0.16	0.09	0.07	0.07	0.07	0.09	0.12	0.13	0.16	0.16	0.05	0.05	0.06	0.05
Udaipur	0.22	0.2	0.12	n.a.	0.05	0.06	0.06	n.a.	0.16	0.17	0.2	n.a.	0.04	0.05	0.09	n.a.
Vietnam9293	0.18	0.18	0.13	0.18	0.04	0.05	0.06	0.01	0.08	0.1	0.09	0.1	0.01	0.02	0.03	0.01
Vietnam9798	0.2	0.2	0.15	0.11	0.08	0.07	0.08	0.09	0.15	0.16	0.17	0.18	0.02	0.04	0.06	0.09

Urban																	
Bangladesh	n.a.	n.a.	n.a.	n.a.	n.a.	n.a.	n.a.	n.a.	n.a.	n.a.	n.a.	n.a.	n.a.	n.a.	n.a.	n.a.	n.a.
Brazil	0.27	0.19	0.15	0.11	0.07	0.07	0.07	0.06	0.16	0.17	0.19	0.23	0.04	0.06	0.06	0.07	0.1
East Timor	0.17	0.18	0.16	0.14	0.06	0.08	0.07	0.05	0.14	0.16	0.18	0.22	0.04	0.03	0.03	0.03	0.02
Ecuador	0.2	0.18	0.14	0.11	0.06	0.07	0.07	0.07	0.14	0.15	0.18	0.21	0.06	0.07	0.07	0.08	0.08
Hyderabad	0.17	0.14	0.1	0.09	0.07	0.07	0.07	0.07	0.19	0.21	0.23	0.21	0.03	0.04	0.04	0.04	0.04
Indonesia00	0.11	0.12	0.1	0.07	0.05	0.06	0.06	0.05	0.18	0.21	0.24	0.27	0.08	0.07	0.07	0.07	0.07
Indonesia93	0.15	0.15	0.14	0.1	0.06	0.07	0.07	0.1	0.19	0.19	0.21	0.23	0.1	0.08	0.08	0.07	0.06
Indonesia97	0.1	0.12	0.11	0.09	0.08	0.08	0.07	0.08	0.18	0.19	0.22	0.24	0.1	0.1	0.1	0.09	0.07
Ivory Coast	0.09	0.09	0.1	0.08	0.06	0.06	0.07	0.06	0.17	0.17	0.16	0.21	0.05	0.05	0.05	0.05	0.04
Mexico	0.19	0.18	0.14	0.14	0.09	0.08	0.08	0.08	0.17	0.19	0.24	0.27	0.05	0.06	0.06	0.07	0.08
Nicaragua	0.21	0.2	0.15	0.1	0.07	0.07	0.08	0.07	0.15	0.16	0.19	0.24	0.05	0.05	0.05	0.06	0.08
Pakistan*	0.11	0.1	0.07	0.07	0.07	0.07	0.08	0.08	0.14	0.14	0.17	0.16	0.04	0.04	0.04	0.04	0.06
Panama	n.a.	0.23	0.18	0.13	n.a.	0.06	0.07	0.06	n.a.	0.17	0.17	0.22	n.a.	0.03	0.03	0.05	0.07
Papua New Guinea	0.22	0.2	0.15	0.16	0.11	0.08	0.08	0.04	0.14	0.17	0.21	0.18	0.01	0.04	0.04	0.03	0.01
Peru	0.21	0.18	0.14	0.1	0.08	0.08	0.08	0.04	0.17	0.17	0.21	0.24	0.01	0.04	0.07	0.06	0.08
South Africa	0.03	0.03	0.03	0.03	0.01	0.02	0.02	0.02	0.19	0.2	0.23	0.25	0.09	0.07	0.07	0.07	0.06
Tanzania	0.17	0.18	0.16	0.14	0.08	0.07	0.08	0.07	0.14	0.16	0.19	0.22	0.1	0.06	0.06	0.04	0.03
Udaipur	n.a.	n.a.	0.11	n.a.	n.a.	n.a.	0.11	n.a.	n.a.	n.a.	0.14	n.a.	n.a.	n.a.	n.a.	0.11	n.a.
Vietnam9293	0.14	0.15	0.12	0.09	0.05	0.06	0.06	0.04	0.1	0.11	0.13	0.19	0.01	0.01	0.01	0.03	0.05
Vietnam9798	n.a.	0.14	0.13	0.08	n.a.	0.05	0.08	0.07	n.a.	0.18	0.21	0.25	n.a.	0.08	0.08	0.1	0.11

Table 7A.3   **Out of the individuals age 31 to 50 whose mother is alive**

	Fraction whose father lives in household				Fraction whose mother lives in household			
	< $1	< $2	$2–$4	$6–$10	< $1	< $2	$2–$4	$6–$10
Rural								
Bangladesh	0.14	0.11	0.11	0.09	0.20	0.22	0.25	0.15
Brazil	0.02	0.06	0.15	0.10	0.03	0.09	0.17	0.14
East Timor	0.27	0.08	0.19	0.00	0.11	0.14	0.27	0.29
Indonesia93	0.04	0.04	0.02	0.00	0.11	0.09	0.06	0.05
Indonesia97	0.21	0.12	0.07	0.02	0.24	0.19	0.15	0.14
Indonesia00	0.14	0.14	0.11	0.03	0.25	0.19	0.20	0.13
Ivory Coast	0.31	0.12	0.08	0.00	0.35	0.13	0.10	0.00
Mexico	0.30	0.21	0.14	0.10	0.32	0.21	0.14	0.14
Nicaragua	0.12	0.12	0.13	0.14	0.12	0.13	0.14	0.16
Pakistan	0.27	0.26	0.29	n.a.	0.26	0.27	0.26	n.a.
South Africa	0.39	0.32	0.23	0.10	0.57	0.50	0.36	0.18
Udaipur	0.09	0.11	0.15	n.a.	0.09	0.13	0.16	n.a.
Vietnam92	n.a.	0.16	0.21	0.14	n.a.	0.27	0.25	0.22
Urban								
Brazil	0.13	0.21	0.13	0.07	0.01	0.20	0.16	0.15
East Timor	0.14	0.11	0.15	0.04	0.16	0.12	0.17	0.02
Indonesia93	0.05	0.04	0.03	0.04	0.19	0.15	0.07	0.04
Indonesia97	0.33	0.20	0.12	0.03	0.28	0.30	0.20	0.15
Indonesia00	0.26	0.20	0.11	0.10	0.54	0.29	0.22	0.20
Ivory Coast	0.32	0.16	0.09	0.00	0.34	0.24	0.10	0.00
Mexico	0.17	0.17	0.18	0.07	0.18	0.18	0.15	0.11
Nicaragua	0.17	0.11	0.09	0.07	0.20	0.22	0.21	0.16
Pakistan	0.25	0.25	0.22	0.38	0.23	0.23	0.20	0.30
South Africa	0.39	0.34	0.25	0.10	0.68	0.54	0.34	0.12
Vietnam92	0.18	0.11	0.09	0.00	0.21	0.17	0.14	0.22

References

Banerjee, A., A. Deaton, and E. Duflo. 2004. Wealth, health, and health services in rural Rajasthan. *American Economic Review* 94 (2): 326–30.

Banerjee, A., and E. Duflo. 2007a. The economic lives of the middle class. MIT. Unpublished Manuscript.

———. 2007b. The economic lives of the poor. *Journal of Economic Perspectives* 21 (1): 141–67.

Banerjee, A., E. Duflo, and R. Glennerster. 2006. A snapshot of micro enterprises in Hyderabad. MIT. Unpublished Manuscript.

Deaton, A. 2004. Measuring poverty. In *Understanding poverty,* ed. A. Banerjee, R. Benabou, and D. Mookherjee, 3–16. New York: Oxford University Press.

Frankenberg, E., and L. Karoly. 1995. The 1993 Indonesian family life survey: Overview and field report. The RAND Corporation, Santa Monica, CA, November.

Frankenberg, E., and D. Thomas. 2000. The Indonesia family life survey (IFLS): Study design and results from waves 1 and 2. The RAND Corporation, Santa Monica, CA. DRU-2238/1-NIA/NICHD, March.

Strauss, J., K. Beegle, B. Sikoki, A. Dwiyanto, Y. Herawati, and F. Witoelar. The third wave of the Indonesia family life survey (IFLS): Overview and field report. WR-144/1-NIA/NICHD, March.

Wagstaff, A. 2002. Poverty and health sector inequalities. *Bulletin of the World Health Organization* 80 (2): 97–105.

World Bank. Living standards measurement study. Available at: http://www.worldbank.org/LSMS/.

Comment   Amitabh Chandra and Heidi Williams

The World Bank estimated that in 2001, 1.1 billion individuals lived under a dollar a day, and over 2.7 billion (approximately half of the world's population) lived on less than two dollars a day. The prevalence of extreme poverty as measured by the fraction of the world's population who live under a dollar a day has been falling, but the toll, as measured by population counts, has been steadily increasing (Bourguignon and Morrisson 2002). Sala-i-Martin (2006) documents that the decline in prevalence is driven largely by improvements in South Asia and East Asia; the past two decades have not seen improvements in Sub-Saharan Africa, the Middle East, Latin America, or Eastern Europe. These sobering facts provoke several sets of immediate and interrelated questions. What causes extreme poverty? What are the effects of living in such poverty? And what policies, microeconomic and macroeconomic, successfully lift people out of these conditions?

In this insightful chapter, Banerjee and Duflo document new facts that illuminate our understanding of the second question. Their analysis uses data from a number of low-income countries (including two new data sets collected by the authors and their colleagues) to study the association between poverty and what is arguably the single most important determinant of welfare: health (in particular, adult mortality). We say most important because even marginal improvement in health, when monetized into dollars using quality-adjusted life years (QALYs) and a societal measure of the willingness to pay for life, will generally dominate improvements in incomes and other measures of well-being. The new facts that emerge from their chapter build on the authors' own previous work (Banerjee and Duflo 2007)

Amitabh Chandra is an assistant professor of public policy at the John F. Kennedy School of Government, Harvard University, and a faculty research fellow at the National Bureau of Economic Research. Heidi Williams is a PhD student in economics at Harvard University.

Chandra gratefully acknowledges support from the National Institute on Aging (NIA PO1-AG19783); Williams gratefully acknowledges support from the National Institute on Aging, Grant Number T32-AG0000186 to the NBER.

in providing insights into the lives of the poor in low-income countries, and also suggest several ways forward for learning about the causes and effects of poverty in low-income countries.

Methods for Measuring Adult Mortality

One reason that so little is known about the correlation between poverty and adult mortality in low-income countries is that many such countries lack a comprehensive death registration system. Registration of deaths is often incomplete, and even when coverage is adequate the data on age is often inaccurate (Hill, Choi, and Timaeus 2005). We tend to have comparatively better data on child mortality in low-income countries, but changes in child mortality measures may correlate poorly with changes in old-age survival. In part due to this lack of high quality data, several broad methods have been developed by demographers to estimate old-age mortality (Hill, Choi, and Timaeus 2005):

1. *Death distribution methods.* If the relationship between deaths and recorded deaths can be estimated, data on recorded deaths can be adjusted and unbiased death rates can be calculated. Demographers have developed methods for such estimation that necessarily rely on simplifying assumptions, but can be designed to account for factors such as migration.

2. *Sample registration systems.* As an example, India's sample registration system has historically been a dual record system consisting of a continuous enumeration of births and deaths by a resident enumerator, and an independent survey every six months. Data from India's system are thought to be of relatively high quality, although attempts to initiate similar systems in other countries are thought to have been less successful.

3. *Census or survey questions concerning household deaths over some reference period.* Although commonly used, this method has a number of potential weaknesses—the method of data collection implies that some deaths will be omitted (such as deaths in single-person households), and deaths in households that dissolve after the death (perhaps due to the death itself) may also be missed.

4. *Indirect methods based on the survival of close relatives.* A variety of methods fall into this category—including methods asking mothers about their children, children about their parents (the so-called "orphanhood" method), widows about their first spouse, and everyone about their siblings.

5. *Intercensal survival methods.* Given data from two censuses, survivorship ratios can be compared to model life table values in order to estimate post-childhood mortality. Concerns with this method often arise due to changes in census coverage and age misreporting.

Each of these methods has strengths and weaknesses. For example, the second method is (at least in some countries, such as India) highly dependent on the quality of local informants—such as barbers, priests, school teachers, and nurses—who inform the first round of enumeration, and is also quite expensive to implement. Moreover, many of these methods do not permit an examination of the relationship between poverty and mortality.

In their chapter, Banerjee and Duflo use a variant of the fourth method—the "orphanhood" method—which has a rich history in the demographic literature, but to the best of our knowledge had not previously been combined with information on household poverty. It is instructive to briefly review the intellectual antecedents of Banerjee and Duflo's contribution. William Brass developed the first formal methods for converting indicators of mortality based on survival of close relatives into standard life table measures. Brass and Hill (1973) and Hill and Trussell (1977) proposed methods for estimating life table survivorship ratios from proportions of respondents in five-year age groups whose mother or father were alive. Rather than attempting to collect ages of the dead relatives, demographers instead estimated these ages based on the ages of respondents (which presumably are reported more accurately than would be the ages of the dead relatives).

Blacker (1977) notes several practical advantages of this orphanhood method: the questions "Is your father alive?" and "Is your mother alive?" are simple, involve no dating or reference period, and can be answered by a straightforward "yes" or "no." Despite these advantages, several potential drawbacks of this method were noted from the outset. For example, if surveyed individuals use the words "mother" and "father" to denote individuals other than their biological parents then bias could result—in part because the process of adoption by foster parents or other relatives may take place precisely due to the adult mortality the researcher is attempting to measure. Carefully worded survey questionnaires attempt to circumvent such issues, although many demographers argue that an "adoption effect" may still be potentially problematic if many children are unaware that the adults who reared them are not their biological parents. A second potential problem is sample selection, in the sense that the mortality experience of nonparents, or of parents whose children have all died, is not represented. Biases could thus arise if parents' survival probabilities are systematically related to their number of living children. Timaeus (1991) argues this effect appears to be small empirically. In terms of reliability, demographer's views on the value of the orphanhood method as a way of estimating adult mortality have varied over time (Timaeus 1991). Blacker (1977) compared some of the early results of the orphanhood method with those from other sources and concluded that the orphanhood method was a cheap and simple way of obtaining a rough index of adult mortality.

New Facts About Poverty and Adult Mortality

It is worth noting from the outset that any empirical study of the relationship between poverty and adult mortality in low-income countries would expect to be plagued by issues of measurement error. Measurement error in how daily per capita consumption or expenditures are constructed, or in the per capita equivalence scales used to differentiate children and adults, should bias the authors against finding support for a poverty-mortality gradient. With this caveat in mind, the author's empirical findings are even more striking.

Based on three panel data sets from Indonesia, Vietnam, and Udaipur (India), we learn that, across all age groups of adults, the extremely poor (those who live at less than one dollar per day) experience substantially higher adult mortality than those less poor who survive at a higher level of consumption (between six and ten dollars per day). Moreover, in all three countries the differential death rate between the extremely poor and the non-poor is largest in magnitude for the oldest of the poor. As noted by the authors, this empirical regularity in the data is especially striking since if the poor are more likely than the non-poor to die at any given age, the surviving old-age poor could have been expected to have been selected for having relatively good health. In terms of more general health measures, older poorer persons are weaker in Udaipur, but this pattern does not appear to hold in the Indonesian data.

As the authors are careful to note, these relationships may or may not reflect a causal association between poverty and health, though they, like us, are tempted to interpret their results as providing at least suggestive evidence of a causal association running in the direction from poverty to health. A principal threat to this causal interpretation of their results is the possibility that adverse health shocks in the past made people sick, destroyed health capital, and compromised their ability to acquire new human capital.

Using Adult Mortality Data to Learn About Health and Well-Being

Banerjee and Duflo's chapter motivates several lines of future research—both through further investigating the particular stylized facts their chapter generates, and through applying the measure of adult mortality they utilize to other areas of economic research.

As long as one believes that at least some portion of this observed correlation is explained by the direction flowing from poverty to health, the results motivate research into the channels that might give rise to this relationship. What is it about extreme poverty that makes it so lethal? Is it behaviors, poor nutrition, an inability to access appropriate medical care, or neighborhood characteristics such as environmental pollution that kill? Is it poverty per se that kills, or is extreme poverty a marker for extremely low rank in the socioeconomic distribution? In other words, would we expect exogenous increases in income to actually improve health? Work by David Cutler, Angus Deaton, and James Smith, among others, has argued that the causal effect of income per se on health may not be as strong as is often argued (see, e.g., Cutler, Deaton, and Lleras-Muney 2006; Smith 1999). Case and Deaton (2008) note that even for countries that have yet to transcend the "epidemiological transition," changes in income are not particularly predictive of improvements in health. One could read these arguments as suggesting that direct cash-transfer programs may not improve health or reduce mortality for those in extreme poverty. But this conclusion would likely be premature: while it is possible that the direct effect of income on health is small even at low levels of income, it is still not known if the relationship is flat at *extremely* low levels of expenditures such as living under a dollar a day—and it is this portion of the distribution that is the focus of Banerjee and Duflo's analysis. Moreover, while the perceived link between income or expenditures and mortality may be weak at the population level, this relationship may exhibit considerable heterogeneity by age, as the elderly may potentially be better able to utilize resources that are made available to them.

Fortunately for researchers interested in these questions, a number of data sets exist that include the types of orphanhood measures utilized by Banerjee and Duflo. If combined with other sources of variation in incomes, we may start to learn more about the precise mechanisms by which extreme poverty kills. The collection of orphanhood measures began in low-income countries in the mid-1960s (see Timaeus [1991] for a discussion), and these types of questions have since been included in several standard surveys including World Fertility Surveys, the World Bank's Living Standards Measurement Study (LSMS) surveys (as utilized by Banerjee and Duflo in their chapter), and in many Demographic and Health (DHS) surveys. The availability of these measures over a relatively long time period offers the potential for these measures to be utilized to construct retrospective studies, potentially in combination with useful natural experiments. For example, studies analogous to Adriana Lleras-Muney's work (2005) using compulsory education laws to study the effect of education on mortality in the United States could be extended to analyze the relationship between education and mortality in low-income countries—perhaps in combination with some natural experiments such as the Indonesian school expansion program analyzed by Duflo (2001). Studies analogous to Stephen Snyder and William Evans' work (2006) using the U.S. social security "notch" to study the effect of income on mortality in the United States could be extended to analyze the relationship between income and mortality in low-income countries—again, potentially in combination with natural experiments such as the South African pension program analyzed by Duflo (2000) and others, or the Indian social banking experiment analyzed by Burgess and Pande (2005). Issues of statistical power may plague researchers' abilities to utilize these adult mortality measures in otherwise interesting contexts, but the potential for interesting studies seems promising.

Beyond utilizing existing surveys to analyze natural experiments retrospectively, these measures could also be utilized in combination with prospective randomized experiments that vary various dimensions of resources available to the extremely poor. Banerjee and Duflo have been tireless pioneers in this area, and through their efforts we have become very optimistic about the ability of experiments to disentangle the relative importance of different causal channels. For both natural and randomized experiments, the resulting estimates may of course be context dependent—what appears to affect mortality among the elderly poor in rural Udaipur may not have the same effects in a Sao Paulo slum—but these measures as well as direct mortality measures (which presumably could be collected in the context of a prospective randomized experiment) could nonetheless begin to paint a picture of the causes and effects of this poverty-adult mortality gradient in low-income countries. Such evidence would ideally shed light on interventions, which could reduce the incidence of avoidable adult deaths in low-income countries.

References

Banerjee, A., and E. Duflo. 2007. The economic lives of the poor. *Journal of Economic Perspectives* 21 (1): 141–67.

Blacker, J. 1977. The estimation of adult mortality in Africa from data on orphanhood. *Population Studies* 31 (1): 107–28.

Bourguignon, F., and C. Morrisson. 2002. Inequality among world citizens: 1820–1992. *American Economic Review* 92 (4): 727–44.

Brass, W., and K. Hill. 1973. Estimating adult mortality from orphanhood. *International Population Conference Liege 1973* 3:111–23.

Burgess, R., and R. Pande. 2005. Do rural banks matter? Evidence from the Indian social banking experiment. *American Economic Review* 95 (3): 780–95.

Case, A., and A. Deaton. 2008. Health and well-being in Udaipur and South Africa. In *Developments in the economics of aging,* ed. D. Wise, 317–58.

Cutler, D., A. Deaton, and A. Lleras-Muney. 2006. The determinants of mortality. *Journal of Economic Perspectives* 20 (3): 97–120.

Duflo, E. 2000. Child health and household resources: Evidence from the South African old-age pension program. *American Economic Review Papers & Proceedings* 90 (2): 393–98.

———. 2001. Schooling and labor market consequences of school construction in Indonesia: Evidence from an unusual policy experiment. *American Economic Review* 91 (4): 795–813.

Hill, K., Y. Choi, and I. Timaeus. 2005. Unconvential approaches to mortality estimation. *Demographic Research* 13 (12): 281–300.

Hill, K., and J. Trussell. 1977. Further developments in indirect mortality estimation. *Population Studies* 31 (2): 313–34.

Lleras-Muney, A. 2005. The relationship between education and adult mortality in the United States. *Review of Economics and Statistics* 72 (1): 189–221.

Sala-i-Martin, X. 2006. The world distribution of income: Falling poverty and . . . convergence, period. *Quarterly Journal of Economics* 121 (2): 351–97.

Smith, J. 1999. Health bodies and thick wallets: The dual relation between health and economic status. *Journal of Economic Perspectives* 13 (2): 145–66.

Snyder, S., and W. Evans. 2006. The effect of income on mortality: Evidence from the social security notch. *Review of Economics and Statistics* 88 (3): 482–95.

Timaeus, I. 1991. Measurement of adult mortality in less developed countries: A comparative review. *Population Index* 57 (4): 552–68.

What's Past Is Prologue
The Impact of Early Life
Health and Circumstance
on Health in Old Age

Anne Case

8.1 Introduction

Recent research finds that early life health has effects on health and economic circumstance from childhood through middle age. Controlling for parental income, education, and social class, this research finds that members of the 1958 and 1970 British birth cohorts who experienced poor health in childhood have significantly lower educational attainment, poorer health, and lower social status as adults. Childhood health and circumstance work both through their impact on initial adult health and economic status, and through the continuing direct effect of prenatal and childhood health in middle age (Case, Fertig, and Paxson 2005). Using height as a marker of childhood health and environment, recent research has also documented a strong and robust relationship between height and cognitive ability both in childhood and adulthood (Abbot et al. 1998; Case and Paxson 2008; Richards and Wadsworth 2004).

The impact of the uterine environment on health in middle age has been examined in a series of papers. (See, for example, Barker [1992]; Barker [1995]; Ravelli et al. [1998].) Many of these conclude that a poor uterine environment leaves individuals at risk for diabetes and cardiovascular dis-

Anne Case is the Alexander Stewart 1886 Professor of Economics and Public Affairs and a Professor of Economics and Public Affairs at the Woodrow Wilson School of Public and International Affairs and the Economics Department at Princeton University, and a research associate of the National Bureau of Economic Research.

This work was funded by NIA grant P01AG005842 and R01 AG20275-01. I thank David Cutler for suggesting the idea of looking at crops, and for sharing data on crop production in the early twentieth Century, and James P. Smith and participants at the NBER Aging Conference at the Boulders, 2007, for helpful comments. Lisa Vura-Weis provided expert research assistance.

ease in middle age, although others argue that there is little evidence that intrauterine health can explain chronic diseases in adulthood (Rasmussen 2001).

Less is known about the impact of early childhood environment on health in old age. In this chapter, we investigate the relationship between health and environment in early childhood and health and functioning in old age, using longitudinal data collected by the Health and Retirement Study (HRS). The HRS gives us an opportunity to document the lasting impact of early life environment on cohort members' quality of life, including self-reported health status, hypertension, difficulties with activities of daily living, and fine and gross motor skills.

We use two markers of health and early life environment. We document the extent to which height, as a measure of early life health and nutrition, is associated with more favorable outcomes in old age. We also investigate whether conditions that might have governed mother's nutrition while pregnant—such as the success of crop production while she was pregnant—are predictive of health in later life, and whether this marker of mother's nutrition can explain the association between height and health outcomes in old age. In addition, we examine the channels through which early life health and nutrition may affect health in later life, by introducing controls for educational attainment and occupational choice.

We find that height is protective of health in the HRS cohort. On average, taller men and women are significantly more likely to report themselves to be in better health, and are significantly less likely to report that a doctor has told them that they have hypertension. They report fewer difficulties with activities of daily living (ADLs), and better fine motor skills. Height appears to become more protective against hypertension, ADLs, and loss of fine motor skills as cohort members age, which is when cohort members face the largest risk of poor outcomes.

We find that height is predicted by the success of the corn crop in the year before birth, and that, taken together, height and corn production both have large and significant effects on HRS cohort member's health in old age. Corn production, which we argue is a broad marker for mother's nutrition, is protective against hypertension and the loss of fine motor skills and large muscle group skills. Corn production also appears to protect cohort members' abilities to carry out activities of daily living. For some markers of health in old age, the association between height and health can be explained by the association between height, education, and occupation. For other markers, we find a continued role for childhood conditions, even with controls for economic outcomes in adulthood.

We will proceed as follows. Section 8.2 presents our conceptual framework. Section 8.3 introduces the data we use on HRS cohort members, and documents the extent to which height is associated with more positive health outcomes in the cohort. Section 8.4 presents evidence that height is significantly correlated with greater educational attainment and higher status occupational choice. Section 8.5 documents the extent to which height and corn production—both markers of early life environment—are associated with better health outcomes for cohort members in later life, and examines the extent to which this can be explained by the association between height and early life nutrition on one hand, and educational and occupational outcomes on the other.

8.2   Conceptual Framework

Our interest in height and crop production stems from the information they carry about health and nutrition in early life, which may affect individuals throughout their lives. The model we use is based on a life course framework, which emphasizes the extent to which health in childhood has lasting effects on adult health—directly, through the impact of health itself, and indirectly, by restricting or enhancing educational attainment and life chances (Kuh and Wadsworth 1993; Case, Fertig, and Paxson 2005).

To illustrate ideas, we divide the life course into three time periods: early childhood (c), young adulthood (y), and older adulthood (a). Early childhood is the period in which height and childhood health are determined; young adulthood is the period when education is completed and an occupation is chosen; and older adulthood is the period under study here, in which HRS cohort members are age fifty and above. We express our measures of health in older adulthood (H_a) as a linear function of indicators of socioeconomic status in young adulthood, here educational attainment and occupational choice (e_y), and a vector of prenatal and childhood characteristics (C), and here adult height and crop production in the cohort member's geographical division in the year prior to the cohort member's birth:

$$(1) \qquad H_a = \alpha_0 + e_y \alpha_e + C \alpha_C + \varepsilon_a.$$

Indicators of socioeconomic status in young adulthood are assumed to be functions of prenatal and childhood characteristics:

$$(2) \qquad e_y = \gamma_{0e} + C \gamma_e + v_y.$$

Substitution of (2) into (1) yields reduced form equations for health in later adulthood.

Parameter estimates from (1) shed light on several issues. Estimates of α_C provide information on whether childhood circumstances have direct effects on outcomes in later adulthood, even controlling for earlier adult outcomes, or whether the effects of childhood circumstances in later adulthood work through their effects on outcomes in younger adulthood. The effects of early life health may only become apparent at older age (Barker 1992, 1995).

Alternatively, childhood circumstances may affect adult outcomes through their effects on educational attainment and social status early in adulthood. Under this alternative, α_C will be zero.

Estimates from (1) and (2) also provide information on the relationship between economic status and health in young and older adulthood. The cross effect of socioeconomic status on future health, α_e, is of particular in-terest. The large literature on the gradient—the positive association between health and economic status—contains a variety of hypotheses on how economic status affects health, and vice versa, with little consensus on which direction is more important (Smith 1999). Pathway models stress the idea that status in young adulthood influences future health (i.e., α_e nonzero), largely through the effects of low economic status on psychosocial stress (Marmot et al. 1991). This literature argues that childhood circumstance and health in early adulthood are generally not qualitatively as important as adult socioeconomic status in determining adult health (i.e., that α_C is relatively less important than α_e). Brunner et al. (1999) state, for example, that "whatever the salient features of the adult socioeconomic environment may be, it seems they are equally or more important than circumstances in childhood" (762) in determining cardiovascular risk among British civil servants.

We use estimates of (1) and (2) to examine which implications of these models find support in the HRS. Some important omissions must be highlighted before we begin. In principle, (1) could also include measures of health in early adulthood. The mechanisms through which early life health and circumstance affect health in old age may work through their effects on health in early adulthood. Unfortunately, markers for early adult health are limited in the HRS. To the extent that we find height and crop production are significant in (1), they may be working through their effects on health in middle life. We are not able to speak to that here. However, we are still able to test whether the *only* channels through which childhood affects health later in life is through socioeconomic status in middle age—that is, whether coefficients on childhood health (α_C) become insignificant when we control for education and occupation. In addition, we have limited information on the socioeconomic status of the households in which HRS cohort members were raised. To the extent that we find crop production is a significant predictor of health outcomes in old age, it may be that crop production affects household resources in childhood, and that household socioeconomic status is the channel through which early life circumstance affects health in old age. We discuss this later, and argue that the timing of crop production is consistent with mother's nutrition (although we certainly cannot rule out other channels).

The parameter estimates of (1) and (2) will be unbiased only under mean independence between the error term in (1) and e_y and C—that is, $E[\varepsilon_a | e_y, C]$ = 0. There are situations under which conditional mean independence may not hold. There may be individual heterogeneity that is not measured by *C*—for example, individuals may have unobserved characteristics that result in both poor health and low socioeconomic status throughout life. Unfortunately, solutions to this problem either require a set of valid instruments for economic status and health at younger ages, or require fixed effect estimation, which in turn requires long panels of data. Neither approach is available to us here (even if we were not skeptical of the ability of instrumental variables to solve these problems, or skeptical of the assumption that coefficients are constant over the life course, which is necessary for the fixed effect analysis).

In the next section, we introduce the HRS data that we use in our analysis, and document the associations between adult height and later life health outcomes that we find in these data. We then turn to our econometric analysis and estimates of equations (1) and (2).

8.3   Height and Health in the HRS Cohort

Our analysis relies on the University of Michigan's longitudinal Health and Retirement Study (HRS), sponsored by the National Institute on Aging. Every two years, the HRS interviews a cohort of men and women in the United States over the age of fifty, in order to gain a better understanding of the physical and mental health, quality of life, and life circumstances of older Americans. (See http://hrsonline.isr.umich.edu for details.) Because some of the health indicators we are interested in were collected for the whole cohort only beginning in wave 3 of the study (1996), we will restrict our analysis to waves 3 to 7 (1996 to 2004). To reduce heterogeneity, we further restrict our analysis to non-Hispanic white men and women ages fifty and above in the HRS for whom no proxy respondent was used.

Summary statistics for this cohort are presented in table 8.1, where we report means of variables of interest for cohort members, in the first and last waves in which they are observed in our sample. Not all cohort members are observed in each wave from waves 3 to 7, and we do not restrict our sample to those who are. For table 8.1 only, the sample is restricted to individuals with nonzero sample weight in their first and last wave. Weighted and unweighted means are very similar, but throughout the analysis we will present results that have been sample weighted.

We examine six broad measures of health and functional limitations that are available in each wave of the HRS from waves 3 to 7. These measures are chosen because of their importance as markers of health, and because they are asked in a manner that makes them comparable across waves. All health measures are constructed such that a higher number can be interpreted as a worse health outcome. *Self-reported health status* is reported in each wave as 1 = excellent, 2 = very good, 3 = good, 4 = fair, 5 = poor. *Hypertension* is an indicator variable that the cohort members report that a doctor has

Table 8.1   **Summary statistics for HRS cohort members**

	Men		Women	
	First	Last	First	Last
Health outcomes and functional limitations				
Self-reported health status	2.57	2.80	2.60	2.85
Hypertension	0.38	0.51	0.38	0.53
Difficulties with activities of daily living	0.17	0.25	0.22	0.34
Large muscle group index	0.83	1.02	1.22	1.42
Fine motor skills	0.11	0.16	0.13	0.19
Gross motor skills	0.25	0.40	0.40	0.62
Childhood and early adult variables				
Height in inches	70.1	70.1	64.1	64.1
Corn production (billions of bushels)	0.38	0.37	0.36	0.36
Completed years of schooling	13.1	13.2	12.6	12.7
White-collar occupation in longest-held job	0.42	0.44	0.50	0.53
Geographic birthplace				
New England	0.07	0.07	0.07	0.07
Mid Atlantic	0.20	0.20	0.19	0.19
East North Central	0.23	0.23	0.22	0.22
West North Central	0.14	0.14	0.13	0.13
South Atlantic	0.12	0.12	0.13	0.13
East South Central	0.07	0.07	0.08	0.08
West South Central	0.08	0.08	0.09	0.09
Mountain	0.03	0.03	0.03	0.03
Pacific	0.06	0.06	0.06	0.06
Number of observations	6,090	6,090	7,439	7,439

Notes: Statistics are presented for the first and last observation (wave) in which the cohort member was observed. Sample is restricted to non-hispanic white men and women ages fifty and above, observed in waves 3, 4, 5, 6, and/or 7. All means are weighted using sample weights. For table 8.1 only, the sample is also restricted to individuals with nonzero sample weight in their first and last observation.

ever told them that they have high blood pressure or hypertension. Difficulties with *activities of daily living* (*ADLs*) are the sum of indicators for whether the cohort member reports difficulty bathing, eating, dressing, walking across a room, or getting out of bed. The *large muscle group* index is constructed as the sum of indicators of difficulty with four activities: sitting for two hours; getting up from a chair; stooping or kneeling or crouching; and pushing or pulling a large object. The *fine motor skills* index is constructed as the sum of indicators of difficulty picking up a dime, dressing, and eating, and the *gross motor skills* index as the sum of indicators of difficulty walking one block, walking across the room, climbing a flight of stairs, and bathing.

That members of the HRS cohort experience decline in these health indicators can be seen by comparing results between individuals' first reports and their last. The prevalence of hypertension, for example, increases from

40 to 50 percent over this period (generally 1996 to 2004) for both men and women. Women start, on average, from a worse health position on all dimensions. However, the declines experienced between the waves are quite similar for men and women.

Our first measure of childhood health and early life nutrition is adult height in inches, which is self-reported in the HRS. We present average heights of cohort members, by geographic region (division) of birth in figure 8.1. On average, men and women born in New England are almost an inch shorter than those born in the Pacific and Mountain states. The HRS cohort members born in later years are taller on average than those born in earlier years, as can be seen in nonparametric regression results presented in figure 8.2 for men and women born in New England and in the Pacific and Mountain states.

Our second measure of early-life nutrition is corn production in the cohort member's geographic birth place (division), in the year prior to his or her birth. These were drawn from the U.S. Department of Agriculture's National Agricultural Statistics Service. The HRS releases information on cohort members' geographic division of birth, and we have assigned to each

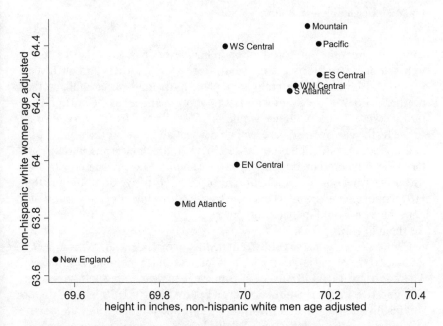

Fig. 8.1   Average heights in inches for women and men by geographic division

Notes: Non-hispanic white adult respondents in the HRS, age adjusted and weighted. States are grouped by division: New England: CT, ME, MA, NH, RI, VT; Mid Atlantic: NJ, NY, PA; East-North Central: IN, IL, MI, OH, WI; West-North Central: IA, KS, MN, MO, NE, ND, SD; South Atlantic: DE, DC, FL, GA, MD, NC, SC, VA, WV; East-South Central: AL, KY, MS, TN; West-South Central: AR, LA, OK, TX; Mountain: AZ, CO, ID, NM, MT, UT, NV, WY; Pacific: CA, OR, WA.

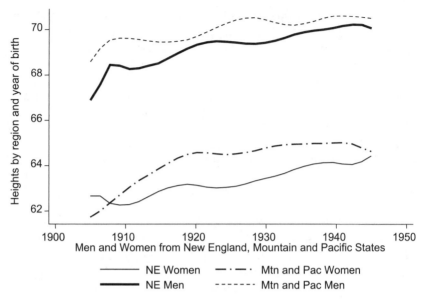

Fig. 8.2 Heights by year of birth

cohort member the corn production in his or her division in the year prior to his or her birth. We chose the year prior to birth, rather than birth year, because corn harvests generally take place in the mid- to late-fall, so that mothers who were pregnant with HRS cohort members in the fall and winter following the corn harvest would be most affected by the harvest prior to the birth year. We also have available wheat and oats production by year and division. Production is correlated between the three crops, and the pattern of results presented following is very similar to what we find when we use either wheat or oat production in place of corn. We do not argue that HRS cohort members' mothers were eating corn while pregnant, but that a good harvest would increase the probability of abundant nutritious foods for them to choose from.

Figure 8.3 presents harvests from the East North Central division, which includes three of the largest "corn belt" states (Ohio, Indiana, and Illinois). There is a great deal of variation from year to year in bushels harvested. The negative trend in production until approximately 1930 may be due to soil fertility depletion, and the upturn in production that followed may be attributable to the introduction of hybrid seeds and greater (and better) use of fertilizer (Bray and Watkins 1964; Crickman 1946). Corn production is sensitive to the amount of heat and rain a region receives during the growing season, and the low production in the early 1930s may also be attributable to years of severe drought (Crickman 1946). Production in the corn belt is an order of magnitude larger than that in many other divisions. In our regres-

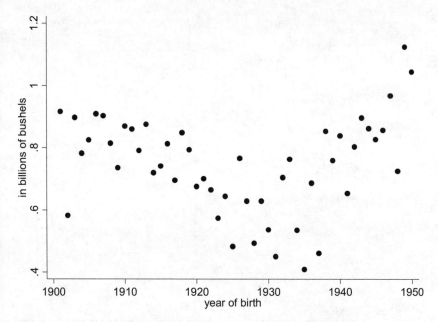

Fig. 8.3   **Corn production in the East North Central Division by year**

sion analysis, we will include a complete set of division indicator variables, so that the impact of corn production in any given year is relative to the mean for that division.

Our measures of socioeconomic status in young adulthood are years of completed schooling and an indicator that the longest held job was a white-collar job (here defined as professional, managerial, sales, clerical, or administrative support).

8.3.1   Health and Functional Status

Figure 8.4 presents a first look at the relationship between height, health, and functional status in the HRS cohort. Figures in the left-hand column present means of the prevalence of hypertension, ADLs, the gross motor skill index, the fine motor skill index, and the large muscle index, by five-year age categories from fifty to fifty-five to ninety-five to one hundred. There is physical decline between each age group, although the patterns vary: reports of hypertension increase markedly until age seventy-five and then level off, for example, while reports of difficulties with activities of daily living are relatively flat until age seventy, and then increase rapidly with age after that point.

Figures in the right-hand column are the coefficients on age category indicators interacted with height, from sample-weighted ordinary least squares (OLS) regressions that include a complete set of age-category indi-

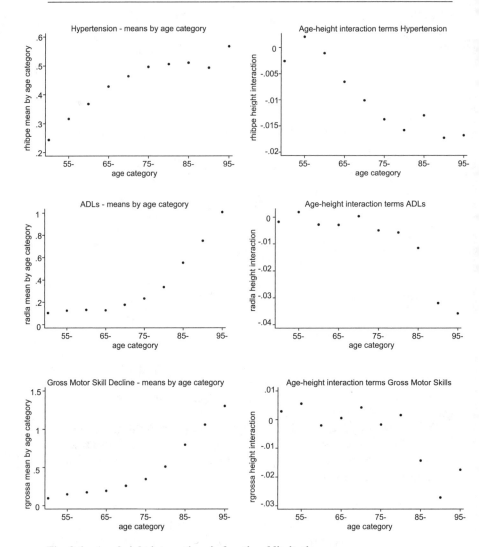

Fig. 8.4   Age-height interactions in functional limitations

cators, wave indicators, and a sex indicator. We find that height is protective against hypertension, ADLs, and loss of gross and fine motor skills. Height becomes protective when cohort members' risk of poor health outcomes becomes elevated. For example, the height-age indicator interaction terms become successively more negative from age category fifty-five to sixty to age category eighty to eighty-five. After that point risk of hypertension has leveled off, and the protection offered by height levels off as well. Similarly, with respect to ADLs, height offers no protection before the age at which

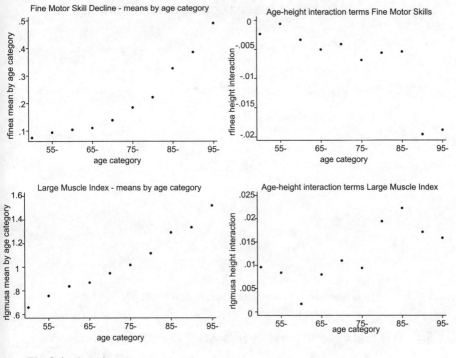

Fig. 8.4   (cont.)

individuals' risk of difficulties becomes nontrivial, after which point the height-age category interaction terms become negative and significant.

For all but one health measure, height appears to be protective, and more so at older ages. One category in which height is not protective is for the large muscle group index. Within this group of tasks, taller people report less difficulty pushing or pulling large objects, and no more or less difficulty than shorter people in sitting for two hours. However, they have significantly greater difficulty stooping, and getting out of a chair.

Figure 8.5 examines the extent to which height is protective of self-reported health status. In all age categories, taller people report better health (a lower number is a better score). The height-age interactions are significant for age categories from fifty to fifty-five through seventy-five to eighty. Beyond that point, there is no difference on average between taller and shorter adults in their self-assessed health. This may reflect selection in who lives past age eighty, a point we may return to in future research.

In summary, height predicts better health and fewer functional limitations in old age along a number of dimensions. We turn now to mechanisms through which height might protect health.

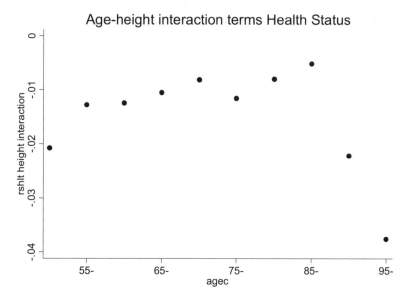

Fig. 8.5   Age-height interactions in self-reported health status

8.4   Health and Nutrition as Determinants of Education and Occupation

In this section, we examine the relationship between childhood conditions, as measured by height and corn production, and outcomes in adulthood. Table 8.2 presents OLS regression results for the HRS cohort, with one observation for each cohort member. We find a positive and significant association between corn production and adult height. On average, a one-standard deviation increase in corn production (.3895) is associated with a one-fifth of an inch increase in final adult height (.20 inches). This result is robust to estimating the height equation separately by division. For example, when estimated separately, we find that a one-standard deviation increase in corn production in East North Central leads to a (.14) inch increase in height there, (.20) in West North Central, (.36) in the Mountain division, and (.24) in the Pacific division, and that the differences between these estimates are not statistically significant.

Height is associated with increased years of education. The association between height and years of schooling is large, and robust to many changes in specification. When estimated separately by sex, results for both men and women show that a one inch increase in height is associated with a 0.10 to 0.12 increase in years of completed schooling, on average. The same is true when we run regressions separately by division (not reported in table 8.2). We find no significant relationship between corn production and years of completed schooling, with or without controls for height—so that although

Table 8.2   The relationship between early life circumstances, education, and occupation

	Dependent variable		
	Height in inches	Years of education	= 1 if longest-held job was in a white-collar occupation
Height in inches	—	.1168	.0093
		(.0085)	(.0015)
Corn production	.5053	−.0434	−.0808
	(.1867)	(.1860)	(.0332)
Female	−5.877	.3601	.1693
	(0.044)	(.0666)	(.0119)
Number of observations	13,775	13,775	13,775

Notes: Coefficients presented from OLS regressions (standard errors in parentheses). Observations weighted using sampling weights. Also included were a complete set of year of birth indicators by five year categories, and a complete set of division of birth indicator variables.

corn production predicts height, it cannot explain any of the association between height and educational attainment.

Height is also positively and significantly associated with respondents' reports that their longest held job was a white-collar job. This is again true for men and women when estimation is carried out by sex, and true when estimation is carried out division by division. Individuals born in years following a bumper corn year in their division are significantly less likely to report white-collar occupations. However, this result is not robust to estimating the white-collar regression separately by division. In no division is the association between corn production in the year before birth significantly associated with white-collar occupations later in life.

In summary, higher corn production in the year prior to birth is associated with greater adult height, and greater adult height is associated with both greater years of schooling and job holding in white-collar occupations. We turn next to estimate the extent to which these earlier life-course outcomes affect health in old age.

8.5   Health and Functional Limitation in Old Age

Table 8.3 presents OLS regression results for the health and functional limitation outcomes discussed before, where each health measure is regressed on height and corn production, with a complete set of indicator variables for cohort members' age, division of birth, sex, and survey wave. Given the results presented in figure 8.4, we allow the impact of height and corn to change with age. There are many possible ways to add flexibility to the impact of height and nutrition. Here, we add interaction terms of height

Table 8.3   **The impact of early life circumstance on health and functional limitations**

	Self-reported health		Hypertension	
Height in inches	−.0141	−.0008	−.0014	.0001
	(.0039)	(.0037)	(.0018)	(.0018)
Height × older	.0037	.0006	−.0115	−.0125
	(.0042)	(.0041)	(.0020)	(.0021)
Corn production (B bushels)	.0021	−.0050	−.0818	−.0815
	(.0694)	(.0681)	(.0345)	(.0346)
Corn production × older	−.0289	−.0203	−.0015	−.0002
	(.0431)	(.0419)	(.0219)	(.0219)
Years of education		−.1059		−.0135
		(.0047)		(.0023)
Education × older		.0305		.0089
		(.0065)		(.0033)
White-collar occupation		−.1930		−.0002
		(.0236)		(.0116)
White-collar × older		.1357		−.0045
		(.0363)		(.0184)
Number of observations	56,831	56,831	56,821	56,821

	Activities of daily living		Fine motor skills	
Height in inches	−.0007	.0025	−.0027	−.0009
	(.0025)	(.0025)	(.0014)	(.0014)
Height × older	−.0046	−.0044	−.0037	−.0037
	(.0026)	(.0026)	(.0016)	(.0016)
Corn production (B bushels)	−.0097	−.0148	.0121	.0087
	(.0382)	(.0380)	(.0226)	(.0227)
Corn production × older	−.0437	−.0437	−.0343	−.0346
	(.0270)	(.0270)	(.0165)	(.0165)
Years of education		−.0250		−.0137
		(.0031)		(.0018)
Education × older		−.0004		.0018
		(.0047)		(.0027)
White-collar occupation		−.0648		−.0324
		(.0134)		(.0076)
White-collar × older		.0217		−.0021
		(.0222)		(.0136)
Number of observations	56,829	56,829	56,829	56,829

	Gross motor skills		Large muscle group index	
Height in inches	.0020	.0080	.0062	.0170
	(.0032)	(.0032)	(.0044)	(.0043)
Height × older	−.0038	−.0042	.0055	.0013
	(.0035)	(.0034)	(.0046)	(.0046)
Corn production (B bushels)	−.0532	−.0604	−.1457	−.1510
	(.0517)	(.0513)	(.0776)	(.0777)
Corn production × older	−.0031	−.0020	.0350	.0447
	(.0360)	(.0359)	(.0482)	(.0479)

Table 8.3   (continued)

	Gross motor skills		Large muscle group index	
Years of education		−.0454		−.0870
		(.0041)		(.0056)
Education × older		.0052		.0499
		(.0061)		(.0074)
White-collar occupation		−.0979		−.1659
		(.0177)		(.0273)
White-collar × older		.0343		.0944
		(.0297)		(.0410)
Number of observations	56,830	56,830	56,821	56,821

Notes: OLS regression coefficients reported (with standard errors in parentheses). Observations weighted using sampling weights. Standard errors allow for correlation in the unobservables for observations for the same person. Included in all regressions are an indicator of sex, and a complete set of age indicator variables, indicators for the survey wave, and indicators for the cohort member's geographical division of birth.

and corn production with indicator variables that the cohort member's age is greater than seventy.

8.5.1   Self-Reported Health Status

The first set of results in table 8.3 report on self-reported health status. Taller cohort members report better health and, consistent with the results in figure 8.5, we find no change with age in the impact of height on self-reported health. Height is strongly predictive of education and occupation, and once we add controls for education and occupation, there is no longer a significant correlation between height and self-reported health. In regressions estimated (results not shown in table 8.3), we find it is the inclusion of a control for years of completed schooling that renders height insignificant. Adding indicators for white-collar occupation does not change the size or significance of the height variables. We interpret these results as being consistent with a model in which the effect of height on self-assessed health works through its effect on education.

On average, the impact of education and occupation on self-reported health is less pronounced for cohort members older than seventy. The interaction terms between education and an indicator for being older than seventy, and the interaction term between white-collar occupation and age above seventy, are both positive and significant. Neither interaction term entirely offsets the protective effects of greater education or having worked in a white-collar job, but their effects are dampened at oldest ages.

8.5.2   Hypertension

Both height and corn production are negatively and significantly related to the probability of reporting hypertension. The effect for height appears at older ages (above age seventy), and is robust to the inclusion of controls for educational attainment and occupation. In contrast, the effect for corn production is equally strong at younger and older ages, and is also robust to the inclusion of other controls.

Education is significantly correlated with hypertension, although like height, its association is weaker above age seventy. Having worked in a white-collar occupation is not associated with hypertension, given controls for age, division of birth, and sex. Using a set of occupational categories (estimated but not reported in table 8.3) we also find that occupation does not change the large and significant relationship between height, corn production, and hypertension. This is inconsistent with hypotheses generated from pathway models that suggest early-life environment only matters through its impact on early adult outcomes (such as occupational choice).

8.5.3   Activities of Daily Living and Fine Motor Skills

Height and nutrition are protective against decline in both ADLs and fine motor skills above age seventy. The ADL index increases on average by 0.01 with each year of age, the fine motor skill index by 0.006. Using this metric, an extra inch of height translates into a rolling-back of the age clock by approximately half a year. The impact of height and nutrition on these health measures are unchanged by the inclusion of education and occupation variables, which themselves have large, significant effects on both indexes at all ages. These results suggest that, whatever the mechanisms are that lead height and corn production to affect ADLs and fine motor skills at older ages, they are not working through education or occupational choice.

8.5.4   Gross Motor Skills and Large Muscle Group Indexes

Neither height nor corn production are significantly associated with the gross motor skill index, while education and white-collar occupations are protective for both older and younger HRS cohort members.

Consistent with figure 8.4, we find height increases the large muscle group index. Taken together, the coefficients on height and height interacted with being an older cohort member are jointly significant (p-value = 0.03) in the second to the last column of table 8.3. We find (results not shown) that this is due to taller cohort members reporting more difficulty crouching or stooping, and more difficulty getting out of a chair. In contrast, corn production is negatively and significantly associated with the large muscle group index, and has its largest effect on reporting being able to push or pull a large object. We find education and white-collar occupation protective for all cohort members, but less so at older ages.

8.6   Discussion

Results presented here are consistent with early life environment having lifelong effects on health. Here, we conclude with three thoughts.

We interpreted corn production in the year prior to birth to be a marker for mothers' nutrition while pregnant. There are other, quite different, interpretations. Crop production in the fall prior to birth, for example, may be a marker for higher socioeconomic status around the time of the child's birth, which may have independent effects on children's outcomes. (Perhaps the house was better heated, for example, or there was money to see a doctor when needed.) However, the timing of the impact of crop production is consistent with the effect working through maternal nutrition. When cohort members are assigned the crop production in the year of their birth (rather than the year prior to birth), we find no effect of corn production on reports of hypertension, and no effect on ADLs. If, as has been argued by Barker (2004), hypertension is especially sensitive to nutrition in utero, then the sensitivity of hypertension to crop production in the year prior to birth may point to crop production being a marker for nutrition.

At oldest ages, it is important to recognize the role that selective mortality may play in the estimation. Less well educated people who survive to age eighty-five may be a more select group than better educated people who survive to that age, for example. Finally, the crop production data by state and year of birth can be matched to several data sets that contain information on state of birth and current (adult) health. It will be useful analyze additional data—both as a cross-check for results here and to investigate additional channels through which early life environment affects adults in older age.

References

Abbott, R. D., L. R. White, G. W. Ross, H. Petrovitch, K. H. Masaki, D. A. Snowdon, and J. D. Curb. 1998. Height as a marker of childhood development and late-life cognitive function: The Honolulu-Asia aging study. *Pediatrics* 102 (3): 602–9.

Barker, D. J. P. 1992. The fetal origins of diseases of old age. *European Journal of Clinical Nutrition* 46 (Supplement 3): S3–9.

———. 1995. Fetal origins of coronary heart disease. *British Medical Journal* 311 (6998): 171–74.

———. 2004. The developmental origins of well-being. *Philosophical Transactions of the Royal Society B* 359:1359–66.

Bray, J. O., and P. Watkins. 1964. Technical change in corn production in the United States, 1870–1960. *Journal of Farm Economics* 46 (4): 751–65.

Brunner, E., B. Shipley, D. Smith, and M. G. Marmot. 1999. When does cardiovascular risk start? Past and present socioeconomic circumstances and risk factors in adulthood. *Journal of Epidemiology and Community Health* 53 (12): 757–64.

Case, A., A. Fertig, and C. Paxson. 2005. The lasting impact of childhood health and circumstance. *Journal of Health Economics* 24 (2): 365–89.

Case, A., and C. Paxson. 2008. Stature and status: Height, ability, and labor market outcomes. *Journal of Political Economy* 116 (3): 499–532.

Crickman, C. W. 1946. Postwar agricultural problems in the corn belt. *Journal of Farm Economics* 28 (1): 243–60.

Kuh, D. J., and M. E. Wadsworth. 1993. Physical health status at 36 years in a British national birth cohort. *Social Science and Medicine* 37 (7): 905–16.

Marmot, M. G., G. D. Smith, S. Stansfeld, C. Patel, F. North, J. Head, I. White, E. Brunner, and A. Feeney. 1991. Health inequalities among British civil servants: The Whitehall II Study. *The Lancet* 337 (8754): 1387–93.

Rasmussen, K. M. 2001. The "fetal origins" hypothesis: Challenges and opportunities for maternal and child nutrition. *Annual Review of Nutrition* 21:73–95.

Ravelli, A. C. J., J. H. P. van der Meulen, R. P. J. Michels, C. Osmond, D. J. P. Barker, C. N. Hales, and O. P. Bleker. 1998. Glucose tolerance in adults after prenatal exposure to famine. *The Lancet* 351:173–77.

Richards, M., and M. E. J. Wadsworth. 2004. Long term effects of early adversity on cognitive function. *Archives of Disease in Childhood* 89:922–27.

Smith, J. P. 1999. Healthy bodies and thick wallets: The dual relationship between health and economic status. *Journal of Economic Perspectives* 13 (2): 145–66.

Comment   James P. Smith

In the last decade, economists have rediscovered health as a fundamental subject of research (Smith 1999). The subsequent research has been instructive and insightful. Not the least among these important contributions has involved documenting the importance of childhood health, not only on subsequent health outcomes during the adult years, but also, and in large part due to this life-course health linkage, on a series of economic outcomes as an adult. These outcomes have included final years of schooling, labor supply, income, and occupational status (Smith 2006). Anne Case with her colleagues has been among the most important contributors in this fast expanding literature with a series of papers documenting these linkages into the early and middle part of the adult years (see (Case, Lubotsky, and Paxson 2002) and (Case, Fertig, and Paxson 2005) for two examples). This chapter extends Anne Case's excellent recent work with Chris Paxson on height and childhood health into much older ages than she has done before by using the Health and Retirement Survey (HRS), which samples a population of Americans who are at least fifty years old (Case and Paxson 2006).

The central thesis of Case and Paxson is that very early childhood health is extremely important for subsequent adult health and SES outcomes. Measuring childhood health is difficult in itself, but combining it with data that measure these outcomes during the adult years is extremely challenging. The key insight of Case and Paxson is that adult height is a particularly

James P. Smith holds the Rand Chair in Labor Market and Demographic Studies at the RAND Corporation.

These comments were written with the support of grants from the National Institute on Aging and were delivered at a NBER conference on the Economics of Aging, Carefree, Arizona, May 2007.

good marker and summary statistic for these early childhood health and environment factors.

In this chapter, Anne Case extends this insight into an analysis of adults at much older ages—age fifty and beyond. Using the Health and Retirement Survey (HRS), Case relates adult height to several health outcomes, including prevalence of hypertension, general health status, measures of functional ability, and measures of muscular and motor skills. She mostly finds that additional height promotes better health in all these dimensions. In particular, and the one I will focus on in my comments, she finds that one is less likely to be hypertensive if you are tall. Generally speaking, Case also reports that these beneficial effects of height on adult health increase with age—that is, there is more of a health benefit to those extra vertical inches the older one is.

While these are important findings indeed, Anne Case is more scientifically ambitious than to leave it just as that. In the second part of her chapter, she takes it all back a step by asking what influences adult height in the first place (and by backward induction, what influences childhood health). She relates crop production in the state of birth around the time the mother was pregnant to these late life health outcomes to see if this helps explain the height to later life health pathway. She reports quite positive results—good crops in year before birth (that is, the time when the baby was in uterus and most sensitive to the nutritional environment of the mother) predicts additional height and also lowers the subsequent likelihood of hypertension.

This is a fine chapter with important new findings that represent a significant contribution to the literature. In my comments, I will raise three questions: (a) do these results generalize beyond hypertension and beyond the HRS; (b) why does the effect of height increase with age; and (c) how robust are the results on crop failures?

Do These Results Generalize Beyond Hypertension and the HRS?

In the original literature linking childhood and inter-uterine environments to subsequent childhood health, two types of diseases were prominent— heart disease (of which hypertension is an important precursor) and diabetes (see Barker 1997). While the HRS is an important data set and is in some ways ideal for what Anne is trying to test, it does have its limitations. In particular, HRS only measures diagnosed disease. A nontrivial segment of the population has a disease, but is not aware of it (Smith 2007). A data set that does measure both diagnosed as well as undiagnosed disease is the National Health and Nutrition Examination Survey (NHANES), where blood pressure is taken on respondents as well as blood samples so that undiagnosed diabetes can be detected. Heights are also measured more accurately than in HRS as respondents' heights (and weights) are actually measured directly in NHANES.

To answer these questions in this subsection of my comments, I apply the

Table 8C.1   Estimated effect of height in a probit model of diagnosed hypertension: NHANES 4, 1999–2002

	df/dx	z	df/dx	z
Overweight	.132	6.15	—	—
Obese	.296	13.9	—	—
Height	.003	0.88	.002	0.81

Note: Also controls for race, ethnicity, gender, age, education, smoking, and exercise.

type of analysis conducted by Anne Case to diabetes. Table 8C.1 contains estimates (partial derivates from a probit model) of the impact of height measured in centimeters on the prevalence of hypertension for a population aged twenty-five to seventy years old. These models were estimated using the combined NHANES for the years 1999 to 2002. The models also include the standard set of other covariates typically included in prevalence models (race, ethnicity, gender, age, smoking, exercise, being overweight, or being obese). But contrary to the thesis in Anne Case's chapter, the estimated effect of adult height is statistically insignificant. Height appears not to matter a whit.

My initial thought was that the contradiction between the results present in Anne Case's chapter and these results summarized in table 8C.1 was a consequence of the other controls included in the model. In particular, the diagnosed hypertensive prevalence model in table 8C.1 includes controls for excessive body mass index (BMI)—either being overweight (BMI between 25 and less than 30) or being obese (30 or more). The construction of BMI (weight in kilograms/[height in meters^2]) has height in the denominator so that the direct effects of height might be suppressed by these BMI controls. Moreover, there is a quite reasonable argument based on the perspective taken by Anne Case that controls for BMI are not appropriate. The reasoning might be that one of the extra benefits of additional height is that it makes one less likely to be obese as an adult.

The results summarized in the rightmost columns of table 8C.1, however, reject this conjecture. In those columns, I list the estimated impacts of height obtained when the overweight and obesity variables were removed from the model. The effect of height remains small and insignificantly different from zero.

But not all is lost. The models in table 8C.1 are prevalence models for diagnosed hypertension (as are the models in Anne Case's chapter). But what we really want to know are the predictors of total hypertension prevalence, including those with undiagnosed diabetes. Fortunately this is possible since the NHANES includes blood pressure tests on their respondents, allowing us to identify those with undiagnosed hypertension and thus total prevalence of hypertension. The models summarized in table 8C.2 are identical to those in table 8C.1 except that the outcome variable is now total hypertension prevalence instead of just diagnosed hypertension as in table 8C.1. Once again the estimated effects of height do not depend on whether or not the overweight and obesity models are included in the models. But height now has, as Anne's chapter argues that it should have, a statistically significant negative impact on the probability of being hypertensive.

The reason is more readily apparent from the probit model listed in table 8C.3. This is a model of the probability that one is an undiagnosed hypertensive given that one is hypertensive (either diagnosed or undiagnosed). Additional height significantly reduces the probability of being undiagnosed so that the diagnosed hypertensive model alone gives a biased perspective on the true impact of height on the probability of being a hypertensive. One of the benefits of additional height, apparently, is that you do the right thing and make certain that any disease you might have is diagnosed and presumably treated.

But not all is regained either. Tables 8C.4, 8C.5, and 8C.6 perform an identical analysis but this time examining diagnosed diabetes, total diabetes, and the probability of undiagnosed diabetes, respectively. In addition to hypertension, diabetes represents an excellent additional test of the early health impacts during childhood (using height as a marker) as it was one of the diseases mentioned by Barker (1997) as a prime candidate for early childhood illness being a marker for later life onset of disease. Just as was the case for hypertension, the effect of height is statistically insignificant for diagnosed diabetes (whether or not the controls for excess weight are included in the model (see table 8C.4). But this time we are not rescued by examining total diabetes prevalence since height remains statistically insig-

Table 8C.2   **Estimated effect of height in a probit model of total hypertension prevalence: NHANES 4, 1999–2002**

	df/dx	z	df/dx	z
Overweight	.135	6.35	—	—
Obese	.273	13.0	—	—
Height	−.006	1.92	−.006	1.91

Note: Also controls for race, ethnicity, gender, age, education, smoking, and exercise.

Table 8C.3   **Estimated effect of height in a probit model of the probability of undiagnosed hypertension: NHANES 4, 1999–2002**

	df/dx	z
Height	−.008	4.28

Note: Also controls for race, ethnicity, gender, age, education, smoking, and exercise.

Table 8C.4   **Estimated effect of height in a probit model of diagnosed diabetes: NHANES 4, 1999–2002**

	df/dx	z	df/dx	z
Overweight	.025	1.90	—	—
Obese	.084	6.22	—	—
Height	–.001	0.86	–.001	0.82

Note: Also controls for race, ethnicity, gender, age, education, smoking, and exercise.

Table 8C.5   **Estimated effect of height in a probit model of total diabetes prevalence: NHANES 4, 1999–2002**

	df/dx	z	df/dx	z
Overweight	.047	3.06	—	—
Obese	.138	8.68	—	—
Height	–.002	1.02	–.002	0.93

Note: Also controls for race, ethnicity, gender, age, education, smoking, and exercise.

Table 8C.6   **Estimated effect of height in a probit model of probability of undiagnosed diabetes: NHANES 4, 1999–2002**

	df/dx	z
Height	.0006	0.69

Note: Also controls for race, ethnicity, gender, age, education, smoking, and exercise.

nificant in that model as well (see table 8C.5). This is, of course, no surprise since height apparently has no effect of the probability of being an undiagnosed diabetic (table 8C.6).

Thus in the end this supplementary evidence from the NHANES is mixed. On the one hand, the data on hypertension, the same disease used by Anne Case, is quite supportive of her hypothesis. On the other hand, the data on diabetes, a disease that in at least my view should yield similar results, does not support the notion that height (a marker for early childhood health) is related to diabetes prevalence. More data and more diseases should be brought to bear on this problem since (as I said earlier) my intellectual sympathies are with the view that Anne Case puts forth so well in her chapter.

Why Does the Effect of Adult Height Grow with Age?

One of the more intriguing findings in this chapter is that the positive association of height with better adult health at older ages appears to become stronger with age. At first reading this result surprised me and my puzzlement remains unresolved. I can think of no really good reason why the pathways that Anne Case is talking about with the delayed effects of better child nutrition on hypertension should show up with greater force at age eighty when the prevalence rates for hypertension are quite high, for example, than at age fifty, when the incidence curve of hypertension is quite steep. In fact, I would have thought that the opposite result was more likely.

Let me offer a potential explanation. Adult heights are not completely fixed after the teenage years, as is often assumed. This assumption is fine for most of the adult life span, but becomes less tenable at really old ages. People actually do "shrink" at older ages and the centimeters begin slowly to disappear. Moreover, it is reasonable to presume that those in poorer health and the frail shrink the most. If shrinkage is sufficiently important, then adult height becomes endogenous, and at least to some degree the causation now runs from poor later life adult health to adult height. In a panel context, we could use, say, height in your fifties or early sixties to control for this problem, but that is not yet an option open to Anne using the HRS. Many of her observations entered this sample when they were quite old and to some extent their adult height may have already reacted to their increasing poor health and frailty.

How Robust Are the Results on Crop Failures?

The second part of the chapter tries to identify the sources of the adult height to adult health relationship. In this part of the chapter, Anne Case relates corn production in the division of birth of respondent while mother was pregnant to these late life health outcomes to see if this helps explain the height to later life health pathway. The basic idea is that good crops in year before birth through better nutrition predicts additional height and thereby lowers hypertension as an older adult.

The results summarized well in Anne Case's chapter, generally speaking, lend good support to her hypothesis. For example, good crops in year before birth predict additional height and lower the prevalence of hypertension as an adult.

This is a very ambitious part of the research agenda and I want first before I raise any questions or doubts to congratulate Anne on her boldness and urge her to continue on this line. One concern that I do have is that this seems to be asking a lot of the data given the real possibility of age reporting problems, especially at very old ages. Isolating precisely the year before pregnancy is difficult given normal age reporting problems, which may be compounded by the fact that bias may also be operating in that older people may say that they are younger than they really are. One possibility does exist to help mitigate this problem. The HRS has matched to social security records where ages are far more precise. These Social Security (SS) match records can be used to get the "true" ages of these respondents. Finding the same results with these ages would say a ton about the robustness of the results.

The second concern I have is the regional basis of the analysis. Even during the period when these HRS respondents were born, I would think that the food market was pretty national, produced in some places but consumed in all. Bad corn crops would show up as more scarce corn and higher prices of corn and their related products everywhere. Corn is also an important feeder crop for animals (like pigs) and these lags would seem longer than just during the term of pregnancy.

Conclusions

It should come as no surprise to those who have read Anne Case's prior work on this topic that she has written yet another fine chapter. I think that the evidence is growing and is quite persuasive about the fundamental importance of very early childhood health on our economic and health lives during the adult years. Anne Case provides some additional evidence in this chapter that these linkages are not just for the middle-aged but also follow us into our post-retirement years. The fact that I raise some questions about the details should not camouflage the fact that at its core I believe the perspective she advances in this chapter and in her prior and (I hope) subsequent work is dead-on right.

References

Barker, D. J. P. 1997. Maternal nutrition, fetal nutrition and diseases in later life. *Nutrition* 13 (9): 807–13.

Case, A., A. Fertig, and C. Paxson. 2005. The lasting impact of childhood health and circumstance. *Journal of Health Economics* 24 (2): 365–89.

Case, A., D. Lubotsky, and C. Paxson. 2002. Economic status and health in childhood: the origins of the gradient. *American Economic Review* 92 (5): 1308–34.

Case, A., and C. Paxson. 2006. Stature and status: Height, ability, and labor market outcomes. NBER Working Paper no. 12466. Cambridge, MA: National Bureau of Economic Research, August.

Smith, J. P. 1999. Healthy bodies and thick wallets: The dual relation between health and economic status. *Journal of Economic Perspectives* 13 (2): 145–67.

———. 2006. The impact of childhood health on adult labor market outcomes. Geary Institute, University College Dublin, Working Paper no. 200814.

———. 2007. Nature and causes of male diabetes trends, undiagnosed diabetes and the SES health gradient. *PNAS Proceedings of National Academy of Sciences* 104 (33): 13225–13231.

Income, Aging, Health, and Well-Being around the World
Evidence from the Gallup World Poll

Angus Deaton

9.1   Introduction

This chapter looks at the effects of income and age on self-reported well-being in more than a hundred countries. I am particularly concerned with self-reports of life satisfaction, of health, and of disability, with how these measures change with age, and with how the effects of age differ across countries according to their level of development and their region of the world. The analysis is based on the Gallup World Poll, which collected data from samples of people in each of 132 countries during 2006. With the exception of Angola, Cuba, and Myanmar, the samples are nationally representative of people age fifteen and older. Because the survey used the same questionnaire in all countries, it provides an opportunity to make cross-country comparisons while, at the same time, providing enough data to permit within-country disaggregation; for example, by age, sex, ethnicity, or education.

The World Poll data are particularly rich in self-reported measures, including a "ladder" question for life satisfaction, questions on whether or not people are satisfied with their state of health, whether they have health problems that prevent them from doing things that people at their age can usually do, whether or not they have confidence in the healthcare or medical system,

Angus Deaton is the Dwight D. Eisenhower Professor of International Affairs and Professor of Economics and International Affairs at the Woodrow Wilson School of Public and International Affairs and the Economics Department at Princeton University, and a research associate of the National Bureau of Economic Research.

I am grateful to the Gallup Organization for providing me access to the Gallup World Poll, and to Tim Besley, Anne Case, Ed Diener, Carol Graham, John Helliwell, Danny Kahneman, David Laibson, Richard Layard, Andrew Oswald, Glenn Phelps, Raksha Arora, and Jim Smith for comments and suggestions. I acknowledge financial support from the National Institute on Aging through grants No. R01 AG20275–01 to Princeton and P01 AG05842–14 to the NBER.

and whether or not they are satisfied with their standard of living. While these measures are far short of those that might appear in a comprehensive health and economics survey for a single country or a group of similar countries, they have the great advantage of having been asked in exactly the same way in all of the countries. The question is not, therefore, whether these self-reports are adequate measures of individual health—they clearly are not—but whether they provide useful measures of *population* health. In particular, it is possible that individual self-reported satisfaction or health measures are more a function of individual personality, individual temperament, or individual expectations than of any objective circumstance, but the same might not be true for the population, or for age groups within it. In consequence, one of my main objectives is to investigate the usefulness of these simple, cheap, and comparable questions as supplemental measures of population or subpopulation health.

I begin with a theoretical discussion of age-effects and income effects on life satisfaction, where life satisfaction is interpreted as period subutility in the economists' standard life cycle model of consumption. Such a formulation essentially assumes that income and happiness are positively linked, but it offers more interesting predictions about the effects of age; for example, that life satisfaction should fall more rapidly with age in countries with higher adult mortality rates (such as in places with high prevalence of HIV-AIDS). Under appropriate and plausible assumptions, the theory also predicts an inverse U-shaped age-profile of utility. I follow this, in section 9.3, with a brief summary of what the happiness literature—including the literature in psychology—says about the relationship between happiness and age.

Section 9.4 turns to the World Poll data. I look first at general life satisfaction based on a ladder question, how it varies with national income, with age, and with age at different levels of national income. Like earlier studies using a smaller range of countries, I find that the citizens of richer countries are on average more satisfied with their lives than the citizens of poorer countries. Unlike most earlier studies, this effect of income is not confined to poor, unhappy countries, but extends right across the range, from Cambodia, Sierra Leone, Togo, Niger, and Chad (which share the unenviable distinction of being in the bottom ten countries both by income and by life satisfaction), to Norway, Switzerland, Denmark, Australia, and Canada (which rank in the top ten according to both income and life-satisfaction). Each doubling of national income is associated with a near one-unit increase in average life satisfaction measured on an 11-point scale from 0 ("the worst possible life") to 10 ("the best possible life"). If anything, the effect of national income on national happiness is somewhat *stronger* in the rich countries than in the poor countries.

Recent growth in national income, unlike income itself, *lowers* average life satisfaction. This result contradicts much earlier literature that argues that improvements in living standards make people better-off, but that the effect wears off over time.

The pattern of life satisfaction at different ages differs according to the level of economic development. In 2006, life satisfaction was much worse among the elderly than among the young in poor and middle-income countries. By contrast, in rich countries, especially the English-speaking rich countries, the elderly were relatively satisfied with their lives, sometimes more satisfied than those in midlife. The elderly in the countries of Eastern Europe and the former Soviet Union are particularly dissatisfied with their lives. I find no evidence from the 2006 cross-sections that life satisfaction declines with age more rapidly in countries where adult mortality is particularly high.

In section 9.5, I show that in almost all countries and for all age groups, satisfaction with health declines with age, and is lowest among the elderly. More interesting is the fact that the rate of deterioration is much faster in poor than in rich countries, and in some of the richest, satisfaction with health actually *rises* toward the end of life. Reports of limiting health conditions behave similarly, worsening much more rapidly with age in poor countries than in rich. It appears that one of the benefits of being rich, or at least of living in a rich country, is that wealth slows the ravages of age on health, or at least on satisfaction with health. While satisfaction with health is higher in places where more people have confidence in their health and medical systems (or vice versa), confidence in the healthcare system is only weakly correlated with gross domestic product (GDP). Particularly remarkable is the position of the largest rich country, the United States, where only 52 percent of the population express themselves satisfied with the healthcare and medical system, a figure that is not only much lower than the comparable figure in any other rich country—for example, in Britain the fraction is 63 percent—but also lower than the fractions in (to take a few examples from many) India, Iran, Sierra Leone, or Malawi. The United States ranks eighty-first among the 115 countries for which these data were collected.

All of the health measures, in levels and in rates of decline with age, are particularly unfavorable in Eastern Europe and the countries of the former Soviet Union. Some of the dissatisfaction with health in these countries can certainly be linked to their recent decline in health and life expectancy. But there have been much larger declines in life expectancy elsewhere associated with the HIV/AIDS epidemic, and people in countries with high prevalence do not express anything like the same levels of dissatisfaction with their health. Indeed, the fraction of Kenyans who are satisfied with their personal health is the same as the fraction of Britons, and is *higher* than the fraction of Americans.

Section 9.6 discusses the usefulness of the satisfaction measures for the purpose of assessing population health and well-being. The ladder question on life satisfaction is strongly correlated with per capita GDP across countries, and increases linearly with the logarithm of income in rich countries as well as poor. However, the links between life satisfaction and life expectancy or HIV prevalence, or even between health satisfaction and these measures, show too many anomalies to make life satisfaction a good indicator of health and income combined. The same would be true for some combination of life satisfaction and health satisfaction. Particularly troubling is the fact that HIV prevalence appears to have little or no effect on the fraction of the population reporting dissatisfaction with their health. Using such a measure to guide or evaluate policy would lead to the unacceptable position that dealing with HIV/AIDS in Africa need not be an urgent priority.

9.2   Life-Satisfaction, Income, and Age: Theoretical Considerations

Economists have devoted a good deal of attention to life cycle behavior. While these theories were designed to predict the life cycle pattern of consumption, saving, and labor supply, they can also be used to think about the life cycle pattern of utility. While it would be a mistake to take these predictions too seriously, they provide a framework for consideration and interpretation.

The life satisfaction question in the World Poll asks people to imagine an eleven-rung ladder where the bottom (0) represents "the worst possible life for you" and the top (10) represents "the best possible life for you." Respondents are then asked to report "on which step of the ladder do you feel you personally stand at the present time?" Such a question might elicit an evaluation of the respondent's complete life, as seen from "the present time," or perhaps more likely, an evaluation of today's contribution to the lifetime stream. From a standard life cycle perspective, complete life utility is

$$(1) \qquad\qquad U = \sum_{0}^{T}(1 + \delta)^{-t}S_t\upsilon(c_t, a_t),$$

where t represents age (or time), and runs from birth (0) to death (T), δ is the rate of time preference, S_t is the survival rate, the probability of surviving from time zero to time t, and $\upsilon(c_t, a_t)$ is the instantaneous utility—or "felicity," to separate it from U—function that depends on consumption at age t and other factors a sometimes referred to as "taste shifters." I follow the standard, but by no means innocuous, assumption that utility is intertemporally additive, which allows us to talk about instantaneous and lifetime utility in a simple way. For someone currently of age t, the part of (1) from the past will be known, with the remainder an expectation. Consumption is chosen so as to maximize (1) subject to a lifetime income and wealth constraint in which money can be moved from one period to another through lending and borrowing, for simplicity at a constant real interest rate r.

In this model, income—together with initial wealth and the interest rate—constrains how much utility is possible, so that, by assumption, higher incomes generate higher utility within each period and for life as a whole. Given this economic definition of happiness, there is no ambiguity about the proposition that income makes people happier. The effects of age, here represented by t, are somewhat more interesting.

Suppose first that life satisfaction is taken to refer to lifetime utility U. In the absence of uncertainty, lifetime utility U does not change over time. With uncertainty, U will change from period to period in response to new information and the changes in consumption induced by that information. For example, under the assumptions of the life cycle permanent income model, consumption follows a random walk, which will induce random changes in U. But there will be no pattern to the changes in consumption, nor in U, so that there should be no systematic change in U with age. Happiness is what *lifetime* circumstances, both past and future, make it to be, and should not change systematically with age. Unless there is perfect risk-sharing across people, consumption inequality—and under some assumptions, utility inequality—will increase with age (see Deaton and Paxson 1994).

If, instead of life time utility U, we interpret the satisfaction questions as referring to instantaneous utility or felicity, there is more scope for variation with age. Given that consumption is optimally set over the life cycle, and taking the certainty case for simplicity, we must have

$$(2) \qquad \upsilon_1(c_t, a_t) = \lambda(1 + \delta)^t(1 + r)^{-t}S_t^{-1},$$

where the subscript 1 denotes the partial derivative of felicity with respect to its first argument—the marginal utility of consumption—and λ is the lifetime marginal utility of wealth, which is independent of age. If the changes over time in consumption, the interest rate, and the discount rate are all relatively small, (2) gives the approximation

$$(3) \qquad \frac{\upsilon_{11}}{\upsilon_1}\Delta c_t + \frac{\upsilon_{12}}{\upsilon_1}\Delta a_t = -r + \delta - \Delta \log S_t,$$

where Δ indicates a change over time, and double partial derivatives are shown as double subscripts. Note that the proportional change in the survival rate is approximately equal to minus the mortality rate, so that (3) can be rewritten

$$(4) \qquad \frac{\upsilon_{11}}{\upsilon_1}\Delta c_t + \frac{\upsilon_{12}}{\upsilon_1}\Delta a_t = -r + \delta + m_t,$$

where m_t is the mortality rate at age t. Note that because we are talking about decision making regarding life cycle consumption, the relevant mortality rates are those in adulthood, not childhood or infancy, and the former vary a good deal less across poor and rich countries than do the latter.

Equation (4) has a number of useful implications. The marginal utility of consumption is positive and declining ($\upsilon_1 > 0$ and $\upsilon_{11} < 0$) so that, if a is constant, consumption will rise over time in response to r and fall in response to impatience or mortality (the survival rate S_t is falling with t). In thinking about the implications for this across countries, it is hard to see why there should be any systematic relationship between the level of national income and the difference between r and the rate of time preference, but there are certainly major differences in adult mortality rates. Provided the factor v_{11}/v_1 does not change too much with age, the optimal lifetime choice of consumption will have faster rates of consumption decline the higher is the mortality rate; the shorter future provides an incentive to consume and be happy now or to "eat, drink, and be merry, for tomorrow we die." Since the mortality rate rises rapidly with age, the rate of consumption decline should accelerate with age to match. Of course, consumption is not utility and the change in utility depends also on what is happening to a_t.

The change in utility is given by

$$(5) \qquad \Delta u_t = v_1 \Delta c_t + v_2 \Delta a_t,$$

and where Δc_t and Δa_t are linked by (4). Making the substitution, and assuming for simplicity that r and δ are equal, we have

$$(6) \qquad \Delta u_t = \frac{v_1^2}{v_{11}} m_t + \left(v_2 - \frac{v_1 v_{12}}{v_{11}} \right) \Delta a_t.$$

The first term shows that mortality has a negative effect on the rate of change of utility, essentially because the rate of consumption decline rises as mortality rises. To think about the second term, suppose we normalize the taste factors a so that more a is associated with higher utility. The obvious interpretation is that a measures the capacity to enjoy consumption—or individual efficiency as a utility machine. Although the life cycle pattern of a will be chosen by the individual, at least in part, it is plausible that it would have an inverse U-shape, rising at first as people accumulate human capital, self-knowledge, and the ability to enjoy themselves—in other words, learn to be happy—and then eventually falling as the capacity to enjoy fails with age. By this view, the marginal utility of consumption is higher when a is higher, so that $v_{12} > 0$. Consumers will adapt their consumption, not to compensate for changes in a, but to take advantage of them by consuming most when a is highest; consumption is higher in those periods of life where it does the most good—in this case, in midlife. Equation (4) shows that, discounting and mortality effects apart, consumption change tracks taste change, and equation (6) shows that the effects on utility are magnified by the addition of the direct utility effects of changes in a. A similar story could be told about children, whose average numbers follow an inverse U-shape, and who, since they are generally purposively chosen might be supposed to enhance utility—although the empirical happiness literature often disputes this; see Argyle (1999); Clark and Oswald (2002); and Layard (2005)—as well as increasing the marginal utility of consumption by providing more opportunities for the parents to spend money to enjoy themselves. Once again, instantaneous utility would be predicted to have an inverse U-shape with age.

A simple explicit example illustrates further. Suppose that we continue to assume that $r = \delta$, and that the utility function takes the form

$$(7) \qquad U = \frac{1}{1 - \rho} \sum_{0}^{T} (1 + \delta)^{-t} S_t (a_t c_t)^{1-\rho},$$

where ρ is a parameter with $0 < \rho < 1$. The quantity a_t in (7) simply acts to augment consumption. For this specification, the rate of change of consumption with age is given by

$$(8) \qquad \Delta \ln c_t = \frac{-1}{\rho} m_t + \frac{1 - \rho}{\rho} \Delta \ln a_t,$$

while happiness—defined here as $(1 - \rho)^{-1} (a_t c_t)^{1-\rho}$—changes with age according to

$$\Delta \ln u_t = \frac{-1 - \rho}{\rho} m_t + \frac{1 - \rho}{\rho} \ln a_t,$$

so that the effect on mortality on the rate of change of happiness is constant, and as the mortality rate rises ever more rapidly with age, the rate of decline of happiness will accelerate. At the same time, if we look across countries with different adult mortality rates, the rate of decline of happiness with age should be higher in the higher mortality countries.

9.3   Insights from the Psychology and Happiness Literatures

The psychology literature takes a different approach to questions of how happiness is affected by income and by age. In particular, there is no basic assumption that income promotes happiness; income is simply one of life's many circumstances that may or may not be associated with happiness.

One thread emphasizes the importance of personality and temperament as determinants of life satisfaction. In the most extreme version, referred to as "set-point" theory, people cannot be *permanently* moved from their personal happiness set-point level, and while changing life circumstances—consumption, income, and even divorce or the death of a loved one—affect life satisfaction, they do so only temporarily. If this strict version is correct, and if the distribution of temperaments is the same in different countries, we should expect to see no difference in average life satisfaction across populations, at least with the exception of populations that have recently experienced a large positive or negative change in their circumstances. More precisely, average life satisfaction across countries should depend *positively* on *changes* in national income, but should not depend on the *level* of national income. Within countries, happiness should be independent of age.

More generally, individual life-satisfaction is taken to depend on some combination of temperament and circumstance, and there has been a lively debate about which circumstances are important, and about which—if any—have permanent as opposed to merely transitory effects. For example, it is often argued that income is relatively unimportant, and relatively transitory compared with family circumstances, unemployment, or health (see Easterlin 2003). Note that even if variations in temperament are more important than circumstances at the individual level, the same need not be true of the population because temperamental differences might average out over populations, though nothing rules out national differences in temperament. If temperament does average out, population measures of life satisfaction could be useful indicators of population well-being, even when they are poor measures for individuals. The conflict between concepts of capabilities or functionings, which are the measures argued for by Sen (1999), and of which health and income are the most important, is *possibly* much more severe for individuals than for nations. By contrast, if the strict form of set-point theory is true, it is impossible to make individuals or nations permanently happier, including through the improvements in national health and national income that would increase capabilities and that are normally seen as the main goals of economic development.

The role of one particular circumstance, income, is of particular interest. Many within-country studies have found only a small effect of income on happiness relative to other life circumstances such as employment or marital status; see, for example, Helliwell (2003) or Blanchflower and Oswald (2004). Kahneman et al. (2005) argue that even these measures *overstate* the effects of income. They suggest that more income may do nothing for happiness, and that the observed correlation between life satisfaction and income comes from a "focusing illusion," induced by the life satisfaction question, which prompts respondents to compare their incomes with some standard, such as their own previous incomes or with the incomes of others. It is therefore possible that, over the long run, increases in income will generate no increase in life satisfaction. This result is consistent with the microlevel evidence from the German Socioeconomic Panel by Di Tella, Haisken-DeNew, and MacCulloch (2005), who regress life satisfaction on income and on several lags of income, and find that life satisfaction adapts completely to income within four years. It is only income *change* that matters, not income itself. At the country level, a long-run zero effect of income is also consistent with the famous findings of Easterlin (1974, 1995) that for those countries for which we have data, happiness does not increase over long time spans, in spite of large increases in per capita income. Such theories and findings are in sharp contrast to the standard economic model developed previously in which more consumption—or more lifetime wealth, or lifetime income—makes people happier.

Whether or not set-point theory works for other circumstances—such as the death of a spouse, or the permanent loss of work—the results for income suggest that there is little or no long-run relationship between national income and national happiness, so that one might reasonably infer that this would also be so across countries, given that most international income differences are long established. But the evidence does not support this inference. Although the United States and Japan may have failed to become happier as they grew richer, poor countries such as India or Nigeria are less happy than rich countries such as the United States or Japan. See, for example, Ingelhart and Klingemann (2000); Graham (2005); Layard (2005); Leigh and Wolfers (2006) or the careful and balanced survey by Diener and Oishi (2000). As Diener and Oishi note, one argument, due to Veenhoven (1991), is that more income improves happiness only until basic needs are met; beyond the point where there is enough income so that people are no longer hungry, their children do not die from readily preventable diseases, and absolute poverty has been eliminated, income does not matter for happiness. While this story seems plausible, they also note that it might be only after these basic needs have been met that the possibilities for intellectual and cultural development can be fully explored. This is akin to Robbins' (1938) account of the Brahmin who claimed to be "ten times as capable of happiness as that untouchable over there."

An important source of previous empirical evidence is the World Values Survey, which covers rich countries, together with a smaller number of poor countries, as well as a group of countries from Eastern Europe and the former Soviet Union. Authors who have worked with these data have tended to conclude that (a) richer countries are happier, (b) the cross-country effect of income on happiness is larger than the within-country effect of income and happiness, and (c) that among the rich countries, there is no relationship between national income and national happiness. (See again Ingelhart and Klingemann [2000, figure 7.2] and Layard [2005, 32], who writes that for "the Western industrial countries, the richer ones are no happier than the poorer.") Findings (a) and (c) are consistent with the basic needs story together with a set-point or adaptive model in rich countries where basic needs are met, while (b) is a consequence of the comparison between poor countries as a group and rich countries as a group. As we shall see, the results from the World Poll are very different.

The literature on the relationship between happiness and age is essentially empirical; Helliwell (2003) and Easterlin (2006) review the literature, including work that finds essentially no effect of age, work that finds that older people are happier, and work that finds a U-shaped profile over the life course. As one might expect, these results are sensitive to which other variables are controlled—health in particular—and to what role is assigned to cohort and period effects when estimating age effects, see Blanchflower and Oswald's reply (2007) to Easterlin.

9.4   Life Satisfaction, Income, and Age: Evidence from the World Poll

Figure 9.1 shows a world map of the life satisfaction measure from the 2006 World Poll data. The numbers for each individual range from 0 to 10, and the shading corresponds to the (sample weighted) averages for the 121 countries used here. The map looks similar to an income plot of the world: North America, Europe, Japan, Australasia, and Saudi Arabia are happy as well as rich, and the really unhappy places on the planet are in sub-Saharan Africa, plus Haiti and Cambodia. The only countries in the bottom twenty according to life satisfaction and that are relatively well-off in income terms are Georgia and Armenia. At the other end, there are two relatively poor places in the happiness top twenty, Costa Rica and Venezuela.

Figure 9.2 summarizes a great deal of information about the relationship between life satisfaction and national income, and about how that relationship changes with age, or equivalently, how the age profile of average life satisfaction varies across countries. The horizontal axis, for all plots, is per capita GDP in 2003 (the nearest year for which there is complete data in the Penn World Table) measured in purchasing power parity (PPP) dollars at 2000 prices. Each circle is a country, with diameter proportional to population, and marks average life satisfaction and GDP for that country. Important countries are labeled; most of the countries of sub-Saharan Africa are

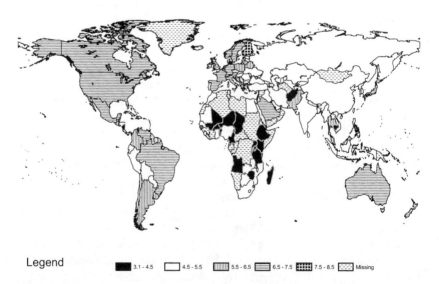

Legend   ▇ 3.1 - 4.5   ☐ 4.5 - 5.5   ⦀ 5.5 - 6.5   ▤ 6.5 - 7.5   ▦ 7.5 - 8.5   ⬚ Missing

Fig. 9.1   Life satisfaction around the world: Population means of 0 to 10

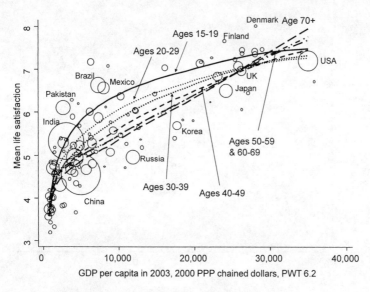

Fig. 9.2   Life satisfaction, per capita GDP, and age

on the bottom left, India and China are the two large circles near the left, the western European countries appear near the upper right, and the United States is the large country on the top right. There are also seven plotted lines on the graph, only six of which are clearly visible. Each of these corresponds to an age group: fifteen to nineteen, twenty to twenty-nine, thirty to thirty-nine, forty to forty-nine, fifty to fifty-nine, sixty to sixty-nine, and seventy and over. For each of these seven groups, and for each country, I calculated the average life satisfaction. Each line is a nonparametric regression plot for one age group of its average life satisfaction against national per capita GDP (taken to be the same for all age groups in the country). These lines can be thought of as a disaggregation by age of the average plot represented by the circles.

As with the map in figure 9.1, life satisfaction increases with GDP per head. The slope is steepest among the poorest countries, where income gains are associated with the largest increases in happiness, but it remains positive and substantial even among the rich countries; it is *not true* that there is some critical level of GDP per capita above which income has no further effect on happiness. Since this result is different from the earlier findings reviewed in the previous section, I investigate it further.

Figure 9.3 plots average happiness against the *logarithm* of income, and this simple transform is enough to make the relationship close to linear. Column (1) of table 9.1 shows the basic regression for the 114 countries for which we have both life satisfaction and per capita PPP GDP from the Penn World Table. The coefficient is 0.850 with an estimated standard error

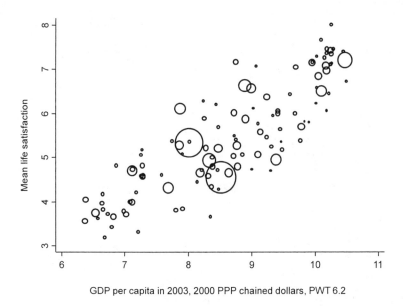

Fig. 9.3   Life satisfaction and the logarithm of GDP per capita

Table 9.1   Cross-country regressions of average life satisfaction on the logarithm of per capita GDP

Income cutoff	(1) None	(2) None	(3) y < 12,000	(4) y ≥ 12,000	(5) y ≥ 20.000	(6) None	(7) None
lny	0.850	−0.859	0.708	1.743	0.617	0.751	0.677
s.e.	(0.051)	(0.778)	(0.085)	(0.287)	(0.649)	(0.081)	(0.064)
(lny)²		0.101					
s.e.		(0.046)					
lny*I(y > 12,000)						0.032	
s.e.						(0.021)	
lny*I(y > 20,000)							0.073
s.e.							(0.018)
R²	0.716	0.728	0.480	0.521	0.040	0.722	0.752
Number of countries	114	114	78	36	24	114	114

Notes: y is real chained GDP per capita in 2003 in 2000 international $ from the Penn World Table version 6.2. I(y > 12,000) is an indicator variable that is 1 if y is greater than 12,000, similarly for I(y > 20,000). Regressions are not weighted by population. s.e. = standard error.

of 0.051. Using the same sample, the quadratic in column (2) improves the fit only slightly; the *t*-value on the squared term is only 2.2. Note too that the quadratic term has a *positive* sign, so that the effect of log income on life satisfaction is estimated to *increase* at higher levels of income per head. Columns (3) and (4) split the sample at $12,000; figure 9.2 shows that this is a level that splits the poor and middle-income countries from the rich countries. Once again, the slope in the upper income countries is higher, although it has a large estimated standard error. If we restrict the sample to the twenty-four countries whose per capita GDP is above $20,000, the estimated slope is 0.617 with a standard error of 0.649, which is clearly consistent both with a zero slope, and with a slope that is the same as the slope in the poor countries; visual inspection of figure 9.3 shows that the latter is the obvious conclusion. The final two columns address the same question in a slightly different way, interacting the term in log income with, first in column (6), and indicator that per capita income is above $12,000, and then second in column (7), an indicator that per capita income is above $20,000. In both cases, the interaction term is estimated to be positive, and is significantly different from zero in the final column.

These results support the visual impression in figure 9.3 that the logarithmic fit with a constant slope is adequate for all countries, rich or poor, and if there is any evidence for deviation, it is small and in the direction of the slope being higher among the richer countries.

Why are these results so different from those studies that have concluded that, among the rich countries, national income has no effect on national life satisfaction? Figure 9.4 shows the data that supports these findings, taken from the 1981, 1990, and 1996 waves of the World Values Surveys, with each country marked by its three letter "isocode" as used by the Penn World Table and World Bank. For comparability with the World Poll, I have included

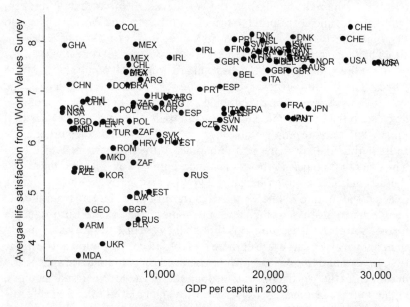

Fig. 9.4   Life satisfaction and national income from the World Values Surveys: 1981, 1990, and 1996

only countries that appear in both sources, and I have excluded regions or cities. Even so, figure 9.4 reproduces the main features of previous analyses. There is a steep relationship between happiness and income on the left of the graph, which becomes much flatter among the rich countries on the right. To see how this relates to the World Poll data, note four points: (a) apart from South Africa (ZAF) and Korea (KOR), *all* of the countries at the bottom left are in Eastern Europe or were once part of the Soviet Union, including Moldova, Ukraine, Armenia, Belarus, Russia, Bulgaria, Latvia, Estonia, Azerbaijan, Bosnia and Herzegovina, Macedonia, Romania, Estonia, and Slovakia; (b) if we look at the few long-term poor countries in the sample, Ghana, China, Philippines, Bangladesh, India, Peru, and the Dominican Republic, they all are much happier than the Eastern European countries; (c) as a consequence of (a) and (b), the sharply curved nature of the happiness to income relationship comes, not so much from the poor countries, but from the Eastern European and former Soviet countries, whose unhappiness is almost certainly not primarily due to their low incomes; (d) figure 9.4, unlike figure 9.3, shows income on an absolute, rather than a logarithmic scale. Once the transformation is made, the happiness to log income relationship is close to linear except, once again, for the countries of Eastern Europe (see also Leigh and Wolfers [2006]).

Figure 9.5 combines the World Poll and World Values Survey (WVS) data using a logarithmic scale for income; it is identical to figure 9.3 with the WVS data overlaid. The World Poll data are shown as heavy solid circles and correspond to the right-hand scale; the World Values Survey data in broken, lighter circles and correspond to the left-hand scale. The World Poll uses an 11-point scale (0 to 10) and the World Values Surveys a 10-point scale (1 to 10.) The most important difference between the two surveys is that all the points at the bottom left of the diagram are World Poll points, mostly from Africa. The World Poll covers many more very poor countries than do the World Values Surveys and the happiness and income data for these countries lie close to the line for middle-income and rich countries alike. Otherwise, the two data sets are more notable for their similarities than their differences. India and China are richer and unhappier in the more recent World Poll, which perhaps comes not from substance, but from the fact that the World Poll is a national sample whereas the WVS, particularly the earlier rounds, selected Indian and Chinese (and Nigerian) samples largely from literate people in urban areas. At the same time, some of the Eastern European and former Soviet countries, unhappy though they are in 2006, are less unhappy than in the earlier surveys. But there is no broad contradiction between the two surveys, and the World Values Surveys provide no evidence against the finding from the World Poll that, throughout the range of national incomes, higher average incomes are associated with higher levels of average life satisfaction.

It is of course possible that income is standing in for something else,

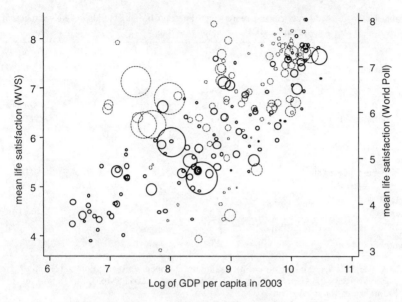

Fig. 9.5   **Life satisfaction and log per capita income, World Poll and World Values Surveys compared**

such as relative income, income relative to expectations or to past income (growth), or for other variables correlated with income, of which health is plausibly the most important. Indeed, the international pattern of life satisfaction in relation to per capita GDP is very similar to the pattern between life expectancy and income, first documented by Preston (1975).

Table 9.2 investigates the growth and health stories. Column (1) regresses average life satisfaction on the logarithm of income in 2003 and the average growth rate of income from 2000 to 2003. Note that this is mechanically equivalent to regressing life satisfaction on the logarithms of income in both 2000 and 2003, or indeed to regressing life satisfaction on the logarithm of income in 2000 and its growth from 2000 to 2003. The addition of growth to the regression does not eliminate the effect of income in levels, so that there is no evidence that the effect of income is spurious, picking up only the correlation between income and its growth rate. It is not true that it is only the growth of income that matters, not its level. Secondly, and more surprisingly, at any given level of income, economic growth is associated with *lower* reported levels of life satisfaction, a result that seems inconsistent with any of the accounts in the literature, although see Diener, Diener, and Diener (1995), who also find a negative effect of growth on happiness in an international sample of college students, though not in their national samples. Indeed, this is one of the most puzzling and surprising results in this chapter.

Table 9.2   Cross-country regressions of average life satisfaction on levels and lags of per capita GDP and on life expectancy

Income cutoff	(1) None	(2) None	(3) None	(4) $y < 12,000$	(5) $y \geq 12,000$
ln y 2003	0.860	0.890	0.910	0.698	1.297
s.e.	(0.049)	(0.053)	(0.110)	(0.173)	(0.359)
Growth rate 2000–2003	–4.47	–3.65	–4.64	–3.50	–8.02
s.e.	(1.41)	(1.58)	(1.39)	(1.52)	(5.76)
Growth rate 1990–2000		–3.32			
s.e.		(2.51)			
Life expectancy 2000			–0.009	0.001	0.038
s.e.			(0.011)	(0.014)	(0.046)
LE 2000–LE 1990			0.047	0.036	–0.074
s.e.			(0.019)	(0.022)	(0.120)
R^2	0.740	0.763	0.757	0.556	0.582
Number of countries	114	103	114	78	36

Notes: See table 9.1. Among the countries that are dropped between columns (2) and (3) are Azerbaijan, Belarus, Georgia, Kazakhstan, Lithuania, Latvia, Moldova, Tajikistan, and Ukraine. s.e. = standard error.

Note that growth from 2000 to 2003 is the change in log income divided by three, so that the regression in column (1) can also be interpreted as a levels regression in which log income in 2003 attracts a negative coefficient, and log income in 2000 a positive one, with their sum remaining at 0.860. Essentially these data cannot tell which year's income is the most important one, a finding that is confirmed by adding further lags of log income (not shown). Yet in all of these alternative specifications, the sum of the coefficients on the lags remains roughly constant, which is consistent with life-satisfaction responding to the long-term average income, as in a permanent-income model of life satisfaction. Column (2) also shows that the precise period of income growth is not important, and that the model does just as well assigning the negative effects of growth to the three years from 2000 to 2003, or the decade from 1990 to 2000, or some combination of the two. The addition of earlier growth rates does nothing to enhance or change these results.

It is also worth noting that the coefficients on growth, even when divided by three, are larger in absolute value than the coefficient on the current level of income. This implies that a regression of life satisfaction on lagged income and current growth will still show a negative effect of growth; the coefficient on lagged income is the same as that on current income in the original regression. This finding rules out the possibility that the negative effect of growth comes from identifying those countries whose current income overstates their long-run income, and who should therefore be less happy than those who have been richer for longer. However we count it, income makes countries happy and income growth makes them unhappy.

The countries of Eastern Europe and of the former Soviet Union have some of the lowest levels of life satisfaction in the world, much lower than warranted by their incomes. The upheavals associated with the fall of communism are likely factors, though they do not show up in the regressions as working through the fall in incomes, if only because these countries were not among the countries with the worst growth record from 2000 to 2003. Consideration of earlier growth rates is not possible, because many of the countries did not exist in 1990, and are therefore excluded from the regression in column (2) (see the footnote to the table). But given the robustness of the estimated negative effects of growth between columns (1) and (2), it seems most likely that it is features of the transition other than declines in income that are responsible for dissatisfaction with life.

Columns (3), (4), and (5) investigate the role of life expectancy and its rate of change. Because life expectancy is the standard period measure, formed from current survival rates, it is *not* a long-term measure that changes only slowly in response to changes in the epidemiological and social environment. There were twenty-eight countries in the sample whose life expectancies fell from 1990 to 2000. Eighteen of these are in sub-Saharan Africa—as are all of the double-digit declines—one is Iraq (sanctions and Saddam Hussein), and the other nine are countries of the former Soviet Union, including Russia itself. (Note that estimates of life expectancy are available for these countries in 1990, although income estimates are not.) Yet the table shows that life expectancy plays a very limited role in explaining international variations in life satisfaction. The introduction of the life expectancy variables has only a small effect on the estimated effects of income, so that it is not true that income is standing proxy for life expectancy. Life expectancy itself does not show up significantly in any of the regressions, though the increase in life expectancy from 1990 to 2000 has a significant positive effect on average life satisfaction. The estimated coefficient is 0.047, which would exert a sizable negative effect on life satisfaction in countries in sub-Saharan Africa with large declines in life expectancy, such as Botswana (–20 years), Zimbabwe (–19 years), or South Africa (–16 years), but cannot explain the low levels of life satisfaction in the former Soviet Union (FSU) countries where the declines were much smaller, such as Russia (–2 years).

I have repeated the life satisfaction and health regressions using infant and child mortality measures instead of, and in addition to, life expectancy. These generate no new insights, largely because of the strong interrelations between the three measures in a single cross-section. Indeed, in the poorest and highest mortality countries, among whom the variation in life expectancy is largest, life expectancy is often imputed using measures of infant and child mortality, so it is not surprising that the data should be unable to separate out their effects, if indeed they exist.

I have also experimented with a measure of the HIV prevalence rate (taken from the World Development Indicators). Although this is certainly measured with error, it reliably identifies those countries most severely affected, and to ensure that is the case, I constructed a dummy variable that identifies the thirteen countries with an estimated 2003 prevalence of 5 percent or more, namely Botswana, Burundi, Cameroon, Haiti, Kenya, Mozambique, Malawi, Nigeria, Rwanda, South Africa, Tanzania, Zambia, and Zimbabwe. Whether added to the regressions in column (1) or column (3) of table 9.2, the dummy attracts a small and insignificant coefficient (not shown). This is surely an extraordinary finding, that reported life satisfaction is unaffected by a plague whose severity is unparalleled in modern times. And even if people do not know that they are HIV positive, it is hard to believe that their satisfaction with life is unaffected when more than a fifth of adults are infected, and when burials of the victims are a daily occurrence.

Figure 9.2 shows that the relationship between life satisfaction and income differs across the age groups or, perhaps more obviously, that the relationship between life satisfaction and age depends on the level of development. Most notably, among the low- and middle-income countries, reported life satisfaction declines as people age. However, among the rich countries, the lines come together, and eventually cross so that, among the world's richest countries, there is no monotone relationship between life satisfaction and age. Figure 9.6 explores these regularities in more detail for the transition countries among which there is an almost uniform picture of life satisfaction declining with age, sometimes quite sharply. (These graphs show unconditional averages of life satisfaction with age with neither standardization

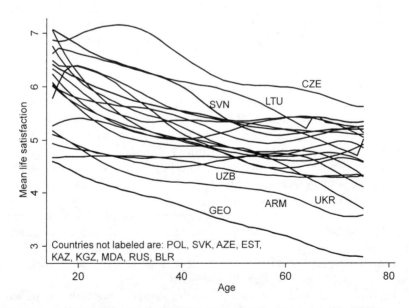

Fig. 9.6   Declining life-satisfaction with age in Eastern Europe and the FSU

nor controls.) Whatever aspects of the transition it is that make people unhappy, the effects appear to be much more pronounced among the elderly. Perhaps it is they who have suffered the adverse consequences of disruption, who were most satisfied with their old lives, and who cannot expect to live long enough to see any improvements that might occur in the future. For them, there is only transition, no promised land.

Figure 9.7 shows similar age profiles of life satisfaction for the rich English-speaking countries of the world. Not only are these people generally much happier than people in the previous figure, but their life satisfaction is, in most cases, U-shaped in age. Because of our inability to control for cohort or period effects, we cannot tell whether these U-shapes are age effects for people in the English-speaking countries, or some mixture of period and cohort effects. The results from other countries (not shown here) suggest that there is no general (unconditional) U-shape for life satisfaction with age in the 2006 cross-section. Not only is life satisfaction declining with age in the countries in figure 9.4, but there is also somewhat milder (and less uniform) decrease with age in Latin America. There is no systematic pattern in the countries of Africa, Asia, or Western Europe other than Britain and Ireland. The obvious explanation is that there are period or cohort effects that are specific to countries or to groups of countries. The age-related decline in life satisfaction in Eastern Europe and the Former Soviet Union (FSU) in figure 9.4 is unlikely to be a pure age effect, but is probably more

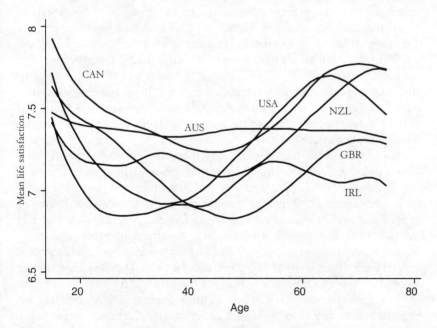

Fig. 9.7   U-shaped life satisfaction in rich English-speaking countries

an interaction of a period effect (the transition) that was particularly hard on the elderly. In the rich English-speaking countries, the relatively high satisfaction of the elderly might be linked to the substantial intergenerational transfers from young to old in those countries, though this explanation would also hold for much of the rich world. The lack of a decline in happiness with age in sub-Saharan Africa is also hard to reconcile with its generally high rates of adult mortality.

I have replicated the income results in tables 9.1 and 9.2 by age group, and the results are qualitatively similar to those for all age groups combined. For each of the age groups, the level of national income is an important positive determinant of life satisfaction, and the rate of growth of income a negative determinant. In further work, when the individual income numbers from the World Poll are more developed, it may be possible to use the data to look at income distribution across age groups, or indeed to compare the within-national effects of income on happiness with those estimated here from the international comparisons.

9.5   Perceptions of Health, Disability, and Health Systems

I now turn from overall life satisfaction to satisfaction with health. World Poll respondents are asked whether they are satisfied or dissatisfied with the state of their personal health. The next question is whether they "have any health problems that prevent you from doing any of the things people of your age usually do," again with a dichotomous answer, yes or no. I refer to this as the disability question. Figures 9.8 (for health satisfaction) and 9.9 (for disability) are drawn in the same way as figure 9.2, plotting the fraction satisfied with their health or the fraction with a disability against average per capita income, for everyone together—the circles with diameters proportional to population—or separately by age—the fitted nonparametric curves. In figure 9.9, for disability, the circles are drawn separately for two of the age groups, ages thirty to thirty-nine (solid circles), and ages sixty to seventy (broken circles).

These figures show that people are less often disabled and are more likely to be satisfied with their health in richer countries, and that, less surprisingly, they become more disabled and less healthy as they age. As was the case for life satisfaction, the rate at which things get worse with age is greater in poor and middle income countries than in rich countries, where income seems to provide some protection against the effects of aging. Indeed, at the top right of figure 9.8, the fifty to fifty-nine age group is *less* satisfied with its health than is either of the two older groups. There is even a similar reversal for reported disabilities between the fifty to fifty-nine and sixty to sixty-nine group in figure 9.9. It is most improbable that these reversals can be attributed to any objective health conditions or disabilities. Perhaps the fifty to fifty-nine group is particularly intolerant of the first signs of aging.

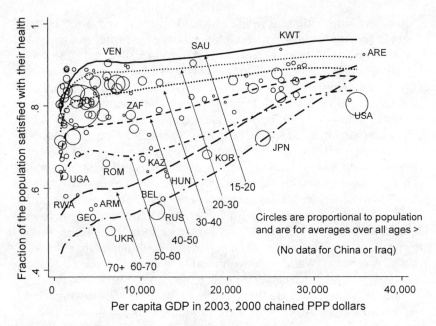

Fig. 9.8   Health satisfaction, age, and income

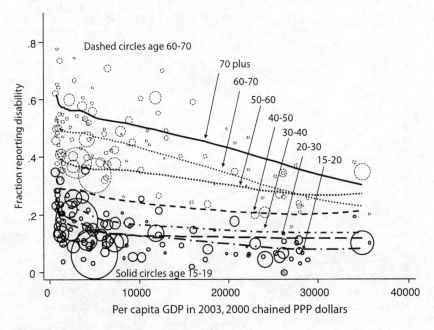

Fig. 9.9   Disability, age, and income

In health satisfaction, as in life satisfaction, the countries of Eastern Europe and the former Soviet Union report extraordinary low levels. Ukraine (rank 1), Russia (3), Georgia (4), Armenia (5), Belarus (6), Moldova (8), Hungary (9), Latvia (12), Estonia (14), Romania (15), and Kazakhstan (17) are eleven of the twenty worst countries in the world in health satisfaction, ranking alongside much higher mortality countries such as Haiti (2), Rwanda (7), Uganda (10), Burundi (11), Cambodia (14), Chad (16), Benin (18), and Cameroon (19). (South Korea is twentieth, for no immediately obvious reason.) In all of these countries, the fraction of people reporting themselves satisfied with their health is between a half and two-thirds, which is worth contrasting with the situation in some of countries worst hit by the HIV/AIDS epidemic: Tanzania (70 percent), Zimbabwe (75 percent), Botswana and South Africa (both 78 percent), and Kenya (82 percent). Indeed, the percentage of Kenyans satisfied with their health is the same as the proportion of Britons, and is a percentage point higher than the fraction of Americans. While objective mortality rates have an effect on health satisfaction, at least in changes if not in levels, so do other factors, and the declines in life expectancy in the countries of the former Soviet Union have clearly had a much larger effect on reported life satisfaction than have the much larger declines in life expectancy in the African countries affected by HIV/AIDS.

The way in which health satisfaction declines with age is illustrated for two sets of countries in figures 9.10 and 9.11 the former shows five selected

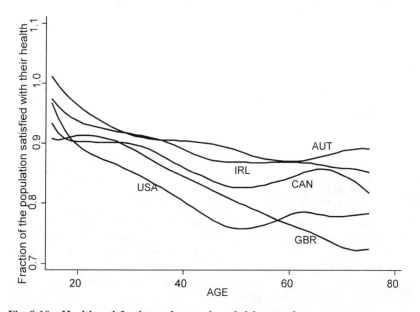

Fig. 9.10   Health satisfaction and age, selected rich countries

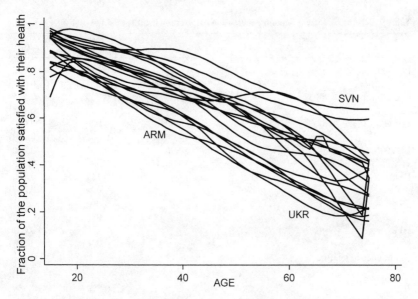

Fig. 9.11   Health satisfaction and age, Eastern Europe and FSU

rich countries, including the United States and Britain, while the latter shows the Eastern European and FSU countries. In the fifteen to nineteen age group, almost everyone is satisfied with their health. In the rich countries, satisfaction falls relatively slowly, and in the United States, actually *improves* with age after age fifty, (probably coincidentally) overtaking the generally more stoical British at around the age at which the respective age-specific mortality curves cross. In the Eastern European and FSU group, health satisfaction falls very rapidly with age, and very large fractions of the elderly report themselves as dissatisfied with their health.

Table 9.3 explores the correlates of health satisfaction, following the same general procedures as in tables 9.2 and 9.3. Column (1) shows, consistently with the figures, that the fraction of people satisfied with their health is higher in higher income countries, although even allowing for the fact that the scale is a tenth as large, the effect is a good deal smaller than for life satisfaction. As was the case for life satisfaction, recent economic growth is *negatively* associated with health satisfaction conditional on the level of GDP per capita. In column (2), the level of life expectancy has no effect on health satisfaction, although increases in life expectancy between 1990 and 2000 are associated with higher health satisfaction. Because declines in life expectancy are associated either with HIV/AIDS (itself mostly in sub-Saharan Africa), or with the transition countries of Eastern Europe, I have constructed three dummy variables, one for the Eastern European countries, one for sub-Saharan Africa, and one for HIV prevalence that has already been described. The first of these dummies ("east") attracts a negative and

Table 9.3   Cross-country regressions of average health satisfaction

	(1)	(2)	(3)	(4)
ln y 2003	0.0219	0.0472	0.0156	0.0127
s.e.	(0.006)	(0.014)	(0.014)	(0.014)
Growth rate 2000–2003	–1.346	–1.384	–0.722	–0.725
s.e.	(0.225)	(0.219)	(0.238)	(0.231)
Life expectancy 2000		–0.003	–0.000	–0.000
s.e.		(0.001)	(0.002)	(0.002)
LE 2000–LE 1990		0.007	0.001	0.000
s.e.		(0.002)	(0.003)	(0.003)
East			–0.137	–0.118
			(0.024)	(0.024)
SSA			–0.056	–0.041
			(0.034)	(0.034)
HIV			0.015	–0.001
			(0.036)	(0.035)
Confidence in healthcare				0.121
				(0.045)
R^2	0.303	0.357	0.529	0.559
Number of countries	112	112	112	112

Notes: East is a dummy that is one for Eastern Europe and the Former Soviet Union, SSA is a dummy that is one for sub-Saharan Africa, and HIV is a dummy that is one if the estimated prevalence of HIV/AIDS is greater than 5 percent among fifteen to forty-nine-year-olds. s.e. = standard error.

significant coefficient, the second (sub-Saharan Africa) an insignificantly negative one, and the third (HIV) a coefficient that is neither negative nor significant. With these dummies included, the change in life expectancy no longer has any effect, and the significance of the income variables is also reduced. This is perhaps not surprising given the evidence in figure 9.6, where it is clear that the poor health satisfaction in the transition countries could not be attributed entirely to the objective decrease in life expectancy. These results also reinforce the fact that even high levels of HIV prevalence do not much affect the health satisfaction reports, certainly not in proportion to their dire effects on mortality. I have also interacted the dummies with the change in life expectancy (results not shown) to test the possibility that the changes in life expectancy have different effects in the different areas, or with different causes, but the estimated effects are neither significant nor informative.

One variable that does predict average health satisfaction is what people think of their healthcare system. The World Poll asks people to report whether or not they have confidence in their health care or medical system. The average of this for each country is entered in the last row of the last column of table 9.3, where it has a large and statistically significant coefficient. Of course, because this is itself a subjective response, we do not know whether it is a better or worse indicator of the actual performance of the healthcare system than health satisfaction is itself a good indicator of objective health. Put differently, both health satisfaction and healthcare confidence may be functions of third factors, which themselves vary by region, time, or age group. And it would certainly be unwarranted to interpret the last column of the table as evidence that the healthcare system is effective in delivering health.

The degree of confidence in the healthcare system varies widely from country to country, and although it is correlated with income—see figure 9.12—the correlation is weak. Note particularly the astonishingly low confidence that Americans in 2006 had in their healthcare and medical system. Almost all the inhabitants of rich countries are well-satisfied with their healthcare and medical systems; that the United States is an exception in this regard is well-known, see Davis et al. (2007), who find also that the United States does not lag in the *effectiveness* of healthcare, but does in other dimensions such as equity, access, and safety. Experience is much more diverse among the poor countries of the world, but people in some poor countries (such as Vietnam, Thailand, Malaysia, and Cuba) have great confidence in the healthcare system, and the majority of poor countries do much better than does the United States, even if they deliver much worse health outcomes. The ranking of the United States in the World Poll (81 out of 115) is even worse than in the World Health Organization (WHO) (2000), though

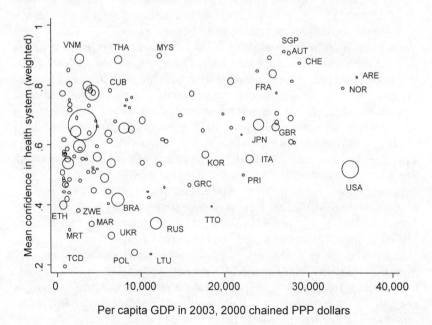

Fig. 9.12   Satisfaction with health care and income

it should be noted that the WHO's methodology has been robustly challenged by several commentators (see in particular Williams [2001]).

Given the high correlation between the subjective evaluations in different domains, here between personal health and the healthcare system, it is worth returning to life satisfaction and asking whether we can "explain" life satisfaction in terms of health satisfaction. This follows Easterlin (2006), who relates overall life satisfaction to satisfactions in the various domains and thus aggregating satisfactions into an overall evaluation. Certainly, if we repeat the regressions in table 9.2 with health satisfaction on the right-hand side, there is a large (close to 4) and statistically significant coefficient, and with this variable added, life expectancy, the change in life expectancy, and the rate of economic growth lose their significance. While such regressions are useful for understanding the life satisfaction responses (though one might just as well argue for regressing health satisfaction on life satisfaction), they are less useful for deciphering the relationship between the satisfaction reports and the objective circumstances of life.

9.6 Discussion

The currently dominant approach for measuring population well-being is based on Sen's ideas of measuring people's abilities to function, or their capabilities to lead a life worth living. Without health, there is very little that people can do and, without income, health alone does little to enable people to lead a good life. Other factors, such as education or the ability to participate in society, are important too, although income and health tend to get the primary attention in evaluations of development progress, for example in the Millennium Development Goals. For many reasons, elaborated by Sen and others, self-reports of satisfaction with life, with income, or health are given little weight. People may adapt to misery and hardship, and cease to see it for what it is. They do not necessarily perceive their lack of freedom as a problem; the child who is potentially a great musician but never has a chance to find out will not express her lack of satisfaction, and whole groups can be taught that their poor health, or their lack of political participation, are natural or even desirable aspects of a good world.

Some of these issues have an empirical as well as philosophical component, and it is possible that reports of life satisfaction, at least on average, provide a clear-eyed aggregate of the different components of peoples' capabilities. Some of the results in this chapter are quite supportive of that position, much more so than I had originally expected. In particular, the very strong international relationship between per capita GDP and life satisfaction suggests that, on average, people have a good idea of how income, or the lack of it, affects their lives. It is simply not true that the people of India are as satisfied with their lives as the people of France, let alone Denmark, nor is it true that people in sub-Saharan Africa, or Afghanistan, Iraq, or

Cambodia, are as happy as people in India. Beyond that, the misery of many of the countries of Eastern Europe and the former Soviet Union seems plausible enough, as does the special misery of the elderly in those countries. As a result, the map in figure 9.1 clearly corresponds in broad detail to what an overall map of capabilities might look like, always supposing we could construct such a thing.

But when we turn to health and its effects on life satisfaction, the poll results diverge from what would be required in the capabilities approach. Longer life expectancy surely enables people to do more with their lives yet, conditional on income, it has no apparent effect on life satisfaction. Instead, it is *changes* in the expectation of life that seem to have an effect, no matter whether life expectancy is high or low. Even satisfaction with health, a much more focused question, is not related to life expectancy, though in some specifications it is sensitive to changes in life expectancy, consistent with a focusing illusion for health. The extraordinary low health satisfaction ratings for Eastern Europe and the countries of the former Soviet Union are a testament, not to their poor population health, but to the effects of a decline in health among a population that was used to a better state of affairs. It is also the case that in the rich countries it is people in their fifties, not in their sixties or seventies, who report the least satisfaction with their health and the highest level of disability. Again, this is a group whose health is actually much better than that of their elders, but who are experiencing health problems for the first time; perhaps it is not poor health that is hard to bear, but the first intimations of mortality. In the poor countries, and particularly in Africa, where the joint evolution of man and parasites has ensured that, for hundreds of thousands of years, morbidity has been a constant companion throughout life (Iliffe 1995), health satisfaction declines rapidly with age. But this does not mean that health satisfaction is a good indicator of health capabilities in the poorest countries. That it is not so is demonstrated by the fact that countries with high rates of HIV prevalence do not systematically report poorer health status, a finding that is in line with earlier reports that self-reported health measures are often better in places where people are sicker, and presumably more adapted to being sick (Sen 2002; Chen and Murray 1992).

In spite of the positive relationship between life satisfaction and national income, and in spite of the plausibility of unhappiness and health dissatisfaction in the countries of Eastern Europe, neither life satisfaction nor health satisfaction can be taken as reliable indicators of population well-being, if only because neither adequately reflects objective conditions of health.

Even if this conclusion is accepted—and for a different view see Graham (2005)—the satisfaction questions are clearly of interest in their own right, as is the analysis of their correlates. These are among the best measures that we have of an important aspect of human experience, and we need to understand what and why they are. In this respect, this analysis of the World Poll data has confirmed a number of earlier findings, but has yielded some new and different results. One surprising finding is figure 9.3, the close to linear relationship across countries between average life satisfaction and the logarithm of income per head. There is no evidence that the cross-country effects of income vanish among the richer countries. It is also true that life satisfaction responds to changes in circumstances, though the effects of economic growth are *negative* and not positive, as would be predicted by previous discussion and almost all previous microbased empirical evidence. Health satisfaction, in contrast, responds very weakly to (perhaps unsatisfactory) objective measures of health, though there is a response of the correct sign to changes in life expectancy, at least in some specifications.

The 2006 within-country age profiles of life satisfaction are quite different from country to country, sometimes declining, sometimes exhibiting a U-shape, and sometimes showing no particular pattern. But in the 2006 cross-sections, there is a systematic tendency for both life and health satisfaction to decline more rapidly with age in poorer countries. As with many other things, wealth helps buffer the effects of aging on at least the perception of good health and the good life.

References

Argyle, M. 1999. Causes and correlates of happiness. In *Well-being: The foundations of hedonic psychology,* New York: Russell Sage. ed. D. Kahneman, E. Diener, and N. Schwarz, 353–73.
Blanchflower, D. G., and A. Oswald. 2004. Well-being over time in Britain and the USA. *Journal of Public Economics* 88 (7–8): 1359–86.
———. 2007. Is well-being U-shaped over the life-cycle? NBER Working Paper no. 12935. Cambridge, MA: National Bureau of Economic Research, February.
Chen, L., and C. Murray. 1992. Understanding morbidity change. *Population and Development Review* 18 (September): 481–504.
Clark, A., and A. Oswald. 2002. Well-being in panels. University of Warwick, Department of Economics. Working Paper.
Davis, K., C. Schoen, S. C. Schoenbaum, M. M. Dory, A. L. Holmgren, J. L. Kriss, and K. K. Shea. 2007. Mirror, mirror on the wall: An international update on the comparative performance of American health care. Fund Report of the Commonwealth Fund, vol. 59, May. New York: The Commonwealth Fund.
Diener, E., M. Diener, and C. Diener. 1995. Factors predicting the subjective well-being of nations. *Journal of Personality and Social Psychology* 69 (5): 851–64.
Diener, E., and S. Oishi. 2000. Money and happiness: Income and subjective well-being across nations. In *Culture and subjective well-being,* ed. E. Diener and E. M. Suh, 185–218. Cambridge, MA: MIT Press.
Deaton, A., and C. Paxson. 1994. Intertemporal choice and inequality. *Journal of Political Economy* 102 (3): 437–67.
Di Tella, R., J. Haisken-DeNew, and R. MacCulloch. 2005. Happiness adaptation to income and to status in an individual panel. Working Paper, October.

Easterlin, R. A. 1974. Does economic growth improve the human lot? In *Nations and households in economic growth: essays in honor of Moses Abramovitz,* ed. P. A. David and M. W. Reder, 89–125. New York: Academic Press.

———. 1995. Will raising the incomes of all increase the happiness of all? *Journal of Economic Behavior and Organization* 27 (1): 35–48.

———. 2003. Explaining happiness. *Proceedings of the National Academy of Science* 100 (19): 11176–83.

———. 2006. Life cycle happiness and its sources: Intersections of psychology, economics, and demography. *Journal of Economic Psychology* 27 (4): 463–82.

Graham, C. 2005. Insights on development from the economics of happiness. *World Bank Research Observer* 20 (2): 201–31.

Helliwell, J. F. 2003. How's life? Combining individual and national variables to explain subjective well-being. *Economic Modeling* 20 (2): 331–60.

Iliffe, J. 1995. *Africans: The history of a continent.* Cambridge: Cambridge University Press.

Inglehart, R., and H.-D. Klingemann. 2000. Genes, culture, democracy, and happiness. In *Culture and subjective well-being,* ed. E. Diener and E. M. Suh, 165–83. Cambridge, MA: MIT Press.

Kahneman, D., A. B. Krueger, D. Schkade, N. Schwarz, and A. A. Stone. 2006. Would you be happier if you were richer? A focusing illusion. *Science* 312 (5782): 1908–10.

Layard, R. 2005. *Happiness: Lessons from a new science.* New York: The Penguin Press.

Leigh, A., and J. Wolfers. 2006. Happiness and the human development index: Australia is not a paradox. *The Australian Economic Review* 39 (2): 176–84.

Preston, S. H. 1975. The changing relation between mortality and level of economic development. *Population Studies* 29:231–48.

Robbins, L. 1938. Interpersonal comparisons of utility: A comment. *Economic Journal* 43 (4): 635–41.

Sen, A. K. 1999. *Development as freedom.* New York: Knopf.

———. 2002. Health: Perception versus observation. *British Medical Journal* 324 (7342): 860–1.

Veenhoven, R. 1991. Is happiness relative? *Social Indicators Research* 24:1–34.

Williams, A. 2001. Science or marketing at WHO? A commentary on "World Health 2000." *Health Economics* 10:93–100.

World Health Organization. 2000. *World health report 2000—Health systems, improving performance.* Geneva: WHO.

Comment   Amitabh Chandra and Heidi Williams

Many questions in economics are motivated by the question of what circumstances or public policies make individuals better or worse off. Traditionally, economists have relied on revealed preference arguments to motivate the

Amitabh Chandra is an assistant professor of public policy at the John F. Kennedy School of Government, Harvard University, and a faculty research fellow at the National Bureau of Economic Research. Heidi Williams is a PhD student in economics at Harvard University.

Chandra gratefully acknowledges support from the National Institute on Aging (NIA P01-AG19783); Williams gratefully acknowledges support from the National Institute on Aging, Grant Number T32-AG0000186 to the NBER.

idea that these questions can be answered by studying data on people's observed choices. Dating back at least to the work of Richard Easterlin (1974), an alternative and complementary literature has developed that focuses on studying data on subjective self-reports of individuals' well-being—for example, questions that are roughly of the form: "Would you say you are very happy, happy but not very happy, unhappy but not very unhappy, or very unhappy?"

Building on Easterlin's seminal work in this area, a large literature has developed that uses these types of "happiness" measures to study a variety of questions—ranging from whether divorcing couples become happier after their marriage dissolves (Gardner and Oswald 2006) to whether the narrowing of the gender gap (broadly construed) has led to increases in happiness among women (Stevenson and Wolfers, forthcoming). But arguably the main focus of this economics of happiness literature has been on the question that Easterlin initially addressed—namely, on studying the relationship between income and happiness. In what is thought to be the first analysis of this relationship, Easterlin (1974) noted that although average gross domestic product (GDP) per capita rose between 1975 and 1997 in the United States, mean reported happiness remained relatively flat.

In an insightful and thoughtful chapter, Angus Deaton brings fresh perspective to the economics of happiness literature. Deaton's analysis is based on the newly available Gallup World Poll data, which covers a large number of countries and includes data that is nationally representative for persons age fifteen and older; the latter feature is arguably an important improvement from previously used data sources, which often only sample urban and literate populations. Deaton uses this data to reexamine the Easterlin puzzle as well as many of the other classic questions in the economics of happiness literature. Importantly, despite noting a powerful association between life satisfaction and income, he notes that the association between health satisfaction and health (measured as life expectancy and HIV prevalence) is tenuous. Deaton concludes that these small correlations between subjective measures and real health outcomes should temper our proclivity to conclude that subjective well-being measures are reliable indicators of population health.

Are Subjective Well-Being Measures Useful Summary Measures of Social Welfare?

Deaton examines the cross-country relationship between average life satisfaction and life expectancy (table 9.2), and finds that life expectancy and changes in life expectancy play limited roles in explaining international cross-sectional variations in average reported life satisfaction. Income displays a persistent and robust role in predicting life satisfaction, and it does not appear to be a statistical surrogate for life expectancy. Deaton notes that measures of infant mortality, child mortality, and HIV prevalence explain little of the variation in reported life satisfaction. When he examines the analogous relationship between average health satisfaction (rather than life satisfaction) and life expectancy (table 9.3), he finds that life expectancy and changes in it play a limited role in explaining international variations in average reported health satisfaction.

Deaton correctly notes that these results are at odds with the view that subjective health should be at least partially correlated with core measures of objective health. His results raise questions about whether subjective well-being measures can serve as useful summary indicators of human welfare in international comparisons. Similar questions were raised by Betsey Stevenson and Justin Wolfers (2007), who noted that by many objective measures of well-being (for example, real wages, educational attainment, and control over fertility) the lives of women in the United States have improved dramatically over the past thirty-five years. Yet measures of subjective well-being indicate that women's happiness has declined over that period both in absolute terms and relative to male happiness. The authors document this stylized fact in a wide variety of data sets, and show that the trend holds across demographic groups—for both working and stay-at-home moms, for both married and divorced women, for both young and old women, and across the education distribution. These findings raise questions about the legitimacy of using subjective well-being measures to assess the impacts of broadscale social changes.

Examining Links between Measures of Subjective Well-Being and "Real" Outcomes

Di Tella and MacCulloch (2006) review the literature on what subjective measures of well-being are actually measuring and argue that elicitations of happiness almost surely provide a measure of true internal utility at the individual level. The authors acknowledge that there is clearly some noise in measurement, but their interpretation is that the signal-to-noise ratio in the available data is sufficiently high to make empirical research productive. As evidence, they cite cross-sectional and panel studies, which suggest that unemployed individuals tend to report low happiness scores (Clark and Oswald 1994; Winkelmann and Winkelmann 1998), suggesting that happiness surveys are capturing something meaningful about "true" utility.

Others who have noted the value of subjective measures of health include Blanchflower and Oswald (2008), who use cross-country data and provide evidence that "happier" countries report systematically lower levels of (albeit, self-reported) hypertension, or high blood pressure. As noted by the authors, objective hypertension measures would be valuable for this analysis but are not available for all countries in their sample. A natural and useful extension of this type of analysis would be to ask whether changes in "real" health measures affect changes in measures of subjective well-being. For example, one can imagine using micro-level empirical data to directly test the hypothesis that changes in life expectancy affect measures of subjective well-being. Variation in life expectancy may be usefully generated by within-person differences generated when individuals learn the results of medical diagnostic tests—for example, genetic tests that give information on an individual's probability of being diagnosed with breast cancer. Clearly, there would be two components to such an exercise—first to measure the short-run response on subjective health, and also to measure the longer-run response. This latter reaction may, in theory, be smaller than the former if individuals adapt to changes in objective health status over time.

If the results of such micro-level empirical studies provide evidence that changes in health translate into changes in subjective well-being, one could then explore potential explanations that could reconcile these micro-level estimates with the types of macro-level evidence provided by Deaton—which suggested little if any relationship between changes in life expectancy and measures of subjective well-being. Finding an association in micro-analysis that is not present in the macro-analysis could be reconciled through a model that included some form of country level differences in health temperament, reference-dependent preferences, or sample-selection. The first theory would suggest that there is an idiosyncratic, country-specific, "fixed effect" in how subjective health is reported. The presence of such an effect could, in principal, mask a macro relationship between subjective and objective health. Of course, if these idiosyncratic differences in temperament were truly fixed, the lack of a macro-level association between subjective and objective health would reemerge if the regression was estimated in changes (something that would be possible with panel data). An alternative theory, as discussed by Di Tella and MacCulloch (2006), is that many researchers—beginning with Easterlin himself in his original 1974 article—have suggested that subjective well-being measures may be capturing some form of reference-dependent preferences (which in a cross-section would be statistically indistinguishable from country fixed effects in temperament). In the context of studying the relationship between income and self-reported measures of subjective well-being, several recent studies have suggested that individuals' self-reported well-being may depend on their consumption or income relative to some reference group (see, for example, Clark [2003] and Luttmer [2005]). Analogously in the context of life expectancy instead of income, if individuals' utility was modeled as a function of their life expectancy relative to the life expectancy of some reference group, it is possible that a positive correlation between life expectancy and reported well-being at the individual level could be consistent with there being no or even a negative correlation at the aggregate level. A negative correlation between life expectancy and reported well-being at the aggregate level could arise if decreases in life expectancy associated (for example) with HIV decreased average life expectancy, but the actual individuals affected by HIV who themselves have lower life expectancy are less likely to be captured by surveys than are non-HIV affected individuals. This hypothesis is arguably ruled out by the sampling scheme of the Gallup data, which promises representative samples. But to the extent to which sicker individuals are less likely to complete these surveys, or are more likely to be hospitalized, it is not difficult to see that sample-selection is a third theory that may offer an explanation for the observed facts.

In the absence of additional empirical evidence that changes in objective measures of well-being (such as life expectancy) are correlated with changes in subjective measures of well-being, we agree with Deaton that it seems difficult to argue that these subjective measures of well-being can serve as useful summary measures of social welfare that can be used to guide policy. For example, if one policy was found to raise subjective measures of well-being but leave infant mortality unchanged, and an alternative policy was found to reduce infant mortality rates but leave subjective measures of well-being unchanged, one would need to take a stance on which measures should be given more weight in a social welfare function. It seems difficult to argue that subjective well-being measures should be valued over "real" measures such as infant mortality, at least in the absence of much more empirical evidence on these questions.

References

Blanchflower, D., and A. Oswald. 2008. Hypertension and happiness across nations. *Journal of Health Economics* 27 (2): 218–33.

Clark, A. 2003. Unemployment as a social norm: Psychological evidence from panel data. *Journal of Labor Economics* 21 (2): 323–51.

Clark, A., and A. Oswald. 1994. Unhappiness and unemployment. *Economic Journal* 104 (424): 628–59.

Di Tella, R., and R. MacCulloch. 2006. Some uses of happiness data in economics. *Journal of Economic Perspectives* 20 (1): 25–46.

Easterlin, R. 1974. Does economic growth improve the human lot? Some empirical evidence. In *Nations and households in economic growth: Essays in honor of Moses Abramovitz,* ed. P. David and M. Reder, 89–125. New York and London: Academic Press.

Gardner, J., and A. Oswald. 2006. Do divorcing couples become happier by breaking up? *Journal of the Royal Statistical Society Series A* 169 (2): 319–36.

Luttmer, E. 2005. Neighbors as negatives: Relative earnings and well-being. *Quarterly Journal of Economics* 120 (3): 963–1002.

Stevenson, B., and J. Wolfers. Forthcoming. The paradox of declining female happiness. *American Economic Journal: Economic Review.*

Winkelmann, L., and R. Winkelmann. 1998. Why are the unemployed so unhappy? Evidence from panel data. *Economica* 65 (257): 1–15.

IV

Retirement Saving

10

The Rise of 401(k) Plans, Lifetime Earnings, and Wealth at Retirement

James M. Poterba, Steven F. Venti, and David A. Wise

Over the past two-and-a-half decades there has been a fundamental change in the way people save for retirement in the United States. There has been a rapid shift from saving through employer-managed defined benefit (DB) pensions to defined contribution (DC) retirement saving plans that are largely controlled by employees. Just two or three decades ago, employer-provided DB plans were the primary means of saving for retirement in the United States. But since that time, 401(k) and other personal retirement accounts have become the principal form of retirement saving in the private sector. More than 80 percent of private retirement plan contributions in 2000 and 2001 were to 401(k) and other personal accounts. The DB plans have remained an important form of retirement saving for federal employees and for state and local employees, although even for these employees personal retirement accounts are becoming increasingly important. Contributions to personal retirement plans accounted for only 12 percent of total contributions to Federal pension plans in 2000, but had increased to 17 percent by 2004. We do not have quantitative data on state and local DC

James M. Poterba is president and CEO of the National Bureau of Economic Research and the Mitsui Professor of Economics at the Massachusetts Institute of Technology. Steven F. Venti is the DeWalt Ankeny Professor of Economic Policy and a professor of economics at Dartmouth College, and a research associate of the National Bureau of Economic Research. David A. Wise is the John F. Stambaugh Professor of Political Economy at the John F. Kennedy School of Government, Harvard University, and director of the program on aging at the National Bureau of Economic Research.

This research was supported by the U.S. Social Security Administration (SSA) through grant #10-P-98363-1-02 to the National Bureau of Economic Research. Funding was also provided by the National Institute on Aging, through P01 AG005842 to the National Bureau of Economic Research. The findings and conclusions expressed are solely those of the authors and do not represent the views of SSA, any agency of the Federal Government, or the NBER.

plans but anecdotal evidence suggests that contributions to these plans are growing rapidly as well. This transition to personal retirement saving has important implications for the well-being of the elderly and perhaps for design changes in Social Security as well.

In Poterba, Venti, and Wise (2007a), we described the rise of 401(k) plans and the implications of this rise for the flow of assets into and out of 401(k) plans over the next four decades. In Poterba, Venti, and Wise (2007b) we described the decline in DB plans and assessed the implications of the decline for the flow of assets into and out of DB plans over the next four decades. Our projections suggest that the average (over all persons) present value of real DB benefits at age sixty-five achieved a maximum in 2003, when this value was $72,637 (in year 2000 dollars), and then began to decline. The projections also suggest that by 2010 the average level of 401(k) assets at age sixty-five will exceed the average present value of DB benefits at age sixty-five. Thereafter the value of 401(k) assets grows rapidly, attaining levels much greater than the historical maximum present value of DB benefits. If equity returns between 2006 and 2040 are comparable to those observed historically, by 2040 average projected 401(k) assets of all persons age sixty-five will be over six times larger than the maximum level of DB benefits for a sixty-five-year-old achieved in 2003 (in year 2000 dollars). Even if equity returns average 300 basis points below their historical value, we project that average 401(k) assets in 2040 would be 3.7 times as large as the value of DB benefits in 2003.

These analyses consider changes in the aggregate level of pension assets. Although the projections indicate that the *average* level of retirement assets will grow very substantially over the next three or four decades, it is also clear that the accumulation of assets in 401(k)-like plans will vary across households. Whether a person has a 401(k) plan is strongly related to income. Low-income employees are much less likely than higher-income employees to be covered by a 401(k) or similar type of tax-deferred personal account plan. Thus, in this chapter we focus on the accumulation of 401(k) assets by lifetime earnings deciles. Because we are interested in the relationship between Social Security wealth and the future change in 401(k) assets, we also consider the accumulation of 401(k) assets by Social Security wealth deciles. We consider in particular how the combined accumulation of Social Security and 401(k) assets will change over the next three-and-a-half decades.

In section 10.1 we set out background data that helps to put in context the projections we present in this chapter. In section 10.2 we set out the method that we use to project 401(k) assets. In section 10.3 we describe the average level of 401(k) assets for cohorts that attain retirement age in each year through 2040. In section 10.4 we describe the rise in 401(k) assets by lifetime earning deciles and by Social Security wealth deciles and then consider how the total of Social Security and 401(k) assets will change between 2000 and 2040.

10.1   Background

We describe first the relationship between age and earnings, and current 401(k) eligibility and participation rates. We then describe current levels of dedicated retirement assets—Social Security and private pensions—for persons near retirement age.

Table 10.1 shows 401(k) plan eligibility and participation rates by annual earnings and by age in 2003, based on data from the Survey of Income and Program Participation (SIPP). The table shows 401(k) eligibility and participation rates for families that have been created by matching SIPP data for persons. The "age" of the family is the age of the reference person. A family participates in (is eligible for) a 401(k) plan if either spouse participates in (is eligible for) a 401(k) plan. The sample is restricted to families with positive earnings in 2003. These eligibility and participation rates pertain to all employer-based 401(k)-like saving plans, but exclude participation in Keogh and individual retirement account (IRA) plans. Eligibility rates do not differ much by age. But families with low earnings are much less likely than families with higher earnings to be covered by 401(k) plans. Over 87 percent of families with earnings greater than $100,000 per year were eligible for a 401(k) plan; less than 36 percent of families with earnings less than $25,000 per year were eligible. Participation follows a similar pattern. About 80 percent of families with annual earning over $100,000 participate; about 20 percent of families with earnings less than $25,000 participate.

It is likely that in the future 401(k) participation rates will also vary by earnings and thus the level of 401(k) assets will vary by earnings. In other words, there is likely to be a strong relationship between lifetime earnings

Table 10.1   401(k) eligibility and participation, by age and earnings

		Age		
Earnings	< 35	35–50	50–65	All
		Eligibility		
< $25k	33.6	37.8	34.0	35.2
25–50	65.0	66.1	64.1	65.2
50–100	79.9	81.3	78.0	80.1
> $100k	86.7	88.4	85.6	87.2
All	56.4	64.0	56.5	59.6
		Participation		
< $25k	17.4	23.5	20.0	20.4
25–50	47.8	50.5	50.6	49.7
50–100	65.8	70.5	67.5	68.6
> $100k	75.1	81.3	80.6	80.0
All	40.4	51.0	44.1	45.9

Source: Author's calculations from the 2003 SIPP.

and 401(k) assets. Thus, the level of 401(k) assets relative to Social Security wealth will also vary greatly among families. In particular, the ratio of 401(k) assets to the present value of Social Security benefits is likely to be highest among families with greater Social Security benefits.

Table 10.2 shows average dedicated retirement assets in 2000 for households with heads sixty-three to sixty-seven by "*lifetime* earnings" deciles. Unlike table 10.1, this table includes families in which no member is employed, as well as families that include an employed person. Dedicated retirement assets include DB and 401(k) pension wealth as well as Social Security wealth and balances in IRA and Keogh plans. These estimates are based on data from the Health and Retirement Study (HRS). They pertain to families comprised of persons for whom the HRS obtained Social Security earnings records. The earnings are corrected for the Social Security earnings limit, as described in the appendix. The calculations for each asset category are also explained in the appendix.

There are several key features of the data. First, the category "401(k) assets" includes all 401(k)-like plans, such as 403(b) plans, 457 plans, employee stock option plans, supplemental retirement accounts, thrift saving plans, stock and profit-sharing plans, money purchase plans, as well as traditional employer-provided DC plans. Second, for this age group in particular, 401(k) and IRA assets must be considered jointly. A large fraction of assets in IRA plans are "rollovers" from 401(k) plans. Many new retirees "rollover" 401(k) assets into an IRA plan when they retire or have "rolled over" 401(k) assets into an IRA in the past when they changed jobs. For example, 89 percent of flows into IRA accounts were rollovers in 1996, 89 percent in 1997, 93 percent in 1998, 95 percent in 1999, and 96 percent were rollovers in 2000.[1] In the subsequent analyses we present projections of 401(k) assets, including assets that would have been rolled over into IRA accounts. Third, the sum of 401(k) and IRA assets is large, greater than average DB assets for all deciles combined. But even for the lower lifetime earnings deciles the amounts in personal retirement accounts are substantial. Recall that IRA and 401(k) plans were introduced in 1982 so that households whose heads were sixty-three to sixty-seven in 2000 could have contributed for (at most) eighteen years to such plans. Copeland (2004) reports that persons with IRA accounts in 2001 had contributed an average of 8.2 years and persons with 401(k) plans in 2001 had contributed an average of 7.2 years.

Fourth, both dedicated retirement assets and total wealth increase noticeably with lifetime earnings, as would be expected. Following, we consider the ratio of assets and total wealth to lifetime earnings and find that this ratio does not show a systematic relationship to lifetime earnings.

Table 10.3 is similar to table 10.2 except that the deciles are defined by Social Security wealth (the discounted present value of expected Social

---

1. See Figure 5 of Holden et al. (2005).

Table 10.2   Mean household assets by lifetime earnings decile, HRS respondents age 63 to 67 (year 2000 dollars)

Lifetime earnings decile	Sum of lifetime earnings	SS wealth	DB pension wealth	401(k) assets	IRA and Keogh assets	401(k) + IRA and Keogh assets	Total dedicated retirement assets[a]	Other nonretirement nonhousing assets	Home equity	Total wealth
1	70,993	74,074	65,372	168	23,157	23,325	162,771	79,037	59,948	301,756
2	341,717	97,345	42,877	989	11,162	12,151	152,373	57,763	49,415	259,551
3	622,660	109,638	76,101	4,363	19,492	23,855	209,593	103,125	65,070	377,788
4	950,451	131,219	72,846	18,528	29,523	48,051	252,117	88,598	79,012	419,726
5	1,336,716	176,401	89,382	12,010	31,994	44,004	309,787	141,396	94,958	546,142
6	1,722,307	196,484	73,890	20,745	66,958	87,703	358,077	154,865	90,008	602,949
7	2,063,969	225,868	94,841	23,210	67,263	90,473	411,182	229,444	96,835	737,461
8	2,398,018	244,630	118,559	12,166	95,415	107,581	470,770	221,927	121,249	813,946
9	2,760,500	260,767	129,356	36,990	116,659	153,649	543,772	264,321	136,891	944,984
10	3,565,347	279,080	151,608	124,323	295,400	419,723	850,412	540,170	203,659	1,594,241
All	1,612,059	181,373	92,288	26,098	77,716	103,814	377,475	191,457	100,833	669,765

[a]Sum of DB, 401(k), SS, IRA, and Keogh assets.

Table 10.3 Mean household assets by Social Security wealth, HRS respondents age 63 to 67 (year 2000 dollars)

Social Security wealth decile	Sum of lifetime earnings	SS wealth	DB pension wealth	401(k) assets	IRA and Keogh assets	401(k) + IRA and Keogh assets	Total dedicated retirement assets[a]	Other nonretirement nonhousing assets	Home equity	Total wealth
1	580,433	4,130	102,978	4,689	30,909	35,598	142,707	114,801	76,699	334,207
2	439,816	63,202	45,689	3,638	15,744	19,382	128,272	77,025	46,049	251,347
3	809,662	104,223	77,392	13,945	25,255	39,200	220,815	67,327	53,617	341,760
4	1,196,148	144,732	84,379	19,690	50,006	69,696	298,806	130,049	84,076	512,931
5	1,413,009	185,295	89,797	18,934	47,513	66,447	341,540	142,331	108,009	591,880
6	1,693,391	220,624	53,015	26,382	54,731	81,113	354,752	179,014	96,581	630,347
7	2,053,137	243,583	78,149	19,908	72,888	92,796	414,527	198,514	98,891	711,932
8	2,469,990	260,405	121,052	33,613	122,325	155,938	537,395	272,371	131,956	941,722
9	2,641,173	275,658	125,599	78,679	168,943	247,622	648,878	393,285	148,379	1,190,542
10	2,820,765	311,403	144,801	41,332	188,555	229,887	686,091	339,298	163,932	1,189,321
All	1,612,059	181,373	92,288	26,098	77,716	103,814	377,475	191,457	100,833	669,765

[a]Sum of DB, 401(k), SS, IRA, and Keogh assets.

Security benefits) instead of lifetime earnings. A noticeable feature of these data is that households in the lowest Social Security wealth decile have relatively large personal pension wealth—$138,576 in non-Social Security dedicated retirement assets, compared to $88,697 for households in the lowest lifetime earnings decile. In addition, this group has an average of $334,207 in total wealth, somewhat greater than the total wealth of households in the lowest lifetime earnings decile. This apparent anomaly is, in part, a consequence of our measurement of lifetime earnings, which is based on Social Security earnings records. Some households were likely not eligible for Social Security over their entire working lives. Thus, in some years a person may have worked in a job not covered by the Social Security system. Earnings in these years are not included in the Social Security earnings records and thus not included in our measure of lifetime earnings. Thus, actual earnings may be greater than measured earnings, particularly in the lowest lifetime earnings decile.

Finally, in table 10.4 we show ratio of dedicated retirement assets to lifetime earnings and the ratio of total wealth to lifetime earnings. We consider these ratios by lifetime earnings decile (the left three columns of the table) and by Social Security wealth decile (the right three columns of the table). Recall that our "lifetime earnings" are based on earnings reported to the Social Security Administration. Persons who were never covered by Social Security are not in the data. Persons who were covered by Social Security for only a portion of their working lives are in the data, but for some their actual earnings may be considerably larger than Social Security earnings. The difference between actual and Social Security earnings is likely to be the

Table 10.4   **Ratio of dedicated retirement assets to Social Security lifetime earnings and ratio of total wealth to lifetime earnings, by lifetime earnings decile and by Social Security wealth decile**

Lifetime earnings decile	Dedicated retirement assets	Total wealth	Social Security wealth decile	Dedicated retirement assets	Total wealth
1	2.29	4.25	1	0.25	0.58
2	0.45	0.76	2	0.29	0.57
3	0.34	0.61	3	0.27	0.42
4	0.27	0.44	4	0.25	0.43
5	0.23	0.41	5	0.24	0.42
6	0.21	0.35	6	0.21	0.37
7	0.20	0.36	7	0.20	0.35
8	0.20	0.34	8	0.22	0.38
9	0.20	0.34	9	0.25	0.45
10	0.24	0.45	10	0.24	0.42
All	0.23	0.42	All	0.23	0.42

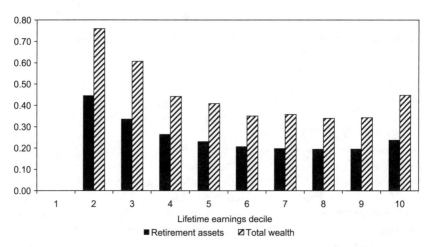

Fig. 10.1   Ratio of retirement assets to lifetime earnings and ratio of total wealth to lifetime earnings, by lifetime earnings decile

greatest for persons with low reported Social Security earnings, as discussed following.

Consider first the ratios by lifetime earnings decile, which are graphed in figure 10.1 (excluding the data for the lowest decile). The ratio of dedicated retirement assets to lifetime earnings (shown as dark bars in the figure) in the fourth to the tenth deciles varies only between 0.20 and 0.27. The variation in the ratio of total wealth to lifetime earnings is, to us, also surprisingly small over the fourth to the tenth deciles, ranging from 0.34 to 0.45. These data suggest that when dedicated retirement assets at age sixty-five are compared to lifetime earnings, the "retirement replacement rate" does not vary greatly by lifetime income. The data also seem to suggest that the total "saving rate" (including Social Security, housing wealth, and nonretirement financial assets) may not vary greatly by lifetime earnings deciles and in particular that the saving rate may not increase systematically with lifetime earnings. However, we emphasize the accumulation of retirement assets and not the saving rate as typically measured. There has been considerable analysis of this issue by others and we do not pursue the question further here.[2]

Since we are particularly interested in the relationship between Social Security wealth and other assets, we want to consider the ratios for deciles defined by Social Security wealth. They are shown in the last three columns of table 10.4 and are graphed in figure 10.2. The ratio of dedicated retirement assets to lifetime earnings within Social Security wealth deciles ranges

---

2. Gustman and Steinmeier (1999) and Venti and Wise (1998) find a relatively flat wealth to lifetime earnings profile. Dynan, Skinner, and Zeldes (2004) find an upward sloping profile. They also present a comprehensive review of the literature on this topic.

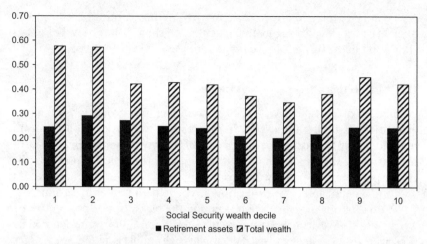

Fig. 10.2   Ratio of retirement assets to lifetime earnings and ratio of total wealth to lifetime earnings, by Social Security wealth decile

from a low of 0.20 in the seventh decile to 0.29 in the second decile, with no systematic pattern by decile. The ratio of total wealth to lifetime earnings ranges from 0.35 in the seventh decile to 0.58 in the first decile. Families with the lowest Social Security wealth accumulate more total wealth (relative to lifetime earnings) than families with greater Social Security wealth.

From table 10.4 it can be seen that lifetime earnings by Social Security wealth decile differ from lifetime earnings by lifetime earnings deciles. For example, the average of lifetime earnings in the lowest lifetime earnings decile is $70,993, but the average of lifetime earnings for families in the lowest Social Security wealth decile is $580,433. That is, many families with the lowest Social Security wealth have lifetime earnings well above the lowest lifetime earnings decile; the average within the lowest Social Security wealth decile is just below the average in the third earnings decile. Again, this apparent anomaly seems to be due to persons who were not covered by Social Security over their entire working lives and thus had low Social Security wealth even though they had substantial lifetime earnings over the period that earnings were reported to the Social Security Administration.

In the subsequent sections of this chapter we consider how the rise of 401(k) plans will change the accumulation of assets at retirement. In particular we consider how 401(k) assets within lifetime earning deciles and within Social Security wealth deciles will change over time. For the purposes of this chapter we assume that future generations of retirees will receive the same Social Security benefits, and thus have the same Social Security wealth, as current retirees (in year 2000 dollars). Of course, the Social Security benefit formula will likely be different for retirees in 2040 than for retirees in 2006. We begin in the next section by explaining how we project 401(k) assets in the future. We then describe projections by lifetime earnings decile and by Social Security wealth decile. In particular, we show how the level of assets shown in tables 10.2 and 10.3 change with the rise in 401(k) assets.

10.2   Projecting 401(k) Assets at Retirement

In Poterba, Venti, and Wise (2007a), we developed projections of aggregate 401(k) assets in future years. In this chapter, we consider how the accumulation of 401(k) assets varies across families with different lifetime earnings histories. In this section, we borrow liberally from the discussion in the earlier paper to explain how the projections are developed, but here we add additional detail about the projection of participation rates by earnings.

We first set out the calculations that are the basis for our projections of 401(k) wealth. We denote persons by the subscript i. Cohorts are denoted by subscript c. Associated with each person in each cohort is a lifetime earnings profile. The earnings of person i in cohort c at age a are denoted by $E_{ci}(a)$. The zero-one indicator that person i in cohort c participates in a 401(k) plan at age a is denoted by $P_{ci}(a)$, the rate of return earned on 401(k) assets that were held at the beginning of the year when the person attained age a is denoted by $R_{ci}(a)$, and the contribution rate is denoted by C (expressed as a proportion of earnings). The value of the 401(k) assets held by person i in cohort c at age a is given by

$$(1) \qquad W_{ci}(a) = \sum_{t=0}^{a} \left\{ \prod_{j=0}^{t} [1 + R_{ci}(a - j)] \right\} C_{ci}(a - t),$$

where $C_{ci}(a - t) = E_{ci}(a - t) \cdot P_{ci}(a - t) \cdot c$. This calculation is made for every person (i.e., earnings history) for every age in every cohort. In practice, separate calculations are made for wealth in stocks and bonds and the assumed rates of return do not vary by individual. In particular, the 401(k) wealth of person i in cohort c at sixty-five is given by

$$(2) \qquad W_{ci}(65) = \sum_{t=0}^{65} \left\{ \prod_{j=0}^{t} [1 + R_{ci}(65 - j)] \right\} C_{ci}(65 - t).$$

This accumulation is calculated for each person (earnings history) in our sample.

We then obtain the average wealth held by the population of all persons age sixty-five for a cohort c. To do this we need to know how many persons of type i are in the population. Denote the number of persons with lifetime earnings profile i in cohort c at age sixty-five by N_{ci} (to be determined by population projections). Then the average of 401(k) assets held by all persons in cohort c at age sixty-five is given by

$$(3) \qquad \overline{W}_c(65) = \sum_{i} \left(\frac{N_{ci}(65)}{\sum_{j=1}^{j} N_{cj}(65)} \right) \cdot W_{ci}(65),$$

where J is the number of persons (earnings histories) in the sample. In practice, we do not have population forecasts associated with each earnings history in the sample. Instead, we project total assets using population projections for groups of persons with the same demographic characteristics. The Office of the Actuary of the Social Security Administration has developed population projections by calendar year and age and by gender and marital status. Each earnings history in our sample can also be identified by the gender and marital status of the person. We first calculate the average of $W_{ci}(65)$ separately for each of the four gender-marital status pairs and denote this average by $\overline{W}_{c,gm}$. Then the average wealth at sixty-five for each cohort is determined by

$$
(4) \qquad \overline{W}_c(65) = \sum_{gm} \left(\frac{N_{c,gm}(65)}{\sum_{j=1}^{GM} N_{c,j}(65)} \right) \cdot \overline{W}_{c,gm}(65),
$$

where the sum is over the four gm (gender-marital-status groups) and the number of persons in each of these groups is taken from the Social Security Administration demographic projections.

To implement these calculations we need to develop projections of future 401(k) participation rates and earnings and we need to make assumptions about future 401(k) contribution rates, rates of return, cash-out probabilities, and 401(k) withdrawals. We begin by describing projections of average 401(k) participation rates for each cohort. We then describe the other assumptions that are needed to obtain estimates of 401(k) asset accumulation.

10.2.1   Average Participation Rates

We use data from the SIPP to track the spread of 401(k) plans over the past two decades and to develop projections of future 401(k) assets. Various SIPP surveys enable us to collect data on participation in (and eligibility for) 401(k) plans in 1984, 1987, 1991, 1993, 1995, 1998, and 2003. Each SIPP survey is a random cross-section sample of the population. The cross-section data can be used to create "synthetic" cohorts. For example, to construct cohort data for the cohort that was age twenty-five in 1984 we use the 1984 panel to obtain data for persons twenty-five in that year, the 1987 panel to obtain data for persons who were twenty-eight in that year, the 1991 panel to obtain data for persons who were thirty-two in that year, and so forth. The cohort that was twenty-five in 1984 was forty-four in 2003. We sometimes label a cohort by the age of the cohort in 1984 and sometimes by the year in which the cohort attains age sixty-five. For example, the cohort that is age twenty-five in 1984 attains age sixty-five in 2024 and is referred to as the C25 or the R2024 cohort. The unit of observation in the SIPP is an individual and our projections of 401(k) participation rates are made at the individual level. For some later analyses we aggregate individual-level results to show projections for families.

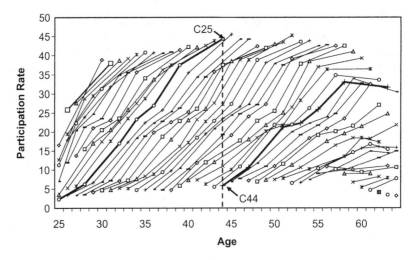

Fig. 10.3   **Person participation rate by cohort**

We begin with historical participation rates for individuals by cohort, as shown in figure 10.3. The earliest SIPP data are for 1984 and the most recent data are for 2003. We will use these data to project 401(k) participation at ages twenty-five through sixty-five for a large number of cohorts, ranging from the cohort that attains age sixty-five in 1982 through the cohort that attains age sixty-five in 2040. Only a few of the cohorts (shown in the bottom right of figure 10.3) had attained age sixty-five by 2003. Thus, for all but a few of the cohorts we must project participation rates from the last observed age in 2003 to age sixty-five.

The participation rate is the eligibility rate times the participation rate given eligibility. The future eligibility rate will depend in particular on the spread of 401(k) plans to small employers. We know that eligibility rates have increased very rapidly over the past two decades, and that participation, given eligibility, increased substantially over the 1984 to 2003 period, as shown in Poterba, Venti, and Wise (2007a). We have not found a compelling way to formally project future rates of eligibility or participation conditional on eligibility. Thus, we have simply made "plausible" assumptions about future participation rates and use them to project future cohort participation rates for persons in cohorts not covered in the SIPP data.

Simple extrapolations of the cohort data are likely to yield implausibly large participation rates. Consider, for example, the participation rates at age forty-four highlighted by the vertical dashed line in figure 10.3. The C44 cohort attained age forty-four in 1984 and had a participation rate of 5.8 percent at that time. The C25 cohort attained age forty-four in 2003, nineteen years later, and had a participation rate of 44.3 percent. On average, the participation rate at age forty-four increased about 2 percentage points with each successively younger cohort. Were this rate to continue, the participation rate of the C12 cohort at age forty-four (that the C12 cohort will attain in 2016) would be 70.3 percent (44.3 + 13 × 2). We suspect that this estimate of the future participation rate is too high, because 401(k) plans have already diffused through the segments of the corporate population that have workforces that find these plans most attractive, and that have the lowest per-employee administrative costs of implementing a plan.

Estimation of cohort effects by fitting the aforementioned profiles shows some compression with successively younger cohorts. In addition, figure 10.3 suggests that within cohorts, the increase in participation rates was lower between the last two data points for each cohort, 1998 and 2003, than for earlier intervals of comparable length. These features of the data suggest that the rate of growth of 401(k) participation may be slowing.

To recognize the apparent compression in the cohort effects and the apparent decline in the rate of within-cohort increase in participation rates, we make future projections for each cohort based on its observed 2003 participation rate. We assume that the annual increase in future participation rate will be smaller than that between 1998 and 2003. In particular, we assume that the future annual rate of increase declines by 0.12 percent per year. With this assumption, the projected future participation rates for the C25 and the C12 cohorts would be as shown in figure 10.4, which also shows the actual participation rates for these cohorts in 2003 and earlier years. Based

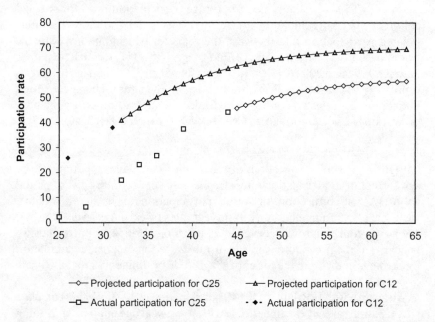

Fig. 10.4   Projected participation rates for cohorts C25 (R2024) and C12 (R2037)

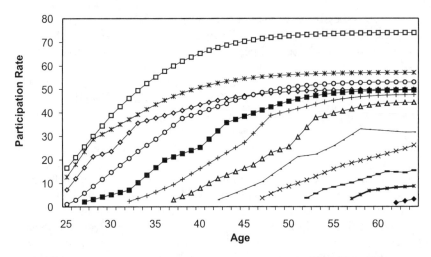

Fig. 10.5   Interpolated (1982–2003) and projected (2004–2040) participation rates for selected cohorts

on these projections, the participation rate of the C12 cohort when it attains age forty-four in 2016 would be 61.7 percent, compared to 44.3 percent for the C25 cohort, which attained age forty-four in 2003. At age sixty-four, the participation rate would be 56.6 percent for the C25 cohort and 69.4 percent for the C12 cohort.

Figure 10.5 shows the projected average participation rates for selected cohorts from C11 (R2038) to C64 (R1985). The figure also shows the interpolated participation rates between the years for which data are available prior to 2003. The decline in the rate of growth of 401(k) participation between 1998 and 2003 (the last two years for which SIPP data are available) is noticeable for many of the cohorts shown in the figure. The figure shows projections for selected cohorts. The projection algorithm we use includes projections for all cohorts from C65 (R1984) through C9 (R2040).

10.2.2   Participation Rates by Earnings

Figure 10.5 shows projections of the average 401(k) participation rate by age and cohort. Participation rates also increase with earnings, given age and cohort. As with projections of average participation rate by age and cohort, we know of no compelling way to project rates by earnings level. Thus, we use a procedure that we believe yields plausible results. In particular, we believe that the procedure yields plausible variation in asset accumulation by earnings, indicating the order of magnitude of differences that are likely to occur.

We begin with SIPP data on 401(k) participation in 2003. We first calculate participation rates by earnings decile within five-year age intervals beginning

Table 10.5   **Actual and fitted participation probabilities by age interval and earnings decile within age interval, from the 2003 SIPP**

	Age interval								
Earnings decile	25–30	30–35	35–40	40–45	45–50	50–55	55–60	60–65	All
	Actual probabilities								
1 (lowest)	12.9	17.3	17.3	16.9	20.4	19.7	18.0	10.7	17.1
2	21.8	22.1	20.5	24.4	25.0	26.7	28.2	23.8	23.8
3	23.3	25.7	30.3	33.2	34.0	41.4	35.5	29.1	31.4
4	25.8	34.8	38.3	40.4	48.7	43.4	42.7	45.5	39.2
5	32.8	44.2	43.9	49.0	54.3	49.8	57.0	39.8	46.5
6	39.3	41.7	48.8	54.5	49.9	54.2	51.7	44.4	48.3
7	45.5	49.3	57.0	60.4	59.9	56.5	59.0	53.8	55.2
8	51.9	55.7	57.7	65.3	56.7	63.7	60.1	56.6	58.6
9	54.4	60.0	62.9	66.2	66.3	60.6	67.7	62.1	62.5
10 (highest)	55.7	62.3	69.8	69.0	70.1	74.5	72.6	62.0	67.2
All	36.6	41.8	45.2	48.3	49.0	49.7	49.8	43.2	45.4
	Fitted probabilities								
1 (lowest)	11.5	14.3	16.4	18.4	18.9	19.3	19.4	15.2	16.5
2	18.0	21.8	24.4	26.9	27.5	28.1	28.2	22.9	24.6
3	24.8	29.2	32.3	35.1	35.8	36.4	36.5	30.5	32.4
4	31.0	36.0	39.2	42.3	43.0	43.7	43.8	37.3	39.4
5	36.6	41.8	45.2	48.3	49.0	49.7	49.8	43.2	45.4
6	41.5	46.8	50.2	53.4	54.0	54.7	54.8	48.2	50.4
7	45.8	51.2	54.7	57.7	58.4	59.1	59.2	52.6	54.9
8	50.0	55.4	58.8	61.8	62.4	63.1	63.2	56.8	59.0
9	54.3	59.6	62.9	65.8	66.5	67.1	67.2	61.0	63.1
10 (highest)	59.0	64.2	67.4	70.1	70.7	71.3	71.4	65.5	67.5
All									

with age twenty-five to age thirty and ending with age sixty to age sixty-five. These rates are shown in the top panel of table 10.5. One feature of these data that we rely on in making projections is that the average participation rate within an age interval is typically close to the fifth decile participation rate within that interval. And the overall participation rate is close to the overall participation rate for the fifth decile. We fit these participation rates with a probit model, allowing estimation of separate coefficients by earnings decile within each of the eight five-year age intervals. We then calculate the probit coefficients for each earnings decile for the average participation rates (over all age groups). These probit coefficients are shown by the markers in figure 10.6. The average effects can be fitted very well by a third-order polynomial as shown in the figure.

The fitted relationship between average participation rates by earnings decile can be used to fit the participation rates for each of the age intervals.

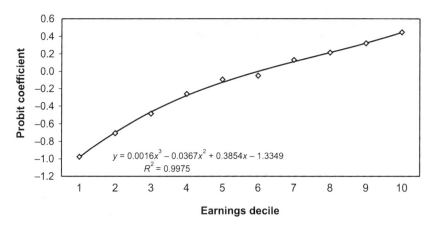

Fig. 10.6   Probit coefficients for average of age interval participation rates, by earnings decile in 2003

For example, suppose we want to estimate the participation rates for persons in the sixty to sixty-five age interval. We follow this procedure: first, we determine the constant term in the polynomial fit (figure 10.6) such that the predicted probability for the fifth decile for the sixty to sixty-five age interval is equal to the average probability for this age interval (0.432). Then using this constant term, we use the polynomial to determine the probit coefficient for each of the other earnings deciles. The corresponding fitted participation probabilities are shown under the sixty to sixty-five heading in the second panel of table 10.5. The fitted probabilities for each of the other age intervals are also shown in the second panel of the table. We judge that, on average, the fitted participation rates by age interval are rather close to the actual participation rates.

These estimated probit coefficients are used to project 401(k) participation rates by earnings decile for a given age within a cohort in future years. In particular, we assume that the *average* projected participation rate (as discussed in the previous section and illustrated in figure 10.5) corresponds to the participation rate of the fifth earnings decile. Consider, for example, the participation rates at age sixty. Figure 10.5 shows the projected average (over all earnings deciles) participation rate at age sixty for several cohorts. We want to project participation rates for each earnings decile at age sixty for each of these cohorts. Following the procedure described before, we first determine the constant term in the polynomial fit (in figure 10.5) such that the participation rate in the fifth earnings decile is equal to the average projected participation rate. Then using the polynomial with this constant term, we predict the participation rate for each of the earnings deciles. Table 10.6 shows the projected participation rates for persons age sixty in cohorts retiring in 2000, 2010, 2020, 2030, and 2040. The average projected rate is

Table 10.6   **Illustration: Projected participation rates at age 60 by earnings decile for three cohorts—R2000, R2020, and R2040**

	Cohort		
Earnings decile	R2000	R2020	R2040
All	43.4	60.7	74.1
1 (lowest)	15.3	27.9	41.6
2	23.0	38.2	53.0
3	30.6	47.3	62.1
4	37.5	54.7	68.9
5	43.4	60.7	74.1
6	48.4	65.5	78.0
7	52.8	69.5	81.2
8	57.0	73.0	83.9
9	61.2	76.5	86.4
10 (highest)	65.7	80.0	88.8

shown in the first row of the table, labeled "All." The remaining rows show projected participation rates for each earnings decile. The probit procedure insures that the projected participation rates by earnings decile are in the 0 to 1 interval. The increase in the participation rate in the tenth decile is from 65.7 in 2000 to 88.8 percent in 2040. The implied increase in the first decile is rather large, from 15.3 in 2000 to 41.6 percent in 2040. Thus, there is some compression of the variation in participation rates by earnings decile. Whether this implication in particular is plausible depends on the spread of 401(k) plans to small firms with low-wage employees over the next three or four decades. Clearly, the results depend on the participation rate and other assumptions we have made.

10.2.3   Asset Allocation and Rate of Return

We assume that 60 percent of 401(k) contributions are allocated to large-capitalization equities and 40 percent to corporate bonds. The projections use actual annual pretax returns through 2005. Beginning in 2006, we make projections based on two rate of return assumptions. First, we assume that the average annual nominal return on equities is 12 percent and that the average nominal return on corporate bonds is 6 percent. Ibbotson Associates (2006) reports that the historical arithmetic mean of pretax returns on long-term corporate bonds has been 6.2 percent per year, while large-capitalization stocks have returned an average of 12.3 percent over the period 1926 to 2005. Second, we assume that the rate of return on equities is 300 basis points less than the historical rate. These returns are the pretax returns available on a portfolio with no management fees. We have not as yet accounted for asset management fees. The average dollar weighted management fee on stock funds is currently about 70 basis points.

10.2.4   Job Separation, Lump Sum Distributions, and Cashouts

At age twenty-five each person is assigned to a 401(k) job based on the participation probability for that person's age, cohort, and earnings. In subsequent years each person either remains in the 401(k) job or leaves the 401(k) job. Job separation rates are estimated from the 1998 SIPP for five-year age intervals. These rates are shown in the first column of table 10.7. Separation rates are allowed to vary by age, but not by time in job. Estimated annual rates range from a high of 23 percent for the youngest workers to 12.1 percent for workers age fifty to fifty-four. After leaving a 401(k) job persons enter a pool of "non-participants." In each year, members of this pool are selected for a new 401(k) job at a rate that makes the overall participation rate for persons of a particular age and cohort equal to the projected probability for that age and cohort. A similar projection algorithm, with an identical treatment of transitions in and out of 401(k) participation, is described in Poterba, Venti, and Wise (2001).

The probability that a 401(k) accumulation is cashed out is determined by the job separation rate, the probability that the employees take a lump sum distribution (LSD), and the probability that a lump sum distribution is cashed out rather than rolled over into an IRA. That is, the probability of a cashout is given by:

$$\text{Pr [cashout]} = \text{Pr [job separation]} \times \text{Pr [LSD]} \times \text{Pr [LSD cashout]}.$$

The probabilities associated with each of the components of the cashout decision are shown in table 10.7.

When employees separate from a job they may choose to keep their accu-

| Table 10.7 | Cashout: Probability of job separation, probability of LSD \| job separation, and probability of cashout \| LSD |

Probability of job separation[a]		Probability LSD | separation[a]	Probability cash out | LSD[b]	
			Size of distribution	Percent of dollars cashed-out
Age	Percent	Percent		
25–29	23.0	57	< $1,000	77.2
30–34	15.6	57	1,000–2,000	67.7
35–39	15.6	57	2,000–5,000	49.6
40–44	13.6	57	5,000–10,000	52.8
45–49	13.9	57	10,000–15,000	39.1
50–54	12.1	57	15,000–25,000	37.8
55–59	12.5	57	25,000–50,000	28.8
60–64	15.7	57	50,000–100,000	8.2
			> $100,000	10.2
All	15.1	57.0		27.2

[a]Authors' calculation based on SIPP data.
[b]From Hurd, Lilliard, and Panis (1998), based on HRS data.

mulation with their old employer or they may decide to take a LSD. The SIPP only provides information on the disposition of a LSD. Thus, we are unable to obtain the probability of a LSD given job separation by age from the SIPP. We use the average rate of 57 percent obtained by Hurd, Lilliard, and Panis based on data from the Health and Retirement Study (HRS). On average, the probability of a cashout in a given year is $(.151) \times (.570) \times (.272) = 0.0234$.

This cashout probability differs from the probability in Poterba, Venti, and Wise (2001). In that paper, the average was about 0.0108. The principle reason for the difference is the job separation rates. In the earlier chapter we used estimates based on retrospective information in the HRS. The average separation rate based on that source was 0.048, compared to the average rate of 0.151 based on the SIPP estimates.[3] In the earlier paper our average estimate of the (probability of a LSD) × (probability of cashout | LSD) was 0.226. The average of these two components used here is somewhat smaller: $(.570) \times (.272) = 0.155$.

10.2.5   Withdrawals

The projections reported here assume a crude withdrawal scheme. Annual withdrawals are assumed to be 2 percent of balances between ages sixty-five and seventy-and-a-half. At older ages, the amount withdrawn from the 401(k) is (1/Remaining Life Expectancy) times the 401(k) balance. These withdrawal assumptions likely overstate amounts withdrawn from 401(k) plans. Berkshadker and Smith (2005) show that over 50 percent of current IRA holders do not make their first withdrawal before age seventy.

10.2.6   Earnings

To estimate the 401(k) contributions of a cohort, we need to determine the earnings and the contribution rates of cohort members. The key to developing an earnings history is access to a long time series of earnings by a single individual or a family. We use the HRS, which provides linked Social Security earnings histories for respondents who agreed to the link. These data represent earnings histories for a sample of individuals who were between the ages of fifty-two and sixty-one in 1992. The implicit assumption in our analysis is that the distribution of earnings histories that will be realized by younger cohorts will be similar to the earnings histories of the HRS respondents.

To develop earnings histories for younger cohorts we begin with the Social Security earnings histories of the HRS respondents, available for the years 1961 through 1991.[4] Earnings for 1992 through 2000 are obtained directly from HRS respondents. We begin with the earnings of the cohorts that

---

3. The estimate of 15.1 percent is approximately 5 percent lower than estimates reported by Stewart (2002), based on Current Population Survey data.

4. We used a two-limit tobit specification (with a separate equation for each year) to impute SS earnings for persons censored at the upper Social Security earnings limit.

attained age sixty-five in 1998, 1999, and 2000. We obtain lifetime earnings for all single persons that attained age sixty-five in these years and for all persons in two-person families in which the male partner attained age sixty-five in these years. The earnings of the 1998 cohort are "aged" two years and the earnings of the 1999 cohort are "aged" one year, based on the Social Security average wage index. We then treat these earnings histories as a random sample of the earnings of the cohort that attained age sixty-five in 2000 (the "R2000" cohort). The sample reports actual earnings histories, including years with zero earnings, so it recognizes that individuals may not be employed in some years. We implicitly assume that the employment rate and the distribution of employment by age are similar for future cohorts as for past ones. (The "R2000" cohort contains some female spouses who were not sixty-five in 2000.)

To make projections for the earnings of younger cohorts, we inflate the "R2000" sample using the intermediate earnings growth assumptions reported in the 2005 Annual report of the Board of Trustees of the Social Security Administration. Similarly, to project a sample of earnings for older cohorts we deflate the earning of the "R2000" cohort based on the Social Security average wage index. This method does not account for any potential change in the relative earnings of high- and low-wage persons.

10.2.7   Contribution Rate

We assume a contribution rate of 10 percent of earnings, including both the employee and the employer contributions. There are several sources of information on contribution rates. Data from the 2003 SIPP are shown by age interval in table 10.8. The overall median of the total of employee and employer contributions is 9.8 percent. The employee and employer medians are 5.7 percent and 3.0 percent, respectively. The overall mean is 12.6 percent. The mean rates may be substantially affected by reporting errors.

Table 10.8   **Employee and employer 401(k) contribution rates as a percent of earnings, for individuals, based on 2003 SIPP**

Age	Employee Mean	Employee Median	Employer Mean	Employer Median	Total Mean	Total Median
25–29	6.8	5.0	4.6	3.0	11.4	9.0
30–34	7.7	5.2	4.6	3.0	12.4	9.3
35–39	7.9	5.8	4.7	3.0	12.5	9.7
40–44	7.8	5.7	4.6	3.0	12.4	10.0
45–49	8.0	6.0	4.8	3.0	12.8	10.0
50–54	8.6	6.0	4.3	3.0	13.0	10.0
55–59	9.1	6.0	4.6	3.0	13.7	10.0
60–64	8.7	6.0	4.6	3.0	13.3	10.0
All	8.0	5.7	4.6	3.0	12.6	9.8

Poterba, Venti, and Wise (1998) reported contribution rates based on the 1993 Current Population Survey (CPS). The average employee contribution rate was 7.1 percent and the average employer rate was 3.1 percent. The 1998 Form 5500 data show that about 32 percent of dollars are contributed by employers, which is roughly consistent with the 2003 SIPP median percent and with the 1993 CPS values. Holden and VanDerHei (2001) analyzed the responses to an Employee Benefit Research Institute (EBRI)-Investment Company Institute (ICI) survey and report that in 1999 the average total contribution rate was 9.7 percent. Cunningham and Engelhardt (2002) report that, based on HRS data, the average employee contribution rate was 6.6 percent in 1991, which is again generally consistent with the estimates based on SIPP and on CPS data.

For several reasons, however, the contribution rate in future years is uncertain. One reason for uncertainty about future contribution rates is the effect of increases in contribution limits. Legislation over the past several years has increased contribution limits very substantially and now future increases are indexed to inflation. Our projections assume that contributions as a percent of salary will be unaffected by the rising limits. In part, the effect of rising limits depends on how many participants are constrained by the contribution limits now and whether fewer participants or more participants will be constrained by future limits. Holden and VanDerHei (2001) report that in 1999, 11 percent of participants with incomes over $40,000 contributed at the legislated maximum, 13 percent of those with incomes between $70,000 and $80,000 did, and 18 percent of those with incomes between $80,000 and $90,000 contributed at the legislated maximum. Thus, one question is how wage growth will interact with rising limits to affect the proportion of persons at the limit. Even though the limits have increased and are now indexed to the Consumer Price Index (CPI), wages are likely to increase faster than the CPI. The Social Security Administration assumes future wage growth of 3.9 percent and future inflation of 2.8 percent. The legislated maximum, however, may not be the effective limit for many employees. Holden and VanDerHei (2001) report that 52 percent of participants in 1999 faced employer imposed limits below the legislated maximum. The number of participants that is constrained by these limits is unknown. And how the limits set by employers might change in the future is also unknown.

In addition, we have not accounted for the recent Pension Protection Act of 2006 that gives employers latitude to set more "saving friendly" defaults in 401(k) plans. Beshears et al. (2008) survey some of the recent evidence on how changing defaults for enrollment, contribution rates, and asset allocation can significantly increase retirement saving through 401(k) plans. Thus, our 401(k) projections may underestimate the actual accumulation of assets in these plans. Finally, the legislated increases in contribution limits may affect participant decisions of how much "should" be saved for retirement. The government-set limits may serve to "frame" employee decisions.

10.3   Average 401(k) Assets at Retirement

The 401(k) projection algorithm discussed previously is based on the earnings histories and contribution rates of persons. In this section we present results based on these data. In the next section, we combine results for persons to present projected asset accumulation for families. The average *per person* of 401(k) assets at age sixty-five (in 2000 dollars) is shown in figure 10.7, for cohorts attaining age sixty-five in years 1982 through 2040 (R 1982 to R2040). Two profiles are shown, one assuming the average historical rate of return for equities and the other assuming the historical rate less 300 basis points. The projected average of 401(k) assets increases very substantially over the next thirty-five years. If the historical rate of return on equities is assumed, the average increases from about $29,000 in 2000, to $137,000 in 2020, to $452,000 by 2040 (all in year 2000 dollars). Assuming the historical rate of return on equities less 300 basis points, the average increases from $29,000 in 2000 to $269,000 by 2040. The projected increase is due to the increase in the participation rates of younger cohorts, to real wage growth, and to the increase in the number of years that 401(k) contributions were possible for successively younger cohorts. The 401(k) program effectively began in 1982 so cohorts retiring before 2020 were unable to make contributions early in their working lives. Persons who attained age sixty-five in 2000 could have contributed to a 401(k) plan for (at most) eighteen years and on average contributed for a little over seven years. For the cohort that will attain age sixty-five in 2040, 401(k) plans will have been available over the entire working life.

Figure 10.8 shows the average of 401(k) assets at retirement for persons who *have 401(k)* plans. For persons with plans, the average increases from

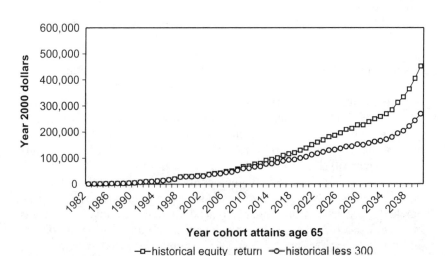

Year cohort attains age 65

–□–historical equity return   –○–historical less 300

Fig. 10.7   Average 401(k) assets at age 65, by year of retirement, all persons

about $87,000 in 2000 to $580,000 by 2040, assuming historical rates of equity return, and to $335,000 assuming historical returns less 300 basis points.

For comparison, the maximum average (over all persons) of the present value of DB benefits at age sixty-five was about $73,000, attained in 2003. Thereafter benefits in DB plans decline, based on the projections in Poterba, Venti, and Wise (2007b). The comparison is shown in detail in figure 10.9 that is the same as figure 10.7 but with the addition of the DB projections.

To check our projection algorithm, we compared our estimate of the

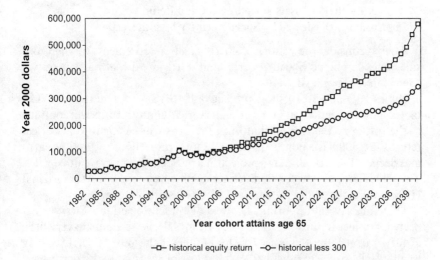

Fig. 10.8   Average 401(k) assets at age 65 for persons with a 401(k), by cohort

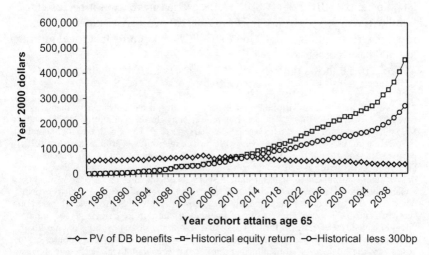

Fig. 10.9   Average 401(k) assets at age 65 and the PV of DB benefits at age 65, all persons

mean 401(k) assets of persons who attained age sixty-five in 2000 with the mean 401(k) assets of HRS respondents between the ages of sixty-three and sixty-seven in 2000. The HRS mean (for persons) is $25,892, compared to our projected mean of $29,708. However, the mean 401(k) balance in the HRS excludes amounts that were originally accumulated in 401(k) plans but later rolled into IRAs; our projected 401(k) balance includes amounts that were rolled over into an IRA. Thus, it appears that our projection is quite plausible compared to the HRS mean.

10.4   Future 401(k) Assets at Retirement by Lifetime Earnings Decile and by Social Security Wealth Decile

We first consider projections of 401(k) assets at retirement. We then consider how combined Social Security and 401(k) wealth at retirement will change in the coming decades.

Tables 10.9 and 10.10 show projected 401(k) assets at retirement. The tables show projections assuming that historical equity returns will continue in the future and assuming that future returns will be equal to historical returns less 300 basis points. Table 10.9 shows projections by lifetime earnings deciles. Table 10.10 shows projections by Social Security wealth deciles. The tables show assets for families, determined by reforming the original HRS families for whom the earnings histories were obtained.

There are several important features of these projections. First, as expected, families in the lowest lifetime earnings decile accumulate very little in 401(k) assets.[5] But this is not true for families in the lowest Social Security wealth decile. Some families in the lowest Social Security wealth decile have substantial lifetime earnings (as explained before) and on average accumulate substantial 401(k) assets. Second, the average increase in 401(k) assets of families is very large—from $43,764 in 2000 to $575,117, assuming historical rates of return, and from $43,764 to $348,284, assuming historical returns less 300 basis points.

Table 10.11 shows the ratio of 401(k) assets in 2040 to 401(k) assets in

---

5. Most of the "families" in the lowest lifetime earnings decile are single women and all have zero or very low earnings. The mean lifetime earnings for families in this decile is about $70,000, or an average of $1,700 (in year 2000 dollars) per year. Those with zero lifetime earnings accumulate no 401(k) wealth. Others, with low and intermittent earnings, have low 401(k) participation rates and if they do participate have high cash-out rates. Thus, they accumulate little or no 401(k) wealth as well. However, many families in this decile are not poor. Despite zero or low lifetime earnings, many have substantial Social Security wealth. This is because many are apparently widowed or divorced and, although they are not entitled to Social Security benefits based on their own earnings, they are entitled to substantial Social Security wealth based on survivor benefits. However, our measure of lifetime earnings for these single-person families does not include the earnings of the former spouse, so our algorithm does not generate 401(k) balances for the surviving spouse. In principal, these "401(k)-poor" surviving spouses could be assigned the 401(k) assets of their former spouses, but we cannot do this because the former spouse left the household before reaching age sixty-five in 2000 and is thus not in our sample.

Table 10.9   **Mean projected 401(k) assets for cohorts retiring in 2000, 2010, 2020, 2030, and 2040, by lifetime earnings decile, for families (in year 2000 dollars)—historical equity return and historical return less 300 basis points**

	Cohort (year attains age 65)				
Lifetime earnings decile	R2000	R2010	R2020	R2030	R2040
	Assuming historical equity rate of return				
1 (lowest)	0	158	366	1,372	3,688
2	627	3,405	7,100	21,917	50,857
3	3,532	12,421	28,647	47,770	128,600
4	8,506	29,355	57,614	120,706	274,958
5	19,437	82,367	166,268	272,135	489,558
6	37,215	92,391	203,597	390,004	644,261
7	48,740	112,424	300,917	508,402	822,220
8	68,860	177,574	361,543	647,329	947,474
9	83,385	186,913	434,814	622,449	1,134,979
10 (highest)	166,405	343,137	577,632	895,179	1,242,580
All	43,764	104,159	213,632	353,106	575,117
	Assuming historical equity rate of return less 300 basis points				
1 (lowest)	0	147	335	810	2,072
2	627	3,158	5,908	13,638	31,625
3	3,532	11,542	22,996	31,442	81,916
4	8,506	26,995	46,223	81,744	172,671
5	19,437	75,555	128,920	179,540	292,902
6	37,215	84,785	156,523	253,293	382,988
7	48,740	102,944	230,322	333,852	484,933
8	68,860	162,660	277,968	424,948	560,366
9	83,385	170,459	335,284	417,112	680,937
10 (highest)	166,405	315,294	454,171	614,789	785,150
All	43,764	95,487	165,699	235,388	348,284

2000. The ratios are shown by lifetime earnings decile in the top panel of the table and by Social Security wealth decile in the bottom panel. Ratios are shown for historical rates of equity return and for historical rates less 300 basis points. The *relative* increase between 2000 and 2040 is substantially greater for the lowest lifetime earnings deciles than for the highest deciles (excluding the lowest decile for which projected 401(k) assets are zero in 2000). The ratios range from 81.1 in the second decile to 7.5 in the tenth decile, assuming historical rates of return and from 50.4 in the second decile to 4.7 in the tenth decile, assuming historical rates of return less 300 basis points.

The large relative increase for families in the lowest earnings deciles is due in large part to the very low assets in 2000. The large increase between 2000 and 2040 among families in the lowest lifetime earnings interval may be especially sensitive to our assumptions about the spread 401(k) partici-

Table 10.10   Mean projected 401(k) assets for cohorts retiring in 2000, 2010, 2020, 2030, and 2040, by Social Security wealth decile, for families (in year 2000 dollars)—historical rate of return and historical rate less 300 basis points

Social Security wealth decile	Cohort (year attains age 65)				
	R2000	R2010	R2020	R2030	R2040
Assuming historical equity rate of return					
1	6,552	19,577	50,967	83,375	147,153
2	1,079	7,584	13,337	25,568	84,322
3	22,631	49,828	103,310	186,639	337,767
4	22,623	51,521	82,494	163,541	247,881
5	15,188	44,150	116,633	199,554	353,425
6	23,592	78,883	185,703	302,433	523,799
7	39,964	130,346	247,766	492,913	792,127
8	66,531	167,486	398,453	571,714	975,052
9	102,415	222,430	413,099	728,271	1,082,121
10	136,842	269,395	526,433	774,407	1,198,301
All	43,764	104,159	213,632	353,106	575,117
Assuming historical equity rate of return less 300 basis points					
1	6,552	18,013	39,642	53,388	89,574
2	1,079	7,022	11,000	17,191	52,321
3	22,631	45,798	81,065	126,900	207,786
4	22,623	47,353	64,765	111,164	156,241
5	15,188	40,588	90,753	131,134	210,784
6	23,592	72,332	143,977	198,485	312,788
7	39,964	119,473	189,323	319,429	462,750
8	66,531	152,689	306,398	380,269	583,300
9	102,415	203,970	322,565	487,597	663,471
10	136,842	247,269	408,920	526,464	738,273
All	43,764	95,487	165,699	235,388	348,284

pation to lower-income workers. Nonetheless, the projections suggest very large increases in 401(k) retirement assets for families in all but the lowest lifetime earnings decile. Even in the second lifetime earnings decile projected assets by 2040 are quite large, $50,857 compared to $627 in 2000, assuming historical rates of equity returns.

The relative increase in 401(k) assets by Social Security wealth decile follows a very different pattern. Assuming that 401(k) assets increase with lifetime earnings, the pattern reflects the lifetime earnings of families in each Social Security wealth decile. There are several noticeable features of the relative increases between 2000 and 2040. First, the growth of 401(k) assets is substantial in all Social Security wealth deciles. Second, there is no systematic pattern of the increase in 401(k) assets by Social Security wealth decile. Although the lowest relative increase is for the tenth decile and the highest for the second decile (assuming historical rates of return), there is no pattern in the growth rates of 401(k) assets in the second through tenth

Table 10.11   **Ratio of 401(k) assets in 2040 to assets in 2000, for families, by lifetime earnings decile, and by Social Security wealth decile—historical rate of equity return and historical rate less 300 basis points**

Decile	Historical rate of return	Historical less 300
	Lifetime earnings deciles	
1	—	—
2	81.1	50.4
3	36.4	23.2
4	32.3	20.3
5	25.2	15.1
6	17.3	10.3
7	16.9	9.9
8	13.8	8.1
9	13.6	8.2
10	7.5	4.7
All	13.1	8.0
	Social Security wealth deciles	
1	22.5	13.7
2	78.1	48.5
3	14.9	9.2
4	11.0	6.9
5	23.3	13.9
6	22.2	13.3
7	19.8	11.6
8	14.7	8.8
9	10.6	6.5
10	8.8	5.4
All	13.1	8.0

Social Security wealth deciles. The same findings hold if we assume historical return on equity less 300 basis points.

One of our principal goals has been to understand how the rapid increase in 401(k) assets will change the combined level of Social Security and 401(k) assets. There are of course other assets that can be used for support in retirement, but Social Security wealth and 401(k) assets will be the principal dedicated retirement assets. Table 10.12 shows the sum of Social Security and 401(k) saving at age sixty-five in years 2000, 2010, 2020, 2030, and 2040 for each decile of the lifetime earnings distribution. These projections assume that real Social Security benefits will remain constant at their 2000 level. The top panel of the table shows the sum of retirement assets assuming historical rates of equity returns; the bottom panel shows the sum assuming historical rates less 300 basis points. The increase in the sum of Social Security wealth and 401(k) assets is large for all lifetime income deciles, except for the first decile. The average of the sum of Social Security wealth and 401(k) assets increases from $225,593 in 2000 to $756,956 in 2040, assuming historical

Table 10.12   **Social Security wealth plus projected 401(k) assets for cohorts retiring in 2000, 2010, 2020, 2030, and 2040, by lifetime earnings decile, for families (in year 2000 dollars)—historical equity return and historical return less 300 basis points**

Lifetime earnings decile	Cohort (year attains age 65)				
	R2000	R2010	R2020	R2030	R2040
	Assuming historical equity return				
1	71,189	71,347	71,555	72,561	74,877
2	98,524	101,302	104,997	119,814	148,754
3	113,997	122,886	139,112	158,235	239,065
4	147,720	168,569	196,828	259,920	414,172
5	198,267	261,197	345,098	450,965	668,388
6	231,846	287,022	398,228	584,635	838,892
7	275,279	338,963	527,456	734,941	1,048,759
8	312,926	421,640	605,609	891,395	1,191,540
9	343,158	446,686	694,587	882,222	1,394,752
10	445,310	622,042	856,537	1,174,084	1,521,485
All	225,593	285,988	395,461	534,935	756,946
	Assuming historical equity return less 300 basis points				
1	71,189	71,336	71,524	71,999	73,261
2	98,524	101,055	103,805	111,535	129,522
3	113,997	122,007	133,461	141,907	192,381
4	147,720	166,209	185,437	220,958	311,885
5	198,267	254,385	307,750	358,370	471,732
6	231,846	279,416	351,154	447,924	577,619
7	275,279	329,483	456,861	560,391	711,472
8	312,926	406,726	522,034	669,014	804,432
9	343,158	430,232	595,057	676,885	940,710
10	445,310	594,199	733,076	893,694	1,064,055
All	225,593	277,316	347,528	417,217	530,113

rates of return and from $225,593 to $530,113, assuming historical rates of return less 300 basis points (all in year 2000 dollars). Table 10.13 shows comparable results for each decile of the Social Security wealth distribution.

To help compare the increases across the lifetime earnings deciles, the top panel of table 10.14 shows the ratio of the sum of Social Security wealth and 401(k) assets in 2040 to the sum of Social Security wealth and 401(k) assets in 2000 for each lifetime wealth decile. The first column of the table shows the ratios assuming historical rates of return and the second column shows the ratios assuming historical rates less 300 basis points. On average, families in 2040 are projected to have 3.36 times as much as Social Security and 401(k) wealth in 2040 as they had in 2000. In all but the first two deciles, real retirement assets more than double between 2000 and 2040. However, the projections suggest essentially no growth of total retirement assets among

Table 10.13   **Social Security wealth plus projected 401(k) assets for cohorts retiring in 2000, 2010, 2020, 2030, and 2040, by Social Security wealth decile, for families (in year 2000 dollars)—historical equity return and historical return less 300 basis points**

Social Security wealth decile	Cohort (year attains age 65)				
	R2000	R2010	R2020	R2030	R2040
	Assuming historical equity return				
1	11,473	24,498	55,888	88,296	152,074
2	65,101	71,606	77,359	89,590	148,344
3	127,176	154,373	207,855	291,184	442,312
4	168,124	197,022	227,995	309,042	393,382
5	201,465	230,427	302,910	385,831	539,702
6	244,505	299,796	406,616	523,346	744,712
7	283,749	374,131	491,551	736,698	1,035,912
8	326,950	427,905	658,872	832,133	1,235,471
9	378,004	498,019	688,688	1,003,860	1,357,710
10	448,204	580,757	837,795	1,085,769	1,509,663
All	225,593	285,988	395,461	534,935	756,946
	Assuming historical equity return less 300 basis points				
1	11,473	22,934	44,563	58,309	94,495
2	65,101	71,044	75,022	81,213	116,343
3	127,176	150,343	185,610	231,445	312,331
4	168,124	192,854	210,266	256,665	301,742
5	201,465	226,865	277,030	317,411	397,061
6	244,505	293,245	364,890	419,398	533,701
7	283,749	363,258	433,108	563,214	706,535
8	326,950	413,108	566,817	640,688	843,719
9	378,004	479,559	598,154	763,186	939,060
10	448,204	558,631	720,282	837,826	1,049,635
All	225,593	277,316	347,528	417,217	530,113

families in the very lowest earnings decile. The projected increase is 50 percent among families in the second lifetime earnings decile. The same patterns hold assuming historical returns less 300 basis points.

The bottom panel of table 10.14 shows the ratio of assets in 2040 to assets in 2000 for each Social Security wealth decile. The increases for each of the Social Security wealth deciles exhibit striking uniformity, except for the first decile. The increase in the first decile is very large. Again, this apparently anomalous ratio for the lowest Social Security wealth decile reflects the relatively low level of projected 401(k) assets in 2000. The ratios are shown in figure 10.10 for all but the first decile. If historical equity returns continue in the future, the sum of Social Security wealth and 401(k) assets will more than double between 2000 and 2040, for all Social Security wealth deciles. If future equity returns are equal to the historical average less 300

Table 10.14   Ratio of the sum of Social Security and 401(k) assets in 2040 to the sum of Social Security and 401(k) assets in 2000 by lifetime earnings decile and by Social Security wealth decile—historical rates of equity returns and historical rates less 300 basis points

Decile	Historical rate of return	Historical rate of return less 300 basis points
Lifetime earnings deciles		
1	1.05	1.03
2	1.51	1.31
3	2.10	1.69
4	2.80	2.11
5	3.37	2.38
6	3.62	2.49
7	3.81	2.58
8	3.81	2.57
9	4.06	2.74
10	3.42	2.39
All	3.36	2.35
Social Security wealth deciles		
1	13.25	8.24
2	2.28	1.79
3	3.48	2.46
4	2.34	1.79
5	2.68	1.97
6	3.05	2.18
7	3.65	2.49
8	3.78	2.58
9	3.59	2.48
10	3.37	2.34
All	3.36	2.35

basis points the ratio will be greater than 1.5 in all deciles. Thus, the rise of 401(k) plans significantly bolsters total retirement saving for families with low Social Security wealth as well as for families with high Social Security wealth. Similar patterns emerge (although the magnitudes are lower) if we assume that future equity returns are 300 basis points less than their historical average.

10.5 Summary and Discussion

We have projected the accumulation of 401(k) assets for families retiring through 2040. Our goal has been to understand how the rise of personal retirement saving plans will change the wealth of persons at retirement. In particular, we compare the sum of Social Security wealth and 401(k) assets for families that attain age sixty-five in 2000 to the sum of Social Security

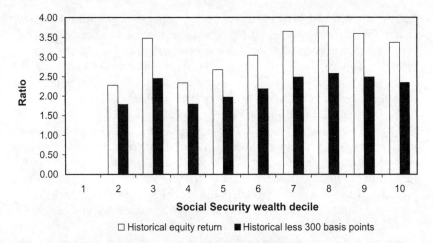

Fig. 10.10   Ratio of the sum of Social Security wealth + 401(k) assets in 2040 to the sum in 2000, for Social Security wealth deciles, by equity return

wealth and 401(k) assets in 2040. We consider the growth of retirement assets by Social Security wealth decile as well as by lifetime earnings decile. Because the projections are based on a series of assumptions with uncertain validity, the projections are subject to considerable uncertainty. We believe, however, that the projections provide a reasonable indicator of how the rise in 401(k) plans will affect the total retirement assets of future retirees.

We have not emphasized DB pension benefits in these calculations because our projections indicate that the proportion of retirement saving in DB plans will decline substantially in the coming decades. In addition we have not emphasized IRA assets, primarily because we are unable to distinguish assets accumulated from IRA contributions from rollovers from 401(k) to IRA accounts. Our 401(k) projections include such rollovers.

The 401(k) system is not yet fully mature. A person who retired in 2000, for example, could have contributed to a 401(k) for at most eighteen years and the typical 401(k) participant had only contributed for a little over seven years. Even current retirees could have contributed only in the latter half of their working lives. Nonetheless, the current accumulation of 401(k) assets is substantial. Projections in Poterba, Venti, and Wise (2007a) show that in 2007 401(k) assets at age sixty-five were over 60 percent of the total of 401(k) and DB assets. By 2040, the projections show that 401(k) assets will be between 4.30 and 6.85 times as large as DB assets. The private pension system is moving from a DB to a personal account system and workers who retire three decades from now will have had the opportunity to contribute to a 401(k) plan over their entire working lives (as many as forty years in our projections).

How will the maturing of the 401(k) system affect the sum of the Social

Security wealth and 401(k) assets of future retirees? Our projections show that if the historical rate of equity return continues in the future then, on average, the sum of family Social Security wealth plus the 401(k) assets of retirees will more than triple between 2000 and 2040 (in year 2000 dollars). If the equity return is equal to the historical rate less 300 basis points, the sum of these retirement assets will more than double.

We find that the rate of growth of the sum of Social Security wealth and 401(k) assets is surprisingly uniform across deciles of the distribution of lifetime earnings. Assuming historical rates of equity return, we find that the sum of these retirement assets more than doubles between 2000 and 2040 for all but the first two deciles of the distribution of lifetime earnings. Our projections also show little growth in the sum of Social Security and 401(k) assets for families in the lowest decile of lifetime earnings; the projected growth for families in the second decile is 50 percent.

We emphasize the projected growth of the sum of Social Security wealth and 401(k) assets for each Social Security wealth decile. We find substantial increases in each decile. Assuming historical rates of return, the sum of these retirement assets at age sixty-five in 2040 ranges from a low of 228 percent to a high of 378 percent of the sum in 2000 (excluding the larger increase for the first decile). If the future rate of return on equities is equal to the historical rate less 300 basis points, the sum of Social Security wealth and 401(k) assets at age sixty-five in 2040 ranges from 179 percent to 258 percent of the sum in 2000, depending on the Social Security wealth decile.

Appendix

Tables 10.2 and 10.3 present components of wealth by lifetime earnings decile and by Social Security wealth decile. These components are calculated for all single-person families age sixty-three to sixty-seven and for all two-person families with male head age sixty-three to sixty-seven in 2000. The calculations are all based on Health and Retirement Study (HRS) data.

Lifetime earnings are calculated using the Social Security earnings records for the years 1951 to 1991 and HRS respondent reported earnings for the years 1992 to 2000. A tobit specification is used for each year to impute earnings for persons constrained by the Social Security earnings limit. Earnings in each year are converted to year 2000 dollars using the Social Security average wage index and then summed to obtain lifetime earnings. Respondents that do not have matching Social Security earnings records are not included in tables 10.2 and 10.3.

401(k) wealth is our estimate of 401(k) wealth obtained from HRS respondents and pertains to balances in plans on the respondent's current job as well as on former jobs.[6] The estimate includes assets in all 401(k)-like plans, including assets in traditional employer-provided DC plans. Each HRS respondent is asked if they have a pension plan and, if so, whether it is "Type A" (benefits are usually based on a formula involving age, years of service, and salary), "Type B" (money is accumulated in an account for you), or "both." Associated with the latter two responses is a follow-up question asking for the plan balance.

DB wealth is the sum of pension wealth from two sources. If the respondent is employed in 1998 then DB wealth on the *current* job is calculated as the present value of expected benefits, assuming that the respondent will continue to work to the normal retirement age.[7] These present value calculations (made by HRS staff) are based on features of the pension plan obtained from the employer. These estimates of pension wealth are only available for 1998, so the present value in 2000 is obtained by assuming that DB wealth grew 4 percent per year from 1998 and 2000. DB wealth from *prior* jobs is based on respondent-reported receipt of "pension and annuity benefits" in 2000. We calculate the mortality-adjusted present value of pension income for each person in the household reporting such income in 2000. We assume that the pension income reported in 2000 remains constant in the future. We also assume a 3 percent real discount rate and we use a unisex life table. No adjustments are made for survivor benefits or for cost-of-living adjustments that are common in state and local pensions.

Social Security wealth is the present value of Social Security benefits in 1992, assuming that the respondent continued to work until the normal retirement age.[8] These estimates of Social Security wealth are only available in 1992 dollars so we convert these values to year 2000 dollars using the CPI.

Other components of total wealth, including IRA balances and housing equity, are reported values from the 2000 wave of the HRS.

References

Beshears, J., J. Choi, D. Laibson, and B. Madrian. 2008. The importance of default options for retirement saving outcomes: Evidence for the United States. In *Lessons from pension reform in the Americas,* ed. S. J. Kay and T. Sinha, 59–87. Oxford: Oxford University Press.

6. See documentation for the HRS data file "Imputations for Pension-Related Variables," v1.0, June 2005.
7. See documentation for the HRS data file "Imputations for Pension Wealth, v2.0," December 2006.
8. These data were obtained from the HRS restricted use data file "Summary of Earnings and Projected Benefits."

Bershadker, A., and P. A. Smith. 2006. Cracking open the nest egg: IRA withdrawals and retirement finance. *Proceedings of the 98th Annual Conference on Taxation* 98 (winter): 73–83.

Copeland, C. 2004. Retirement accounts and wealth, 2001. *EBRI Notes* 25 (5): 5–12.

Cunningham, C. R., and G. V. Engelhardt. 2002. Federal Tax policy, employer matching, and 401(k) saving: Evidence from HRS W-2 records. *National Tax Journal* 55 (3): 617–45.

Dynan, K., J. Skinner, and S. Zeldes. 2004. Do the rich save more? *Journal of Political Economy* 112 (2): 397–444.

Gustman, A., and T. Steinmeier. 1999. Effects of pensions on savings: Analysis with data from the Health and Retirement Study. *Carnegie-Rochester Conference series on Public Policy* 50 (June): 271–324.

Holden, S., K. Ireland, V. Leonard-Chambers, and M. Bogdan. 2005. The Individual Retirement Account at age 30: A retrospective. *Perspective* (Investment Company Institute) 11 (1): 1–21.

Holden, S., and J. VanDerHei. 2001. Contribution behavior of 401(k) plan participants. *EBRI Issue Brief* 238 (October): 1–20.

Hurd, M., L. Lillard, and C. Panis. 1998. An analysis of the choice to cash out pension rights at job change or retirement. RAND Discussion Paper no. DRU-1979-DOL.

Ibbotson Associates. 2006. Stocks, bonds, bills, and inflation. Ibbotson Associates, Morningstar, Inc.

Poterba, J., S. Venti, and D. A. Wise. 1998. Implications of rising personal retirement saving. In *Frontiers in the economics of aging,* ed. D. A. Wise, 125–172. Chicago: University of Chicago Press.

———. 2001. Preretirement cashouts and foregone retirement saving: Implications for 401(k) asset accumulation. In *Themes in the economics of aging,* ed. D. A. Wise, 23–58. Chicago: University of Chicago Press.

———. 2007a. New estimates of the future path of 401(k) assets. NBER Working Paper no. 13083. Cambridge, MA: National Bureau of Economic Research, May.

———. 2007b. The decline of defined benefit retirement plans and asset flows. NBER Working Paper no. 12834. Cambridge, MA: National Bureau of Economic Research, January.

Stewart, J. 2002. Recent trends in job stability and job security: Evidence from the March CPS. U.S. Department of Labor, Office of Employment and Unemployment Statistics. Working Paper no. 356.

Venti, S., and D. Wise. 1998. The cause of wealth dispersion at retirement: Choice or chance? *American Economic Review* 88 (2): 185–91.

Comment   Robert J. Willis

This chapter is the third in a sequence of papers by this team that investigates the implications of the growth of 401(k) plans as the major source of pension wealth in the United States. Since I also served as discussant of the

Robert J. Willis is a professor of economics at the University of Michigan, where he is also a research scientist at the Institute for Social Research and a research associate of the Population Studies Center.

earlier papers, I will use my discussion to provide some context on the overall project as well as specific comments on this chapter.

The first two papers (Poterba et al. 2005; Poterba, Venti, and Wise 2009), focus on the trade-off between risk and returns faced by individual households in the Health and Retirement Study (HRS) cohort who use 401(k) plans to save for retirement. In their analysis, they calculate probability distributions of retirement wealth under alternative portfolio allocations of annual contributions to bonds and stocks using simulations based on the historical distribution of annual stock market returns. They establish that portfolios with a high share of stocks (nearly) stochastically dominate those with bonds. Using these probability distributions to evaluate the expected utility of the alternative investment strategies, they find that all-stock portfolios would be preferred by all but extremely risk averse persons, as would be expected from the puzzlingly high equity premium. To incorporate the possibility that the future will differ (modestly) from the past, they also analyze the expected utilities of alternative portfolios under the assumption that returns will be 300 basis points lower than the historical mean. Even in this case, portfolios dominated by stocks tend to have higher expected utility for persons with moderate degrees of risk aversion or significant amounts of other wealth such as Social Security. Including human capital and flexible labor supply (including delayed retirement) as another means to offset risky stock returns would only strengthen this conclusion.

In contrast to their previous papers, the current chapter provides actuarial projections for successive cohorts to 2040 of 401(k) wealth and defined benefit (DB) wealth by deciles of lifetime earnings or Social Security wealth with no allowance for risk apart from considering the effect of projections in which the mean rates of return are either assumed to be at slightly less than their historical nominal averages of 12.6 percent for large cap stocks and 6.2 percent for long-term corporate bonds or, alternatively, with returns on both assets that are 300 basis points lower. These projections document the rapid growth of 401(k) plans across cohorts since they were introduced in 1982 and project that this growth will continue into the future, albeit at an eventually slowing rate, tending toward an equilibrium with high, but not universal coverage characterized by substantial differentials in participation across socioeconomic groups. On average, they project that the total dedicated financial resources available to individuals and households will be far larger than would have been the case had there been continued reliance on DB plans, even in the scenario in which stock returns are 300 basis points lower than their historical average.

The chapter itself is primarily devoted to describing in detail the methods, data, and assumptions used to carry out the projections. As would be expected from this team, the projections are done carefully and, in situations in which there are data problems, as seems to be true of lifetime earnings in the lowest decile, or no obviously sound model on which to base projections, such as cross-cohort growth in participation rates in 401(k) plans, the issues and, for the most part, their approaches in dealing with them are laid out clearly. However, despite the fact that their projections show a dramatic change in the level and composition of retirement resources for future cohorts, they provide very little discussion of likely behavioral responses of households and public policy to these changes. In addition, as I noted earlier, they do not consider the role of uncertainty about stock returns at either the micro or macro level. In my remaining comments, I will speculate about behavioral responses and the role of uncertainty.

Over the next forty years, using the U.S. Social Security Administration (SSA) assumptions employed by Poterba, Venti, and Wise (henceforth, PVW) of 3.9 percent future nominal wage growth and 2.8 percent inflation rate, real wages will be about 1.5 times as high in 2040 as they are now and, given some neutrality assumptions, the lifetime earnings of cohorts reaching age sixty-five in 2040 will also be about 1.5 times as large as the lifetime earnings of cohorts reaching retirement in 2000. Assuming that future returns to stocks and bonds equal their historical returns, PVW project that real retirement wealth will be 2.8 to 3.5 times as high for those in the top six deciles of the lifetime earnings distribution for cohorts retiring in 2040 compared to those retiring in 2000. With stock returns lowered by 300 basis points they project that retirement wealth will still be 2.0 to 2.5 times as large for this subgroup. Even those in the second decile are projected to have retirement wealth that grows more rapidly than real lifetime earnings.

Is it plausible to believe that the U.S. retirement landscape will evolve according to the PVW projections? At first glance, it may seem unlikely that people would shift such a large portion of their lifetime resources toward the end of life. The reason for the projected rapid growth of retirement resources is the high rate of return of both stocks and bonds relative to projected defined benefits either from a pay-as-you-go Social Security program or from private DB plans together with the assumption that contribution rates of future cohorts will be similar to current cohorts. Of course, given certainty of rates of return, a DB plan could promise to pay a flow of benefits during retirement that has exactly the same present value that a DC plan with the same asset base could pay. In the past, however, promised DB benefits have not risen in proportion to assets when, as in the 1990s, returns have been unusually large. Rather, in such a situation, firms have sought to reduce contributions to their pension funds because they are not needed to maintain solvency. The shift from DB to DC plans reflects not only a shift in who bears the risk of variable asset returns, but also a shift from provision for retirement as part of a collective wage bargain to a matter of individual household saving decisions.

While the PVW projections do not allow for it, it seems quite possible that individuals managing their own 401(k) participation and contribution rates might also reduce contributions if fund balances are growing too rapidly. More generally, in order to understand the implications of the shift to 401(k) plans, we need to have better estimates of the elasticity of lifetime savings with respect to expected rates of return to put in place of the zero elasticity implicit in the PVW projections. In a similar vein, another response to an overly rapid accumulation of 401(k) balances might be earlier retirement. Such a response would require a "re-reversal" of the recent rise in retirement age that appears to have broken the long-term decrease in retirement age from the mid-nineteenth century until around 1995, as documented by Costa (2000). One possible reason for the recent increase in retirement age, of course, is that people believe that the latter part of the life cycle will require substantially more retirement resources than in the past, in part because they expect to live longer and, more importantly, because of the growth in both the cost and efficacy of medical care. The PVW projections suggest that the shift toward 401(k) plans may generate resources to accommodate increasing needs for medical care in old age. On the other hand, pay-as-you-go financing of Medicare reduces the connection between incentives for retirement saving and demand for medical care. All of this suggests that it would be fruitful to embody more behavioral responses and alternative policy scenarios into projections of the sort presented by PVW.

In thinking forty years into the future and beyond, everyone agrees that uncertainty is enormously important but, as in this chapter, it is often ignored because it is so difficult to think about a reasonable way to deal with it in quantitative terms. Nonetheless, I think that one cannot think about implications of the spread of 401(k) assets as the major form of dedicated retirement wealth for much of the population without thinking about the role of uncertainty. In the previous two papers by PVW (plus Joshua Rauh) that I mentioned at the beginning of my comments, they showed convincingly that the expected utility from retirement portfolios invested in risky assets like stocks tends to be higher than safer portfolios invested in bonds for all but the most risk averse households, based on historical returns in the stock market.

At the cost of a lot of effort, the simulations in the current chapter could have utilized the same methodology utilized in the earlier papers to calculate the projected distribution of expected utilities at retirement of successive cohorts of Americans as 401(k) plans spread. I have a strong expectation—doubtless shared by PVW—that such an effort would not alter the main findings of the current chapter with its much simpler assumptions about future rates of return. The reason is implicit in the equity premium puzzle: namely, historical stock returns are puzzlingly high relative to returns on safe assets and, consequently, projected future values of portfolios dominated by stocks using historical returns will tend to dominate alternative mechanisms for providing retirement resources.

The key question is whether historical returns provide a reliable guide to the level of expected returns and degree of long-term risk faced by households in current and future cohorts who are entrusting their financial well-being in retirement to accumulations in their 401(k) accounts. While professors like me (and the authors) who have participated in 403(b) plans during their careers have done extremely well with portfolios dominated by stock, it appears that the broad population represented in the Health and Retirement Study has a more pessimistic view of stock returns, as reflected by their answers to the question: "By next year at this time, what is the percent chance that mutual fund shares invested in blue chip stocks like those in the Dow Jones Industrial Average will be worth more than they are today?" For instance, Gabor Kézdi and I have found that, on average, HRS respondents think that the probability of a stock market gain over one year is 48 percent (as compared to a probability of 73 percent based on historical data) and that they believe the variability of returns is also larger than the historical record shows (Kézdi and Willis 2007). Indeed, the professors themselves may not believe that the future will be like the past. For example, rare disasters (Barro 2006) or the evolution of the "hidden structure" of the economy (Weitzman 2007) create considerably greater uncertainty than is contained in the historical record of stock prices used in the first two PRVW (Poterba, Rauh, Venti, and Wise) papers, to say nothing of the virtual certainty assumed in the current chapter. These papers suggest that the equity premium reflects this excess risk, perhaps inadequately.

The picture painted by PVW of a prosperous future of retirees living on their 401(k) wealth may be the most reasonable point estimate, but there is some chance (not easily estimable) that it will be wildly off the mark. People who have roughly equal expected lifetime utility during the accumulation phase of the life cycle but choose different portfolio mixes may end up with very different levels of living in retirement. In the PVW scenario, those who put their eggs in the equity basket will end up far richer during retirement than their fellow cohort members who choose inflation-adjusted bonds. On the other hand, persistent downside macro risks of the sort emphasized by Barro and Weitzman may give those on the pessimistic fringe the last laugh. However the economy evolves, large inequalities in retiree resources may create strong political pressure for redistribution. Pay-as-you-go financing of Social Security and Medicare, as proponents often note, provides an insurance benefit that is more valuable the higher the true riskiness of the real economy. Fortunately, both households and government have flexibility to make substantial adjustments in choices and policies as elements of the hidden structure of the economy are revealed or disasters occur. This flexibility reduces the private and social costs of long-term risks, allowing economists analyzing the welfare effects of the spread of 401(k) plans to put more weight on the happy scenario that is described in this chapter, despite the possibility of lurking disasters.

References

Barro, R. 2006. Rare disasters and asset markets in the twentieth century. *Quarterly Journal of Economics* 26 (7–8): 1075–92.
Costa, D. 2000. *The evolution of retirement.* Chicago: University of Chicago Press.
Kézdi, G., and R. J. Willis. 2007. Stock market expectations and portfolio choice of American households: Work in progress. Paper presented at conference on Subjective Probabilities and Expectations: Methodological Issues and Empirical Applications to Economic Decision-making. 7–8 September, Jackson Lake Lodge, Wyoming.
Poterba, J. M., J. Rauh, S. F. Venti, and D. A. Wise. 2005. Utility evaluation of risk in retirement saving accounts. In *Analyses in the economics of aging,* 2005 Series: (NBER-C) National Bureau of Economic Research Conference Report, ed. D. A. Wise, 13–58. Chicago: University of Chicago Press.
Poterba, J. M., J. Rauh, S. F. Venti, and D. A. Wise. 2009. Life-cycle asset allocation strategies and the distribution of 401(k) retirement wealth. In *Developments in the economics of aging,* ed. D. A. Wise, 15–56. Chicago: University of Chicago Press.
Weitzman, M. L. 2007. Subjective expectations and asset-return puzzles. *American Economic Review* 97 (4): 1102–30.

11

The Impact of Employer Matching on Savings Plan Participation under Automatic Enrollment

John Beshears, James J. Choi, David Laibson, and
Brigitte C. Madrian

Companies have used a variety of approaches to encourage participation in employer-sponsored savings plans. The most common approach, the provision of an employer matching contribution, is now offered by the vast majority of large firms (Profit Sharing Council of America 2006). Even with a match, however, savings plan participation rates are often surprisingly low (Choi, Laibson, and Madrian 2005), and empirical studies of matching contributions' effect on plan participation have uniformly found relatively small effects (Andrews 1992; Papke and Poterba 1995; Papke 1995; Bassett, Fleming, and Rodrigues 1998; Kusko, Poterba, and Wilcox 1998; Choi et al. 2002; Even and Macpherson 2005; Duflo et al. 2006; Engelhardt and Kumar 2007).

John Beshears was a PhD Candidate in Business Economics Harvard University when this chapter was written, and is currently a Visiting Fellow in Aging Research at the NBER. James J. Choi is an assistant professor of finance at Yale School of Management and a faculty research fellow of the National Bureau of Economic Research. David Laibson is the Robert I. Goldman Professor of Economics and Harvard College Professor at Harvard University, and a research associate of the National Bureau of Economic Research. Brigitte C. Madrian is the Aetna Professor of Public Policy and Corporate Management at the Kennedy School of Government, Harvard University, and a research associate of the National Bureau of Economic Research.

The findings and conclusions expressed are solely those of the authors and do not represent the views of SSA, National Institute on Aging, the National Science Foundation, any other agency of the U.S. Federal Government, the RRC, or the NBER. We thank Hewitt Associates for their help in providing the data. We are particularly grateful to Pam Hess, Yan Xu, and Lori Lucas at Hewitt for their help with this project. Neel Rao provided excellent research assistance. We appreciate the helpful feedback of Dan McFadden and seminar participants at the National Bureau of Economic Research. The authors acknowledge financial support from the National Institute on Aging (grant R01-AG021650 and P01-AG005842) and the U.S. Social Security Administration (funded as part of the Retirement Research Consortium grant #10-M-98363-1-01). Beshears acknowledges financial support from a National Science Foundation Graduate Research Fellowship. Laibson also acknowledges support from the National Science Foundation (HSD 0527516).

Automatic enrollment is an alternative mechanism for increasing savings plan participation. In a standard opt-in enrollment scheme, employees must actively elect to participate in the plan if they wish to contribute. In contrast, under automatic enrollment, employees are enrolled in their employer's savings plan at a default contribution rate and asset allocation unless they actively make an alternative choice. Relative to the standard opt-in approach, automatic enrollment dramatically increases plan participation, particularly among younger, low-tenure, and lower-income employees (Madrian and Shea 2001; Choi et al. 2002, 2004; Beshears et al. 2008). The participation rate increase at one year of tenure is as much as 60 percentage points.

All of the companies in which automatic enrollment has been studied to date have also offered an employer matching contribution. In principle, the match gives most employees a strong reason not to opt out of participation (and indeed, few do). But some extensions of automatic enrollment, such as the Automatic individual retirement account (IRA) proposal in the United States, do not include a matching contribution. The extent to which automatic enrollment's effectiveness relies on the presence of a match is an open question. Without a match, the opt-out rate could be much higher, since participation incentives are greatly reduced. On the other hand, if employee inertia drives the automatic enrollment participation effect, we might expect high participation rates even without a matching contribution.

We estimate the employer match's impact on savings plan participation under automatic enrollment in two ways. First, we study a large firm (Company A) using automatic enrollment that replaced its employer match (25 percent on the first 4 percent of pay contributed) with an employer contribution equal to 4 percent of pay plus an annual profit-sharing contribution. The employer contribution in the new regime was not contingent on the employee's contributions. We find that among new hires with six months of tenure, savings plan participation rates decreased by, at most, 5 to 6 percentage points after the firm eliminated the employer match, and overall average employee contribution rates fell by 0.65 percent of pay.

Second, we pool data on savings plan participation at nine firms with automatic enrollment. We use variation in the match structure both across and within firms to identify the relationship between participation rates and the match. This analysis is potentially confounded by firm-level omitted variables but still offers suggestive evidence. We find that a 1 percentage point decrease in the maximum potential match as a fraction of salary is associated with a 1.8 to 3.8 percentage point decrease in plan participation at six months of eligibility. Thus, moving from a typical matching structure of 50 percent on the first 6 percent of pay contributed to no match at all would reduce savings plan participation under automatic enrollment by 5 to 11 percentage points. These results, along with those for Company A discussed before, lead us to conclude that automatic enrollment participation rates are positively related to match generosity, but the magnitude of this effect is modest.

Section 11.1 describes the savings plan and data for Company A. In section 11.2, we analyze the impact of Company A's change from a matching contribution to a noncontingent contribution. Section 11.3 examines the relationship between plan participation and the employer match amount at nine firms with automatic enrollment. Section 11.4 concludes.

11.1 Savings Plan and Data for Company A

Company A is a Fortune 500 company in the information sector. We will consider this firm's employee savings outcomes from January 1, 2002 through December 31, 2005. Table 11.1 lists the salient features of Company A's 401(k) plan. Plan eligibility is restricted to employees age twenty-one or older. Full-time employees who satisfy this age requirement are immediately eligible to participate, while part-time employees are eligible only after reaching one year of service and having worked 1,000 hours. Because of eligibility differences between full- and part-time employees, we restrict our analysis to full-time employees who are eligible for the plan.[1] Throughout the sample period, full-time employees were automatically enrolled in the 401(k) plan. After thirty days of service, employees who did not make an active enrollment election were enrolled at a contribution rate of 3 percent of salary allocated entirely to a money market fund. The plan offered six other investment options, including employer stock.

Until December 31, 2003, the company made matching contributions at a rate of 25 percent on employee contributions up to 4 percent of pay for employees who had attained at least one year of service and 1,000 hours of work (thus, the maximum possible employer match was 1 percent of pay). The maximum contribution rate over this time period was 25 percent of pay. On January 1, 2004, the company discontinued the employer match and replaced it with an employer contribution of 4 percent of pay plus an annual profit-sharing contribution that was not guaranteed in advance. In 2004 and 2005, this profit-sharing contribution was 5 percent of salary. The employer contributions in the new regime were not contingent upon the employee's contributions. The company also reduced the maximum employee contribution rate to 15 percent of pay at this time. Throughout the entire sample period, employees were also subject to IRS annual dollar

1. We do not observe full- or part-time status directly in our data. In order to screen out part-time employees, we eliminate those who did not become eligible for the plan within two months of hire. Even though full-time employees were immediately eligible upon hire, we keep employees with up to a two-month eligibility lag to allow for the possibility of administrative delays.

Table 11.1   401(k) Plan features at Company A

Eligibility	
Eligible employees	Age 21 +

Eligibility to make employee
    contributions
	Full-time employees: Immediately upon hire
	Part-time employees: After 1 year of service
	    and 1,000 hours

Eligibility for employer contributions	After 1 year of service and 1,000 hours

Automatic enrollment	Full-time employees automatically enrolled after
	    30 days at a 3% contribution rate allocated to
	    a money market fund

Employee contributions	Before 1/1/2004: Up to 25% of pay After 1/1/2004: Up to 15% of pay

Employer contributions	Before 1/1/2004: Employer match of 25% on first
	    4% of pay contributed by employee
	Starting 1/1/2004: Noncontingent employer
	    contribution of 4% of pay plus profit-sharing
	    contribution

Match vesting	Immediate
Other	
Loans	Available
Hardship withdrawals	Available; limited to one per year
Investment choices	7 options including employer stock

Source: Summary Plan Descriptions.

contribution limits.[2] Those employees classified as "highly compensated" for IRS nondiscrimination testing purposes were potentially subject to stricter contribution rate limits, and for this reason we exclude them from the following analysis.

Our employee-level data come from Hewitt Associates, a large U.S. benefits administration and consulting firm. We have a series of year-end cross-sections of all Company A employees from 2002 through 2005. These cross-sections contain demographic information such as birth date, hire date, gender, and compensation. They also contain 401(k) variables such as the initial plan eligibility date, current participation status, initial plan participation date, a monthly contribution rate history, and year-end asset allocation and total balances.

Our analysis compares two Company A employee cohorts. The "match cohort" contains plan-eligible full-time employees hired between January 1, 2002 and June 30, 2003. The "no-match cohort" contains plan-eligible full-time employees hired between January 1, 2004 and June 30, 2005. We exclude employees hired between July 1, 2003 and December 31, 2003 because these

---

2. In the sample we analyze, only eight out of 645 employees contributed enough in a year to plausibly be constrained by the IRS annual dollar contribution limits. The results we report do not account for this censoring, but they are unaffected if we exclude these eight employees from the analysis.

employees were hired under the old regime (employer match), but the point at which we measure participation and contribution outcomes for our analysis is after the switch to the new regime (a noncontingent employer contribution). Because our primary outcome variables—plan participation and employee contribution rates—are measured at six months of tenure, both cohorts are further limited to include only individuals whose employment at the company lasted for at least six months.

Company A made several significant acquisitions during our sample period. Unfortunately, our data do not identify those employees who joined the firm as a result of these acquisitions. To minimize the potentially confounding influence of these acquisitions, we make three further restrictions to our sample. First, we exclude employees who lived in states where the acquired companies were headquartered. Second, we exclude employees whose initial appearance in our data set does not correspond to their year of hire (e.g., we exclude employees who are first observed in our data in the 2004 cross-section but who are listed as being hired before 2004).[3] Third, we exclude employees whose hire dates are revised by more than one calendar month across different year-end cross-sections.

Our final sample contains 645 employees: 293 in the match cohort and 352 in the no-match cohort.

11.2   Savings Plan Outcomes under Automatic Enrollment with and without an Employer Match: Company A

We begin our analysis by comparing means across the match and no-match cohorts. We first consider plan participation, which we define as having a positive (nonzero) employee contribution rate. The first row of table 11.2 shows that 89.1 percent of match-cohort employees were participating in the savings plan at six months of tenure. In contrast, the six-month participation rate for the no-match cohort is 80.7 percent. This 8.4 percentage point difference in participation rates across the two cohorts is statistically significant and relatively stable from two months of tenure onward. The second row of table 11.2 shows average employee contribution rates at six months of tenure (including nonparticipants with a contribution rate of 0). Given the decline in plan participation, it is not surprising that the average contribution rate also falls from 3.60 percent to 2.89 percent of salary after the elimination of the employer match. This 0.71 percent drop is statistically significant and driven both by the participation decline and a reduction in the average contribution rate conditional on participation from 4.04 percent to 3.58 percent of pay. The 0.46 percent drop in the conditional average

---

3. We make one exception to this second criterion. There are twenty-two employees who first appear in our data in the year-end 2003 cross-section with December 2002 hire dates. We include these employees in the sample because their absence from the 2002 data is likely due to administrative delays in processing new employees at year-end rather than due to an acquisition.

Table 11.2   Summary statistics on savings plan outcomes and demographic characteristics for employees at Company A

	Match cohort (Hired 1/1/2002 through 6/30/2003)	Nonmatch cohort (Hired 1/1/2004 through 6/30/2005)	t-statistic for difference
Savings plan outcomes (at six months tenure)			
Participation rate	89.1%	80.7%	2.95
Average contribution rate (all employees)	3.60%	2.89%	3.01
Average contribution rate (participants only)	4.04%	3.58%	1.86
Demographic characteristics			
Fraction female	51.5%	45.7%	1.47
Average age	33.21	31.83	2.07
Annual salary (2004 dollars)	$49,167	$40,343	2.93
Sample size	$N = 293$	$N = 352$	

Source: Authors' calculations. The sample includes non-highly-compensated, full-time, savings-plan-eligible employees. Growth in seasonally adjusted average weekly earnings for private sector workers from the Current Employment Statistics survey is used to deflate employee salaries to 2004 dollars.

contribution rate, however, is only statistically significant at the 10 percent level and is partly explained by the concurrent reduction in the maximum allowable contribution rate from 25 percent to 15 percent of pay.

Figure 11.1 shows the distribution of employee contribution rates at six months of tenure for the two cohorts separately. We see that the transition from the employer match to the noncontingent contribution was associated with a decrease in the fraction of employees contributing, at most, positive rates.[4] More than two-thirds of employees in both cohorts contribute at the 3 percent default contribution rate, consistent with previous research on how automatic enrollment affects the employee contribution rate distribution (Madrian and Shea 2001; Choi et al. 2002, 2004; Beshears et al. 2008). In contrast to previous research, we observe very few employees contributing at the 4 percent match threshold (only 2 percent of employees in the match cohort and 1 percent of employees in the nonmatch cohort for whom the match threshold is no longer relevant). There are several plausible explanations for why so few employees in the match cohort are at the match threshold. First, the employees at Company A are observed at only six months of tenure, which does not give them much time to switch from the default contribution rate to the match threshold (or another contribution rate of their choosing). Second, because the match threshold was only 1 percentage point above the default rate, participants' incentive to increase their contribution rate to the match threshold was much weaker than in other

4. The decline in the fraction of employees contributing at a rate greater than 15 percent in the nonmatch cohort is an artifact of the reduction in the maximum allowable contribution rate from 25 percent to 15 percent of pay that coincided with the switch from a matching contribution to a noncontingent contribution.

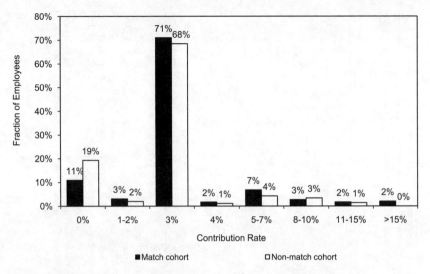

Fig. 11.1   Distribution of contribution rates with and without and employer match at six months of tenure: Company A

firms studied (Carroll et al. 2009). Finally and perhaps most importantly, employees were not eligible to receive matching contributions until having completed one year of service, so most of the benefits from contributing at the match threshold did not accrue to employees at six months of tenure.

Of course, the transition from an employer match to a noncontingent contribution may have been accompanied by other changes at Company A that caused the savings plan choice differences between the two cohorts. Table 11.2 shows that relative to the nonmatch cohort, the match cohort was disproportionately female, somewhat older, and had a higher average salary.[5] Not controlling for these differences could make the participation decline due to the employer match elimination look larger than it really was.

Table 11.3 shows the results of regressions that include demographic explanatory variables. The first two columns show the coefficients from a linear probability regression of savings plan participation at six months of tenure on an indicator for having been hired with an employer match in place, gender, age, and income in 2004 dollars. In column (1), we control linearly for age and income, whereas in column (2) we include age and income

5. We deflated the salaries of employees in both cohorts to 2004 dollars using the growth in seasonally adjusted average weekly earnings for private sector workers from the Current Employment Statistics survey. Part of the difference in average age and income between the cohorts might be the result of an internship program that took place in the second half of the sample period. Compared to other employees, interns probably have weaker motives to participate in the 401(k) plan. To make sure that the presence of interns is not driving our results, we drop the twenty-nine employees in the sample with incomes of less than $10,000 and redo our analysis. The qualitative results do not change.

Table 11.3   Effect of the employer match on savings plan outcomes under automatic enrollment: Company A

	Participation (OLS) (1)	Participation (OLS) (2)	Participation (probit) (3)	Participation (probit) (4)	Employee contribution rate (tobit) (5)	Employee contribution rate (tobit) (6)
Match cohort	0.0670**	0.0603**	0.0653**	0.0543**	0.6769**	0.6394**
	(0.0284)	(0.0271)	(0.0274)	(0.0251)	(0.2725)	(0.2679)
Female	0.0750***	0.0353	0.0679**	0.0268	0.5159**	0.3860
	(0.0284)	(0.0275)	(0.0275)	(0.0244)	(0.2738)	(0.2720)
Age						
Years	0.0003		-0.0007		0.0056	
	(0.0019)		(0.0018)		(0.0181)	
Linear spline	No	Yes	No	Yes	No	Yes
Income (2004 USD)						
$1,000	0.0014***		0.0020***		0.0214***	
	(0.0004)		(0.0005)		(0.0040)	
Linear spline	No	Yes	No	Yes	No	Yes
Sample size	$N = 645$	$N = 645$	$N = 645$	$N = 645$	$N = 645$	$N = 645$

Source: Authors' calculations.

Notes: Standard errors are in parentheses. The sample includes non-highly-compensated, full-time, savings-plan-eligible employees. Growth in seasonally adjusted average weekly earnings for private sector workers from the Current Employment Statistics survey is used to deflate employee salaries to 2004 dollars. All specifications include a constant. The dependent variable in columns (1) to (4) is a binary indicator for savings plan participation. The dependent variable in columns (5) to (6) is the employee's (censored) savings plan contribution rate (including zeros). Columns (3) to (4) report the marginal effects from a probit regression holding all variables fixed at their means. Columns (5) to (6) report the marginal effects from a tobit regression holding all variables fixed at their means. In the case of binary variables, the marginal effects in columns (3) to (6) are reported for a change from zero to one. The age spline has knots at thirty, forty, and fifty years, and the income spline has knots at $20,000, $40,000, $60,000, and $80,000. When linear splines for age and income are included in a regression, marginal effects are calculated holding age and income at their means (as opposed to holding the variables that make up the splines each fixed at their individual means).

***Significant at the 1 percent level.

**Significant at the 5 percent level.

splines.[6] The estimated 6.0 to 6.7 percentage point participation impact of having a match is statistically significant and somewhat lower than the raw 8.4 percentage point difference seen in table 11.2. A probit specification (columns [3] and [4]) yields estimated employer match marginal effects of 5.4 to 6.5 percentage points, also statistically significant. Columns (5) and (6) list the marginal effects from a tobit regression of employee contribution rates, which are censored below at zero and above at 25 percent (the match cohort) or 15 percent (the nonmatch cohort). Eliminating the employer match at Company A is associated with a contribution rate decline of about 0.66 percent of salary, an effect that is statistically significant and only slightly less than the 0.71 percent raw effect in table 11.2.

In summary, controlling for demographic differences between the match and nonmatch cohorts reduces but does not eliminate the estimated impact of the employer match under automatic enrollment. Note that these estimates represent the *combined* effect of removing the match and replacing it with a noncontingent contribution. The replacement of a match with a (relatively larger) noncontingent contribution generates a substitution effect that discourages employee contributions and a *net* income effect that also discourages employee contributions. Employee contributions are no longer subsidized and the employee has more total savings (employee plus employer contributions) for any given employee contribution.[7] Our estimates provide an *upper bound* of the effects due *solely* to the removal of the employer match, since the simultaneous introduction of the noncontingent employer contribution generates an income effect that suppresses employee contributions.[8]

Our analysis also sheds light on the question of savings crowd-out. Our estimates provide an upper bound on the negative participation effects due *solely* to the introduction of the noncontingent contribution, since the simultaneous elimination of the match is likely to have discouraged employee participation.[9]

One limitation of many savings studies that use administrative data is the inability to address potentially offsetting (or reinforcing) changes in savings

6. The age spline has knots at thirty, forty, and fifty years, and the income spline has knots at $20,000, $40,000, $60,000, and $80,000.

7. The employee loses a 25 percent match on contributions up to 4 percent of income but gains both a noncontingent employer contribution equal to 4 percent of income and a noncontingent profit-sharing contribution.

8. On the other hand, there are some plausible reasons that the introduction of the noncontingent contribution could *increase* employee contributions. Employees might view it as a signal that their expected future income growth has fallen. Alternatively, employees could interpret the noncontingent contribution as implicit advice that their optimal savings rate is higher than they previously believed.

9. A match unambiguously increases participation in a two-period model. Opposite effects are possible in models with more periods. However, the empirical literature on matching generally finds positive participation effects. Note that even in a two-period model, matching need not increase the average employee contribution due to the substitution effect.

behavior *outside* of the account being studied. This caveat applies here as well. Employees have additional assets outside their 401(k) plan, and some employees also have other savings plan assets within Company A, which has an employee stock ownership plan (ESOP). However, most of the employees in our nonmatch sample are not eligible to participate in the ESOP (employees must have one year of service to be eligible). Moreover, the plan is nonelective; the company makes ESOP contributions on an annual basis to all employees who are eligible. With more years of data, it might be possible to assess the extent to which changes in ESOP balances across the two cohorts affect employees' 401(k) choices at Company A.[10] Unfortunately, the data are not presently available to undertake such an analysis, and we do not observe any other financial assets of this company's employees.

11.3   Employer Matching Level and Savings Plan Participation under Automatic Enrollment at Nine Companies

We now broaden our analysis to explore the relationship between the generosity of the employer match and savings plan participation under automatic enrollment at nine companies. We use variation in the employer match structure both within and across firms for identification. However, because of the potential existence of firm-level omitted variables, the following results must be interpreted with caution.

Table 11.4 describes the match structure at the nine companies used in our analysis. The match rate varies from no match at Company A (beginning in 2004 for the nonmatch cohort) to a 133 percent match on the first 6 percent of pay at Company I. Conditional on offering a match, the match threshold ranges from 2 percent of pay for employees with less than one year of tenure at Company F to 7 percent of pay at Company B. Two companies have changes in their employer match over our sample period: Company A (analyzed in sections 11.2 and 11.3), which replaced its employer match of 25 percent on the first 4 percent of pay contributed with a noncontingent employer contribution in January 2004; and Company B, which gradually increased its match rate from 60 percent to 62 percent to 65 percent on the first 7 percent of pay contributed.

For this section's analysis, we use data that are identical in structure to the Company A data described in section 11.2. We pool employees at the nine firms who are observed in at least one of the year-end cross-sections from 2002 through 2005.[11] Our sample is limited to employees at these firms

---

10. Madrian and Shea (2001), who first documented large participation increases following automatic enrollment in a 401(k) savings plan, find no evidence of offsetting savings behavior in the Employee Stock Purchase Plan (ESPP) of the company they studied.

11. Three firms did not have data available for all four years. We drop three additional firm-years because different employees within a company were offered different matches in these years and we are unable to identify which employees were offered which match.

Table 11.4   401(k) Eligibility and match structure at nine companies with automatic enrollment

Firm	Eligibility	Match structure	Maximum match	Auto. enroll. details	Years	Demographics
A	Must be age 21 +. FT: immediately eligible. PT: eligible after 1 yr. and 1,000 hrs. Match or noncontingent contribution after 1 yr. and 1,000 hrs.	Before 01/04: 25% on first 4% of pay. After 01/04: None; 4% noncontingent contribution + profit-sharing contribution	Before 01/04: 1% After 01/04: 0%	Default: 3% rate, money market fund When: 30 days	2002–2005	Yes
B	FT: immediately eligible. PT: 1,000 hrs. in a 12-month period. All participants eligible for match.	Before 01/04: 60% on first 7% of pay 01/04–01/05: 62% on first 7% of pay After 01/05: 65% on first 7% of pay	Before 01/04: 4.2% 01/04–01/05: 4.34% After 01/05: 4.55%	Default: 3% rate, pre-mixed portfolio When: 30 days	2003–2005	Yes
C	All employees immediately eligible. Participants eligible for match after 1 year.	75% on first 6% of pay	4.5%	Default: 3% rate, balanced fund When: 30 days	2002–2005	Yes
D	FT: immediately eligible. PT: 1,000 hrs. in a 12-month period. All participants eligible for match.	< 1 yr. tenure: 35% on first 6% of pay ≥ 1 yr. tenure: 70% on first 6% of pay	4.2%	Default: 3% rate, balanced index fund When: 31 days	2002–2005	Yes
E	All employees immediately eligible to contribute and receive a match.	100% on first 3% of pay	3%	Default: 2% rate, money market fund When: 30 days	2002–2004	No
F	All employees immediately eligible to contribute and receive a match.	< 1 yr. tenure: 100% on first 2% of pay ≥ 1 yr. tenure: 100% on first 6% of pay	6%	Default: 2% rate, money market fund When: Immediate	2003–2005	Yes
G	All employees immediately eligible to contribute and receive a match.	60% on first 6% of pay	3.6%	Default: 4% rate When: 30 days	2002	Yes
H	All employees immediately eligible. Participants eligible for match after 1 yr.	100% on first 6% of pay	6%	Default: 6% rate, money market fund When: Immediate	2002–2004	No
I	FT: immediately eligible. PT: ineligible. All participants eligible for match.	133% on first 6% of pay	8%	Default: 3% rate, near-term portfolio When: 60 days	2002 2004 2005	No

Note: FT: Full-time employees; PT: Part-time employees.

who meet the following criteria: they became eligible for their employer-sponsored savings plan between January 1, 2002 and June 30, 2005; they became eligible when they were between twenty-one and sixty-five years of age; they became eligible when automatic enrollment was in effect; and they did not leave the company within six months of becoming eligible. Unlike the analysis in sections 11.2 and 11.3, we do not attempt to filter out part-time employees because we are unable to identify them for some of the companies.

To assess the relationship between the employer match and savings plan participation under automatic enrollment, we run a linear probability regression[12] of savings plan participation at six months of eligibility[13] on age, income in 2004 dollars, gender, and the generosity of the employer match. Our key dependent variable of interest is the maximum employer match (as a fraction of income) that a participant can receive by contributing at the match threshold and fulfilling all match-related service requirements, given the match structure in place at six months of eligibility. The maximum employer match does not necessarily correspond to the matching contribution an employee could receive after only six months of eligibility. For example, the maximum employer match as just defined at Company D is 4.2 percent of pay (a 70 percent match on the first 6 percent of pay), even though employees with less than one year of tenure can receive a match of at most 2.1 percent of pay (a 35 percent match on the first 6 percent of pay). Table 11.4 lists the maximum employer match used in our regression for each of the nine firms.

Our employer match variable definition rests on the assumption that employees are forward-looking with respect to the match when making their decision about whether to opt out of savings plan participation under automatic enrollment. Given that the service requirement to obtain the maximum employer match is at most one year in our sample, we feel that this assumption is appropriate. Only three of our nine firms (companies A, C, and H) have matches linked to tenure. We also assume that the match rate changes within companies A and B were surprises that were not known to employees in advance, since we define the maximum employer match using the match structure in place at the time we measure participation.

Because our maximum employer match variation is largely across-firm variation, we are precluded from putting firm-level fixed effects in these regressions. We do, however, calculate Huber-White standard errors with clustering at the firm level.

12. Even though our dependent variable is binary, we use a linear probability regression rather than a probit in order to facilitate the graphical display of the results in figure 11.2.
13. Instead of measuring participation at six months of tenure, as done earlier for Company A, we measure participation after six months of eligibility because some firms' employees are not immediately eligible upon hire. For most employees in the sample, however, six months of tenure and six months of eligibility are equivalent.

Table 11.5   **The effect of the employer match on savings plan participation under automatic enrollment**

	Full sample		Companies with control data	
	(1)	(2)	(3)	(4)
Maximum match	2.7818***	2.1995***	3.7519***	1.7784***
	(0.6131)	(0.3257)	(0.2623)	(0.4290)
Gender				
Female	No	0.0021	No	0.0075
		(0.0059)		(0.0072)
Indicator for gender missing	No	−0.3254	No	No
		(0.6318)		
Age				
Linear spline	No	Yes	No	Yes
Indicator for age missing	No	−0.4109	No	No
		(0.2125)		
Income (2004 USD)				
Linear spline	No	Yes	No	Yes
Indicator for income missing	No	0.4882***	No	No
		(0.1128)		
Constant	0.7778***	0.1722	0.7536***	0.2281
	(0.0271)	(0.1254)	(0.0028)	(0.1265)
Sample size	$N = 44{,}279$	$N = 44{,}279$	$N = 35{,}895$	$N = 35{,}895$

Source: Authors' calculations.

Notes: Huber-White robust standard errors with clustering by firm are reported in parentheses. The sample includes savings plan-eligible employees ages twenty-one to sixty-five. All regressions are linear probability regressions. The dependent variable is a binary indicator for savings plan participation. The maximum match is the maximum fraction of income an employee can receive in matching contributions by contributing at the match threshold and fulfilling all service requirements, given the match structure in place when the employee had six months of 401(k) eligibility. The coefficient on the maximum match represents the percentage point increase in the participation rate when employees are offered an additional 1 percent of their salary in matching contributions. The spline for age has knots at thirty, forty, and fifty years, and the spline for income has knots at $20,000, $40,000, $60,000, and $80,000. Growth in seasonally adjusted average weekly earnings for private sector workers from the Current Employment Statistics survey is used to deflate employee salaries to 2004 dollars.

***Significant at the 1 percent level.

Column (1) in table 11.5 gives the coefficient estimates from the regression previously described when no other control variables are included. In this specification, decreasing the maximum employer match by 1 percent of salary is associated with a plan participation reduction at six months of eligibility under automatic enrollment of 2.8 percentage points. This is somewhat smaller than the 5 to 6 percentage point decline observed at Company A when it eliminated its employer match. However, as noted earlier, the Company A estimate is an upper bound on the true effect of match removal, since the match was replaced with a noncontingent employer contribution that is theoretically expected to decrease participation.

Figure 11.2 displays the regression results from the first column of table

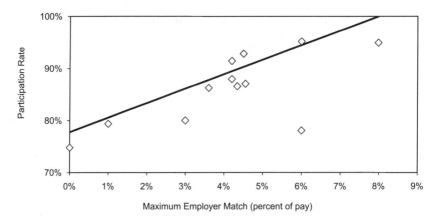

Fig. 11.2   Relationship between the employer match and savings plan participation under automatic enrollment at nine firms

Notes: Each point represents the raw participation rate among individuals who are employed by a given firm with the specified match amount. Participation is defined as having a positive employee contribution rate at six months of eligibility. The match amount is defined as the maximum fraction of income an employee can receive in employer matching contributions by contributing at the match threshold and fulfilling all service requirements, given the match structure in place when the employee had six months of 401(k) eligibility. The slope and intercept of the fitted line are given by the coefficients on the match amount and the constant in column (1) of table 11.5.

11.5 graphically. Every data point in figure 11.2 corresponds to a group of employees that shares the same firm and maximum employer match (firms whose match changes over time are represented in the graph by more than one data point). The maximum match is on the *x*-axis, and the raw savings plan participation rate is on the *y*-axis. The regression line from the first column of table 11.5 is also shown. Figure 11.2 shows that the positive relationship between the maximum match and participation estimated in table 11.5 is robust and does not seem to be driven by outliers.

In column (2) of table 11.5, we add control variables, using linear splines for age and income as well as indicator variables for missing gender, age, and income data.[14] The inclusion of demographic controls reduces the estimated impact of the employer match slightly: decreasing the maximum employer match by 1 percent of salary is associated with a 2.2 percentage point decline in participation, rather than the 2.8 percentage point decline shown in column (1).

Most of the individuals for whom gender, age, or income data are missing come from three firms. Therefore, we restrict the sample in column (3)

---

14. The results are qualitatively similar if we use linear controls for age and income rather than splines.

to the six firms for which we can construct demographic controls.[15] When we run the regression without control variables—as in column (1)—on this restricted sample, the estimated impact of the employer match increases relative to that in column (1); participation declines by 3.8 percentage points when the maximum match decreases by 1 percent of pay. This suggests that there are some differences between the companies in our sample for which we do and do not have demographic data.

Finally, in column (4), we add the demographic control variables to the regression restricted to companies with demographic information. Just as in the full sample, adding demographic controls to this restricted sample reduces the estimated impact of the employer match. Across all of the specifications in table 11.5, the coefficient on the maximum employer match ranges from 1.8 to 3.8, indicating that decreasing the maximum employer match by 1 percent of salary reduces savings plan participation at six months of eligibility under automatic enrollment by 1.8 to 3.8 percentage points.

11.4   Conclusions

Automatic enrollment is an increasingly important feature of the retirement savings landscape. A recent survey of large U.S. firms found that 36 percent already automatically enroll new employees, and 55 percent of firms without automatic enrollment say that they are very likely or somewhat likely to adopt it within a year (Hewitt Associates 2007). To date, all the automatic enrollment savings plans that have been studied have had an employer match. The U.S. pension regulations encourage the use of matching through safe harbor clauses; firms can avoid nondiscrimination testing if they have a sufficiently generous match. However, there is *also* a safe harbor for noncontingent employer contributions.[16]

This chapter aims to address how effective automatic enrollment might be in the absence of an employer match. Using two estimation strategies, one based on the substitution of the employer match with a noncontingent employer contribution, and the other based primarily on variation in the employer match across firms, we find that participation rates under automatic enrollment decline only modestly when the employer match is eliminated or reduced. The switch from a matching contribution to a noncontingent contribution at Company A caused the plan participation rate at six months of tenure to drop by 5 to 6 percentage points. In a sample of nine

15. Even within those companies for which we have demographic information, some employees are nonetheless missing this information. We drop these employees with missing demographic data from the regressions in columns (3) and (4).

16. To obtain safe harbor status, the plan must provide either a matching contribution equal to 100 percent of contributions up to 1 percent of pay and 50 percent of contributions for the next 5 percent of pay, or a noncontingent contribution of 3 percent of pay.

firms with automatic enrollment, decreasing the employer match amount by 1 percent of pay was associated with a 1.8 to 3.8 percentage point decrease in the plan participation rate at six months of eligibility. Collectively, these results imply that moving from a typical matching structure of 50 percent on the first 6 percent of pay contributed to no match at all would reduce savings plan participation under automatic enrollment by 5 to 11 percentage points. Interestingly, these results are similar to the employer match effect on participation estimated by Engelhardt and Kumar (2007) in a sample of older employees, most of whom were not subject to automatic enrollment.

Therefore, the success of automatic enrollment at increasing participation in employer-sponsored savings plans does not appear to rely much on having an employer match. It thus seems likely that automatic enrollment will also be effective at increasing participation in other contexts that do not naturally lend themselves to a matching contribution.

These results also suggest that companies with automatic enrollment need not offer a match in order to achieve broad-based participation. However, the employer match may be valuable for reasons other than the inducement that it creates to participate. For example, as a tax-favored form of compensation, the employer match may be important in the recruiting and retention of employees even if it does not have a large impact on savings plan participation.

However, the experience of Company A suggests that some of the purposes served by an employer match could be achieved with a noncontingent employer contribution as well. The merits of an employer match versus a noncontingent contribution likely hinge not only on their average impact on savings plan outcomes (e.g., lower participation with a noncontingent contribution), but also on their distributional impact. For example, a noncontingent contribution will likely increase total savings for those employees least inclined to save, but its effects elsewhere in the savings distribution are ambiguous, since a match tends to cause herding at the match threshold. This herding may either increase or decrease savings, depending on how high the match threshold is and what savings rate employees would have chosen in the absence of a match.

References

Andrews, E. S. 1992. The growth and distribution of 401(k) plans. In *Trends in pensions 1992*, ed. J. Turner and D. Beller, 149–76. Washington, DC: U.S. Department of Labor, Pension, and Welfare Benefits Administration.

Bassett, W. F., M. J. Fleming, and A. P. Rodrigues. 1998. How workers use 401(k) plans: The participation, contribution, and withdrawal decisions. *National Tax Journal* 51 (June): 263–89.

Beshears, J., J. J. Choi, D. Laibson, and B. C. Madrian. 2008. The importance of default options for retirement savings outcomes: Evidence from the United States. In *Lessons from pension reform in the Americas,* ed. S. J. Kay and T. Sinha, 59–87. New York: Oxford University Press.

Carroll, G. D., Choi, J. J., D. Laibson, B. C. Madrian, and A. Metrick. 2009. Optimal defaults and active decisions. *Quarterly Journal of Economics,* forthcoming.

Choi, J. J., D. Laibson, and B. C. Madrian. 2005. $100 bills on the sidewalk: Suboptimal saving in 401(k) plans. NBER Working Paper no. 11554. Cambridge, MA: National Bureau of Economic Research, August.

Choi, J. J., D. Laibson, B. C. Madrian, and A. Metrick. 2002. Defined contribution pensions: Plan rules, participant decisions, and the path of least resistance. In *Tax policy and the economy* 16, ed. J. Poterba, 67–114. Cambridge, MA: MIT Press.

———. 2004. For better or for worse: Default effects and 401(k) savings behavior. In *Perspectives in the economics of aging,* ed. D. Wise, 81–121. Chicago: University of Chicago Press.

Duflo, E., W. Gale, J. Liebman, P. Orszag, and E. Saez. 2006. Savings incentives for low- and middle-income families: Evidence from a field experiment with H&R Block. *Quarterly Journal of Economics* 121:1311–46.

Engelhardt, G. V., and A. Kumar. 2007. Employer matching and 401(k) saving: Evidence from the Health and Retirement Study. *Journal of Public Economics* 91:1920–43.

Even, W. E., and D. A. Macpherson. 2005. The effects of employer matching in 401(k) plans. *Industrial Relations* 44 (3): 525–49.

Hewitt Associates. 2007. *Survey findings: Hot topics in retirement 2007.* Lincolnshire: Hewitt Associates LLC.

Kusko, A., J. Poterba, and D. Wilcox. 1998. Employee decisions with respect to 401(k) plans. In *Living with defined contribution pensions: Remaking responsibility for retirement,* ed. O. Mitchell and S. Schieber, 98–112. Philadelphia: University of Pennsylvania Press.

Madrian, B., and D. Shea. 2001. The power of suggestion: Inertia in 401(k) participation and savings behavior. *Quarterly Journal of Economics* 116 (4): 1149–87.

Papke, L. E. 1995. Participation in and contributions to 401(k) pension plans. *Journal of Human Resources* 30 (2): 311–25.

Papke, L. E., and J. M. Poterba. 1995. Survey evidence on employer match rates and employee saving behavior in 401(k) plans. *Economics Letters* 49:313–17.

Profit Sharing Council of America. 2006. *49th annual survey of profit-sharing and 401(k) plans.* Chicago: Profit Sharing Council of America.

Comment   Daniel McFadden

The rise of 401(k) plans as a channel for providing retirement incomes to employees makes enrollment in these plans increasingly important for the welfare of future retirees. The authors utilize persuasive natural experiments to quantify behavioral response to key 401(k) plan features: whether the default is automatic enrollment unless the employee opts out or nonenroll-

Daniel McFadden is the E. Morris Cox Professor of Economics at the University of California, Berkeley, and a research associate of the National Bureau of Economic Research.

ment unless the employee opts in, whether there is employer matching of contributions or an unconditional employer contribution, and the default contribution rate for enrollees. Classical theory of rational life cycle savings implies that response to tax-qualified savings plans will depend critically on circumstances and intertemporal preferences (with matching or unconditional employer savings contributions inducing income and intertemporal substitution effects), but rational consumers should display no partial or incomplete adjustment that leaves final choices dependent on defaults. The authors' findings of significant default effects reinforces an extensive behavioral literature that shows that consumers are inconsistent in their transactions that trade certain consumption today for uncertain consumption in the future. These inconsistencies may be due to separate "mental accounts" for current and future consumption, difficulty in consistently evaluating risky prospects, time-inconsistent hyperbolic discounting, or breakdowns in decision making due to lack of attention and procrastination.

Natural questions for social planners dealing with default-sensitive consumers is what aspects of savings instruments *are* significant in influencing retirement savings behavior, and how defaults and other savings plan features can be designed to minimize the regret that consumers have at retirement when they review their past savings behavior. Note that inattention and incomplete optimization are bad for consumers who would otherwise be intertemporally consistent, but can be protective in circumstances where defaults avoid the excesses of faulty expectations and instant gratification. The authors find that employer matching of contributions to a 401(k) plan and unconditional employer 401(k) contributions both increase participation rates, but their effect on participation is small relative to the effect of opt-in versus opt-out. Then, adding or dropping matching or unconditional contributions to a 401(k) plan are not as critical as the opt-in or opt-out default. An additional question that would be interesting to answer if the authors' data permitted would be whether total 401(k) savings from both employer and employee contributions, and total savings taking into account all consumer intertemporal transactions, including purchase and financing of housing and other assets, increase as the result of employer matching or unconditional 401(k) contributions. Lack of consumer adjustment from defaults suggests that the answer would be affirmative. Then, to the extent that people undersave for retirement, employer 401(k) matching or unconditional contributions will increase consumer welfare more than the same payment in current wages.

Rational Saving Behavior

At retirement, a large majority of consumers state that they regret that they did not save more. Also, consumption typically falls upon retirement, although whether this is inconsistent with rational life cycle planning depends on the nature of preferences for goods versus leisure. These observations are consistent with a tacit assumption in the chapter that most consumers do undersave. However, in defining the baseline against which various tax-qualified savings plans and consumer responses are to be judged, it is worth reviewing what a textbook Fisherian analysis of savings says about participation in such plans, and their impact on total savings.

The instruments for intertemporal allocation available to consumers are purchase of consumer durables (e.g., home ownership) with secured (e.g., mortgage) financing; credit card debt and other unsecured borrowing; and purchase of financial assets through conventional and tax qualified saving. Each channel for borrowing or saving carries its own rate of return (RoR), credit restrictions, and risk characteristics. Rational saving behavior is the result of optimal life cycle planning in the face of income endowments and the available instruments for intertemporal transactions. Then, rational savings will depend on current wealth and future income expectations, age and mortality expectations, family status (e.g., other wage earners, children), the available transaction instruments, and the applicable marginal RoR.

The Intertemporal Budget Set

Consider a simple model with a working period and a retirement period, each thirty years long, and consider annual consumption at the representative ages forty-five and seventy-five for work and retirement. Abstract from buffer stock and diversification motives induced by risk, liquidity motives induced by transactions costs, and asset portfolio and consumption adjustments in response to life event shocks within the working and retirement eras. This is a gross oversimplification, but enough remains to clarify some key features of rational saving. Let Y_0 and Y_1 denote, respectively, endowments of working income now and retirement income in the future. Retirement consumption will be determined by Y_1 and by voluntary saving and borrowing. Let t denote the marginal income tax rate, and assume for simplicity that it is independent of income level or period, and that capital gains are taxed the same as ordinary income. Let home ownership during the working years represent the single available consumer durable. Let C_0 and C_1 denote, respectively, working period consumption and retirement period consumption net of housing services and taxes.

Assume that the rental rate on housing available to both workers and retirees is R. Assume that all retirees rent, and that workers either rent, or buy and occupy a house at purchase price H with a mortgage M. Owners amortize their mortgage over the working years, and sell when they retire. Assume that a minimum house price H^* is required to provide the same services as a rental, and $H > H^*$ is a consumer durable investment. There are three other channels for intertemporal transactions: conventional savings (S), tax-qualified savings (Q) in a 401(k) plan, and unsecured borrowing (B). Let r_S, r_M, and r_B denote the respective annual interest rates on saving, secured mortgage borrowing, and unsecured borrowing, and let r_H

denote the annual housing rate of capital gains less maintenance. Let $a_k \equiv r_k/[1 - (1 + r_k)^{-30}]$ denote an annual payment over thirty years that has unit present value at interest rate r_k. Note that one unit of an asset in period 0 that has an annual interest rate r_k yields a future value $(1 + r_k)^{30}$ in period 1, and the present value of a unit annual payment over 30 years at interest rate r_k is $p_k = 1/a_k$. In the absence of risk or tax factors that induce an equity premium or discount, rent R in housing market equilibrium when landlords discount at the interest rate r_S satisfies $H^* = R/a_S + H^*(1 + r_H)^{30}/(1 + r_S)^{30}$.

Empirically, working consumers have high discount rates; to reflect this, we assume that consumers discount at rate r_B. This implies that consumers facing a market interest rate lower than r_B will choose to consume more when working than when retired. For the two-period representation of the consumer's problem, assume that the initial equity $H - M$ in a house is annualized within period 0 to $(H - M)a_B$, and that the receipts $(1 + r_H)^{30}H$ from a house sale in period 1 are annualized within period 1 to $(1 + r_H)^{30}Ha_B$. A mortgage M that is amortized over the span of period 0 has annual payments $a_M M$, with $1 - (1 + r_M)^{T-30}$ giving the fraction of $a_M M$ that is mortgage interest in year T. The annualized value at the rate r_B of the mortgage interest payments is $a_M[1 - a_B(1 + r_M)((1 + r_M)^{-30} - (1 + r_B)^{-30})/(r_B - r_M)]M \equiv a_1 M$; this is a deduction from taxable income. Unsecured annual borrowing of $a_B B/(1 + r_B)^{30}$ during the working period leads to a balance B repaid with annual payments $a_B B$ during retirement.

If a 401(k) plan has a unconditional employer contribution $Q^{\#}$ and a matching rate λ, then the employee with an annual contribution Q in the working period receives an annual taxable return of $(Q^{\#} + Q(1 + \lambda))(1 + r_S)^{30}$ in the retirement period. Credit constraints are an income-determined bound $(B \leq y Y_0)$ on unsecured borrowing, income and house value bounds $(M \leq \alpha Y_0$ and $M \leq \beta H)$ on a mortgage, and a cap $(Q \leq Q^*)$ on tax-qualified savings. The case that a 401(k) plan is not available will correspond to $Q^{\#} = Q^* = 0$. This notation is summarized in table 11C.1.

Let D denote a discrete variable that is one if the consumer buys a house, and zero if she rents. Taking into account the rules that the 401(k) contribution and mortgage interest expense are deductible from taxable income in period 0, and all 401(k) saving is taxed when withdrawn, representative working period and retirement period annual consumption satisfy

$$C_0 = Y_0 - t(Y_0 - Q) + Ba_B/(1 + r_B)^{30} - S - Q$$
$$- (1 - D)R - D(a_M M + a_B(H - M) - ta_1 M),$$

$$C_1 = (1 - t)(Y_1 + (1 + r_S)^{30}S + (1 + r_S)^{30}(Q^{\#} + Q(1 + \lambda)))$$
$$+ tS - R - a_B B + Da_B H((1 - t)(1 + r_H)^{30} + t).$$

A home purchaser will benefit from obtaining the maximum possible mortgage if

Table 11C.1   **Channels for intertemporal transactions**

Channel	Quantity	Interest rate	Credit constraint
Conventional saving	S	r_S	none
House purchase	H	r_H	$H \geq H^*$
Mortgage	M	r_M	$M \leq \min\{\beta H, \alpha Y_0\}$
Revolving credit	B	r_B	$B \leq \gamma Y_0$
Tax qualified 401(k) saving	Q	r_S	$Q \leq K$

$$\partial C_0 / \partial M = a_B + t a_I - a_M > 0.$$

For example, at tax rate $t = 0.3$ and real annual interest rates $r_B = 0.10$ and $r_M = 0.05$, one has $a_B = 0.106$, $a_M = 0.065$, $a_I = 0.034$, and $\partial C_0 / \partial M = 0.051$. The after-tax RoR for the intertemporal transaction instrument S is $\text{RoR}_S = -(\partial C_1 / \partial S)/(\partial C_0 / \partial S) = (1 - t)(1 + r_S)^{30} + t$. Similarly, the after-tax RoR for B and Q are, respectively, $\text{RoR}_B = (1 + r_B)^{30}$ and $\text{RoR}_Q = (1 + \lambda)(1 + r_S)^{30}$. The present value of postponing taxes implies $\text{RoR}_Q > \text{RoR}_S$. Continuing the numerical example with $\lambda = 1$ gives $\text{RoR}_B = 17.45$, $\text{RoR}_Q = 4.85$ when $\lambda = 1$ and $\text{RoR}_Q = 2.43$ when $\lambda = 0$, and $\text{RoR}_S = 2.00$. The housing after-tax RoR for $H > H^*$ with a maximum mortgage unconstrained by income is $\text{RoR}_H = a_B[t + (1 - t)(1 + r_H)^{30}]/[\beta a_M + (1 - \beta)a_B - \beta t a_I]$. When the mortgage is constrained by income ($H > \alpha Y_0/\beta$ and $M = \alpha Y_0$), the housing RoR is $\text{RoR}_{H0} = t(1 - t)(1 + r_H)^{30}$. In the example, when $r_H = 0.02$ and $\beta = 0.7$, the RoR are $\text{RoR}_H = 2.88$ and $\text{RoR}_{H0} = 1.57$. The ranking of RoR_H relative to RoR_Q and RoR_S is quite sensitive to the tax rate, the expected rate of capital gains less maintenance for housing, and λ. Note that unconditional employer contributions $Q^\#$ to a 401(k) plan are equivalent to a shift in retirement income.

Because the various instruments for saving or borrowing have different RoR and restrictions, these equations in each of the two conditions $D = 0$ and $D = 1$ define a convex budget set with piecewise linear boundaries. The overall budget set is then the possibly nonconvex union of these two conditional budget sets. The rational consumer will seek the efficient boundary of the overall budget set, and will always save at the highest available post-tax RoR and borrow at the lowest available post-tax RoR. When the best available borrowing RoR exceeds the best available saving RoR, the rational consumer will gain by reducing borrowing and saving dollar for dollar until one is zero. This gives the Fisherian exclusionary rule that a rational consumer will never a borrower *and* lender be, except possibly for investment channels like housing that lever the purchase with mortgage borrowing, and give the combination favorable tax treatment. The optimal intertemporal allocation for the rational consumer will be at a node, or on a line segment between nodes at which only one intertemporal channel is not constrained at a boundary. Thus, consumers who maximize utility with positive unsecured borrowing will have zero conventional saving, and will not respond to incremental new 401(k) savings channels whose RoR is lower than their effective RoR on debt. It is more efficient for them to pay down debt if an incremental change in tastes or income endowment leads them to want to postpone some consumption. Consumers who have positive conventional savings at their utility maximum will enroll in a 401(k) plan when it becomes available, and this portfolio shift will reduce conventional saving. It is also possible that consumers who have invested in owner-occupied housing beyond the level necessary for basic housing services will enroll in a 401(k) plan when it becomes available, and reduce their housing investment. Whether these offsets are partial or complete will depend on income and substitution effects. Only consumers at a node in the budget set where they are neither borrowers nor savers will have unambiguously higher savings after introduction of a 401(k) channel. In no case will the opt-in or opt-out default on a 401(k) plan influence the rational consumer's final position.

The clear-cut implications from the Fisherian exclusionary rule will be relaxed in reality when some instruments are used for liquidity to reduce transactions costs, and/or when instruments are risky and the benefits of diversification offset loss in expected return. However, it is difficult to avoid the implication that in general it is rational for borrowers facing high marginal RoR to pay down debt rather than carry both debt and voluntary 401(k) contributions. Then, 401(k) defaults that induce high participation rates may misdirect consumers who should instead be reducing debt, although the consumer who irrationally undersaves and does not offset induced tax-deferred saving with increased debt may benefit from the precommitment and be better off than with no savings at all.

Rational Intertemporal Optimization

For further discussion within the simple Fisherian framework of savings behavior, and the income and substitution effects induced by 401(k) plans, it is useful to represent the budget set graphically. Figure 11C.1 illustrates the overall budget set for typical values.[1] The budget set for renters is the area southwest of the line segments through a, b, c, d. Node c corresponds to no tax-qualified or conventional savings and no borrowing. The segment c-d corresponds to unsecured borrowing to the maximum at d. The segment b-c corresponds to 401(k) contributions to a maximum at b, and the segment a-b corresponds to conventional saving. The budget set for owners is the area southwest of the line segments through e, f, g, h, i. Node h corresponds to a minimum house purchase with a maximum mortgage, and no other saving or borrowing. The segment h-i corresponds to unsecured borrowing

---

1. Numerical values are $Y_0 = 150$, $Y_1 = 50$, $H^* = 200$, $Q^\# = 4$, $Q^* = 4$, $t = 0.3$, $\alpha = 2$, $\beta = 0.7$, $\gamma = 1$, and $\lambda = 1$. The interest rates are $r_B = 0.1$, $r_M = 0.05$, $r_S = 0.03$, and $r_H = 0.02$.

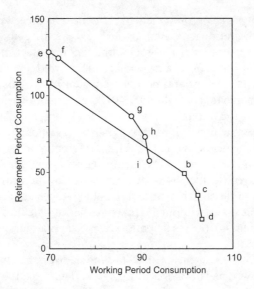

Fig. 11C.1   Fisherian budget set

to a maximum at i. The segment g-h corresponds to 401(k) contributions to a maximum at g. The segment f-g corresponds to a consumer durable investment in housing, with maximum mortgage financing, to a maximum at f where the income constraint on a mortgage binds. The segment e-f corresponds to conventional saving. The union of the renter and owner budget sets is not convex—linear combinations of b and h are not attainable. Note that nodes a and i are interior to the budget set, as are various points reached by combinations of borrowing or saving at less than the best available RoR.

A population of consumers with varying rates of impatience will maximize preferences among the exposed nodes and line segments of the given overall budget set. The more impatient rent, and the more patient own. (Heterogeneity in wealth and the intertemporal distribution of income endowments will induce heterogeneity in overall budget sets, and this will also contribute to heterogeneity in optimal choices.) In the example in the figures, consumers who optimize as renters at the node c or on the segment c-d, or optimize as owners at h or on the exposed part of the line segment h-i, will not contribute voluntarily to a 401(k) plan. Note that these conclusions are quite sensitive to the relative position of the node h and the line segment a-b; increases in the 401(k) employer match rate or a higher contribution ceiling Q^*, or an increase in r_S, may shift h to the southwest of the a-b segment so that it is no longer efficient to be a homeowner without savings.

Now consider the impact of changes in features of the 401(k) plan. First, rational consumers treat an increase in an unconditional employer contribution to a 401(k) plan as a component of retirement income, with no substitution effect on discretionary saving. In the usual case that current and future consumption are both normal goods, the income effect of an increased 401(k) unconditional contribution will reduce period 0 voluntary savings, but increase total savings and period 1 consumption. Second, increasing the employer match rate on voluntary 401(k) contributions increases RoR_Q, or the slopes of the a-h and b-c segments in the figures. The substitution effect will increase contribution rates of consumers whose optima are on the g-h or b-c line segments, and may induce participation of some consumers located at the nodes h and b. The income effect in the normal goods case will offset some of the increased savings induced by the substitution effect. If the increase in the matching rate moves the budget sets around in a way that makes some nodes without 401(k) contributions inefficient, there could be a nonmarginal 401(k) participation response to a marginal increase in the matching rate.

The nature of heterogeneity of tastes and endowments among rational consumers, as well as tax rates and RoR, will determine the overall population impact of changes in 401(k) features. The example in the figures does not necessarily describe the dominant effect. However, the example serves to illustrate the point that universal participation in 401(k) plans, even with significant matching, is not necessarily rational, and that the overall impact of 401(k) plan parameters must be assessed in terms of overall life cycle consequences. The important next step after showing that consumers adjust only partially from defaults is to establish that it is second-best welfare-maximizing to select defaults that increase participation. Even if this step is true for most, it is a significant research problem to define welfare when consumer behavior does not reveal consistent preferences, to determine who the winners are when a policy changes defaults, and to determine how defaults should be targeted to consumer segments to approximate a second-best welfare maximum.

Conclusions

I conclude with some observations on sources and consequences of behavioral inconsistencies, their impact on "happiness" broadly defined, and the ease with which these errors can be controlled to increase consumer welfare through defaults, framing, and education. There seem to be two major categories of deviations from life cycle rationality. First, there are errors that arise from lack of attention, procrastination, faulty perceptions, and careless optimization. These are "mechanical" errors in preference maximization that may either be overcome through consumer education, or finessed through framing and defaults. The consumer may be aware of these shortcomings in her decision process, and recognize that defaults, precommitments, or other interventions facilitate her decisions and increase her happiness. In the case of 401(k) choices, the use of enrollment windows, penalties for delay, and rewards for immediate response may focus attention and discourage procrastination. Consumers are also more likely to attend to employer unconditional contributions or matching if they are marketed as attention-getting "bargains" for the consumer, or framed to deflect attention from current cost.

Second, there are errors that arise from mistakes in anticipating the consumer's own tastes, particularly time-inconsistent impatience, asymmetric loss aversion, and genuine instabilities in tastes, including phenomena such as physical or emotional health-linked tastes that cannot be anticipated from the consumer's current state. Here, intervention is more difficult, both because the consumer may resist changes that appear to reduce current utility, and because in the absence of stable preferences it is difficult to make unambiguous judgments about consumer welfare. Further, interventions to encourage saving have to counter the active, sharp marketing practices of financial institutions that profit from exploiting consumers' intertemporal irrationality and drive for instant gratification through overselling of credit cards, subprime mortgages, and equity loans. Laboratory lottery experiments in which both the utility and the probability of payoffs are ambiguous seem to offer the best possibility of testing consumer acceptance of information or procedures that reduce ambiguity, encourage strategic planning, or build resistence to marketing appeals for instant gratification.

References

Benhabib, J., and A. Bisin. 2005. Modeling internal commitment mechanisms and self-control: A neuroeconomics approach to consumption-saving decisions. *Games and Economic Behavior* 52 (2): 460–92.

Laibson, D. I., A. Repetto, and J. Tobacman. 2005. Self-control and saving for retirement. In *Social Security reform: Financial and political issues in international perspective,* ed. A. Razin and R. Brooks, 73–143. Cambridge: Cambridge University Press.

Shefrin, H. M., and R. H. Thaler. 1988. The behavioral life-cycle hypothesis. *Economic Inquiry* 26 (4): 609–43.

———. 1997. An economic theory of self-control. In *Culture, social norms, and economics, Vol. 1: Economic Behavior,* ed. M. Casson, 471–85. Cheltenham: Elgar.

Thaler, R. 1985. Mental accounting and consumer choice. *Marketing Science* 4: 199–214.

12

Housing Price Volatility and Downsizing in Later Life

James Banks, Richard Blundell, Zoë Oldfield,
and James P. Smith

In this chapter we will document and model the housing transitions of the elderly in two countries—England and the United States. One important form of these transitions involves downsizing, but there remains considerable controversy even about what the facts are about downsizing at older ages. This controversy stems partly from the absence until recently of long panel data on the housing wealth and circumstances of elderly households. It may also flow from a relatively narrow view of what downsizing is for the purposes of empirical modeling—selling a home and becoming a renter. Other dimensions that are now possible to analyze include selling a home to move into a smaller place either as a renter or owner, or moving in with family or friends, renting out rooms, or simply reducing maintenance and repairs (see Davidoff 2004).

Thus, in addition to the transition into renting, we will document and model the factors associated with downsizing across several of these relevant dimensions.[1] We will examine the extent to which these transitions are

James Banks is deputy research director at the Institute for Fiscal Studies and a professor of economics at University College, London. Richard Blundell is research director of the Institute for Fiscal Studies and a professor of economics at University College, London. Zoë Oldfield is a senior research economist at the Institute for Fiscal Studies. James P. Smith holds the RAND Chair in Labor Market and Demographic Studies at the RAND Corporation.

The authors gratefully acknowledge the financial support of a grant from the National Institute on Aging. Blundell and Banks also acknowledge cofunding from the ESRC Centre for the Microeconomic Analysis of Public Policy at IFS. Smith benefited from the expert programming assistance of David Rumpel. The usual disclaimer applies. This chapter was prepared for presentation at the Boulders Economics of Aging Conference in Carefree, Arizona in May 2007. We very much appreciate the useful and constructive comments of our discussant, Steve Venti, as well as the other participants at the conference.

1. Less immediately transparent forms of downsizing—reducing additions and repairs or renting out rooms—will be dealt with, to the extent that data allow, in subsequent research.

coincident or near other salient events such as retirement or widowhood by estimating models for the empirically important types of housing transitions over multiple waves of our panel data. While other literature has looked at some of these transitions in the United States, the contribution of our analysis, in addition to broadening the empirical analysis to include multiple downsizing measures, is to exploit the longer sample periods now available to look at transitions over a longer horizon where we are more likely to see evidence of downsizing if it does exist in the data. We also provide, to our knowledge, the first systematic comparison of downsizing behavior between the United States and Britain, where there has been much less empirical evidence on downsizing to date.[2]

A second contribution of this chapter is to discuss and model the potential role of house price volatility, which we have previously studied for younger households' home ownership and housing consumption decisions (Banks, Blundell, and Smith 2003a, Banks et al. 2006) in the housing decisions of the elderly. In addition to any type of downsizing in housing consumption that may occur, some housing transitions at older ages may reflect an attempt to escape from the risk associated with a highly price volatile asset, given the relatively short remaining life span. For example, housing price risk at older ages may encourage moving to less price volatile areas but leave intact ownership status as well as the level of real housing consumption. Among those who do sell their homes to buy another, we will therefore also document the transitions between housing price safe and volatile areas even if home size does not change.

Because it places the future flow of nonhousing consumption at risk, greater housing price risk provides an incentive to reduce housing consumption more quickly (at an earlier age) or equivalently to downsize in all forms. Greater (mean preserving) price risk increases the probability that individuals will want to increase their savings in safe assets. Because holding a house in a volatile area is not a safe asset, this implies that the desire to downsize is greater when house price risks are higher. These effects will be mitigated to the extent households have annuitized incomes.

Because housing price volatility is temporally and spatially variable, our empirical analysis will document the importance of the role of house price volatility using comparable panel data analysis for the United States and Britain. One reason motivating our choice of comparison countries is the significant differences in housing price variability between these two countries—Britain has considerably higher house price volatility, with the relatively safe regions having comparable volatility to the most risky regions of the United States (see Banks et al. [2006] for example). Consequently, if volatility matters, one might expect differences in downsizing behavior across countries.

---

2. For an exception, see Disney, Henley, and Stears (2002), which looked at housing wealth and savings trajectories for older households in the United Kingdom between 1988 and 1994.

Of course there may be many other differences between the two countries and hence, in contrast to the descriptive evidence comparing the two countries, our empirical analysis will exploit within-country regional and time series variation in volatility to identify the effects of volatility on downsizing behavior. This distinction between these two approaches turns out to be important. At the broadest level, our descriptive comparison of the two countries reveals less downsizing behavior in Britain than in the United States—a result at odds with the idea that higher volatility should lead to greater downsizing. Once we look within country and also control for other covariates, however, we find a positive correlation between downsizing and volatility in the United States, and a qualitatively similar although statistically weaker effect within Britain. This suggests that other differences between the two countries are driving the international differences, and some potential factors are discussed briefly in the spirit of topics for future research.

A third contribution of our chapter is to examine more generally the long contested issue of whether households in both countries at sufficiently old age reduce their consumption. In particular the question we ask is whether consumption of housing declines in addition to any changes induced by a set of demographic changes producing smaller households and the decision to retire from the labor force. Because housing is an important component of total consumption and is usually believed to be one of the components most resistant to any downward changes, our finding of a downward path of housing consumption adds important evidence to the more general debate on the nature of consumption trajectories at older ages.

This chapter is divided into six sections. Section 12.1 outlines and discusses implications from a simple theoretical model of the impact of housing price variability on life cycle choices regarding housing decisions with an emphasis on its implications for downsizing during late life. Section 12.2 describes the data sources used in both Britain and the United States. Section 12.3 documents the principal facts about the extent of different forms of late life downsizing in both countries and their possible relation to housing price variability within and between Britain and the United States. In section 12.4 we summarize the predictions to be tested and provide the results of the empirical tests of our model. Section 12.5 uses the results of previous sections to present and discuss age trajectories of housing consumption at older ages in the two countries. In section 12.6 we present our conclusions.

12.1 Theoretical Model

Economic theory has implications about the possibility of downsizing at older ages for a number of reasons. As families progress through the life cycle, the demand for the consumption of housing services is likely to fall. For example, it is a standard implication of life cycle models that at sufficiently older ages as mortality risks rise, total household consumption (of which housing is an important part) will fall with age. While the extent of the actual fall in total household consumption remains a matter of active debate, it appears to be the case that at sufficiently older ages household consumption does indeed fall with age, most likely reflecting the combined influences of time preferences and mortality risk. When total consumption falls, housing consumption should also fall since if it did not, all reductions in total consumption would have to take place in nonhousing consumption alone.

12.1.1   The Demographic Ladder

The second and perhaps more immediately apparent reason that one might expect reductions in housing consumption at older ages are demographic. One useful description of the demographic forces is the housing ladder, which we see as demographically driven as individuals marry and form families with children aging and growing in their housing needs. Eventually people complete their family building with older children starting to leave home to go off on their own. Figure 12.1, panel A, depicts this demographic process by plotting by age for the United States three dimensions of the demographic ladder—the fraction of families who had completed their family, the fraction of families who ever have had a child at least five years old, and the fraction of families who currently have a child at least five years old in the household.[3] A parallel set of graphs are provided for Britain in figure 12.1, panel B.

The demographic housing life cycle can be divided into five broad stages. In the first stage, an individual lives with their parents; in the second, they form partnerships; and in the third, they go on to have children and complete their family size. In the remainder of the life cycle, in stage four, children leave home, and the final stage is widowhood. At each stage, there is a decision to buy or rent and a decision about a minimum level of housing consumption necessary to meet needs. The demography depicted in figure 12.1, which are remarkably similar in both countries, indicates that housing demand will grow during the early and middle parts of life, but may then reverse as children leave home and go off on their own.

Because the fraction of families with a child over age five in the household peaks around age forty in both countries, the fraction of families with children under age eighteen will peak in the mid-fifties and the demographically driven demand for housing should peak at this age or before. Multiple children should matter as well in housing demand. Further reductions in housing demand at older ages will flow from divorce and/or widowhood as people enter the final stage of life without a partner.

---

3. This figure plots the cumulative fraction of individuals who completed their family size by age. This was obtained from data on individuals age fifty and over by taking the age at which they had their last child as being the age they completed their family.

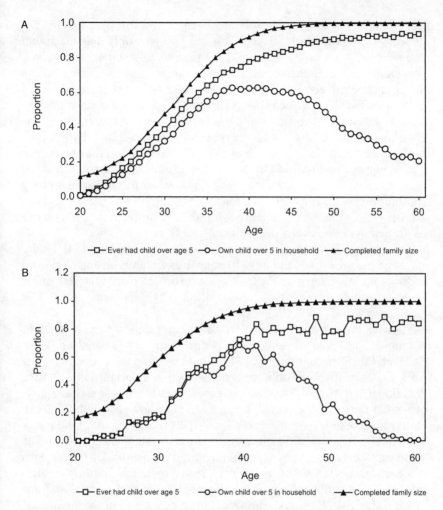

Fig. 12.1   The demographic ladder: *A*, United States; *B*, United Kingdom

12.1.2   Housing Price Risk

The third factor that may influence decisions to downsize concerns the influence of housing price risk. In an earlier paper (Banks et al. 2006), we investigated the influence of housing price risk on the decision to own a home during the rising upward part of the demographic housing ladder. To summarize, one possible solution to the changing housing demand over the life cycle is to simply purchase the amount of housing one requires at each stage, but high transactions costs serve as an effective barrier to that strategy.

Another solution would be to rent in the early stages and then purchase the "right," presumably larger, home when family size is complete. The difficulty with that strategy is that housing price volatility may mean that you are priced out of this market at the time when you need to purchase your family home. Because there are no market insurance devices that can insure against this risk, one can only self-insure against the future housing price volatility. To provide this insurance, a household wishes to hold an asset with a value correlated with house prices they will face in the future. Holding housing equity essentially provides some insurance against high house prices later. Since, in the absence of a formal market, the only way to obtain housing equity is to buy a house, to insure themselves, individuals must purchase a house earlier than they may have wanted based on housing consumption demographic needs alone. Thus, the more volatile house prices are, the greater the insurance motive of owning a house in the early phases of the demographic ladder depicted in figure 12.1.

This chapter is motivated by an extension of our model into the older stages of the life cycle—the stage that involves children leaving home and widowhood. Are people willing to downsize in order to fund their retirement consumption, and how is this decision affected by the presence of volatile house prices?

The integration of housing price risk into a single theoretical framework is complex, and even algebraic closed-form solutions will only be possible under certain forms of preferences. Ideally, however, we want such a framework to use relatively flexible preferences (such as Constant Relative Risk Aversion [CRRA]) that also have some minimum housing needs or requirement that must be met in each period, and such analytical solutions can be hard to come by. We have confirmed the predictions that follow in a numerical simulation of a simple three-period model of the later stages of life to capture the stages of the demographic ladder identified in the previous section, with CRRA utility, house price risk, a minimum housing requirement that rises and then falls with the housing ladder, and a simplified form of mortality risk. For the purposes of this chapter, and in the absence of analytical results, we focus instead on intuitive descriptions of the mechanisms in play.

The first thing to note is that the model is not symmetric with regard to the role of volatility in early as opposed to late life. In the rising phrase of the housing ladder, individuals want to self-insure so that they will not be forced to live in a house that is too small when their housing demand is high in midlife. In volatile areas, expected price volatility induces one to move into home ownership at a younger age and hence, to reduce consumption of other goods.

On the later rungs of the household ladder, however, housing is no longer required in order to meet an insurance need. Instead, when household size is no longer expected to rise, housing reverts to a more straightforward risky asset which individuals (if they are risk averse) may wish to avoid Put simply, in the later stages of life or the downsize of the housing ladder, one may want to release some housing consumption to consume other goods. Greater housing price risk (whether in the form of greater house equity for a given level of risk, or greater risk for a given level of equity) puts that decision at risk, thereby encouraging homeowners in more price volatile areas to either downsize more rapidly than they might have wanted, to rent, or to move to areas with less house price volatility. Another option is equity withdrawal or reverse mortgages, which not only provide some insurance against mortality risk but also slowly reduces uncertainty about the equity. But like many annuities this market is quite thin, perhaps due to standard adverse selection issues.

Downsizing essentially involves cashing in housing equity. You want to do this because you want to use housing wealth to finance future nonhousing consumption, but as with any approaching asset realization, an optimal path would be to gradually reduce risk and move into safe assets to avoid exposure to shocks at the time of realization that will have permanent effects. (This is a mechanism directly analogous to the prediction in the pensions literature that as retirement approaches the optimal pension portfolio is to gradually switch out of stocks and into bonds.)

There are, of course, many good reasons why individuals may not want to downsize. One is that they may have build up a "habitual" demand for this house as they may over time have fitted it to their tastes, or they may want children to return to the home in which they were raised. The cost of not downsizing is that all other consumption may have to absorb more of the fall.

If you do decide to downsize, the specific timing may be coordinated with other salient events—indeed, our description of the housing ladder is event-specific as opposed to age- or time-specific. One event may be retirement, since one's work is location-specific even if there is housing price risk. The other is widowhood or other forms of marital dissolution where, at a minimum, the old house may be too big. Thus, any downsizing that does take place may be correlated with retirement, widowhood, or divorce and our empirical analysis will need to allow for these transitions.

In the previous discussion we have not addressed the issue that, conditional on location, house price volatility may not be avoidable by switching to the rental sector, since rental prices may be more volatile as well in such areas, which may indeed generate a demand for owner-occupation to avoid rent risk (see Sinai and Souleles 2005). Several things are worth mentioning here. First, the mechanisms previously discussed relate to stock of housing wealth as opposed to the flows of period-by-period housing costs associated with ownership or rental, respectively. Although once mortgages are paid off, the risk associated with house price fluctuations for homeowners is all related to the value of assets and not post-housing cost incomes, so the relative comparison of ownership to rental is changed in favor of owner-occupation. The fact that horizons are shorter would weaken the importance of such an effect.

Second, in our framework, switching from an owner to a renter is just one way that an individual can choose to downsize. This means that our framework is compatible with that of Sinai and Souleles because individuals who wish to avoid both rental risk and house price risk can do so by downsizing in ways in which they can remain an owner occupier. Finally, even when it comes to homeownership itself, in contrast to the up stage of the ladder the prediction here is that more volatility would lead to lower ownership rates—a mechanism that would work against that previously described, if anything. To the extent that the previous two considerations do not totally remove the relevance of rental price risk (relative to ownership) in volatile areas, we may be underestimating the effect of volatility in our empirical models.

12.1.3   Other Risks

Of course, other risks that may or may not be correlated with house price risk may also matter for households' housing and downsizing decisions. Perhaps the two most natural to think of are income risk and mortality or morbidity risk. On the assumption that most downsizing takes place at or after retirement, income risk is most likely of only second-order importance since there is no earnings risk and large fractions of the incomes of retired households may well have some degree of inflation protection.

More important is likely to be health risks, and there are several ways in which additional health risk may also affect housing wealth and nonhousing wealth accumulation and decumulation decisions at older ages. Especially when health insurance is not complete, it increases the risks of additional out-of-pocket expenditures, particularly at the tails, which should encourage additional precautionary savings.

Before retirement, morbidity risk also shows up as one of the determinants of income risk and thus will have effects similar to those described in the previous section. Holding a risky asset such as housing when prices are highly volatile may be a dubious strategy when one faces additional health risk. A spread in pure mortality risk (making it more likely you will live longer as well as shorter) will make risk-averse agents engage in more precautionary savings in all forms in face of an added risk of living too long. This effect will depend both on the extent to which retirement incomes have been annuitized (which varies a great deal across our countries) and the importance of any bequest motive that might exist. We will not incorporate health risk into this chapter but note that it is an important topic (on which we are gradually gaining a better empirical understanding) for inclusion in future drafts.

12.2   Sources of Data

This research will rely on microdata from the United States and Britain. For the United States, we will use the Health and Retirement Study (HRS) and primarily the Panel Survey of Income Dynamics (PSID). For Britain, we will use the British Household Panel Survey (BHPS). Besides the standard set of demographics on age, schooling, family income, marriage, and other aspects of family building, outcomes information available in all these surveys include several aspects of housing choice—ownership, size of house, and value of house.

HRS   This research uses a set of surveys of the over-age fifty population: the original Health and Retirement Study (HRS-original) and the Assets and Health Dynamics of the Oldest Old (AHEAD). The HRS-original is a national sample of about 7,600 households (12,654 individuals) with at least one person in the birth cohorts of 1931 to 1941 (about fifty-one to sixty-one years old at baseline). The AHEAD includes 6,052 households (8,222 individuals) with at least one person born in 1923 or earlier (seventy or over in 1993). Follow-ups have taken place at two-year intervals.

The HRS housing section includes wave-by-wave data about tenure (renter or owner), value and purchase price of the home, outstanding mortgages (and hence, home equity) and monthly mortgage payments, whether the household refinanced since the last interview, other fixed payments (e.g., property taxes, fuels, etc.), rents (if a renter), and number of rooms. Information is also available on second homes. In this chapter, HRS is used simply to confirm the principal patterns of changing housing demand obtained from the PSID during later life.

The Panel Study of Income Dynamics   The PSID has gathered almost thirty years of extensive economic and demographic data on a nationally representative sample of approximately 5,000 (original) families and 35,000 individuals who live in those families. Details on family income and its components have been gathered in each wave since the inception of PSID in 1967. Starting in 1984 and in five-year intervals until 1999, PSID asked questions to measure household wealth. Starting in 1997, the PSID switched to a two-year periodicity, and wealth modules are now part of the core interview.

In each wave, the PSID asks detailed questions on family size and composition, schooling, education, age, and marital status. State of residence is available in every year and individuals are followed to new locations if they move. Unlike other American wealth surveys, PSID is representative of the complete age distribution. Yearly housing tenure questions determine whether individuals own, rent, or live with others. Questions on value and mortgage were asked in each wave of the PSID. Renters are asked the rent they pay, and both owners and renters are asked the number of rooms in the residence. Health conditions and timing of onset were added in 1999.

British Household Panel Survey   The BHPS has been running annually since 1991 and, like the PSID, is also representative of the complete age distribution. The wave 1 sample consisted of some 5,500 households and 10,300 individuals. The BHPS contains annual information on individual and household income and employment, as well as a complete set of demographic variables, and has several other features to recommend it. There is an extensive amount of information on mortgages and housing (including number of rooms) that enables us to measure housing wealth in each wave of the data.[4] Regional variation in ownership and housing wealth accumulation will be essential in our tests and the data will provide us with sufficient observations per year in each region to carry out our tests.

12.2.1   Housing Price Volatility

For the United States, housing price data to measure housing price risk were obtained from the Office of Federal Housing Enterprise Oversight (OFHEO) House Price Index. This data contain quarterly and yearly price indexes for the value of single-family homes in the United States in the individual states and the District of Columbia.[5] This data use repeat transactions for the same houses to obtain a quality constant index and is available for all years starting in 1974. All yearly housing prices by state are reported relative to those that prevailed in 1980. By 1995 there were almost 7 million repeat transactions in the data so that the number of observations for each state is reasonably large. No demographic data are available with this index.

For Britain, regional house price data to measure housing price risk will be obtained from the Nationwide Building Society House Price series, which is a quarterly regional house price series going back to 1974. Rather than use a repeat sales index, the prices are adjusted for changes in the mix of sales to approximate a composition constant index, and are also seasonally adjusted.

As with our previous paper (Banks et al. 2006), housing volatility is defined using a moving five-year window. That is, our measure of volatility is the standard deviation of the house price around its trend in the five years prior to the observation. What should matter for individual decisions, of course, is the conditional variance of expected house prices over the individuals' horizon and in this respect our measure is only crude, intending simply to capture that the recent past might be used as a prediction of the future.

---

4. With the exception of 1992, when house value was only collected for those living at new addresses.
5. For details on this data see Calhoun (1996).

Nevertheless, sensitivity analysis in previous papers revealed the empirical conclusions to be broadly unaffected by choice of window-length within reasonable ranges, and subject to the constraints of, and subsequent impacts on, the amount of time series variation available. Finally, with regard to picking out regional as opposed to time series variation in volatility, we are confident that the measure picks out the risky from the safe regions both within and across countries.

12.3   Establishing the Facts

Even the basic question of whether housing is downsized as people age is not well answered in the literature. For example, Venti and Wise (2001) concluded, based on the AHEAD data in the United States, that after controlling for transitions into widowhood and nursing homes, the elderly do not generally reduce housing equity as they age. Yet Sheiner and Weil (1992) estimated that among households entering old age owning a home, just 41 percent still own when the surviving spouse dies.

One source of the differences that emerge in the current literature is that moving out of home ownership is only but one form downsizing may take. Individuals may sell the original family home to move into a smaller one while remaining owners are either in the same or a different general location. They can also remain homeowners even if the size of the home is the same but move to a less expensive and less volatile place. They may also invest less in upkeep of their home, an implicit form of downsizing, or rent a room out. Or, they may move into the home of another relative (especially children) or have them move into their own home, perhaps with shared ownership. The years around labor market retirement and the death of a spouse may be especially important ones for these transitions. Very little is currently known about the magnitude and reasons for these broader cumulative transitions or about any international differences that might exist. In this section, we document the principal empirical facts around these issues in both the United States and the United Kingdom.

12.3.1   Home Ownership Rates at Older Ages

Especially at older ages, most Americans are homeowners. Based on multiple waves of the PSID, table 12.1, panel A, presents tenure status for individuals by age of the household head for ten-year age groups starting at age fifty, concluding with a residual category of those eighty-plus years old. Using the same format, panel B lists parallel data derived from the BHPS for individuals in Britain. For both countries, the data are also stratified by whether or not the household lives in an area characterized by volatile housing prices.

Table 12.1, panel A, shows that slightly more than 80 percent of all American individuals over age fifty are homeowners. Approximately one

Table 12.1   Tenure status for individuals by age of head of family

	50–59	60–69	70–79	80+	Total
	A United States				
Owner	83.0	83.1	77.5	65.5	80.5
Renter	15.0	14.6	19.2	28.8	16.7
Other	1.9	2.3	2.5	6.7	2.8
Risky areas					
Owner	77.2	74.9	68.4	57.4	73.7
Renter	21.2	22.9	29.9	36.1	24.4
Other	1.6	2.2	1.7	4.6	2.0
Nonrisky areas					
Owner	85.1	85.8	79.9	68.3	81.8
Renter	11.8	12.8	16.2	26.2	14.2
Other	2.2	2.4	3.9	7.4	3.0
	B United Kingdom				
Owner	76.5	71.0	63.2	48.2	67.6
Renter	19.7	25.3	31.8	42.5	27.5
Other	3.8	3.7	5.1	9.3	4.9
Risky areas					
Owner	78.7	74.7	66.2	50.6	70.5
Renter	17.4	21.9	29.2	39.4	24.7
Other	3.9	3.4	4.7	10.1	4.8
Nonrisky areas					
Owner	72.3	64.0	57.8	43.5	62.2
Renter	24.2	31.7	36.5	48.6	32.8
Other	3.5	4.3	5.8	7.9	4.9

Sources: Panel A: PSID—(1968–1999), weighted individual level data. Panel B: BHPS—(1991–2004), weighted individual level data.

in every six Americans in this age group are renters, while a relatively small fraction are in the catch-all "other categories" that largely consist of living with relatives or in a nursing home. Among older Americans, there is a gradual decline in the fraction who are homeowners across age groups post-age seventy. Below age seventy, homeownership rates are about 83 percent—above age eighty the rate is 66 percent. Most of the decline in the probability of owning a home appears as an increase in renting but some of it, particularly among those over age seventy, reflects an increase in the likelihood of living with others or in a nursing home.

For British individuals over age fifty (summarized in panel B of table 12.1), the probability of being a homeowner is about 13 percentage points lower than that of American individuals, a deficit mostly offset by a higher probability of renting. There is a much sharper negative age pattern in Britain compared to the United States across the age groups depicted in table 12.1. Among those in their fifties, for example, there is less than a 7 percentage point difference in homeownership rates between the two countries—by ages eighty and over the likelihood of owning a home is 17 percentage points lower in Britain compared to the United States. As documented in Banks, Blundell, and Smith (2003), this sharp negative age gradient in homeowning rates in Britain largely reflects cohort effects and the sale at subsidized rates of government-owned council housing.

In the United States, homeownership rates are much higher in nonrisky housing price locales than in the risky ones. One might be tempted to attribute this difference to the fact that housing prices are also considerably higher in the risky places, but that temptation is deterred by the fact that the reverse pattern appears to be the case in Britain even though housing prices in Britain are also higher in the more volatile housing price places.

12.3.2   Changes in Housing Tenure with Age

Our principal concern in this chapter involves not homeownership status per se but rather the transitions in tenure that takes place at older ages. The very pronounced cohort effects in housing status in Britain documented in the previous section indicate that it would be perilous to attempt to read housing transitions from cross-sectional age housing tenure patterns, especially in Britain. Instead, in this section we will highlight the salient transitions using the panel nature of the data in the United States and Britain.

Since much of the existing research on downsizing at older ages focuses on the decision to sell one's original home and become a renter, we begin with the transitions conditional on originally being a homeowner. Table 12.2 examines these tenure transitions in the United States (using the PSID) and Britain (using the BHPS) for a subpopulation who are at least fifty years old and who were originally homeowners in the initial period. Because the extent of the transitions that place will depend on the length of the window during which we allow households to adjust their status, the data are presented for three different durations between the waves of the panel—two years apart, five years apart, and ten years apart. All tenure transitions are presented separately for risky and nonrisky price areas. Finally, table 12.3 organizes the data in precisely the same way for those who were initially renters.

These two-year transitions may illustrate why there is some skepticism about downsizing being an important dimension of behavior at older ages. Across a two-year period, only 11 percent of American homeowners move and only one in twenty relocate during a single year. Such mobility is even less in Britain, where only about 6 percent of British homeowning households relocate over a two-year horizon. However, as we allow the number of years between the survey waves to expand, the extent of mobility taking place increases significantly. To illustrate, over a decade, almost one in every three American homeowners who were at least fifty years old moved out of an originally owned home. Among those Americans who did move, however, 71 percent of them remained homeowners by purchasing another home. Another 22 percent of them became renters while the rest do a col-

Table 12.2   Housing transition among owners in the United States and in the United Kingdom

	All	Risky	Nonrisky
Two-year transitions			
United States			
Owner, Owner, No move	88.9	89.4	88.7
Owner, Owner, Moved	8.0	7.7	8.1
Owner, Renter	2.2	2.3	2.1
Owner, Other	0.9	0.6	1.0
United Kingdom			
Owner, Owner, No move	94.0	93.7	94.8
Owner, Owner, Moved	4.2	4.5	3.5
Owner, Renter	1.2	1.2	1.2
Owner, Other	0.6	0.6	0.5
Five-year transitions			
United States			
Owner, Owner, No move	80.0	79.8	80.1
Owner, Owner, Moved	14.3	14.7	14.1
Owner, Renter	4.2	4.4	4.2
Owner, Other	1.5	1.1	1.6
United Kingdom			
Owner, Owner, No move	86.5	86.1	87.3
Owner, Owner, Moved	10.7	11.2	9.6
Owner, Renter	2.1	2.0	2.3
Owner, Other	0.7	0.7	0.8
Ten-year transitions			
United States			
Owner, Owner, No move	68.2	65.6	69.0
Owner, Owner, Moved	22.7	26.0	21.7
Owner, Renter	6.8	6.5	6.9
Owner, Other	2.3	1.8	2.5
United Kingdom			
Owner, Owner, No move	76.1	75.6	77.3
Owner, Owner, Moved	20.2	20.8	19.0
Owner, Renter	2.8	2.6	3.0
Owner, Other	0.9	1.0	0.7

Source: U.S. data based on PSID for all years 1968–1999—Population ages fifty and over. UK data are based on BHPS. All data are weighted and are individual level data.

lection of things, including moving in with family members or into group dwellings.

Mobility among homeowners is clearly less in Britain for older households. Across the same ten-year span between survey waves, about one in every four British homeowners relocated compared to about one in three American households. In these simple tabulations, in neither Britain nor the United States does an owner's propensity to sell a home appear to depend on whether one lives in a housing price risky or nonrisky locale.

Table 12.3   **Housing transitions among renters in the United States and in the
United Kingdom**

	All	Risky	Nonrisky
Two-year transitions			
United States			
Renter, Renter, No move	61.1	68.5	56.8
Renter, Renter, Moved	27.0	22.7	29.4
Renter, Owner	9.8	6.8	10.2
Renter, Other	3.0	2.0	3.6
United Kingdom			
Renter, Renter, No move	88.2	87.9	90.1
Renter, Renter, Moved	6.6	7.5	5.4
Renter, Owner	4.0	4.0	3.9
Renter, Other	0.6	0.7	0.6
Five-year transitions			
United States			
Renter, Renter, No move	59.0	64.6	56.3
Renter, Renter, Moved	28.5	26.8	29.3
Renter, Owner	8.4	6.7	9.2
Renter, Other	4.1	1.9	5.2
United Kingdom			
Renter, Renter, No move	76.6	75.3	78.5
Renter, Renter, Moved	14.3	15.7	12.3
Renter, Owner	8.0	7.8	8.3
Renter, Other	1.1	1.2	0.9
Ten-year transitions			
United States			
Renter, Renter, No move	28.2	37.1	22.5
Renter, Renter, Moved	43.5	39.5	46.0
Renter, Owner	24.2	20.9	26.2
Renter, Other	4.2	2.5	5.2
United Kingdom			
Renter, Renter, No move	59.8	58.7	61.4
Renter, Renter, Moved	24.1	24.7	23.4
Renter, Owner	14.6	14.8	14.2
Renter, Other	1.4	1.8	1.0

Source: U.S. data based on PSID for all years 1968–1999—Population ages fifty and over. UK
data are based on BHPS. All data are weighted and are individual level data.

Table 12.3 demonstrates that—not surprisingly—renters in both countries are far more mobile than owners. Across the ten year survey interval,
72 percent of American renters moved at least once compared to 40 percent
of British renters, so that once again British households are less mobile than
their American counterparts. Most of these originally renting households
remain so and simply settle into another apartment or flat. But a little more
than one in every four American renters who do relocate over age fifty subsequently become homeowners—the comparable British number is one-third.

While these transitions rates were similar between risky and nonrisky areas for homeowners, it appears that renters in nonrisky areas are more likely to move in the United States.

Table 12.4 displays patterns of housing tenure transitions by ten year age groups for those owners who are at least age 50, and table 12.5 does the same for those who were originally renters. In the United States, until after eighty, roughly two-thirds of homeowners do not move to another place over a ten-year window. However, among those who do move, a growing fraction of them do not purchase another home. Rather, they increasingly

Table 12.4   Housing transition among owners by age of head (of family)—ten year transitions

	50–59	60–69	70–79	80 plus
United States				
Overall				
Owner, Owner, No move	70.8	70.2	62.9	42.8
Owner, Owner, Moved	24.5	20.6	15.5	12.9
Owner, Renter	3.6	6.3	12.2	38.0
Owner, Other	1.1	2.9	5.8	6.3
Risky areas				
Owner, Owner, No move	64.5	65.7	74.9	46.9
Owner, Owner, Moved	29.2	25.4	10.9	18.6
Owner, Renter	4.8	7.5	10.9	25.5
Owner, Other	1.6	1.5	3.4	9.0
Nonrisky areas				
Owner, Owner, No move	70.8	70.2	62.9	42.8
Owner, Owner, Moved	24.5	20.6	15.2	12.9
Owner, Renter	3.6	6.3	16.2	38.0
Owner, Other	1.1	2.9	5.8	6.3
United Kingdom				
Overall				
Owner, Owner, No move	73.5	74.0	81.1	79.0
Owner, Owner, Moved	24.2	22.9	15.2	11.8
Owner, Renter	1.7	1.9	3.2	7.1
Owner, Other	0.6	1.1	0.6	2.1
Risky areas				
Owner, Owner, No move	73.2	73.5	81.1	76.1
Owner, Owner, Moved	24.7	23.2	15.3	13.9
Owner, Renter	1.4	2.0	2.9	7.9
Owner, Other	0.7	1.3	0.8	2.2
Nonrisky areas				
Owner, Owner, No move	74.1	75.3	80.8	84.5
Owner, Owner, Moved	23.0	22.2	14.9	7.8
Owner, Renter	2.5	1.7	3.9	5.7
Owner, Other	0.4	0.7	0.3	2.1

Source: U.S. data based on PSID for all years 1968–1999—Population ages fifty and over. UK data are based on BHPS 1991–2004. All data are weighted and are individual level data.

Table 12.5   **Housing transition among renters by age of head—ten year transitions**

	50–59	60–69	70–79	80 plus
United States				
Overall				
Renter, Renter, No move	21.6	31.1	41.4	26.9
Renter, Renter, Moved	40.6	47.0	41.8	56.4
Renter, Owner	33.3	17.1	12.0	8.2
Renter, Other	4.6	2.9	4.9	8.4
Risky areas				
Renter, Renter, No move	30.7	39.4	51.7	37.3
Renter, Renter, Moved	38.8	41.1	37.3	44.5
Renter, Owner	27.5	18.5	8.0	8.4
Renter, Other	3.0	1.1	3.0	9.8
Nonrisky areas				
Renter, Renter, No move	15.3	25.7	35.3	22.6
Renter, Renter, Moved	41.9	50.7	44.4	61.1
Renter, Owner	37.2	19.5	14.4	8.2
Renter, Other	5.7	4.0	5.9	7.8
United Kingdom				
Overall				
Renter, Renter, No move	45.5	61.2	61.5	71.0
Renter, Renter, Moved	27.0	23.6	25.5	20.3
Renter, Owner	26.1	13.8	11.3	7.6
Renter, Other	1.4	1.5	1.7	1.1
Risky areas				
Renter, Renter, No move	43.4	54.3	64.3	72.5
Renter, Renter, Moved	26.0	24.6	27.7	19.5
Renter, Owner	28.3	18.3	6.4	7.5
Renter, Other	2.3	2.9	1.6	0.5
Nonrisky areas				
Renter, Renter, No move	48.9	69.1	57.5	69.0
Renter, Renter, Moved	28.5	22.4	22.2	21.3
Renter, Owner	22.6	8.6	18.6	7.7
Renter, Other	0.0	0.0	1.8	1.9

Source: U.S. data based on PSID for all years 1968–1999. Population ages fifty and over. UK data are based on BHPS. All data are weighted and are individual level data.

move into rental properties and, to a lesser extent, into either assisted living or to stay with family members. The probability of a homeowner moving into a rental property is far less in Britain than in the United States and it is a good deal less likely at older ages for a homeowner in Britain to subsequently become a renter.

In the United States and in Britain, renters become increasingly less mobile with age, once again with an important exception noted for those aged eighty through eighty-nine in the United States. Compared to 22 percent of American renters in their fifties, 41 percent of American renters in their seventies stay in the same place over a ten-year horizon. Across all age groups, many more American renters relocate in the nonrisky areas compared to the risky ones.

Table 12.5 demonstrates that a good deal of the additional mobility among renters in the United States in nonrisky areas involves larger movements from renter to owner status (compared to the risky areas). To this point, we have emphasized the incentives involved in these housing decisions from the point of view of owners. However, the arguments are completely symmetric. From the perspective of those who were originally renters, changing from being a renter to an owner of housing in a house price risky area would make little sense indeed. That transition is less problematic in places where housing price risk is less problematic. Thus, our model predicts that mobility of owners should be higher in housing price risky areas but mobility of renters should be the reverse—that is, mobility will be higher among renters in the nonrisky areas.

12.3.3   Changes in the Number of Rooms

In addition to changing ownership status—the most commonly used measure of downsizing—another form may involve selling an existing home and buying a new one that is spatially smaller or constitutes less housing consumption in other ways. One definition of objective home size available in all our data sets is the number of rooms. Using the PSID for those ages fifty or more, table 12.6 examines changes in the number of rooms of the primary dwelling among those who changed residences between the waves of the data. These patterns are presented by type of area (whether a risky price area or not), initial type of housing tenure (owner or renter), and three time durations between the PSID waves—two, five, and ten years.

These data indicate convincingly that among older Americans, once they decide to relocate, they do tend to move into a smaller dwelling. On average, the new house is around 0.7 of a room smaller than the prior one, a scaling down of about 16 percent, using rooms as the metric. This tendency to downsize is almost entirely due to a movement to smaller places among those who were initially homeowners. Moreover, most of that reduction in size is due to those who change in housing tenure from owner to renter—a new rental dwelling that is on average two-and-a-third rooms smaller than the prior owned one. But—especially as the duration between the waves of the PSID increases—even those who remain homeowners purchase a new home that is on average about one-third of a room smaller.

At least in these univariate descriptive statistics, this tendency of American homeowners to downsize their house at older ages appears to be somewhat stronger if they originally lived in a risky housing price area. This is especially the case among those homeowners who sell and then buy another home. Using the ten-year interval horizon, the change in the number of rooms is twice as high in the risky areas when homeowners buy another

Table 12.6   **Change in number of rooms among movers—PSID ages fifty and over by number of years**

	Delta no. of rooms		
	2 years	5 years	10 years
Overall			
Owners	-0.574	-0.739	-0.817
Owners-renters	-2.016	-2.102	-2.149
Owners-new owners	-0.191	-0.319	-0.395
Renters	-0.004	-0.084	-0.176
Renters-owners	0.692	0.639	0.631
Renters-new renters	-0.151	-0.311	-0.527
Risky areas			
Owners	-0.776	-0.970	-0.992
Owners-renters	-2.219	-2.358	-2.670
Owners-new owners	-0.383	-0.558	-0.641
Renters	-0.094	-0.211	-0.357
Renters-owners	0.336	0.413	0.348
Renters-new renters	-0.158	-0.339	-0.629
Nonrisky areas			
Owners	-0.517	-0.668	-0.756
Owners-renters	-1.943	-2.023	-2.114
Owners-new owners	-0.137	-0.242	-0.308
Renters	0.034	-0.025	-0.078
Renters-owners	0.818	0.727	0.764
Renters-new renters	-0.158	-0.297	-0.470

Source: PSID ages fifty and over (1968–1999) rooms limited to eight. All data are weighted and are individual level data.

home. In nonrisky areas, there is little difference in size of dwelling among renters, but renters do appear to downsize in the risky area.

One limitation of the PSID is that sample sizes become thin once one stratifies by age. Tables 12.7 and 12.8 list similar data on the changing number of rooms associated with housing mobility for two HRS cohorts where relatively long horizons are possible to track housing changes. Table 12.7 provides data from the original HRS cohort (those fifty-one to sixty-one years old in 1992), while table 12.8 does the same for the AHEAD cohort (those seventy-plus years old in 1993.) These two cohorts are of particular interest since the first captures transitions associated with the pre-retirement years while the second focuses on the nature of post-retirement mobility.

During the pre-retirement years, we do find a tendency of Americans to downsize, but this is concentrated completely on homeowners and appears to be more pronounced in the price risky places. Over a ten year time horizon, homeowners who lived in price risky areas when they moved reduced the size of their dwelling by 1.6 rooms if they became a renter and half a

Table 12.7   Change in number of rooms among movers—original HRS cohort by number of years

	Delta no. of rooms		
	2 years	6 years	10 years
Overall			
Owners	−0.298	−0.214	−0.796
Owners-renters	−1.276	−0.779	−1.191
Owners-new owners	−0.152	−0.134	−0.758
Renters	0.310	0.149	0.323
Renters-owners	1.180	0.633	0.919
Renters-new renters	−0.120	−0.206	−0.319
Risky areas			
Owners	−0.352	−0.234	−0.805
Owners-renters	−1.008	−0.659	−1.632
Owners-new owners	−0.268	−0.169	−0.668
Renters	0.123	0.025	−0.054
Renters-owners	1.411	0.753	0.477
Renters-new renters	−0.360	−0.442	−0.498
Nonrisky areas			
Owners	−0.250	−0.210	−0.793
Owners-renters	−1.348	−0.821	−0.996
Owners-new owners	−0.078	−0.124	−0.787
Renters	0.381	0.204	0.537
Renters-owners	1.085	0.599	1.126
Renters-new renters	−0.132	−0.084	−0.191

Source: HRS—original cohort ages 51–61—rooms unlimited. All data are weighted and are individual level data.

room on average if they remained a homeowner. The comparable figures for those in less housing price risky areas were about a one-room reduction if they became a renter and a .8 reduction if they remained a homeowner—about half as large as the amount of downsizing taking place among those living in the price risky areas.

If anything, these size reductions appear to be even larger in the post-retirement AHEAD cohort who are examined in table 12.8. Conditional on relocation, there is a tendency to move to a smaller place even if one remains a homeowner. This tendency is much stronger among those who initially resided in a place with a lot of housing price risk.

The comparable data on number of rooms for the sample ages fifty-plus in Britain are contained in table 12.9 based on data from the BHPS. Downsizing at older ages characterizes households in both countries, although it is a less pervasive phenomenon in Britain than in the United States. The term "less pervasive" applies not only to a smaller probability of changing residences at all older ages in Britain, but also to a smaller change in the size of dwelling, given that a move takes place. If we compare tables 12.6 and

Table 12.8   **Change in number of rooms among movers—HRS Ahead cohort by number of years**

	Delta no. of rooms		
	2 years	4 years	8 years
Overall			
Owners	−0.509	−0.578	−0.646
Owners-renters	−2.039	−1.829	−1.619
Owners-new owners	−0.231	−0.389	−0.507
Renters	0.126	−0.073	−0.002
Renters-owners	0.748	0.636	0.951
Renters-new renters	−0.297	−0.046	−0.300
Risky areas			
Owners	−0.789	−0.800	−0.807
Owners-renters	−2.695	−2.001	−2.362
Owners-new owners	−0.242	−0.489	−0.387
Renters	0.178	0.174	0.166
Renters-owners	1.054	1.352	1.041
Renters-new renters	−0.261	−0.405	−0.540
Nonrisky areas			
Owners	−0.424	−0.508	−0.592
Owners-renters	−1.848	−1.731	−1.434
Owners-new owners	−0.228	−0.355	−0.554
Renters	0.105	−0.171	−0.091
Renters-owners	0.586	0.361	0.872
Renters-new renters	−0.311	−0.485	−0.167

Source: HRS—AHEAD Cohort—rooms unlimited. All data are weighted and are individual level data.

12.9, the changes in number of rooms are almost half as large in Britain compared to the United States. The principal difference lies in the switch from owner to renter status, where the reduction in number of rooms in Britain is 1.4 compared to 2.2 in the United States. As was the case in America, the magnitude of the downsizing that takes place is somewhat larger in the housing price risky areas of Britain compared to places with more stable housing prices.

12.3.4   Escaping Housing Price Volatility

Even when older householders remain homeowners and stay in a home of approximately the same size, they can avoid some of the costs of housing price risk by moving to places where housing prices are less volatile. The data contained in table 12.10 (panel A for the United States and panel B for Britain) indicate that this is precisely what takes place. For those who moved, this table measures the difference in our measure of housing price risk (the standard deviation in housing prices) between the area where they originally lived and the area to which they moved. Thus, a positive nega-

Table 12.9   Change in number of rooms among movers—UK (BHPS) by number of years

	Delta no. of rooms		
	2 years	5 years	10 years
Overall			
Owners	−0.629	−0.586	−0.449
Owners-renters	−0.558	−1.176	−1.442
Owners-owners	−0.876	−0.472	−0.314
Renters	−0.396	−0.486	−0.442
Renters-owners	−0.036	−0.103	−0.019
Renters-renters	−0.615	−0.704	−0.699
Risky areas			
Owners	−0.683	−0.613	−0.466
Owners-renters	−0.861	−1.286	−1.593
Owners-owners	−0.636	−0.493	−0.322
Renters	−0.433	−0.502	−0.456
Renters-owners	0.048	0.079	0.105
Renters-renters	−0.695	−0.792	−0.795
Nonrisky areas			
Owners	−0.484	−0.521	−0.293
Owners-renters	−0.906	−0.964	−1.140
Owners-owners	−0.335	−0.416	−0.409
Renters	−0.333	−0.461	−0.421
Renters-owners	−0.158	−0.345	−0.195
Renters-renters	−0.460	−0.541	−0.560

Source: BHPS—rooms unlimited. All data are weighted and are individual level data.

tive number indicates that the area that they left was characterized by more housing price volatility than the area to which they moved—that is, the household was reducing their exposure to housing price risk. In addition to age stratification, the data in table 12.9 (based on the PSID) and table 12.10 (based on the BHPS) are stratified by whether one was originally an owner or a renter and within each housing tenure type by the housing tenure type to which one moved. Additional data for the American sample based on the two HRS cohorts are provided in the appendix, table 12A.1. In these tables, the American units of volatility were defined as ten times the British units.

There are a number of salient patterns, foremost of which is that after age fifty, when they do move, people move on average to a place with less housing price volatility. The tendency of Americans to move to less price volatile areas peaks during the dominant retirement years (ages sixty to sixty-nine) and actually reverses after age eighty. This may not be surprising since housing decisions at very old age may have more to do with attempts to provide care for the elderly when they become frailer. This would include moving to assisted living communities and to live with relatives.

Second, as predicted by the theory, the tendency to move to areas with

Table 12.10   **Differences in housing price volatility by state among movers by age group**

	50–59	60–69	70–79	80+	Total
		A United States			
Two-year transitions					
All owners who move	0.055	0.065	−0.007	−0.008	0.044
Owner to renter	0.074	0.062	0.003	0.005	0.017
Owner to owner	0.064	0.070	−0.017	0.003	0.053
All renters who move	0.020	0.062	0.032	−0.002	0.033
Renter to renter	0.009	0.055	0.017	0.002	0.023
Renter to owner	0.054	0.097	0.015	0	0.074
All movers	0.042	0.062	0.008	−0.005	0.038
Five-year transitions					
All owners who move	0.090	0.072	0.014	−0.010	0.066
Owner to renter	0.047	−0.025	0.006	−0.014	0.011
Owner to owner	0.096	0.095	0.009	−0.075	0.081
All renters who move	0.033	0.104	0.048	−0.000	0.055
Renter to renter	0.011	0.072	0.025	−0.014	0.032
Renter to owner	0.073	0.199	0.163	−0.008	0.116
All movers	0.070	0.078	0.027	−0.004	0.060
Ten-year transitions					
All owners who move	0.152	0.067	0.011	−0.023	0.102
Owner to renter	0.118	−0.029	0.029	−0.041	0.030
Owner to owner	0.160	0.094	0.013	0.193	0.127
All renters who move	0.058	0.103	0.108	−0.097	0.074
Renter to renter	0.027	0.048	0.111	−0.103	0.043
Renter to owner	0.102	0.252	0.084	−0.187	0.138
All movers	0.121	0.075	0.038	−0.016	0.091
PSID Ages 50+ 1968–1999					
		B United Kingdom (BHPS)			
Two-year transitions					
All owners who move	0.015	0.020	0.014	0.018	0.016
Owner to renter	0.020	0.018	0.015	0.023	0.019
Owner to owner	0.014	0.021	0.013	0.011	0.016
All renters who move	0.014	0.020	0.025	0.020	0.019
Renter to renter	0.014	0.022	0.028	0.022	0.021
Renter to owner	0.015	0.016	0.019	0.017	0.016
All movers	0.015	0.020	0.019	0.019	0.017
Five-year transitions					
All owners who move	0.036	0.038	0.035	0.041	0.037
Owner to renter	0.056	0.039	0.028	0.056	0.045
Owner to owner	0.034	0.038	0.037	0.026	0.035
All renters who move	0.028	0.037	0.045	0.028	0.035
Renter to renter	0.030	0.042	0.044	0.039	0.038
Renter to owner	0.027	0.026	0.046	0.006	0.029
All movers	0.033	0.038	0.040	0.035	0.036
Ten-year transitions					
All owners who move	0.076	0.079	0.076	0.086	0.078
Owner to renter	0.087	0.087	0.068	0.096	0.085
Owner to owner	0.075	0.079	0.078	0.080	0.077
All renters who move	0.077	0.069	0.069	0.069	0.072
Renter to renter	0.078	0.073	0.070	0.071	0.073
Renter to owner	0.075	0.063	0.066	0.066	0.069
All movers	0.076	0.077	0.073	0.078	0.076

less price volatility is far more prevalent among homeowners than among renters. The difference for Americans in the pre- and post-standard deviation of housing prices is six times larger among homeowners compared to renters. Among homeowners, there is almost no change in volatility if the one changes status from being an owner to a renter, but a very large one if one remains a homeowner.

These data on the change in housing price volatility associated with a move are also arrayed by the length of the time transition between the surveys. The longer the time duration between the surveys the greater the difference in location-specific price volatility associated with the move. This effect is particularly large among those who were originally in their fifties. In this age group, the longer the time duration examined the more likely the move is associated with the retirement decision, where other factors are less likely to play a major role.

With this consideration in mind, table 12A.1 presents a similar array of data for two important cohorts in the HRS data. The first is the original HRS cohort, those who were fifty-one to sixty-one years old in 1992. This cohort was largely in the immediate pre-retirement phrase of the life cycle when the survey began. The second is the AHEAD cohort, a random sample of individuals who were at least seventy years old in 1970. Most of these individuals were in the post-retirement phase of life. Individuals in both cohorts tend to move to less price volatile locations when they do move, especially if they were originally homeowners and especially if they remain homeowners after the move. However, the escaping of price volatility is much larger in the pre-retirement cohort, especially as the duration of time between the survey snapshots increases. One reason that this effect is smaller in the post-retirement AHEAD cohort is that many of them have already moved after retirement to a less price volatile place.

Table 12.10, panel B, lists parallel numbers for Britain. Just as in the United States, British citizens also tend to move to less volatile housing areas if they do decide to move, but on average the escape from volatility is less dramatic there than in the United States. In spite of this similarity, there are some important differences between the two countries as well. For example, the escape from volatility in Britain appears not to vary substantially by age and also appears to be as large among renters as among owners.

12.4   Model Estimates

We will estimate a number of empirical models that relate to the downsizing decisions at older ages. These models include the following for those who did change residences across the waves of the data (i.e., movers): the change in the number of rooms, the change in the price volatility of the location in which one lives, and the change in the value of the house (for those who remained homeowners). Since these models condition on the decision to move, we also use the full sample to estimate a probit model of the decision to change residence (where our dependent variable takes a value of one if the individual moves) and the change in the number of rooms. Having these two models side by side allows us to distinguish between the effects of variables on the probability of moving and then conditional on that probability, the probability that one downsizes housing. These models are also combined into a single model of downsizing at older ages.

We include in all models the following sets of demographic variables—a set of five-year age dummies beginning at ages fifty to fifty-four, with those ages eighty and over the reference group, the change in the number of people living in the house, three marital status transitions (married-single, single-married, single-single with married-married as the omitted group), and children living at home transitions (kids-no kids, no kids-kids, no kids-no kids with kids-kids as the omitted group). The marital and child transition variables tell us, conditional on the changes in the number of residents, whether the type of resident matters. For example, one might suspect that children would matter more than spouses in these transitions since they might have a bigger impact on the number of rooms. Because not all transitions from married to single are the same, we also include a dummy variable for whether or not one became widowed across the waves.

The probability of moving and hence, the possibility of downsizing, may be related to work transitions including retirement that take place at these ages. Therefore, a set of work transitions are included in these models (work-no work, no work-work, no work-no work with work-work as the omitted category). Unlike the demographic variables above which are common to the family unit, the work variables are individual level variables.

The economic variables include the ln of real annual income and education, measured by years of schooling. In the United States education is separated into three groups—thirteen to sixteen years of schooling, sixteen or more years of schooling, and with twelve or fewer years the reference group. In Britain we construct broadly comparable groups based on educational qualifications—the lowest education (reference) group are those with compulsory schooling only, the middle group has some post-compulsory schooling or vocational qualifications but less than a college degree, and the final group has college degrees or higher.

We also include a measure of baseline house value (for homeowners only) and home equity and baseline housing price volatility. A linear time trend is part of all models. The data used for estimation are based on a sample of individuals ages fifty and more using the PSID for the United States (for all years 1968 to 1999) and the BHPS for Britain (years 1993 to 2004).[6]

---

6. Although the BHPS sample began in 1991, data on house value was only collected for those who were interviewed at a new address in 1992. Since our models are based on differences, we effectively have data starting in 1993.

12.4.1   The Probability of Moving

Table 12.11 (panel A for the United States and panel B for the United Kingdom) list estimated derivatives and the associated z statistics obtained from probit models of the probability of changing residence (leaving aside the issue of changing areas or locations for the time being). For each country, models are estimated across three time horizons—one, five, and ten years.

If we examine first the set of transition variables included in the model (marriage, kids, and work), the reference group (married-married, kids-kids, and work-work) is generally the one least associated with residential mobility. Next in line tends to be the other category, which also does not involve a transition between states over the time period under consideration (single-single, no kids-no kids, and no work-no work). The higher effect compared to the reference group may reflect lagged effects of transitions into the single, no kids, or no work states. If a marriage transition did take place, the demographic one most likely to lead to higher residential mobility is from single to married. Compared to the transition from married to single of which it is a part, becoming widowed is less likely to result in mobility, presumably since it is not necessary that someone move in this case. The impact of kids leaving home on mobility appears to be larger in the United States than it is in Britain. The estimated magnitude of these demographic transitions effects do not change significantly with the time horizon over which the effects are estimated. The two work transitions are about equally likely to induce additional mobility in both countries. The results are generally remarkably similar in the two countries with the principal transitional difference taking place in the dimension of the kids at home variables.

We next describe the estimated impacts of the economic variables included in the models. Several dimensions of economic resources are measured, including ln household income, education, whether or not one is initially a homeowner, house value, and home equity among homeowners. Statistically significant positive education and income effects are estimated for both countries, effects that increase in size with the duration of the horizon. Given the stage of the life cycle that we are examining, income is not a proxy for job market opportunities in alternative labor markets. These are more likely income effects that capture the ability to finance moves and the ability to purchase amenities associated with localities that are no longer tied to jobs.

Consistent with the previous descriptive tables, homeowners in both countries are less mobile than renters even after controlling for this set of economic and demographic variables. However, conditional on being a homeowner in both countries, mobility rises with the value of the house but declines with home equity when both variables are in the model. One interpretation of the home value effect (in addition to the normal income effect mentioned previously) is that as the value of the home goes up, people

Table 12.11   **Probit models of the probability of moving between waves**

	Horizon					
	One year		Five years		Ten years	
	df/dx	t	df/dx	t	df/dx	t
A United States						
Education 13–15 baseline	.027	6.81	.035	5.31	.042	4.37
Education ≥ 16 baseline	.021	5.16	.044	6.41	.043	4.45
Year at baseline	−.001	7.69	−.004	12.98	−.007	13.00
Age 50–54	.036	6.16	.010	0.91	−.090	3.65
Age 55–59	.020	3.54	−.019	1.69	−.118	4.86
Age 60–64	.004	0.81	−.036	3.30	−.129	5.38
Age 65–69	−.006	1.03	−.062	5.79	−.157	6.68
Age 70–74	−.013	2.37	−.055	4.95	−.158	6.59
Age 75–79	−.013	2.10	−.073	6.10	−.150	5.85
ln income at baseline	.007	5.04	.011	3.81	.018	4.08
Volatility at baseline	−.001	5.38	−.001	3.43	−.000	0.98
Married/single	.149	13.54	.164	16.55	.144	12.21
Single/married	.345	16.63	.343	17.88	.331	13.59
Single/single	.025	7.44	.060	9.21	.065	6.63
Became widowed	−.007	2.13	−.016	2.45	.001	0.06
Kids/no kids	.085	11.02	.085	11.69	.106	11.72
No kids/kids	.110	9.82	.144	10.49	.125	6.91
No kids/no kids	.038	14.97	.087	17.39	.113	13.95
Change in household size	−.002	0.84	−.004	1.55	.004	1.54
Work/not work	.063	10.65	.075	12.03	.057	7.72
Not work/work	.057	7.21	.072	5.55	.102	4.79
Not work/not work	.028	9.67	.047	9.11	.067	8.47
Owner	−.396	20.81	−.506	21.82	−.548	20.12
ln house value (baseline)	.033	11.11	.042	8.56	.047	6.88
ln home equity (baseline)	−.051	20.89	−.061	14.71	−.055	9.47
(Have negative home equity)	−.149	16.33	−.208	12.82	−.197	8.44
B United Kingdom						
Education—compulsory level only	.012	3.46	.048	5.48	.085	4.41
Education—A levels	.001	0.43	.027	3.46	.046	2.60
Year at baseline	.001	2.01	.001	0.87	.004	0.69
Age 50–54	.013	2.97	.064	5.18	.075	2.68
Age 55–59	.012	2.81	.058	4.94	.092	3.51
Age 60–64	.003	0.69	.034	3.03	.042	1.73
Age 65–69	−.005	1.38	.026	2.38	.019	0.80
Age 70–74	−.007	1.99	.002	0.22	.025	1.13
Age 75–79	−.003	0.89	−.002	0.20	.022	0.97
ln income at baseline	.000	0.09	.010	2.16	.020	1.92
Volatility at baseline	.035	1.17	.084	1.03	.242	1.53
Married/single	.175	7.69	.294	11.01	.241	5.56
Single/married	.262	10.66	.342	12.12	.232	5.43
Single/single	.005	2.08	.020	3.27	−.001	0.04
Became widowed	−.029	4.65	−.099	5.84	−.144	3.81
Kids/no kids	.015	1.55	−.020	1.52	−.072	2.54
No kids/kids	.023	1.16	.012	0.29	.060	0.81
No kids/no kids	.005	1.19	−.010	0.86	−.063	2.03
Change in household size	.003	1.42	.005	1.31	.012	1.71
Work/not work	.039	6.83	.052	5.79	.077	4.35
Not work/work	.025	3.47	.054	3.46	.061	1.87
Not work/not work	.008	3.16	.020	2.64	.030	1.66
Owner	−.036	3.32	−.081	3.15	−.077	1.47
ln house value (baseline)	.015	3.73	.050	5.54	.039	2.14
ln home equity (baseline)	−.013	3.96	−.051	7.27	−.051	3.24
(Have negative home equity)	−.027	2.58	−.076	2.48	−.095	1.37

are consuming a lot of housing relative to their income, inducing them to want to downsize their house. Conditional on the value of the house, an increase in home equity is equivalent to a reduction in the stock and flow of mortgage payments, which makes it less likely that people move to reduce those payments.

We estimate positive but statistically weak impacts of price volatility on mobility in Britain. One reason for not being able to estimate volatility effects in Britain may be that there are much fewer years over which to estimate the volatility effect in Britain, a point which will become a theme in what follows. Particularly for the longer differences, the time series variation is extremely limited in the British sample—with twelve years of data we have $t = 2$ for a ten-year difference—and since our identification of the volatility effects depends on time-series as well as regional variation, there is only a very limited extent to which we could detect volatility effects.

We estimate a negative effect of price volatility in the United States; that is, higher price volatility is associated with a lower probability of moving. As explained before, there is no unambiguous prediction of the effect of price volatility on the geographic mobility. On the one hand, higher price volatility should encourage owners to move in order to either downsize or escape the volatility. On the other hand, higher price volatility makes renters more constrained in their moves since they should not be eager to change their tenure status by buying a house. To test this idea, we ran separate models in the United States for the ten-year horizon for owners and renters. The estimated effect (derivative) of volatility on mobility was 0.001 ($z = 3.26$) for owners and –0.003 ($z = 5.92$) for renters. These results also suggest that it may be more appropriate to estimate the models on alternative forms of transitions (owners-owners, owners-renters, renters-owners, or renters-renters), for the predictions differ.

Conditional on the attributes included in the model (which include incomes that will be growing with time), negative mobility time trends are estimated in the United States and no time trends in Britain. Finally, especially as the horizon expands to the ten-year interval, we find that in the United States those ages eighty and over are the most mobile. This no doubt reflects the increasing necessity of moving into assisted living arrangements or moving in with relatives as individuals' health deteriorates at very old age. However, among the other age groups, those in their fifties are the most mobile, with mobility falling until people are in their early seventies. In contrast, mobility in Britain is lowest among those eighty or more years old and peaks among those in their late fifties.

12.4.2   The Change in the Number of Rooms—Movers

The decision to move at older ages does not necessarily imply that downsizing of housing is occurring. For that to be true, those who do move would have to reduce their housing consumption in some form. The most direct quantitative measure of housing consumption available in both countries is the number of rooms per dwelling. Table 12.12 (panel A for the United States and panel B for Britain) list estimated coefficients and the associated t = statistics obtained from ordinary least squares (OLS) models of the change in the number of rooms per dwelling estimated across a sample of movers. Once again, models are estimated across three time horizons—one, five, and ten years.

Demographic attributes of the household are not surprisingly strong predictors of the magnitude of housing demand. Reductions in the size of household (the dominant direction of change during this phase of the life cycle) are strongly associated with reductions in the number of rooms. The impact of people moving out also depends on the types of people who are leaving. In the United States, having no remaining children at home or having a spouse leave the home reduces the size of the house while entry does the opposite. In the United States, the difference between spouses and no children are not all that large, suggesting that this is not simply a bedroom effect. Lag effects of prior exit are no doubt operating as well since the no spouse-no spouse and no kid-no kid are both associated with reductions in the size of the dwelling. Conditional on changes in the number of household members, these demographic composition effects associated with children are much smaller and less consistent in Britain compared to the United States. Marriage effects are more similar in the two countries.

However, while work transitions were strongly correlated with mobility in both countries, they have little impact on the size of the dwelling unless they are also accompanied by demographic changes in the household structure. The extent of downsizing, at least as measured in this dimension, appears to increase with age in both countries. This age pattern becomes particularly steep after age seventy, when the evidence appears to support reductions in housing consumption with age.

Moreover, the age patterns of downsizing in housing consumption that occur are by and large independent of the other demographic and work transitions (marital status, work status, and kids at home status) in the sense that these estimated age patterns are about the same when all the demographic and work transitions are excluded from the model. Thus, these age patterns lend support to the most basic prediction of the life cycle model that at sufficiently old ages total consumption, of which housing is a very important part, will tend to decline. We return to this point again in section 12.5.

Not only is higher household income associated with higher mobility at older ages, it also is associated, particularly in Britain, with a reduced likelihood of reducing the size of the dwelling once one does move. Given the general desire to downsize at older ages, families in their present houses have more housing than they really need at this stage of their lives. Not downsizing puts the load on other forms of nonhousing consumption to fall. Essentially the amenities of a "too large" house (family memories,

Table 12.12   **Models of changes in number of rooms between waves**

	Horizon					
	One year		Five years		Ten years	
	Coefficient	t	Coefficient	t	Coefficient	t
	A United States—Movers					
Education 13–15 baseline	.048	0.95	.065	1.39	.069	1.38
Education ≥ 16 baseline	.055	0.97	.097	1.98	.115	2.21
Year at baseline	−.001	0.41	−.008	3.65	−.008	2.80
Age 50–54	.521	6.95	1.023	13.40	1.413	12.82
Age 55–59	.455	6.15	1.039	13.84	1.399	12.80
Age 60–64	.526	7.59	1.018	13.66	1.247	11.44
Age 65–69	.486	6.47	.842	11.08	1.059	9.58
Age 70–74	.373	4.69	.672	8.47	.675	5.85
Age 75–79	.347	3.98	.328	3.68	.291	2.30
ln income at baseline	.079	4.34	.124	6.47	.121	5.56
Volatility at baseline	−.006	2.89	−.011	6.23	−.016	8.40
Married/single	−.649	7.06	−.478	8.72	−.565	10.60
Single/married	.248	2.22	.483	5.90	.479	5.51
Single/single	−.210	4.84	−.319	7.76	−.445	9.68
Became widowed	−.050	1.10	−.032	0.81	.019	0.47
Kids/no kids	−.592	7.14	−.588	11.48	−.718	14.28
No kids/kids	.352	3.22	.348	4.18	.600	6.61
No kids/no kids	−.119	3.13	−.324	8.61	−.529	11.84
Change in household size	.310	12.74	.304	21.03	.267	19.83
Work/not work	.068	1.02	−.031	0.76	.025	0.62
Not work/work	−.026	0.28	.070	0.83	.014	0.13
Not work/not work	.067	1.76	.094	2.59	.048	1.16
Owner	−.026	0.19	.131	1.00	.565	3.93
ln house value (baseline)	−.150	4.59	−.204	6.50	−.298	8.68
ln home equity (baseline)	−.068	2.48	−.070	2.57	−.008	0.27
(Have negative home equity)	−.294	2.62	−.202	1.82	.032	0.26
Constant	−.538	2.38	−1.178	5.06	−1.483	5.49
	B United Kingdom—Movers					
Education—compulsory level only	−.292	1.72	−.130	1.32	−.171	1.30
Education—A levels	−.046	0.27	.180	1.90	.098	0.76
Year at baseline	.039	1.89	.019	0.91	−.063	1.19
Age 50–54	.460	1.84	.559	3.58	1.332	6.50
Age 55–59	.388	1.63	.649	4.32	.879	4.55
Age 60–64	−.117	0.48	.322	2.16	.912	4.83
Age 65–69	−.170	0.69	.439	2.96	.708	3.71
Age 70–74	−.043	0.17	.154	1.02	.573	3.19
Age 75–79	−.036	0.14	.032	0.21	.654	3.56
ln income at baseline	.434	4.83	.230	4.05	.296	3.76
Volatility at baseline	.954	0.53	.406	0.37	−1.882	1.52
Married/single	−.250	0.63	−.281	1.51	−.495	2.04
Single/married	.381	1.25	.640	3.82	.856	4.01
Single/single	.062	0.50	−.055	0.69	.048	0.43
Became widowed	.460	0.71	.860	3.17	1.415	4.29
Kids/no kids	−.164	0.37	−.164	0.98	.112	0.53

Table 12.12   (continued)

	Horizon					
	One year		Five years		Ten years	
	Coefficient	t	Coefficient	t	Coefficient	t
No kids/kids	−.326	0.47	−.361	0.85	−.057	0.14
No kids/no kids	−.212	0.84	−.530	3.76	−.420	2.08
Change in household size	.643	8.12	.380	9.32	.498	9.94
Work/not work	−.252	1.19	−.231	2.24	.002	0.02
Not work/work	.560	1.93	−.029	0.17	.266	1.23
Not work/not work	−.079	0.51	−.002	0.02	.113	0.83
Owner	1.53	2.82	1.35	4.37	.875	2.41
ln house value (baseline)	−.497	2.09	−.256	2.21	.071	0.59
ln home equity (baseline)	.071	0.38	−.074	0.86	−.267	2.55
(Have negative home equity)	.979	0.85	−.608	1.39	.081	0.16
Constant	−4.644	4.89	−2.664	4.20	−2.652	2.44

associations with old neighbors, etc.) can be thought of as a luxury good, which the more well-to-do are more able to afford.

In the United States, there is limited evidence of a net impact of education on the size of the house with some tendency for less educated British households to downsize more, even conditional on their lower incomes. Increases in the value of the initial owned home tends to lead to a larger decrease in the size of the dwelling, suggesting that when a lot of resources are tied up in the house, there is a greater tendency to downsize at older ages. The same is true when one has a lot of equity in the home, although this effect is only found in Britain at the ten-year horizon.

In the United States, consistent with the theory outlined before, living in a more price volatile area does encourage additional downsizing among those who do move. There appears to be little effect in Britain, although one obtains the expected negative point estimate of the effect at the ten-year horizon, albeit only with a t-value of 1.5.

12.4.3   The Change in the Number of Rooms—Full Sample

In the previous two sections, we estimated separate models for the probability of changing residences at older ages and the change in the number of moves conditioned on being a mover. The advantage of the two-part model is that we can more easily detect whether variables have differential effects on mobility and the consequences of that mobility for housing consumption. We have already seen that in a number of cases the estimated effects are even of different sign. In this section, we ignore that separation by estimating the effect of covariates on the changing number of rooms over the full sample of respondents. Since most people in fact do not move at all at older ages, these estimated effects will of course be necessarily smaller. In table 12.13,

Table 12.13 **Models of changes in number of rooms between waves**

	Horizon					
	One year		Five years		Ten years	
	Coefficient	t	Coefficient	t	Coefficient	t
	A United States—All					
Education 13–15 baseline	.012	1.04	.024	1.38	.006	0.25
Education ≥ 16 baseline	.017	1.41	.045	2.54	.096	3.74
Year at baseline	−.000	0.23	−.001	1.55	.002	1.21
Age 50–54	.085	4.93	.433	13.96	.914	14.05
Age 55–59	.076	4.49	.414	13.60	.890	13.76
Age 60–64	.075	4.50	.404	13.40	.843	13.08
Age 65–69	.073	4.39	.376	12.38	.761	11.73
Age 70–74	.063	3.64	.305	9.66	.619	9.25
Age 75–79	.050	2.67	.227	6.60	.430	5.98
ln income at baseline	.010	2.34	.040	5.30	.048	4.17
Volatility at baseline	−.001	1.35	−.003	4.34	−.006	6.01
Married/single	−.212	7.34	−.273	11.02	−.377	12.25
Single/married	.292	6.06	.286	6.35	.346	5.87
Single/single	−.055	4.87	−.165	9.36	−.252	9.70
Became widowed	.016	1.33	.058	3.25	.073	2.94
Kids/no kids	−.131	6.32	−.220	11.76	−.388	16.18
No kids/kids	.055	1.83	.083	2.43	.268	5.54
No kids/no kids	−.029	3.65	−.136	10.13	−.277	12.70
Change in household size	.128	17.78	.175	28.15	.176	24.21
Work/not work	−.015	0.90	−.053	3.33	−.053	2.68
Not work/work	−.010	0.43	−.002	0.05	−.032	0.56
Not work/not work	.004	0.44	.002	0.15	−.037	1.79
Owner	.062	2.04	.169	3.37	.408	5.60
ln house value (baseline)	−.033	4.49	−.089	7.42	−.150	8.59
ln home equity (baseline)	.005	0.67	.004	0.35	.011	0.74
(Have negative home equity)	.011	0.40	−.021	0.49	.036	0.58
Constant	−.097	1.85	−.463	5.09	−.876	6.07
	B United Kingdom—All					
Education—compulsory level only	−.016	1.08	−.059	2.51	−.103	2.10
Education—A levels	−.011	0.80	.035	1.62	.101	2.25
Year at baseline	.003	1.72	.008	1.74	−.022	1.27
Age 50–54	−.007	0.38	.078	2.39	.373	5.22
Age 55–59	.004	0.24	.070	2.29	.193	2.93
Age 60–64	−.014	0.80	.027	0.93	.225	3.64
Age 65–69	.001	0.05	.032	1.11	.174	2.88
Age 70–74	−.007	0.41	−.016	0.58	.081	1.44
Age 75–79	−.005	0.29	−.009	0.30	.074	1.31
ln income at baseline	.025	3.21	.063	4.74	.120	4.36
Volatility at baseline	.227	1.75	.294	1.28	−.480	1.16
Married/single	−.095	1.31	−.405	6.16	−.555	5.12
Single/married	−.027	0.38	.333	5.02	.446	4.28
Single/single	.001	0.11	−.006	0.32	.025	0.67
Became widowed	.203	2.44	.548	6.95	.897	6.99
Kids/no kids	.046	1.11	−.013	0.33	.024	0.30

Table 12.13   (continued)

	One year		Five years		Ten years	
	Coefficient	t	Coefficient	t	Coefficient	t
No kids/kids	−.140	1.60	−.055	0.44	.229	1.16
No kids/no kids	−.017	0.84	−.072	2.07	−.215	2.64
Change in household size	.111	9.64	.152	13.35	.227	11.91
Work/not work	−.045	2.14	−.079	3.31	−.106	2.33
Not work/work	.016	0.57	.009	0.22	.051	0.60
Not work/not work	−.012	1.02	−.009	0.43	−.005	0.10
Owner	.108	2.86	.272	4.20	.483	3.60
ln house value (baseline)	−.019	1.00	−.034	1.27	−.016	0.32
ln home equity (baseline)	−.003	0.17	−.016	0.75	−.066	1.51
(Have negative home equity)	.015	0.15	−.244	2.01	−.204	0.92
Constant	−.256	3.16	−.696	4.87	−.844	2.27

panels A and B present the results of these empirical models for the United States and Britain, respectively.

Not surprisingly, the estimated impacts of demographic variables resemble those estimated over the mover sample, but at much diminished magnitude. The size of these demographics associated with family-related transitions tends to increase with the time duration of the window in which a move can take place. In both countries, the transition from married to single is associated with a smaller dwelling, while the reverse is true when people change from the single life to a married one. Two differences between the two countries in the impact of the demographic transitions are first that widowhood has no impact on the size of the house in Britain, while it tends to reduce the number of rooms in the United States. Second, the transitions associated with children appear to have no effect in Britain, but kids leaving home do promote some downsizing in the United States. The only consistent impact of work transitions on the size of the dwelling in either country is that the transition from work to no work (presumably during these ages mostly retirement) leads to a smaller house.

Higher incomes strongly discourage downsizing in both countries with somewhat larger estimated impacts in Britain. This implies that the increase in probability of moving is offset by the fact the move is less likely to reduce the size of the dwelling. Across the full sample, higher home values encourage downsizing in the United States, but there is no effect in Britain. Home equity appears to have little impact in either country. Once again the estimated patterns with age indicate that housing consumption does decline with age, a decline that cannot be explained by the other demographic and work transitions included in these models. These adjusted age patterns of downsizing appear to be larger in the United States than they are in Britain. On net, higher housing price volatility encourages downsizing in the United States with statistically significant effects in Britain.

12.4.4   Changes in House Price

In addition to the number of rooms, the other dimension of housing consumption that we can measure in both countries is the change in the value of the house among those who move. By necessity, the sample over which these models are estimated are homeowners who moved but who remained homeowners. These models are presented in table 12.14 (panel A for the United States and panel B for Britain). In order to control for any state- or region-wide capital gains in housing, these models include two additional variables that are not in the change in rooms equation. The first is the percent change in the real price of housing in the state of origin over the horizon used in the regression (measured as the delta in the geometric means) and the second is whether or not one changed state of residence when a move took place. Not surprisingly, individual level changes in house values when people move are positively correlated with area-wide real housing price changes.

A useful comparison is to compare the results for the two dimensions of downsizing—change in number of rooms among movers (table 12.12) and change in home price (table 12.14). Taking into account that sample sizes are much smaller in the model for the change in ln home value specification, the results for the United States are generally similar but statistically weaker than for the change in number of rooms. In particular, becoming single or having the final child leave home, and more generally reductions in the number of people living in the household, are all associated with a move to a less expensive home. There is little association of the value of the home with any of the work transitions. Most important, volatility at baseline has the expected negative coefficient in both the change in rooms and change in ln home value models, but it is less statistically significant in the home value specification. Perhaps the biggest difference is that income effects are much weaker in the change in home value model in the United States. If anything, the results in Britain are weaker still where we encounter a lack of precision on our estimates of the volatility terms and weaker income effects than in the model for the change in rooms.

12.4.5   Reducing Price Volatility

We have argued that, from an exposure to house price risk point of view, one alternative to downsizing is to protect your assets in housing by moving to a less price volatile housing area. Table 12.15 models the change in housing price volatility among movers for the United States and Britain. The outcome variable is measured as current housing price volatility minus volatility in the new location, so that positive values imply a movement to a less housing price volatile area. The same set of variables that entered the

Table 12.14   **Models of change in Ln value of house between waves**

	One year		Five years		Ten years	
	Coefficient	t	Coefficient	t	Coefficient	t
A United States—Homeowners who are movers						
Education 13–15 baseline	−.018	0.51	.004	0.12	.063	1.77
Education ≥ 16 baseline	−.008	0.21	−.046	1.48	.039	1.16
Trend	−.001	0.46	−.001	0.91	−.013	5.69
Age 50–54	.070	1.03	.097	1.27	.124	0.98
Age 55–59	.011	0.17	−.027	0.36	.056	0.44
Age 60–64	.050	0.76	.039	0.52	.103	0.82
Age 65–69	.026	0.38	.033	0.43	.143	1.13
Age 70–74	.017	0.24	−.003	0.03	.013	0.10
Age 75–79	.045	0.57	−.109	1.24	−.075	0.53
ln income at baseline	.029	1.98	−.014	0.92	−.016	0.92
Volatility at baseline	−.004	2.42	−.004	2.89	−.002	1.51
Married/single	−.143	1.62	−.217	4.48	−.229	4.74
Single/married	.031	0.37	.056	0.87	.136	1.90
Single/single	−.060	1.41	−.125	3.08	−.011	0.24
New widow	.100	2.02	.048	1.20	−.031	0.75
Kids/no kids	−.096	1.51	−.159	3.92	−.182	4.37
No kids/kids	−.118	1.30	.316	4.52	.393	4.92
No kids/no kids	−.041	1.39	−.106	3.43	−.142	3.66
Delta state house price	.608	8.78	.545	13.21	.475	11.80
Changed state	−.044	1.06	.137	5.01	−.127	4.51
Constant	−.218	1.41	.367	2.24	.368	1.73
B United Kingdom—Homeowners who are movers						
Education 13–15 baseline	.044	0.64	.054	1.60	.105	1.94
Education ≥ 16 baseline	−.006	−0.08	.101	3.22	.121	2.39
Trend	.002	0.14	.006	0.43	.019	0.50
Age 50–54	.204	1.50	.289	4.46	.250	2.39
Age 55–59	.231	1.74	.252	4.02	.198	1.96
Age 60–64	.068	0.52	.226	3.60	.183	1.86
Age 65–69	.116	0.81	.205	3.21	.133	1.34
Age 70–74	.091	0.65	.145	2.20	.109	1.07
Age 75–79	.099	0.68	.085	1.25	.062	0.61
ln income at baseline	.064	1.69	.024	1.22	.081	2.41
Volatility at baseline	−.725	0.77	.258	0.63	−.276	0.47
Married/single	−.139	0.70	.432	5.75	−.505	4.13
Single/married	−.045	0.31	.094	1.45	.219	2.06
Single/single	−.072	1.18	.038	1.20	−.059	1.05
New widow	.055	0.17	.442	3.92	.496	2.79
Kids/no kids	−.020	0.10	−.074	1.29	−.099	1.14
No kids/kids	−.451	1.58	.015	0.09	−.148	0.84
No kids/no kids	.026	0.24	−.048	0.96	−.144	1.73
Change in household size	.114	2.38	.116	6.63	.047	1.90
Work/not work	−.152	1.62	−.138	3.99	−.081	1.57
Not work/work	.063	0.47	−.039	0.67	.038	0.39
Not work/not work	.005	0.07	−.015	0.44	.013	0.21
Delta region house price	.309	0.68	.838	9.22	.903	6.61
Changed region	−.163	2.71	−.122	4.21	−.019	0.42
Constant	−.721	1.76	−.398	1.58	−1.010	1.68

Table 12.15   **Models of change in volatility between waves**

	Horizon					
	One year		Five years		Ten years	
	Coefficient	t	Coefficient	t	Coefficient	t
A United States—Movers						
Education 13–15 baseline	−.102	1.04	−.276	2.52	−.505	3.84
Education ≥ 16 baseline	−.028	0.25	−.496	4.33	−1.01	7.43
Year at baseline	.002	0.43	−.002	0.32	−.007	0.94
Age 50–54	.263	1.83	.434	2.44	.547	1.92
Age 55–59	.303	2.14	.549	3.14	.689	2.43
Age 60–64	.275	1.93	.627	3.61	.596	2.11
Age 65–69	.354	2.45	.347	1.96	.327	1.14
Age 70–74	−.027	0.17	.253	1.37	.348	1.16
Age 75–79	.178	1.07	.310	1.49	.215	0.66
ln income at baseline	.073	2.10	.298	6.71	.509	8.98
Married/single	−.329	1.85	−.046	0.36	.002	0.01
Single/married	−.069	0.31	−.253	1.32	.020	0.09
Single/single	−.130	1.55	−.011	0.11	.116	0.96
Became widowed	.043	0.49	.097	1.07	.113	1.05
Kids/no kids	.392	2.44	.579	4.84	.332	2.53
No kids/kids	.059	0.28	.242	1.24	.344	1.45
No kids/no kids	.163	2.23	.292	3.32	.160	1.37
Change in household size	.074	1.62	.051	1.51	.037	1.06
Work/not work	.499	3.85	.801	8.23	.550	5.31
Not work/work	.233	1.34	.207	1.05	.279	0.99
Not work/not work	.252	3.41	.300	3.52	.193	1.78
Owner	−.302	1.14	−.636	2.09	−1.32	3.52
ln house value (baseline)	.080	1.28	.188	2.57	.375	4.18
ln home equity (baseline)	.074	1.40	.137	2.13	.052	0.65
(Have negative home equity)	.297	1.37	.597	2.30	.225	0.69
Constant	−1.316	3.02	−4.055	7.45	−5.568	7.91
B United Kingdom—Movers						
Education—compulsory level only	−.000	0.09	.001	0.57	.001	0.42
Education—A levels	−.001	0.61	.001	0.38	−.000	0.28
Year at baseline	.003	15.48	.016	78.48	.038	54.77
Age 50–54	−.006	1.98	.003	1.17	−.003	0.81
Age 55–59	−.007	2.56	.001	0.50	−.007	1.88
Age 60–64	−.005	1.90	.002	1.15	−.000	0.10
Age 65–69	−.004	1.5	−.000	0.12	.003	0.84
Age 70–74	−.002	0.71	−.000	0.21	.002	0.74
Age 75–79	−.004	1.55	−.000	0.03	.006	1.68
ln income at baseline	−.001	0.55	.000	0.57	.004	2.61
Married/single	.002	0.31	−.003	0.95	−.002	0.54
Single/married	−.001	0.31	.002	0.85	.010	2.63
Single/single	−.001	0.75	.002	1.29	.005	2.26
Became widowed	.001	0.09	.010	2.43	.002	0.33
Kids/no kids	.010	1.78	.003	1.27	−.006	1.53
No kids/kids	−.010	1.14	−.001	0.22	−.018	2.47
No kids/no kids	−.004	1.12	.002	0.73	−.005	1.35

Table 12.15   (continued)

	One year		Five years		Ten years	
	Coefficient	t	Coefficient	t	Coefficient	t
Change in household size	.002	1.99	−.000	0.63	−.002	2.14
Work/not work	−.002	0.86	−.002	0.96	−.003	1.41
Not work/work	−.008	2.07	.004	1.65	.004	1.00
Not work/not work	−.001	0.52	.000	0.10	.001	0.41
Owner	−.009	1.34	.009	1.99	.001	0.21
ln house value (baseline)	.004	1.20	−.004	2.10	−.001	0.51
ln home equity (baseline)	−.002	0.87	.001	1.06	−.001	0.45
(Have negative home equity)	−.019	1.32	.004	0.60	−.007	0.74
Constant	−.017	1.43	−.201	−22.26	−.571	34.66

(Header spanning "One year", "Five years", "Ten years" is: **Horizon**)

room downsizing model are included in this model for escaping housing price volatility. Examining first table 12.15, panel B, we can see immediately why it is so difficult to obtain an effect for housing price volatility in Britain. Given the short time span over which models are estimated, there is a very strong time trend in volatility that dominates everything else included in the model. Conditional on this trend (where price volatility is increasing over time), there are little remaining systematic associations with price volatility in Britain.

Given the longer number of years available for analysis, coupled with more systematic and larger differences between the volatile and less volatile areas, more interesting results were obtained for the U.S. model summarized in table 12.15, panel A. A positive coefficient in these models indicates that a variable is associated with moving to an even less price volatile area. To begin with, we see that many of the demographic transition variables associated with other forms of downsizing are also important here. Most importantly, the transition of the last child leaving home is associated with a greater tendency to move to a less housing price volatile area, and those families whose children have already left home (the kids-no kids group) are also more likely to search out a less price volatile area than those whose children remain in the home. Once again, we interpret this as a lagged effect of children leaving home prior to the baseline year since the subsequent decision to relocate may not be instantaneous. Second, those households who either are retired or who become retired are also likely to reduce the housing volatility associated with the place where they decide to reside by more.

In contrast to some of the other measures, however, we do not find significant effects of changes in marital status or widowhood, even over the longest time period horizons. Finally, we find contrasting education and income effects that are somewhat hard to interpret—conditional on income, the more educated are less likely to reduce their house price volatility, which is somewhat of a puzzle, although the effect of income would be to offset this unconditionally, since those with higher incomes tend to reduce their house price volatility by more. Since the age coefficients tend to become less positive after age groups fifty-five to fifty-nine and sixty to sixty-four, the tendency to seek out places in less volatile areas peaks in that age group.

12.5   Consumption Trajectories at Older Ages

One of the more hotly debated issues regarding life cycle patterns of consumption with age concerns is whether households reduce their consumption at older ages. The importance of the debate stems in part from the fact that it is a basic implication of the life cycle model that such consumption declines should occur, in part due to rising rates of age-specific mortality at older ages. Of course, there are other reasons for consumption to fall with age, particularly related to the shrinking of households as children leave home and widowhood becomes more common. Thus, the question to ask is whether consumption declines in addition to any changes induced by a set of demographic changes producing smaller households and the decision to retire from the labor force. Housing is an important component of total consumption and is believed to be resistant to any downward changes. Thus, we argue that evidence showing a downward path of housing consumption adds important evidence to this debate.

To provide such evidence, figure 12.2, panel A, plots the change in the number of rooms across age bands that is estimated in the models for movers in table 12.12. Figure 12.2, panel B, provides similar plots except in this case the sample consists of all households whether or not they change residence (i.e., the models estimated in table 12.13). For the purposes of these plots, we used the models estimated over the five-year horizon. The declines in housing consumption documented in this section would be even larger if we used instead estimates obtained from the ten-year horizon. For figure 12.2, we plot the estimated age trajectories obtained while controlling for other transitions between waves (i.e., the models in tables 12.12 and 12.13, respectively), and also the trajectories estimated from a more restricted model with the demographic and employment status transition variables excluded. In each country the changes are normalized around the value for the fifty to fifty-four age group in the models without any controls for demographic and work transitions.

Figure 12.2, panel A, demonstrates that there exists in both countries a clear decline in housing consumption (as measured by the change in the number of rooms) for movers, a decline that appears to accelerate after age sixty-five. Except for very old ages (ages seventy-five and older) this decrease in housing consumption appears to be roughly similar in both countries. After age seventy-five, the decrease in the number of rooms is clearly larger in the United States, presumably reflecting the decline in the number of rooms

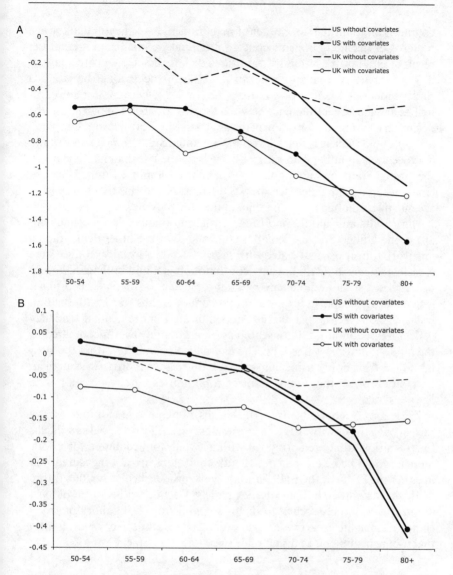

Fig. 12.2   Normalized change in number of rooms by age: *A*, Movers only; *B*, All households

associated with widowhood in the United States and the absence of any such association in Britain. These declines in housing consumption are not trivial—about one room in the United States and half a room in Britain.

If we control for the other demographic and work transitions and all other covariates included in the models in table 12.12, the age patterns are very much the same, indicating declining housing consumption with age in both countries of about the same order of magnitude. This indicates that the age patterns of declining housing consumption that we document are not the result of either work or family transitions that are associated with aging.

The age patterns that are plotted in figure 12.2, panel B, for all households (independent of whether they move or not over the five-year horizon) dramatize a much larger difference between the two countries. In particular, the decline in housing consumption with age across this more relevant sample of all households is clearly much larger in the United States than it is in Britain. The decline in number of rooms with age is a little less than half a room in the United States and about one-twentieth of a room in Britain. The principal reason for the differences between panels A and B is that households are much less mobile in Britain than in the United States.

Our results indicate that housing consumption appears to decline with age in the United States, even after controlling for the other demographic and work transitions associated with age that would normally produce such a decline. No such fall in housing consumption is found in Britain, largely because British households are much more likely to stay in their original residence. The important question that cannot be answered with data on housing alone is whether these results indicate a more general tendency of less reduction in total household consumption in Britain compared to the United States at older ages. The alternative possibility is that the British adjust their nonhousing consumption downward more than American households do so that the patterns of total household consumption with age are similar.

There may of course be other transitions, not controlled for in our analysis, driving the downwards trajectories observed. The principal candidates for transitions that are correlated with age and not accounted for in our models would be health related. Health conditions are not measured well in either the PSID or the BHPS and we will consider them instead in future work that uses the HRS and ELSA panels. Declines in health in old age are of course closely related to the principal factor (rising mortality risk) emphasized in life cycle models that produce the decline in consumption so that it may be difficult to disentangle these effects in practice.

12.6   Conclusions

In this chapter, we examined and modeled several types of housing transitions of the elderly in two countries—Britain and the United States. One important form of these transitions involves downsizing of housing consumption, the importance of which among older households is still debated. We find that on balance—looking over a number of dimensions over a number of transition intervals—downsizing is an important part of life for many older households in both countries. For example, over a decade, almost one in every three American homeowners who were at least fifty years old moved out of their originally owned home. And mobility is much higher in both countries (and in particular in the United States) among renters. Moreover, when they do move, we find that on average households in both countries tend to downsize their housing consumption. This downsizing takes multiple forms, including reductions in the number of rooms per dwelling and the value of the home. There is also evidence that this downsizing is greater when house price volatility is greater and, in addition, that American households also try to escape housing price volatility by moving to places that experience significantly less housing price volatility.

Our comparative evidence in the descriptive tables in section 12.3 also suggests that there is less evidence of downsizing in Britain than in the United States, although a note of caution is appropriate here because we have a considerably smaller sample and a different (and shorter) time period in Britain. Nevertheless, given differences in house price volatility across the countries this is a result that is, on the surface, contrary to the predictions of our simple theoretical discussion. Looking within country, however, we find the expected positive correlation between volatility and downsizing (although this correlation is weaker in Britain where we have less variation in volatility to exploit). This in turn suggests that other factors must account for the differences in the average levels of downsizing across the two countries. Possible candidates would include the role of lower mobility in general in Britain. While this is only an incomplete explanation since mobility is itself an outcome measure and one indicator of downsizing, if households are moving less often (and their children and grandchildren are also less likely to move) then there will be less downsizing, to the extent that the number of rooms and a reduction in house value only change on moving.

Hence, other explanations might lie in transactions costs associated with moving in Britain (where stamp duties are levied on house sales and the fixed costs associated with house sales are both high and somewhat uncertain)— the nature of bequests and inheritance tax bases, and the role of housing wealth in other economic institutions such as the means test for long-term care. However, such mechanisms are unlikely to be the full explanation since mobility in Britain is particularly low among renters. In addition, to the extent that retirement-related mobility yields movements outside Britain— to Spain and France, as opposed to Florida and Arizona, for example—such transitions are not captured in our data, although the empirical importance of such transitions in Britain is still likely to be relatively limited. Finally, it is certainly the case that even in the least volatile regions of Britain there is still considerable volatility, so the possibility of avoiding house price volatility altogether is somewhat limited. Such explanations should be considered as topics for future research.

Appendix

Table 12A.1   Differences in housing price volatility by state among movers in HRS samples

A HRS original cohort—ages 51–61: Transitions over number of years		
	2 years	10 years
All owners who move	0.078	0.149
Owner to renter	0.035	0.092
Owner to owner	0.084	0.158
All renters who move	0.049	0.066
Renter to renter	0.042	0.069
Renter to owner	0.058	0.050
All movers	0.069	0.128

B AHEAD original cohort ages 70+: Eight-year transitions			
	70–79	80+	Total
All owners who move	0.035	–0.020	0.022
Owner to renter	–0.007	–0.073	–0.022
Owner to owner	0.041	0.054	0.048
All renters who move	–0.030	0.132	0.001
Renter to renter	–0.004	0.059	0.007
Renter to owner	–0.031	0	–0.027
All movers	0.018	0.011	0.020

References

Banks, J., R. Blundell, Z. Oldfield and J. P. Smith. 2006. Housing price volatility and housing ownership over the life-cycle. Institute for Fiscal Studies Research Report, December.

Banks, J., R. Blundell, and J. P. Smith. 2003a. Financial wealth inequality in the United States and Great Britain. *Journal of Human Resources* 38 (2): 241–79.

———. 2003b. Wealth portfolios in the US and the UK. In *Perspectives on the economics of aging,* ed. D. Wise, 205–46. Chicago: University of Chicago Press.

Calhoun, C. A. 1996. OFHEO house price indexes: HPI technical description, March 1996. Washington, DC: Office of Federal Housing Enterprise Oversight. Available at http://www.fhfa.gov/webfiles/896/hpi_tech.pdf

Davidoff, T. 2004. Maintenance and the home equity of the elderly. Fisher Center for Real Estate and Urban Economics Paper no. 03-288. University of California, Berkeley, Haas School of Business.

Disney, R., A. Henley, and G. Stears. 2002. Housing costs, house price shocks and savings behaviour among older households in Britain. *Regional Science and Urban Economics* 32 (September): 607–25.

Sheiner, L., and D. Weil. 1992. The housing wealth of the aged. NBER Working Paper no. 4115. Cambridge, MA: National Bureau of Economic Research, July.

Sinai, T., and N. S. Souleles. 2005. Owner-occupied housing as a hedge against rent risk. *Quarterly Journal of Economics* 120 (2): 763–89.

Venti, S. F., and D. A. Wise. 2001. Aging and housing equity: Another look. In *Perspectives on the economics of aging,* ed. D. Wise, 127–80. Chicago: University of Chicago Press.

Comment   Steven F. Venti

Housing is the largest single asset in the portfolios of most households in the United States and the United Kingdom. This chapter takes up, once again, the important question of what happens to housing as households age. The analysis is very well done, so much so that I have nary a complaint about their methods. The findings first add to the large and growing body of evidence that housing eventually declines at older ages. This finding is shown to be robust to the choice of four different ways to measure housing. The authors then address a more unsettled and perhaps more important question: why do households downsize? I will devote most of my comments to what their findings tell us about the motives for housing decumulation.

Housing is a peculiar asset because it has both consumption and investment aspects. This dual role makes it difficult, as a matter of theory, to pin down what motivates households to accumulate, hold, and—at some point in the life cycle—to decumulate housing assets. Of particular importance is the lack of consensus on whether retired households intend to spend-down home equity to replace earnings or whether they want to hold on to housing assets for other purposes. Most financial planners consider most nonhousing assets such as IRAs, pensions, and financial assets as "saving" for retirement in the sense that these assets will be used to replace earnings to finance general consumption in retirement. A typical target, recognizing that consumption may fall after retirement, is that income from savings should replace 80 percent of pre-retirement earnings. When it comes to housing the treatment of housing assets is more ambiguous. Some financial advisors "count" housing assets as saving for retirement; others do not. Similarly, some financial software programs designed to help investors set retirement goals include housing wealth; others do not. And the vast academic literature on the "adequacy of saving" has been equally inconsistent (see, e.g., Bernheim 1992; Engen, Gale, and Uccello 1999; Gustman and Steinmeier 1999, and Scholz, Seshadri, and Khitatrakun 2006). Some studies ignore housing wealth, some include it, and others assume some arbitrary fraction of housing wealth should be considered among the assets that will be used to finance consumption in retirement.

Steven F. Venti is the DeWalt Ankeny Professor of Economic Policy and a professor of economics at Dartmouth College and a research associate of the National Bureau of Economic Research.

If households are asked whether they plan to decumulate housing assets to finance consumption in retirement they invariably answer "no." Survey data on planning shows that most households do not plan to move out of their houses. Unless they refinance or take advantage of reverse mortgages—both rare among the elderly—they do not plan to downsize. For example, in the 2004 Health and Retirement Study (HRS), respondents were asked the question: "What are the chances that you will sell your house to finance your retirement?" They were asked to respond using a scale ranging from zero to 100 where zero equals absolutely no chance and 100 equals absolutely certainty. The responses are graphed in figure 12C.1 for all respondents and in figure 12C.2 for respondents over the age of sixty-five. The majority of respondents who own homes do not anticipate selling their house to finance consumption. Over three quarters of those over the age of sixty-five and owning homes do not plan to sell their homes to finance consumption in retirement. Another survey, by the American Association of Retired Persons (AARP 2003), asked a sample of persons a similar question: "How likely do you think it is that you will be able to stay in your current home for the rest of your life?" The results, shown in figure 12C.3, show that over 80 percent of owners and over 80 percent of all persons over the age of sixty-five believe it is likely that they will remain in their current residence the rest of their lives. These respondents not only do not plan a housing transition to finance general consumption, but also do not anticipate a shock that will force them to downsize.

Although households may not plan to run down housing assets, whether they actually do is an empirical question. This chapter provides a great deal of information to address this question. Briefly, the study uses two surveys, the Panel Study of Income Dynamics (PSID) in the United States and the

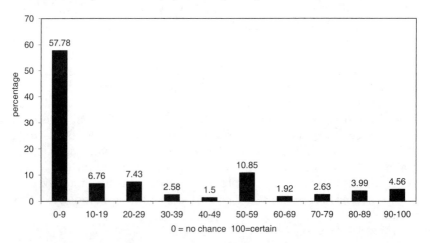

Fig. 12C.1   **What are the chances that you will sell your house to finance retirement? (all respondents)**

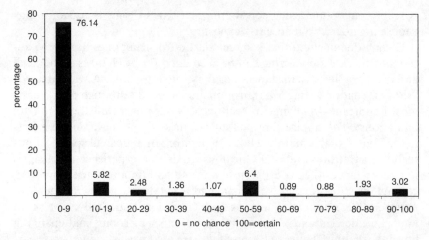

Fig. 12C.2   **What are the chances that you will sell your house to finance retirement? (over age 65)**

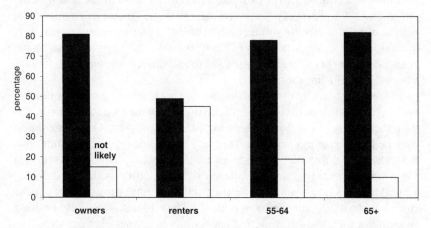

Fig. 12C.3   **How likely do you think it is that you will be able to stay in your current home for the rest of your life?**

British Household Panel Survey (BHPS) in the United Kingdom to study the housing transitions linked to downsizing. An improvement over past work is that four measures of housing transition are used. These are whether a household moves and then, conditional on a move, the change in the number of rooms, the change in the value of the house, and the change in house price volatility. For each measure, some downsizing is observed at older ages. The extent of downsizing is in the same range as that found in previous studies that focused only on homeownership or home equity (see, for example, Venti and Wise [2004] or Heiss and Börsch-Supan [2005]). The change in house price volatility is a particularly novel feature. In some models greater volatility puts nonhousing consumption at risk so some households may choose to relocate to reduce risk exposure.

Having documented that some modest downsizing does occur, the authors then ask if downsizing can be accounted for by changes in financial and demographic circumstances faced by the household. A wide array of "shocks" that may trigger a transition are included (although perhaps the most important—a change in health status—is not included due to data limitations). The empirical results suggest these shocks have similar effects in the United States and the United Kingdom. In almost all specifications the lowest transition rates are for households that experience no changes in circumstances (i.e., continuously married, continuously with children, continuously working, etc.). A change in marital status is by far the most important determinant of moving and, conditional on a move, is also an important determinant of changing the number of rooms and changing housing wealth. Changes in household size also have strong effects, particularly on the number of rooms. A recent change in house price volatility had little effect on transitions in either country. This result is somewhat surprising since previous research has identified this factor as an important source of transitions for younger households. However, escaping volatility should not be a concern for the elderly, who do not plan to move unless there is a strong bequest motive or a desire to extract home equity to finance nonhousing consumption.

These results clearly show that downsizing is associated with major events such as widowhood, divorce, or job change. How are we to reconcile this with the finding that households do not plan to downsize? One explanation may be that households neither want nor plan to downsize, but underestimate the probability they will face an event that will force them to readjust their housing in the future. An alternative explanation is that households view (and use) housing to insure themselves against catastrophic shocks that they recognize may occur later in life. They do not plan to use housing wealth, but they know it is there if needed. They neither plan nor expect to ever use their housing wealth in much the same way that most purchasers of automobile accident insurance, if asked, would say they neither plan nor expect to ever make a claim. In this case housing may best be viewed as an asset of last resort, not to be counted among the assets funding the 80 percent replacement rate promoted by financial advisors, but still available if hit by a shock in late life.

Both of these explanations for downsizing in the absence of a stated plan to do so suggest that households that do not experience significant changes in financial or demographic circumstances should not be expected to reduce housing in any dimension. A nice feature of the regression specification is that the authors include a set of age variables that allow us to determine if households downsize in the absence of shocks. Unfortunately, no clear pattern emerges from these estimates. For example, after controlling for the effects of shocks, table 12.13 shows the number of rooms declines steeply with age in the United States but the decline is much more modest (and not statistically significant after age sixty) in the United Kingdom. And after controlling for shocks, table 12.14 shows there is essentially no decline in home value in the United States, but home values in the United Kingdom decline rather steadily with age.

In general, the estimated age effects are different for physical and financial dimensions of downsizing and different for the United Kingdom and the United States. One possible explanation, as the authors acknowledge, is that health care costs and changes in health conditions are not accounted for in these estimates. Perhaps the biggest financial shock that older persons in the United States may face is large out-of-pocket health expenditures, including nursing home expenses. Skinner (2007) estimates that about 6 percent of U.S. households faced out-of-pocket medical expenses in excess of half of their income in a single year (2004) and this percentage is expected to increase rapidly in the future. De Nardi, Jones, and French (2005) show how health expenses rising with age will accelerate the drawdown of all assets. Whether health costs and changing health conditions can explain the decline in housing at older ages in the United States and the United Kingdom is a possibility the authors plan to address in future work using the HRS and English Longitudinal Study of Aging (ELSA).

In summary, the results of this study clearly show that downsizing of housing occurs in several dimensions in both the United States and United Kingdom. Events such as widowhood, a change in marital status, a change in number of children, or a change in work status are shown to trigger housing transitions. Whether downsizing is completely accounted for by these changes in financial and demographic circumstances is still an unresolved issue, leaving open the question of how housing fits into the life cycle planning process. The authors have made substantial progress advancing our understanding of downsizing by older households. Their future work using survey data (HRS and ELSA) that contain better measures of health care costs and conditions should complete our understanding of what motivates households to downsize.

References

American Association of Retired Persons. 2003. These four walls. . . . Americans 45+ talk about home and community. Research Report. Matthew Greenwald and Associates, May.

Bernheim, B. D. 1992. Is the baby boom generation preparing adequately for retirement? Technical Report, Merrill Lynch. Princeton, NJ.

De Nardi, M., J. Jones, and E. French. 2005. Differential mortality, uncertain medical expenses, and the saving of elderly singles. Federal Reserve Bank of Chicago Working Paper no. 2005-13.

Engen, E. M., W. G. Gale, and C. E. Uccello. 1999. The adequacy of household saving. *Brookings Papers on Economic Activity,* Issue no 2: 65–187. Washington, DC: Brookings Institution.

Gustman, A. L., and T. L. Steinmeier. 1999. Effects of pensions on savings: Analysis with data from the Health and Retirement Study. *Carnegie-Rochester Conference Series on Public Policy* 50 (June): 271–324.

Heiss, F., M. Hurd, and A. Börsch-Supan. 2005. Healthy, wealthy and knowing where to live. In *Analyses in the economics of aging,* ed. D. Wise, 241–80. Chicago: University of Chicago Press.

Scholz, J. K., A. Seshadri, and S. Khitatrakun. 2006. Are Americans saving "Optimally" for retirement? *Journal of Political Economy* 114 (4): 607–43.

Skinner, J. 2007. Are you sure you are saving enough for retirement? NBER Working Paper no. 12981. Cambridge, MA: National Bureau of Economic Research, March.

Venti, S. F., and D. A. Wise. 2004. Aging and housing equity: Another look. In *Perspectives in the economics of aging,* ed. D. Wise, 127–81. Chicago: University of Chicago Press.

V

Medicare

The Narrowing Dispersion
of Medicare Expenditures
1997 to 2005

Jay Bhattacharya, Alan M. Garber, and
Thomas MaCurdy

13.1   Introduction

The projected gap between Medicare revenues and expenditures has growing immediacy with the implementation of the Part D drug benefit and the
looming bankruptcy of the Hospital Insurance Trust Fund, which is used
to make Medicare Part A payments. However, concerns about the sustainability of Medicare are not new, and over the past twenty-five years several
important legislative initiatives to control the growth in Medicare spending
have been passed into law. The adoption of Medicare's Prospective Payment
System in the 1980s, for example, not only transformed the hospital care of
Medicare patients, but influenced hospital reimbursement by private payers
as well. Among the most far-reaching legislative initiatives since then was
the passage of the Balanced Budget Act (BBA) of 1997.

Most of the changes in the BBA were intended to cut reimbursements
rather than to change mechanisms of payment, but they were more than
minor modifications of existing payment policies. The changes included
direct reductions to the Prospective Payment System (PPS) inpatient hospital annual operating update and PPS inpatient capital payments, affect-

Jay Bhattacharya is an associate professor of medicine at Stanford University School of Medicine and a research associate of the National Bureau of Economic Research. Alan M. Garber
is a staff physician at the VA Palo Alto Health Care System; director of the Center for Health
Policy and Center for Primary Care and Outcomes Research (CHP/PCOR), and the Henry J.
Kaiser, Jr. Professor and Professor of Medicine as well as Professor, by courtesy, of Economics,
of Health Research and Policy, and of Economics in the Graduate School of Business, Stanford
University; and a research associate of the National Bureau of Economic Research. Thomas
MaCurdy is a professor of economics at Stanford University, a senior fellow at the Hoover
Institution, and a research associate of the National Bureau of Economic Research.

ing nearly all hospitals that cared for Medicare inpatients. Cuts in indirect medical education (IME) payments and direct medical education (DME) payments were felt by teaching institutions, while changes in formulas for disproportionate share (DSH) payments had their greatest effects on hospitals that cared for the indigent and uninsured. The BBA also expanded the Medicare transfer policy (which reduces payments for transfers of short-term acute patients in ten Diagnosis Related Groups who were discharged to a Skilled Nursing Facility, PPS-exempt facilities, or to a home health agency). There were also changes in the structure of payment, such as the implementation of prospective payment systems for outpatient hospital, skilled nursing facilities, and home health agencies, and the creation of Medicare + Choice managed care plans, with efforts to improve geographic adjustments to payments for such plans.

Although not all the BBA features were implemented immediately, and its provisions were modified—and in some cases, weakened—in the Balanced Budget Refinement Act (BBRA) of 1999, its effects were felt by hospitals and other providers. Reportedly hospital margins shrunk, and home health service used dropped dramatically, with a large reduction in the number of home health service providers (Wilensky 2000).

The BBA effects on hospitals may be difficult to assess fully because there were contemporaneous changes in payments from private insurers, many working in the same direction. We seek here to investigate how BBA may have affected trends in Medicare expenditures for beneficiaries. At least in the immediate post-BBA period, the most important effects were on inpatient services and home health services, where the intention was unambiguously to reduce Medicare payments. Other features, such as the introduction of prospective payment for some outpatient services and the creation of Medicare + Choice plans, were clearly intended to provide new payment mechanisms with the prospect for long-term expenditure control, but were not necessarily designed to reduce near-term expenditures.

Our interest focuses on the effects of BBA on the dispersion of Medicare expenditures. That is, we seek to learn whether following the implementation of the BBA expenditures grew more or less rapidly for high-expenditure Medicare beneficiaries than for people who used few Medicare-covered services. The growth in per-beneficiary expenditures slowed after implementation of the BBA but its effects on the dispersion of expenditures have been little studied. In particular, did the BBA selectively reduce cost growth at the high end, where many of its features were directed? Did growth slow evenly among all Medicare beneficiaries? And were the effects different for men and women, or blacks and whites? The changes in disproportionate share payments, for example, would have been felt predominantly by hospitals providing care for the poor, and thus might have led to greater changes in expenditures for blacks than whites.

We describe changes in cohort patterns of expenditures between 1997 and

2005, describing growth in per capita expenditures at different percentiles for different subgroups.

13.2   Data and Methods

Our primary data source is the Medicare Beneficiary Annual Summary File (BASF). The BASF is a data set that contains comprehensive information on Medicare expenditures for 100 percent of all Medicare enrollees who are not enrolled in a Medicare Advantage (HMO) plan. Expenditures include all sources of Medicare expenditures, including Part A, Part B, physician expenditures, home health expenditures, and skilled nursing facilities (thought not Part D, since it was not implemented until 2006). The BASF also includes a comprehensive set of chronic disease indicators for each individual in the file. No individual leaves our sample until death.

13.2.1   Description of the Data

The BASF data are derived from annual enrollment and claims data collected by the Centers for Medicare and Medicaid Services (CMS). These are administrative data used by CMS to verify eligibility and to process hospital and physician claims for payment on behalf of Medicare beneficiaries. Enrollment data capture eligibility and demographic information at a point-in-time (typically July 1st of each calendar year). Claims data are requests for payment for a particular service provided during a given period of time, and they include information on the ICD-9-CM diagnosis and procedure codes, CPT-4/HCPCS codes, revenue center codes, provider type/specialty, Medicare reimbursement, third-party payments, beneficiary copayments, and deductibles. Claim formats vary depending on the type of provider and whether the claims were processed by a fiscal intermediary (hospital insurance under Part A) or a carrier (supplemental medical insurance under Part B). Only those beneficiaries enrolled in Medicare fee-for-service generate claims data.

Claims data in raw format are not useful for analyses of beneficiary utilization and expenditures over time because such an analysis requires aggregating enrollment, service use, program payments, and beneficiary payments across claims, service types, and dates of service. Information on diagnoses and procedures need to be summarized for analyses of beneficiaries with particular conditions and treatments. Enrollment data capturing point-in-time status must be validated and made consistent to reflect continuous enrollment status in Medicare fee-for-service and managed care.

To convert these data into a format useful for conducting analyses of beneficiary utilization and expenditures over time, we created utilization and expenditure files that summarize data on all nonmanaged care Medicare beneficiaries in each year between 1997 and 2005 inclusive. These data contain the beneficiaries' enrollment status, including Part A and Part B enrollment and mortality using date of death information from linked Social Security records. These data also contain utilization and expenditure data by service type, including inpatient hospital, skilled nursing facility (SNF), home health agency, hospice, outpatient hospital, physician (including clinical lab), and durable medical equipment. Expenditure data include Medicare program payments, third-party payments, and beneficiary payments (copayments and deductibles), with indicators supplied signaling assigned diagnosis-related group (DRG) (for inpatient hospital and SNF) or principal diagnosis (home health, outpatient hospital, and physician). In this chapter, we focus our attention on total Medicare expenditures per capita, which is a sum of expenditures from all these categories over the whole year.

13.2.2   Chronic Disease Indicators

For some of our analyses, we need detailed information on the health status of Medicare patients. Rather than rely on self-reports, we instead use diagnostic code data in claims records to generate objective information on the presence of chronic disease. This information is derived from looking at patterns of longitudinally-linked claims records for a single individual. The basic idea in deriving chronic condition indicators is that if an individual has a past claim with the diagnosis listed, then that individual can be presumed to have that chronic condition. The procedures associated with implementing this basic idea obviously involve a lot of attention to detail, however.

For the purpose of creating risk adjustment scores for payment to managed care programs, CMS has endorsed a methodology for assigning chronic disease indicators (called hierarchical conditional categories, or HCCs). We adopt this methodology to develop chronic disease indicators here. Pope et al. (2004) describe this methodology in some detail; we refer interested readers there, focusing here on only a few important details.

To assign HCCs for a Medicare enrollee in 1997, we examine diagnostic codes in Medicare claims in the prior two years. Once an enrollee is assigned a chronic disease indicator, that same enrollee is recorded with the same indicator in subsequent years. The list of conditions is derived from a longer and more detailed list of chronic conditions called CCs, which is itself derivative of the well-known ICD-9 coding system.

Clearly, this method of assigning chronic disease indicators is imperfect. Biases can arise from many different sources. In the 1970s, when large administrative data sets recording hospital claims data for patient discharges first became available, it was natural for researchers to want to use them to estimate some outcomes of interest, such as mortality rates associated with particular diseases. However, distrust of coding accuracy, given empirical backing by a series of influential studies by the Institute of Medicine (1977a, 1977b, 1980), likely played a role in discouraging investigators from using these data sets in such a manner. One of these studies (Institute of Medicine 1977b) found for the National Hospital Discharge Survey that the discharge diagnosis listed in the data set agreed with a controlled, expert reabstraction of the medical chart only an average of 73.2 percent of the time. Qualitatively similar results were found for Medicare claims data.

With the introduction of the prospective payment system and DRG reimbursement for Medicare claims, the additional concern arose that hospitals might game the reporting of patient diagnosis in order to increase payment for cases. Hsia et al. (1988) found that for a sample of 7,050 Medicare case records from 239 hospitals, the reabstracted diagnosis disagreed with that in the data set 20.8 percent of the time. Of these discrepancies, a statistically significant 61.7 percent favored the hospital financially. Additionally, Iezzoni et al. (1988) found that for a set of records from fifteen Boston hospitals, cases that presented as potential acute myocardial infarction (AMI) were commonly recorded as AMI even if further investigation revealed some other disease process. This was especially common for tertiary care teaching hospitals.

Recent scholarship has been cautiously optimistic about the improving quality of the Medicare administrative database diagnostic information. For example, another case record reabstraction study conducted by Fisher et al. (1992) explicitly attempted to replicate the Institute of Medicine study with the 1985 Medicare claims database. They found that the accuracy had modestly improved by 5 percentage points, relative to the earlier study.

While reabstraction studies have generally found diagnostic discrepancies on the order of 20 percent or more, the Medicare data set has performed better when other approaches are used to verify its external validity. Using Medicare claims and enrollment data from 1983 to 1986, Whittle et al. (1991a) estimated the incidence rate of breast, lung, and colon cancer and the rate of their surgical resection among the elderly population. They compared these estimates to those derived independently using a different survey instrument by the National Cancer Institute's Surveillance, Epidemiology, and End Results (SEER) program. The SEER data come from nine regional registries, accounting for 10 percent of the U.S. population. They found that the Medicare incidence rates were within 6 percent of SEER estimates, but that Medicare resection rates were 12 percent to 27 percent lower than SEER rates. One possible explanation for the discrepancy in resection rates is that practice patterns outside of SEER regions differ from those inside. However, they found that the Medicare resection estimates within SEER regions are not statistically different from those outside SEER regions for lung and colon cancer.

McBean, Babish, and Warren (1993) also estimated lung cancer incidence from Medicare data and compared the result to SEER estimates for the years 1986 to 1987. With the assumption that SEER estimates have no sampling variance, they found that SEER identified a statistically significant 5.9 percent more cases than did Medicare. However, the population incidence estimates were similar, with 274.2/100,000 calculated for SEER and

264.7/100,000 for the Medicare data. In contrast to Whittle et al. (1991a) they found that age-adjusted cancer incidence rates calculated using Medicare data were about 10 percent higher for patients residing outside SEER regions than inside.

In a more comprehensive study, McBean, Warren, and Babish (1994) repeated their previous work for the years 1986 to 1990, and for six different cancers. For breast, colon, lung cancer, and corpus uteri, they found that SEER and Medicare data estimates differed by less than 5 percent, while they differed by less than 8 percent for prostate and esophagus cancer. They found no uniform pattern in the differences between incidence rates inside and outside SEER regions. They concluded that Health Care Financing Administration (HCFA) data should be used to augment SEER monitoring of cancer incidence.

One potential explanation for the different conclusions reached by the reabstraction studies and the SEER studies is that while case abstracters may have trouble replicably assigning a very specific code, they have little problem assigning a broad diagnosis, like lung cancer. Hospitals are also less likely to misreport broad diagnostic designations for financial gain because the likelihood of detection by review agencies is higher than when fine diagnostic distinctions are misrepresented. If this is indeed the case, then studies using Medicare administrative databases to track broad diagnostic categories, such as HCCs, are more plausible than those that make use of finer diagnostic information.

These concerns aside, a large number of articles use Medicare Part A administrative data to estimate various epidemiological quantities of interest. Among such applications include estimates of: mortality rates after radical prostatectomy for prostate cancer patients (Mark 1994); in-hospital mortality after a stroke (May and Kittner 1994); resection rates and associated long-term mortality rates for colon cancer (Whittle et al. 1992) and lung cancer (Whittle et al. 1991b); post-myocardial infarction (MI) mortality rates, reinfarction rates, and likelihood of undergoing coronary artery bypass grafting (CABG) and/or percutaneous transluminal coronary angioplasty (PTCA) (Udvarhelyi et al. 1992); and structural shifts in the mortality rates associated with CABG and PTCA over time (Peterson et al. 1994). Finally, this data set has been popular in the health services literature as well for myriad uses such as the estimation of regional variation in readmission rates for various diseases (Fisher et al. 1994) among many other applications. It is necessarily beyond the scope of this chapter to review all of these papers.

13.2.3   Methods

In this chapter, we track changes in the distribution of Medicare expenditures over the period 1997 to 2005. Program payments are funds paid by the Medicare program on behalf of the beneficiary. Expenditures include third-party payments, in addition to beneficiary copayments and deductibles. Hereafter, we will refer to the sum of program payments and expenditures as simply expenditures. Among the statistics we track, we include mean expenditures as well as first, fifth, tenth, twenty-fifth, fiftieth, ninetieth, ninety-fifth, and ninety-ninth percentiles. We examine trends in the distribution of expenditures for different demographic and clinical subgroups of patients. To conduct these subgroup analyses, we first select all Medicare enrollees in each year that are members of the subgroup and then calculate summary statistics on expenditures for those members. We report changes in these summary statistics in two ways: absolute changes in real expenditures over the 1997 to 2005 period and per annum growth rates in expenditures. All results are reported in constant 2005 dollars.

In addition to trends in these summary statistics, we develop smoothed estimates of how the distribution of Medicare expenditures has changed over time. To track changes in mean expenditures, we estimate ordinary least squares (OLS) regression equations in which expenditures are a smooth function of the age of the respondent and the year of the observation. To track changes in the percentiles, we estimate quantile regressions (see Koenker and Hallock 2001) in which the key dependent variables are also smooth functions of age and year. In the remainder of this section, we make clear what we mean by "smooth functions." In this discussion, we will focus on how mean expenditure changes, but the smoothing method we use applies just as well in the quantile regression setting.

Constructing age-specific profiles of costs invariably runs into a problem of sample size. Even in a large, nationally representative sample such as the Medicare Current Beneficiary Survey (MCBS), the sample size at a single age turns out to be quite small to construct reliable estimates, especially for some of the smaller subgroup analyses that we conduct. To address this problem, we rely on the idea that Medicare expenditures should change smoothly across ages.

To describe the method we use to produce smooth age-specific prevalence functions—the overlap polynomial method[1]—it is helpful to introduce some notation. Each observation i, taken in $year_i$, consists of information about i's Medicare expenditures $expend_i$ and age_i.[2] Given these data, we estimate the following model of Medicare expenditures:

(1) $$expend_i = c + g_1\,(age_i,\, \beta_1) + g_2\,(year_i,\, \beta_1).$$

The g functions allow Medicare expenditures to flexibly vary with the year of observation and the age-cohort of the respondent. Age-cohort enters the model through g_1, which is specified using an overlap polynomial:

---

1. See MaCurdy, Green, and Paarsch (1990); MaCurdy and Garber (1993); and Bhattacharya, Garber, and MaCurdy (1997).

2. It is possible to adapt this method to use other covariates.

$$(2) \qquad g_1(\text{age}_i) = \sum_{j=0}^{K} \left(\Phi\left(\frac{\text{age}_i - k_{j+1}}{\sigma_1} \right) - \Phi\left(\frac{\text{age}_i - k_j}{\sigma_i} \right) \right) p_j(\text{age}_i; \beta_{1j}),$$

where $p_j(\text{age}_i; \beta_{1j}) j = 0, \ldots, K + 1$ are all nth-order polynomial in age$_i$. The knots are $k_0 \ldots k_{K+1}$, and σ_1 is a smoothing parameter, which in addition to n, are all fixed before estimation. We use first-degree polynomials. Though we experimented with higher-order polynomials, we find that they add to the costs of computation with no change in the final projections.

With this smoothing technique, the knots define age intervals. When the smoothing parameter approaches zero, the age profile over each interval simply equals the within-interval average expenditures. In this case, the age profile reduces to a step function, where each step equals the within-interval average disability.[3] As the smoothing parameter increases, the estimator uses increasingly more information from outside each interval. In the extreme, as the smoothing parameter approaches infinity, there is no meaningful distinction between any two intervals. Allowing nonzero values of the smoothing parameters eliminates the sharp discontinuity of the growth rates at the knots. One advantage of overlapping polynomials over traditional splines is that the function and all its derivatives are automatically continuous at the knots without imposing any parameter restrictions.

In addition to an overlap polynomial for age, we also include another overlap polynomial, g_2, for year to flexibly allow for changes in the age-prevalence relationship over time. Here, the knots are $m_j, j = 0, \ldots, M$, the smoothing constant is σ_2, and q_j are the polynomials. As before, experimentation led us to use first-order polynomials in year.

$$(3) \qquad g_2(\text{year}_i) = \sum_{j=0}^{M} \left(\Phi\left(\frac{\text{year}_i - m_{j+1}}{\sigma_2} \right) - \Phi\left(\frac{\text{year}_i - m_j}{\sigma_2} \right) \right) q_j(\text{year}_i; \beta_{2j}).$$

The object of the estimation is to obtain consistent estimates for β_1 and $\beta_2 - \beta_1$ and $\hat{\beta}_2$, respectively. Using these estimates, it is straightforward to generate age-specific expenditure profiles representative for any particular year. Let $\rho_{t,a}$ be the predicted expenditures among a-year olds in year t. Then,

$$(4) \qquad \rho_{t,a} = \frac{1}{N} \sum_i [\hat{c} + g_1(\text{age}_i, \hat{\beta}_1) + g_2(\text{year}_i, \hat{\beta}_2)].$$

In some specifications, we are interested in how cohort profiles in Medicare expenditures have changed over time. For these specifications, we include interaction terms like:

---

3. When this is the case, $\Phi(.)$ reduces to an indicator function equal to zero if age $< k_j$ and one if age $\geq k_j$. Thus, the first term of the sum, $(\Phi((\text{age}_i - k_1)/\sigma_1) - \Phi((\text{age}_i - k_0)/\sigma_1))p_0$, equals p_0 when $k_0 < \text{age} \leq k_1$, and zero otherwise. Between k_0 and k_1, the rate of disability is given by p_0, which in turn depends on the parameters $\beta_{1,0}$.

$$\sum_{j=0}^{M} \left(\Phi\left(\frac{\text{year}_i - m_{j+1}}{\sigma_2} \right) - \Phi\left(\frac{\text{year}_i - m_j}{\sigma_2} \right) \right) q_j(\text{age}_i; \beta_j) \quad \text{and}$$

$$\sum_{j=0}^{M} \left(\Phi\left(\frac{\text{age}_i - m_{j+1}}{\sigma_2} \right) - \Phi\left(\frac{\text{age}_i - m_j}{\sigma_2} \right) \right) q_j(\text{year}_i; \beta_j).$$

Including terms like this is necessary because a specification like (1) imposes that cohort trends in expenditures are all parallel to each other. However, because age, cohort, and year are linearly related, it is not possible to estimate a full set of interaction terms. MaCurdy and Garber (1993) provide details on what restrictions are necessary and on how to recover cohort trends from specifications like the one shown previously.

13.3 Results

Table 13.1 shows how per capita expenditures on Medicare patients grew over the period 1997 to 2005. The BASF data confirm the finding from other data sources that per capita Medicare expenditures grew at 4.29 percent per annum over this period (see Bhattacharya and Lakdawalla 2006). Since all these figures are adjusted for inflation with the standard consumer price index, this represents a real growth in Medicare expenditures. This mean growth rate, however, hides important facts in the evolution of Medicare expenditures.

One of these facts, evident in table 13.1, is that the upper tail of the expenditure distribution actually shifted left between 1997 and 2000. The ninetieth percentile of the expenditure distribution decreased from $15,348 in 1997 to $15,011 in 2000; the ninety-fifth percentile decreased from $27,218 to $26,556; and the ninety-ninth percentile decreased from $59,325 to $58,215. Even mean expenditures declined between 1997 and 1999. Presumably these declines can be attributed to the effects of the 1997 Balanced Budget Act (BBA). The declines were short-lived, though. The expenditure distribution started shifting to the right in 2000 (after passage of the BBRA) and continued to do so in every percentile and in every year through 2005.

Despite the decline between 1997 and 2000, there has been growth in per capita Medicare expenditures across the whole distribution of expenditures (save the left tail) between 1997 and 2005. For instance, median per capita expenditures grew by $842; the ninetieth percentile grew by $5,821; and the ninety-ninth percentile grew by $74,808. Looking at these absolute dollar increases alone, it would appear that there were larger increases at the upper end of the distribution than there were at the lower end. But as a proportion of initial 1997 expenditures for each percentile, the upper end of the distribution actually grew more slowly than the lower end. For instance, the median grew at 10.06 percent per annum while the ninetieth and ninety-ninth percentiles grew at only 3.52 and 2.94 percent per annum. Median

Table 13.1 Per capita Medicare expenditure, by year

	1997	1998	1999	2000	2001	2002	2003	2004	2005	Change 2005–1997	Annual change (%)
p1	$0	$0	$0	$0	$0	$0	$0	$0	$0	$0	0.00
p5	$0	$0	$0	$0	$0	$0	$0	$0	$0	$0	0.00
p10	$0	$0	$0	$0	$0	$0	$0	$0	$0	$0	0.00
p50	$730	$777	$845	$948	$1,101	$1,191	$1,309	$1,452	$1,572	$842	10.06
p90	$15,348	$14,718	$14,475	$15,011	$16,439	$17,403	$18,568	$20,092	$21,169	$5,821	4.10
p95	$27,218	$26,262	$25,762	$26,556	$28,806	$30,356	$31,895	$34,265	$35,892	$8,674	3.52
p99	$59,325	$57,943	$57,015	$58,215	$62,491	$65,441	$67,210	$71,633	$74,808	$15,483	2.94
Mean	$5,175	$5,048	$5,020	$5,222	$5,719	$6,040	$6,377	$6,864	$7,240	$2,066	4.29
Observations (millions)	27.9	27.3	27.1	27.4	28.2	29.0	29.5	29.8	29.6		

expenditures more than doubled over the 1997 to 2005 period. This was not the case for the upper percentiles.

The implications of these changes are that the Medicare per-capita expenditure distribution shifted to the right and that relative differences in expenditures between the lowest and highest parts of the distribution (leaving aside zeroes in the lowest percentiles) shrank. The fastest growth occurred in the middle of the distribution, while the upper end grew only modestly. This updates the trend reported by MaCurdy and Geppert (2005) for years prior to 1997. In one sense, inequality in Medicare expenditures has been declining: the distribution of per capita Medicare expenditures, conditional on having some expenditures at all, has been narrowing since 1997.

In another sense, inequality has been rising. Differences between expenditures for the care of black and white Medicare beneficiaries inequality has been increasing. Table 13.2, shows changes between 1997 and 2005 in the distribution of Medicare expenditures separately for black and white males and black and white females. For white males and white females, the real per annum mean growth rate in Medicare expenditures was 4.13 percent and 4.55 percent. By contrast, the analogous growth rates for black males and black females were 3.59 percent and 3.31 percent per annum. For whites, conditional on spending something, there was growth throughout the expenditure distribution. Given the results we report in table 13.1, it is unsurprising that the

Table 13.2   Medicare expenditure, by sex and race

	White		Black		Other race	
	Change 2005–1997	Annual change (%)	Change 2005–1997	Annual change (%)	Change 2005–1997	Annual change (%)
A Males						
p1	$0	0.00	$0	0.00	$0	0.00
p5	$0	0.00	$0	0.00	$0	0.00
p10	$0	0.00	$0	0.00	$0	0.00
p50	$785	9.93	$519	9.98	$416	11.42
p90	$5,721	4.00	$6,252	3.42	$5,236	4.82
p95	$8,526	3.41	$10,544	3.32	$8,631	3.79
p99	$16,225	3.05	$23,402	3.30	$18,148	3.16
Mean	$1,997	4.13	$2,135	3.59	$1,823	4.40
B Females						
p1	$0	0.00	$0	0.00	$0	0.00
p5	$0	0.00	$0	0.00	$0	0.00
p10	$39	n.a.	$0	0.00	$0	0.00
p50	$943	10.30	$840	9.48	$625	10.26
p90	$5,992	4.34	$5,315	2.77	$5,473	5.06
p95	$8,702	3.70	$8,570	2.66	$8,258	3.78
p99	$13,916	2.84	$19,199	2.75	$15,731	2.94
Mean	$2,124	4.55	$2,089	3.31	$1,932	4.65

fastest growth for blacks and whites occurred at the middle of their respective distributions (about 10 percent per annum for whites and 9.5 to 10.3 percent per annum for blacks at the median). Growth was slower at the upper tails for everyone, though less in general for blacks than whites. To summarize, Medicare expenditure differences between blacks and whites grew over this period while the distribution of Medicare expenditures narrowed for each group.

Table 13.3 charts the increase in expenditures for men and women in different age groups rather than of different races. The most striking result in table 13.3 is that ninety-five-to ninety-nine-year-olds—both men and women—had the large increases in mean Medicare expenditures relative to younger Medicare populations between 1997 and 2005. For men, sixty-five to sixty-nine-year-olds had the smallest increase at the mean—3.67 percentage points per annum. For women, eighty-five to eighty-nine-year-olds had the smallest increase at the mean—3.84 percent per annum. For all age-sex groups, the biggest proportionate increases in Medicare expenditures occurred in the lower end of the distribution (conditional on any expenditures). Indeed, eighty-five to eighty-nine-year-old men had an increase of 31.6 percent at the tenth percentile. Similarly, seventy- to seventy-four and ninety-five to ninety-nine-year-old women and ninety- to ninety-four-year-old men at the tenth percentile spent nothing in 1997 but spent positive amounts in 2005.

Table 13.4 offers another perspective on the relationship between aging and per capita Medicare expenditures. We organize the data by cohort of birth (rather than by age), and we follow the expenditure distributions of three cohorts between 1997 and 2005. For the oldest cohort we examine (born in 1912), mean and median expenditures increased by 7.5 percent and 3.9 percent per annum, which was less than the analogous increases for the 1922 and 1932 birth cohorts. The sharpest increases occurred for the youngest (born in 1932) cohort's expenditure distribution. Its median expenditures went up by 10.9 percent per annum.

Figures 13.1 and 13.2 organize these data visually using the smoothing technology that we describe in the methods section. In these figures, we plot both the age-expenditure profile in 2001 and the cohort-specific trends for the 1912, 1922, and 1932 cohorts in each year between 1997 and 2005. Figure 13.1 plots these objects at the ninetieth, ninety-fifth, and ninety-ninth percentiles, while figure 13.2 plots them at the mean and median. In each case, the cohort profiles are steeper than the age-expenditure profiles. For instance, the ninety-ninth percentile of expenditures for seventy-nine-year-olds in 2001 was less than the ninety-ninth percentile for seventy-nine-year-olds in 2002. It is evident from these figures and from table 13.4 that the youngest cohorts experienced the sharpest growth in Medicare expenditures.

The fact that the population of the oldest old experienced the smallest increases in per capita Medicare expenditures is consistent with the finding

Table 13.3   Medicare expenditure, by age category

	Ages 65–69		Ages 70–74		Ages 75–79		Ages 80–84		Ages 85–89		Ages 90–94		Ages 95–99		Ages 100+	
	Change 2005–1997	Annual change (%)	Change 2005–1997	Annual change (%)	Change 2005–1997	Annual change (%)	Change 2005–1997	Annual change (%)	Change 2005–1997	Annual change (%)	Change 2005–1997	Annual change (%)	Change 2005–1997	Annual change (%)	Change 2005–1997	Annual change (%)
							A Males									
p1	$0	0.00	$0	0.00	$0	0.00	$0	0.00	$0	0.00	$0	0.00	$0	0.00	$0	0.00
p5	$0	0.00	$0	0.00	$0	0.00	$0	0.00	$0	0.00	$0	0.00	$0	0.00	$0	0.00
p10	$0	0.00	$0	0.00	$0	0.00	$22	19.15	$88	31.57	$101	n.a.	$0	0.00	$0	0.00
p50	$344	9.91	$677	9.91	$1,031	9.56	$1,170	7.70	$1,360	6.85	$1,819	7.53	$2,730	17.50	$0	0.00
p90	$2,895	3.48	$4,852	3.83	$6,731	4.02	$7,405	3.75	$8,059	3.71	$8,545	3.83	$10,117	4.98	−$530	−6.67
p95	$5,423	2.97	$7,505	3.15	$9,687	3.44	$10,463	3.38	$10,744	3.34	$10,405	3.29	$11,831	4.05	−$180	−0.26
p99	$14,374	3.06	$16,157	3.00	$17,990	3.04	$18,397	3.01	$17,440	2.90	$15,388	2.76	$15,413	3.07	$5,142	2.00
Mean	$1,221	3.67	$1,780	3.96	$2,366	4.17	$2,572	3.88	$2,823	3.83	$3,130	4.06	$3,988	5.89	$63	0.57
							B Females									
p1	$0	0.00	$0	0.00	$0	0.00	$0	0.00	$0	0.00	$0	0.00	$0	0.00	$0	0.00
p5	$0	0.00	$0	0.00	$0	0.00	$0	0.00	$17	n.a.	$0	0.00	$0	0.00	$0	0.00
p10	$0	0.00	$25	n.a.	$106	36.24	$133	21.98	$145	18.16	$121	17.08	$90	n.a.	$0	0.00
p50	$581	11.29	$871	11.05	$1,068	10.02	$1,149	8.62	$1,173	7.24	$1,345	7.24	$1,889	12.16	$0	0.00
p90	$3,906	5.30	$5,199	4.66	$5,863	3.95	$6,546	3.63	$7,460	3.69	$8,423	4.01	$10,014	5.09	$1,733	2.75
p95	$6,166	3.80	$7,708	3.64	$8,655	3.42	$9,298	3.29	$9,955	3.33	$10,532	3.53	$12,005	4.29	$4,125	2.90
p99	$13,423	3.03	$14,467	2.89	$15,410	2.85	$14,902	2.71	$14,488	2.69	$12,866	2.52	$12,692	2.70	$8,429	2.56
Mean	$1,490	4.68	$1,940	4.66	$2,227	4.36	$2,375	3.98	$2,561	3.84	$2,858	4.08	$3,553	5.50	$521	2.45

Table 13.4　　　Medicare expenditure by year and cohort (selected years)

Year	p1	p5	p10	p50	p90	p95	p99	Mean
				Born in 1912				
1997	$0	$0	$37	$1,572	$22,191	$33,641	$63,468	$7,322
2000	$0	$0	$67	$1,704	$21,200	$32,364	$62,752	$7,139
2002	$0	$0	$111	$2,123	$24,555	$37,164	$70,256	$8,267
2005	$0	$0	$154	$2,795	$29,718	$43,950	$79,846	$9,950
Change 2005–1997	$0	$0	$117	$1,223	$7,527	$10,309	$16,378	$2,629
% Annual change	0%	0%	19.5%	7.5%	3.7%	3.4%	2.9%	3.9%
				Born in 1922				
1997	$0	$0	$0	$825	$15,408	$27,793	$61,918	$5,323
2000	$0	$0	$0	$1,078	$15,150	$27,137	$60,582	$5,397
2002	$0	$0	$11	$1,354	$17,506	$30,997	$68,524	$6,248
2005	$0	$0	$25	$1,797	$21,254	$36,463	$78,402	$7,496
Change 2005–1997	$0	$0	$25	$972	$5,846	$8,670	$16,484	$2,173
% Annual change	0%	0%	n.a.	10.2%	4.1%	3.5%	3.0%	4.4%
				Born in 1932				
1997	$0	$0	$0	$267	$6,484	$16,142	$47,148	$3,009
2000	$0	$0	$0	$354	$6,560	$15,804	$46,510	$3,069
2002	$0	$0	$0	$472	$7,571	$17,952	$52,426	$3,526
2005	$0	$0	$0	$612	$9,488	$21,578	$60,961	$4,237
Change 2005–1997	$0	$0	$0	$346	$3,003	$5,437	$13,813	$1,228
% Annual change	0%	0%	0%	10.9%	4.9%	3.7%	3.3%	4.4%

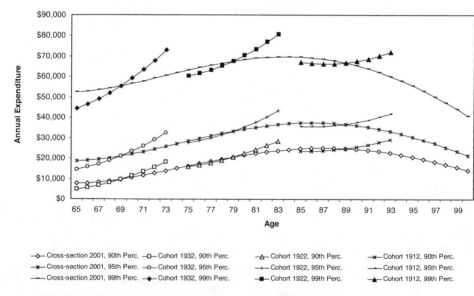

Fig. 13.1　Smoothed annual Medicare expenditure, 1912, 1922, and 1932 cohorts—90th, 95th, and 99th percentiles

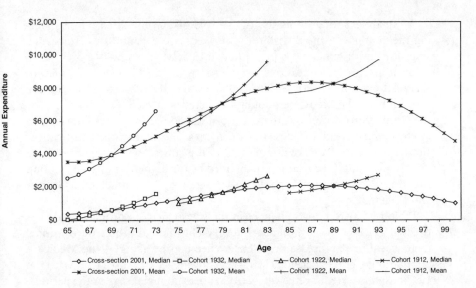

Fig. 13.2   Smoothed annual Medicare expenditure, 1912, 1922, and 1932 cohorts—median and mean

reported by Manton, Gu, and Lamb (2006) that this group has experienced a decline in disability prevalence over this period. Disabled individuals are substantially more likely than nondisabled individuals to have high Medicare expenditures (see Goldman et al. 2005). Similarly, the fact that the youngest cohorts have experienced the sharpest increases in per capita Medicare expenditures is consistent with the finding reported by Lakdawalla, Bhattacharya, and Goldman (2004) that disability rates have been increasing over parts of this period in the near-elderly population. As these near-elderly individuals age into Medicare, they will naturally raise per capita expenditures for the youngest Medicare enrollees.

One conclusion suggested by the numbers in table 13.2 is that men and women had similar increases in per capita Medicare expenditures even if the distribution of expenditures for men shifted to the right a bit more than the distribution for women. Tables 13.3 and 13.4 show that the latter impression is an artifact of the age distribution of men and women in the Medicare program. Since men, on average, die at earlier ages than women, the proportion of women in the population who are older than eighty-five years of age is larger than the analogous proportion for men. Of course, we have seen that older populations had smaller increases in per capita Medicare expenditures over this period. So comparisons between men and women that are unadjusted for age, such as table 13.2, will be biased toward showing greater increases in expenditures for men than for women just because Medicare men tend to be younger than Medicare women.

We turn next to a discussion of the role of chronic disease in explaining the changes in the distribution of Medicare expenditures. To set the stage for this discussion, we present table 13.5, which shows the prevalence of various chronic conditions in subgroups of the Medicare population averaged over the whole 1997 to 2005 period. The most common chronic conditions in the Medicare population include cataracts (27.95 percent of the population), coronary atherosclerosis (20.85 percent), atrial fibrillation (16.69 percent), and diabetes (16.04 percent). The low prevalence of cancer survivors in the Medicare population—for example, only 1.9 percent have a history of lung/GI cancer—is explained by the high mortality rate among Medicare cancer patients in the year of diagnosis (see Bhattacharya, Garber, and Miller 2006).

Table 13.5 also reports changes in the prevalence of chronic disease between 1997 and 2005. For nearly every chronic condition we examine, there was a rise in disease prevalence reflecting the aging of the Medicare population over this period. The largest prevalence increases relative to the 1997 baseline were for renal disease (93.4 percent increase over the period), osteoporosis (96.4 percent increase), osteoarthritis (57.0 percent increase), depression (53.2 percent increase), diabetes (37.6 percent increase), and dementia (35.5 percent increase). Several conditions—unstable angina, cataracts, myocardial infarction, stroke, and hip fracture/dislocation—actually declined in frequency over the period. Qualitatively, the pattern of changes in disease frequency was similar for men and women.

Chronic disease prevalence increases show no obvious relation to changes in the distribution of per capita Medicare expenditures shown on the right side of table 13.6. For instance, myocardial infarction (heart attacks), which decreased in prevalence over this period, had a sharp $1,350 increase in mean expenditures. By contrast, mean expenditures on cataracts, which also showed a decrease in prevalence, had a modest $260 increase over the period. Conversely, the average expenditures on osteoporosis patients, which saw large increase in prevalence, had the lowest increase in mean per capita expenditures ($144). For nearly every condition we examine, expenditures toward the lower end of the expenditure distribution grew sharply, while expenditures toward the upper tails increased less sharply. That no one with a chronic condition had zero expenditures is an artifact of the way in which the chronic disease indicators are constructed—we inferred the presence of a chronic disease from claims files, so a claim (and hence expenditures) were required to detect chronic disease.

13.4   Conclusions

After 1997, the growth in expenditures among the highest percentiles of users of Medicare-reimbursed care was less than the rate of growth at the lower percentiles (among those with any expenditures at all). Thus, the

Table 13.5   Chronic condition frequencies 1997–2005 (% of population)

	Whole population			Males			Females		
	1997 (%)	2005 (%)	% Change	1997 (%)	2005 (%)	% Change	1997 (%)	2005 (%)	% Change
Lung/upper GI/Other severe cancer	1.77	1.84	4.36	2.25	2.20	−2.01	1.44	1.58	9.83
Breast/prost/colorectal/other cancer	9.39	10.22	8.90	12.22	13.35	9.22	7.47	7.95	6.41
Diabetes	16.04	22.06	37.55	16.35	22.92	40.17	15.83	21.44	35.44
Renal disease	3.20	6.18	93.38	3.88	7.18	85.09	2.73	5.45	99.49
Atrial fibrillation	16.69	19.41	16.29	18.11	21.20	17.11	15.73	18.10	15.07
Rheum arthritis/inflamed connective tissue	3.73	4.14	10.83	2.40	2.57	6.88	4.63	5.28	13.94
Osteoarthritis of hip or knee	5.99	9.40	57.03	4.65	7.12	53.05	6.90	11.07	60.53
Osteoporosis and other bone/cartilage	8.30	16.29	96.37	2.89	5.05	74.38	11.95	24.48	104.75
Dementia/cerebral degeneration	7.04	9.54	35.50	5.65	7.67	35.78	7.99	10.91	36.56
Depression	4.37	6.70	53.15	2.89	4.32	49.37	5.38	8.43	56.77
Congestive heart failure	14.31	14.78	3.32	14.18	14.93	5.28	14.39	14.68	1.97
Myocardial infection	1.56	1.55	−0.79	1.91	1.78	−6.90	1.32	1.38	4.32
Unstable angina	4.80	3.76	−21.65	5.66	4.37	−22.83	4.22	3.32	−21.31
Coronary atherosclerosis	20.85	23.34	11.93	25.04	28.96	15.69	18.02	19.25	6.82
Heart infection	0.49	0.58	18.57	0.52	0.59	12.35	0.46	0.57	23.21
Ischemic or unspecified stroke	5.45	5.12	−6.01	5.49	5.03	−8.42	5.42	5.19	−4.27
COPD	13.43	14.71	9.56	15.64	15.99	2.23	11.94	13.79	15.52
Glaucoma	10.08	12.22	21.22	8.78	10.62	20.96	10.97	13.39	22.11
Cataract	27.95	27.70	−0.89	24.58	25.27	2.82	30.22	29.46	−2.52
Hip fracture/dislocation	2.03	1.71	−15.96	1.09	0.97	−11.06	2.67	2.25	−15.92

Table 13.6   Annual percent changes in per capita Medicare expenditures by disease: 1997–2005

Chronic conditions	p1 (%)	p5 (%)	p10 (%)	p50 (%)	p90 (%)	p95 (%)	p99 (%)	Absolute annual change in mean
Lung/upper GI/other severe cancer	9.82	9.77	8.80	4.58	4.05	3.66	3.00	$966
Breast/prost/colorectal/other cancer	9.70	9.00	8.78	4.03	3.73	3.62	3.14	$444
Diabetes	16.38	11.47	10.39	5.88	2.50	2.40	2.58	$327
Renal disease	8.69	7.05	5.53	0.53	1.31	1.32	1.64	$348
Atrial fibrillation	11.52	10.11	9.62	4.48	2.92	2.79	2.80	$518
Rheum arthritis/inflamed connective tissue	15.58	11.30	10.66	8.58	3.30	2.90	2.57	$449
Osteoarthritis of hip or knee	22.13	12.47	11.62	7.19	2.93	2.85	2.65	$381
Osteoporosis and other bone/cartilage	10.29	6.29	5.74	3.26	1.23	1.36	1.57	$144
Dementia/cerebral degeneration	9.02	6.21	6.05	3.25	2.63	2.45	2.60	$488
Depression	15.61	10.03	9.55	5.73	2.86	2.56	2.61	$547
Congestive heart failure	14.51	11.38	10.49	4.79	3.25	3.07	3.07	$699
Myocardial infection	7.42	10.67	6.11	4.85	3.84	3.82	3.94	$1,350
Unstable angina	11.38	10.97	10.15	5.38	3.55	3.58	3.74	$983
Coronary atherosclerosis	13.13	10.77	10.62	5.29	2.85	2.74	2.71	$457
Heart infection	11.92	9.98	8.86	4.08	3.30	3.38	3.42	$1,213
Ischemic or unspecified stroke	9.63	7.48	7.12	3.30	3.03	3.01	3.22	$663
COPD	19.51	11.63	11.28	5.19	3.47	3.22	2.99	$585
Glaucoma	n.a.	16.19	12.78	8.79	4.10	3.53	2.94	$304
Cataract	n.a.	19.25	13.02	7.55	3.83	3.29	2.82	$260
Hip fracture/dislocation	12.92	11.32	12.13	5.56	3.78	3.51	3.46	$1,203

overall dispersion in expenditures fell over time. This trend was diminished, at least temporarily, after the implementation of the BBRA. These findings suggest that the main effects of the BBA of 1997 came about as expected. Admission to the hospital—even once in a year—is enough to move a beneficiary into a relatively high expenditure category. Most of the provisions of the BBA that were likely to lead to immediate reductions in expenditures, such as the revisions to hospital payments, would have had greatest impact on high-cost beneficiaries. Other nonhospital provisions, such as restrictions on home health service payments, would also affect primarily high-cost users. The provisions that might lead to long-term expenditure reductions for beneficiaries who do not use inpatient or outpatient services heavily, such as those who are relatively young and do not have chronic diseases, did not necessarily have large effects in the near term. For example, a shift to prospective payment for outpatient services might reduce payments for office visits in the long term, but typically a transition to such a payment system includes relatively generous payments initially. These changes, of course, depend not only on the mechanism of payment but the level of payment.

Changes in expenditures varied by age and other characteristics. A great deal of compression in the expenditure distribution occurred at advanced ages: cross-sectional analyses reveal that expenditures increased least sharply on average for the oldest beneficiaries. Though cohort growth rates outpaced the cross-sectional growth in expenditures for every cohort we examined, younger cohorts had sharper increases than the oldest cohort. These changes reflect a variety of influences, an important one being reductions in payments for home health services, which are disproportionately used by the very old. They also reflect, to a large degree, changes in disability and disease prevalence in the these populations.

Although there are important differences between expenditures for men and women, who have different levels of expenditures, the trends in expenditure growth rates were similar for both. By contrast, post-BBA expenditure growth for blacks at the upper percentiles and at the mean of expenditures was lower than for whites. Throughout the time period, mean, median, ninetieth, and ninety-fifth percentiles of expenditures for blacks were generally greater than the levels for whites, which is consistent with the worse health of blacks on average.

Although these results cannot be definitively traced to any specific aspects of policy, they followed a far-reaching attempt to limit the growth of Medicare expenditures. They suggest that expenditure growth was altered most in the areas targeted by BBA. They also suggest that piecemeal changes—those that target only some components of Medicare—cannot be assumed to control overall expenditure growth, since substitution of services can offset some of the savings. In the case of the BBA, the appropriate concentration on high expenditures is likely to have led to a compression of the expenditure distribution, which has implications for all policies that depend upon not only the level of expenditures but their variance, a critical consideration in expansions of insurance coverage.

References

Bhattacharya, J., A. M. Garber, and T. MaCurdy. 1997. Cause-specific mortality among Medicare enrollees. In *Inquiries in the economics of aging,* ed. D. Wise, 311–26. Chicago: University of Chicago Press.

Bhattacharya, J., A. M. Garber, and Miller. 2006. Progress against cancer among elderly Americans. Stanford University. Unpublished Manuscript.

Bhattacharya, J., and D. Lakdawalla. 2006. Does Medicare benefit the poor? *Journal of Public Economics* 90 (1–2): 277–92.

Fisher, E. S., J. E. Wennberg, T. A. Stukel, and S. M. Sharp. 1994. Hospital readmission rates for cohorts of Medicare beneficiaries in Boston and New Haven. *New England Journal of Medicine* 331 (15): 989–95.

Fisher, E. S., F. S. Whaley, W. M. Krushat, D. J. Malenka, C. Fleming, J. A. Baron, and D.C. Hsia. 1992. The accuracy of Medicare's hospital claims data: Progress has been made, but problems remain. *American Journal of Public Health* 82 (2): 243–8.

Garber, A., and T. MaCurdy. 1993. Nursing home discharges and the exhaustion of Medicare benefits. *Journal of the American Statistical Association* 88:727–36.

Goldman, D. P., B. Shang, J. Bhattacharya, A. M. Garber, M. Hurd, G. F. Joyce, D. Lakdawalla, C. Panis, and P. Shekelle. 2005. Health and spending of the future elderly: Consequences of health trends and medical technology. *Health Affairs.* Web Exclusive, 26 September.

Hsia, D.C., M. Kurushat, A. B. Fagan, J. A. Tebbutt, and R. P. Kusserow. 1988. Accuracy of diagnostic coding for Medicare payments under the prospective-payment system. *New England Journal of Medicine* 318:352–5.

Iezzoni, L. I., S. Burnside, L. Sickles, M. A. Moskowitz, E. Sawitz, and P. A. Levine. 1988. Coding of acute myocardial infarction: Clinical and policy implications. *Annals of Internal Medicine* 109 (9): 745–51.

Institute of Medicine. 1977a. *Reliability of hospital discharge abstracts.* Washington, DC: National Academy of Sciences.

———. 1977b. *Reliability of Medicare hospital discharge records.* Washington, DC: National Academy of Sciences.

———. 1980. *Reliability of national hospital discharge survey data.* Washington, DC: National Academy of Sciences.

Koenker, R., and K. Hallock. 2001. Quantile regression. *Journal of Economic Perspectives* 15:143–56.

Lakdawalla, D., J. Bhattacharya, and D. Goldman. 2004. Are the young becoming more disabled? *Health Affairs* 23 (1): 168–76.

Manton, K. G., X. Gu, and V. L. Lamb. 2006. Change in chronic disability from 1982 to 2004/2005 as measured by long-term changes in function and health in the U.S. elderly population. *Proceedings of the National Academy of Science* 103 (48): 18374–9.

MaCurdy, T., and J. Geppert. 2005. Characterizing the experiences of high-cost users in Medicare. In *Analyses in the economics of aging,* ed. D Wise, 79–128. Chicago: University of Chicago Press.

MaCurdy, T., D. Green, and H. J. Paarsch. 1990. Assessing empirical approaches for analyzing taxes and labor supply. *Journal of Human Resources* 25 (3): 415–90.

Mark, D. H. 1994. Mortality of patients after radical prostatectomy: Analysis of recent Medicare claims. *Journal of Urology* 152 (3): 896–8.

May, D. S., and S. J. Kittner. 1994. Use of Medicare claims data to estimate national trends in stroke. *Stroke* 25 (12): 2343–7.

McBean, A. M., J. D. Babish, and J. L. Warren. 1993. Determination of lung cancer incidence in the elderly using Medicare claims data. *American Journal of Epidemiology* 137 (2): 226–34.

McBean, A. M., J. L. Warren, and J. D. Babish. 1994. Measuring the incidence of cancer in elderly Americans using Medicare claims data. *Cancer* 73 (9): 2417–25.

Peterson, E. D., J. G. Jollis, J. D. Bebchuk, E. R. DeLong, L. H. Muhbaier, D. B. Mark, and D. B. Pryor. 1994. Changes in mortality after myocardial revacularization in the elderly: The national Medicare experience. *Annals of Internal Medicine* 121 (12): 919–27.

Pope, G. C., J. Kautter, R. P. Ellis, A. S. Ash, J. Z. Ayanian, L. I. Iezzoni, M. J. Ingber, J. M. Levy, and J. Robst. 2004. Risk adjustment of Medicare capitation payments using the CMS-HCC model. *Health Care Financing Review* 25 (4): 119–41.

Udvarhelyi, I. S., C. Gatsonis, A. M. Epstein, C. L. Pashos, J. P. Newhouse, and B. J. McNeil. 1992. Acute myocardial infarction in the Medicare population: Process of care and clinical outcomes. *Journal of the American Medical Association* 268 (18): 2530–6.

Whittle, J., E. P. Steinberg, G. F. Anderson, and R. Herbert. 1991a. Accuracy of Medicare claims data for estimation of cancer incidence and resection rates among elderly Americans. *Medical Care* 29 (12): 1226–36.

———. 1991b. Use of Medicare claims data to evaluate the outcomes of elderly patients undergoing lung resection for lung cancer. *Chest* 100:729–34.

———. 1992. Results of colectomy in elderly patients with colon cancer, based on Medicare claims data. *American Journal of Surgery* 163 (6): 572–6.

Wilensky, G. 2000. The Balanced Budget Act of 1997: A current look at its impact on patients and providers. Testimony before the Subcommittee on Health and Environment, Committee on Commerce, U.S. House of Representatives. July 19.

Comment   Jonathan Skinner

A key to solving the problem of runaway growth in the U.S. Medicare program's expenditures (and for health care expenditures more generally) is a better understanding of the dynamic process by which health care costs continue their march upward. Yet little is known about patterns of growth, nor do we know who is actually receiving the additional care. So this study

Jonathan Skinner is the John Sloan Dickey Third Century Professor in Economics at Dartmouth College, professor of community and family medicine at Dartmouth Medical School, and a research associate of the National Bureau of Economic Research.

is particularly timely in providing a much-needed perspective on patterns of growth and the distribution of Medicare expenditures during the past decade. Their primary result is that the distribution of health care expenditures narrowed between 1997 and 2005, in the sense that Medicare expenditures grew fastest (in percentage terms) for those low in the distribution of health care spending in contrast to those in the top 5 or 10 percent of the spending distribution.

There are several methodological advances used in this chapter. The first is the use of polynomial smoothing methods to impose continuous and differentiable patterns of change in expenditures across age and year. A priori, we would not expect expenditures to jump from one age to the next, and this adjustment is a flexible (if somewhat complex) approach to providing a clearer picture of the relevant distributional trends.

The second is to take seriously the potential for secular changes in the health status of the elderly Medicare population by the use of HCCs (hierarchical conditional categories). These use past evidence of chronic illnesses which can then be used to adjust for subsequent use of medical care. As the authors note, the use of administrative data for clinical information has a somewhat checkered past, and the HCCs represent a step forward by using detailed claims data on previous reasons for having been admitted to the hospital or seen by a physician in previous years. But there is a tension in risk adjustment between using too little or too much information about what was actually done to the patient.

For example, suppose one is trying to ask the question: How much does a "high cost" patient in 1997 actually cost compared to the equivalent "high cost" patient in 2005? Suppose that over this time period, the prevailing standard of care causes the identical patient to be treated for more things. Then one could tend to overcorrect for past "health status" because health status is coded only if one actually is treated. Nonetheless, the HCC approach is clearly the most inclusive approach, and some of the more surprising results in this chapter come from their tabulations of patterns of growth in HCC-measured chronic illnesses.

But adjusting for risk is very unlikely to explain why they find the substantial narrowing of the distribution of Medicare expenditures. Most likely, it has something to do with the year in which their analysis begins, 1997—the last halcyon year of unfettered Medicare spending before the Balanced Budget Act of 1997 (BBA97) clamped down by placing limits on reimbursements, particularly for high-cost users of home health care.

Figure 13C.1 shows the rise and partial fall of the Medicare home health care industry. Home health care billing grew rapidly from under $5 billion in 1990 to more than $20 billion in 1997, before dropping rapidly to under $10 billion by 2000. (These figures are all in constant 2005 dollars.) An important restriction on home health care imposed by the BBA97 was to set upper limits on how often one could bill for an individual patient, and it

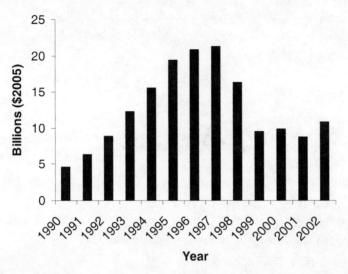

Fig. 13C.1   Medicare home health care expenditures, 1990–2002 (billions of 2005$)
Source: http://www.devicelink.com/mddi/archive/03/12/006.html.

was not difficult prior to 1997 for some patients to be billed for home health care daily for the entire year, for more than $30,000 annually. Thus, the narrowing of the distribution in Medicare expenditures during this period is most likely the direct consequence of the policy change. Starting the time series analysis in an earlier year could help to uncover how much of the tightening in the distribution was simply undoing the former excesses of a program that had become a prime vehicle for fraud—one study by the General Accounting Office suggested that 40 percent of the billings were "inappropriate" (Havemann 1997)—as opposed to secular changes in the distribution of Medicare expenditures.

The authors also provide intriguing results showing changes over time in both the prevalence of chronic illness and spending conditional on having the disease. There were clear differences in growth rates, but I could not think of reasons *why* some diseases, such as osteoporosis or renal disease, should grow so much faster than others. That greater efforts were made to diagnosis these diseases among less severely ill patients is suggested by the much lower than average growth rates in these two diseases—just 3.3 percent for osteoporosis and 0.5 percent for renal disease at the median. Clearly, a topic for future research is accounting, for the extent to which health care costs have risen because of increasing prevalence of chronic disease, increased diagnosis of those diseases, and treatment conditional on having the disease.

A much harder problem is to determine the causes of growth in expenditures. Simply attributing health care costs to "technology growth" begs the

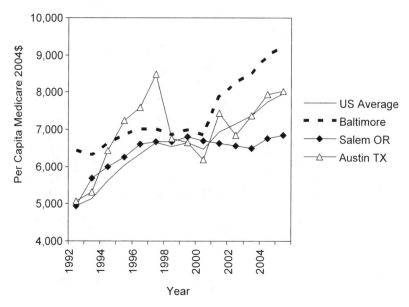

Fig. 13C.2   Medicare per capita growth rates in selection hospital referral regions
Source: www.dartmouthatlas.org and author's calculations.

question of why growth rates in expenditures are so large, or why they are not even larger (Chandra and Skinner 2008). Furthermore, why did some regions seem to adopt cost-increasing technology, or more accurately, why did cost-increasing technology appear to diffuse so rapidly in some regions compared to others?

Figure 13C.2 shows growth rates in per capita real Medicare expenditures (2005$) from the Dartmouth Atlas database. There is one problem with the Continuous Medicare History Survey (CMHS), on which these numbers are based, and that is double-counting of a small fraction of the records during 1998 to 2000, and Centers for Medicare and Medicaid Services (CMS) staff suggested a 10 to 15 percent adjustment downward for these estimates. I used a 10 percent adjustment because it appeared to smooth the aggregate, shown in the solid line. The cost-saving influence of the BBA can be seen in the flattening of growth from about 1997 to 2001, where it resumed its upward trend. But what is interesting is that not all hospital referral regions (HRRs) (see www.dartmouthatlas.org) followed the same growth rates. As shown in figure 13C.2, BBA97 was an inflection point for Salem, OR, growth rates moderated and have not really taken off since then. By contrast, Baltimore has experienced rapid growth in per capita Medicare expenditures, and hence, substantially higher growth rates over the relevant period. Austin, Texas displayed a much different pattern; their expenditures were growing rapidly prior to 1997 (with home health care a prime suspect), but since then has come down in costs and followed the national trend. Who is getting the marginal spending in Baltimore (relative to Salem)—the patient at the fiftieth percentile or the ninety-fifth percentile? And why have Baltimore hospitals made a conscious decision to expand capacity? Is it possible that the over-sixty-five population in Baltimore was constrained in getting the health care they needed prior to 1997?

Of course, we cannot say much about causality by looking at growth rates, and making inferences about the impact of expenditures on outcomes is problematic. But it is presumably something we would like to know when evaluating health care cost growth. McKnight (2006) used the BBA97 as an exogenous shock to study how the cutbacks in home health care affected actual health outcomes, and did not find significant effects on health. In the longer term, we would also like to know how a change in the distribution of health care spending affects health: is spending more on low-cost patients (relative to high-cost patients) a better use of our health care dollars?

References

Chandra, A., and J. Skinner. 2008. Technology growth and cost growth in U.S. health care. Dartmouth College. Unpublished Manuscript, February.

Havemann, J. 1997. Fraud is rife in home care for the elderly; Medicare investigators find 40% of services unjustified. *Washington Post,* July 29.

McKnight, R. 2006. Home care reimbursement, long-term care utilization, and health outcomes. *Journal of Public Economics* 90 (1–2): 293–323.

Skinner, J., and W. Zhou. 2006. The measurement and evolution of health inequality: Evidence from the U.S. Medicare population. In *Public policy and the income distribution,* ed. A. Auerbach, D. Card, J. Quigley, 288–316. New York: Russell Sage.

Mind the Gap! Consumer Perceptions and Choices of Medicare Part D Prescription Drug Plans

Florian Heiss, Daniel McFadden, and Joachim Winter

14.1 Introduction

Medicare Part D provides prescription drug coverage through Medicare-approved plans sponsored by private insurance companies and health maintenance organizations (HMOs). This new program is part of the current trend toward consumer-directed health care. However, making optimal, or even just reasonable, decisions in the Part D market is difficult for seniors. They face uncertainty with respect to their future health status and drug costs, and a rather complicated benefit schedule with a coverage gap and other peculiar institutional features of the Part D program, as well as a large number of available plans with features that vary along several dimensions. How seniors decide whether to enroll in Medicare Part D, and what plans they select, is therefore not only of crucial importance for public policy, but

Florian Heiss is an assistant professor of economics at the University of Munich. Daniel McFadden is the E. Morris Cox Professor of Economics at the University of California, Berkeley, and a research associate of the National Bureau of Economic Research. Joachim Winter is a professor of economics at the University of Munich.

We thank Abby Block, Carol Kelly, and Audrey McDowell of CMS, Dana Goldman of RAND, and Richard Suzman of NIA for information and comments. Helpful comments were also obtained from Amy Finkelstein and Arie Kapteyn; from conference participants at the AEA Annual Meeting in Chicago, IL (January 2007), the NBER Conference on the Economics of Aging, Carefree, AZ (May 2007), the Workshop on the Economics of Aging at Collegio Carlo Alberto, Turin (May 2007), and from seminar participants at the University of Mannheim and the ifo Institute, Munich. Dedicated research assistance was provided by Byung-hill Jun, Carlos Noton, and Gregor Tannhof. This research was supported by the Behavioral and Social Research program of the National Institute on Aging (grants P01 AG 05842-18 and R56 AG026622-01A1), with additional support from the E. Morris Cox Fund at the University of California, Berkeley. The authors are solely responsible for the results and conclusions offered in this chapter.

also an informative experiment on how consumers behave in real-world decision situations with a complex, ambiguous structure and high stakes.

In the week before Medicare Part D enrollment began in November 2005, we conducted a survey of Americans age sixty-five and above, termed the Retirement Perspectives Survey (RPS), to study information, perceptions, and preferences regarding prescription drug use, cost, and insurance. After the initial enrollment period closed on May 15, 2006, we reinterviewed the same respondents to elicit their actual Medicare Part D decisions for 2006. In addition, we presented hypothetical choice tasks with experimental variation of plan features. In a third wave of our survey, we reinterviewed our respondents in March and April 2007 to collect data about their experiences in the first year of Medicare Part D and their choices for 2007.[1]

We found in our first interview of eligible seniors in November 2005 that despite the complexity of the program's competing plans, which can differ in premiums and coverage, a majority of the Medicare population had at least some knowledge of Part D and intended to enroll. However, low-income, less educated elderly with poor health or some cognitive impairment were significantly less informed, and we concluded at that time that they might fail to take advantage of the new program; see Winter et al. (2006). In our May 2006 survey following the initial enrollment period, we confirmed that Medicare had met its target of 90 percent coverage in the Medicare-eligible population; see Heiss, McFadden, and Winter (2006). However, we also found that sizable numbers of elderly people remain uncovered.

Consumer opinions about Part D were mixed just after the initial enrollment period in May 2006. Majorities were troubled by the deductible and gap provisions of Standard Part D coverage, and found it difficult to determine the current and future formularies of the plans they evaluated. Asked the question, "Does your experience with Medicare Part D leave you more satisfied or less satisfied with the Medicare program?" 58.1 percent said they were less satisfied. Asked the question, "Does your experience with Medicare Part D leave you more satisfied or less satisfied with the political process in Washington that produced this program?" 74.7 percent said they were less satisfied. These responses indicated substantial dissatisfaction with the design and administration of the program at that point in time. This raises a more general issue: Consumers are often skeptical about markets, and suspicious of their organizers (McFadden 2006). This may lead consumers to question market solutions to public good allocation problems despite the attractions of consumer-directed choice. This seems to have been the case for Part D. We did not re-ask general opinion questions regarding Part D in 2007, but surveys by the Kaiser Family Foundation find that levels of dissatisfaction with the Part D program have fallen from 55 percent at its

---

1. In what follows, the three waves of the Retirement Perspectives Survey are referred to as RPS-2005, RPS-2006, and RPS-2007, respectively.

inception to 34 percent at the end of 2006, with remaining dissatisfaction focused on the complexity of the program, formularies, the gap, and tedious appeals procedures.

In this chapter, we study the actual enrollment decisions made in the initial enrollment period for the Medicare Part D program. In most of our analysis, we concentrate on "active deciders," the eligible individuals in our sample who did not have prescription drug coverage in November 2005 that was automatically converted to Part D coverage or equivalent in 2006 (e.g., automatic coverage through their current or former employer's health program, the Veterans Administration, or Medicaid). The first part of our analysis is descriptive; its intention is to study whether choices were related to the salient features of the program and the economic incentives they generated. We look at whether active deciders enrolled in Part D or not, at the timing of enrollment, and at the choice of plans. We stress the role of 2005 prescription drug use, health risks, related expectations, and subjective factors in the demand for prescription drug insurance.

In the second part, we develop a stylized intertemporal optimization problem faced by an individual without other prescription drug coverage during the initial enrollment period. We calibrate, solve, and simulate this model using data on the dynamics of health status and chronic conditions as well as drug use and expenditure taken from the Medicare Current Beneficiary Survey (MCBS). This normative analysis allows us to characterize optimal intertemporal decision making rules in the presence of risk. We then combine these results with our own data to study the rationality of decisions in the Medicare Part D initial enrollment period.

We generally find that seniors' choices respond to the incentives provided by their own health status and the market environment as predicted by our intertemporal optimization model. However, there is also evidence that seniors overreacted to some of the salient features of the choice situation, particularly 2006 costs and benefits, and were insufficiently sensitive to future cost and benefit consequences of their current decisions. We find that the proportion of individuals who do not attain the optimal choice is relatively small, but some of this is due to the fact that enrollment was clearly immediately beneficial for 81.7 percent of the population, and was intertemporally optimal for 97.5 percent. Given these program features, there was limited opportunity for error. Consumers were less consistently rational in their choices among plans, often selecting inexpensive plans in circumstances where plans with more expensive and comprehensive coverage were actuarially favorable.

The remainder of this chapter is structured as follows. In section 14.2, we describe the new Medicare Part D prescription drug benefit and the plans offered by private insurers during the initial enrollment period from November 2005 through May 2006. The existing literature on Medicare Part D, and on the demand for health insurance plans more generally, is reviewed briefly in section 14.3. We then introduce our primary source of data, the Retirement Perspectives Survey (section 14.4). Section 14.5 contains our descriptive analysis of decisions in the initial enrollment period. In section 14.6, we develop, calibrate, and simulate an intertemporal optimization model of the Medicare Part D enrollment decision, and we evaluate the rationality of observed decisions. Section 14.7 takes a preliminary look at the data from the final wave of our survey to characterize first-year experiences with Part D. Section 14.8 contains some concluding remarks.

14.2   The Medicare Part D Prescription Drug Benefit

The Centers for Medicare and Medicaid Services (CMS) within the U.S. Department of Health and Human Services administer health insurance coverage for older Americans via the Medicare program. The Medicare Modernization Act of 2003 (MMA) was enacted to extend coverage for prescription drugs to the Medicare population. Beginning in 2006, the new Medicare Part D benefit reduced the financial burden of prescription drug spending for beneficiaries, especially those with low incomes or extraordinarily high ("catastrophic") out-of-pocket drug expenses. The CMS administers this program, subsidizing outpatient prescription drug coverage offered by private sponsors of drug plans that give beneficiaries access to a standard prescription drug benefit.[2] Critical parameters in determining Standard plan benefits are the plan formulary, the beneficiary's annual pharmacy bill for drugs in the plan formulary, the beneficiary's true out-of-pocket (TrOOP) payments for these covered drugs and threshold for catastrophic coverage, and the average monthly premium. In the benefits formula, expenditures for drugs not in the plan formulary are *not* counted in the pharmacy bill or in TrOOP payments. Part D premiums are also excluded from TrOOP payments. The Standard Medicare Part D plan had the following benefit schedule in 2006:

- The beneficiary has an annual deductible of $250.
- The beneficiary pays 25 percent of drug costs above $250 and up to $2,250. The TrOOP payment is then $750 for a beneficiary whose pharmacy bill has reached $2,250.
- The beneficiary pays 100 percent of drug costs above $2,250 and up to a TrOOP payment of $3,600; this is referred to as the *coverage gap* or *doughnut hole*. The TrOOP threshold of $3,600 is attained at a drug bill of $5,100.
- The beneficiary pays 5 percent of drug costs above a drug cost threshold of $5,100, at which the TrOOP threshold level is achieved; this is referred to as *catastrophic* coverage.

2. See http://www.medicare.gov/medicarereform/drugbenefit.asp.

- Monthly premiums vary with plan sponsor and area, but a national average premium determined by CMS (and used in determining its subsidy) is a publicly available indicator of plan cost to beneficiaries.

Figure 14.1 shows the 2006 benefit schedule as a function mapping the total yearly drug bill into TrOOP cost. Standard plan coverage in 2007 and 2008 has the same structure, with table 14.1 showing the adjustments of plan parameters to reflect market base premiums and inflation in drug prices. Section 14.5.3 provides a calculation of the actuarial value of Standard plan benefits, based on a projection by CMS in 2005 of the distribution of 2006 drug costs for the full Medicare-eligible population. This calculation shows that the 2006 expected drug cost in this population was $245.03 per month. If enrollment in the Part D Standard plan had been universal, the expected benefit would have been $128.02 per month, or $91.13 net of the monthly average premium of $37 anticipated in 2005, and the expected TrOOP cost would have been $117.01 per month. The actual monthly average premium

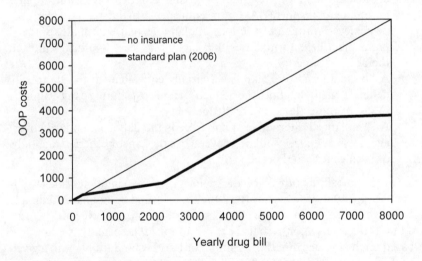

Fig. 14.1   Part D standard plan

Table 14.1   **Medicare Part D standard plan parameters**

	Year		
	2006 $	2007 $	2008 $
Deductible	250	265	275
Gap threshold	2,250	2,400	2,510
Catastrophic coverage TrOOP threshold	3,600	3,850	4,050
National average base premium	32.20	27.35	27.93

of $32.20 in 2006 was lower than anticipated; we interpret this as the result of lower drug costs arising from pharmacy benefit management and drug price negotiations by sponsors, resulting in 2006 average drug cost of $215.85 per month, an expected benefit of $111.74 per month, or $79.55 net of the premium, and TrOOP cost of $104.11 per month.

The Medicare Part D plans sponsored by private insurance firms may differ from the Standard plan in their premiums and other plan features, provided that their benefits for any drug cost are, on average, at least as high as those of the Standard plan. Enhancements may include coverage for the $250 deductible and for the gap in the standard plan. The CMS classifies the stand-alone prescription plans that are available under Medicare Part D in four categories (see Bach and McClellan 2006, 2313):

- The "standard benefit" is a plan with the statutorily defined coverage, deductible, gap, and cost sharing.
- An "actuarially equivalent" plan is one that has the same deductible and gap as the standard plan, but has different cost sharing (such as copayment tiers for preferred drugs and generic drugs rather than a percentage copayment). Actuarial equivalence to the standard plan may be achieved through restrictions in plan formularies, but all approved plans must have formularies that include at least two drugs in each therapeutic category.
- A "basic alternative" plan is actuarially equivalent to the statutorily defined benefit, but both the deductible and cost sharing can be altered. (Most of these plans have no deductible.)
- An "enhanced alternative" plan exceeds the defined standard coverage—for example, by offering coverage in the gap for generic drugs only, or both generic and branded drugs.

One important feature of Medicare Part D is the penalty for late enrollment. Individuals who enroll after May 15, 2006 and do not have creditable coverage from another source face a late enrollment penalty fee of 1 percent a month for every month that they wait to join. The penalty is computed based on the average monthly premium of Part D standard plans in a given year. This rule was put in place to reduce adverse selection, and as our analysis in section 14.6 confirms, it provides a strong incentive for eligible consumers to enroll in 2006 rather than wait to join when health problems develop and drug costs rise.

Section 14.5.3 describes the market for alternative plans: the CMS subsidy program and its impact on pricing, and the composition of plans offered in 2006 through 2008, and chosen in 2006 and 2007. More details on the Medicare Part D prescription drug benefit can be found on the CMS website and in Bach and McClellan (2005). The political controversy surrounding its introduction is reflected in two back-to-back papers in the *New England Journal of Medicine*—Bach and McClellan (2006) and Slaughter (2006).

14.3   Related Literature

The new Medicare Part D prescription drug benefit, and choice of health plans more generally, have been studied by numerous authors. In this section, we briefly review those papers that are more directly related to our analysis.

Hall (2004) provides an empirical analysis of how much Medicare beneficiaries value prescription drug benefits. Using a nested logit specification and data from the Medicare HMO program, she estimates parameters of demand for drug benefits and calculates estimates of consumer surplus and marginal cost. The premium elasticity is estimated to be –0.15 to –0.32. Further, her results indicate that Medicare beneficiaries are willing to pay about $20 per month on average for prescription drug benefits and are willing to pay $28 to increase their brand-name coverage by $100. Her study also provides empirical evidence for adverse selection and moral hazard effects. She finds that adding a prescription drug benefit raises HMO costs by $146 per person per month, and raising brand-name coverage by $100 costs $100. These cost estimates are higher than the corresponding welfare estimates. Hall argues that this discrepancy is probably due to either the HMOs experiencing adverse selection or regulation of the HMOs that lead them to offer benefits inefficiently combined with moral hazard on the part of beneficiaries.

Huskamp et al. (2003, 2005) provide empirical analysis of the effects of three-tier prescription drug formularies that have been adopted by health plans and employers in an effort to control rising prescription drug costs. Huskamp et al. (2003) examine the impact of changes in two employer-sponsored health plans on the use of three specific drugs. They find that different changes in formulary administration may have dramatically different effects on drug use and spending; in some cases patients even discontinue therapy. Huskamp et al. (2005) estimate econometric models of the probability of selecting drugs assigned to the third tier (with the highest copayment requirement) of a three-tier plan and compute changes in out-of-pocket spending. They find that implementation of the three-tier formulary resulted in some shifting of costs from the plan to patients. They argue that the savings from increased bargaining power from plans may well be substantial.

Joyce et al. (2002) analyze the impact of pharmacy benefit changes implemented by employers and health insurance providers, using data on a large cross-section of employers with different pharmacy benefit designs. Joyce et al. find that moving from a two-tier to a three-tier formulary, increasing existing copayments or coinsurance rates, and requiring mandatory generic substitution, all would result in a reduction in plan payments and total pharmacy spending. Goldman et al. (2004) investigate the effects of such plan changes on the demand for specific drug classes. They find that a doubling of copayments was associated with reductions in the use of eight classes. The largest decreases occurred for nonsteroidal antiinflammatory drugs and antihistamines, which are both often used intermittently to treat symptoms. The reduction in use of medications for individuals in ongoing care was more modest.

Moran and Simon (2006) estimate how retirees' use of prescription medications responds to changes in their incomes. They find that lower-income retirees exhibit considerable income sensitivity in their use of prescription drugs, using data from the 1993 wave of the Study of Asset and Health Dynamics Among the Oldest Old (AHEAD). Their estimates indicate that a $1,000 increase in post-retirement income (in 1993 dollars) for those in the low education and lower-income group would increase the number of prescription medications used in a typical month by approximately 0.55 prescriptions per household. Yang et al. (2004) investigate how insurance affects medical care utilization, and subsequently, health outcomes over time. They develop a dynamic model of these variables, and use longitudinal individual-level data from the 1992 to 1998 Medicare Current Beneficiary Survey to estimate these effects. Their simulations indicate that over five years, expanding prescription drug coverage would increase drug expenditures by between 12 percent and 17 percent. However, other health care expenditures would only increase slightly, and their results suggest that the mortality rate would decrease. Several studies look at the economic incentives provided by the new Medicare Part D prescription drug benefit, including Lucarelli (2006) and McAdams and Schwarz (2006). Frakt and Pizer (2006) and Simon and Lucarelli (2006) describe the plans that were available in 2006. The latter paper also contains a hedonic regression that relates plan premiums to plan features.

There are also several papers that discuss whether Medicare Part D provides sufficient coverage to all older Americans, and in particular the effect of the coverage gap. Stuart, Simoni-Wastila, and Chauncey (2005) argue that discontinuities in the drug benefit will affect people with greater-than-average medical need disproportionately (which by itself is not surprising). More interestingly, they argue that those affected by the coverage gap will reduce their medication use and spending. Donohue (2006) discusses the potential impact of Medicare Part D on the demand for drugs that are used persistently at high expected cost, such as certain psychotropic medications. Her study stresses the close relation between known chronic conditions (and the medications taken for them) and plan choice.

We are aware of only a few empirical studies of individuals' actual behavior during the Part D initial enrollment period.[3] The Health and Retirement Study (HRS) contained questions on prescription drug use, expenditure,

---

3. Health insurance and health plan choices have of course been studied in many other situations. Buchmueller (2006) presents estimated the premium (price) elasticity of health plan demand and reviews other papers on the effect of price on health plan choice.

and Part D decisions in several of its surveys in 2005 and 2006, but results are not yet available. Hurd et al. (2007) conducted hypothetical choice experiments with a sample of individuals from the American Life Panel.[4] They obtain the ranking of several hypothetical prescription drug plans with varying cost and payment schedules. Using data on the respondent's actual drug expenditure, they can also calculate the expected out-of-pocket costs for each of the hypothetical plans. They find that the correspondence between the preference and cost rankings is low. They speculate that respondents do not know the full cost of their drugs and so cannot know what the out-of-pocket cost would be. Another explanation they give for the stated preferences is that respondents anticipate that with some probability their prescription drug requirements will change and take into account the insurance aspects of the plans.

Another recent study of demand for Medicare Part D plans that uses official CMS data is Cubanski and Neuman (2006). Neuman et al. (2007) report results from a national survey that was conducted in 2006 to investigate Part D coverage, but that paper has a more narrow scope than this chapter. Where comparable, their results seem to be in line with ours.

Finally, several recent empirical studies address adverse selection and/or moral hazard in health insurance markets and the difficult problem of how to distinguish among these two effects in observed market data; in particular, Abbring et al. (2003), Bajari, Hong, and Khwaja (2006), Fang, Keane, and Silverman (2006). A particularly interesting empirical study by Shang and Goldman (2007) uses data from the Medicare Current Beneficiary Survey (MCBS) to show that exogenous variations in prescription drug coverage are associated with differences in prescription drug use. Those with prescription drug coverage use more drugs but spend less on other health care services, indicating that there is a substitution effect between prescription drugs and other health services.

14.4   The Retirement Perspectives Survey (RPS)

The Retirement Perspectives Survey is a research project conducted by the authors and collaborators[5] to study the feasibility of using Internet survey designs in elderly populations, and using treatments embedded in surveys to detect and mitigate survey response errors. Beginning in 2005, the continuing methodological research objectives have been combined with a substantive focus on consumer choices and experience in the Medicare Part D prescription drug program.

---

4. The American Life Panel, an internet panel maintained by RAND, Santa Monica, is in many respects similar to the Knowledge Networks Panel we used to collect the data for the Retirement Perspectives Survey.

5. Other study investigators are Rowilma Balza, Frank Caro, Byung-hill Jun, Rosa Matzkin, and Teck Ho.

The three waves of the Retirement Perspectives Survey in 2005, 2006, and 2007 used a panel of individuals maintained by Knowledge Networks (KN), a commercial survey firm. The members of the KN Panel are enrolled using random digit dialing sampling to obtain a pool that is representative of the U.S. noninstitutionalized population in terms of demographics and socioeconomic status. Participants are provided with web TV hardware to use to respond to periodic survey elicitations with content from both commercial and academic clients. The KN Panel members are compensated for participation. The RPS respondents are somewhat younger, more educated, healthier, and computer-literate than the underlying population.[6] For example, about half the panel members use the Internet, compared with about a third in the corresponding population. Sample weighting is used to adjust for attrition in the recruitment and retention process, and for nonresponse to specific surveys.

The first wave of our study, RPS-2005, was conducted in November 2005, just before the initial enrollment period for the new Medicare Part D prescription drug benefit began. This survey focused on prescription drug use and intentions to enroll in the new Medicare Part D program. Additional questions focused on long-term care, and a sequence of questions was designed to obtain simple measures of respondents' risk attitudes. The RPS-2005 questionnaire also contained some embedded experiments on information processing and response behavior in consumer surveys (see McFadden, Schwarz, and Winter [2006] for a discussion of these experiments). In May 2006, after the initial enrollment period had ended, we administered the second wave (RPS-2006). For this survey, we recontacted the Medicare eligible respondents of RPS-2005 and elicited their prescription drug insurance status as well as their Part D decisions, including plan choice. RPS-2007 was conducted in March and April 2007; its sample consisted of reinterviews of earlier RPS respondents plus refreshment cases. The RPS interviews required about thirty minutes for completion in 2005 and 2007, and about twenty minutes in 2006. Most socioeconomic and demographic variables were provided by Knowledge Networks as background on panel members, and were not requested again in the RPS questionnaires.

Table 14.2 contains sample sizes and participation rates for the various RPS waves and segments. Participation rates from the KN panel were gener-

---

6. Dennis (2005) details the RPS-2005 sampling protocol and weighting. The initial RDD sample was drawn using U.S. Government standards, with about 50 percent of drawn numbers linkable to an address and selected for further sampling. An extended effort was made to contact selected numbers and solicit participation; an overall participation rate of 56 percent using supplied web TVs was attained among address-linked numbers. The resulting KN panel was representative of the U.S. population except for some oversampling of the four largest states, the cities of Chicago and Los Angeles, and minority households. In addition, rural households not covered by MSN TV (about 8 percent) were not sampled. One adult per household was sampled, independently of household size.

Table 14.2   Sample selection criteria and response rates, RPS 2005–2007

			RPS 2007		
	RPS 2005	RPS 2006	64 and older		
Age selection criteria	50 and older	63 and older[a]	Reinterview	Refreshment	Total
Completed RPS 2005		Yes[b]	Yes[b]	No	
Completed RPS 2006			No Yes	No	
KN members contacted	5,879	2,598	217 1,704	1,250	3,171
Completed interviews	4,738	2,137	165 1,526	1,020	2,711
Response rate[c]	80.6%	82.3%	76.0% 89.6%	81.6%	85.5%

[a]In addition, RPS 2005 respondents younger than sixty-three years were contacted for RPS 2006 if they said that they are on Medicare.

[b]Completion of RPS 2005 was required for this subsample.

[c]The cooperation rate is defined as the number of completed interviews as a proportion of the number of KN Panel members contacted.

ally rather high. For the first wave (RPS-2005), we contacted almost 6,000 KN Panel members age fifty and older, and 80.6 percent of those invited to participate completed the questionnaire. For RPS-2006, we contacted only KN members who had completed RPS-2005 and were age sixty-three years or older at the time of the interview (or in a few cases were younger but already on Medicare). The participation rate was again rather high at 82.3 percent. Finally, for RPS-2007 we used two samples: reinterviews of earlier RPS respondents (i.e., those who had completed either RPS-2005 only or both RPS-2005 and RPS-2006), and a refreshment sample of KN Panel members who had not participated in any prior RPS wave. The participation rate among these groups was the highest for those who had completed both RPS-2005 and RPS-2006 (89.6 percent) and slightly below the other rates for those who had completed RPS-2005 but missed RPS-2006 (76.6 percent). The participation rate for the refreshment sample was 81.5 percent and thus well in line with that in the comparable RPS-2005 sample. In private correspondence, KN indicated that the participation rates that were achieved for the RPS surveys were slightly above those typically observed in other studies that use the KN Panel; this is attributed to the highly topical subject of the surveys.

In sections 14.5 and 14.6, we use data from the RPS-2006 "core sample." This sample consists of 1,569 respondents who were sixty-five or older in May 2006, eligible for Part D, interviewed in both RPS-2005 and RPS-2006, and had no item nonresponse on key variables. Item nonresponse rates are generally very low in the KN Panel (less than 5 percent for most questions considered in this chapter). Most variables used in our analysis are based directly on the corresponding survey question. The key pharmacy bill variables (for 2005, 2006, and 2007) are measures of what the annual out-of-pocket drug costs would be for a person without any prescription drug insurance. They are constructed using procedures described later.

Descriptive statistics of key variables in the RPS samples are reported in table 14.3, along with corresponding statistics from the 2004 wave of the Health and Retirement Study (HRS).[7] We present both unweighted and weighted statistics. The RPS samples shown in this table are the 2005 full sample, the 2005/06 core sample, and the 2007 full sample. Table 14.3, panel A, compares the RPS-2005 full sample, which is based on a random selection of KN panel members age fifty and older, with the full HRS 2004 sample. The weighted RPS-2005 full sample is very similar to the weighted HRS sample with respect to key demographic variables. This is an expected result of the weighting protocols used in each survey.[8] The distribution of self-rated health in the RPS-2005 full sample is comparable to HRS-2004; but more compressed with fewer responses in the extreme categories. This difference may arise from both response effects and sampling issues. The HRS uses an auditory format (CATI) and RPS is a visual format, and both auditory sequence and visual range have small but predictable effects on response.[9] Sample selection is a factor, as the KN population is noninstitutionalized and sufficiently functional to follow the web TV protocol, while the HRS follows its panel subjects even when they are disabled or institutionalized. Third, the impact of weighting on the marginal distributions of key demographic variables is much stronger in HRS than in RPS; this is due to the complicated multicohort sample design of HRS. For an extended discussion of the role of weighting in the analysis of RPS data, see McFadden et al. (2006). Table 14.3, panel B, contains descriptive statistics for the 2005/06 core sample and the 2007 full sample, and the comparable HRS 2004 population age sixty-five and over. The core sample contains all RPS respondents who participated in both RPS-2005 and 2006 and who were older than sixty-five and on Medicare in 2005, while RPS-2007 contains all continuing RPS participants age sixty-five and older, refreshed with a new sample of KN panelists age sixty-five and over. This table shows that there are only minor variations in the distributions of key demographic variables across the three RPS subsamples.

The RPS data has been augmented with three other sources of data. First, the MCBS provides data on pharmacy bills for a four-year rolling panel with about 10,000 beneficiaries per year; we use the year 2000 to 2003 surveys. The MCBS data are currently available only through 2004, but CMS provided

---

7. We use the RAND version F of the HRS data.
8. The RPS sample responses were weighted by ranking iteratively to age interacted with the following demographic variables: gender, race/ethnicity, education, Census region, Income, and Internet Access.
9. Auditory respondents are slightly biased toward the last category mentioned, and visual respondents are slightly biased against the extremes of a range.

Table 14.3   **Descriptive statistics**

	A HRS 2004 and RPS 2005/06			
	HRS 2004 (Full sample)		RPS 2005 (Full sample)	
	Unweighted (%)	Weighted (%)	Unweighted (%)	Weighted (%)
Gender				
Female	57.6	54.1	53.8	54.0
Male	42.4	45.9	46.2	46.0
Race				
White	80.9	85.6	80.1	77.9
Non-white	19.1	14.4	19.0	21.3
Age				
50–60	28.5	44.2	45.3	46.0
61–70	34.4	26.6	30.1	27.7
71–80	23.0	19.2	19.0	19.3
81–90	12.0	8.9	5.3	6.5
> 90	2.1	1.0	0.3	0.4
Education				
Less than HS	27.9	22.8	12.0	17.3
High school	30.9	30.3	35.4	33.8
More than HS	41.2	46.9	52.6	48.8
Income				
< $20K	29.6	24.9	19.5	21.0
$20K–$60K	41.5	39.4	48.7	44.9
> $60K	28.9	35.7	31.8	34.1
SRHS				
Excellent	11.3	13.2	9.4	8.8
Very good	27.1	29.3	34.7	33.3
Good	31.3	30.9	34.8	35.3
Fair	20.8	18.5	16.2	17.4
Poor	9.5	8.1	4.9	5.1
Number of observations	19,279		4,738	

	B HRS 2004, RPS 2005/06, and RPS 2007					
	HRS 2004 (age 65 and older)		RPS 2005/06 (Core sample)		RPS 2007 (Full sample)	
	Unweighted (%)	Weighted (%)	Unweighted (%)	Weighted (%)	Unweighted (%)	Weighted (%)
Gender						
Female	57.4	57.1	56.0	57.4	56.6	57.2
Male	42.6	42.9	44.0	42.6	43.4	42.8
Race						
White	83.7	89.2	85.8	81.1	86.7	81.7
Non-white	16.3	10.8	12.5	17.1	11.7	16.9
Age						
50–60						
61–70	35.6	32.9	38.4	35.2	32.3	31.5
71–80	39.9	44.2	47.7	48.4	51.6	49.1
81–90	20.9	20.6	13.1	15.2	15.0	18.3
> 90	3.6	2.3	0.9	1.1	1.1	1.1

(*continued*)

Table 14.3   (continued)

	B HRS 2004, RPS 2005/06, and RPS 2007					
	HRS 2004 (age 65 and older)		RPS 2005/06 (Core sample)		RPS 2007 (Full sample)	
	Unweighted (%)	Weighted (%)	Unweighted (%)	Weighted (%)	Unweighted (%)	Weighted (%)
Education						
Less than HS	32.8	29.6	12.6	25.9	12.4	23.5
High school	32.5	33.7	41.7	36.6	42.1	37.6
More than HS	34.7	36.7	45.7	37.4	45.6	38.9
Income						
< $20K	36.1	34.0	23.5	28.8	23.5	26.1
$20K–$60K	45.6	46.6	58.1	52.4	58.4	53.8
> $60K	18.3	19.4	18.5	18.8	18.1	20.0
SRHS						
Excellent	8.4	8.9	6.1	5.6	3.5	3.1
Very good	25.4	26.8	31.9	27.8	29.7	26.6
Good	32.4	33.4	40.0	42.4	42.4	43.3
Fair	23.1	21.6	17.9	19.4	19.9	22.0
Poor	10.6	9.3	4.1	4.8	0.044	5.0
Number of observations	11,113		1,569		2,711	

an early release in 2005 of projected pharmacy bills in 2005 and 2006, adjusted for drug prices and for sample undercounting. Providers of Part D plans used this information for actuarial calculations of the expected cost of alternative plans, and we do as well. Second, we assembled data on median retail prices of about 100 of the most heavily used drugs in 2006, and 200 of the most heavily used drugs in 2007, primarily from secondary sources such as the American Association of Retired Persons (AARP) website. We used these data to estimate the pharmacy bill of each RPS respondent, based on the inventory of drugs that they report taking, and imputing the cost of drugs with missing prices. We mapped respondent estimates obtained in this way into the 2006 MCBS distribution of pharmacy bills by matching the empirical distribution of RPS bills to quantiles of the MCBS distribution. We followed the same procedure in 2007, with an adjustment for drug price levels. Details on our construction of pharmacy bills can be found in Winter et al. (2006). Third, we use U.S. standard life tables, classified by gender—but not by race—to predict mortality.

14.5   Consumers' Decisions in the Initial Enrollment Period

In this section, we describe the enrollment decisions of the "active deciders" among the RPS-2006 respondents, the RPS-2006 core respondents who were not automatically enrolled in a Part D plan because of prior coverage by a provider that coordinated with Medicare, such as an employer health plan or a Medicare Advantage plan, or because of Medicaid, military, or veteran status. We look at three aspects of these respondents' decisions: whether they enrolled, when they enrolled, and what plan they chose. This analysis is descriptive, but it nevertheless sheds light on how consumer's behavior responds to the economic incentives in the Medicare Part D market.

14.5.1   Features of Respondents

In the RPS-2006 core sample of 1,569 respondents, 443 respondents are classified as *active deciders*. Among those, 349 (78.6 percent) enrolled in a Part D stand-alone plan; 94 (21.4 percent) remain uncovered. Table 14.4 summarizes the enrollment status of all 1,569 core respondents, along with breakdowns along various demographic dimensions as well as year 2005 drug use and expenditure. Of the 349 active deciders who enrolled, 319 provided the exact name of their plan, allowing us to determine plan features such as premium and gap coverage from the landscape of plans provided by CMS.

14.5.2   Enrollment and Enrollment Timing

The expected payoff of enrolling in a Part D stand-alone plan consists of two components: the expected current value (CV) (defined as expected 2006 benefits less 2006 premiums) and the expected present value (PV) of the benefit of avoiding premium penalties in case of future enrollment. The PV component involves future events and choices, and is difficult to evaluate. However, a positive CV is already a sufficient condition for enrollment for risk-neutral or risk-averse consumers, so it is useful to see whether enrollment reacts to factors that influence CV.

As noted before, the initial enrollment period began on November 15, 2005 and ended on May 15, 2006. Coverage in the initial enrollment period began in the month after enrollment (in January 2006 if already enrolled in 2005). Thus, decisions in the initial enrollment period have a second dimension—consumers not only had to decide whether to sign up for a Part D stand-alone plan, they had to choose when to sign up. To characterize the timing dimension, we consider a stylized description of the decision problem.

An individual decides at the beginning of the enrollment period whether to enroll early (Nov/Dec 2005), late (May 2006), or not at all. Let p denote the yearly premium and PV the expected present value of the option of avoiding a premium penalty for enrollment in Part D after 2006. We leave PV unspecified for the purpose of the current descriptive analysis, and specify it fully in the intertemporal optimization model presented in section 14.6. Let c_y denote the pharmacy bill in year y. For the current analysis, assume that these bills have a normal random effects stochastic structure, with censor-

Table 14.4   Prescription drug insurance status after the initial enrollment period

	No coverage	Automatic	Private	Part D	Total
Observations	94	827	299	349	1,569
%	5.99	52.71	19.06	22.2	100.0
2005 drug costs (dollars)					
Mean	1,411.3	2,574.2	2,610.6	2,766.9	2,554.3
1st quartile	0.0	748.0	685.4	843.9	685.4
Median	93.8	1,996.5	1,671.4	1,981.4	1,878.8
3rd quartile	1,492.5	3,479.6	3,330.1	3,333.2	3,338.4
Total prescription drug cost in 2005					
$0	39.4	10.6	12.0	9.7	12.4
$1 to $250	16.0	6.9	7.7	6.6	7.5
$251 to $1,000	9.6	9.7	10.7	8.9	9.7
$1,001 to $2,250	20.2	27.8	29.1	32.7	28.7
$2,251 to $5,100	8.5	32.4	27.8	29.2	29.4
$5,101 or more	6.4	12.6	12.7	12.9	12.3
Total number of prescription drugs taken in 2005					
No drugs	38.3	10.5	12.0	9.7	12.3
1 or 2 drugs	34.0	24.4	30.4	29.2	27.2
3 or more drugs	27.7	65.1	57.5	61.0	60.5
Self-reported health status					
Excellent	20.2	5.3	7.0	6.6	6.8
Very good or good	62.8	71.7	69.9	73.0	71.1
Poor or fair	17.0	23.0	23.1	20.4	22.1
Age class					
70 years or younger	38.3	42.3	39.1	45.9	42.3
71 to 75 years	37.2	27.6	27.4	24.4	27.4
76 years or more	24.5	30.1	33.4	29.8	30.3
Sex					
Male	35.1	50.1	36.5	38.7	44.0
Female	64.9	49.9	63.6	61.3	56.0
Education class					
More than high school	38.3	49.0	42.8	42.4	45.7
High school or less	61.7	51.0	57.2	57.6	54.3
Income class					
$20,000 or less	30.9	20.9	31.1	28.1	25.1
$20,001 to $60,000	58.5	58.7	51.5	56.5	56.8
$60,001 or more	10.6	20.4	17.4	15.5	18.2

Notes: "Private" includes prescription drug coverage as part of a Medicare Advantage program. "Part D" includes only Part D stand-alone plans.

ing below at zero; that is, there is a latent bill $c_y^* = \mu + \eta\lambda + \zeta_y\gamma$, where μ is a mean, η is a persistent individual standard normal random effect, the ζ_y are independent i.i.d. standard normal disturbances, λ and γ are standard deviations, and $c_y = \max\{0, c_y^*\}$. We fit this model by maximum likelihood to 2005 and 2006 RPS pharmacy bills, with top-censoring of bills at $12,000 to reduce the influence of extreme outliers that may be mismeasured, and estimate $\mu = 2{,}027.7$, $\lambda = 2{,}672.5$, and $\gamma = 1{,}759.9$. In a Monte Carlo simulation of 8,000 bills for 2005 and 2006, c_y has mean \$2,548, standard deviation \$2,469, and a correlation of 0.61 between 2005 and 2006 bills. The probability of a zero bill is 0.26 in the simulation, higher than the observed probability of 0.15, with conditional probabilities of 0.61 of a zero bill in 2006 given a zero bill in 2005, and of 0.12 of a zero bill in 2006 given a positive bill in 2005.

Assume that to first-order, individuals cannot control the timing of drug bills during the year. Suppose latent monthly bills satisfy $c^*_{yt} = (\mu + \eta\lambda)/12 + \zeta_{yt}\gamma/(12)^{1/2}$, where the ζ_{yt} are i.i.d. standard normal monthly disturbances. Then the sum of latent monthly bills over twelve months gives the model shown previously for the annual latent bill, $c^*_y = \mu + \eta\lambda + \zeta_y\gamma$. Similarly, the latent bill for the last seven months of 2006 is $c^*_{6-12:06} = 7(\mu + \eta\lambda)/12 + \zeta_{6-12:06}\gamma^*$, where $\zeta_{6-12:06}$ is standard normal and $\gamma^* = \gamma(7/12)^{1/2} = 1{,}344.0$. Assume that the realized bill for this seven month period is again censored, $c_{6-12:06} = \max\{0, c^*_{6-12:06}\}$. The sum of left-censored latent variables is at least as large as the left-censored sum of latent variables, so that the assumption that both the full year and the seven-month bills can be represented as left-censored normals is an approximation.

Assume that consumers know the persistent component of their latent annual bill, $c^\# = \mu + \eta\lambda$. The expected annual bill given $c^\#$ is then $Ec_y = \int_0^\infty c\phi((c - c^\#)/\gamma)dc/\gamma = c^\#\Phi(c^\#/\gamma) + \gamma\phi(c^\#/\gamma)$. Under the Medicare Part D Standard plan in 2006, the benefits formula is

(1) $B(c) = 0.75 \cdot \min\{2{,}000, \max(0, c - 250)\} + 0.95 \cdot \max(0, c - 5{,}100)$,

where c is the pharmacy bill covered by the plan. The expected current benefit from enrollment for the full year, given $c^\#$, is

$$
\begin{aligned}
CV_{12} &= \mathbf{E}B(c_{06}) - 12p \\
&= 0.75 \int_{250}^{2{,}250} (c - 250)\phi((c - c^\#)/\gamma)dc/\gamma + 1{,}500 \cdot \Phi((c^\# - 2{,}250)/\gamma) \\
&\quad + 0.95 \int_{5{,}100}^{\infty} (c - 5{,}100)\phi((c - c^\#)/\gamma)dc/\gamma - 12p \\
&= -12p + 0.75(c^\# - 250)(\Phi((c^\# - 250)/\gamma) - \Phi((c^\# - 2{,}250)/\gamma)) \\
&\quad + 1{,}500 \cdot \Phi((c^\# - 2{,}250)/\gamma) \\
&\quad + 0.75\gamma(\phi((c^\# - 250)/\gamma) - \phi((c^\# - 2{,}250)/\gamma)) \\
&\quad + 0.95(c^\# - 5{,}100)\Phi((c^\# - 5{,}100)/\gamma) + 0.95\gamma\phi((c^\# - 5{,}100)/\gamma).
\end{aligned}
$$

Let $c^\% = 7c^\#/12$. The expected current benefit from enrollment for the last seven months is

$$CV_7 = \mathbf{E}B(c_{6-12:06}) - 7p$$

$$= 0.75 \int_{250}^{2,250} (c - 250)\phi((c - c^{\%})/\gamma^*)dc + 1,500 \cdot \Phi((c^{\%} - 2,250)/\gamma^*)$$

$$+ 0.95 \int_{5,100}^{\infty} (c - 5,100)\phi((c - c^{\%})/\gamma^*)dc - 7p$$

$$= -7p + 0.75(c^{\%} - 250)(\Phi((c^{\%} - 250)/\gamma^*) - \Phi((c^{\%} - 2,250)/\gamma^*))$$

$$+ 1,500 \cdot \Phi((c^{\%} - 2,250)/\gamma^*)$$

$$+ 0.75\gamma^*(\phi((c^{\%} - 250)/\gamma^*) - \phi((c^{\%} - 2,250)/\gamma^*))$$

$$+ 0.95(c^{\%} - 5,100)\Phi((c^{\%} - 5,100)/\gamma^*)$$

$$+ 0.95\gamma^*\Phi((c^{\%} - 5,100)/\gamma^*).$$

Figure 14.2 gives the values of CV_{12} and CV_7 plotted against 2006 expected pharmacy bill. Empirically, we find that if $CV_{12} > CV_7$, which occurs at expected 2006 pharmacy bills above \$950, then $CV_{12} > 0$ and early enrollment is optimal. However, if $CV_7 > CV_{12}$, then there is a more complicated decision on whether to enroll late or not at all, depending on whether $CV_7 + PV$ is positive. A myopic consumer who ignores PV will not enroll at an expected pharmacy bill below \$300; increasing PV would lower this threshold.

When allowing individuals to decide month by month whether to enroll or delay enrollment, new information may make enrollment beneficial in the middle of the enrollment period. However, the probability of significant new information within a few months is low, so one would expect peaks of enrollment at the beginning of the enrollment period (for people who immediately

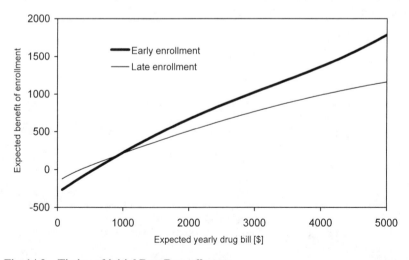

Fig. 14.2   **Timing of initial Part D enrollment**

benefit) and at the end where avoiding the penalty becomes relevant. The distribution of months in which the sample of RPS respondents enrolled is shown in figure 14.3. As expected, there are peaks at the beginning and at the end of the initial enrollment period (even though November 2005 and May 2006 each had only fifteen "enrollment days").

For further analysis, the sample is split into four groups of respondents. Details can be found in table 14.5. As argued before, individuals with high drug costs should sign up early, those with intermediate drug costs or high present value of the penalty should sign up late, and for the others, it might be rational not to sign up at all. The distribution of drug costs differs significantly between the four groups. Conditional means, medians, and tenth and ninetieth percentiles are also presented in table 14.5. The empirical cumulative distributive functions (CDFs) are given in figure 14.4; pairwise

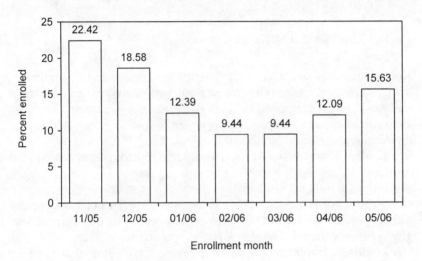

Fig. 14.3   Distribution of enrollment month

Table 14.5   Distribution of the month of Part D enrollment among active deciders

	November–December	January–March	April–May	Not enrolled	Total
Observations	139	106	94	94	433
%	32.1	24.5	21.7	21.7	100.0
2005 drug costs (dollars)					
Mean	3,376.8	2,802.9	1,887.0	1,411.3	2,486.2
1st decile	685.4	142.5	0.0	0.0	0.0
Median	2,364.7	1,968.0	1,140.4	93.8	1,614.0
9th decile	7,095.7	5,477.9	5,279.8	3,117.1	5,477.9

Notes: Ten respondents without information on the enrollment month are excluded.

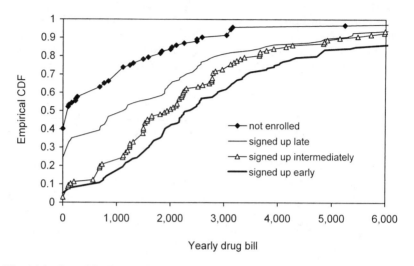

Fig. 14.4   Drug bill distribution by enrollment

Kolmogorov-Smirnov tests confirm that they are statistically significantly different from each other (all pairwise p-values are smaller than 0.01 except for "early" versus "intermediate," which has $p = 0.07$). Current drug costs appear to have a strong impact on enrollment, especially on early enrollment by December 2005 and additional enrollment by March 2006. Additional late enrollment in April or May does not seem to strongly depend on 2005 drug costs.

Next, we present results from logit models for enrollment with dummies for categories of drug costs. A specification with splines and a semiparametric specification with an additive nonparametric function of drug costs give essentially the same results. A few socioeconomic variables are added. Odds ratios for enrollment are presented in the first column of table 14.6.[10] Drug costs in 2005 are very strong predictors of enrollment. Younger seniors (under seventy years of age) are more likely to enroll. As might be expected, those in "excellent" Self-Reported Health Status (SRHS) are less likely to enroll, even controlling for drug costs. Poor or fair (SRHS) also decreases the enrollment probability relative to the intermediate SRHS category, which may indicate that those in poor health had more difficulty in evaluating the program and completing the enrollment process.

The table also shows results from logit models of enrollment timing. As argued before, the rational decision whether to enroll early mainly depends on whether the individual expects immediate benefits in 2006, since delay-

10. Consider a binomial logit model $P = 1/(1 + \exp(-\beta_0 - \beta_1 D))$, where D is a dummy variable with coefficient β_1, and β_0 summarizes the effect of other covariates. Then, $P/(1 - P) = \exp(\beta_0 + \beta_1 D)$ is called the *odds,* and the ratio of the odds when $D = 1$ and $D = 0$, equal to $\exp(\beta_1)$, is called the *odds ratio.*

Table 14.6   **Logit analysis of the active enrollment decision**

	Enrollment	Enrollment by March 06	Late enrollment given not enrolled by March 06
2005 drug costs (reference category is $0)			
$1 to $250	1.5898	3.0426**	1.064
$251 to $1,000	4.53***	5.84***	2.65*
$1,001 to $2,250	7.33***	13.48***	2.42*
$2,251 to $5,100	16.48***	17.12***	4.62***
$5,101 or more	9.74***	12.47***	2.55
p-value for F-test	(< 0.0001)	(< 0.0001)	(0.0728)
Socioeconomic variables			
71 to 75 years	0.4498**	0.8006	0.4835*
76 years or more	0.72	0.89	0.78
Female	0.73	1.10	0.49**
High school or less	0.67	0.98	0.58
Income less than $30,000	0.88	0.97	0.78
SRHS excellent	0.37**	0.87	0.26***
SRHS poor or fair	0.45**	0.94	0.34**
p-value for F-test	(0.0193)	(0.9933)	(0.0152)
Observations	432	432	188

Notes: Coefficients reported in this table are odds ratios; all covariates are coded as dummy variables.
***Significant at the 1 percent level.
**Significant at the 5 percent level.
*Significant at the 10 percent level.
(For a two-sided *t*-test.)

ing enrollment until the deadline in May did not cause a premium penalty. Then, the decision to enroll early should depend primarily on expected drug costs in 2006, which are highly correlated with drug costs in 2005. The second column of table 14.6 shows logit results for early enrollment (defined as being enrolled by March 2006). The results are as expected for rational individuals. Drug costs in 2005 are a very strong predictor of early enrollment, while the sociodemographic variables have no significant impact. Late enrollment within the initial enrollment period is rational for individuals who do not expect immediate benefits in 2006 but want to avoid the penalty. The present value of avoiding the penalty depends on the whole trajectory of future drug costs. Those are also correlated with 2005 drug costs but weaker than 2006 costs. In addition to that, individual expectations, tastes, and the understanding of the penalty and its expected present value drive the decision whether to enroll late or not at all, given that early enrollment is not beneficial.

The final column of table 14.6 shows logit results for whether individuals enroll late (April or May 2006), given that they did not enroll early (by March 2006). Note that this is not a structural behavioral model since it ignores self-selection. The results show that among those not enrolled early, 2005 drug costs do predict late enrollment, but only weakly. On the other hand, socioeconomic variables become important predictors. They may reflect health and other expectations, information, and/or tastes. Taken together, the models in table 14.6 show that the strong predictive power of drug costs for total enrollment (column [1]) is mainly driven by early enrollers (column [2]), while the enrollment differentials by socioeconomic variables are mainly driven by late enrollers (column [3]). This is consistent with a view that most individuals understood at least the gross attributes of the initial enrollment alternatives and the incentives they faced.

14.5.3   The CMS Subsidy, and Enhanced Plan Features and Premiums

The mechanism used by CMS to subsidize Part D plan sponsors determines the premiums for the Standard plan, and affects the cost to sponsors of offering enhanced plans. Key features of the mechanism are established in the Medicare Prescription Drug Improvement and Modernization Act (MMA) of 2003. Descriptions of the mechanism are given in Congressional Budget Office (CBO) (2004), CMS (2005), Medpac (2006), and Simon and Lucarelli (2006). The essential features of the benefit formulas and subsidy mechanism are summarized here for completeness.

The CMS subsidy of plan sponsors has two components: a direct subsidy, paid prospectively, and reinsurance of a share of catastrophic benefits, paid retrospectively. The prospective payments include risk adjustments for the sponsor's enrollee mix that are intended to neutralize adverse selection, and premium subsidies for qualified low-income enrollees. A key feature of the subsidy mechanism is that sponsors submit bids annually to CMS for their anticipated costs of providing benefits to a representative Part D enrollee, including administrative costs and return on capital, but excluding reinsurance of catastrophic benefits. The CMS then processes these bids to produce a national base premium that covers 25.5 percent of the prospective national average total benefits and administrative cost of a representative Part D enrollee (including reinsurance cost), and an associated base direct subsidy equal to the national average bid less the base premium. Premiums for individual plans are then set to the plan's bid less the base direct subsidy. As a consequence, each plan has a premium that when added to the base direct subsidy equals the plan's bid, and the plan bid determines its premium. The principle behind the Part D market design is that competition for enrollees should limit the ability of plan sponsors to profit from increasing their bids, encourage cost-saving, and drive bids toward actual long-run cost.[11]

---

11. Two phenomena may lead to outcomes that are not strictly competitive. First, the Part D market is dominated by two firms, Humana and United Healthcare (AARP), with a fringe of smaller rivals. These firms have sufficient market power to influence the national average bid, and the consequent CMS direct subsidy. Second, the churn rate for enrollees is low, and this created incentives for sponsors to offer low initial premiums to establish large enrollee bases whose relative immobility might later be exploited to shelter their plans from competition.

The notation we use to describe the Standard plan benefit is defined in table 14A.1 in the appendix.

As indicated by these formulas, if an enrollee has an annual pharmacy bill (APB), then she will receive a basic benefit (BB) equal to 75 percent of the APB above a deductible of DED, up to gap threshold (GTH).[12] In the gap above this threshold, the enrollee pays all pharmacy costs until her APB reaches the catastrophic pharmacy bill threshold (CTH) at which her true out-of-pocket (TrOOP) cost reaches TTH, after which she is entitled to a catastrophic benefit CB, equal to 95 percent of the APB above CTH.[13] The TrOOP formula is TrOOP = min{TTH,APB − BB} + 0.05 · CPB. Classes of drugs excluded from Part D coverage, and drugs not in the plan formulary, are *not* counted in the APB used in the TrOOP calculation. Part D premiums are also excluded from TrOOP. The plan sponsor can influence the APB and benefits under this schedule through its formulary, through incentives to physicians and pharmacies to substitute generic for branded drugs, and through the prices of covered drugs it negotiates with pharmaceutical companies.[14]

The notation in table 14A.2 will be used to detail the subsidy mechanism. The key steps by CMS in determining the direct subsidy are the averaging of sponsor bids for standard and actuarially equivalent plans to form the national average bid (NBID), an estimate by CMS of the proportion r of catastrophic reinsurance in total benefit and administrative cost, and from this an estimate of national average total cost NTC = NBID/$(1 − r)$. The base annual premium (BAP) is mandated to equal 25.5 percent of NTC. The base direct subsidy then equals 74.5 percent of NTC, less the expected catastrophic reinsurance. If a plan bid equals NBID, then its premium equals BAP. More generally, the plan annual premium (APR) equals the base annual premium plus the difference between the plan bid and the national average bid, APR = BAP + BID − NBID, or zero if this expression is negative. The quantities NBID and BAP are unknown to the sponsor at the time bids are submitted, and are largely outside the sponsor's influence. By construction, when APR is positive, the prospective revenue,

---

12. Actuarially equivalent plans have the same DED and GTH, and alternative cost-sharing arrangements (e.g., copayment tiers for generic, preferred branded, and nonpreferred branded drugs, rather than a percentage copayment) that yield the same expected BB. Basic alternative plans also yield the same expected BB, but can alter both the deductible and cost-sharing arrangements; they typically have a zero deductible.

13. Enrollees in the gap are entitled to the established prices for formulary drugs.

14. The CMS requires that each sponsor appoint a Pharmacy and Therapeutics (P&T) Committee of physicians and pharmacists to determine its formulary, requires that "formularies must include drug categories and classes that cover all disease states," stipulates that "each category or class must include at least two drugs (unless only one drug is available for a particular category or class, or only two drugs are available but one drug is clinically superior to the other for a particular category or class), regardless of the classification system that is utilized," and reviews compliance with these requirements and additional conditions to ensure that the formulary does not substantially discourage enrollment in the plan by beneficiaries with certain disease states; see CMS (2006, "Chapter 6: Part D Drugs and Formulary Requirements").

base direct subsidy plus the plan average premium, satisfies BDS + APR = $(0.745 - r) \cdot$ NBID/$(1 - r)$ + BAP + BID − NBID = BID. If APR = 0, then prospective revenue exceeds the plan bid. Then, the sponsor's bid determines its premium, and its position in the competition for enrollees, and prospectively it expects revenue to be at least as large as its bid.

The actual direct subsidy to a plan sponsor is determined by adjusting its bid for the case mix of its enrollees, with the objective of neutralizing adverse selection. Each member of the population of prospective enrollees (submitted by the sponsor) is given a risk weight, using a prescription drug hierarchical condition category (RxHCC) specified by CMS that depends on diagnoses, sex, age, and disabled status. They are averaged to obtain a RxHCC weight, which then multiplies the plan's bid. Other enrollee mix factors are applied to account for low-income and institutionalized status. The result is a case-mix adjusted plan bid. The actual plan direct subsidy PDS then equals the case-mix adjusted plan bid less the enrollee premium,

PDS = BID $\cdot$ [RxHCC weight]
$\cdot$ [Low-income and institutionalized-status weight] − APR.

If the plan has a nationally representative case mix, then the adjustment weights are one, and PDS equals BDS. More generally, to the extent that the case-mix weights accurately capture differences in benefit costs attributable to observable patient characteristics, the weighting will neutralize adverse selection, removing the incentive for the sponsor to selectively discourage enrollment or reenrollment by patients with observed characteristics that are associated with high benefit costs. The RxHCC classification system and risk factor models are described in Robst, Levy, and Ingber (2007).[15]

There are additional adjustments to CMS subsidies that provide prospective payments for low-income premium subsidies and catastrophic reinsurance, with reconciliation after the end of each year. Finally, there are "symmetric risk corridors" that reduced risk to sponsors via a profit-sharing arrangement in the initial years of operation of the new Part D market; this feature is designed to disappear over time.

Next consider enhanced alternative plans that provide gap coverage, and

15. Risk adjustment weights are effective in neutralizing adverse selection incentives if each observationally distinguishable patient group has the same risk-weight deflated expected benefit cost to the sponsor. They will not be completely effective if the sponsor finds groups that, in interaction with its formulary and benefit schedule, have higher or lower deflated expected benefit cost. The models used to obtain risk weights explain a relatively low proportion of the variance in annual pharmacy bills. This is not in itself a barrier to effective neutralization, but it leaves opportunities for data mining that may identify groups for whom deflation is imperfect. In particular, risk adjustment weights tuned to neutralize adverse selection for universal Standard plan benefits are unlikely to neutralize adverse selection incentives in extended plan benefits, or even in Standard plan benefits once nonenrollment and selection among plans makes Standard plan benefits nonuniversal. Sponsors seeking to profit from imperfect neutralization are likely to look for diagnostic interactions that are not captured by the RxHCC classification, higher-order interactions that are omitted from the essentially linear additive models used by CMS to calculate the risk weights, and statistical inaccuracies.

the CMS subsidies they receive. Three coverage levels have been offered by these plans: all formulary drugs, more restrictively generic drugs, and even more restrictively "preferred" generic drugs. These plans extend the basic coverage copayment terms into the gap. These plans are affected by a feature of the MMA that specifies a TrOOP threshold for catastrophic benefits, and excludes supplemental premium payments from the calculation of TrOOP. Then, enhanced coverage that lowers TrOOP increases the pharmacy bill threshold CTH for catastrophic benefits, and reduces the reinsurance component of the CMS subsidy. Consequently, there is in effect a tax on gap coverage that partly offsets the CMS subsidy. Recognizing this disincentive to enhanced plans, CMS established a Part D payment demonstration to "allow private sector plans maximum flexibility to design alternative prescription drug coverage." This demonstration allows some classes of sponsors of enhanced plans to select a "capitated option" and receive an "actuarially equivalent" capitated payment for catastrophic coverage in lieu of catastrophic reinsurance. Excluded from the demonstration are PACE and employer-subsidized plans. The capitated payment is determined by calculating the case-mix adjusted reinsurance payments expected for enrollees in the extended plan if they had instead been enrolled in the standard plan.

Sponsors electing capitation have Flexible Capitation and Fixed Capitation options. Under the flexible option, catastrophic coverage does not commence until TrOOP reaches TTH. Then there is a range of APB above the standard plan CTH ($5,100 in 2006) where TrOOP is below TTH, and the beneficiary copayment is the same as in the basic benefit range (25 percent) rather than the catastrophic copayment rate of 5 percent. This reduces the value of the extended benefit relative to the standard plan, but increases the pool of revenue the sponsor can use to reduce the supplementary premium for extended benefits. Under the fixed capitation option, catastrophic coverage commences at the standard plan threshold CTH, and the TrOOP threshold is ignored.

To evaluate extended plans offering generic coverage, it is necessary to determine the share of generic drugs in the APB. Utilizing 1,833 observations on specific drugs used by respondents in RPS-2007, their generic classification, and their average market prices, we regress the share of generics in drug expenditures on the reciprocal of APB for APB satisfying $1 < APB < $10,000 and obtain an intercept of 0.341 (SE = 0.009) and a slope coefficient of 3.183 (SE = 0.560). Then, the estimated generic expenditure share is over 50 percent for low APB, but in the gap where this allocation affects extended benefits and TrOOP, it is near 34 percent. Our generic expenditure shares are similar in pattern but somewhat higher than those found several years earlier by Dana Goldman in a sample of age sixty-five and over retirees from a large firm.[16] We cannot determine whether this is due to the limitations of the drug information collected in RPS-2007, or is the result of recent generic

16. Private communication.

competition in several popular drug categories, and incentives to physicians and pharmacists from Part D sponsors to dispense generics.

14.5.4   Plan Choice

Next, we turn to plan choice of those core respondents who enrolled in a Medicare Part D stand-alone plan. We examine both choices across different types of plans, and choice of sponsor within plans of a given type. We do not consider choices of Medicare Advantage (MA) plans, which involve broader health care decisions, including choice of HMO or fee-for-service care. Table 14.7 reproduces summary information from a CMS website for consumers that provides a landscape of alternative stand-alone plans. This website contains a "plan finder" for consumers that identifies plans with formularies that include the consumer's current drugs, and for each of these plans estimate the consumer's expected TrOOP in the coming year.[17] The average number of distinct plans available in a state was 42.5 in 2006, 54.7 in 2007, and 53.4 in 2008. In 2006, the number of plans available in the various states ranged from seventeen to fifty-two. Between 2006 and 2008, the share of Standard or actuarially equivalent plans available has remained around one-third, the share of basic alternative plans that eliminate the deductible has fallen from 51 percent to 38 percent, the share of enhanced plans that offer gap coverage for generics has risen from 13 percent to 29 percent, and the share of enhanced plans that offer gap coverage for all formulary drugs has fallen from 2.5 percent to near zero. Average monthly premiums have decreased slightly from 2006 for Standard and actuarially equivalent plans, and enhanced plans that cover the deductible, and have increased substantially for enhanced plans offering gap coverage for generics.[18] The average premium for enhanced plans with full gap coverage shows a major increase between 2006 and 2007, and in 2008 this coverage was unavailable except for one plan in Florida. One interpretation of these observations is that providers of plans with full coverage experienced higher than expected drug bills in 2006 due to adverse selection and/or moral hazard, and adjusted their plans accordingly.

We asked the RPS Part D enrollees what plan they chose using a two-stage procedure during which they were first presented with a list of plan providers active in their state, and then with a list of plans offered by that firm. Information on all available plans' features comes from a database available on the CMS website. Because of variations in plan formularies as

17. The plan finder is a useful tool for consumers, but by concentrating on current drug use, it facilitates myopic choice in which the consumer ignores the risks of altered drug requirements in the future.
18. There is an actuarial relationship between the average Standard plan premium calculated and posted by CMS as part of their determination of the subsidy to plan sponsors, and averages calculated from posted premiums on the CMS website. However, due to features of the CMS calculation, particularly adjustments for health risk in the projected population of beneficiaries of a plan, the averages are not identical.

Table 14.7   **Types of plans, all plans available (excluding territories)**

	Share (%)			Average premium ($/mo)		
	2006	2007	2008	2006	2007	2008
Standard or actuarially equivalent benefit	34.0	31.1	32.8	$30.75	$27.70	$28.41
No or reduced deductible, no gap coverage	50.6	40.0	38.0	$37.92	$31.93	$33.12
Gap coverage for generics	12.9	27.5	29.2	$48.13	$51.03	$63.34
Gap coverage for generics and brand-name drugs	2.5	1.4	0.0	$61.88	$96.92	$49.40
Total	100.0	100.0	100.0	$37.36	$36.71	$40.39
Average number of plans per state	42.5	54.7	53.4			

well as plan features such as copay and tier arrangements, deductible, and gap coverage for generics or for all drugs, individuals face a complex set of alternatives. However, plans can be switched annually with no cost other than the time and bother. Unless individuals choose plans strategically to reduce the burden of future switching, plan choice should depend only on expected benefits in 2006.

For 316 of the 349 respondents with individual stand-alone insurance (92 percent) in 2006, the information that subjects provide in RPS is sufficient to identify the specific plan they chose. Table 14.8 shows the distribution of drug costs by enrollment status and plan features. "Cheapest plan" indicates whether the individual enrolled in the plan with the lowest premium available in his or her state. Figure 14.5, panel A, shows the distribution of the premiums of all 2,166 plans that were available for 2006, stratified into four coverage classes: standard plans, actuarially equivalent plans, and two types of enhanced plans (one with gap coverage only for generic drugs, the other with gap coverage for generic and brand drugs). As expected, premiums are higher for the enhanced plans. More importantly, there is considerable variation in plan premiums in each coverage class. Figure 14.5, panel B, shows similar distributions for those plans that were chosen by the RPS respondents. A comparison of the two figures shows that RPS respondents tended to choose cheaper plans in each of the categories, and also to concentrate on a few plans in each category, in particular among the equivalent plans. The plan that was in highest demand in this group was the United Healthcare plan endorsed by AARP, which had a 30 percent share among RPS respondents who enrolled in a stand-alone plan (see table 14.9). The market shares we obtained from RPS-2006 data are well in line with those computed using official CMS data by Cubanski and Neuman (2006, table 1).

Table 14.10 shows results from ordinary least squares (OLS) and quantile regressions for chosen plan premiums, using the same covariates as in table 14.6. Higher pharmacy bills substantially increase chosen plan premiums, especially in the lower part of the APB distribution. The socioeconomic variables have almost zero explanatory power. Table 14.11 presents odds ratios

Table 14.8   2006 enrollment decisions, plan attributes, and 2005 drug costs

| | | | 2005 drug costs | |
	Observation	Column %	Mean	Median
Total	1,569	0.0	2,554.3	1,878.8
Enrollment of active deciders				
No	94	21.2	1,411.3	93.8***
Yes	349	78.8	2,766.9	1,981.4
Information on chosen plan				
No	31	8.9	2,801.9	2,168.9
Yes	318	91.1	2,763.4	1,934.5
Cheapest plan				
Yes	252	79.2	2,882.3	2,142.5**
No	66	20.8	2,309.7	1,497.0
Monthly premium				
$20 or less	93	29.2	2,248.0	1,492.5***
$21 to $30	141	44.3	2,822.0	1,898.6
$31 or more	84	26.4	3,235.9	2,544.5
Deductible				
Yes	117	36.8	2,650.3	1,878.8
No	201	63.2	2,829.3	2,010.8
Gap coverage				
No	288	90.6	2,679.5	1,883.5***
Yes	30	9.4	3,569.7	3,449.9

***Significant at the 1 percent level.
**Significant at the 5 percent level.
(Corresponding to tests of equal medians.)

from logit regressions where the dependent variables are various classifications of choice among "cheap" or "bare-bones" plans versus the remainder. A cheap plan is defined in the first column as one with a premium less than $10/month, in the second column as the cheapest of all available plans in the respondent's state, and the third column as a Part D Standard plan (with no deductible or gap coverage). A high ABP substantially decreases the probability of enrolling in a cheap or "bare-bones" plan. Tables 14.10 and 14.11 support the proposition that individuals who enroll in order to avoid the penalty but do not expect immediate benefits rationally choose cheap or "bare-bones" plans since there is no monetary cost to switching plans in future years.

Table 14.12 reports market shares and average premiums for those plans that were chosen by RPS respondents in 2006 and 2007. The changes between 2006 and 2007 are similar to those observed on the supply side (table 14.7). In particular, demand for plans with full gap coverage almost vanished in our sample.

To analyze the impact of the CMS subsidy mechanism on premiums and the value of alternative plans to beneficiaries, we utilize the distribution of

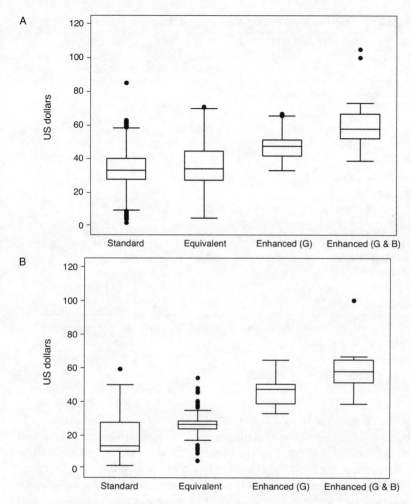

Fig. 14.5 Premiums of Part D plans by coverage type: *A,* All plans available for 2006; *B,* Plans chosen by RPS 2006 respondents

Table 14.9   Top five plans purchased by RPS 2006 respondents

Rank	Plan name	N	Share (%)	Mean premium (dollars)	Plan type
1	AARP Medicare Rx Plan	93	29.15	25.95	Equivalent
2	Humana PDP Standard	66	20.69	8.96	Standard
3	Humana PDP Enhanced	18	5.64	13.67	Equivalent
4	Humana PDP Complete	12	3.76	53.93	Enhanced (G & B)
5	Pacificare Saver Plan	10	3.13	24.63	Equivalent
	Other plans	120	37.62	33.59	
Total		319	100	25.63	

Table 14.10   **Regression analysis of premiums of chosen Part D plans**

		Quantile regression: Percentiles		
	OLS	Median	20th	80th
2005 drug costs (reference category is $0)				
$1 to $250	7.31*	9.18***	3.01	2.26
$251 to $1,000	1.94	4.50**	3.95	−0.16
$1,001 to $2,250	8.84***	9.88***	9.58**	2.63
$2,251 to $5,100	13.12***	11.65***	14.74***	12.97***
$5,101 or more	10.42***	10.97***	12.50**	2.95
Socioeconomic variables				
71 to 75 years	−0.07	0.02	4.43	−2.13
76 years or more	0.84	−1.22	4.79	−1.11
Female	−1.44	−1.67*	−1.72	−1.09
High school or less	−0.45	0.15	−1.42	0.94
Income less than $30,000	−1.57	0.96	−0.06	−1.82
SRHS excellent	1.97	1.98	7.95	2.82
SRHS poor or fair	−0.15	0.63	−4.64	3.07
Constant	18.51***	16.78***	5.41	29.44***
Observations	318	318	318	318

Notes: All covariates are coded as dummy variables. OLS = ordinary least squares.
***Significant at the 1 percent level.
**Significant at the 5 percent level.
*Significant at the 10 percent level.
(For a two-sided test.)

2006 APB estimated by CMS from the Medicare Current Beneficiary Study (MCBS). Table 14.13 gives this distribution of the eligible population, and gives the benefits at selected APB for the Standard plan and alternatives. The second panel of the table gives the calculation of the Standard plan premium when the national average bid is based on this distribution and includes an allowance of 13 percent of benefits paid to cover administrative costs. It also gives the catastrophic reinsurance payments, direct subsidy, base and annual premiums, and net expected benefits from the Standard plan and alternatives. These calculations assume that the premiums on each plan are set to cover sponsor benefit payments and administrative costs if the full eligible population enrolled in this plan.

Using the MCBS distribution yields an expected annual pharmacy cost of $2,940 and Standard plan benefits of $1,536. The Standard plan monthly premium is near $37, the number anticipated by CMS in 2005. The expected benefit net of premiums for the Standard plan is then $1,094, the implied Medicare subsidy of Part D. The net expected benefits of extended plan alternatives are all less than that for the Standard plan, to be expected since the extended benefits and administrative overhead must be covered by the supplementary premiums. Of course, these plans may still be preferred by

Table 14.11   **Logit odds ratios of choosing a cheap plan**

	Low monthly premium (< $10)	Cheapest plan available	Standard plan
2005 drug costs (reference category is $0)			
$1 to $250	0.251*	0.452	0.312*
$251 to $1,000	0.336*	0.641	0.451
$1,001 to $2,250	0.092***	0.279***	0.298***
$2,251 to $5,100	0.110***	0.122***	0.290***
$5,101 or more	0.211**	0.219**	0.295**
Socioeconomic variables			
71 to 75 years	0.871	0.633	0.802
76 years or more	0.807	0.667	0.637
Female	1.368	0.965	1.149
High school or less	1.409	1.101	0.926
Income less than $30,000	0.748	1.109	1.249
SRHS excellent	0.195	0.391	0.426
SRHS poor or fair	0.888	1.815	1.438
Observations	318	318	318
Percent "yes"	11.0	20.8	35.2

Notes: Coefficients reported in this table are odds ratios; all covariates are coded as dummy variables.
***Significant at the 1 percent level.
**Significant at the 5 percent level.
*Significant at the 10 percent level.
(For a two-sided test.)

Table 14.12   **Types of plans chosen by RPS respondents**

	Share (%) 2006	2007	Average premium ($/month) 2006	2007
Full deductible, no gap coverage	36.3	26.2	17.0	17.8
no/reduced deductible, no gap coverage	54.3	59.9	26.6	28.0
Gap coverage for generics	4.8	13.2	46.1	56.5
Gap coverage for generics and brand-name drugs	4.6	0.6	60.8	102.8
Total	100.0	100.0	25.6	29.6

consumers who are risk averse or who have information on their prospective drug use that the sponsor does not know or cannot use. Full deductible and gap coverage has a substantially lower net expected benefit, due to the implicit tax imposed by the delay in catastrophic coverage until the TrOOP threshold is reached. Generic gap coverage without capitation is also

Table 14.13   Total benefits for alternative plans (MCBS cost distribution, 2006)

	CDF for eligible population	Standard plan	Full deductible and gap coverage	Generic gap coverage, no capitation	Generic gap coverage, flexible capitation	Generic gap coverage, fixed capitation
Benefits at annual pharmacy bill (APB, average = $2,940)						
$0	14.56%	$0	$0	$0	$0	$0
$250	19.46%	$0	$188	$0	$0	$0
$2,250	50.65%	$1,500	$1,688	$1,500	$1,500	$1,500
$5,100	83.70%	$1,500	$3,825	$2,229	$2,229	$2,229
$6,200	88.77%	$2,545	$4,650	$2,594	$2,594	$3,274
$15,000	99.09%	$10,905	$11,370	$10,954	$10,954	$11,634
$40,000	99.95%	$34,655	$35,120	$34,704	$34,704	$35,384
Expected benefit	EB	$1,536	$2,222	$1,656	$1,656	$1,751
Catastrophic coverage						
Catastrophic threshold	CTH	$5,100	$14,400	$6,080	$6,080	$5,100
Catastrophic pharmacy bill	CPB	$574	$83	$438	$438	$574
Reinsurance	$RI = 0.8*CPB$	$459	$66	$350	$459	$459
Costs						
Administrative	ADM	$200	$289	$215	$215	$228
Sponsor cost	$SC = EB + ADM - RI$	$1,277	$2,445	$1,521	$1,413	$1,519
Total cost	$TC = SC + RI$	$1,736	$2,511	$1,872	$1,872	$1,978
Subsidy, based on standard coverage						
RI share of total cost	$r = RI/TC$	0.26	(same as Standard Plan)			
Direct subsidy	$DS = (0.745 - r)*TC$	$834	(same as Standard Plan)			
Annual premium	$APR = SC - DS$	$442	(same as Standard Plan)			
	APR/month	$36.89	(same as Standard Plan)			
Total premium and net benefits						
Supplemental premium	$SPR = SC - DS - APR$	$0	$1,168	$244	$136	$242
	SPR/month	$0.00	$97.31	$20.37	$11.32	$20.20
Total premium	$TPR = APR + SPR$	$442	$1,610	$686	$578	$684
Net expected benefit	$= EB - TPR$	$1,094	$611	$969	$1,078	$1,066

affected by this implicit tax, but the impact is smaller because 100 percent copayment for branded drugs increases TrOOP rapidly in the gap.

The actual experience in 2006 was a national average Standard plan premium of $32.20 rather than $36.89, indicating that in some combination, sponsors anticipated lowering APBs through formulary control, incentives to use generic drugs, and lower drug prices obtained by negotiation with pharmaceutical companies, and were willing to accept below normal recovery of administrative costs in order to recruit large enrollment bases. To reflect this, table 14.14 adjusts the MCBS APB distribution to reproduce the 2006 observed Standard plan premium. This is done by first approximating the MCBS cumulative distribution function by a log normal distribution with a point mass at zero, $F_{MCBS}(APB) = 0.1456 + 0.8544 \cdot \Phi((\log(APB) - \mu)/\sigma)$, with parameters $\mu = 7.87$ and $\sigma = 0.77$ obtained by matching the 50 percent and 90 percent quantiles. Then, μ is adjusted (to $\mu = 7.70$) to yield the Standard plan premium of $32.20. The overall levels of net benefits are lower in table 14.14 than table 14.13, as are supplementary premiums, but the comparisons between plans are essentially the same.

The expected benefit and premium calculations in tables 14.13 and 14.14 assumed that the entire eligible population enrolled in the plan being examined. In fact, consumers will choose among plans given their information on prospective APB. This creates the potential for adverse selection in which people with low APB in 2005 do not enroll, and those with high APB choose plans with extended gap coverage. This selection increases the sponsor cost of enrolled extended plan beneficiaries, and lowers the sponsor cost of enrolled Standard plan beneficiaries if the diversion of high APB enrollees to extended plans offsets the loss of low-APB nonenrollees. To assess the impact of plan selection, we assume that enrollees faced the plan, premium, and benefit schedules in table 14.14. We make a computationally convenient rough approximation to the conditional distribution of an enrollee's 2006 APB given her 2005 APB. With probability 0.61, $APB_{2006} = APB_{2005}$, and with probability 0.39, APB_{2006} has the distribution of the full Part D eligible population. This implies a correlation of 0.61 between APB_{2005} and APB_{2006}, corresponding to our estimate from section 14.3 of this chapter of the correlation between RPS-2005 and RPS-2006 APB. With this distributional assumption, the expected benefit to an enrollee in a specified plan equals 0.61 times the net benefit if $APB_{2006} = APB_{2005}$, plus 0.39 times the expected net benefit for the full Medicare-eligible population. We assume that the enrollee chooses the plan that maximizes her conditional expected net benefit. Table 14.15 gives the calculated premiums and plan shares, and for comparison, RPS active decider enrollment shares in 2006. In this table, the observed average Standard plan premium is lower than the national average; this reflects selection in which enrollees choose low-premium plans. The calculated and observed premiums for generic gap coverage are comparable. However, the observed premium for full gap coverage is substantially

Table 14.14   Total benefits for alternative plans (modified approximate cost distribution, 2006)

	CDF for eligible population	Standard plan	Full deductible and gap coverage	Generic gap coverage, no capitation	Generic gap coverage, flexible capitation	Generic gap coverage, fixed capitation
Benefits at annual pharmacy bill (APB, average = $2,590):						
$0	14.56%	$0	$0	$0	$0	$0
$250	14.75%	$0	$188	$0	$0	$0
$2,250	57.24%	$1,500	$1,688	$1,500	$1,500	$1,500
$5,100	87.66%	$1,500	$3,825	$2,229	$2,229	$2,229
$6,200	91.99%	$2,545	$4,650	$2,594	$2,594	$3,274
$15,000	99.41%	$10,905	$11,370	$10,954	$10,954	$11,634
$40,000	99.99%	$34,655	$35,120	$34,704	$34,704	$35,384
Expected benefit	EB	$1,341	$1,949	$1,447	$1,447	$1,517
Catastrophic coverage						
Catastrophic threshold	CTH	$5,100	$14,400	$6,080	$6,080	$5,100
Catastrophic pharmacy bill	CPB	$371	$33	$270	$270	$371
Reinsurance	$RI = 0.8*CPB$	$296	$26	$216	$296	$296
Costs						
Administrative	ADM	$174	$253	$188	$188	$197
Sponsor cost	$SC = EB + ADM - RI$	$1,219	$2,176	$1,419	$1,339	$1,418
Total cost	$TC = SC + RI$	$1,515	$2,203	$1,635	$1,635	$1,714
Subsidy, based on standard coverage						
RI share of total cost	$r = RI/TC$	0.2	(same as Standard Plan)			
Direct subsidy	$DS = (0.745 - r)*TC$	$832	(same as Standard Plan)			
Annual premium	$APR = SC - DS$	$386	(same as Standard Plan)			
	APR/month	$32.20	(same as Standard Plan)			
Total premium and net benefits						
Supplemental premium	$SPR = SC - DS - APR$	$0	$957	$200	$120	$199
	SPR/month	$0.00	$79.78	$16.70	$10.01	$16.57
Total premium	$TPR = APR + SPR$	$386	$1,343	$586	$506	$585
Net expected benefit	$= EB - TPR$	$955	$606	$860	$941	$932

Table 14.15   2006 total monthly premiums and plan shares

	Monthly premium		Plan share	
Plan	Calculated ($)	Observed ($)	Calculated (%)	Observed (%)
None	0.00	0.00	14.8	12.7
Standard and actuarially equivalent	32.20	30.80	55.5	79.1
Full deductible and gap coverage	111.98	61.90	7.9	4.0
Generic gap coverage				
All	—	48.10	21.8	4.2
No Capitation	48.90	—	0.0	—
Flexible Capitation	42.21	—	17.1	—
Fixed Capitation	48.77	—	4.7	—

below the calculated break-even level. An important factor is that in 2006, many sponsors did not offer generic gap coverage plans, a supply constraint that limited demand for these plans.

Despite the fact that the observed premium for extended coverage was substantially below the calculated premium, the calculated shares in table 14.15 underestimate the observed Standard plan share, and overestimate the observed extended plan shares. For generic gap coverage, availability of plans was a factor. There may also have been confusion on the part of enrollees regarding the added benefits of extended coverage, and a tendency in the face of ambiguity to choose low-price "bargains."

The pattern of calculated choice among plans leads to substantial adverse selection. People with APB_{2005} below $250 do not enroll. Those with APB_{20005} between $250 and $3,000 enroll in the Standard plan. Those with APB_{2005} between $3,000 and $5,000 enroll in generic gap coverage with flexible capitation, those between $5,000 and $7,800 enroll in full deductible and gap coverage, and those above $7,800 enroll in generic gap coverage with fixed capitation. Generic gap coverage without capitation is never chosen. As a result of the diversion of high APB enrollees to enhanced plans, Standard plans save more on the sponsor share of catastrophic benefits than they lose on low-APB nonenrollees, and are calculated to earn positive profits. In contrast, extended plans are selected by people who on the basis of APB_{2005} predict that they will gain more from benefits than the premium cost, despite the loading produced by administrative costs and the implicit tax on noncapitated extended coverage. While a major fraction of the actual benefits paid to high-APB enrollees is recaptured by sponsors through case-mix adjustments to the prospective capitated payment by CMS in lieu of reinsurance, the 15 percent sponsor share of catastrophic pharmacy bills is not fully captured by risk-adjusted prospective direct subsidies, since the risk-adjustment weights do not depend on historical pharmacy bills and therefore cannot capture all the information used by enrollees in selecting among plans. Calculation shows that if consumers allocate themselves among plans as previously described, then the Standard plan would show a profit of about $17 per enrollee per month, full deductible and gap coverage and generic coverage with flexible capitation would both show a loss of about $12 per enrollee per month, and generic coverage with fixed capitation would break even.

One would expect the Part D market to adjust to the success and profitability of alternative plans. In particular, if consumer plan choice follows the previous calculations, then one would expect unprofitable or unpopular plans such as full gap coverage, and generic gap coverage with no capitation or flexible capitation, to raise premiums substantially or exit the market. In particular, full gap coverage appears to be in a death spiral in which increasingly expensive plans would be demanded by a shrinking fraction of the population who can expect to benefit at the high added premium, and falling share will lead to its extinction. Generic gap coverage may also face a death spiral. The forces acting against extinction are that extended plans offer insurance to risk-averse consumers, and some aid in managing personal budgets through the calendar year, and that sponsors may recognize some benefit in managing their case mix through separating equilibria in which there is some cross-subsidization across plans, but these may be insufficient to overcome adverse selection when sponsors are prohibited from discriminating among potential enrollees on the basis of past APB.

The market penetration and profitability of plans is very sensitive to plan mix and the workings of selection. Table 14.16 gives calculated plan shares and profitability with various mixes of plans in the market. If the unprofitable full gap coverage plans becomes extinct, or all unprofitable extended plans become extinct, then generic gap coverage with fixed capitation becomes unprofitable, and may then begin its own adverse selection death spiral.

Table 14.16   Plan shares and profitability with alternative plan mixes

| Market environment | Standard | Full | Generic by type of capitation | | |
			None	Flexible	Fixed
All present					
Share	55.5%	7.9%	0.0%	17.1%	4.7%
Profit	$17	–$12	$0	–$13	$0
Full gap plan extinct					
Share	55.5%	—	0.0%	18.1%	11.5%
Profit	$17	—	—	–$13	–$6
Full, generic/none, and generic/flexible					
plans extinct					
Share	76.3%	—	—	—	23.7%
Profit	$17	—	—	—	–$17

14.5.5   Market Hedonics of Part D Plans

The evolution of the Part D market can be pictured as a sequential hedonic equilibrium in which sponsors announce the features and premiums
of the plans they will provide in the coming year, consumers then choose
among the available plans to maximize their preferences, and the process
repeats itself in following years, with sponsors having additional information on market shares and profit history of offered plans and on the strategies of rivals. Anderson, De Palma, and Thisse (1996) discuss the economic
theory and econometrics of oligopolistic markets with products that are
differentiated in hedonic space, and Heckman, Matzkin, and Nesheim
(2003) analyze equilibrium in such markets, and the econometric issues of
identifying and estimating market structure. The Part D market has several
characteristics that simplify hedonic analysis. First, CMS rules fix the schedule for offering plans, and substantially restrict the range of plans that can
be offered. As a result, sponsors do not have significant opportunities to
revise offerings in response to the plans offered by rivals, or in response to
current consumer behavior, but they can learn from history. A feature that
the Part D market shares with many markets where consumers must renew
or switch contracts is the prospect for substantial consumer inertia, which
creates incentives for sponsors to capture market share with "loss-leader"
prices, and then profit from price increases later that will not induce much
switching; see Jenkins et al. (2005). Opportunities for sponsors to conduct
limited-time, limited-area offers to test plans experimentally are precluded
by CMS regulations, although national sponsors may learn about price
response from state-by-state pricing. The Part D market has a few large
sponsors, with a fringe of smaller ones. We anticipate that this market will
approach an equilibrium with some price leadership, but sufficient impact
of the fringe to attain roughly competitive pricing, with frontier plans priced
near their marginal cost, and inefficient plans losing market share or migrat-
ing toward the frontier in successive years.

It is conceivable that in 2006 many sponsors offered plans inside the
efficiency frontier because consumer hedonic values and rival strategies
were unknown. We observe that in the 2007, there was less variety and less
price variation across comparable plans, and anticipate that the trade-offs
in features of frontier plans will move toward trade-offs in consumer side
hedonic values.

For a more detailed look at the features of chosen plans, we present estimates of both the implicit price and the willingness to pay for those features
in 2006 and in 2007. The attributes we study are:

- *No deductible:* Plan offers benefits without the $250 deductible of the
  standard plan.
- *Gap coverage (generics):* Generic drugs are covered in the coverage gap
  of the standard plan.

- *Gap coverage (brand-name drugs):* In addition to generics, brand-name drugs are also covered in the coverage gap.
- *Top 100 drugs uncovered:* Number of top 100 drugs missing in the formulary (available in 2006 only).
- *Top 100 with authorization:* Number of top 100 drugs only covered after authorization or step therapy (available in 2006 only).
- *Drug tiers:* Plan divides drugs into tiers with differing copays.

We first estimate the implicit supply prices of these attributes based on a hedonic regression for the 2,166 plans offered in the fifty-one states in 2006.[19] For state s, company c, and plan p, the premium pr_{scp} is specified as

$$(2) \qquad pr_{scp} = \alpha_{sc} + \mathbf{x}_{scp}\boldsymbol{\beta} + u_{scp},$$

with $\mathbf{x}_{scp}$ denoting the vector of plan attributes listed in table 14.7. The regression includes fixed effects for state/company combinations so that the implicit prices $\boldsymbol{\beta}$ are identified by plans with different features offered by the same company in the same state. Results for 2006 plans are reported in the first column of table 14.17. Sponsors priced coverage (of 75 percent of the cost of covered drugs, or equivalent) of the $250 deductible at $7.42 per month, generic gap coverage at $8.29 per month, and full (generic and branded drugs) gap coverage at $31.09 per month. From table 14.14, the actuarial added cost of deductible coverage is approximately $11.40 per month, of generic gap coverage with flexible capitation is $10.01 per month, and of full gap coverage is $79.78 per month.[20] To the extent that adverse selection led consumers to choose deductible or gap coverage only if they were likely to benefit from it, these figures underestimate actuarial costs. We conclude that extended deductible and generic gap coverage were priced below their actuarial costs to sponsors, although perhaps within a range where formulary control, negotiated drug prices, and low marginal administrative costs might be sufficient to break even. On the other hand, full gap coverage was apparently substantially underpriced by sponsors.

The price of a large formulary was 95 cents per additional drug from the top 100. Sponsors charge $6.63 per month for plans that place drugs on tiers, which have the ambiguous effect of reducing copayments for generic drugs, and increasing copayments for non-preferred branded drugs. Finally, sponsors do not reduce premiums for plans requiring prior authorization for some drugs. The attributes in table 14.17 explain 74 percent of the variance

19. Simon and Lucarelli (2006) present a hedonic analysis of Part D plans that uses a database they collected that includes various plan characteristics that are not part of the publicly available CMS database we use.

20. A representative consumer has a 85.3 percent change of an APB above $250, and a 12.3 percent chance of an APB above $5,100. Then, a benefit of 75 percent of the deductible, or $187.50, will be realized with probability 85.3 percent, and this benefit will be recovered by the sponsor due to delay in reaching the TrOOP threshold with probability 12.3 percent. Then, the expected value of deductible coverage is $11.40 per month.

Table 14.17   **Implicit prices of, and willingness-to-pay for, Part D stand-alone plan attributes**

		Willingness to pay		
	Implicit price	All	Low costs	High costs
No deductible	7.42***	14.13***	15.03***	13.28***
Gap coverage (generics)	8.29***	2.72	–2.58	7.18
Gap coverage (brand-name drugs)	31.09***	20.25***	22.60***	19.63***
Drug tiers	6.63***	–11.21***	–12.02***	–9.91*
Top 100 drugs uncovered	–0.95***	–1.40***	–0.90***	–2.08***
Top 100 with authorization	–0.04	–1.01***	–1.04***	–1.08***
Constant	31.56***			
R2 (within)	0.74			
Var(α)/Var($\alpha + u$)	0.76			
Corr(α,xβ)	–0.42			

Notes: See text for definition of plan attributes and explanation of regressions.
***Significant at the 1 percent level.
**Significant at the 5 percent level.
*Significant at the 10 percent level.
(For a two-sided *t*-test.)

of the premium within companies and states. The variance of the company/ state fixed effects is more than three times the variance of the remaining i.i.d. error. Interestingly, the correlation between these fixed effects and the explained premiums is negative, so plans offered by "expensive" companies in "expensive" states tend to have inferior measured attributes.

Consider the demand side of the hedonic market for plans and willingness to pay (WTP) for plan attributes. Table 14.12 shows that deductible coverage was popular with consumers, but gap coverage was not, despite full gap coverage being offered at premiums substantially below break-even levels for sponsors. Even if full gap coverage had been offered with fixed capitation to avoid the implicit tax from a delayed catastrophic threshold, it would still have had a break even monthly supplementary premium above $50, well above the observed hedonic supply price. Thus, the lack of interest by consumers in this coverage indicates that capitation to reduce premiums would have been insufficient to make full gap coverage viable. The RPS data shows that consumers who selected gap coverage tended to have large pharmacy bills that increased once they were enrolled. Thus, adverse selection and moral hazard both appear to be working to make extended plans with gap coverage unprofitable for sponsors.

To determine consumer WTP for plan attributes, we assume that the utility to consumer i of plans $j = 1, \ldots, J$ available in his or her state depends on plan attributes and the premium,

(3)
$$U_{ij} = \mathbf{x}_j \boldsymbol{\gamma} + pr_j \delta + \varepsilon_{ij}.$$

The error terms, ε_{ij}, are specified as i.i.d. Extreme Value Type 1 random variables, leading to a multinomial logit model of choice.[21] The WTP is defined as the amount of premium increase that exactly offsets the increase of an attribute by one unit, so that the total utility (and therefore the choice probability) remains unaffected.[22] This model is first estimated for the sample of the 316 individuals for whom we can identify the chosen plan, assuming identical WTP. Then, the same model is estimated adding full interactions between the attributes and an indicator for respondent 2005 drug costs above the median. These models can be interpreted as allowing values to vary with expected need. Consumers with low drug costs may be more sensitive to premium, and less sensitive to extended features of the plans, than consumers with high drug costs. The results for the WTP and implicit price estimates are shown in the last three columns in table 14.17.

For all respondents without value differentiation by pharmacy cost, the WTP for deductible coverage is $14.13 per month. Limited gap coverage is valued at $2.72 per month, and full gap coverage is valued at $20.25 per month. For each of the top 100 drugs not in the formulary, the value of a plan is decreased by $1.40. Requiring authorization or step therapy for a drug decreases the value of a plan by $1.01. Consumers dislike drug tiers, valuing them at –$11.21 per month. In the last two columns of table 14.17, comparing consumers with low and high drug costs in 2005, we find that those with high drug costs place a higher values on limited gap coverage and an expansive formulary, and are less deterred by drug tiers.

Compare supply-side hedonic prices in 2006 and the corresponding demand side WTP. For coverage of the $250 deductible, price ($7.42) was below cost ($11.40), which was below value ($14.13). Then, consumers should view this coverage favorably and choose it, while sponsors push price increases for deductible coverage to cover their costs. What we see instead in table 14.7 is some exit of plans offering deductible coverage, and relatively stable prices. For generic gap coverage, value ($2.72) was below price ($8.29), which was below cost ($10.01). For full gap coverage, value ($20.25) was below price ($31.09), which was below cost ($79.78). Then, many consumers should view this coverage unfavorably, with the possible exception of consumers with moderately high APB who can benefit from full gap coverage, but are unlikely to reach APB levels where the delayed catastrophic threshold taxes these benefits away, or consumers with very high APB who can benefit from plans with fixed capitation. There groups created adverse selection that made full gap coverage actuarially more costly, and this coverage even more

---

21. See McFadden (1984) and McFadden and Train (2000). It would be preferable to implement a flexible mixed multinomial logit choice model of taste heterogeneity, which could be used to study the development of the hedonic market, including possible separating equilibria with clusters of plans competing for different segments of consumers. Data limitations preclude this generalization.

22. The WTP for the kth component of x is calculated as $-\gamma_k/\delta$.

unprofitable for sponsors. Then, in 2007 one would expect declining supply, reduced demand, and increased prices for full gap coverage.

For generic gap coverage, average WTP is below the hedonic price, but for consumers with high drug costs, WTP is near the hedonic supply price. Thus, there may be substantial demand for generic gap coverage by high APB users. As noted in the discussion of table 14.16, the presence of full gap coverage plans in the market may mask the potential unprofitability of generic gap plans with fixed capitation, but with the extinction of full gap plans, sponsors are likely to experience losses from their generic gap plans.

Other plan features where there are substantial discrepancies between price and value are drug tiers and authorization requirements. Unless sponsors find cost savings that allow significant reductions in the prices of these features, one would expect most plans to drop these features.

For comparability across the 2006 and 2007 plan years, we repeat the hedonic analysis of plans and of WTP, with a restricted set of plan attributes that are measured in both periods. The results are given in table 14.18. There are only minor changes in the estimated values of the retained attributes of 2006 plans when those attributes not available for 2007 are omitted. The only dramatic shifts between 2006 and 2007 are substantial increases in the prices of generic gap coverage from \$8.99 to \$18.23 and full gap coverage from \$31.10 to \$38.76. Then, full gap coverage remained priced well below cost, while generic gap coverage price rose above cost levels before adjustment for adverse selection. In contrast, WTP for generic or full gap coverage

Table 14.18   **Implicit prices of, and willingness-to-pay for, Part D stand-alone plan attributes**

	Implicit price		Willingness to pay (all)	
	2006	2007	2006	2007
No deductible	10.12***	6.22***	13.94***	24.81***
Gap coverage (generics)	8.99***	18.23***	1.12	0.50
Gap coverage (brand-name drugs)	31.10***	38.76***	26.53***	19.31**
Drug tiers	3.41***	4.17***	−13.11***	−19.78***
Constant	26.26***	23.51***		
R2 (within)	0.60	0.77		
Var(α)	12.04	8.57		
Var(u)	8.34	8.01		
Corr(α,xβ)	−0.40	−0.08		

Notes: See text for definition of plan attributes and explanation of regressions.
***Significant at the 1 percent level.
**Significant at the 5 percent level.
*Significant at the 10 percent level.
(For a two-sided *t*-test.)

changed little from 2006 to 2007, and remain well below the hedonic prices for these features.

To investigate further how WTP for gap coverage varies with current drug expenditure, we estimated additional models with an interaction between splines of current drug bills and the gap coverage dummies. The estimated parameters are omitted here; instead we show implied WTPs for 2006 and 2007 as functions of 2005 and 2006 drug bill in figure 14.6, panels A and B, respectively. Panel A shows that there is a strong effect of 2005 drug expenditure on WTP for gap coverage in the plan choices for 2006. In particular, once the current drug bill exceeds about $3,000, WTP is significantly positive. This finding matches well with the location of the coverage gap (which

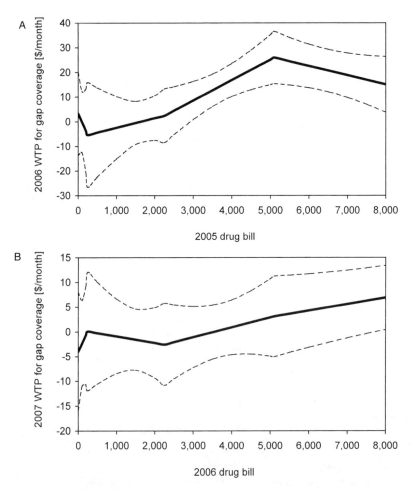

Fig. 14.6   WTP for gap coverage by drug bill: *A*, 2006 choice; *B*, 2007 choice.
Note: The dotted line corresponds to the 95 percent confidence bands.

Table 14.19   **Drug bill by 2006 enrollment**

	Observations	Mean in 2005	Mean change 2005–2006	Median in 2005	Median change 2005–2006
Total	1,318	2,577.2	440.4***	1,878.8	190.8***
No coverage	83	1,270.4	652.8*	110.7	0.0
Automatic	688	2,584.0	613.1***	1,979.1	276.6***
Private	248	2,712.0	49.9	1,659.1	146.3**
Part D	299	2,812.8	307.8	2,034.4	120.5*
Part D, by type of plan					
Unknown type	24	2,574.0	454.0	2,165.5	0.0
Standard plan	99	2,654.7	169.3	1,898.6	120.5
No deductible	146	2,814.9	80.7	1,934.5	30.0
Gap coverage	30	3,515.2	1,753.5***	3,110.0	1,256.8***

***Significant at the 1 percent level.
**Significant at the 5 percent level.
*Significant at the 10 percent level.
(For a two-sided t-test.)

starts at \$2,250). We conclude that gap coverage will attract a limited subpopulation with high drug bills, which may result in escalating prices and further adverse selection. The effect of drug expenditure on WTP is much weaker in the choices for 2007; one explanation is that few consumers in our data considered switching plans for 2007 and even fewer actually switched (we will come back to this issue in section 14.7). Thus, it is not surprising that plan attributes do not explain 2007 plan choices well.

Important questions are the impact of drug use on enrollment and plan choices, and consequent adverse selection, and the impact of prescription drug insurance on drug use. Table 14.19 gives the mean and median pharmacy bills of RPS respondents classified by their prescription drug insurance status in 2006, and the change in pharmacy bills from 2005 to 2006 classified by insurance status. The 2005 pharmacy bills were substantially lower for consumers who chose no coverage in 2006 than for covered consumers. Consumers with automatic, private, or Part D stand-alone coverage have comparable 2005 pharmacy bills. Because the share of nonenrollees is quite low, the effect of adverse selection in enrollment is small. Pharmacy bills rise in 2006 (compared with 2005) for enrollees in all types of Part D plans, and strikingly for those enrolling in plans with gap coverage and those with automatic enrollment, which often incorporates gap coverage. This is strong evidence of a moral hazard in which gap coverage induces additional drug use. This puts pressure on the profitability of current plans offering gap coverage. Whether this induced drug use is productive in lowering other medical costs and promoting health cannot be assessed yet in the RPS population, although there is other evidence that at least selective promotion of drug use can lower overall medical costs; see Goldman and Philipson (2007). Table

14.19 shows that for consumers without drug coverage, median pharmacy bills do not change from 2005 to 2006. However, their mean pharmacy bills increase significantly, indicating that a tail of this group experienced health problems and significant drug needs in 2006. This underscores the risks and the value of Part D insurance, even for this healthy group.

14.6   The Utility Option Value of Enrolling in Medicare Part D

In this section, we consider the dynamic stochastic programming problem faced by an individual with the option of enrolling now in a Medicare Part D prescription drug plan, or delaying enrollment. An individual who enrolls now gains current insurance coverage, and preserves the option value of later coverage at a nonpenalized premium. An individual who delays has no current insurance coverage, and faces a premium penalty if he or she enrolls later, but if current drug use is sufficiently low, may still come out ahead by waiting until health conditions warrant. We ask whether observed enrollment decisions are "rational" in the sense of consistency with optimization of a dynamic stochastic program that minimizes the expected present value of lifetime out-of-pocket and insurance premium expenditures, noting that genuine "irrationalities" may result if the individual fails to act in their own self-interest given their beliefs, or if they fail to have "rational expectations" regarding future events, but spurious claims of irrationality could result if we misspecify their dynamic programming problem.

Medicare Part D embeds a substantial government subsidy, so that at market premiums it is actuarially favorable for most seniors. As a consequence, all risk-averse seniors with significant current prescription drug costs will find delayed enrollment "out of the money." Seniors meeting this criterion are clearly irrational if they fail to enroll.[23] However, healthy seniors with sufficiently low current drug costs face a more difficult choice, weighing the expected net cost of immediate enrollment against the likelihood of future health problems and drug needs, and the expected present value of penalized premiums from delayed enrollment. A saving remnant in the difficulty of the choice facing healthy seniors is that the expected cost of a mistake is low, so that these consumers may justifiably give the choice limited attention, and make a casual or default choice. Elements of a rational decision on enrollment for these individuals will be socioeconomic status, age, gender, the degree of risk aversion, their discount rates, and their beliefs about future health, mortality, and prescription drug needs and costs, given current health.

23. We classify rejection of actuarially favorable insurance as "irrational" behavior. In principle, an individual could be risk-loving and rationally decline actuarially favorable insurance. We have not formally tested this possibility, but believe that as an explanation of Part D enrollment choices it would be inconsistent with other behavior and with stated preferences among hypothetical lotteries.

An individual who enrolls in Part D may also face choices among alternative plans that differ in premiums, coverage, and degree of risk protection. It is possible to embed the Part D enrollment decision in a more general framework for modeling dynamic decisions on health, including decisions on the use of optional preventative or palliative drugs, and the effects of drug use on health outcomes. We will outline this modeling framework, but will not implement all its elements in our current analysis. The major pieces of our analysis are a dynamic stochastic programming model for the enrollment decision, and an econometric hidden Markov model for the dynamics of health and drug use status. Section 14.6.1 provides a general framework for studying consumers' life cycle economic and health decisions. Section 14.6.2 describes the hidden Markov model we specify and estimate for health and drug cost dynamics. In section 14.6.3, we describe the dynamic programming model we use to study Part D enrollment decisions, and present the results of a simulation study of rational decisions. Section 14.6.4 contrasts rational and observed Part D enrollment decisions of RPS respondents.

14.6.1 Modeling Consumer Lifetime Health and Economic Dynamics

The life cycle of a consumer can be described as a series of periods (e.g., years) at which economic and health states are realized, and economic and health choices are made. Broadly, the consumers' problem is to make these choices to maximize well-being, subject to the impact of choices on the evolution of economic and health states. In general, economic and health choices influence both current satisfaction and the evolution of the individual's state.

In general form, a model of health dynamics may specify a vector of health states and indicators, as well as economic state variables, a decision set that includes economic alternatives on consumption, saving, and insurance, and health alternatives including use of preventative and palliative drugs, equations of motion that determine the evolution of economic and health states as functions of medical technology, and health care and lifestyle choices. We describe the dynamics of health in terms of latent "health capital," whose evolution depends on the technology for health maintenance, stochastic health risks, behavior, and inputs of resources that treat or prevent problems. The concept of health capital was introduced by Grossman (1972). His model with a depreciation rate that increases with age captures some of the life cycle dynamics of health, but McFadden (2005) suggests that health capital may be more like the stock of water in a reservoir, so that (a) early in life the body's self-repair and replenishment mechanisms are usually adequate to maintain the stock near capacity; (b) with age, natural replenishment diminishes and more budgeted investment is needed to maintain the stock; and (c) the technology of depreciation may induce losses that are not proportional to stock, and are relatively larger when the stock is small, old, and worn. This analogy provides a simple explanation as to why health expenditures can be low when we are young and health capital is high, and can rise sharply as we age and the remaining stock of health capital diminishes.

This chapter models health capital as one-dimensional, with SRHS, a five-point semantic differential from "poor" to "excellent," as an indicator. More generally, health capital may be fundamentally multidimensional (e.g., cardiovascular, gastrointestinal, crystallized and fluid mental, respiratory, and skeletal-muscular capital), with multiple indicators such as health conditions, biomarkers, Activities of Daily Living (ADLs), and Instrumental Activities of Daily Living (IADLs). This approach to describing health raises a number of interesting questions for future research. Are different types of health capital complements or substitutes? Can consumers rebalance their portfolios of health capital stocks through the life cycle to minimize health problems? Can individuals report self-rated cardiovascular or respiratory health status more reliably than a single overall self-rated health status? How predictive are various health capital levels for incidence of health problems or death?

A preliminary question for our analysis is the reliability of SRHS as an indicator of health capital. Adams et al. (2003) find in an analysis of AHEAD data that Poor/Fair SRHS is predictive of future incidence of health conditions and of mortality, but the Good/Very Good/Excellent gradient is not predictive. This may be a reporting effect, or if SRHS is a good indicator of health capital, may reflect sharply diminishing productivity of health capital above a threshold. This chapter also finds that Poor/Fair SRHS is strongly associated with clinical depression, and strongly associated with a dwelling rated Poor/Fair, even with statistical control for overall socioeconomic status. This suggests that reporting effects may influence SRHS. The SRHS may also be susceptible to justification effects; see Baker, Stabile, and Deri (2004). Our treatment of SRHS can tolerate some reporting effects, but it does not attempt to identify and remove them.

The evidence from Heiss (2006) is that persistent unobserved components are present in the evolution of health capital. There may be heterogeneity across individuals in the technologies available for health maintenance and in initial endowments of health capital; these individual differences reflect what is often designated the latent "robustness" or "frailty" of the individual. In the current model, we assume that all such differences are captured by our dynamic specification for latent health capital. More critically, in this chapter we assume that the evolution of health capital is not influenced by feedbacks from consumer choices on health insurance, prescription drug use, or other economic or health-relevant decisions. We believe this is reasonable for the analysis of insurance and drug use over a two-year period, but future research that looks more broadly at questions of interactions and feedbacks between health outcomes and consumer behavior, particularly between prescription drug use and incidence of health problems, will have to look closely at the determination of health capital.

A general model of the life cycle well-being of consumers requires specification of a felicity function of current consumption and health status that incorporates risk preferences. In general, some consumption expenditures and health states enter felicity directly, and others are inputs to the technology that determines the evolution of health. For example, palliative drugs to relieve the effects of specific health conditions such as arthritis or depression will enter felicity, while therapeutic drugs to treat health conditions such as diabetes and preventative drugs to treat conditions such as hypertension will enter the equation of motion for health capital. A future research question is whether insurance programs such as Part D will selectively encourage the use of preventative drugs, and improve compliance with therapeutic regimens. A research challenge is to determine how felicity is influenced by health conditions, and the extent to which individuals rationally manage the risks of future health conditions. Behavioral research suggests that humans do poorly in anticipating the disutility of health impairments and pain, and adapt to these impairments when they occur (the "hedonic treadmill"), so that it will be challenging to construct predictive models of health risk management that assume rational planning; see Kahneman and Snell (1990) and Gilbert et al. (1998).

Our analysis of Part D enrollment decisions isolates a single component of overall felicity, the pharmacy out-of-pocket cost and drug insurance premium cost, and assumes that consumers seek to minimize the expected present value of this cost. We assume that consumers are risk-neutral, but this assumption can be relaxed within our model framework.

14.6.2 A Hidden Markov Model for Health Dynamics

We model health dynamics as an annual process with the timing convention that events for a survivor at the end of the old year unfold in the following sequence: (a) If the individual has not previously enrolled in Part D, an enrollment decision is made. If there are plan choices, the individual decides whether to switch to a new plan. (b) A new year health capital state is determined. (c) Survivor status, SRHS, and pharmacy bill are determined for the year, but part-year SRHS and pharmacy bills are discarded for individuals who do not survive the entire year.[24] (d) Net out-of-pocket pharmacy costs are calculated, taking into account insurance coverage and plan. (e) Finally, felicity for the new year, equal to the negative of the current value of Part D premiums plus out-of-pocket pharmacy costs, is determined. We initialize the dynamics at age sixty-four, so that all consumers who reach age sixty-five and become eligible for Medicare have a prior year health capital state.

We adapt the econometric specification of Heiss (2006, 2008) for the

---

24. Lack of monthly data, and inconsistent reporting in year of death due to the discrete timing of surveys and limited proxy information, make it impractical to implement a monthly dynamic model.

dynamics of health capital; see Heiss et al. (2009) for a similar model. Let $R^*(n,t)$ denote the latent "robustness" of respondent n in year t, and $H^*(n,t)$ denote the latent health capital of this respondent. Assume that robustness follows a stationary AR(1) process, and that latent health capital is determined by robustness plus an exogenous drift,

$$(4) \qquad R^*(n,t) = \rho R^*(n,t-1) + (1-\rho^2)^{1/2}u_0(n,t) \quad \text{and}$$

$$H^*(n,t) = \alpha_0 x(n,t) + R^*(n,t),$$

where $x(n,t)$ is a vector of exogenous variables such as age and gender, and the $u_0(n,t)$ are i.i.d. standard normal.[25] Robustness is assumed to be standard normal at age sixty-four. Then, $R^*(n,t)$ is a stationary process, and if one directly observed R^* in two or more periods without censoring, its off-diagonal covariances identify the parameter ρ. However, because mortality depends on R^*, the density of R^* conditioned on survival is influenced by selection at ages greater than sixty-four.

Suppose that one observes mortality/morbidity status $d(n,t)$ in year t, and for survivors with $d(n,t) = 1$, one observes SRHS in five categories from "poor" to "excellent," and pharmacy bills (PB) in twelve categories. These satisfy the mappings,

$$(5) \qquad d(n,t) = \mathbf{1}(x(n,t)\alpha_1 + \gamma_1 H^*(n,t) + u_1(n,t) > 0),$$

$$(6) \quad \text{SRHS}(n,t) = m_2 \text{ if } \theta_{2,m-1} \le \gamma_2 H^*(n,t) + u_2(n,t) < \theta_{2,m}$$
$$\text{for } m_2 = 1, \ldots, 5,$$

$$(7) \qquad \text{PB}(n,t) = m_3 \text{ if } \theta_{3,m-1} \le x(n,t)\alpha_3 + \gamma_3 H^*(n,t) + u_3(n,t) < \theta_{3,m}$$
$$\text{for } m_3 = 1, \ldots, 12,$$

where the $u_j(n,t)$ are i.i.d. logistic disturbances, and the threshold parameters satisfy $\theta_{2,0} = \theta_{3,0} = -\infty$, and $\theta_{2,5} = \theta_{3,12} = +\infty$. Equation (6) requires one additional normalization of the location relative to the thresholds, which is accomplished, for example, by imposing $\theta_{2,3} = 0$, or equivalently by requiring that the sample mean of H^* at age sixty-four be zero. We continue to assume that the vector $x(n,t)$ is exogenous, but note that the model could be extended to accommodate predetermined variables in x such as previous year's pharmacy bill. We assume there is no autocorrelation in the disturbances entering the equations for SRHS and PB. This is a strong restriction that forces latent health capital to account for all persistence random effects, such as persistent random reporting effects in SRHS. One limitation of the current model specification is that it cannot account for feedbacks from pre-

25. This modeling choice specifies the form of depreciation of health capital and excludes feedbacks from health care and behavior to health capital depreciation or restoration. In light of the previous discussion of the forms that health capital might take, an interesting research question is whether alternative specifications of health capital dynamics give better fits to observed health dynamics.

scription drug use to health outcomes. These are potentially important, but are unlikely to be observed in a short panel. The model (4) through (7) can be estimated by maximum likelihood or generalized method of moments. Note that, as specified, these equations of motion do not depend on behavior such as the Part D enrollment choice, so that issues of endogeneity do not arise. While it would be possible to carry out simulated maximum likelihood estimation directly in our short panel, a more practical and stable method that also works in long panels is a sequential algorithm similar to the Kalman filter; see Heiss (2008).

Given the value of $H^*(n,t)$, the outcome $d(n,t)$ has a binomial logit probability. Further, the independence of $u_j(n,t)$ implies that given $H^*(n,t)$, mortality occurs "at random," so that conditioned on survival, SRHS and PB are independent and their probabilities are ordered logit. Let $y(n,t)$ denote the observed events "$d(n,t) = 0$" in the case of mortality and "$d(n,t) = 1$, SRHS $= m_2$, PB $= m_3$" in the case of survival, and observations m_2 and m_3 for SRHS and PB, respectively, and let $\Pr(y(n,t)|H^*(n,t))$ denote the conditional probability of $y(n,t)$ given $H^*(n,t)$. The likelihood contribution of individual n can then be expressed as

$$(8) \qquad L(n) = \int \ldots \int \prod_{t=1}^{T} Pr[y(n,t)|H^*(n,t)]$$

$$f_{1\ldots T}[H^*(n,1), \ldots, H^*(n,T)] dH^*(n,1) \ldots dH^*(n,T),$$

where $f_{1\ldots T}$ is the density of $[H^*(n,1), \ldots, H^*(n,T)]$. Absent mortality, this density would be multivariate normal density with mean vector $(\alpha_0 x(n,1), \ldots, \alpha_0 x(n,T))$ and covariance matrix Σ with elements $\Sigma_{ij} = \rho^{|i-j|}$. However, mortality causes it to be modified by selection. As discussed by Heiss (2008), the structure of such models allows us to write this likelihood contribution as the product of conditional likelihoods,

$$(9) \qquad L(n) = \int \Pr(y(n,1)|H^*(n,1)) f_1(H^*(n,1)) dH^*(n,1)$$

$$\times \prod_{t=2}^{T} \int \Pr(y(n,t)|H^*(n,t))$$

$$f_{t|1,\ldots,t-1}(H^*(n,t)|y(n,1), \ldots, y(n,t-1)) dH^*(n,t),$$

where $f_{1\ldots J}$ is the marginal density for the first period, and $f_{t|1,\ldots,t-1}$ is the conditional density for period t given observed outcomes prior to t. These densities would be normal if there were no selection and the conditioning was on past values of H^*, but are modified from this specification by selection and by conditioning on observed events. Equation (9) allows a sequential approximation of the likelihood contribution in the spirit of the Kalman filter. Start with the outcome probability of the first period. The conditional density $f_{2|1}$ needed for the second period is approximated in two steps. First, account for the information $y(n,1)$ contains on $H^*(n,1)$ using the model for $\Pr(y(n,t)|H^*(n,t))$ and Bayes' rule. In the second step, account for the shocks u_0 using the transition model (4). This procedure is repeated recursively until all T observations are included. Heiss (2008) discusses this approach and the sequential Gaussian quadrature algorithm used for the estimation of our model in more detail.

14.6.3   Data and Estimation Results

The data used to estimate the model of health and drug expenditure dynamics come from the Medicare Current Beneficiary Survey (MCBS) collected by CMS; in particular, the Cost and Use files for years 2000 to 2003. The MCBS is a rotating panel based on a stratified random sample of about 12,000 Medicare beneficiaries in each cohort. An individual is observed for at most three years (together with a preliminary interview, resulting in at most four observations). The MCBS includes information on demographics, socioeconomic status, health status, and utilization as well as cost of medical care (including physician services, inpatient hospital services, and prescription drugs). Self-reported events are validated by Medicare claims. A study by Poisal (2003) suggests that there is some underreporting in self-reported prescription drug expenditure in the MCBS. We do not address this issue here.

Table 14.20 shows the maximum likelihood parameter estimates of the full model. It includes age splines, a dummy variable for high education (more than high school), and a dummy variable for noncaucasian respondents in all equations. The model is estimated separately by gender. Ceteris

Table 14.20   Parameter estimates

	Males		Females	
Mortality				
Nonwhite	0.309**	(0.127)	–0.083	(0.117)
High education	–0.734***	(0.094)	–0.706***	(0.089)
Latent health	1.336***	(0.061)	1.728***	(0.057)
Drug bill				
Nonwhite	–0.271	(0.301)	–0.683***	(0.246)
High education	–1.133***	(0.209)	–1.232***	(0.185)
Latent health	6.124***	(0.175)	6.228***	(0.150)
SRHS				
Nonwhite	0.370***	(0.065)	0.465***	(0.052)
High education	–0.914***	(0.044)	–0.847***	(0.039)
Latent health	0.877***	(0.025)	0.910***	(0.022)
Latent robustness				
Correlation ρ	0.967***	(0.004)	0.963***	(0.003)

Notes: All equations also include age splines.

***Significant at the 1 percent level.

**Significant at the 5 percent level.

(Parameters significantly different from zero.)

paribus, nonwhite females use less drugs than white females. Independent of gender, highly educated respondents use less drugs and report better self-rated health. The latent component enters all equations significantly and its correlation from one year to the next is high (.97 for males and .96 for females), but the null hypothesis of time-constant latent "robustness" is clearly rejected by a likelihood ratio test ($p < 0.001$).

14.6.4   Simulation of Health Trajectories

Since the model parameters are difficult to interpret directly, a few simulations of the trajectories help to understand the model and its implications. All results are for white males with a high school degree or less unless stated otherwise.

Figure 14.7 illustrates the dynamic features of the latent robustness R^*. It shows its mean for the surviving population given starting values at the median, the tenth, and ninetieth percentile. While the three lines tend to converge, they remain distinct. Technically, this is due to the high serial correlation in R^*, and to the differential effects of mortality. Intuitively it means that someone who is very healthy at age sixty-five will be still relatively healthy at age ninety, compared to someone who was in worse health at sixty-five. Selection due to mortality shifts the distribution markedly at higher ages.

Figure 14.8 shows survival probabilities for the same hypothetical individuals with initial latent health at the median, the twenty-fifth, and seventy-fifth percentile. The differences are strong. While only half of the unhealthy survive past age seventy, half of the average individuals survive to age eighty, and almost half of the very healthy survive to age ninety.

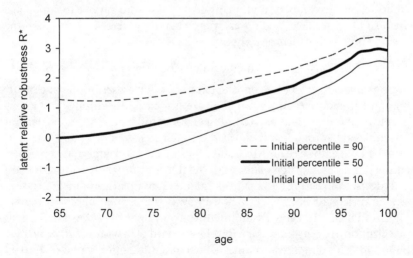

Fig. 14.7   Persistence and selectivity: Latent robustness by age

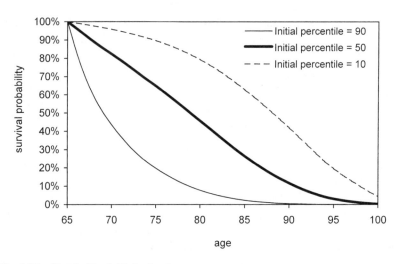

Fig. 14.8   Survival by initial robustness

Figure 14.9 shows the average drug bill by age. The thick black line represents cross-sectional averages in the MCBS sample. If anything, the average drug bills decrease with age, as those with health conditions requiring high drug use are selected out by mortality. The thin black line shows the simulation results from the estimated model. It represents the average simulated drug bill for the surviving population. The decline over time appears mostly as a selection effect: the healthy use less drugs and are more likely to survive to a higher age. This effect is illustrated by the thin lines. They show the simulated drug bill of the population surviving to age seventy, seventy-five, eighty, eighty-five, ninety, and ninety-five. Those who survive to a high age are also likely to have used fewer drugs when they were sixty-five than the average population alive at sixty-five.

14.6.5   The Consumer's Dynamic Stochastic Program

Consumers face an open enrollment period for prescription drug insurance at the end of each year. If they are not currently enrolled, they may decide to enroll, or default to continued nonenrollment. (About 60 percent of seniors are automatically enrolled through employer or union, VA, military, Federal employee, or Medicaid programs.) If consumers are currently enrolled, they may switch plans, or by default continue in their current plan. This decision structure allows us to simulate an optimal enrollment decision strategy in a relatively straightforward way. We ignore plan choice in analyzing enrollment strategies, assuming the only options of a consumer are no prescription drug insurance or a Part D standard plan with a market average premium. This simplification may understate the option value of Part D enrollment, but the effect will be small. Since the consumer can switch plans

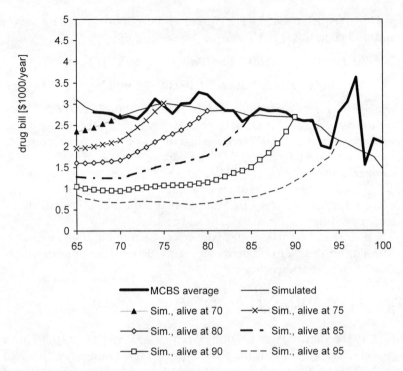

Fig. 14.9   Drug bill by age

annually, plan choice conditioned on current enrollment and health capital does not require strategic preparation. Since the added features of extended plans are not subsidized, they will be actuarially unfair to their enrollees in market equilibrium once administrative overhead costs are added. Then, the possibility is remote that a risk-neutral consumer will in the future encounter circumstances where extended plans offered at market premiums are substantially better values than the standard plan, and these additional plans will add little to the option value of enrollment for healthy consumers.

Let $t = 1, \ldots, T$ denote years past age sixty-four, so that at $T = 35$, an individual is age 100, which we assume is the maximum attainable age. Let $H^*(n,t)$, $d(n,t)$, $SRHS(n,t)$, and $PB(n,t)$ denote, respectively, latent health capital, a survival indicator, self-rated health status, and pharmacy bill for consumer n in year t, and assume that they are determined by (4) through (7). Let $E(n,t)$ be an indicator for enrollment in a Part D plan in year t, and let

$$(10) \qquad CNE(n,t) = \sum_{s=1}^{t} (1 - E(n,s))$$

denote the cumulative years of nonenrollment (CNE) at the end of year t. (All consumers age sixty-four and over start with zero CNE in 2005 when the

Part D market first opened.) The current net benefit from Part D standard plan enrollment, from (1), is

(11) $CV(n,t) = 0.75 \cdot \min\{2{,}000, \max(PB(n,t) - 250{,}0)\}$

$$+ 0.95 \cdot \max(PB(n,t) - 5{,}100{,}0) - (1 + 0.12 \cdot CNE(n,t)) \cdot 12p,$$

where p is the monthly premium and the factor $(1 + 0.12 \cdot CNE(n,t))$ is the premium penalty for delayed enrollment. We assume that the standard plan benefit schedule and premium remain fixed in real terms into the future. We assume that at the time of an enrollment decision at the end of year $t - 1$, consumers know $H^*(n,t-1)$, $SRHS(n,t-1)$, $PB(n,t-1)$, and $CNE(n,t-1)$, and can predict perfectly all future values of exogenous variables x, but do not know the future shocks that determine health capital, health status, pharmacy bills, and survival in year t and beyond.

The objective of the risk-neutral consumer of age $\tau - 1$ in 2005 is to choose an enrollment strategy to maximize the expected present value of the future stream of current net benefits,

(12) $$E_{t-1} \sum_{t=\tau}^{T} \left[\prod_{s=\tau}^{t} d(n,s) \right] \beta^{\tau-t} E(n,t) \cdot CV(n,t),$$

subject to the known initial conditions $H^*(n,\tau - 1)$, $SRHS(n,\tau - 1)$, $PB(n,\tau - 1)$, and $CNE(n,\tau - 1) = 0$, and to the equations (4) through (7), (10), and (11). Let $V(H^*,CNE,x,t)$ denote a valuation function, giving the optimized expected present value of the future stream of current net benefits from age t on, starting from state variables H^* and CNE and the exogenous variables x. Then, V is defined by backward recursion, with

(13) $V(H^*(n,T-1),CNE(n,T-1),x,T)$

$$= \max_{E(n,T)=0,1} E_{T-1} d(n,T) \cdot E(n,T) \cdot CV(n,T),$$

and

(14) $V(H^*(n,t-1),CNE(n,t-1),x,t)$

$$= \max_{E(n,t)=0,1} E_{t-1} d(n,t) \{ E(n,t) \cdot CV(n,t) + \beta \cdot V(H^*(n,t),CNE(n,t),x,t) \},$$

where $d(n,t)$ and $CV(n,t)$ are given by (4) through (7), (10), and (11), and $\beta < 1$ is a rate of time impatience.

Discretize the distribution of the health state with K nodes, so $H^*(n,t) \in \{h_1, \ldots, h_K\}$. These nodes can be thought of as draws from the marginal distribution of H^*. Equation (4) then translates into transition probabilities $P_{jk} = \Pr(H^*(n,t) = h_j \mid H^*(n,t-1) = h_k)$ for any $j,k = 1, \ldots, K$.

The decision problem is now solved using backward induction from $T = 100$. For each possible configuration $CNE(n,T-1) \in \{0, \ldots, 34\}$ and $H^*(n,T-1) \in \{h_1, \ldots, h_K\}$, and x, solve (13). Then, recursively, given the previously obtained valuation function $V(H^*(n,t),\text{CNE}(n,t),x,t)$ and each possible configuration $\text{CNE}(n,t-1) \in \{0, \ldots, t-1\}$ and $H^*(n,T-1) \in \{h_1, \ldots, h_K\}$, and x, solve (14). The final result is a table of optimal strategies for individuals age sixty-four and over for each possible configuration of state variables and exogenous variables they may face. An optimal strategy is obtained for an individual of age $\tau - 1$ in 2005 with health capital $H^*(n,\tau-1)$ by look-up for these state variables and $\text{CNE}(n,\tau-1) = 0$.

We give simulations from this dynamic stochastic program for illustrative combinations of socioeconomic characteristics. Figure 14.10, panel A, shows net benefits of enrollment for sixty-five-year-old white males with a high school degree or less who are choosing whether to enroll into a standard plan that costs \$240 a year. The discount rate is set to 5 percent per year. The abscissa represents the relative value of H^*. The very healthy are located on the left, and the very unhealthy on the right. The thin solid upward sloping line shows the expected immediate net benefit of enrollment. It is negative for the healthiest 14 percent of this population. The dotted line shows the expected present value of penalty savings. It is driven by two effects: worse health increases the probability of future enrollment and decreases further life expectancy. These two effects have offsetting effects regarding the expected present value of penalty savings.

In the simulation, the extremely healthy have a low present value of future penalty savings because they have a good chance never to enroll. Present value of penalty savings increases as health gets worse. The tenth percentile already has a very high probability of future enrollment. However, as health worsens further, life expectancy and therefore also the present value of penalty savings decreases markedly. The top thick solid line is the total net benefit of enrollment, the sum of the other two lines. It is positive for all but the healthiest 2 percent. Then, according to our model, 98 percent of this population should enroll.

Panel B of figure 14.10 shows the same graph as panel A for the same population but with the additional restriction that in the previous year, the individual did not use any drugs. This population only has an 8 percent chance that they will end up with a drug bill that makes enrollment immediately beneficial. But at the same time, the further life expectancy is quite high for this group and there is a good chance that they will eventually end up with a sizable drug bill, the expected present value of the penalty savings is high enough to make enrollment beneficial for more than 80 percent.

Panel C of figure 14.10 shows the simulation results for the same population as panel A, but for the age of eighty instead of sixty-five. The expected immediate benefits are similar to those of the sixty-five-year-olds, but due to the lower further life expectancy, the present value of future benefit savings is lower, resulting in a rational enrollment rate of only 60 percent.

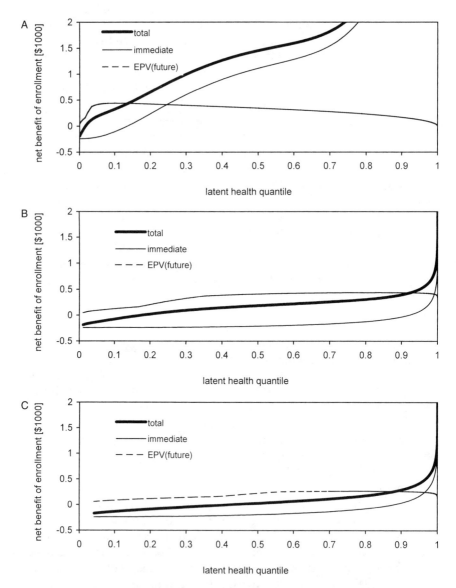

Fig. 14.10 Simulated benefit of enrollment: *A,* Sixty-five-year-old white males with a high school degree or less; *B,* Sixty-five-year-old white males with a high school degree or less, zero previous drug bill; *C,* Eighty-five-year-old white males with a high school degree or less, zero previous drug bill

14.6.6   Predicted and Observed Part D Enrollment
Decisions of RPS Respondents

We have run the same simulation presented for illustrative individuals in section 14.6.5 for all active deciders in RPS. The result is a probability that enrollment is rational according to our model, which represents the share of people with the same age, previous year's drug bill, SRHS, and demographics who have a positive net benefit. Furthermore, we impute the enrollment share if individuals only look at the next year's outcome and the expected benefit of enrollment, split into the immediate benefit and the present value of saved penalties.

Table 14.21 shows the overall descriptive statistics of these values. In total, 97.5 percent should enroll if they are fully rational, and for 81.7 percent this is even immediately beneficial. On average, the immediate benefit is $1,116 and the present value of future benefit savings is $299. In table 14.22, these averages are classified by the actual enrollment decisions of the RPS respondents. (For this table, enrollment is defined as either a Part D stand-alone plan or a Medicare Advantage plan with Part D prescription drug coverage.) Respondents who have a larger probability that enrollment is rational do have a higher enrollment rate. But using the fully rational rule given by our model, 93.4 percent of those who did not enroll should have enrolled.

Table 14.23 shows actual and simulated enrollment by health and socio-

Table 14.21   Simulation results: Descriptives

	Mean	5th	95th
Enrollment share			
Fully rational	97.5%	81.7%	100.0%
Myopic	81.7%	7.8%	100.0%
Benefit of enrollment			
Total	$1,413	$148	$3,989
Immediate	$1,116	–$163	$3,813
Future	$299	$110	$447

Table 14.22   Simulated vs. actual enrollment

		Enrollment share		Benefit of enrollment		
Actually enrolled?	Observations	Fully rational (%)	Myopic (%)	Total ($)	Immediate ($)	Future ($)
Total	653	97.5	81.7	1,413	1,116	299
Yes	558	98.2	85.8	1,510	1,217	295
No	95	93.4	57.6	845	523	324

Table 14.23   Simulation results by individual characteristics

	Observations (%)	Enrollment share			Benefit ($1,000)	
		Actual (%)	Rational (%)	Myopic (%)	Immediate	Future
2005 drug bill						
Bill = 0	15.8	64.1	84.3	12.7	−136	335
0 < bill ≤ 250	8	71.2	99.6	63.1	144	392
250 < bill ≤ 1,000	9.7	84.1	100.0	88.8	408	348
1,000 < bill ≤ 2,250	29.9	90.3	100.0	98.3	782	327
2,250 < bill ≤ 5,100	25.4	95.2	100.0	100.0	1,573	256
Bill > 5,100	11.3	91.9	100.0	100.0	3,997	163
SRHS						
Excellent	9.2	68.3	90.6	53.8	302	341
Very good	32.5	82.5	96.8	73.7	690	330
Good	37.1	90.5	98.6	87.7	1,279	290
Fair	17.3	87.6	99.5	95.4	1,700	250
Poor	4	92.3	99.6	95.6	2,410	245
Age						
≤ 70	44.1	87.5	98.4	80.8	1,239	351
70 < age ≤ 75	28	80.9	97.0	78.2	872	313
> 75	27.9	86.8	96.5	86.5	1,165	202
Gender						
Male	36.1	85.6	95.5	77.5	1,002	281
Female	63.9	85.4	98.6	84.1	1,180	309
Education						
High school or less	59.1	84.7	97.2	82.2	1,069	300
More than high school	40.9	86.5	97.9	81.0	1,183	298
Race						
White	90	85.0	97.3	81.0	1,105	297
Other	10	89.2	99.1	87.6	1,215	314

demographic and health variables. Only respondents who have not used any drugs in 2005 have a reasonable probability to be better off not enrolling, according to the rational model. The myopic decision rule implies only 12.7 percent enrollment with a zero previous drug bill. The actual enrollment in this group is with 64.1 percent between the rational and the myopic rule. For higher drug bills, the probability that enrollment is rational is essentially one. Higher 2005 drug bills are clearly correlated with both myopically optimal and actual enrollment.

Table 14.24 compares estimates from reduced-form models of actual and rational enrollment. The previous drug bill is the most important determinant of both. Also, both are lower for respondents with excellent SRHS. The other predictors are hardly significant for actual enrollment. Rational enrollment is lower for the older because of the lower life expectancy over which the present value of avoided penalties accumulate. Highly educated

Table 14.24   Reduced-form regressions: Actual and rational enrollment

	Logit model		OLS on log odds[a]	
	actual enrollment		rational enrollment	
0 < bill ≤ 250	0.241	(0.380)	5.827***	(0.207)
250 < bill ≤ 1,000	1.156***	(0.417)	6.730***	(0.105)
1,000 < bill ≤ 2,250	1.657***	(0.323)	7.036***	(0.083)
2,250 < bill ≤ 5,100	2.473***	(0.472)	7.099***	(0.082)
Bill > 5,100	1.920***	(0.548)	7.110***	(0.089)
SRHS excellent	−0.775**	(0.335)	−0.556***	(0.116)
SRHS fair/poor	−0.499	(0.359)	0.082*	(0.045)
70 < age ≤ 75	−0.526*	(0.283)	−0.171***	(0.046)
> 75	−0.275	(0.308)	−0.615***	(0.079)
Female	−0.169	(0.255)	0.419***	(0.054)
More than high school	0.354	(0.252)	0.307***	(0.050)
Nonwhite	0.222	(0.426)	0.038	(0.070)

Note: Standard errors in parentheses.
[a]Dependent variable $= \log(P/(1 - P))$, where P represents the rational enrollment probability, trimmed at 0.9999.
***Significant at the 1 percent level.
**Significant at the 5 percent level.
*Significant at the 10 percent level.

individuals have a higher life expectancy. The same is true for females and they tend to use more drugs. Race does not play any role.

Table 14.25 shows parameter estimates from more logit models of enrollment. Specification (1) only includes the simulated rational enrollment probability as an explanatory variable. Its coefficient is highly significantly positive—on average, respondents who have a high enrollment probability in our model are more likely to actually enroll. Specification (2) adds the dollar-value of enrollment, split into immediate and future benefits. High immediate benefits increase the enrollment probability, whereas future benefits do not seems to have an effect. Specification (3) also includes the simulated enrollment probability if respondents only care about the immediate benefits. Its coefficient comes out highly significantly and all other variables lose their explanatory power. Adding sociodemographic variables in specification (4) does not qualitatively change the results. Adding the 2005 drug bill, in addition, leads to a collinearity problem: the four simulated values and the 2005 drug bill are too highly dependent to statistically decide which of the groups of variables drive the results. While single t-tests of these nine variables do not reject the hypothesis that they are equal to zero, a Wald test of the hypothesis that they are all zero is clearly rejected (a chi-square test statistic with 9 degrees of freedom is 46.94, giving significance $p < 0.0001$). Overall, the results indicate that respondents are very well aware of the (simple) fact that enrollment is more beneficial with a higher drug bill, but

Table 14.25   **Logit models for actual enrollment**

	(1)	(2)	(3)	(4)	(5)
Rational enrollment	5.530***	3.877***	−0.289	−0.656	−0.297
	(1.155)	(1.494)	(1.873)	(2.002)	(2.053)
Immediate benefits		0.468**	0.166	−0.040	−0.022
		(0.212)	(0.177)	(0.203)	(0.244)
Future Benefits		−1.389	−0.267	−3.618	−1.641
		(1.724)	(1.775)	(2.898)	(3.200)
Myopic enrollment			1.894***	2.160***	0.692
			(0.514)	(0.530)	(1.645)
SRHS excellent				−0.757**	−0.767**
				(0.353)	(0.369)
SRHS fair/poor				−0.416	−0.522
				(0.337)	(0.344)
$70 < \text{age} <\, = 75$				−0.725**	−0.626*
				(0.322)	(0.336)
Age > 75				−0.817*	−0.536
				(0.496)	(0.547)
Female				−0.089	−0.122
				(0.270)	(0.285)
More than high school				0.240	0.321
				(0.254)	(0.286)
Nonwhite				0.207	0.222
				(0.447)	(0.450)
$0 < \text{bill} <\, = 250$					0.027
					(0.940)
$250 < \text{bill} <\, = 1,000$					0.766
					(1.318)
$1,000 < \text{bill} <\, = 2,250$					1.145
					(1.456)
$2,250 < \text{bill} <\, = 5,100$					1.847
					(1.522)
Bill > 5,100					1.200
					(1.708)
Observations	653	653	653	653	653
Log-likelihood	−259.4	−250.6	−244.0	−238.5	−235.0

Note: Standard errors in parentheses.
***Significant at the 1 percent level.
**Significant at the 5 percent level.
*Significant at the 10 percent level.

do not seem to understand the (complicated) consequences of the penalty for late enrollment.

14.7   Plan Satisfaction and Switching: First Results from RPS-2007

The analysis presented in this chapter so far focused mostly on data from RPS-2005 and RPS-2006. As discussed in section 14.3, we interviewed the

RPS respondents for a third time in April 2007 to ask them about their plan choices for 2007 as well as their satisfaction with their 2006 plan. In this section, we investigate plan satisfaction and switching very briefly. The number of observations is larger than in our earlier analysis since we can also use answers from respondents in the 2007 refreshment sample (for whom we do not have 2005 and 2006 data).

We asked the RPS respondents about their satisfaction with their 2006 Part D stand-alone plans, both overall and with respect to five plan features. Each question was answered on a five-point scale (poor, fair, good, very good, excellent). The results are summarized in table 14.26, where we report the proportion of respondents who were dissatisfied ("poor" or "fair" ratings). Overall, 17.6 percent are dissatisfied with their plans. The dimension that attracts the most negative ratings is gap coverage—47.2 percent say that they are dissatisfied with this feature. The rating is even worse for those respondents who say that they actually hit the gap; among them, 66.3 percent are dissatisfied with having a gap in their coverage. In contrast, customer service does not seem to be a major cause of dissatisfaction.

Table 14.27 summarizes the Part D enrollment status of those respondents who have a stand-alone plan for 2007. Of these respondents, 91.2 percent already had coverage in 2006. The majority (62 percent) did not consider switching, and another 18.4 percent considered switching but stayed with their plan. Only 10.7 percent switched plans. The fact that only relatively few respondents considered switching, and even fewer actually switched, is important since switching is costless and many plans changed one or more

Table 14.26   **Dissatisfaction with current Part D plan**

	"Poor" or "fair" rating (%)
Overall	17.6
Premium	23.5
Gap coverage	47.2
Deductible	25.8
Formulary	19.4
Customer service	12.7

Table 14.27   **Switching of Part D stand-alone plans**

	Observations	Share (%)
Enrolled in the same plan in 2006 and . . .		
. . . did not consider switching	323	62.0
. . . considered switching	96	18.4
Switched plans	56	10.7
Not enrolled in 2006	46	8.8
Total	521	100.0

of their attributes—not only premiums but also such features as deductibles, gap coverage, formularies, and so forth. We have not performed a formal analysis, but it is conceivable that switching would have been optimal for more than just about 10 percent of consumers. Thus, it seems that there is a lock-in effect, and so it may have been a good strategy for plan providers in this repeated-interaction market to offer cheap plans in the first period and then to increase premiums and/or reduce plan quality over time. (For instance, one plan that was very popular in 2006 has seen a substantial premium increase from 2006 to 2007, which was hotly debated in the popular press.) We cannot investigate this issue further, but this is certainly an important area for future research on consumer and firm behavior in "consumer-directed" health care markets.

Finally, we estimated logit models for the dependent variables "considered switching plans" and "switched plans" (table 14.28). The number of observations is rather small because these models require information on the features of the chosen plans in both 2006 and 2007. Having a plan with no deductible in 2006 has a negative effect on whether a respondent considers switching. Also, an increase in the premium of the 2006 plan in 2007 made respondents consider a switch. When we add plan dissatisfaction, defined as in table 14.26, it also has a positive and strong effect on considering a switch. These variables have similar effects on the actual switching decision. Comparing both models, the switching decision appears to be better explained by the variables in our model, and the effects are generally intuitive. Thus, even though arguably too few consumers switch plans, the switching decision itself is well in line with the underlying economics incentives.

Table 14.28   **Logit models for plan switching**

		Considered switching		Switched	
2006 characteristics	Premium	1.023	1.032	1.086**	1.098**
	No deductible	0.353**	0.373**	0.252**	0.264*
	Gap coverage	0.486	0.436	0.007**	0.006*
2006–2007 change	Premium	1.062	1.068*	1.183**	1.201**
	No deductible	0.514	0.512	0.608	0.734
	Gap coverage	1.640	1.498	0.808	0.790
Dissatisfaction with plan			3.994***		5.798***
Constant		0.319**	0.178***	0.018***	0.007***
Number of observations		197	190	197	190

Notes: Coefficients reported in this table are odds ratios.
***Significant at the 1 percent level.
**Significant at the 5 percent level.
*Significant at the 10 percent level.
(For a two-sided *t*-test.)

14.8   Conclusions

The introduction of Medicare Part D—the most significant expansion of the Medicare program since its inception—had several political goals, most importantly to provide access to affordable drug coverage to all Medicare beneficiaries (in particular to the chronically ill) and to create a "competitive, transparent marketplace offering a wide array of benefits" (Bach and McClellan 2005). Medicare Part D also exemplifies the trend toward consumer-directed healthcare, giving consumers more choice but also confronting them with difficult decisions. The complexity of the program was a great source of concern before its introduction. Consumers were quite confused about the Part D program before enrollment began, with 40 percent knowing little or nothing about what the program offered (according to our earlier estimates; see Heiss, McFadden, and Winter [2006]).

In this chapter, we investigated in great detail how older Americans made their decisions in the enrollment periods for the first two years of the new Medicare Part D prescription drug benefit. We analyzed data from three waves of the Retirement Perspectives Survey (RPS), which we designed specifically to obtain information on older Americans' health status and expenditures, their preferences, and their prescription drug insurance choices before and after the introduction of Medicare Part D. The main purpose of our analysis was to understand how consumers react to the economic incentives embedded in Medicare Part D. This is an important research question that goes much beyond the more pressing public policy issue of how successful the program was in terms of the goals stated before. It is our view that understanding whether and how consumers react to economic incentives in complex health insurance markets is an important part of the process of optimally designing social insurance programs such as Medicare Part D. This chapter can be interpreted as a first step in that direction.

Our analysis proceeded in several steps. We began by looking at how consumers reacted to the incentives operating in the first year of Part D. Specifically, we asked whether and when eligible consumers without prescription drug coverage from other sources enrolled in Medicare Part D. Given the structure of the program, expected drug costs for the first year should be by far the most important determinant of those decisions. Our analysis confirms this: enrollment, and particularly early enrollment (i.e., before January 1, 2006) seems to be driven almost entirely by 2005 drug costs (which should be a good predictor of 2006 drug costs) and very little by other variables. Also, those consumers who enrolled late in the initial enrollment period have had lower drug expenditure in 2005 than those who enrolled early. Overall, these results suggest that consumers' choices can be approximated well already by a very simple model with static expectations and myopic decisions in which only current drug costs play a role. That observed choices can be explained by such a simple model may be not surprising since

CMS's information campaign as well as advertisements by plan providers stressed exactly those immediate costs and benefits of enrolling in a Part D.

Next, we investigated plan choices of those individuals who enrolled in a Part D stand-alone plan. While in a full structural model, the enrollment and the plan choice decisions cannot be separated, we believe it is a reasonable approximation of actual choice behavior to consider these decisions separately. Our analysis of plan choices was based on a comparison of the implicit prices of various plan features (estimated using a simple hedonic regression model and CMS data on all plans offered) and consumers' willingness to pay for those features (estimated using a discrete choice model and RPS data on actual plan choices). We found that implicit prices and WTPs match up surprisingly well. In particular, WTP for "coverage in the gap" is significantly positive for those consumers whose 2005 drug bills put them in the coverage gap.

The overall conclusion from this first part of our analysis is that consumers respond to the *immediate* incentives that are induced by their current health status and drug expenditures combined with the salient, widely publicized features of the Medicare Part D program. However, this is only half of the story since, in an attempt to counter potential adverse selection problems, the designers of Medicare Part D introduced a penalty for late enrollment. This feature makes the enrollment decision a dynamic one. In the second part of our analysis, we thus analyze whether consumers also react to the *intertemporal* incentives provided by Medicare Part D. To this end, we developed a dynamic model of health status and drug expenditure, which we estimated using data from the Medicare Current Beneficiary Survey (MCBS) and an intertemporal optimization model of Medicare Part D enrollment decisions that could be used to predict optimal enrollment decisions in our sample. Our model predicts that some consumers for whom enrollment in 2006 did not have positive value should nevertheless have enrolled in order to avoid future penalties. Under the assumptions we made, not enrolling in 2006 would have been rational only for 2.5 percent of our sample, according to our simulations. This finding reflects the combined effects of the subsidies to the program and the penalty for signing up after first becoming eligible.

We conclude from our analysis that the Medicare Part D market has been, on the whole, a tactical success. It has achieved high enrollment levels, and through tight control of products in the market has assured that rates of consumer deception and fraud are low. It has led to competition among sponsors that has kept premiums low, and succeeded in applying competitive pressure to lower drug prices and encourage use of generic substitutes. In the annual open enrollment period, consumers can switch away from plans that provide unsatisfactory service, a choice that has option value and influences sponsor behavior even if it is not commonly exercised. However, adverse selection appears to be in the process of extinguishing most of the extended plan alternatives that would offer consumers wide choice. Strategically, it remains to be seen whether this market dominated by two large sponsors will remain vigorously competitive, whether the risk weighting methods used by CMS will be effective in neutralizing adverse selection, particularly for extended plans, and consumers will be sufficiently alert to use their ability to switch to discipline poor service. It is clear that the administrative cost of operating a Medicare prescription drug benefit through a market rather than through a mandatory single-product system (such as Medicare Part A) is higher than the best-run single-payer systems around the world. The question for society is whether the efficiencies of production and the consumer benefits of choice actually achieved in this market are sufficient to justify its higher administrative cost, and if so whether the organization and administration of the Part D market is a good model for other areas of health care.

We end by mentioning directions for future research on Medicare Part D and on consumer-directed health care and insurance markets more generally. One issue that deserves more attention is whether consumers' decision are rational. However, any analysis of this issue, including our attempt in this chapter, is necessarily restricted by the need to make strong assumptions about preferences and expectations. Another important aspect of the market for Medicare Part D plans is adverse selection and moral hazard, the extent to which they hinder market efficiency, and the extent to which they can be neutralized through mechanism design. We have provided some first insights in this chapter on these questions, but more research is needed here as well. Next, market structure and firm behavior are interesting in its own right, and they may also interact with consumer behavior (for instance, the fact that few consumers switched plans between 2006 and 2007 may indicate that a pricing strategy with low premiums in 2006 and then increases for 2007 would have been very effective). Finally, as we already noted, we hope that the models we developed and estimated in this chapter will prove useful in the design of future health insurance reforms, including periodic reappraisal of the Medicare Part D program itself.

Appendix

Table 14A.1   Standard plan benefits

Notation	Description	Comments
APB	Annual pharmacy bill	Enrollee characteristic
TrOOP	True out-of-pocket cost of enrollee	Enrollee characteristic
DED	Deductible ($250 in 2006)	Part D parameter
GTH	Gap threshold ($2250 in 2006)	Part D parameter
TTH	TrOOP threshold for catastrophic benefits ($3,600 in 2006)	Part D parameter
BB	Basic benefit, 75 percent of APB above DED, up to GTH	$BB = 0.75 \max\{0,\min\{APB,GTH\} - DED\}$
CTH	Catastrophic pharmacy bill threshold ($5,100 in 2006)	$CTH = TTH + 0.75 \cdot (GTH - DED)$
CPB	Catastrophic pharmacy bill	$CPB = \max\{0,APB - CTH\}$
CB	Catastrophic benefit, 95 percent of CPB	$CB = 0.95\ CPB$

Table 14A.2   CMS subsidy per enrollee

Notation	Description	Comments	National average
ADM	Administrative costs (overhead plus return on capital)	Industry standard: 15 percent of benefits	
TC	Total benefit and administrative cost, including reinsurance	$TC = BB + CB + ADM$	NTC
RI	Federal catastrophic reinsurance ($r = 0.27$ in 2006)	$RI = 0.8 \cdot CPB$	$NRI = r \cdot NTC$
BID	Sponsor bid to CMS for expected benefit payments plus administrative costs, excluding reinsurance	$BID = TC - RI = BB + 0.15 \cdot CPB + ADM$	NBID
BAP	Base annual premium	$BAP = 0.255 \cdot NTC = 0.255 \cdot NBID/(1 - r)$	
BDS	Base direct subsidy	$BDS = (0.745 - r) \cdot NTC = (0.745 - r) \cdot NBID/(1 - r)$	
APR	Plan annual premium	$APR = \max\{0,BAP + BID - NBID\}$	
PDS	Plan direct subsidy	Base direct subsidy, risk adjusted for case mix	
SPR	Supplementary premium	Supplement for extended plans	

References

Abbring, J. H., P.-A. A. Chiappori, J. J. Heckman, and J. Pinquet. 2003. Adverse selection and moral hazard in insurance: Can dynamic data help to distinguish? *Journal of the European Economic Association* 1 (2–3): 512–21.

Adams, P., M. D. Hurd, D. McFadden, A. Merrill, and T. Ribeiro. 2003. Healthy, wealthy, and wise? Tests for direct causal paths between health and socioeconomic status. *Journal of Econometrics* 112 (1): 3–56.

Anderson, S., A. De Palma, and J. Thisse. 1996. *Discrete choice theory of product differentiation.* Cambridge, MA: MIT Press.

Bach, P. B., and M. B. McClellan. 2005. A prescription of a modern Medicare program. *New England Journal of Medicine* 353: 2733–35.

———. 2006. The first months of the prescription-drug benefit: A CMS update. *New England Journal of Medicine* 354: 2312–14.

Bajari, P., H. Hong, and A. Khwaja. 2006. Moral hazard, adverse selection and health expenditures: A semiparametric analysis. NBER Working Paper no. 12445. Cambridge, MA: National Bureau of Economic Research, August.

Baker, M., M. Stabile, and C. Deri. 2004. What do self-reported, objective, measures of health measure? *Journal of Human Resources* 39 (4): 1067–93.

Buchmueller, T. 2006. Price and the health plan choices of retirees. *Journal of Public Economics* 25 (1): 81–101.

Centers for Medicare and Medicaid Services (CMS). 2006. Medicare Prescription Drug Benefit Manual. Available at: http://www.cms.hhs.gov/PrescriptionDrug CovContra/.

———. 2005. Instructions for the Part D payment demonstration. Centers for Medicare and Medicaid Services, Technical Report.

Congressional Budget Office (CBO). 2004. A detailed description of CBO's cost estimates for the Medicare prescription drug benefit. Technical Report, CBO.

Cubanski, J., and P. Neuman. 2006. Status report on Medicare Part D enrollment in 2006: Analysis of plan-specific market share and coverage. *Health Affairs* 26 (1): w1–w12.

Dennis, J. M. 2005. *Field report for the retirement perspectives survey.* Menlo Park, CA: Knowledge Networks, Inc.

Donohue, J. 2006. Mental health in the Medicare Part D drug benefit: A new regulatory model? *Health Affairs* 25 (3): 707–19.

Fang, H., M. P. Keane, and D. Silverman. 2006. Sources of advantageous selection: Evidence from the Medigap insurance market. NBER Working Paper no. 12289. Cambridge, MA: National Bureau of Economic Research, June.

Frakt, A. B., and S. D. Pizer. 2006. A first look at the new Medicare prescription drug plans. *Health Affairs* 25 (4): w252–w261.

Gilbert, D. T., E. C. Pinel, T. D. Wilson, S. J. Blumberg, and T. Wheatley. 1998. Immune neglect: A source of durability bias in affective forecasting. *Journal of Personality and Social Psychology* 75 (3): 617–38.

Goldman, D. P., G. F. Joyce, J. J. Escarce, J. E. Pace, M. D. Solomon, M. Laouri, P. B. Landsman, and S. M. Teutsch. 2004. Pharmacy benefits and the use of drugs by the chronically ill. *Journal of the American Medical Association* 291 (19): 2344–50.

Goldman, D., and T. Philipson. 2007. Integrated insurance design in the presence of multiple medical technologies. *American Economic Review, Papers and Proceedings* 97 (2): 427–32.

Grossman, M. 1972. On the concept of health capital and the demand for health. *Journal of Political Economy* 80 (2): 223–55.

Hall, A. E. 2004. Estimating the demand for prescription drug benefits by Medicare beneficiaries. MIT and NBER. Unpublished Manuscript.

Heckman, J., R. Matzkin, and L. Nesheim. 2003. Estimation and simulation of nonadditive hedonic models. NBER Working Paper no. 9895. Cambridge, MA: National Bureau of Economic Research, August.

Heiss, F. 2006. Dynamics of self-rated health and selective mortality. University of Munich. Unpublished Manuscript.

———. 2008. Sequential numerical integration in nonlinear state-space models for microeconometric panel data. *Journal of Applied Econometrics* 23 (3): 373–89.

Heiss, F., A. Börsch-Supan, M. Hurd, and D. Wise. 2009. Pathways to disability: Predicting health trajectories. In *Health at older ages: The causes and consequences of declining disability among the elderly,* ed. D. Cutler and D. A. Wise, 105–50. Chicago: University of Chicago Press.

Heiss, F., D. McFadden, and J. Winter. 2006. Early results: Who failed to enroll in Medicare Part D, and why? *Health Affairs* 25 (5): w344–w354.

Hurd, M., A. Kapteyn, S. Rohwedder, and A. van Soest. 2007. Knowledge of drug costs and insurance plan choice. Paper presented at the American Economic Association (AEA) Annual Meeting. January, Chicago.

Huskamp, H. A., P. A. Deverka, A. M. Epstein, R. S. Epstein, K. A. McGuigan, and R. G. Frank. 2003. The effect of incentive-based formularies on prescription-drug utilization and spending. *New England Journal of Medicine* 349 (23): 2224–32.

Huskamp, H. A., R. G. Frank, K. A. McGuigan, and Y. Zhang. 2005. The impact of a three-tier formulary on demand response for prescription drugs. *Journal of Economics and Management Strategy* 14 (3): 729–53.

Jenkins, M., P. Liu, R. Matzkin, and D. McFadden. 2005. The browser war: Econometric analysis of Markov perfect equilibrium in markets with network effects. University of California, Berkeley. Unpublished Manuscript.

Joyce, G. F., J. J. Escarce, M. D. Solomon, and D. P. Goldman. 2002. Employer drug benefit plans and spending on prescription drugs. *Journal of the American Medical Association* 288 (14): 1733–39.

Kahneman, D., and J. Snell. 1990. Predicting utility. In *Insights in decision making,* ed. R. Hogarth, 295–310. Chicago: University of Chicago Press.

Lucarelli, C. 2006. An analysis of the Medicare prescription drug benefit. Cornell University. Unpublished Manuscript.

McAdams, D., and M. Schwarz. 2006. Perverse incentives in the Medicare prescription drug benefit. NBER Working Paper no. 12008. Cambridge, MA: National Bureau of Economic Research, February.

McFadden, D. 1984. Econometric analysis of qualitative response models. In *Handbook of econometrics, vol. II,* ed. Z. Griliches and M. D. Iniriligator, 1395–1457. Amsterdam: North-Holland.

———. 2005. Comments on Case-Deaton "Broken down by work and sex: How our health declines." In *Analyses in the economics of aging,* ed. D. Wise, 185–212. Chicago: University of Chicago Press.

———. 2006. Free markets and fettered consumers. *American Economic Review* 96 (1): 5–29.

McFadden, D., F. Heiss, B. Jun, and J. Winter. 2006. On testing for independence in weighted contingency tables. *Medium for Econometric Applications* 14 (2): 11–18.

McFadden, D., N. Schwarz, and J. Winter. 2006. Measuring perceptions and behavior in household surveys. University of California, Berkeley. Unpublished Manuscript.

McFadden, D., and K. Train. 2000. Mixed MNL models for discrete response. *Journal of Applied Econometrics* 15 (5): 447–70.

Medpac. 2006. Part D payment system. Available at: www.medpac.gov.

Moran, J. R., and K. I. Simon. 2006. Income and the use of prescription drugs by the elderly: Evidence from the notch cohorts. *Journal of Human Resources* 41 (2): 411–32.

Neuman, P., M. K. Strollo, S. Guterman, W. H. Rogers, A. Li, A. M. C. Rodday, and D. G. Safran. 2007. Medicare prescription drug benefit progress report: Findings from a 2006 national survey of seniors. *Health Affairs* 26 (5): w630–w643.

Poisal, J. A. 2003. Reporting of drug expenditures in the MCBS. *Health Care Financing Review* 25 (2): 23–36.
Robst, J., J. Levy, and M. Ingber. 2007. Diagnosis-based risk adjustment for Medicare prescription drug plan payments. *Health Care Financing Review* 28 (4): 15–30.
Shang, B., and D. P. Goldman. 2007. Prescription drug coverage and elderly Medicare spending. NBER Working Paper no. 13358. Cambridge, MA: National Bureau of Economic Research, September.
Simon, K. I., and C. Lucarelli. 2006. What drove first year premiums in stand-alone Medicare drug plans? NBER Working Paper no. 12595. Cambridge, MA: National Bureau of Economic Research, October.
Slaughter, L. M. 2006. Medicare Part D: The product of a broken process. *New England Journal of Medicine* 354 2314–15.
Stuart, B., L. Simoni-Wastila, and D. Chauncey. 2005. Assessing the impact of coverage gaps in the Medicare Part D drug benefit. *Health Affairs* 10 (April): w167–w179.
Winter, J., R. Balza, F. Caro, F. Heiss, B. Jun, R. Matzkin, and D. McFadden. 2006. Medicare prescription drug coverage: Consumer information and preferences. *Proceedings of the National Academy of Sciences of the United States of America* 103 (20): 7929–34.
Yang, Z., D. B. Gilleskie, and E. C. Norton. 2004. Prescription drugs, medical care, and health outcomes: A model of elderly health dynamics. NBER Working Paper no. 10964. Cambridge, MA: National Bureau of Economic Research, December.

Comment   Amy Finkelstein

This is a fascinating and extremely timely chapter analyzing the elderly's enrollment choices in the new Medicare Part D prescription drug program. The new Medicare prescription drug benefit, which began in 2006, arguably represents the largest single expansion in social insurance in the United States since 1965. It is therefore an extremely important program to understand in its own right. In addition, the authors' findings have interesting implications more broadly for how to think about the optimal design of social insurance programs.

The chapter focuses on individuals' decisions during the initial enrollment period (November 15, 2005 to May 15, 2006). It investigates the determinants of both whether an individual enrolls during this period, and the timing of enrollment conditional on enrollment. The chapter provides both positive and normative analysis of the elderly's choices. I discuss each in turn, and their implications for the optimal design of social insurance, particularly for offering choice within a social insurance program.

Amy Finkelstein is a professor of economics at the Massachusetts Institute of Technology and a research associate of the National Bureau of Economic Research.

Descriptive Analysis

The chapter begins by presenting new data from a survey that the authors designed and conducted. The survey contains information on whether individuals enroll during the initial enrollment period, and if so whether they enrolled early or late within this initial enrollment period. Individuals who enroll after the end of the initial enrollment period and did not have coverage from another source face a late enrollment penalty. This late penalty is designed to reduce adverse selection by encouraging individuals to enroll at the beginning of the program rather than waiting until they develop health problems. The survey also contains information on the individuals' prior year drug costs, their self-reported health status, and various socioeconomic characteristics.

Early enrollment is rational for individuals with high expected drug costs. Consistent with this incentive structure, the authors find that expected drug costs are strongly predictive (in the expected direction) of early enrollment. Late enrollment within the initial enrollment period is rational for individuals with intermediate drug costs or a high present value of the penalty; the incentives for late enrollment (conditional on not enrolling early) therefore depend not only on expected drug costs but also on other characteristics of the individuals, such as their preferences (for example, risk aversion) and their understanding of the penalty system. Again consistent with this incentive structure, the authors find that socioeconomic variables (which may well proxy for preferences or understanding of the penalty system), are the main drivers of the late enrollment decision; expected drug costs are only weakly predictive of late enrollment.

These twin results provide extremely nice examples of the difference between single dimensional and multidimensional selection problems. Standard adverse selection models of insurance markets (such as Rothschild and Stiglitz [1976] consider single dimensional selection; they assume that individuals differ only in their private information about their risk type (here, their expected drug costs). In such models, those who have private information that they are higher risk (higher expected drug costs) will self-select into the insurance market.

The authors' results indicate that the early enrollment decision appears to follow these standard models and reflect a single dimensional selection problem: those who expect to be higher risk are more likely to enroll early. By contrast, the late enrollment decision appears to be driven by factors other than expected risk type, such as preferences and cognition. This is consistent with a growing body of empirical work suggesting that, in many insurance markets, the selection problem may be multidimensional. As a result, differences in nonrisk characteristics of the individual can be as or more important than their private information about their risk type in predicting insurance decisions. Several recent empirical papers have found substantial evidence of unobserved (by the insurance company) preference heterogeneity that is an important determinant of insurance decisions. Examples include automobile insurance (Cohen and Einav 2007), long-term care insurance (Finkelstein and McGarry 2006), reverse mortgages (Davidoff and Welke 2005), Medigap (Fang, Keane, and Silverman 2006), and annuities (Einav, Finkelstein, and Schrimpf 2007). Interestingly, many of these insurance markets are for the elderly. Indeed, in the case of Medigap, which provides private health insurance to supplement some of the (other) gaps in Medicare, Fang, Keane, and Silverman (2006) find that cognitive ability is an important determinant of insurance coverage. Likewise, the authors here conjecture that some of their socioeconomic variables may proxy for cognitive understanding of the penalty for late enrollment.

When selection into an insurance market is based on multiple dimensions of private information—that is, preferences as well as risk type—a market may suffer from adverse selection even if expected risk type is not positively correlated with the coverage decision (Finkelstein and McGarry 2006). Detecting adverse selection empirically thus becomes more difficult once the possibility of multiple dimensions of private information (and hence of selection) is recognized (Chiappori et al. 2006; Finkelstein and Poterba 2006).

The presence of multiple dimensions of private information also raises interesting questions regarding optimal design of social insurance. Mandatory social insurance is the canonical solution to the problem of adverse selection in insurance markets (e.g., Akerlof 1970). Yet, as emphasized by Feldstein (2005) (among others), mandates are not necessarily welfare improving when individuals differ in their preferences. When individuals differ in both their preferences and their (privately known) risk types, mandates may involve a trade-off between the allocative inefficiency produced by adverse selection and the allocative inefficiency produced by imposing a uniform, "one size fits all" program on individuals whose optimal insurance coverage varies. Whether and which mandates can increase welfare thus becomes an empirical question. Analyzing the welfare consequences of different mandates in turn requires estimation of the joint distribution of individuals' (privately known) preferences and (privately known) risk type (Einav, Finkelstein, and Schrimpf 2007).

Normative Analysis

The second part of the chapter is a normative analysis of whether individuals' enrollment decisions are "rational." Specifically, the authors investigate whether individuals' behavior matches the predictions of an optimal dynamic stochastic programming problem that they develop and estimate. They find that, on the margin, individuals seem to understand the (simple) fact that an increase in expected drug costs increases the benefits from enrollment. However, they also find that the level of enrollment is lower than the optimal level that they estimate, and that individuals are less aware of the (complicated) consequences of the penalty of late enrollment.

As the authors point out, any discrepancy between the actual choice and the predicted choice may reflect a failure of rational expectations, a failure of optimization, and/or a failure of the model they have specified. To the extent that the discrepancies the authors find reflect either a failure of rational expectations or a failure of individuals to optimize appropriately, these findings also have implications for the benefits of allowing choice within social insurance programs. In particular, it becomes important to distinguish between differential behavior across individuals that reflects real differences in underlying preferences as opposed to differences in behavior that reflect "mistakes." The former suggests some benefits from allowing individuals choice within social insurance, while the latter suggests that there may be some value to restricting choice. The authors' interesting findings suggest that an important direction for future work—both for Medicare Part D and for other social insurance programs more generally—is distinguishing between "true" preference heterogeneity and failures of rationality.

References

Akerlof, G. 1970. The market for "Lemons": Quality uncertainty and the market mechanism. *Quarterly Journal of Economics* 84 (3): 488–500.
Cohen, A., and L. Einav. 2007. Estimating risk preferences from deductible choice. *American Economic Review* 97 (3): 745–88.
Chiappori, P.-A., B. Jullien, B. Salanie, and F. Salanie. 2006. Asymmetric information in insurance: General testable implications. RAND Journal of Economics 37 (4). (Available online.)
Davidoff, T., and G. Welke. 2005. Selection and moral hazard in the reverse mortgage market. University of California, Berkeley, Haas School of Business. Unpublished Manuscript.
Einav, L., A. Finkelstein, and P. Schrimpf. 2007. The welfare cost of asymmetric information: Evidence from the U.K. annuity market. NBER Working Paper no. 13228. Cambridge, MA: National Bureau of Economic Research, July.
Fang, H., M. Keane, and D. Silverman. 2006. Sources of advantageous selection: Evidence from the Medigap insurance market. NBER Working Paper no. 12289. Cambridge, MA: National Bureau of Economic Research, June.
Feldstein, M. 2005. Rethinking social insurance. NBER Working Paper no. 11250. Cambridge, MA: National Bureau of Economic Research, April.
Finkelstein, A., and K. McGarry. 2006. Multiple dimensions of private information: Evidence from the long-term care insurance market. *American Economic Review* 96 (4): 938–58.
Finkelstein, A., and J. Poterba. 2006. Testing for adverse selection with "unused observables." NBER Working Paper no. 12112. Cambridge, MA: National Bureau of Economic Research, March.
Rothschild, M., and J. E. Stiglitz. 1976. Equilibrium in competitive insurance markets: An essay on the economics of imperfect information. *Quarterly Journal of Economics* 90 (4): 630–49.

Contributors

Steven J. Atlas
General Medicine Division
Massachusetts General Hospital
50 Staniford Street, 9th floor
Boston, MA 02114

Abhijit V. Banerjee
Department of Economics, E52-252d
Massachusetts Institute of Technology
50 Memorial Drive
Cambridge, MA 02142-1347

James Banks
Institute for Fiscal Studies
7 Ridgmount Street
London WC1E 7AE England

John Beshears
Department of Economics
Harvard University
Littauer Center
Cambridge, MA 02138

Jay Bhattacharya
117 Encina Commons
Center for Primary Care and Outcomes
   Research
Stanford University
Stanford, CA 94305-6019

Richard Blundell
University College London
Gower Street
London WC1E 6BT, England

Axel Börsch-Supan
Mannheim Research Institute for the
   Economics of Aging
University of Mannheim
Building L13, 17
D-68131 Mannheim, Germany

Anne Case
367 Wallace Hall
Princeton University
Princeton, NJ 08544

Amitabh Chandra
John F. Kennedy School of
   Government
Harvard University
79 JFK Street
Cambridge, MA 02138

James J. Choi
Yale School of Management
135 Prospect Street
New Haven, CT 06520-8200

David M. Cutler
Department of Economics
Harvard University
1875 Cambridge Street
Cambridge, MA 02138

Angus Deaton
328 Wallace Hall
Woodrow Wilson School
Princeton University
Princeton, NJ 08544-1013

Esther Duflo
Department of Economics E52-252G
Massachusetts Institute of Technology
50 Memorial Drive
Cambridge, MA 02142

Amy Finkelstein
Department of Economics, E52-357
Massachusetts Institute of Technology
50 Memorial Drive
Cambridge, MA 02142

Alan M. Garber
PCOR/CHP
Stanford University
117 Encina Commons
Stanford, CA 94305-6019

Edward L. Glaeser
Department of Economics
315A Littauer Center
Harvard University
Cambridge, MA 02138

Florian Heiss
Department of Economics
University of Munich
Ludwigstr. 28 (RG)
D-80539 Munich, Germany

Michael Hurd
RAND Corporation
1776 Main Street
Santa Monica, CA 90407

Arie Kapteyn
RAND Corporation
1776 Main Street
Santa Monica, CA 90407-2138

David Laibson
Department of Economics
Harvard University
Littauer Center
Cambridge, MA 02138

Adriana Lleras-Muney
Department of Economics
9373 Bunche Hall
University of California, Los Angeles
Los Angeles, CA 90095

Erzo F. P. Luttmer
John F. Kennedy School of
  Government
Harvard University
79 John F. Kennedy Street
Cambridge, MA 02138

Thomas MaCurdy
Department of Economics
Stanford University
Stanford, CA 94305-6072

Brigitte C. Madrian
John F. Kennedy School of
  Government
Harvard University
79 John F. Kennedy Street
Cambridge, MA 02138

Daniel McFadden
University of California, Berkeley
Department of Economics
549 Evans Hall #3880
Berkeley, CA 94720-3880

Zoë Oldfield
Institute for Fiscal Studies
7 Ridgmount Street
London WC1E 7AE, England

James M. Poterba
National Bureau of Economic
  Research
1050 Massachusetts Ave
Cambridge, MA 02138

John B. Shoven
Department of Economics
Stanford University
579 Serra Mall at Galvez Street
Stanford, CA 94305-6015

Jonathan Skinner
Department of Economics
6106 Rockefeller Hall
Dartmouth College
Hanover, NH 03755

James P. Smith
RAND Corporation
1776 Main Street
Santa Monica, CA 90401-3208

Arthur van Soest
Netspar, Tilburg University
PO Box 90153
5000 LE Tilburg, the Netherlands

Steven F. Venti
Department of Economics
6106 Rockefeller Center
Dartmouth College
Hanover, NH 03755

Heidi Williams
Department of Economics
Harvard University
Littauer Center
Cambridge, MA 02138

Robert J. Willis
University of Michigan
Economics Department
611 Tappan Street
Ann Arbor, MI 48109-1220

Joachim Winter
Department of Economics
University of Munich
Ludwigstr. 28 (RG)
D-80539 Munich, Germany

David A. Wise
John F. Kennedy School of
   Government
Harvard University
79 John F. Kennedy Street
Cambridge, MA 02138

Author Index

Aarts, L. J. M., 37
Abbott, R. D., 211
Abbring, H. ., 421
Akerlof, G., 483
Anderson, S., 449
Andrews, E. S., 311
Apkarian, A. V., 147, 161
Atlas, S. J., 146, 154, 157, 160
Autor, D., 64, 163

Babish, J. D., 391, 392
Bach, P. B., 418, 475
Bajari, P., 421
Baker, M., 458
Baliki, M. N., 147, 161, 162
Banerjee, A., 169, 170, 171, 207
Banks, J., 64, 160, 338, 341, 346, 347
Barker, D. J. P., 106, 211, 213, 227, 229, 231
Barro, R., 308
Bassett, W. F., 311
Benitez-Silva, H., 60, 147, 161
Bernheim, B. D., 379
Beshears, J., 291, 312, 316
Bhattacharya, J., 393n1, 401
Blacker, J., 205
Blanchflower, D. G., 146n1, 161, 242, 244, 265
Blöndal, S., 40
Blundell, R., 338, 347
Bombardier, C., 161
Börsch-Supan, A., 43, 53, 63, 64, 66, 93n1, 381

Bound, J., 64
Bourguignon, F., 203
Brass, W., 205
Bray, J. O., 218
Brock, W. A., 123
Brunner, E., 214
Buchmueller, T., 420n3
Burgess, R., 207
Burkhauser, R. V., 37, 63, 64

Calhoun, C. A., 346n5
Carroll, G. D., 317
Case, A. C., 106, 108, 121, 123, 145, 150, 207, 211, 213, 228
Casey, C. Y., 162
Chandra, A., 410
Chauncey, D., 420
Chen, L., 261
Chernew, M., 101
Chiappori, P.-A., 483
Chibnall, J. T., 163
Choi, J. J., 311, 312, 316
Choi, Y., 204
Chou, R. A., 145, 161
Christakis, N. A., 123
Clark, A., 265, 266
Cohen, A., 483
Copeland, C., 274
Costa, D., 106, 108, 307
Crane, J., 123
Crickman, C. W., 218
Cubanski, J., 420, 439

Cunningham, C. R., 291
Cutler, D. M., 18, 32, 33n1, 101, 102, 145, 206

Davidoff, T., 337, 483
Davis, K., 259
Deaton, A., 108, 145, 150, 170, 171n2, 206
De Jong, P. R., 37
DeMarzo, P. M., 126
De Nardi, M., 383
Dennis, J. M., 422n6
De Palma, A., 449
Deri, C., 458
Deyo, R. A., 154, 161
Diener, C., 249
Diener, E., 243, 249
Diener, M., 249
Disney, R., 338n2
Di Tella, R., 242, 265, 266
Donohue, J., 420
Duflo, E., 169, 170, 171, 204, 207, 311
Duggan, M., 64, 163
Durlauf, S. N., 123
Dynan, K., 278n2

Easterlin, R. A., 242, 243, 264
Einav, L., 483
Ellison, G., 125
Engelhardt, G. V., 291, 311
Engen, E. M., 379
Evans, W. N., 124, 129, 130, 207
Even, W. E., 311

Fang, H., 421, 483
Farah, M. J., 162
Farrell, P., 121
Farrelly, M. C., 124, 129, 130
Feldstein, M., 483
Fertig, A., 106, 211, 213, 228
Finkelstein, A., 483
Fisher, E. S., 391, 392
Fleming, M. J., 311
Fogel, R. W., 106
Fowler, J. H., 123
Frakt, A. B., 420
Frankenberg, E., 171n1, 182
French, E., 383
Fuchs, V. R., 18, 121
Fudenberg, D., 125

Gale, W. G., 379
Garber, A., 393n1

Gardner, J., 264
Gawande, A., 161, 162
Geha, P. Y., 147, 161
Geppert, J., 397
Gerorge, L., 126
Gilbert, D. T., 459
Glaeser, E., 123, 124, 127, 163
Glennerster, R., 171
Gluck, J., 154
Goda, G. S., 27, 32
Goldman, D. P., 401, 419, 421
Graham, C., 243, 261
Green, D., 393n1
Groot, W., 51
Grossman, M., 457
Gruber, J., 40, 53, 54, 58, 63
Gu, X., 401
Gustman, A., 278n2, 379

Hackman, D. A., 162
Hadler, N. M., 163
Hagen, K. B., 154
Haisken-DeNew, J., 242
Hall, A. E., 419
Hallock, K., 393
Havemann, J., 409
Heckman, J. J., 69, 449
Heiss, F., 381, 414, 458, 459, 460, 461, 475
Helliwell, J. F., 242, 243
Henley, A., 338n2
Hesselius, P., 43
Hill, K., 204, 205
Holden, S., 24n1, 291
Hong, H., 421
Hurd, M., 381, 421
Huskamp, H. A., 419
Hyslop, D. R., 69

Iezzoni, L. I., 391
Iliffe, J., 261
Ingelhart, R., 243

Jenkins, M., 449
Jones, J., 383
Joyce, G. F., 419
Jürges, H., 43

Kahneman, D., 145, 160, 242, 459
Kapteyn, A., 75, 146, 152, 162
Karoly, L., 171n1
Katz, F., 123
Keane, M. P., 421, 483

Keller, R. B., 154
Kézdi, G., 308
Khitatrakun, S., 379
Khwaja, A., 421
Kittner, S. J., 392
Klevmarken, N. A., 43
Klingemann, H.-D., 243
Koenker, R., 393
Krause, N., 154
Krueger, A. B., 145, 146, 148n3, 160, 161
Kuh, D. J., 213
Kumar, A., 311
Kusko, A., 311
Kuziemko, I., 123

Laibson, D., 311
Lakdawalla, D., 401
Lamb, V. L., 401
Layard, R., 243
Leigh, A., 243, 248
Liebman, J. B., 32
Lleras-Muney, A., 102, 145, 207
Lubotsky, D., 228
Lucarelli, C., 420, 434, 450n19
Lurie, J. D., 146, 157
Luttmer, E., 266

MacCulloch, R., 242, 265, 266
Macpherson, D. A., 311
MaCurdy, T., 393n1, 397
Madrian, B. C., 311, 316, 320n10
Manski, C., 123, 141
Manton, K. G., 101, 401
Mark, D. H., 392
Marmot, M. G., 214
Matzkin, R., 449
May, D. S., 392
McAdams, D., 420
McBean, A. M., 391, 392
McClellan, M. B., 418, 475
McFadden, D., 414, 422, 452n21, 457, 475
McGarry, K., 483
McKnight, R., 411
Meara, E., 32, 33n1
Melzack, R., 147
Menendez, A., 122
Miller, G., 161
Mokdad, A. H., 109
Montgomery, E. B., 124, 129, 130
Moran, J. R., 420
Morrisson, C., 203
Murray, C., 261

Nagi, S. Z., 103
Nataraj, S., 27
Nesheim, L., 449
Neuman, P., 421, 439
Nicoletti, C., 64n1

Oishi, S., 243
Oleinick, A., 154
Oswald, A., 242, 244, 264, 265

Paarsch, H. J., 393n1
Pande, R., 207
Papke, L. E., 311
Patrick, D. L., 161
Paxson, C., 106, 211, 213, 228
Peracchi, F., 64n1
Peterson, E. D., 392
Pizer, S. D., 420
Poisal, J., 462
Poterba, J. M., 272, 280, 282, 291, 293, 301, 305, 311, 483
Preston, S. H., 249

Rasmussen, K. M., 212
Ravelli, A. C. J., 211
Rege, M., 163
Richards, M., 211
Richards, S., 32, 33n1
Robbins, L., 243
Rodrigues, A. P., 311
Rothschild, M., 482

Sacerdote, B., 123, 124, 127, 163
Sala-i-Martin, X., 203
Scarpetta, S., 40
Scheinkman, J., 123, 124, 127, 163
Scholz, J. K., 379
Schrimpf, P., 483
Schultz, G. P., 26
Schwarz, M., 420, 422
Sen, A. K., 47, 51, 242, 261
Seshadri, A., 379
Shang, B., 421
Shea, D., 312, 316, 320n10
Sheiner, L., 18, 347
Shoven, J. B., 20, 27, 32
Silverman, D., 421, 483
Simon, K. I., 420, 434, 450n19
Simoni-Wastila, L., 420
Sinai, T., 343
Skinner, J., 278n2, 383, 410
Slaughter, L. M., 418

Slavov, S. N., 32
Smith, J. P., 75, 146, 153, 162, 182, 206, 214,
   228, 229, 338, 347
Smyth, S., 32
Snell, J., 459
Souleles, N. S., 343
Stabile, M., 458
Stapleton, D. C., 63
Stears, G., 338n2
Steinmeier, T., 278n2, 379
Stevenson, B., 264, 265
Stiglitz, J. E., 482
Stone, A. A., 145, 146, 148n3, 161
Strauss, J., 171
Stuart, B., 420
Swensson, B., 432

Tait, R. C., 163
Telle, K., 163
Thisse, J., 449
Thomas, D., 171n1, 182
Timaeus, I., 204, 205, 207
Topa, G., 123
Tosteson, T. D., 146, 157
Train, K., 452n21
Trussell, J., 205
Tsui-Wu, Y., 154

Uccello, C. E., 379

VanDerHei, J., 291
Van Soest, A., 75, 146, 153, 162
Vayanos, D., 126

Vella, F., 69
Venti, S. F., 272, 278n2, 280, 282, 291, 293,
   301, 305, 347, 381
Verbeek, M., 69
Verbrugge, L., 103
Vortruba, M., 163

Waddell, G., 154
Wadsworth, M. E. J., 211, 213
Wagstaff, A., 171
Waldfogel, J., 126
Warren, J. L., 391, 392
Watkins, P., 218
Weber, H., 157
Weil, D., 347
Weinstein, J. N., 146, 157
Weitzman, M. L., 308
Welke, G., 483
Whittle, J., 391, 392
Wilcox, D., 311
Wilensky, G., 388
Willis, R. J., 308
Winkelmann, L., 265
Winkelmann, R., 265
Winter, J., 414, 422, 426, 475
Wise, D. A., 40, 53, 54, 58, 63, 272, 278n2,
   280, 282, 291, 293, 301, 305, 347, 381
Wolfers, J., 243, 248, 264, 265

Yang, Z., 420

Zeldes, S., 278n2
Zweibel, J., 126

Subject Index

Page numbers followed by f or t refer to figures or tables, respectively.

Activities of daily living (ADL), 226

adult mortality, measure of, 177–82

age: alternative measures of, 2–3, 17–18; effects of income and, on self-reported well-being, 235–38; life satisfaction and, 9; literature on alternative ways of measuring, 18; of mortality milestones, 18–20, 19f

age pyramids, poor and, 172–77

age-specific mortality rates: in India, 186f; in Indonesia, 182–83; in Vietnam, 183–86

aging, poor and: data sources for, 171; in India, 187–93; in Indonesia, 193–95; introduction, 169–71; youth and, 172–77

automatic enrollment, 312; with and without employer matching, 315–20; employer matching level and savings plan participation at nine companies, 320–25

back pain, 154–60, 162

Balanced Budget Act (BBA) (1997), 12–13, 13–14, 387–88

Beneficiary Annual Summary File (BASF), 389

British Household Panel Survey (BHPS), 345, 346

childhood health: disability and, 105–6, 107f; impact of, 211–13

chronic disease indicators, 390–92

corn production: conceptual framework for height and, 213–15; height and, 212

Defined benefit (DB) pensions, 271–72

Defined contribution (DC) retirement saving plans, 271

disability: childhood health and economic status and, 105–6, 107f; by education, theories of, 105–14; education and, 101–4; empirical analysis of, 114–18; factors explaining education gradient in, 118–19; interaction with medical system and, 111–12; living arrangements and, 112–14; medical conditions and, 109–11; occupation and, 108, 108f; perceptions of, 254–60

disability benefits: expenditures on and self-reported male work disability, 67, 67t; public expenditure on, 65–66, 66f

disability insurance programs, 3; effects of, 53–54; enrollment by European country, 46f; enrollment by European country and gender, 46f; enrollment rate predictions for, controlling for demographics and health, 50–53; explaining microdata variations of enrollment in, 47–53; introduction to, 37–41; United States vs. European countries, 38, 39–40f; variation in spending across countries for, 3–4

disability trends: drinking and, 109, 110f; education and, 4–7, 101–4; health behaviors and, 5–6; obesity and, 5, 108–9, 110f; smoking and, 5–6, 108–9, 110f
drinking, disability trends and, 109, 110f

economic circumstances: health and, 7–10; mortality and, 8
education: disability trends and, 4–7, 101–4; health and nutrition as determinants of, 222–23; prevalence of pain and, 6–7, 145–47
employer matching, 315–25
employer-sponsored savings plans, 311–13; automatic enrollment and, 320–25; for Company A, 313–20
English Longitudinal Study on Aging (ELSA), 40, 41–47
European Community Household Panel (ECHP), 64–65

Family Life Surveys, 171
fine motor skills, 226
401(k) plans, 271–72; average assets, at retirement, 292–94; eligibility and participation, by age and earnings, 273–80, 273t; future assets at retirement, by lifetime earnings decile and by Social Security wealth decile, 294–300; projecting assets, at retirement, 280–91

gross motor skills, 226

happiness literature, 241–44
health: economic circumstances and, 7–10; functional limitation in old age and, 223–26; height and, 8, 212–13; height in HRS cohort study and, 215–21; nutrition as determinants of education and occupation and, 222–23; perceptions of, 254–60
Health and Retirement Study, U.S. (HRS), 40, 146, 212, 345; height and health in, 215–22; prevalence of pain in, 147–54
health behaviors: disability and, 108–9, 110f; disability trends and, 5–6; peers and, 6
health systems, perceptions of, 259–60
height: conceptual framework for corn production and, 213–15; corn production and, 212; health and, 8, 212–13; and health in HRS cohort study, 215–21
house price volatility, 337–39, 346–47; data

sources, 345–46; establishing facts of, 347–60; model estimates of, 360–76; reducing, 370–74; theoretical model of, 339–44
housing equity, 10, 12
hypertension, 225–26

income, effects of, on self-reported well-being, 235–38
India: age-specific mortality rates in, 186f; aging, health, and poverty in, 187–93
Indonesia: age-specific mortality rates in, 182–83; aging, health, and poverty in, 193–95
Indonesian Family Life Survey, 182–83

labor force participation rates, 3, 24–30; older workers and, 63–64
labor market institutions, variation in, 65–68
large muscle group indexes, 226
life satisfaction, 236–38; age and, 9; evidence from World Poll, 244–54; health and, 8–9; insights from psychology and happiness literatures and, 241–44; theoretical considerations, 238–41
living arrangements, disability and, 112–14
Living Standard Measurement Surveys (LSMS), 171

Maine Lumbar Spine Study, 146, 154–60
medical conditions, disability and, 109–11
medical systems, interactions with, disability and, 111–12
Medicare, 12–14; chronic disease indicators, 390–92; data for, 389–90; introduction, 387–89; methods use for study of, 392–95; results of study of, 395–402
Medicare Part D, 12; consumers' decisions in initial enrollment period, 426–56; introduction, 413–16; literature on, 419–21; prescription drug benefit, 416–18; satisfaction with, 472–74; utility option value of enrolling in, 456–72
mortality milestones, 18–20, 19f
mortality risk, 2, 20, 21f; economic circumstances and, 8; remaining life expectancy and, 21–23, 22f

Nationwide Building Society House Price series, 36
nutrition, as determinant of education and occupation, 222–23

obesity, disability trends and, 5, 108–9, 110f
occupation: disability and, 108, 108f; health
    and nutrition as determinants of, 222–
    23
older workers: disability among, and educa-
    tion, 101–2; labor force participation
    rates and, 63–64

pain, prevalence of: discussion of results of,
    160–63; education and, 6–7, 145–47; in
    Health and Retirement Study, 147–54;
    in Maine Lumbar Spine Study, 154–60
Panel Study of Income Dynamics (PSID),
    64–65, 345–46
peers, health behaviors and, 6, 123–24
poor, the: age pyramids of, 172–73; age-
    specific mortality rates of, 182–86; data
    sources for, 171; introduction, 169–71;
    parents of, 177–82. *See also* India;
    Indonesia; Vietnam, age-specific mor-
    tality rates in
population aging, in United States, 23–24,
    23f
prescription drug benefit. *See* Medicare
    Part D
Prospective Payment System (PPS), 387

remaining life expectancy (RLE), 2, 17–18;
    mortality risk and, 21–23, 22f
repetition strain injury (RSI), 162–63
retirement: average assets at, 292–94; future
    assets at, by lifetime earnings decile and
    Social Security wealth decile, 294–300;
    projecting assets at, 280–81
Retirement Perspectives Survey (RPS),
    421–26; consumers' decisions in initial

enrollment period, 426–56; utility
    option value of enrolling in, 456–74
retirement savings accounts, 10–12
Roland-Morris Questionnaire, 163–64

self-reported health status, 225
self-reported work disability: expenditures
    on disability insurance and male, 67,
    67t; model of, 68–70; results, 70–72;
    simulations, 72–76
set-point theory, 241–44
smoking, disability trends and, 5–6, 108–9,
    110f
smoking, social interactions and: introduc-
    tion, 123–35; variability of, 134–36
smoking time series, 137–40
social interactions, smoking and: direct
    tests, 128–34; empirical tests of, 126–
    28; introduction, 123–25; sources of,
    125–26
Social Security: long careers and, 27, 28;
    possible reforms for, 27–30
Surveillance, Epidemiology, and End
    Results (SEER) program, 391–92
Survey of Health, Aging and Retirement in
    Europe (SHARE), 40, 41–47

Udaipur, India, poverty in, 171, 187–93
United States, population aging in, from
    present to 2050, 23–24, 23f

Vietnam, age-specific mortality rates in,
    183–86

World Poll, 244–54
World Values Survey, 248